Lecture Notes in Computer Scie

T0238540

Commenced Publication in 1973
Founding and Former Series Editors:
Gerhard Goos, Juris Hartmanis, and Jan van Leeuwen

Kiriakos N. Kutulakos (Ed.)

Trends and Topics in Computer Vision

ECCV 2010 Workshops
Heraklion, Crete, Greece, September 10-11, 2010
Revised Selected Papers, Part II

 Springer

Volume Editor

Kiriakos N. Kutulakos
University of Toronto
Department of Computer Science
10 King's College Road, Toronto, ON M5S 3G4, Canada
E-mail: kyros@cs.toronto.edu

ISSN 0302-9743   e-ISSN 1611-3349
ISBN 978-3-642-35739-8   e-ISBN 978-3-642-35740-4
DOI 10.1007/978-3-642-35740-4
Springer Heidelberg Dordrecht London New York

Library of Congress Control Number: 2012954151

CR Subject Classification (1998): I.4, I.5, I.2.10, I.2, H.5, H.3

LNCS Sublibrary: SL 6 – Image Processing, Computer Vision, Pattern Recognition,
and Graphics

Typesetting: Camera-ready by author, data conversion by Scientific Publishing Services, Chennai, India

Printed on acid-free paper

Springer is part of Springer Science+Business Media (www.springer.com)

Preface

This volume contains the proceedings of four workshops held in conjunction with the 11th European Conference on Computer Vision:

- Workshop on Color and Reflectance in Imaging and Computer Vision
- Workshop on Media Retargeting
- Workshop on Reconstruction and Modeling of Large-Scale 3D Virtual Environments
- Workshop on Computer Vision on GPUs

All workshops took place in Heraklion, Crete, Greece, during September 10–11, 2010.

September 2010   Kiriakos N. Kutulakos

Workshop on Color and Reflectance in Imaging and Computer Vision (CRICV 2010)

Organizing Committee

Theo Gevers	University of Amsterdam
Kostas Plataniotis	University of Toronto
Joost van de Weijer	Univérsitat Autonoma de Barcelona
Todd Zickler	Harvard University

Program Committee

Elli Angelopoulou	University of Erlangen-Nuremberg
Robert Benavente	Univérsitat Autonoma de Barcelona
Hwann-Tzong Chen	National Tsing Hua University
Mark Drew	Simon Fraser University
Christine Fernandez-Maloigne	University of Poitiers
Graham Finlayson	University of East Anglia
David Forsyth	University of California, Berkeley
Clement Fredembach	Canon Information System Research
Peter Gehler	Max Planck Institute
Jan-Mark Geusebroek	University of Amsterdam
Takahiko Horiuchi	Chiba University
Rei Kawakami	University of Tokyo
Reiner Lenz	Linkoping University
Rastislav Lukac	Epson Canada
Marcel Lucassen	University of Amsterdam
Yoshitsugu Manabe	Nara Institute of Science and Technology
Jiri Matas	Czech Technical University
Gerard Medioni	University of Southern California
Gloria Menegaz	University of Verona
Antonio Robles-Kelly	Canberry Research Lab
Raimondo Schettini	University of Milan Bicocca
Ilan Shimshoni	University of Haifa
Sabine Susstrunk	EPFL
Robby Tan	Utrecht University
Alan Tremeau	Université Jean Monnet
Maria Vanrell	Univérsitat Autonoma de Barcelona
Alessandro Rizzi	University of Milan
Sang Wook Lee	Sogang University
Kuk-Jin Yoon	Gwangju Institute of Science and Technology

Workshop on Media Retargeting (MRW 2010)

Organizing Committee

Thomas Deselaers	ETH Zürich
Olga Sorkine	New York University
Alexander Hornung	Disney Research Zürich

Program Committee

Ariel Shamir	The Interdisciplinary Center, Herzliya
Shai Avidan	Adobe Systems
Tong-Yee Lee	National Cheng-Kung University
Wojciech Matusik	Disney Research Zürich
Markus Gross	ETH Zürich, Disney Research Zürich
Johannes Kopf	Microsoft Research
Roland Flemming	MPI Tübingen
Daniel Keysers	Google
Philippe Dreuw	RWTH Aachen University
Luciano Sbaiz	Google
Miki Rubinstein	Massachusetts Institute of Technology
Carsten Rother	Microsoft Research
Christoph Lampert	Institute of Science and Technology Austria
Victor Lempitsky	Oxford University
Theo Gevers	University of Amsterdam
Wolf Kienzle	Microsoft Research
Florrent Perronin	Xerox Research Center Grenoble

Sponsoring Institutions

The Media Retargeting Workshop was sponsored by Disney Research and supported by the European Association for Computer Graphics.

Workshop on Reconstruction and Modeling of Large-Scale 3D Virtual Environments (RMLE 2010)

Organizing Committee

Suya You   University of Southern California
Charalambos Poullis   Cyprus University of Technology
Michael Wand   Saarland University, MPI Informatik

Program Committee

Adrien Bartoli	Université Blaise-Pascal
Ajmal Saeed Mian	University of Western Australia
Avideh Zakhor	University of California, Berkeley
Christos Gatzoulis	University of Cyprus
Daniel G. Aliaga	Purdue University
Gerard Medioni	University of Southern California
Gerhard Roth	University of Ottawa
Guanghui Wang	University of Windsor
Ioannis Stamos	City University of New York
Jan-Michael Frahm	University of North Carolina, Chapel Hill
John Zelek	University of Waterloo
Jun Takamatsu	Nara Institute of Science and Technology
Luc Van Gool	ETH Zürich
Marc Pollefeys	ETH Zürich
Martial Hebert	Carnegie Mellon University
Noah Snavely	Cornell University
Patrick Flynn	University of Notre Dame
Philippos Mordohai	Stevens Institute of Technology
Shinsaku Hiura	Osaka University
Sudipta Sinha	Microsoft Research
Suresh Lodha	University of California, Santa Cruz
Svetlana Lazebnik	University of North Carolina, Chapel Hill
Ulrich Neumann	University of Southern California
Voicu Popescu	Purdue University
Wolfgang Förstner	University of Bonn
Yiorgos Chrysanthou	University of Cyprus
Zhigang Zhu	City University of New York

Workshop on Computer Vision on GPUs (CVGPU 2010)

Organizing Committee

Jan-Michael Frahm   University of North Carolina, Chapel Hill
Marc Pollefeys   ETH Zürich
Horst Bischof   Graz University of Technology

Web Chair

Pierre Fite-Georgel   University of North Carolina, Chapel Hill

Referees

Brian Clipp	Mohammed Hussein	Nicolas Pinto
Daniel Cremers	Renaud Keriven	Thomas Pock
James Fung	Reinhard Koch	Sudipta Sinha
David Gallup	Oliver Kutter	Jan Woetzel
Justin Hensley	P.J. Narayanan	Christopher Zach

Table of Contents – Part II

Workshop on Reconstruction and Modeling of Large-Scale 3D Virtual Environments

Workshop on Computer Vision on GPUs

Table of Contents – Part I

First International Workshop on Parts and Attributes

Third Workshop on Human Motion Understanding, Modeling, Capture and Animation

International Workshop on Sign, Gesture and Activity

Estimating Shadows with the Bright Channel Cue

Alexandros Panagopoulos[1], Chaohui Wang[2,3], Dimitris Samaras[1],
and Nikos Paragios[2,3]

[1] Image Analysis Lab, Computer Science Dept., Stony Brook University, NY, USA
[2] Laboratoire MAS, École Centrale Paris, Châtenay-Malabry, France
[3] Equipe GALEN, INRIA Saclay - Île-de-France, Orsay, France

Abstract. In this paper, we introduce a simple but efficient cue for the extraction of shadows from a single color image, the bright channel cue. We discuss its limitations and offer two methods to refine the bright channel: by computing confidence values for the cast shadows, based on a shadow-dependent feature, such as hue; and by combining the bright channel with illumination invariant representations of the original image in a flexible way using an MRF model. We present qualitative and quantitative results for shadow detection, as well as results in illumination estimation from shadows. Our results show that our method achieves satisfying results despite the simplicity of the approach.

1 Introduction

Shadows are an important visual cue in natural images. In many applications they pose an additional challenge, complicating tasks such as object recognition. On the other hand, they provide information about the size and shape of the objects, their relative positions, as well as about the light sources in the scene. It is however difficult to take advantage of the information provided by shadows in natural images, since it is hard to differentiate between shadows, albedo variations and other effects.

The detection of cast shadows in the general case is not straightforward. Shadow detection, in the absence of illumination estimation or knowledge of 3D geometry is a well studied problem. [1] uses invariant color features to segment cast shadows in still or moving images. [2] suggests a method to detect and remove shadows based on the properties of shadow boundaries in the image. In [3,4], a set of illumination invariant features is proposed to detect and remove shadows from a single image. This method is suited to images with relatively sharp shadows and makes some assumptions about the lights and the camera. Camera calibration is necessary; if this is not possible, an entropy minimization method is proposed to recover the most probable illumination invariant image. In [5], a method for high-quality shadow detection and removal is discussed. The method, however, needs some very limited user input. Recently, [6] proposed a method to detect shadows in the case of monochromatic images, based on a series of features that capture statistical properties of the shadows.

K.N. Kutulakos (Ed.): ECCV 2010 Workshops, Part II, LNCS 6554, pp. 1–12, 2012.
© Springer-Verlag Berlin Heidelberg 2012

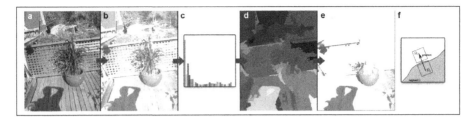

Fig. 1. Bright channel: a. original image (from [3]); b. bright channel; c. hue histogram; d. confidence map; e. refined bright channel; f. confidence computation: for a border pixel i of segment s, we compare the two patches oriented along the image gradient

In this paper, we discuss the estimation of cast shadows in a scene from a single color image.

We first propose a simple but effective image cue for the extraction of shadows, the *bright channel*, inspired from the dark channel prior [7]. Such a cue exploits the assumption that the value of each color channel of a pixel is limited by the incoming radiance, but there are pixels in an arbitrary image patch with values close to the upper limit for at least one color channel.

Then we describe a method to compute confidence values for the cast shadows in an image, in order to alleviate some inherent limitations of the bright channel prior. We process the bright channel in multiple scales and combine the results. We also present an alternative approach for refining the bright channel values, utilizing a Markov Random Field (MRF) model. The MRF model combines the initial bright channel values with a number of illumination-invariant representations to generate a labeling of shadow pixels in the image.

We evaluate our method on the dataset described in [6] and measure the accuracy of pixel classification. We also provide results for qualitative evaluation on other images, and demonstrate an example use of our results to perform illumination estimation with a very simple voting procedure.

This paper is organized as follows: Sec. 2 introduces the bright channel cue; Sec. 3 presents a way to compute confidences for cast shadows and refine the bright channel; Sec. 4 describes an MRF model to combine the bright channel with illumination-invariant cues for shadow estimation, followed by experimental results in Sec. 5. Sec. 6 concludes the paper.

2   Bright Channel Cue Concept

To define the bright channel cue, we consider the following observations:

- The value of each of the color channels of the image has an upper limit which depends on the incoming radiance. This means that, if little light arrives at the 3D point corresponding to a given pixel, then all color channels will have low values.
- In most images, if we examine an arbitrary image patch, the albedo for at least some of the pixels in the patch will probably have a high value in at least one of the color channels.

From the above observations we expect that, given an image patch, the maximum value of the r, g, b color channels should be roughly proportional to the incoming radiance. Therefore, we define the *bright channel*, I_{bright} for image $\mathbf{I}$ in a way similar to the definition of the dark channel [7]:

$$I_{bright}(i) = max_{c \in \{r,g,b\}} \left(max_{j \in \Omega(i)} (I^c(j)) \right) \tag{1}$$

where $I^c(j)$ is the value of color channel c for pixel j and $\Omega(i)$ is a rectangular patch centered at pixel i. We form the bright channel image of $\mathbf{I}$ by computing $I_{bright}(i)$ for every pixel i.

2.1 Interpretation

Let us assume that a scene is illuminated by a finite discrete set $\mathcal{L}$ of distant light sources. Each light source j ($j \in \mathcal{L}$) is described by its direction $\mathbf{d}_j$ and intensity α_j. We assume that the surfaces in the scene exhibit Lambertian reflectance. Let $\mathcal{G}$ be the 3D geometry of the scene and $\mathbf{p}$ be a 3D point imaged at pixel i. We can express the intensity $I(i)$ of pixel i as the sum of the contributions of the light sources that are not occluded at point $\mathbf{p}$:

$$I(i) = \rho(\mathbf{p})\eta(\mathbf{p}), \tag{2}$$

$$\eta(\mathbf{p}) = \sum_{j \in \mathcal{L}} \alpha_j \left[1 - c_\mathbf{p}(\mathbf{d}_j)\right] \max\{-\mathbf{d}_j \cdot \mathbf{n}(\mathbf{p}), 0\}, \tag{3}$$

where $\rho(\mathbf{p})$ is the reflectance (albedo) at $\mathbf{p}$, $\mathbf{n}(\mathbf{p})$ is the normal vector at $\mathbf{p}$ and $c_\mathbf{p}(\mathbf{d}_j)$ is the occlusion factor for direction $\mathbf{d}_j$ at $\mathbf{p}$:

$$c_\mathbf{p}(\mathbf{d}_j) = \begin{cases} 1, \text{ if ray from a light to } \mathbf{p} \text{ along } \mathbf{d}_j \text{ intersects } \mathcal{G} \\ 0, \text{ otherwise} \end{cases} \tag{4}$$

Here we are interested in the illumination component $\eta(\mathbf{p})$. One should note, though, that it cannot be calculated directly since the reflectance $\rho(\mathbf{p})$ above is unknown. The definition of the bright channel, $I_{bright}(i)$ produces a natural lower bound for $\eta(\mathbf{p})$:

$$I(i) \leq I_{bright}(i) \leq \eta(\mathbf{p}). \tag{5}$$

Eq. 5, combined with our observations above, means that the bright channel $I_{bright}(i)$ can provide an adequate approximation to the illumination component $\eta(\mathbf{p})$.

An example of the bright channel of an image is shown in Fig. 1.

2.2 Post-processing

Assuming that at least one pixel in a patch $\Omega(i)$ is fully illuminated, one would observe high values in at least one color channel. However, due to low reflectance or exposure, only in few cases this maximum value is actually the full intensity (1.0). As a result, the values of I_{bright} appear slightly darker than our expectation for η. Thus it is natural to assume that, for any image $\mathbf{I}$, at least β % of the pixels are fully illuminated, and their correct values in the bright channel should be 1.0. This assumption can be easily encoded through sorting the values $I_{bright}(i)$ of pixels in descending order, and choosing the value lying at β %, I_{bright}^{β}, as the white point. Then, we can adjust the bright channel values as:

$$\dot{I}_{bright}(i) = min\left\{\frac{I_{bright}(i)}{I_{bright}^{\beta}}, 1.0\right\} \qquad (6)$$

The second concern of the bright channel is that the dark regions in the bright channel image appear shrunk by $\kappa/2$ pixels, where $\kappa \times \kappa$ is the size of the rectangular patches $\Omega(i)$. This can be explained if the max operation in Eq. 1 is seen as a dilation operation. We correct this by expanding the dark regions in the bright channel image by $\kappa/2$ pixels, using an *erosion* morphological operator [8]. An example of the adjusted bright channel is shown in Fig. 1.b.

3   Robust Bright Channel Estimation

The value of the bright channel cue heavily depends on the scale of the corresponding patch and does not always provide a good approximation of $\eta(\mathbf{p})$ at scene point $\mathbf{p}$. For example, a surface with a material of dark color, which is larger in the image than the patch size used to compute the bright channel cue, will appear dark in the bright channel, even if it is fully illuminated. On the other hand, shadows that are smaller than half the patch size will not appear in the bright channel. We present a method to remedy these problems by computing the bright channel cue in multiple scales, and by computing a confidence value for each dark area in the bright channel image.

3.1   Computing Confidence Values

Since surfaces with dark colors can appear as dark areas in the bright channel, even if they are fully illuminated, we seek a way to compute a confidence that each dark area is indeed dark because of illumination effects. In this paper we are particularly interested in cast shadows.

We first obtain a segmentation Υ of the bright channel image, and we seek to compute a confidence value for each segment. This computation is based on the following intuition: Let Ω_1 and Ω_2 be two $m \times n$ patches in the original image, lying on the two sides of a border caused by illumination conditions (Fig. 1.f). If we compute the values of some feature f_I, which characterizes cast shadows, for both patches and compare them, we expect to find that the difference $\Delta f = f_I(\Omega_1) - f_I(\Omega_2)$ is consistent for all such pairs of patches taken across shadow borders in the scene. On the other hand, the difference Δf will be inconsistent across borders that can be attributed to texture or other factors.

The use of a simple feature like hue is enough to effectively compute a set of confidence values for each segment of the segmentation Υ of the bright channel.

Let $\Delta f_I^{hue}(\Omega_1, \Omega_2)$ be the difference in hue between neighboring patches Ω_1 and Ω_2, where Ω_1 lies inside a cast shadow while Ω_2 lies outside. We expect $\Delta f_I^{hue}(\Omega_1, \Omega_2)$ to be consistent for all pairs of patches Ω_1 and Ω_2 on the border of that shadow.

If patches Ω_1 and Ω_2 are chosen to lie on the two sides of the border of a shadow, then all $\Delta f_I^{hue}(\Omega_1, \Omega_2)$ along this border will lie close to a value μ_k that depends on the hue of the light sources that are involved in the formation of this shadow border. If we model the deviations from this value μ_k due to changes in albedo, image noise, etc., with a normal distribution $\mathcal{N}(0, \sigma_k)$, the hue differences $\Delta f_I^{hue}(\Omega_1, \Omega_2)$ will follow a normal distribution:

$$\Delta f_I^{hue}(\Omega_1, \Omega_2) \sim \mathcal{N}(\mu_k, \sigma_k) \tag{7}$$

The distribution of all $\Delta f_I^{hue}(\Omega_1, \Omega_2)$ across all segment borders in segmentation Υ is modeled by a mixture of normal distributions. The parameters of this mixture model are, for each component k, the mean μ_k, the variance σ_k and the mixing factor π_k. We use an Expectation-Maximization algorithm to compute these parameters, while the number of distributions in the mixture is selected by minimizing a quasi-Akaike Information Criterion (QAIC). The confidence for segment $s \in \Upsilon$ is then defined as:

$$p(s) = \frac{1}{|\mathcal{B}_s|} \max_k \sum_{i \in \mathcal{B}_s} P_k\left(\Delta f_I^{hue}(\Omega_1(i), \Omega_2(i))\right), \tag{8}$$

where $\mathcal{B}_s$ is the set of all border pixels of segment s, k identifies the mixture components, and, for patches $\Omega_1(i)$ and $\Omega_2(i)$ on the two sides of border pixel i, $P_k\left(\Delta f_I^{hue}(\Omega_1(i), \Omega_2(i))\right)$ is the probability density corresponding to Gaussian component k (weighed by the mixture factor π_k).

We take advantage of one more cue to improve the estimation of $p(s)$: we expect that, for every neighboring pair Ω_1, Ω_2, with Ω_1 lying inside the shadow and Ω_2 outside, the value of each of the three color channels will be decreasing to the direction of Ω_1:

$$\frac{1}{|\Omega_1|} \sum_{i \in \Omega_1} I^c(i) - \frac{1}{|\Omega_2|} \sum_{i \in \Omega_2} I^c(i) < 0, \forall c \in \{r, g, b\} \tag{9}$$

If the percentage of patch pairs that violate this assumption for segment s is bigger than θ_{dec}, we set $p(s)$ to 0.

3.2 Multi-scale Computation

We mentioned earlier the trade-off associated with the patch size κ used to compute the bright channel cue. One can overcome this limitation through computating the bright channel in multiple scales and combining the results. The term "scale" refers here to the patch size $\kappa \times \kappa$.

For each scale j of a total N_s scales, a confidence value is computed for each pixel. We combine the confidences from all scales in a final confidence map, by setting the final confidence of each pixel i to

$$p_s(i) = \left(\prod_{j=0}^{N_s} p_s^{(j)}(i) \right)^{\frac{1}{N_s}},$$ (10)

where $p_s^{(j)}(i)$ is the confidence of segment s at scale j, and s is the segment to which pixel i belongs at scale j. Notice that the segmentation is different at each scale, since it is performed on the bright channel values, which depends on κ. We set the bright channel value of any pixel i with confidence $p_s(i) < \xi$ to 1.0. For the rest of the pixels, the final bright channel value is the value computed with the smallest patch size κ_j.

Fig. 1 shows that the use of confidence values significantly improves the results of the bright channel. While the unfiltered bright channel included every dark surface in the image, the result after computing the confidence values includes mainly values related to shadows. These measurements will be used for a global formulation that involves optimal cast shadows detection and illumination estimation in the next section.

4   An MRF Model for Shadow Detection

In this section we present an alternative method to refine the bright channel values, by combining them with well-known illumination-invariant representations of the input image. Graphical models can efficiently fuse different cues within a unified probabilistic framework. Here we describe an MRF model which fuses a number of different shadow cues to achieve higher quality shadow estimation. In this model, the per-pixel shadow values are associated on one hand with the recovered bright channel values, and on the other with a number of illumination invariant representations of the original image.

4.1   Illumination Invariants

Separating shadows from texture is a difficult problem. In our case, we want to reason about gradients in the original image and attribute them to either changes in shadow or to texture variations. For this purpose, we use three illumination-invariant image representations. Ideally, an illumination-invariant representation of the original image will not contain any information related to shadows. Having such a representation, we can compare gradients in the original image with gradients in the illumination-invariant representation to attribute the gradient to either shadows/shading or texture. Having identified shadow borders this way, we can produce a set of labels identifying shadows in the original image.

Illumination-invariant image cues are not sufficient in the general case, however, and more complicated reasoning is necessary for more accurate shadow detection. An example of this can be seen in Fig.2, which shows the illumination invariant features we use for an example image. Edges due to illumination, although dimmer, are still noticeable, while some texture edges are not visible.

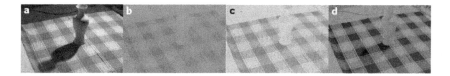

Fig. 2. Illumination invariant images: a) original image, b) normalized rgb, c) $c_1c_2c_3$, d) the 1d illumination invariant image obtained using the approach in [4]. Notice that in all three illumination invariant images, the shadow is much less visible than in the original.

4.2   Illumination-Invariant Cues

Photometric color invariants are functions which describe each image point, while disregarding shading and shadows. These functions are demonstrated to be invariant to a change in the imaging conditions, such as viewing direction, object's surface orientation and illumination conditions. Some examples of photometric invariant color features are normalized RGB, hue, saturation, $c_1c_2c_3$ and $l_1l_2l_3$ [9]. A more complicated illumination invariant representation specifically targeted to shadows is described in [4]. Other interesting invariants that could be exploited are described in [10], [11], [12]. In this work, three illumination-invariant representations are integrated into our model: normalized rgb, $c_1c_2c_3$ and the representation proposed in [4] (displayed in Fig. 2). It is however very easy to add or substitute more illumination invariant representations.

The $c_1c_2c_3$ invariant color features are defined as:

$$c_k(x, y) = \arctan \frac{\rho_k(x, y)}{max\{\rho_{(k+1)mod3}(x, y), \rho_{(k+2)mod3}(x, y)\}} \tag{11}$$

where $\rho_k(x, y)$ is the k-th RGB color component for pixel (x, y).

We only use the $1d$ illumination invariant representation proposed in [4]. For this representation, a vector of illuminant variation e is estimated. The illumination invariant features are defined as the projection of the log-chromaticity vector x' of the pixel color with respect to color channel p to a vector $e^\perp$ orthogonal to e:

$$I' = \mathbf{x}'^T e^\perp \tag{12}$$

$$x'_j = \frac{\rho_k}{\rho_p}, k \in 1, 2, 3, k \neq p, j = 1, 2 \tag{13}$$

and ρ_k represents the k-th RGB component.

These illumination invariant features assume narrow-band camera sensors, Planckian illuminants and a known sensor response, which requires calibration. We circumvent the known sensor response requirement by using the entropy-minimization procedure proposed in [3] to calculate the illuminant variation direction e. Futhermore, it has been shown that the features extracted this way are sufficiently illumination-invariant, even if the other two assumptions above are not met ([4]).

4.3 The MRF Model

In this section we describe an MRF model that models the relationship of a brightness cue such as the bright channel with the illumination invariant cues, in order to obtain a shadow label for each pixel. Intuitively, through this MRF model we seek to obtain labelings that correspond to shadow edges where there is a transition in the bright channel value, but no significant transition/edge appears at the same site of an illumination-invariant representation of the image.

The proposed MRF has the topology of a 2D lattice and consists of one node for each image pixel $i \in \mathcal{P}$. The 4-neighborhood system [13] composes the edge set $\mathcal{E}$ between pixels. The energy of our MRF model has the following form:

$$E(\mathbf{x}) = \sum_{i \in \mathcal{P}} \phi_i(x_i) + \sum_{(i,j) \in \mathcal{E}} \psi_{i,j}(x_i, x_j), \tag{14}$$

where $\phi_i(x_i)$ is the singleton potential for pixel nodes and $\psi_{i,j}(x_i, x_j)$ is the pairwise potential defined on a pair of neighbor pixels. The singleton potential has the following form:

$$\phi_i(x_i) = \left(x_i - \dot{I}_{bright}(i) \right)^2, \tag{15}$$

where $\dot{I}_{bright}(i)$ is the value of the bright channel for pixel i. The pairwise potential has the form:

$$\psi_{i,j}(x_i, x_j) = (x_i - x_j)^2 \left(min_k \{ I_{invar}^{(k)}(i) - I_{invar}^{(k)}(j) \} \right)^2, \tag{16}$$

where $I_{invar}^{(k)}(i)$ is the value of the k-th illumination invariant representation of the image at pixel i. Note that our MRF model is modular with respect to the illumination invariants used. Other cues can easily be integrated.

The latent variable x_i for pixel node $i \in \mathcal{P}$ represents the quantized shadow intensity at pixel i. We can perform cast shadows detection through a minimization over the MRF's energy defined in Eq. 14:

$$\mathbf{x}^{opt} = \arg \min_{\mathbf{x}} E(\mathbf{x}) \tag{17}$$

To minimize the energy of this MRF model we can use existing MRF inference methods such as TRW-S [14], the QPBO algorithm [15,16] with the fusion move [17], etc. The latter was used for the experimental results presented in the next section.

5 Experimental Validation

In this section we present qualitative and quantitative results with the bright channel, and we show further results in an example application in illumination estimation from shadows.

Fig. 3. Results with images from the dataset by [6]. From left to right: the original image; the (unrefined) bright channel; the bright channel refined using confidence estimation; the bright channel refined using the MRF model; the ground truth. These examples show advantages and weaknesses of the two refinement methods.

5.1 Quantitative Evaluation

We evaluated our approach on the dataset provided by [6], which contains 356 images and the corresponding ground truth for the shadow labels. In order to convert the bright channel values to a 0-1 shadow labeling, we used simple thresholding. The pixel classification rates are presented in table 1. Example results can be found in Fig. 3. Fig. 5 shows a case where our algorithm fails, due to very large uniformly dark surfaces.

Table 1. Pixel classification results for the unrefined bright channel (using a single patch size $\kappa = 6$ pixels); the bright channel refined using confidence values and 4 scales; our MRF model with the bright channel (using a single patch size $\kappa = 6$ pixels); and our MRF model with pixel brightness in the LAB color space instead of the bright channel for the singleton potentials.

method	classification rate (%)	false positives (%)	false negatives (%)
bright channel	83.52	13.16	3.31
bright channel + confidence	84.61	11.21	4.17
bright channel + MRF	85.88	8.83	5.28
brightness + MRF	52.53	46.31	1.15

5.2 Simple Illumination Estimation

We can use the bright channel image to perform illumination estimation from shadows. As a proof of concept, we describe a very simple voting method in Algorithm 1, which is in most cases able to recover an illumination estimate given simple 3D geometry of the scene.

The idea is that, shadow pixels that are not explained from the discovered light sources vote for the occluded light directions. The pixels that are not in

---

Algorithm 1. Voting to initialize illumination estimate

Lights Set: $\mathcal{L} \leftarrow \varnothing$
Direction Set: $\mathcal{D} \leftarrow$ all the nodes of a unit geodesic sphere
Pixel Set: $\mathcal{P} \leftarrow$ all the pixels in the observed image
loop
    votes[$\mathbf{d}$] $\leftarrow$ 0, $\forall \mathbf{d} \in \mathcal{D}$
    for all pixel $i \in \mathcal{P}$ **do**
        for all direction $\mathbf{d} \in \mathcal{D} \setminus \mathcal{L}$ **do**
            if $I_{bright}(i) < \theta_S$ **and** $\forall \mathbf{d}' \in \mathcal{L}, c_i(\mathbf{d}') = 0$ **then**
                if $c_i(\mathbf{d}) = 1$ **then** votes[$\mathbf{d}$] $\leftarrow$ votes[$\mathbf{d}$] $+ 1$
            else
                if $c_i(\mathbf{d}) = 0$ **then** votes[$\mathbf{d}$] $\leftarrow$ votes[$\mathbf{d}$] $+ 1$
    $\mathbf{d}^* \leftarrow \arg\max_{\mathbf{d}}(votes[\mathbf{d}])$
    $\mathcal{P}_{\mathbf{d}^*} \leftarrow \{i | c_i(\mathbf{d}^*) = 1 \text{ and } \forall \mathbf{d} \neq \mathbf{d}^*, c_i(\mathbf{d}) = 0\}$
    $\alpha_{\mathbf{d}^*} \leftarrow median \left\{ \frac{1 - I_{bright}(i)}{\max\{-\mathbf{n}(\mathbf{p}(i)) \cdot \mathbf{d}^*, 0\}} \right\}_{i \in \mathcal{P}_{\mathbf{d}^*}}$
    if $\alpha_{\mathbf{d}^*} < \epsilon_{\alpha}$ **then**
        stop the loop
    $\mathcal{L} \leftarrow \mathcal{L} \cup (\mathbf{d}^*, \alpha_{\mathbf{d}^*})$

---

shadow vote for the directions that are not occluded. After discovering a new light source direction, we estimate the associated intensity using the median of the bright channel values of pixels in the shadow of this new light source. The process of discovering new lights stops when the current discovered light does not have a significant contribution to the shadows in the scene. To ensure even sampling of the illumination environment, we choose the nodes of a geodesic sphere of unit radius as the set of potential light directions [18]. The results of the voting algorithm are used to initialize the MRF both in terms of topology and search space leading to more efficient use of discrete optimization. When available, the number of light sources can also be set manually.

Fig. 4. Results with images of cars collected from Flickr. Top row: the original image and a synthetic sun dial rendered with the estimated illumination; Bottom row: the refined bright channel. The geometry consists of the ground plane and a single bounding box for the car.

Fig. 5. A failure case: from left to right, the original image, the bright channel, and the refined bright channel. The uniformly dark road surface is identified as a shadow.

We present results on illumination estimation on images of cars collected from Flickr (Fig. 4). The geometry used in this case was a 3D bounding box representing the car in each image, and a plane representing the ground. The camera parameters were matched by hand so that the 3D model's projection would roughly coincide with the car in the image.

6   Conclusions

In this paper, we presented a simple but effective image cue for the extraction of shadows from a single image, the bright channel cue. We discussed the limitations of this cue, and presented a way to deal with them, by examining the bright channel values at multiple scales and computing confidence values for each dark region using a shadow-dependent feature, such as hue. We further described an MRF model as an alternative way to refine the bright channel cue by combining it with a number of illumination-invariant representations. In the results, we computed the classification accuracy for shadow pixels on a publicly available dataset, we showed examples of the resulting shadow estimates, and we discussed one potential application of the bright channel cue in illumination estimation from shadows. In this application, the low false-negative rate and the relatively accurate shadow estimate we can get from this simple cue makes it possible to tackle a hard problem such illumination estimation with rough geometry information in natural images using simple algorithms such as the voting algorithm we described. In the future, we are interested in incorporating this cue in a more complex shadow detection framework.

Acknowledgments. This work was partially supported by NIH grants 5R01EB7530-2, 1R01DA020949-01 and NSF grants CNS-0627645, IIS-0916286, CNS-0721701.

References

1. Salvador, E., Cavallaro, A., Ebrahimi, T.: Cast shadow segmentation using invariant color features. Computer Vision and Image Understanding 95, 238–259 (2004)
2. Levin, A., Lischinski, D., Weiss, Y.: A closed-form solution to natural image matting. IEEE Transactions on Pattern Analysis and Machine Intelligence 30, 228–242 (2008)

3. Finlayson, G., Drew, M., Lu, C.: Intrinsic Images by Entropy Minimization. In: Pajdla, T., Matas, J. (eds.) ECCV 2004. LNCS, vol. 3023, pp. 582–595. Springer, Heidelberg (2004)

4. Finlayson, G., Hordley, S., Lu, C., Drew, M.: On the removal of shadows from images. IEEE Transactions on Pattern Analysis and Machine Intelligence 28, 59–68 (2006)

5. Shor, Y., Lischinski, D.: The shadow meets the mask: Pyramid-based shadow removal. Computer Graphics Forum 27, 577–586 (2008)

6. Zhu, J., Samuel, K.G.G., Masood, S., Tappen, M.F.: Learning to recognize shadows in monochromatic natural images. In: IEEE Computer Society Conference on Computer Vision and Pattern Recognition, CVPR 2010 (2010)

7. He, K., Sun, J., Tang, X.: Single image haze removal using dark channel prior. In: IEEE Computer Society Conference on Computer Vision and Pattern Recognition, CVPR (2009)

8. Gonzalez, R.C., Woods, R.E.: Digital Image Processing, 3rd edn. Prentice-Hall, Inc. (2006)

9. Gevers, T., Smeulders, A.W.M.: Color based object recognition. Pattern Recognition 32, 453–464 (1997)

10. Geusebroek, J.M., van den Boomgaard, R., Smeulders, A.W.M., Geerts, H.: Color invariance. IEEE Transactions on Pattern Analysis and Machine Intelligence 23, 1338–1350 (2001)

11. van de Weijer, J., Gevers, T., Geusebroek, J.M.: Edge and corner detection by photometric quasi-invariants. IEEE Transactions on Pattern Analysis and Machine Intelligence 27 (2005)

12. Diplaros, A., Gevers, T., Patras, I.: Combining color and shape information for illumination-viewpoint invariant object recognition. IEEE Trans. on Image Processing 15, 1–11 (2006)

13. Boykov, Y., Funka-lea, G.: Graph cuts and efficient n-d image segmentation. International Journal of Computer Vision 70, 109–131 (2006)

14. Kolmogorov, V.: Convergent tree-reweighted message passing for energy minimization. IEEE Transactions on Pattern Analysis and Machine Intelligence 28, 1568–1583 (2006)

15. Hammer, P.L., Hansen, P., Simeone, B.: Roof duality, complementation and persistency in quadratic 0-1 optimization. Mathematical Programming 28, 121–155 (1984)

16. Kolmogorov, V., Rother, C.: Minimizing nonsubmodular functions with graph cuts-a review. IEEE Transactions on Pattern Analysis and Machine Intelligence 29, 1274–1279 (2007)

17. Lempitsky, V., Rother, C., Roth, S., Blake, A.: Fusion moves for markov random field optimization. IEEE Transactions on Pattern Analysis and Machine Intelligence 32, 1392–1405 (2010)

18. Sato, I., Sato, Y., Ikeuchi, K.: Illumination from shadows. IEEE Transactions on Pattern Analysis and Machine Intelligence 25, 290–300 (2003)

Color-Constant Information Embedding

Fan Wang[1] and Roberto Manduchi[2]

[1] Stanford University, Stanford CA 94305, USA
fanw@stanford.edu
[2] University of California, Santa Cruz, Santa Cruz CA 95064, USA
manduchi@soe.ucsc.edu

Abstract. We propose a technique to embed information in the color of a printed surface. One or more reference surfaces are used to help compensate for the color changes due to varying illuminants. Seven different techniques, some of which are novel, are considered for color compensation. Experiments using different performance metrics are presented, providing a comparative assessment of the various algorithms and highlighting the importance of the correct choice of reference surfaces.

1   Introduction

There is a growing interest in technology to embed information in printed matter, in such a way that can be easily accessed by mobile devices such as cell phones. For example, 1-D and 2-D barcodes are often placed in advertisements for products or events, providing a means for anyone with a cell phone equipped with a camera, suitable software, and Internet access, to retrieve more information about the specific product or event. The density of information that can be embedded with this type of markers is limited by the camera resolution and viewing conditions. For example, low illumination requires large exposure time (resulting in motion blur) or high camera gain (resulting in noise). Also, limited depth of field requires precise focusing on the marker, which is sometime problematic with cell phone cameras (for those cell phones that indeed have focusing capabilities).

A simple strategy for adding more information to a marker of a given size is through the use of color. For example, Microsoft's High Capacity Color Barcode (HCCB) technology [1] uses 2-D barcodes enhanced with 4 different colors, resulting in a tremendous increase in the amount of information that can be embedded. By embedding information in a surface's reflectance signature, the spatial density of bars in a marker can be reduced, resulting in better readability from a distance, especially with mobile devices.

Unfortunately, cameras do not take direct reflectance measurements. The color measured by a camera is a function of the reflectance characteristics of the surface as well as of the spectra of the illuminant(s), and of the illumination and viewing geometry. One may partly reduce the influence of these variables by printing markers on Lambertian (opaque) surfaces, but the dependence of the measured color on the illuminant spectrum remains a major impediment to using a large

K.N. Kutulakos (Ed.): ECCV 2010 Workshops, Part II, LNCS 6554, pp. 13–26, 2012.

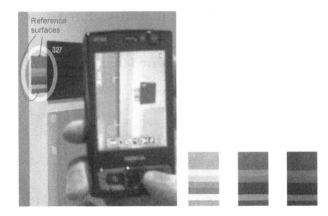

Fig. 1. Left: An example of application of the proposed technique. A marker with 9 color patches (two of which are used for reference) is taken by a cell phone camera. Each color patch contains 7 bits of information. Right: crop-outs from images of the same marker under different illuminants exemplify the dramatic color variations undergone by the patches.

number of colors, as two distinct surfaces may have the same color when lit by different illuminants.

Color constancy is a well known problem, and many partial solutions have been proposed. Our considered application, though, is different from most existing work: rather than normalizing for the unknown illuminant in a general, unconstrained scene, we *design* the marker so as to simplify color constancy. In particular, we add one or more *reference surfaces* next to the unknown, information-carrying surfaces. The color characteristics of the reference surfaces under different illuminants are assumed to be well known (by means of training samples). The idea is that the color of the reference surfaces should give enough information about the illuminant to enable color-constant measurement of the unknown surfaces.

The use of reference surfaces is not new: it is a standard practice in remote sensing, and even regular cameras implement white balancing based on the color of a white surface. Normally, colors are compensated after observation of the reference surface using a diagonal transformation. Although this may be suitable for narrowband channels in multispectral systems, diagonal color compensation is known to be suboptimal for the color matching functions of typical cameras. This is a problem for the quantitative analysis of colors. Thus, in this work we consider several other color compensation algorithm besides the diagonal transformation.

Identifying the unknown, information-carrying surface can be formally expressed as either an *indexing* or a *regression* problem. In the first case, the goal is to determine which among a set of possible surface types best represents the surface in the image. In the second case, we attempt to undo the effect of the specific illuminant, by "rendering" the color of the surface as if seen under a canonical illuminant. In summary, our problem can be expressed as follows:

Problem: Consider an image with R reference surfaces placed coplanar with and close to the "unknown" surface under analysis. All surfaces are Lambertian, and receive light from the same illuminant.

(1) Find the index of the unknown surface within a set of possible surfaces.

(2) Estimate the color of the unknown surface as seen under the canonical illuminant.

We note that the second formulation (regression) is more general in that it addresses the possibility of embedding information via surfaces that are not part of a known data set.

In this contribution, we consider a number of algorithms (some of which are well known, while some are novel) to solve this problem, and present comparative experimental results measuring the accuracy and error using a number R of reference surfaces from 1 to 3.

2 Previous Work

We denote the color of a surface s under illuminant i by $I_{(s)}^{(i)} = [I_{(s),1}^{(i)}, I_{(s),2}^{(i)}, I_{(s),3}^{(i)}]^T$, where $I_{(s),k}^{(i)}$ represents the k-th color channel. A popular model to represent the dependence of the color of the surface to the illuminant is based on the assumption that the spectra of all possible illuminants and of all possible surface reflectances form finite dimensional spaces (of dimension M_i and M_s respectively). For Lambertian (opaque) surfaces, this results in the following bilinear form:

$$I_{(s),k}^{(i)} = \alpha^{(i)T} Q_k \beta_{(s)} \tag{1}$$

where Q_k is an $M_i \times M_s$ matrix with positive entries that only depends on the camera; $\alpha^{(i)}$ only depends on the illuminant and the incidence angle; and $\beta_{(s)}$ only depends on the surface. In particular $\alpha^{(i)}$ and $\beta_{(s)}$ are independent of the color channel k. Let us define

$$\Phi_{(s)} = \left[Q_1 \beta_{(s)} | Q_2 \beta_{(s)} | Q_3 \beta_{(s)} \right] \tag{2}$$

$$\Psi^{(i)} = \left[Q_1^T \alpha^{(i)} | Q_2^T \alpha^{(i)} | Q_3^T \alpha^{(i)} \right]$$

Note that knowledge of $\Phi_{(s)}$ enables *rendering* of the color of the surface s under any illuminant. Tsin *et al.* [2] showed that the matrices $\Phi_{(s)}$ can be estimated using SVD from a collection of images of surfaces under multiple illuminants. A similar idea was presented by Sunkavalli *et al.* [3].

Of special interest are rendering models that use color vectors directly, rather than resorting to an intermediate representation (e.g., the matrices $\Phi_{(s)}$ above). It is well known [4] that if $M_s = 3$, then $I_{(s)}^{(i_2)} = A^{(i_1) \to (i_2)} I_{(s)}^{(i_1)}$, where $A^{(i_1) \to (i_2)} = ((\Psi^{(i_1)})^{-1} \Psi^{i_2})^T$, and we assumed that $\Psi^{(i_1)}$ is full-rank. For a given pair of illuminants, the 3×3 matrix $A^{(i_1) \to (i_2)}$ can be estimated by observation of at least three different surface patches under both illuminants. If the dimension of the reflectance spectra space is further restricted to $M_s = 2$, then it can be shown that the color transformation matrix $A^{(i_1)\to(i_2)}$ can be obtained by measuring the color change of at least two different surfaces.

Finlayson *et al.* [4] showed that, if $M_i = 3$ and $M_s = 2$ (the so–called 3–2 case), only one surface, seen under two different illuminants, is actually needed to estimate $A^{(i_1)\to(i_2)}$. The idea is to perform a suitable change of basis (*spectral sharpening*) in color space: $\hat{I}_{(s)}^{(i)} = T I_{(s)}^{(i)}$ where T is an invertible 3×3 matrix. The columns of T can be chosen as the eigenvectors of the matrix $((\Phi_{(s_1)})^{-1}\Phi_{s_2})^T$, where s_1 and s_2 represent any two different surfaces. It is shown in [4] that in the 3–2 case, the following rendering model applies:

$$\hat{I}_{(s)}^{(i_2)} = D^{(i_1)\to(i_2)}\hat{I}_{(s)}^{(i_1)} \qquad (3)$$

where $D^{(i_1)\to(i_2)}$ is diagonal. Following [4], we will call this a *generalized diagonal* model. Given any two transformed colors $\hat{I}_{(s)}^{(i_1)}$ and $\hat{I}_{(s)}^{(i_2)}$ of the same surface observed under two different illuminants, the k–th diagonal entry of $D_{i_1\to I_2}$ can be computed as $\hat{I}_{(s),k}^{(i_2)}/\hat{I}_{(s),k}^{(i_1)}$.

A simpler version of the previous rendering model, the *diagonal* model, assumes that (3) holds even without the basis change induced by T.

$$I_{(s)}^{(i_2)} = D^{(i_1)\to(i_2)}I_{(s)}^{(i_1)} \qquad (4)$$

It is not difficult to show that this assumption holds true only if each matrix Q_k has only one non–null column.

A different, fully data-driven approach to color constancy was proposed by Miller and Tieu [5]. This algorithm is based on the observation of joint color changes in images due to variation in lighting and other non-geometric camera parameters.

Our stated goal to *index* surfaces in a marker based on the measured color is reminiscent of other color-based indexing techniques (e.g., [6,7]). In contrast with these previous approaches, which focus on the general problem of object recognition in unconstrained environments, our work considers a very precise domain, with contextual information available in the form of reference surfaces.

3   Algorithms

In general, an algorithm to solve the problem stated in the Introduction has three components:

Illuminant estimation: Using the reference surfaces, a representation of the illuminant is obtained.

Surface estimation: A representation of the unknown surface is obtained. This step typically uses the representation of the illuminant found in the previous step.

Rendering/Indexing: The color of the unknown surface is rendered under the canonical illuminant, and the index of the unknown surface in the training data set is found. Indexing is only feasible when the unknown surface is assumed to belong to the training data set.

Below we summarize the algorithms tested in our experiments. The original contributions of this work are marked by the letters [O.C.].

The unknown illuminant (under which the surface is seen) and the canonical illuminant will be denoted by superscripts 'u' and 'c' respectively, while the unknown surface will be denoted by subscript 'u'. Thus, the color of the unknown surface in the image (under unknown illuminant) is $I_{(u)}^{(u)}$, while its color rendered under the canonical illuminant is $I_{(u)}^{(c)}$. We assume that images of a training set of N_s surfaces (which include the references surfaces as well as the unknown surface) under a number N_i of different illuminants (which include the canonical illuminant) have been captured off-line. The color values of the training data set are collected in the following matrices:

$$J_{(s)} = \left[I_{(s)}^{(1)} | I_{(s)}^{(2)} | \dots | I_{(s)}^{(N_i)} \right]^T \ , \ 1 \leq s \leq N_s \tag{5}$$

$$Y^{(i)} = \left[I_{(1)}^{(i)} | I_{(2)}^{(i)} | \dots | I_{(N_s)}^{(i)} \right]^T \ , \ 1 \leq i \leq N_i$$

$$J = \left[J_{(1)} | J_{(2)} | \dots | J_{(N_s)} \right] \ , \ Y = \left[Y^{(1)} | Y^{(2)} | \dots | Y^{(N_i)} \right]$$

We also define:

$$\Phi = \left[\Phi_{(1)} | \Phi_{(2)} | \dots | \Phi_{(N_s)} \right], \Psi = \left[\Psi^{(1)} | \Psi^{(2)} | \dots | \Psi^{(N_i)} \right] \tag{6}$$

$$A = [\alpha^{(1)} | \alpha^{(2)} | \dots | \alpha^{(N_i)}]^T \ , \ B = [\beta_{(1)} | \beta_{(2)} | \dots | \beta_{(N_s)}]^T \tag{7}$$

where the matrices $\Phi_{(s)}$ and $\Psi^{(i)}$ were defined in (2). The bilinear model (1) implies that:

$$J_{(s)} = A\Phi_{(s)} \ , \ Y^{(i)} = B\Psi^{(i)} \ , \ J = A\Phi \ , \ Y = B\Psi \tag{8}$$

Without loss of generality, we assume that the reference surfaces have indices in $[1, 2, \dots, R]$, and therefore their colors under the unknown illuminant are $I_{(1)}^{(u)}, I_{(2)}^{(u)}, \dots, I_{(R)}^{(u)}$.

Algorithm 1: Diagonal Model

Illuminant estimation: The illuminant is characterized by the diagonal rendering matrix $D^{(u) \to (c)}$. To find this matrix, we solve the three least-squares problems:

$$D_{[k]}^{(u) \to (c)} = \arg \min_a \sum_{s=1}^{R} \left(I_{(s),k}^{(c)} - a I_{(s),k}^{(u)} \right)^2 \tag{9}$$

where $D_{[k]}^{(u) \to (c)}$ is the (k, k) entry of the matrix.

Rendering/Indexing: $I^{(c)}_{(u)} = D^{(u)\to(c)}I^{(u)}_{(u)}$. Then indexing is accomplished by finding the surface with the closest color to $I^{(c)}_{(u)}$ among the training surface seen under the canonical illuminant:

$$s_u = \arg\min_{1\le s\le N_s}\|I^{(c)}_{(u)} - I^{(c)}_{(s)}\|^2 \tag{10}$$

Note that this algorithm does not require the "surface estimation" step.

Algorithm 2: Generalized Diagonal Model

This algorithm is identical to Algorithm 1, except that the color vectors are pre-multiplied by a "spectral sharpening" matrix T.

[O.C.] We propose a novel approach to derive a suitable "spectral sharpening" matrix T. We begin by observing that a good matrix T is such that $TY^{(c)}$ is well approximated by $D^{(i)\to(c)}Y^{(i)}$ for all illuminants i in the training data set, where $D^{(i)\to(c)}$ are suitable diagonal matrices. It is easily seen that this is identical to the problem of approximating $Y^{(c)}Y^{(i)\dagger}$ (where $Y^{(i)\dagger}$ is the pseudo-inverse of $Y^{(i)}$) with $T^{-1}D^{(i)\to(c)}T$. Thus, the problem is one of finding the matrix T that produces the best approximate joint diagonalization of the 3×3 matrices $Y^{(c)}Y^{(i)\dagger}$. In our experiments, we solved the joint diagonalization problem using the publicly available Matlab function rjd.m, developed by Jean-Francois Cardoso, which is based on a Jacobi-like iterative technique [8].

Algorithm 3: Surface-to-Surface Diagonal Model [O.C.]

This algorithm is based on the simple observation that, under the same hypothesis in which the diagonal model (4) holds true, the following diagonal relationship holds between the colors of two surfaces s_1, s_2 seen under the same illuminant:

$$I^{(i)}_{(s_2)} = D_{(s_1)\to(s_2)}I^{(i)}_{(s_1)} \tag{11}$$

where $D_{(s_1)\to(s_2)}$ is independent of the illuminant. The proof is trivial, and relies on the fact that diagonal matrices commute.

Surface estimation: The unknown surface is represented by the set of R diagonal matrices $D_{(s)\to(u)}$ mapping the colors $I^{(u)}_{(s)}$ to $I^{(u)}_{(u)}$, where $D_{(s)\to(u),k} = I^{(u)}_{(u),k}/I^{(u)}_{(s),k}$. These matrices represent the relationship between the unknown surface and the reference surfaces in the training data set when seen under the same illuminant.

Rendering/Indexing: The matrices $D_{(s)\to(u)}$ are used to map the color of each reference surface $I^{(c)}_{(s)}$ in the training data set, seen under the canonical illuminant, to a prediction of the color of the unknown surface under the canonical illuminant. These predictions are then averaged together. In formulas:

$$I^{(c)}_{(u)} = \sum_{s=1}^{R} D_{(s)\to(u)}I^{(c)}_{(s)}/R \tag{12}$$

Indexing is accomplished as by (10). Note that this algorithm does not require the "illuminant estimation" step.

Algorithm 4: Surface-to-Surface Multiple Diagonal Model [O.C.]

Illuminant estimation: Rather than considering just the canonical illuminant, as in Algorithms 1 and 2, we look at all illuminants i in the training data set and compute all diagonal matrices $D^{(i)\to(u)}$ mapping the color of any surface under illuminant i to the color of the same surface under the unknown illuminant:

$$D^{(i)\to(u)}_{[k]} = \arg\min_a \sum_{s=1}^{R} \left(I^{(u)}_{(s),k} - aI^{(i)}_{(s),k}\right)^2 \tag{13}$$

Surface estimation: We first render the colors of all surfaces in the data set, as seen under the unknown illuminant:

$$I^{(u)}_{(s)} = \sum_{i=1}^{N_i} D^{(i)\to(u)} I^{(i)}_{(s)} / N_i \tag{14}$$

As in Algorithm 3, the unknown surface is represented by the set of all diagonal matrices $D_{(s)\to(u)}$ mapping the colors $I^{(u)}_{(s)}$ to $I^{(u)}_{(u)}$, where $D_{(s)\to(u),k} = I^{(u)}_{(u),k}/I^{(u)}_{(s),k}$. However, with respect to Algorithm 3, now there are N_s such diagonal matrices.

Rendering/Indexing: This part is identical to Algorithm 3, except that the average prediction $I^{(c)}_{(u)}$ is computed using all N_s images in the data set.

Algorithm 5: Bilinear Model

Let us define $\gamma^{(u)} = (A^\dagger)^T \alpha^{(u)}$ and $\delta_{(u)} = (B^\dagger)^T \beta_{(u)}$, where A, B were defined in (6) and $\alpha^{(u)}$, $\beta_{(u)}$ were defined in (1). Then one easily sees that, as long as $\text{rank}(J) \geq M_i$ and $\text{rank}(Y) \geq M_s$: $I^{(u)}_{(s)} = J^T_{(s)}\gamma^{(u)}$, $I^{(i)}_{(u)} = Y^{(i)T}\delta_{(u)}$. This formulation allows us to express a surface color as a linear function of the training data.

Illuminant estimation: Define $J_{\text{ref}} = \left[J_{(1)}|J_{(2)}|\dots|J_{(R)}\right]$. The unknown illuminant is represented by the vector $\gamma^{(u)}$, where $\gamma^{(u)} = \left(\left[I^{(u)T}_{(1)}|I^{(u)T}_{(2)}|\dots|I^{(u)T}_{(R)}\right]J^\dagger_{\text{ref}}\right)^T$.

Surface estimation: First render all surfaces in the data set, as seen by the unknown illuminant:

$$Y^{(u)} = [J^T_{(1)}\gamma^{(u)}|J^T_{(2)}\gamma^{(u)}|\dots|J^T_{(N_s)}\gamma^{(u)}]^T \tag{15}$$

The unknown surface is represented by the vector $\delta_{(u)}$, computed as follows: $\delta_{(u)} = \left(I^{(u)T}_{(u)}Y^{(u)\dagger}\right)^T$.

Rendering/Indexing: $I^{(c)}_{(u)} = Y^{(c)T}\delta_{(u)}$. Indexing is accomplished as by (10).

Algorithm 6: Bilinear Model (Compact) [O.C.]

A problem with Algorithm 5 is that it requires storage and processing of a conspicuous portion of the training data at run time. In fact, storage requirements and computation would be much lighter if the matrices $\{Q_k\}$ in (1) were available. We introduce in the following an algorithm to estimate matrices $\{\tilde{Q}_k\}$ that are algebraically similar to $\{Q_k\}$. To our knowledge, this is the first time that a direct estimation of these matrices has been proposed.

Let us define: $J_{(s),k} = \left[I_{(s),k}^{(1)}, I_{(s),k}^{(2)}, \ldots, I_{(s),k}^{(N_i)} \right]^T$ and $J_k = \left[J_{(1),k} | J_{(2),k} | \ldots | J_{(N_s),k} \right]$. We observe that $J_k = A Q_k B$ for $1 \leq k \leq 3$. Our algorithm for finding matrices $\{\tilde{Q}_k\}$ that are similar to $\{Q_k\}$ proceeds as follows. We first compute $\tilde{Q}_k(1) = A^\dagger J_k B^\dagger$ for $1 \leq k \leq 3$. Then we iterate the following two steps:

Step 1: For $1 \leq s \leq N_s$, $1 \leq i \leq N_i$, compute:

$$\tilde{\Phi}_{(s)}(n) = \left[\tilde{Q}_1(n)\beta_{(s)} | \tilde{Q}_2(n)\beta_{(s)} | \tilde{Q}_3(n)\beta_{(s)} \right] \tag{16}$$

$$\tilde{\Phi}(n) = \left[\tilde{\Phi}_{(1)}(n) | \tilde{\Phi}_{(2)}(n) | \ldots | \tilde{\Phi}_{(N_s)}(n) \right]$$

$$\tilde{\Psi}^{(i)}(n) = \left[\tilde{Q}_1^T(n)\alpha_{(i)} | \tilde{Q}_2^T(n)\alpha_{(i)} | \tilde{Q}_3^T(n)\alpha_{(i)} \right]$$

$$\tilde{\Psi}(n) = \left[\tilde{\Psi}^{(1)}(n) | \tilde{\Psi}^{(2)}(n) | \ldots | \tilde{\Psi}_{(N_i)}(n) \right]$$

$$\tilde{A}(n) = J\tilde{\Phi}^\dagger(n) \ , \ \tilde{B}(n) = Y\tilde{\Psi}^\dagger(n)$$

Step 2: Compute $\tilde{Q}_k(n+1) = \tilde{A}^\dagger(n) J_k \tilde{B}^\dagger(n)$ $(1 \leq k \leq 3)$.

It is easy to see that at each iteration, the Frobenius norm $e_F(n)$ of the error matrix $J - A\tilde{\Phi}(n)$ can only decrease or remain the same. Step 1 and 2 are iterated until the $e_F(n)/e_F(n-1)$ is lower than a fixed threshold. Note that this algorithm is performed off-line with training data. Once the matrices $\{\tilde{Q}_k\}$ and $\{\tilde{\Phi}_{(s)}\}$ have been computed, on-line color analysis is performed as follows.

Illuminant estimation: Define $\tilde{\Phi}_{\text{ref}} = \left[\tilde{\Phi}_{(1)} | \tilde{\Phi}_{(2)} | \ldots | \tilde{\Phi}_{(R)} \right]$. The unknown illuminant is represented by the vector $\alpha^{(u)}$, computed as follows:

$$\alpha^{(u)} = \left(\left[I_{(1)}^{(u)T} | I_{(2)}^{(u)T} | \ldots | I_{(R)}^{(u)T} \right] \tilde{\Phi}_{\text{ref}}^\dagger \right)^T \tag{17}$$

Surface estimation: The unknown surface is represented by the vector $\beta_{(u)}$, computed as follows:

$$\beta_{(u)} = \left(I_{(u)}^{(u)T} \left[\tilde{Q}_1^T \alpha^{(u)} | \tilde{Q}_2^T \alpha^{(u)} | \tilde{Q}_3^T \alpha^{(u)} \right]^\dagger \right)^T \tag{18}$$

Rendering/Index.: $I^{(c)}_{(u)} = \left[\tilde{Q}_1\beta_{(u)}|\tilde{Q}_2\beta_{(u)}|\tilde{Q}_3\beta_{(u)}\right]^T \alpha^{(c)}$ where $\alpha^{(c)}$ is computed off-line. Indexing is accomplished as by (10).

Note that the matrices $\{\tilde{Q}_k\}$ have dimension $M_i \times M_s$. Appropriate values M_i and M_s can be estimated via eigenvalue analysis. In our experiments, we used $M_i = 12$ and $M_s = 9$.

Algorithm 7: Nearest Neighbor [O.C.]

This algorithm is fully data-driven and doesn't use a model of color formation.

Illuminant estimation: The unknown illuminant is represented by the index i^u defined by $i^u = \arg\min_{1 \leq i \leq N_i} \sum_{s=1}^{R} \|I^{(u)}_{(s)} - I^{(i)}_{(s)}\|^2$.

Surface estimation: The unknown surface is represented by the index s_u defined by $s_u = \arg\min_{1 \leq s \leq N_s}\|I^{(u)}_{(u)} - I^{(i^u)}_{(s)}\|^2$.

Rendering/Indexing: The color of the unknown surface is rendered as seen under the canonical illuminant by $I^{(c)}_{(s_u)}$. The index of the unknown surface is s_u.

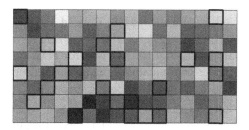

Fig. 2. The $N_s = 128$ surface patches used in the experiments. The 24 patches used for reference are shown with a thick border.

4   Experiments

In order to test our algorithms, we printed a color checkerboard with 512 colors, uniformly sampled in (R,G,B) space. Some of the printed colors were practically indistinguishable from each other, so we selected 128 colors by greedy iterative exclusion from an image of the checkerboard taken by a camera. More precisely, we selected the two patches whose colors (in the image) were most similar, and removed one of them. This operation was repeated until only 128 colors were left. The selected colors are shown in Fig. 2.

Images of the checkerboard were taken under 75 different illumination conditions (one of which is selected as the canonical illuminant). The illumination conditions considered included direct sunlight, diffuse natural light under different overcast conditions, and various types of artificial light (incandescence lamps, neon light, etc.) Two different cameras were used. One was a low-quality camera from a cell phone (Sony Ericsson W580i with white balance set to a fixed value). The other camera was a high-end Canon EOS 350D, producing images in raw (CR2) format. In each image, the color values within a patch (typically covering a few hundred pixels) were averaged together to reduce noise.

The reference colors are chosen from a sample of 24 colors, selected from the 128 colors using k-means. The selected colors are shown with a black border in Fig. 2. Note that this set contains two gray patches. For a given number R, with $1 \leq R \leq 3$, we use all combinations of these 24 colors taken R at a time as reference surface sets. For each choice of reference patch set, all algorithms were tested over each one of the remaining $128 - R$ patches which thus represented the "unknown" patch. In each test, one illuminant is selected, and each unknown patch is analyzed based on the color of the reference patches under the same illuminant.

We devised a cross-validation procedure with a sequence of ten rounds. In each round, half of the illuminants were selected at random to represent the "training" illuminants, meaning that the algorithms were trained based on the color of all surfaces as seen under such illuminants. The algorithms were then tested with each one of the remaining ("test") illuminants. For each test illuminant i chosen in each cross-validation round r, and for each choice of the reference patch set P, we define by *prediction error rate* $E_{\mathrm{p}}^{(i,r,P)}$ the number of unknown patches that were incorrectly indexed by the algorithm, divided by the number of patches considered (in our experiments, 128), and by *rendering error* $E_{\mathrm{r}}^{(i,r,P)}$ the mean (over all considered patches) of the Euclidean error between the rendered color of the unknown patch under canonical illuminant and its correct value. We then compute the average prediction and rendering error $(E_{\mathrm{p,av}}^{(P)}, E_{\mathrm{r,av}}^{(P)})$, along with the maximum prediction and rendering error $(E_{\mathrm{p,max}}^{(P)}, E_{\mathrm{r,max}}^{(P)})$, over all rounds and all illuminants in each round. Note that these values are a function of the choice of reference patch set P. Finally, for each metric considered, we select the reference patch set that minimizes the corresponding error, obtaining $E_{\mathrm{p,av}}$, $E_{\mathrm{r,av}}$, $E_{\mathrm{p,max}}$, or $E_{\mathrm{r,max}}$. We believe that both maximum (worst case) and average errors are important for performance assessment. The results of our experiments are shown in Figs. 3 and 4, along with the optimal reference patches for each metric considered.

4.1   Discussion

When comparing the different algorithms, it is important to bear in mind both performance and computational cost. In terms of implementation, a look-up table could be used to store all possible colors of the reference patches and produce the index of the unknown patch or its color under canonical illumination. Using B bits to represent each color, this table would occupy $2^{RB} \log_2 N_s$ bits of memory for the color indices, and $2^{RB} B$ for the rendered colors. For example, with a 8-bit camera, using $N_s = 128$ as in our experiments and $R = 3$ reference patches, the index table can be stored in 15 Mbytes, while the rendered color table requires 17 Mbytes. This amount of storage is durable even in a hand-held

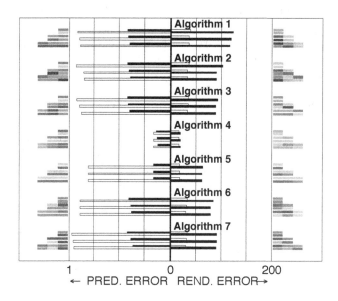

Fig. 3. Results from the experiments using the cell phone camera. For each algorithm, we show results using a number R from 1 to 3 of reference patches. The optimal choice of reference patches for each illuminant and each metric considered is also shown. The left part of the plot shows $E_{p,max}$ (white bars) and $E_{p,ave}$ (black bars). The right part shows $E_{r,max}$ (black bars) and $E_{r,av}$ (white bars).

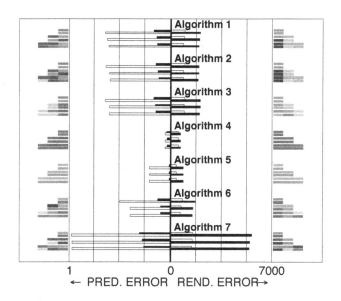

Fig. 4. Results from the experiments using the high-end camera. See caption of Fig. 3

device such as a cell phone. For a larger pixel depth, feasibility of a look-up table depends on the number of reference patches being used.

If online computation is necessary, the fastest techniques are Algorithms 1, 2 and 3, which have negligible complexity. Algorithm 4 and 7 have complexity that is linear with $N_s N_i$. The bulk of complexity of Algorithm 5 is in the computation of the pseudoinverse of a matrix of size $N_s \times 3$ (remember that $N_s = 128$ in our experiments). Algorithm 6 requires computation of the pseudoinverse of a matrix of size $M_s \times 3$ where, as mentioned earlier, M_s was set to 9 in our experiments.

As expected, the tests with the high-end camera produced better accuracy. Note that the the images with this camera had 16 bits per pixel, which explains the higher error values recorded (since each color channels take values from 0 to $2^{16} - 1$). The finer quantization, and a presumably more linear sensor response than the cell phone camera, are likely to account for the better performance of this camera. Note in passing that we have not considered photometric camera calibration, a technique that could improve the quality of the results.

Comparative analysis of the algorithms show that the Algorithms 1, 2 and 3 give similar performances. As expected, the "sharpening" technique of Algorithm 2 improves on the simple diagonal model of Algorithm 1, although only by a small amount. Note that the worst-case scenario prediction error rate $E_{p,max}$ for these algorithms is above 0.5 for both camera. This means that, even with the best choice of reference patches, there exists an illuminant such that half of the patches are misclassified.

The best performing technique is clearly Algorithm 4, which provides the smallest error under all metrics. The worst case prediction error rate $E_{p,max}$ is equal to 0.16 using three reference patches for the camera cellphone case, and 0.03 for the high-end camera. The worst-case rendering error $E_{r,max}$ is equal to 20 for the 8-bit camera and 720 for the 16-bit camera.

The bilinear model (Algorithm 5) gives good results in terms of average errors, but the worst-case prediction error rates are much higher. Its "compact" version (Algorithm 6) gives worse results, likely due to the some inaccuracy in the computation of the matrices $\{Q_k\}$. However, note that Algorithm 6 still performs better than the diagonal models algorithms 1–3, at least for the high-end camera, and has lower complexity than the bilinear model (Algorithm 5). The data-driven approach (Algorithm 7) gives unsatisfactory results overall.

In general, increasing the number of reference patches improves performance, but this improvement is surprisingly small. In fact, in very few cases, adding one more reference patch does not reduce the error at all. In Figs. 3 and 4, these situations lead to some colors being repeated in the optimal reference patch set.

In order to highlight the dependence of the system's performance on the choice of a reference patch, we show in Fig. 5 the values of $E_{r,av}$ for Algorithm 4 for $R = 1$, as a function of the chosen reference patch (all 128 possible patches are considered here, rather than just the 24 shown in Fig. 2) and for a chosen set of training illuminants. Note that the best reference patches have low color saturation values. Indeed, the 20% best performing patches have median saturation equal to 0.5, while the 20% worst performing patches have median saturation equal to 1 (where 'saturation' is defined according to the HSV color space). This confirms the intuitive notion that colors with a broad spectrum are preferable to colors with a narrow spectrum for this application. However, our experiments also shows that white or gray are not necessarily the best reference colors.

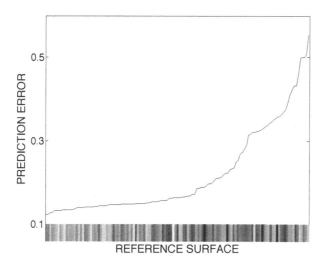

Fig. 5. Values of $E_{p,av}$ for Algorithm 4 with $R = 1$ as a function of the chosen reference patch (images taken by the cell phone camera).

5   Conclusions

Embedding information in printed color is a promising technique, but special care is required to solve the "color constancy" problem. We have presented experimental results comparing seven different algorithms that use one or more reference surfaces to undo the effect of the unknown illuminant. The results, in terms of accuracy and rendering error, are, in our opinion, encouraging. In particular, one of the original algorithms proposed here (Algorithm 4) has excellent accuracy.

Of course, there are other issues besides color constancy that may hinder this approach. For example, printed colors may fade with time unless specialized inks and substrate are used. Noise is also an important factor, especially when the color marker is seen from a distance (resulting in a small foreshortened area) or with low illumination. Still, we believe that this technology has serious potential as a practical means for information embedding, by itself or in conjunction with other techniques such as barcodes.

Acknowledgement. This material is based upon work supported by the National Science Foundation under Grant No. IIS - 0835645.

References

1. Parikh, D., Jancke, G.: Localization and segmentation of a 2D high capacity color barcode. In: Proceedings of the 2008 IEEE Workshop on Applications of Computer Vision (WACV 2008), pp. 1–6. IEEE Computer Society, Washington, DC (2008)
2. Tsin, Y., Collins, R.T., Ramesh, V., Kanade, T.: Bayesian color constancy for outdoor object recognition. In: IEEE Computer Vision and Pattern Recognition (CVPR), pp. 1132–1139 (2001)
3. Sunkavalli, K., Romeiro, F., Matusik, W., Zickler, T., Pfister, H.: What do color changes reveal about an outdoor scene? In: Proc. IEEE CVPR (2008)
4. Finlayson, G., Drew, M., Funt, B.: Diagonal transforms suffice for color constancy. In: Proceedings of Fourth International Conference on Computer Vision, pp. 164–171 (1993)
5. Miller, E., Tieu, K.: Color eigenflows: Statistical modeling of joint color changes. In: Proc. of International Conference on Computer Vision (ICCV), vol. 1, pp. 607–614 (2001)
6. Swain, M.J., Ballard, D.H.: Color indexing. International Journal of Computer Vision 7, 11–32 (1991)
7. Funt, B.V., Finlayson, G.D.: Color constant color indexing. IEEE Transactions on Pattern Analysis and Machine Intelligence 17, 522–529 (1995)
8. Cardoso, J.F., Souloumiac, A.: Jacobi angles for simultaneous diagonalization. SIAM J. Matrix Anal. Appl. 17, 161–164 (1996)

Bi-affinity Filter: A Bilateral Type Filter for Color Images

Mithun Das Gupta and Jing Xiao

Epson Research and Development,
San Jose, California, USA
{mdasgupta,xiaoj}@erd.epson.com

Abstract. We propose a new filter called Bi-affinity filter for color images. This filter is similar in structure to the bilateral filter. The proposed filter is based on the color line model, which does not require the explicit conversion of the RGB values to perception based spaces such as CIELAB. The bi-affinity filter measures the affinity of a pixel to a small neighborhood around it and weighs the filter term accordingly. We show that this method can perform at par with standard bilateral filters for color images. The small edges of the image are usually enhanced leading to a very easy image enhancement filter.

Keywords: Bilateral filter, RGB color filtering, image matting, matting Laplacian.

1   Introduction

Bilateral filter was originally proposed by Tomasi and Manduchi [1]. The principle idea behind such a filtering operation is to combine information from spatial domain as well as feature domain. It can be represented as

$$\mathbf{h}(x) = \frac{1}{k(x)} \sum_{y \in \Omega_x} f_s(x, y) g_r(\mathbf{I}(x), \mathbf{I}(y)) \mathbf{I}(y) \qquad (1)$$

where $\mathbf{I}$ and $\mathbf{h}$ are the input and output images respectively, x and y are pixel locations over the image grid, Ω_x is the neighborhood induced around the central pixel x, $f_s(x, y)$ measures the spatial affinity between pixels at x and y and $g_r(\mathbf{I}(x), \mathbf{I}(y))$ denotes the feature/measurement/photometric affinity. $k(x)$ is the normalization term given by

$$k(x) = \sum_{y \in \Omega_x} f_s(x, y) g_r(\mathbf{I}(x), \mathbf{I}(y)) \qquad (2)$$

The spatial and range filters (f, g respectively), are commonly set to be Gaussian filters

$$f_s(x, y) = exp(\frac{-\|x - y\|_2^2}{2\sigma_s^2}), \quad g_r(u, v) = exp(\frac{-\|u - v\|_2^2}{2\sigma_r^2})$$

K.N. Kutulakos (Ed.): ECCV 2010 Workshops, Part II, LNCS 6554, pp. 27–40, 2012.

parameterized by the variances σ_s, σ_r. The range filter penalizes distance in the feature space and hence the filter has an inherent edge preserving property. Due to this important property bilateral filter has been one of the most widely used filtering techniques within computer vision community.

Bilateral filter is a non-linear filter and as such many researchers have proposed techniques to decompose the non-linear filter into a sum of separable one dimensional filters or similar cascaded representations [2]. Singular value decomposition of the 2D kernel is one such approach which has been proposed by [3,4]. Paris *et al.* [5] proposed an approximation of the bilateral filter by filtering sub-sampled copies of the image with discrete intensity kernels, and recombining the results using linear interpolation.

Recently numerous researches have identified the run-time of the bilateral filter as the critical bottleneck and a few techniques have been proposed which render the filtering operation almost constant time, albeit with larger space requirements [6,7] and behavioral approximations. The research into improving the filter performance heavily relies on the form of the filters which are applied in the range as well as spatial domain. Porikli's method [6] can be entirely broken down to an approximation of a product of a box filter for smoothing and a polynomial or 4th order Taylor series approximation of a Gaussian kernel.

Traditionally, researchers have overlooked one of the most important shortfalls of the bilateral filter, which is a unified handling of multi-channel color images. This is due to the independence assumption within the color channels, such that the filter processes each channel on its own. As a direct consequence, bilateral filter produces color artifacts at sharp color edges. One of the remedies proposed in the original work by Tomasi *et al.* [1] was to convert from RGB space to CIELAB space. According to them, once the image is converted to the CIELAB space the channel wise bilateral filter does not produce such artifacts. We try to investigate further into this weakness and propose a new technique which works at par with the transformed domain techniques which have been the standard practices within the community so far.

2   Color Models

The deterioration of bilateral filter for RGB space seems to indicate that one constant range filter is probably not enough to capture the edge variations in all the channels, and hence a conversion to a suitable space such as CIELAB, which is perceptually more uniform than RGB, is performed. Though this transformation is very fast and can be implemented in hardware, this does not preclude the research in alleviating this necessity. This inherent shortcoming of bilateral filter to work in the RGB space can be traced back to the idea of quantifying the nearness of the color of two pixels within some spatial neighborhood. To determine whether two pixels have the same real world color, the color coordinates of a generic color model are used. Any generic color model assumes either there is no color distortion in the neighborhood, or there is an identical color distortion for all imaging conditions. In practice, when dealing with real world images of an unknown source, these assumptions are rarely true as scene surface color is distorted differently in different images as well as different image regions, depending on the scene and camera settings.

2.1   Color Line Model

The introduction of color lines has been attributed to Omer *et al.* [8], who proposed the idea that the cluster of pixel colors in the RGB space appear to be mostly tubular regions, thereby adhering to the fact that most small regions in natural images can be decomposed into a linear combination of 2 colors. This has the obvious potential in edge preserving filtering domain, since it brings down the estimation problem of a valid range filter from 3 channels to 2.

When looking at the RGB histogram of real world images (Fig. 1), it can be clearly observed that the histogram is very sparse, and it is structured. Color line model exploits these two properties of color histograms by describing the elongated color clusters. It results in an image specific color representation that has two important properties: robustness to color distortion and a compact description of colors in an image. This idea has been used for image matting [9,10], Bayer demosaicing [11] and more recently for image de-noising and de-blurring [12,13]. The matting idea can be further utilized in edge preserving filter applications by removing the constant range filter all-together. The 2 color characteristics of a small patch can be exploited to evaluate the best range variance for the patch itself. This idea is the key intuition behind the new filter introduced in this work.

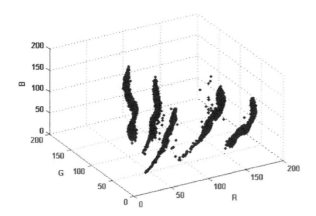

Fig. 1. RGB color histogram adapted from [8]

2.2   Closed Form Matting

The two-color model states that any pixel color I_i can be represented as a linear combination of two colors P and S, where these colors are piecewise smooth and can be derived from local properties within a small neighborhood containing the pixel i.

$$I_i = \alpha_i P + (1 - \alpha_i)S, \quad \forall i \in w, \quad 0 \le \alpha_i \le 1 \tag{3}$$

where w is a small patch. α is called the *matting coefficient*. The patch size is a key parameter in this model, as it is true only for *small* neighborhoods. As the resolution and the size of the images grow, so should the window size as well, to capture a valid neighborhood. For color images, it was proved by Levin et al. [10], that if the color line property is obeyed then the 4D linear model satisfied by the matting coefficient, within a small window, at each pixel can be written as

$$\alpha_i = \sum_c a^c I_i^c + b, \quad \forall i \in w, \quad c \in \{1, 2, 3\} \tag{4}$$

where c is the index over the color channels. Given such a model we can formulate the cost function for evaluating the matting coefficient α. For an image with N pixels we define the cost as

$$J(\boldsymbol{\alpha}, \mathbf{a}, b) = \sum_{k \in N} \left(\sum_{i \in w_k} (\alpha_i - \sum_c a_k^c I_i^c - b_k)^2 + \epsilon \sum_c a_k^{c\,2} \right) \tag{5}$$

where w_k is a small window around pixel k and $\mathbf{a} = \{a_i^c\}$, for all $i = [1, N]$. ϵ is a regularization weight for uniqueness as well as smoothness of the solution.

Theorem 1. *Let $J(\boldsymbol{\alpha}) \doteq \min_{\mathbf{a},b} J(\boldsymbol{\alpha}, \mathbf{a}, b)$, then $J(\boldsymbol{\alpha}) = \boldsymbol{\alpha}^T L \boldsymbol{\alpha}$, where L is an $N \times N$ matrix, whose ij^{th} element is given by*

$$\sum_{k|(i,j) \in w_k} (\delta_{ij} - \frac{1}{|w_k|}(1 + (\mathbf{I}_i - \boldsymbol{\mu}_k)^T \tilde{\boldsymbol{\Sigma}}_k^{-1}(\mathbf{I}_j - \boldsymbol{\mu}_k))) \tag{6}$$

where δ_{ij} is the Kronecker delta, $\boldsymbol{\mu}_k$ is a 3×1 mean vector of colors inside the kth window with both i and j as members, $\mathbf{I}_i$ and $\mathbf{I}_j$ are the color vectors at location i and j, $\tilde{\boldsymbol{\Sigma}}_k = \boldsymbol{\Sigma}_k + \frac{\epsilon}{|w_k|} I_3$, where $\boldsymbol{\Sigma}_k$ is the 3×3 covariance matrix, $|w_k|$ is the cardinality of the window and I_3 is the 3×3 identity matrix.

Proof. We would like to point out that, Levin et al. [10], prove the theorem based on an extension, from a gray scale case. We present the full 3-channel proof which can be readily extended to more channels if necessary.

Rewriting Eq. 5 in a matrix notation, where $\|.\|$ denotes the 2-norm,

$$J(\boldsymbol{\alpha}, \mathbf{a}, b) = \sum_k \|\mathbf{G}_k . \bar{\mathbf{a}}_k - \boldsymbol{\alpha}_k\| \tag{7}$$

where

$$\mathbf{G}_k = \begin{bmatrix} I_1^R & I_1^G & I_1^B & 1 \\ \vdots & \vdots & \vdots & \vdots \\ I_{w_k}^R & I_{w_k}^G & I_{w_k}^B & 1 \\ \sqrt{\epsilon} & 0 & 0 & 0 \\ 0 & \sqrt{\epsilon} & 0 & 0 \\ 0 & 0 & \sqrt{\epsilon} & 0 \end{bmatrix}, \quad \bar{\mathbf{a}}_k = \begin{bmatrix} a_k^R \\ a_k^G \\ a_k^B \\ b \end{bmatrix}, \quad \boldsymbol{\alpha}_k = \begin{bmatrix} \alpha_1 \\ \vdots \\ \alpha_{w_k} \\ 0 \\ 0 \\ 0 \end{bmatrix} \tag{8}$$

Note that another representation of $\mathbf{G}_k$ is possible where the last 3 rows are combined to a single row of the form $[\sqrt{\epsilon} \ \sqrt{\epsilon} \ \sqrt{\epsilon} \ 0]$, but this form leads to an unstable covariance matrix. For known $\boldsymbol{\alpha}_k$, we can solve the least square problem

$$\bar{\mathbf{a}}_k^* = \arg\min \|\mathbf{G}_k.\bar{\mathbf{a}}_k - \boldsymbol{\alpha}_k\| \tag{9}$$
$$= (\mathbf{G}_k^T \mathbf{G}_k)^{-1} \mathbf{G}_k^T \boldsymbol{\alpha}_k \tag{10}$$

Substituting this solution in Eq. 7, and denoting $\mathbf{L}_k = I_{|w_k|+3} - \mathbf{G}_k(\mathbf{G}_k^T\mathbf{G}_k)^{-1}\mathbf{G}_k^T$, where $I_{|w_k|+3}$ is the identity matrix of size $(|w_k| + 3)$, we obtain, $J(\boldsymbol{\alpha}) = \sum_k \|\mathbf{L}_k \boldsymbol{\alpha}_k\| = \sum_k (\boldsymbol{\alpha}_k^T \mathbf{L}_k^T \mathbf{L}_k \boldsymbol{\alpha}_k)$. Making the additional observation that

$$\mathbf{L}_k^T \mathbf{L}_k = (I_{|w_k|+3} - \mathbf{G}_k(\mathbf{G}_k^T\mathbf{G}_k)^{-1}\mathbf{G}_k^T)^T (I_{|w_k|+3} - \mathbf{G}_k(\mathbf{G}_k^T\mathbf{G}_k)^{-1}\mathbf{G}_k^T)$$
$$= I_{|w_k|+3} + \mathbf{G}_k(\mathbf{G}_k^T\mathbf{G}_k)^{-1}\mathbf{G}_k^T\mathbf{G}_k(\mathbf{G}_k^T\mathbf{G}_k)^{-1}\mathbf{G}_k^T - 2\mathbf{G}_k(\mathbf{G}_k^T\mathbf{G}_k)^{-1}\mathbf{G}_k^T$$
$$= I_{|w_k|+3} - \mathbf{G}_k(\mathbf{G}_k^T\mathbf{G}_k)^{-1}\mathbf{G}_k^T = \mathbf{L}_k$$

we can write $J(\boldsymbol{\alpha}) = \sum_k (\boldsymbol{\alpha}_k^T \mathbf{L}_k \boldsymbol{\alpha}_k)$. To complete the proof we need to find the expression for $\mathbf{L}_k|_{i,j}$.

Noting the identity $E[X^2] = \sigma_{XX}^2 + E[X]^2$, denoting the individual channel means $E[R]$ as R, we can write

$$\mathbf{G}_k^T \mathbf{G}_k = |w_k| \left[\overbrace{\underbrace{\begin{pmatrix} \sigma_{RR}^2 + R^2 + \frac{\epsilon}{|w_k|} & \sigma_{RG}^2 + RG & \sigma_{RB}^2 + RB \\ \sigma_{GR}^2 + GR & \sigma_{GG}^2 + G^2 + \frac{\epsilon}{|w_k|} & \sigma_{GB}^2 + GB \\ \sigma_{BR}^2 + BR & \sigma_{BG}^2 + BG & \sigma_{BB}^2 + B^2 + \frac{\epsilon}{|w_k|} \end{pmatrix}}_{A} \overbrace{\begin{pmatrix} R \\ G \\ B \end{pmatrix}}^{D} \\ \underbrace{(R \qquad\qquad G \qquad\qquad B)}_{D^T} \qquad\qquad \underbrace{1}_{C}} \right] \tag{11}$$

where we have divided the matrix into 4 components. Note that $D = \boldsymbol{\mu}_k$ for the kth window. Inverse of the above system can now be written as ([14])

$$(\mathbf{G}_k^T \mathbf{G}_k)^{-1} = \frac{1}{|w_k|} \begin{bmatrix} P & Q \\ R & S \end{bmatrix}$$

$$P = (A - DC^{-1}D^T)^{-1} = (A - DD^T)^{-1}$$

$$= \begin{bmatrix} \sigma_{RR}^2 + \frac{\epsilon}{|w_k|} & \sigma_{RG}^2 & \sigma_{RB}^2 \\ \sigma_{GR}^2 & \sigma_{GG}^2 + \frac{\epsilon}{|w_k|} & \sigma_{GB}^2 \\ \sigma_{BR}^2 & \sigma_{BG}^2 & \sigma_{BB}^2 + \frac{\epsilon}{|w_k|} \end{bmatrix}^{-1} = \tilde{\boldsymbol{\Sigma}}_k^{-1}$$

$$Q = -P(DC^{-1}) = -PD = -\tilde{\boldsymbol{\Sigma}}_k^{-1}\boldsymbol{\mu}_k$$

$$R = -(C^{-1}D^T)P = -D^T P = -\boldsymbol{\mu}_k^T \tilde{\boldsymbol{\Sigma}}_k^{-1}$$

$$S = C^{-1} - R(DC^{-1}) = 1 - RD = 1 + \boldsymbol{\mu}_k^T \tilde{\boldsymbol{\Sigma}}_k^{-1} \boldsymbol{\mu}_k$$

Putting all the terms together, we can write

$$(\mathbf{G}_k^T\mathbf{G}_k)^{-1} = \frac{1}{|w_k|}\begin{bmatrix} \tilde{\boldsymbol{\Sigma}}_k^{-1} & -\tilde{\boldsymbol{\Sigma}}_k^{-1}\boldsymbol{\mu}_k \\ -\boldsymbol{\mu}_k^T\tilde{\boldsymbol{\Sigma}}_k^{-1} & 1+\boldsymbol{\mu}_k^T\tilde{\boldsymbol{\Sigma}}_k^{-1}\boldsymbol{\mu}_k \end{bmatrix} \tag{12}$$

$$\mathbf{G}_k(\mathbf{G}_k^T\mathbf{G}_k)^{-1} = \frac{1}{|w_k|}\begin{bmatrix} (\mathbf{I}_1-\boldsymbol{\mu}_k)^T\tilde{\boldsymbol{\Sigma}}_k^{-1} & 1-(\mathbf{I}_1-\boldsymbol{\mu}_k)^T\tilde{\boldsymbol{\Sigma}}_k^{-1}\boldsymbol{\mu}_k \\ (\mathbf{I}_2-\boldsymbol{\mu}_k)^T\tilde{\boldsymbol{\Sigma}}_k^{-1} & 1-(\mathbf{I}_2-\boldsymbol{\mu}_k)^T\tilde{\boldsymbol{\Sigma}}_k^{-1}\boldsymbol{\mu}_k \\ \vdots & \vdots \\ (\mathbf{I}_{w_k}-\boldsymbol{\mu}_k)^T\tilde{\boldsymbol{\Sigma}}_k^{-1} & 1-(\mathbf{I}_{w_k}-\boldsymbol{\mu}_k)^T\tilde{\boldsymbol{\Sigma}}_k^{-1}\boldsymbol{\mu}_k \\ \sqrt{\epsilon}\tilde{\boldsymbol{\Sigma}}_k^{-1} & \sqrt{\epsilon}\tilde{\boldsymbol{\Sigma}}_k^{-1}\boldsymbol{\mu}_k \end{bmatrix} \tag{13}$$

Right multiplication by $\mathbf{G}_k^T$ yields the final symmetric form, where we show only the ith column for conciseness and ease of understanding

$$\mathbf{G}_k(\mathbf{G}_k^T\mathbf{G}_k)^{-1}\mathbf{G}_k^T \; [:,i] = \frac{1}{|w_k|}\begin{bmatrix} 1+(\mathbf{I}_1-\boldsymbol{\mu}_k)^T\tilde{\boldsymbol{\Sigma}}_k^{-1}(\mathbf{I}_i-\boldsymbol{\mu}_k) \\ 1+(\mathbf{I}_2-\boldsymbol{\mu}_k)^T\tilde{\boldsymbol{\Sigma}}_k^{-1}(\mathbf{I}_i-\boldsymbol{\mu}_k) \\ 1+(\mathbf{I}_3-\boldsymbol{\mu}_k)^T\tilde{\boldsymbol{\Sigma}}_k^{-1}(\mathbf{I}_i-\boldsymbol{\mu}_k) \\ \vdots \\ 1+(\mathbf{I}_{w_k}-\boldsymbol{\mu}_k)^T\tilde{\boldsymbol{\Sigma}}_k^{-1}(\mathbf{I}_i-\boldsymbol{\mu}_k) \\ \epsilon\tilde{\boldsymbol{\Sigma}}_k^{-1}(\mathbf{I}_i-\boldsymbol{\mu}_k) \end{bmatrix}$$

Subtracting from $I_{|w_k|+3}$ and summing over k concludes the proof. Note that $\mathbf{G}_k$ has 3 extra rows, (or C extra rows for general case) for the regularization ϵ. These can be neglected in the final expression since they do not explicitly effect the other computations.   □

3   Bi-affinity Filter

The laplacian matrix $\mathbf{L}$, whose elements are defined in Eq. 6, is called the *matting laplacian* [10]. The usual decomposition of the laplacian matrix into a diagonal matrix and a weight matrix leads to the formulation $\mathbf{L} = \mathbf{D} - \mathbf{W}$. Here $\mathbf{D}$ is a diagonal matrix with the terms $D_{ii} = \#[k|i \in w_k]$ at its diagonal, which represents the cardinality of the number of windows the pixel i is a member of. The individual terms of the weight matrix $\mathbf{W}$, called the *matting affinity*, are given by

$$W_{ij} = \sum_{k|(i,j)\in w_k} \frac{1}{w_k}(1 + (\mathbf{I}_i - \boldsymbol{\mu}_k)^T(\boldsymbol{\Sigma}_k + \frac{\epsilon}{w_k}\mathbf{I}_3)^{-1}(\mathbf{I}_j - \boldsymbol{\mu}_k)) \tag{14}$$

By definition, all the rows of a laplacian matrix sum to zero, which leads to $D_{ii} = \sum_j W_{ij}$. At the local minima the solution $\boldsymbol{\alpha}^\star$ satisfies the first order optimality condition $\mathbf{L}^T \boldsymbol{\alpha}^\star = 0$. So we can write the optimal condition for minimizing $J(\boldsymbol{\alpha})$ as

$$\mathbf{L}^T \boldsymbol{\alpha}^\star = (\mathbf{D} - \mathbf{W})^T \boldsymbol{\alpha}^\star = \begin{pmatrix} D_{11}\alpha_1^\star - \sum_j W_{1j}\alpha_j^\star \\ D_{22}\alpha_2^\star - \sum_j W_{2j}\alpha_j^\star \\ \vdots \qquad \vdots \\ D_{nn}\alpha_n^\star - \sum_j W_{Nj}\alpha_j^\star \end{pmatrix}$$

Substituting $D_{ii} = \sum_j W_{ij}$ into the above system of equations and invoking the first order optimality condition leads to

$$\begin{pmatrix} \sum_j (\alpha_1^\star - \alpha_j^\star)W_{1j} \\ \sum_j (\alpha_2^\star - \alpha_j^\star)W_{2j} \\ \vdots \\ \sum_j (\alpha_n^\star - \alpha_j^\star)W_{nj} \end{pmatrix} = 0 \qquad (15)$$

The effect of this equation is that the affinity W_{ij} for two pixels with the same color (same $\alpha^\star$), is a positive quantity varying with the homogeneity of the local windows containing the pixels i and j as governed by Eqn. 14. But for pixels with different color (different $\alpha^\star$) the affinity is *zero*. In essence the rows of the laplacian matrix $\mathbf{L}$ work as a *zero-sum* filter kernel, after appropriate resizing. For our proposed filter, we replace the range filter of traditional bilateral filter with the appropriate row from the matting laplacian. This leads to the formulation of the *bi-affinity* filter

$$\mathbf{h}_{\sigma,\epsilon}(x) = \frac{\sum_{y \in \Omega_x} f_s^\sigma(x,y)L_{xy}^\epsilon \mathbf{I}(y)}{\sum_{y \in \Omega_x} f_s^\sigma(x,y)L_{xy}^\epsilon} \qquad (16)$$

where we denote the dependence on the user specified parameters σ, ϵ on the filter output. The parameter σ controls the amount of spatial blurring and is same as the spatial filter variance in standard bilateral filter. The parameter ϵ works analogous to the range variance parameter in traditional bilateral filter. Note that the relative weight attributed to the regularization term ϵ, determines the smoothness of the α estimates, which in our work translates to the smoothness of the filtered image. Bilateral filter has an inherent bending effect at the edges, which can be observed in the very simple experiment shown in Fig. 2. Bi-affinity filter does not smooth the edge, due to the affinity formulation which is zero across the edge. This effect can be achieved by bilateral filtering only under infinite range variance.

The calculation of the exact affinity matrix W_{ij} as mentioned in Eqn. 14, involves evaluation over all possible overlapping windows, which contain the center pixel, which is $O(w^3)$, where w is the size of the window. The overall complexity can be reduced by evaluating the affinity over a smaller set of possible windows. In the simplest case, we can evaluate the terms of $W_{i,j}$ locally, thereby counting the contribution of only the local window centered at the current pixel

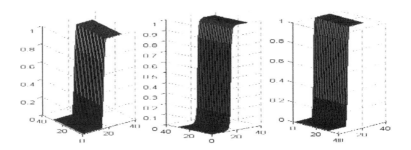

Fig. 2. Left to right: original edge, bilateral filtering, bi-affinity filtering. Note the edge curves slightly for the bilateral result.

(Fig. 3, right), and the complexity is equal to normal bilateral range filter, which is $O(w^2)$. To keep the later comparisons with bilateral filter fair, we define an approximate filter denoted by $\mathbf{h}^l(x)$

$$\mathbf{h}^l(x) = \frac{\sum_{y \in \Omega_x} f_s(x,y) L_{xy}^x \mathbf{I}(y)}{\sum_{y \in \Omega_x} f_s(x,y) L_{xy}^x} \tag{17}$$

which considers only the local window centered around pixel x denoted by L^x. Note that we have dropped the dependence on the user specified parameters σ, ϵ for notational simplicity.

Fig. 3. Left: all possible 3×3 neighborhood windows (brown) for center pixel (red) and neighbor (blue). Right: central window only approximation.

The operations involved in computing the terms L_{ij}'s as mentioned in Eqn. 6, can be decomposed as summation of Gaussian likelihoods over window dependent parameters μ_w, Σ_w. These parameters can be computed by accumulating first and second order sufficient statistics over windows. If memory complexity is not an issue then pre-computing 9 integral images can be an option. These 9 integral images correspond to 3 integral images for each of the channels R, G and B, 3 for RR, GG and BB and the remaining 3 for RG, GB and RB. For 3 channel color images, this is equivalent to storing 3 more images into the memory. For really large images (HDTV etc.) this option might not be the most optimal due to the huge memory overhead. The other method is to collect sufficient statistics for the current window and then updating the statistics for each unit move from top to bottom and left to right, as proposed by the median filtering approach by Huang [15] and then improved by Weiss [16]. Both these methods can now be used to implement the bi-affinity filter.

4 Experiments

The regularization term in the affinity formulation works as an edge smoothness term. For understanding the effect of this term we vary the amount of regularization used for the process and record the PSNR with respect to the original image. We report the results with respect to the window size in Fig. 4. The PSNR degrades for larger window size, which further corroborates the two color model which is valid only for small windows. The regularization term neutralizes the effect of window size to a certain degree as seen by the band of values collecting near PSNR 96DB. This hints at a possible tradeoff between PSNR and edge smoothness. For very small regularization values, the noise across the edge can contribute to the jaggedness of the reconstruction. This effect can be countered by increasing the amount of regularization. But this increase comes at a cost, which is the increased smoothness of the overall image. Empirically, we have obtained good results for larger window sizes by keeping the regularization term relatively larger than proposed in the matting literature. The effect of regularization for fixed window size can be seen in Fig. 5. The edge reconstruction becomes increasingly jagged as the amount of regularization is decreased.

For quantitative comparisons against traditional bilateral filter, we concentrate on the range filter variance of 0.1 to 1 and vary the window size to obtain

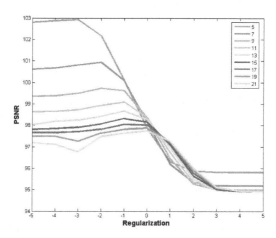

Fig. 4. PSNR with respect to ground truth. The colors depict the window size. The x axis depicts the regularization in log scale such that $\epsilon = 10^x$.

Fig. 5. Effect of regularization term ϵ. From left to right: $\epsilon = 0.0005, 0.005, 0.05, 0.5$. The edge becomes gradually smoother with increasing ϵ as can be seen at the inset images.

the curves in Fig. 6. The PSNR values obtained for our method are within acceptable deviations from those obtained for CIELAB bilateral filter, and surpass the performance at $\epsilon = 1$ and $w = 5$. Also note that Fig. 6 is a zoomed in version of Fig. 4, at x=[-1,0], approximately coinciding with the beginning of the knot.

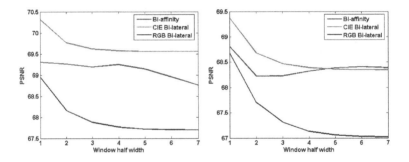

Fig. 6. PSNR comparisons. Left: $\epsilon = \sigma_r = 0.1$, right: $\epsilon = \sigma_r = 1$. $\sigma_d = 5$

In the next experiment, we present comparison of the approximate bi-affinity filter with traditional bilateral filter. This results are illustrated in Fig. 7. The response is very similar even though in our method we do not need any color conversions. For the bilateral filter, the RGB image is converted to CIELAB space and then the filter is applied individually to each channel.

4.1   Image Enhancement and Zooming

The original bi-affinity filter (Eqn. 16), has been derived from the matting laplacian formulation, which has been shown to preserve very minute details which is one of the requirements of matting [10]. In other words, our bi-affinity formulation preserves very intricate details of the image when compared to bilateral filter where only the dominant edges of the image are preserved. In this regard

Fig. 7. Top: left: original image, right: RGB bilateral filter. Bottom: left: CIELAB bilateral filter, $w = 11$, $\sigma_d = 5$, $\sigma_r = 0.1$, right: our method, $\epsilon = 0.1$.

bi-affinity filter can be thought of as preserving all edges, whereas bilateral filter only preserves strong edges. This important feature leads us to one of the most interesting applications of such a filter which is image enhancement and zooming.

Image enhancement techniques try to estimate the high-resolution data from the low-resolution data by estimating the missing information. This leads to numerous formulations, some learning based and some interpolation based. If the missing high-resolution data can be inferred, then it can be added to the interpolated input (which satisfies the data fidelity constraints) to generate the high-resolution image [17]. Given the low-resolution input in Fig. 8, we can interpolate it to the desired high-resolution size, and then add the missing high-resolution info to generate the final high-resolution result. The mean affinity at each pixel, which is the row wise normalized summation of W, contains this missing detail. This detail is shown in Fig. 8, center panel. The bi-affinity filter places a smoothed local affinity weighted kernel at each pixel. The enhancement effect is a byproduct of the filtering formulation and not the main aim of this work. We realize that existing methods, more so the iterative techniques [18], can use a formulation similar to ours to refine the estimate at each step.

Like many other *passive* filtering techniques, e.g. bilateral, bicubic, etc., our method only looks at the low-resolution observation to generate the values of the high-resolution scene. *Active* methods such as Markov random field (MRF) based

Fig. 8. Image enhancement. Left: input image is enlarged by a factor 2 (bicubic interpolation). The mean affinity map for all pixels (center), and the final enhanced image (right).

models, impose neighborhood continuity constraints. We proposed to investigate the details of such a model with the bi-affinity filter as one of its components, as a future work. Additional examples of comparisons against zooming and then post-processing with bilateral filter compared to our technique is shown in Fig. 9.

5   Conclusion and Future Work

In this paper, we have proposed a new edge preserving filter, which works on the principle of matting affinity. We present a full n-channel derivation of the matting laplacian. The formulation of matting affinity allows a better representation of the range filter term in bilateral filter class. The definition of the affinity term can be relaxed to suit different applications. We define an approximate bi-affinity filter whose output is shown to be very similar to the traditional bilateral filter. Our technique has the added advantage that no color space changes are required and hence the images can be handled in their original color space. This is a big benefit over traditional bilateral filter, which needs a conversion to perception based spaces, such as CIELAB to generate better results. The full bi-affinity filter preserves very minute details of the input image, and can be simply extended to an image enhancement application. The implementation of the filter still remains a challenge due to the small window requirement arising from the two color model constraint. We propose a diligent effort in this area, since it is evident that the kernel evaluation can be optimized in more ways than one.

Fig. 9. Image Zooming by a factor 2x. Left column: bi-cubic interpolation + bilateral filter. Right column: our method. Notice the preservation of small details in all the images.

References

1. Tomasi, C., Manduchi, R.: Bilateral filtering for gray and color images. In: ICCV 1998: Proceedings of the Sixth International Conference on Computer Vision, p. 839. IEEE Computer Society, Washington, DC (1998)
2. Wells III, W.: Efficient synthesis of gaussian filters by cascaded uniform filters. IEEE Trans. Pattern Anal. Mach. Intell. 8 (1986)
3. Geusebroek, J., Smeulders, A., van de Weijer, J.: Fast anisotropic gauss filtering. IEEE Transactions on Image Processing 12, 2003 (2002)
4. Lu, W.S., Wang, H.P., Antoniou, A.: Design of two-dimensional digital filters using the singular-value decomposition and balanced approximation method. IEEE Trans. Signal Process. 39, 2253–2262 (1991)
5. Paris, S., Durand, F.: A Fast Approximation of the Bilateral Filter Using a Signal Processing Approach. In: Leonardis, A., Bischof, H., Pinz, A. (eds.) ECCV 2006. LNCS, vol. 3954, pp. 568–580. Springer, Heidelberg (2006)
6. Porikli, F.: Constant time $o(1)$ bilateral filtering. In: IEEE Conference on Computer Vision and Pattern Recognition, CVPR (2008)
7. Yang, Q., Tan, K.H., Ahuja, N.: Real-time o(1) bilateral filtering. In: IEEE Conference on Computer Vision and Pattern Recognition, CVPR (2009)
8. Omer, I., Werman, M.: Color lines: Image specific color representation. In: CVPR (2004)
9. Bando, Y., Chen, B.Y., Nishita, T.: Extracting depth and matte using a color-filtered aperture. ACM Transactions on Graphics 27, 134:1–134:9 (2008)
10. Levin, A., Lischinski, D., Weiss, Y.: A closed form solution to natural image matting. In: CVPR (2006)
11. Bennett, E., Uyttendaele, M., Zitnick, C., Szeliski, R., Kang, S.: Video and Image Bayesian Demosaicing with a Two Color Image Prior. In: Leonardis, A., Bischof, H., Pinz, A. (eds.) ECCV 2006. LNCS, vol. 3951, pp. 508–521. Springer, Heidelberg (2006)
12. Joshi, N., Zitnick, C., Szeliski, R., Kriegman, D.: Image deblurring and denoising using color priors. In: CVPR (2009)
13. Liu, C., Szeliski, R., Kang, S.B., Zitnick, C.L., Freeman, W.T.: Automatic estimation and removal of noise from a single image. PAMI 30, 299–314 (2008)
14. Press, W.H., Teukolsky, S.A., Vetterling, W.T., Flannery, B.P.: Numerical recipes in C: the art of scientific computing, 2nd edn. Cambridge University Press, New York (1992)
15. Huang, T.S.: Transforms and median filters. In: Two-Dimensional Signal Processing II, pp. 209–211. Springer, Berlin (1981)
16. Weiss, B.: Fast median and bilateral filtering. ACM Trans. Graph. 25, 519–526 (2006)
17. Fattal, R.: Image upsampling via imposed edge statistics. In: SIGGRAPH (2007)
18. Irani, M., Peleg, S.: Motion analysis for image enhancement. In: JVCIP (1993)

Photometric Color Calibration
of the Joint Monitor-Camera Response Function

Tobias Elbrandt and Jörn Ostermann

Institut für Informationsverarbeitung
Leibniz Universität Hannover
Appelstraße 9A, 30167 Hannover, Germany
{elbrandt,ostermann}@tnt.uni-hannover.de
http://www.tnt.uni-hannover.de

Abstract. When recording presentations which include visualizations displayed on a monitor or with a video projector, the quality of the captured video suffers from color distortion and aliasing effects in the display area. A photometric calibration for the whole image can not compensate for these defects. In this paper, we present a per-pixel photometric calibration method that solves this problem. We measure the joint monitor-camera response function for every single camera pixel by displaying red, green, and blue screens at all brightness levels and capture them separately. These measurements are used to estimate the joint response function for every single pixel and all three color channels with the empirical model of response (EMoR). We apply the estimated response functions on subsequent captures of the display to calibrate them. Our method achieves a mean absolute error of about 0.66 brightness levels, averaged over all pixels of the image. The performance is also demonstrated with a calibration of a real captured photo, which is hardly distinguishable from the original.

1 Introduction

Recordings of presentations which are based on or make use of a computer monitor or digital video projector often suffer from bad image quality in the recorded presentation screen area. This is due to imperfect color reproduction, aliasing effects and low radiance in these regions. Hence, a calibration of the captured video signal is necessary.

The photometric calibration of cameras is the method to estimate the response function f as the relation between the image irradiance E captured in time t and measured as brightness B.

$$f(Et) = B \tag{1}$$

To calibrate a measured brightness B, the corresponding integrated image irradiance $I = Et$ has to be determined by

$$I = f^{-1}(B) \tag{2}$$

K.N. Kutulakos (Ed.): ECCV 2010 Workshops, Part II, LNCS 6554, pp. 41–49, 2012.

This type of camera image calibration is a vital topic, as it is a precondition for a lot of technology like image stitching, high dynamic range, shape-from-shading, and photometric stereo. Different approaches have been pursued to estimate the aforementioned relation, f. In most cases, parametric models, like gamma curves [1–3] or higher-order polynomials [4] are used. In contrast, a PCA based empirical model which generalizes the response functions of several real-world cameras was developed in [5]. Using a gamma function model gives an advantage, as it is inherently invertible whereas most other approaches make numerical means necessary to determine Eq. (2). Most of the methods only calibrate grayscale images, while [2] differentiates between different color channels.

The calibration of the monitor itself is an important issue for photographers, in order to make displayed photos match the captured ones. The gamma values needed to correctly display photographs taken by a consumer DSLR camera are determined in [6]. To provide a correctly proportional presentation of medical softcopy images, the monitor can be calibrated using a look-up-table measured with a luminance sensor [7].

Our goal is to compensate color distortions and Moiré effects, while capturing images from monitors. In this work, we will focus on the calibration of joint monitor-camera response functions, assuming that the method would be quite similar for a digital video projector. In order to get an understanding of the calibration procedure, we start with a concise description of the system. We divide the estimation of the combined monitor-camera response function in a pre-estimation of the monitor gamma, followed by an accurate estimation of the remaining camera response function for every single pixel, using the eigenvectors of the Empirical Model of Response (EMoR) database [5]. The performed experiments show that this two-step approach has good results. Finally, we apply the estimated calibration parameters to a real photograph. The last section concludes our paper.

2 Method for Calibrating the Joint Monitor-Camera Response Function

Our calibration method calibrates a camera that captures images from an LCD monitor. For this, a camera captures the monitor screen, filled with one of the three color channels, at different brightness levels. First, we analyze the used components, and then describe the calibration procedure.

2.1 Signal Generation and Reception

An ordinary LCD monitor provides a flat screen that can display color images consisting of three color planes – red, green, and blue. Normally, it also features a gamma curve, i.e. the light output is related exponentially to the displayed intensity value. There is always some additional low amplitude noise on the intensity. As the monitor also emits light when displaying only black pixels, the signal is biased. Every monitor pixel is divided into three sub-pixels, one for each of the red, green, and blue color channels. When displaying white color, all sub-pixels are switched on, whereas when displaying green, the red and blue sub-pixels are blocked.

The camera maps light emitted by the monitor onto a two dimensional array of light sensitive camera pixels. In case of a single-chip color camera, which is commonly used, there is a color filter in front of every camera pixel, allowing only light within a certain bandwidth of the light spectrum to pass. The so called Bayer-pattern is the most widely-used sort of color filter arrays, with one red, two green, and one blue color filter for each 2 × 2 pixels. The passbands of the filters overlap a bit, such that the green pixels are also sensitive to the red and blue light spectrum. Some sources of noise between the reception of light and the output of digital values for the camera pixels add a bias and zero-mean noise [8]. While the signal output of every single camera element – apart from being quantized – is proportional to the gathered light, it is often adjusted by the camera to get better images for human eyes.

The combination of monitor and camera adds two effects that substantially influence the signal reception: Since the quantity of light emitted by the monitor pixels decreases with the angle of radiation, the incident light perceived by the camera depends on the viewing angle. Another effect is the Moiré, caused by aliasing due to the rasterization of both the LCD monitor and camera.

Figure 1 illustrates both effects in a graph showing brightness levels measured at adjacent red, green, and blue color elements of one image column, when the camera captured a red, green, and blue monitor screen, respectively. The aliasing causes the waves, while the angle dependent light emission is responsible for the respective base curve. Both influences on a real image can be observed in Fig. 4 a). It is also evident that the waves caused by the aliasing feature different phases. The phase shifts are due to the different spatial positions of both the monitor sub-pixels and the Bayer mosaic of the camera target elements for the three color channels. Comparing the curves of two diagonally adjacent green elements of the Bayer pattern (Fig. 1, right) shows that the aliasing component is rotated about 180° between them.

2.2 Two-Step Calibration Procedure

Considering the analysis above, we pursue the following strategy to calibrate the joint monitor-camera setup:

- Average several captured monitor images to minimize the influence of noise and quantization.
- Measure the response function separately for the base color channels as they measure overlapping bands of the light spectrum.
- Compensate the monitor's gamma separately, as it is not explicitly modeled by the camera response function.
- Calibrate the response function for every single pixel, as it greatly depends on the position.

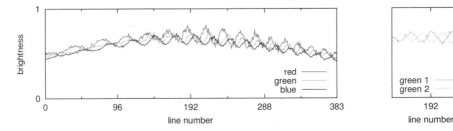

Fig. 1. Left: Brightness levels of the red, green, and blue camera image elements in one column when capturing a red, green, or blue screen, respectively. The Moiré effect is visible in the low amplitude waves, while the base curve shows the general angle dependent light perception. A calibrated camera would show lines with constant brightness levels. Right: The center part of the curves of the two green elements illustrates that the phase shift of the aliasing wave depends on the position of the camera target element.

Compensating the Monitor's Gamma: The **first step** of our method is to analyze and compensate the monitor's gamma. Assuming that both the monitor brightness f_m and the camera response function f_c approximately follow a gamma curve, we can combine both gammas. In addition to the signal biases β of the monitor and camera, this leads to the rough approximation Eq. (3) for the joint monitor-camera response function f_{mc} in relation to the integrated image irradiance I.

$$f_{mc}(I) = f_c(f_m(I)) = \lambda_c (\lambda_m I^{\gamma_m})^{\gamma_c} = \lambda I^{\gamma}$$
$$\text{with } \lambda = \lambda_c \lambda_m^{\gamma_c} \text{ and } \gamma = \gamma_c \gamma_m$$
$$f_{mc}(I) = \lambda I^{\gamma} + \beta \tag{3}$$

We display red, green, and blue screens with increasing intensities i, and capture them N times each, as $\hat{C}_{c,i,n}(x,y) \in [0\ldots 255]$, $c \in \{red, green, blue\}$, $i = 0\ldots M\text{-}1$, $x = 0\ldots w_c\text{-}1$, $y = 0\ldots h_c\text{-}1$. The constants w_c and h_c denote the width and height of the camera target, respectively, and the perceived light intensities are quantized to 256 steps. All pixels of the images taken for an intensity are then averaged to the mean captured brightness

$$\hat{B}_c(i) = \frac{1}{w_c h_c N} \sum_{x,y} \sum_{n=1}^{N} \hat{C}_{c,i,n}(x,y). \tag{4}$$

Using these measurements, the parameter sets $\{\lambda, \gamma, \beta\}_c$ for all colors c are determined using a power regression with offset, i.e. the values for λ, γ, and β are estimated to minimize the error between the measurements $\hat{B}_c$ and Eq. (3).

The monitor is now set to the three gamma values calculated. This actually leads to an output signal of the camera, which is *on average*, approximately linear.

Estimating the Monitor-Camera Response Function: For the **second step**, the display-capture procedure described above is repeated, with the camera capturing the now gamma-calibrated monitor. Again, we measure pixel brightness $\hat{C}_{c,i,n}(x,y)$ which are now averaged to:

$$\hat{B}_{c,i}(x,y) = \frac{1}{N} \sum_{n=1}^{N} \hat{C}_{c,i,n}(x,y). \tag{5}$$

Therefore, we have measurements which describe what camera brightness $\hat{B}$ was received at pixel position (x,y), when the screen displayed the color c with intensity i. Depending on the type of the Bayer pattern of the camera, only 1 (red or blue) or 2 (green) measurements of each 2×2 pixels are taken into account. For example, our camera has an RGGB pattern, so we only regard measurements of the red images at positions where both x and y are even, and likewise, the data of the blue raw images are only regarded at positions where both x and y are odd. The green images are only taken into account at the two remaining positions. Hence, only one of three vectors $\hat{f}_c(x,y) = \{\hat{B}_{c,0}, \ldots, \hat{B}_{c,M-1}\}$ remains for each position.

We tested several methods to calibrate images per-pixel using the vectors $\hat{f}_c(x,y)$ and found that EMoR [5] outperformed the other techniques. Grossberg and Nayar unified 201 films and cameras to 25 PCA eigenvectors h_m and an average vector f_0. Using these vectors[1], the measurements $\hat{B}$ are approximated for all positions (x,y) and the respective color channel c with $H = [h_1 \ldots h_{25}]$:

$$a = H^+ \left(\frac{\hat{B} - b_0}{b_1 - b_0} - f_0 \right) \tag{6}$$

$$\tilde{B} = f_0 + Ha \tag{7}$$

Here, $H^+ = \left(H^T H \right)^{-1} H^T$ is the Moore-Penrose inverse of H, and $b_0 = \min(\hat{B})$ and $b_1 = \max(\hat{B})$ are normalization coefficients to map $\hat{B}$ onto the interval $[0 \ldots 1]$. The first two coefficients a_1 and a_2 for the three color channels are shown in Fig. 2 a-c). Figure 2 d) shows the average vector f_0 and the two most significant eigenvectors h_1 and h_2.

Both the measurements $\hat{B}$ and the approximation $\tilde{B}$ provide camera picture brightness B against displayed intensity I on the screen, i.e. $f(I) = B$. In order to calibrate images, we have to invert this relation to $f^{-1}(B) = I$. This has to be done numerically, as no underlying invertible function is known for a linear combination of f_0 and h_i. Our calibration procedure therefore finishes with replacing the intensity of every camera pixel with the value of the corresponding inverted relation $\tilde{B}_c^{-1}(x,y)$. We also calibrated using the set of inverted EMoR PCA vectors $h_1^{\text{inv}}, \ldots, h_{25}^{\text{inv}}$, also provided by the authors.

---

[1] The vector data can be downloaded under http://www.cs.columbia.edu/CAVE/ software/softlib/dorf.php

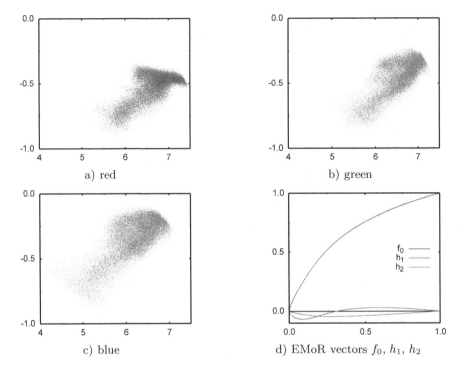

a) red

b) green

c) blue

d) EMoR vectors f_0, h_1, h_2

Fig. 2. Point-clouds of the distributions of the most significant coefficients a_1 and a_2 for the PCA vectors a calculated with Eq. (6) of the color channels a) red, b) green, and c) blue over all pixel positions. It can be observed that the coefficients vary greatly between pixels and color channels. This means that the resulting EMoR approximations diverge between different pixel positions. Fig. d) displays the EMoR average vector f_0 and the most significant vectors h_1 and h_2.

3   Experiments

For our experiments, we captured a Samsung 910T 19" TFT monitor with a Prosilica EC1380C FireWire camera. Both the brightness level of the monitor and the exposure time of the camera were adjusted, such that no signal clipping occurred.

In three loops, full-screen rectangles with increasing intensity from black to full amplitude were displayed on the monitor for the red, green, and bluecolor channels. Each of the screens was captured $N=16$ times and averaged to minimize noise effects, as well as quantization errors. For the first step, we obtained the measurements $\hat{B}_c(i)$. Their approximation with Eq. (3) resulted in the gamma values 2.02, 1.965, and 1.886 for the three channels. The monitor gamma was set to these values.

Then, we repeated the display-capture procedure to receive measurements $\hat{B}_{c,i}(x,y)$, which were then approximated to $\tilde{B}_c(x,y)$ using Eq. (6) and Eq. (7). To get another set of test data $\hat{B}'_{c,i}(x,y)$, this procedure was repeated again.

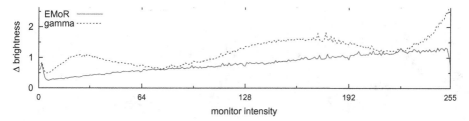

Fig. 3. Root mean square error of the calibration with EMoR and gamma approximation. The errors of both methods rise with increasing intensity level. Comparing the run of the error curve of the gamma approximation with the curves of h_1 and h_2, shown in Fig. 2 d), reveals a certain similarity; these small variations of the response functions from the gamma curve are also covered by EMoR.

We started our evaluation of the calibration procedure itself with ground-truth data. For this purpose, we took the values of the images $\hat{B}'_{c,i}(x,y)$ and calibrated them with $\tilde{B}_c(x,y)$. A perfect calibration should have the result i. The root mean square error (RMSE) between ground-truth i and the calibration results is shown in Figure 3. We included the corresponding graph for a calibration made with an approximated gamma curve; EMoR clearly outperforms the gamma based method, even though both methods are appropriate for our purposes. Table 1 summarizes and compares calibration errors for different techniques. We evaluated the calibrations both with and without a pre-gamma-corrected monitor (step one). The first line displays the results of calibration with per-pixel estimated gamma-curve. Using the measured values $\hat{B}_{c,i}$ directly as a look-up-table, results in the errors shown in the second line; although measured with averaged captures, they are still too noisy to be directly used. A calibration with the inverse EMoR vectors $h_1^{\mathrm{inv}}, \ldots, h_{25}^{\mathrm{inv}}$ is displayed in the second to last line. The direct inversion of the calibration with the approximated $\tilde{B}_{c,i}$ using the above mentioned EMoR vectors $h_1, \ldots, h_{25}$, outperformed the other methods.

After the calibration procedure, we want to show the outcome of our method. For this purpose, we displayed a photograph one color plane after another on the screen and captured it as raw images with the camera. The respective bayer pixels were extracted from each image, e.g. only the even pixel positions of the red capture. These were calibrated using our method, and again put together to

Table 1. Overall measurement of the errors of different calibration procedures. Displayed are the mean absolute error (MAE) and the root mean square error (RMSE) in brightness levels $[0 \ldots 255]$, for calibrations without or with compensation of the monitor's gamma (step one).

method	not gamma corrected		gamma corrected	
	MAE	RMSE	MAE	RMSE
gamma	2.419	3.119	1.103	1.426
look-up-table	0.928	2.213	0.740	1.012
EMoR inverse	1.107	2.558	0.679	0.913
EMoR direct	0.853	2.117	0.662	0.893

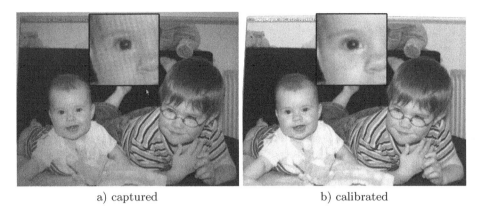

a) captured   b) calibrated

Fig. 4. Photograph a) captured from the screen; the colors are dull and aliasing effects are evident in the colored waves. In the calibrated image b), both effects are compensated. Note that the image is still radially distorted.

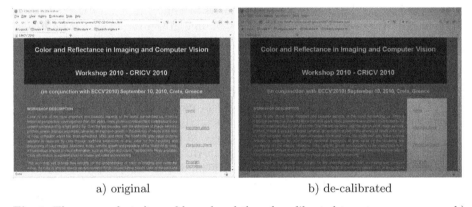

a) original   b) de-calibrated

Fig. 5. The screen shot a) was blurred and then de-calibrated to get an appearance b) as if it was captured by a camera from the monitor

form a calibrated raw image, which was finally demosaiced. The result is shown in Fig. 4. Both the aliasing and color distortions are perfectly compensated.

For the authentic synthesis of scenes including a monitor, a realistic color distortion might be desired for the visible area of the screen. To make an image look like if it was captured by our camera from a monitor, we took a normal screen shot of a browser window (Fig. 5 a), added minor Gaussian blur, and *de-calibrated* it directly with $\tilde{B}_c(x, y)$. The result is shown in Fig. 5 b).

4   Conclusion

We presented a method to calibrate color images from a monitor screen that were captured by a camera. Our calibration procedure works in two steps. First, it estimates the gamma of the monitor, and then it approximates the camera response curve using the EMoR model. Both estimations are performed using camera captures of the monitor, subsequently displaying different brightness levels. The mean absolute error achieved with our method is 0.662 intensity levels, with a root mean squared error of 0.893. With the calibration of a real captured photograph, we showed that undesirable effects, like Moiré and color distortion, are completely compensated.

References

1. Mann, S., Picard, R.W.: On being 'undigital' with digital cameras: Extending dynamic range by combining differently exposed pictures. In: Proceedings of IS&T, pp. 442–448 (1995)
2. Shafique, K., Shah, M.: Estimation of the radiometric response functions of a color camera from differently illuminated images. In: Proceedings of the IEEE International Conference on Image Processing, pp. 24–27 (2004)
3. Debevec, P.E., Malik, J.: Recovering high dynamic range radiance maps from photographs. In: SIGGRAPH, pp. 369–378. ACM (1997)
4. Mitsunaga, T., Nayar, S.: Radiometric self calibration. In: IEEE Computer Society Conference on Computer Vision and Pattern Recognition, vol. 1, pp. 374–380 (1999)
5. Grossberg, M., Nayar, S.: What is the space of camera response functions? In: IEEE Computer Society Conference on Computer Vision and Pattern Recognition, vol. 2, pp. II-602–II-609 (2003)
6. Manders, C., Mann, S.: True images: A calibration technique to reproduce images as recorded. In: Eighth IEEE International Symposium on Multimedia, ISM 2006, pp. 712–715 (2006)
7. Jiquan, L., Jingyi, F., Duchun, L.: Dicom GSDF based calibration method of general LCD monitor for medical softcopy image display. In: The 1st International Conference on Bioinformatics and Biomedical Engineering, ICBBE 2007, pp. 1153–1156 (2007)
8. Healey, G., Kondepudy, R.: Radiometric CCD camera calibration and noise estimation. IEEE Transactions on Pattern Analysis and Machine Intelligence 16 (1994)

Polyakov Action Minimization
for Efficient Color Image Processing

Guy Rosman[1,*], Xue-Cheng Tai[2,3,**], Lorina Dascal[1], and Ron Kimmel[1]

[1] Dept. of Computer Science, Technion, Haifa, Israel
{rosman,lorina,ron}@cs.technion.ac.il
[2] Dept. of Mathematics, Bergen University, Bergen, Norway
tai@math.uib.no
[3] Division of Mathematical Sciences, School of Physical and Mathematical Sciences,
Nanyang Technological University, Singapore

Abstract. The Laplace-Beltrami operator is an extension of the Laplacian from flat domains to curved manifolds. It was proven to be useful for color image processing as it models a meaningful coupling between the color channels. This coupling is naturally expressed in the Beltrami framework in which a color image is regarded as a two dimensional manifold embedded in a hybrid, five-dimensional, spatial-chromatic (x, y, R, G, B) space.

The Beltrami filter defined by this framework minimizes the Polyakov action, adopted from high-energy physics, which measures the area of the image manifold. Minimization is usually obtained through a geometric heat equation defined by the Laplace-Beltrami operator. Though efficient simplifications such as the bilateral filter have been proposed for the single channel case, so far, the coupling between the color channel posed a non-trivial obstacle when designing fast Beltrami filters.

Here, we propose to use an augmented Lagrangian approach to design an efficient and accurate regularization framework for color image processing by minimizing the Polyakov action. We extend the augmented Lagrangian framework for total variation (TV) image denoising to the more general Polyakov action case for color images, and apply the proposed framework to denoise and deblur color images.

Keywords: Laplace-Beltrami, diffusion, optimization, denoising, PDEs.

1 Introduction

Variational, nonlinear diffusion filters have been extensively used in the last two decades for different image processing tasks. Numerical schemes implementing them are designed with an emphasis on accuracy, stability and computational efficiency. While a many of the works on image regularization involve greyscale

---

* This research was partly supported by ISF grant no. 1551/09 and by Rubin Scientific and Medical Fund.
** The research is also supported by MOE (Ministry of Education) Tier II project T207N2202 and IDM project NRF2007IDMIDM002-010.

K.N. Kutulakos (Ed.): ECCV 2010 Workshops, Part II, LNCS 6554, pp. 50–61, 2012.
© Springer-Verlag Berlin Heidelberg 2012

images, only a small portion has made a coherent attempt at regularizing vector-valued signals.

These works, several of which are inspired by [39], describe regularization functionals which operate on vector-valued images. These include the works of Sapiro and Ringach [27], Blomgren and Chan [4], and Sochen et. al. [30], as well as more recent works such as ([34,14]). The Beltrami framework [30] describes a regularizing functional, well suited for color image processing, which can be justified by the Lambertian model of color image formation. The framework considers the image as a 2-manifold embedded in a hybrid spatial-feature space. Regularization of the image in this framework is expressed as minimization of area surface. The Beltrami filter is strongly related to the bilateral filter (see [37], [28], [33], [29], [13], [3]), as well as to the nonlocal means filter, proposed in [1]. Minimization of the associated functional is usually done by evolving the image according to its Euler-Lagrange equation [30]. This evolution, using an explicit scheme, is limited in its time step, resulting in high computational complexity. Another possibility [2] is to perform a fixed-point iteration from the Euler-Lagrange equation. Recently, several approaches were suggested for improving the speed of computation of minimizers for the *Polyakov action* [22]. Those include an approximation of the Beltrami filter kernel [31], as well as employing vector extrapolation techniques [24], or operator splitting methods [11]. For the case of gray-scale images, the projection-based method [8] has been extended to the Polyakov function [5], with no suggestions made for vector-valued images.

In [32], the augmented Lagrangian method [15,23] is used to perform TV regularization of images. In this paper we propose to use a similar constrained optimization for regularization of color images. Instead of discretizing the continuous optimality condition or the resulting Beltrami flow, we minimize the discretized Polyakov action itself. The resulting method is shown to be more efficient and accurate for image denoising and deblurring, compared to existing methods for Beltrami regularization in image processing. In Section 2 we review the Beltrami framework for color image regularization. In Section 3 we extend the coupled constrained optimization approach demonstrated in [32] to regularize color images by the Polyakov action. In Section 4 we display results of using our method for deblurring color images. Section 5 concludes the paper.

2   The Beltrami Framework

We now briefly review the Beltrami framework for non-linear diffusion in computer vision [18,30,38]. The basic notions used in this introduction are taken from Riemannian geometry, and we refer the reader to [12] for further reading.

In the Beltrami framework, images are expressed as maps between two Riemannian manifolds. Denote such a map by $X : \Sigma \to M$, where Σ is a two-dimensional manifold, parameterized by global coordinates (σ^1, σ^2), and M is the spatial-feature manifold, embedded in $\mathbb{R}^{d+2}$, where d is the number of image channels. For example, a gray-level image can be represented as a surface embedded in $\mathbb{R}^3$. The map X in this case is $X(\sigma^1, \sigma^2) = (\sigma^1, \sigma^2, I(\sigma^1, \sigma^2))$, where I is the image intensity. For color images, X is given by $X(\sigma^1, \sigma^2) = (\sigma^1, \sigma^2, I^1(\sigma^1, \sigma^2), I^2(\sigma^1, \sigma^2), I^3(\sigma^1, \sigma^2))$, where I^1, I^2, I^3 are the color components (for example, red, green, blue for the RGB color space).

Next, we choose a Riemannian metric on this surface. Its components are denoted by g_{ij}. The canonical choice of coordinates in image processing uses Cartesian coordinates $\sigma^1, \sigma^2 = x, y$. We denote the elements of the inverse of the metric by superscripts g^{ij}, and the determinant by $g = \det(g_{ij})$.

Once images are defined as Riemannian embeddings, we can look for a measure on this space of embedding maps. Denote by (Σ, g) the image manifold and its metric, and by (M, h) the space-feature manifold and its metric. The functional $S[X]$ characterizes the mapping $X : \Sigma \to M$, and is defined to be

$$S[X, g_{ij}, h_{ab}] = \int d^m \sigma \sqrt{g} \|dX\|^2_{g,h}, \tag{1}$$

where m is the dimension of Σ, g is the determinant of the image metric, and the range of indices is $i, j = 1, 2, ..., \dim(\Sigma)$ and $a, b = 1, 2, ..., \dim(M)$. The integrand $\|dX\|^2_{g,h}$ is given by $\|dX\|^2_{g,h} = (\partial_{x_i} I^a) g^{ij} (\partial_{x_j} I^b) h_{ab}$. We use here Einstein's summation convention: identical indices that appear up and down are summed over. This functional, for $\dim(\Sigma) = 2$ and $h_{ab} = \delta_{ab}$, is known in string theory as the Polyakov action [22], and extends the action functional from classical mechanics to the relativistic case.

In the case of color images, where both the spatial and the color spaces are assumed to be Cartesian, the metric becomes

$$(g_{ij}) = \begin{pmatrix} 1 + \beta^2 \sum_{a=1}^3 (I^a_{x_1})^2 & \beta^2 \sum_{a=1}^3 I^a_{x_1} I^a_{x_2} \\ \beta^2 \sum_{a=1}^3 I^a_{x_1} I^a_{x_2} & 1 + \beta^2 \sum_{a=1}^3 (I^a_{x_2})^2 \end{pmatrix} = G,$$

where a subscript of I^a denotes a partial derivative and the parameter $\beta > 0$ determines the ratio between the spatial and color coordinates. The functional becomes

$$S(X) = \int \sqrt{g} \, d\sigma^1 \, d\sigma^2, \quad g = \det(G) = 1 + \beta^2 \sum_{a=1}^3 \|\nabla I^a\|^2 + \frac{\beta^4}{2} \sum_{a,b=1}^3 \|\nabla I^a \times \nabla I^b\|^2,$$

The role of the cross product term $\sum_{a,b=1}^3 \|\nabla I^a \times \nabla I^b\|^2$ in the regularization was explored in [18],[17]. It penalizes deviations from the Lambertian model of image formation [18], or specifically – misalignment of the gradient directions between color channels.

The functional S is usually minimized by time evolution of the image according to the Euler-Lagrange equations,

$$I^a_t = -\frac{1}{\sqrt{g}} h^{ab} \frac{\delta S}{\delta I^b} = \underbrace{\frac{1}{\sqrt{g}} \operatorname{div}(D \nabla I^a)}_{\Delta_g I^a}, \tag{2}$$

where the matrix $D = \sqrt{g}G^{-1}$. See [30] for explicit derivation. The operator Δ_g generalizes the Laplacian to manifolds, and is called the Laplace-Beltrami operator. Evolution according to these equations result in the Beltrami scale-space.

The functional can also be generalized to the family of functionals

$$\int \sqrt{\beta_1 + \beta_2 \sum_{a=1}^{3} \|\nabla I^a\|^2 + \beta_3 \sum_{a,b=1}^{3} \|\nabla I^a \times \nabla I^b\|^2}, \tag{3}$$

for any positive $\beta_1, \beta_2, \beta_3$. While this approach cannot be explained by the minimal area interpretation, it makes sense in terms of color image restoration, and will be used in the results shown in Figure 4.

In the variational framework, the reconstructed image minimizes a cost-functional of the form

$$\Psi = \frac{\alpha}{2} \sum_{a=1}^{3} \|KI^a - I_0^a\|^2 + S(X),$$

where K is a bounded linear operator. In the denoising case, K is the identity operator $Ku = u$, and in the deblurring case, $Ku = k * u$, where $k(x, y)$ is the blurring kernel. The parameter α controls the smoothness of the solution. This functional has been used for image denoising [30,2] and blind deconvolution [16], and its relation to active contours explored in [6]. We introduce an approach for optimizing the functional Ψ using the augmented Lagrangian method.

3   An Augmented Lagrangian Approach for Beltrami Regularization

In recent years, several attempts have been made of optimizing total variation functionals [26] using dual variables (we refer the reader to [9,7,8,20,35,32,36] and references therein, as well to more references found in the technical report [25]). These algorithms achieved great accuracy and efficiency, and are considered to be among state-of-the-art methods for TV restoration.

Specifically, in [32], total variation regularization is obtained by decoupling the optimization problem

$$\min_{u} \int |\nabla u| + \frac{\alpha}{2} \|Ku - f\|^2 \tag{4}$$

into a constrained optimization problem

$$\min_{u, \mathbf{q}} \int |\mathbf{q}| + \frac{\alpha}{2} \|Ku - f\|^2 \quad s.t. \quad \mathbf{q} = \nabla u, \tag{5}$$

where $\mathbf{q}$ is a auxiliary field, parallel to the gradient of u. This constraint is then incorporated using an augmented Lagrangian penalty function of the form

$\rho_{\mu,r}(u, \mathbf{q}) = \boldsymbol{\mu}^T(\nabla u - \mathbf{q}) + \frac{r}{2}(\|\nabla u - \mathbf{q}\|^2)$. The penalty is used to enforce the constraint $\mathbf{q} = \nabla u$, without making the problem severely ill-conditioned.

We now describe a similar construction for the Polyakov action. Again, it is important to stress we are minimizing the functional itself, rather than discretizing the resulting minimizing PDE as in [30,16,31,2,24,11].

We deal with the case of color images, for which the regularization offered by the Beltrami framework is more meaningful. Specifically, we replace the gradient norm penalty used in TV regularization by the action functional of Equation 1. This is done by replacing the first term in Equation 5 by the term

$$\int \sqrt{1 + \beta^2 \sum_{i \in \{R,G,B\}} \|\mathbf{q}_i\|^2 + \frac{\beta^4}{2} \sum_{i \in \{R,G,B\}} \sum_{j \neq i} \|\mathbf{q}_i \times \mathbf{q}_j\|^2}, \qquad (6)$$

where β is the spatial-intensity aspect ratio, and $\{\mathbf{q}_i\}_{i \in \{R,G,B\}}$ denote components of the field $\mathbf{q}$, parallel to the gradient of each of the image channels. We then trivially extend the rest of the functional to the vectorial (per-pixel) case, obtaining the following functional

$$\mathcal{L}_{BEL}(u, \mathbf{q}, \boldsymbol{\mu}) =$$

$$\int \left\{ \begin{array}{l} \sqrt{1 + \beta^2 \sum_{i \in \{R,G,B\}} \|\mathbf{q}_i\|^2 + \frac{\beta^4}{2} \sum_{i \in \{R,G,B\}} \sum_{j \neq i} \|\mathbf{q}_i \times \mathbf{q}_j\|^2} + \\ \sum_{i \in \{R,G,B\}} \boldsymbol{\mu}_i^T(\mathbf{q}_i - \nabla u_i) + \frac{\alpha}{2}\|Ku - f\|^2 + \frac{r}{2}\sum_{i \in \{R,G,B\}} \|\mathbf{q}_i - \nabla u_i\|^2 \end{array} \right\},$$

which corresponds to Beltrami regularization. The expressions optimizing u and $\boldsymbol{\mu}$ are replaced by their per-channel equivalents, $\{u_i\}$ and $\{\boldsymbol{\mu}_i\}$, for $i \in \{R, G, B\}$. The augmented Lagrangian algorithm for regularizing an image using the Polyakov action is given as Algorithm 1. At each inner iteration k, $\{u_i\}_{i \in \{R,G,B\}}$ is updated in the Fourier domain, as in [32],

---

Algorithm 1. Augmented Lagrangian optimization of the Beltrami framework

1: $\boldsymbol{\mu}^0 \longleftarrow 0$
2: **for** k=0,1,... **do**
3:    Update $\{u_i\}^k$,$\{\mathbf{q}_i\}^k$:

$$(\{u_i\}^k, \{\mathbf{q}_i\}^k) = \text{argmin}_{\{u_i\},\{\mathbf{q}_i\}} \mathcal{L}_{BEL}(\{u_i\}, \{\mathbf{q}_i\}, \{\boldsymbol{\mu}_i^k\}) \qquad (7)$$

   according to Equation 8 and Subsection 3.1.
4:    Update the Lagrange multipliers according to Equation 9
5: **end for**

$$u_i^k = \mathcal{F}^{-1}\left\{ \frac{\alpha\mathcal{F}\{K^*\}\mathcal{F}\{f_i\} - \mathcal{F}\{D_x^-\}((\mu_i^1)^k + r(p_i)^k) - \mathcal{F}\{D_y^-\}((\mu_i^2)^k + r(q_i)^k)}{\alpha\mathcal{F}\{K^*\}\mathcal{F}\{K\} - r\mathcal{F}\{\Delta\}} \right\}, \qquad (8)$$

where $D_x^-, D_y^-, \triangle$ denote the backward derivative along the x and y directions, and the Laplacian operator, respectively, and $\mathcal{F}\{\cdot\}, \mathcal{F}^{-1}\{\cdot\}$ denote the Fourier transform and its inverse, respectively. We explicitly write $\mathbf{q}_i = (p_i, q_i), i \in \{R, G, B\}$, for the components of $\mathbf{q}$ of each color channel, approximating its x and y derivatives, computed using backward differences.

We note that the optimization of u using the Fourier domain resembles, in a sense, the approach taken by [21]. Since, however, it is done with respect to the auxiliary field, iteratively, its effect is suited to the nonlinear nature of the Beltrami flow. An update rule for the auxiliary field $\mathbf{q}_i$ of each channel is described in Subsection 3.1.

According to the augmented Lagrangian method, the Lagrange multipliers $\boldsymbol{\mu}_i$ are updated so as to approximate the optimal Lagrange multipliers,

$$(\boldsymbol{\mu}_i)^k = (\boldsymbol{\mu}_i)^{k-1} + r\left((\mathbf{q}_i)^k - (\nabla u_i)^k\right). \tag{9}$$

Finally, the coefficient r is updated between each outer iteration by multiplying r with a scalar $\gamma > 1$. We note r needs not be very large, thus avoiding ill-conditioning of the functional $\mathcal{L}_{BEL}(u, \mathbf{q}, \mu)$.

3.1   Updating the Auxiliary Field q

For optimizing $\mathbf{q}$, a short inner-loop of a fixed-point solver with *iterative reweighted least squares* (IRLS) allows us to efficiently obtain a solution. In numerical experiments, optimization over $\mathbf{q}$ takes less than half the CPU time of the algorithm. Furthermore, since this problem is solved per pixel, it can be easily parallelized, for example on a GPUs.

The update of $\mathbf{q}_i = (p_i, q_i), i \in \{R, G, B\}$, the components of $\mathbf{q}$ at each pixel, is done by optimizing the function

$$\sqrt{1 + \beta^2 \sum_i (p_i^2 + q_i^2) + \frac{\beta^4}{2} \sum_i \sum_{j \neq i} (p_i q_j - q_i p_j)^2}$$
$$+ \frac{r}{2} \sum_i \|\mathbf{q}_i - (\nabla u_i)\|^2 + \sum_{i \in \{R, G, B\}} (\boldsymbol{\mu}_i^k)^T (\mathbf{q}_i - \nabla u_i),$$

where $(\nabla u)_i = ((u_i)_x, (u_i)_y)^T$ denote the components of the various image channel gradients. Details of the update equations are given in the technical report [25].

4   Results

We now demonstrate the minimization of the Polyakov functional using the augmented Lagrangian method, for various applications. More examples are shown in the Technical report [25].

Scale-Space, Smoothing and Denoising: In Figure 1, results are shown for smoothing an image using various values of α, which in a sense parallel samples along the Beltrami scale-space (defined by the flow). We used the same initial penalty parameter $r = 0.5$, for which the constraints were satisfied after very few iterations. Fixed-point iterations over **q** were limited to 2 inner and 2 outer (IRLS) iterations for each cycle. The number of outer iterations, updating $\boldsymbol{\mu}$, in Figure 1 was 150, although fewer iterations suffice.

A comparison of the results of the augmented Lagrangian method and splitting schemes [11] shows that the augmented Lagrangian method converges faster, as can be seen in Figure 2. In this experiment, α was set for optimal results for both the augmented Lagrangian and the splitting methods. The PSNR plot also demonstrates the more accurate discretization of the proposed method. This can be easily seen in the preservation of edges in Figure 2. Experiments comparing our method to the explicit scheme showed a similar behavior.

Table 1 measures the CPU-time required for several images (shown in Figure 3) for our algorithm, compared to Beltrami filtering with operator splitting techniques. The time step used was the largest possible so as to avoid instabilities and inaccurate operator approximation.

Since the solution obtained by discretizing the functional and by discretizing the resulting Euler-Lagrange equation need not be the same, a different halting condition was used. After measuring the PSNR of each algorithm with respect to the original image, we measured the CPU time each algorithm took to gain 99% of the maximal rise in SNR. While this cannot be done in real applications, it does give us an objective measure of the time it takes to complete the convergence.

The speedups obtained are by at least of a factor of two compared to additive operator splitting (AOS) [19], which is one of the fastest methods for Beltrami regularization [11], even when the time step large enough to cause visible artifacts in the splitting results. The augmented Lagrangian method clearly gave still more accurate results in a shorter CPU time.

Deblurring: Deblurring results using the Beltrami framework are shown in Figure 4, with the blur kernel k a disc of radius 5 pixels. We compare our results to standard deblurring algorithms available in Matlab, as well as to BM3D deblurring [10], and to the FTVd algorithm [35]. Where the algorithms require a regularization parameter other than the noise level, it is empirically set to minimize the mean squared error. For Figure 4, we have chosen to use the functional shown in Equation 3. We set β_1 set to a very small positive constant, and set $\beta_2 = \beta^2, \beta_3 = \frac{\beta^4}{20}$, in order to slightly dampen the strength of the gradient coupling term.

The results clearly demonstrate the accurate deblurring obtained using the regularization offered by the Beltrami framework for natural color images, with slightly better PSNR compared to TV regularization. Beyond PSNR, careful examination of the images show the tendency of Beltrami regularization to avoid artifacts which do not fit the appearance of natural images, and discourage uneven coloring artifacts. This can be seen in Figures 4,5. The same discrepancy between PSNR reading and visual results in color image processing has already been noted by Goldluecke and Cremers [14]. We iterate this word of caution, and refer the reader to the images themselves.

Fruits, noisy   Denoised, $\alpha = 1.00$ Denoised, $\alpha = 0.40$ Denoised, $\alpha = 0.15$

Fig. 1. Smoothing, under various α values, of the Fruits image, with added Gaussian noise with $\sigma = 20$ intensity levels per channel

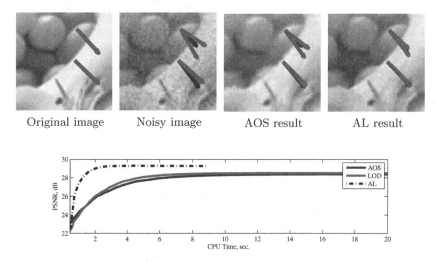

Original image   Noisy image   AOS result   AL result

Fig. 2. A comparison of the results for the AOS scheme, and the augmented Lagrangian method, as well as the PSNR of splitting schemes and the AL method as a function of CPU time. The arrows in the images demonstrate gradient directions at each channel. The graph demonstrates a faster convergence of the augmented Lagrangian method, as well as a more accurate discretization.

Table 1. Comparison of the CPU time required to complete 99% of the rise in SNR

Image	CPU time, AL	CPU time, splitting
Astro	1.77s	3.5s
Fruits	2.97s	7.36s
Lion	21.23s	59.66s
Monarch	3.63s	7.71s

Fig. 3. Images used to compare the computational cost of the augmented Lagrangian and splitting-based Beltrami regularization. Left to right: (a) Astro image. (b) Fruits image. (c) Lion image (d) Monarch image.

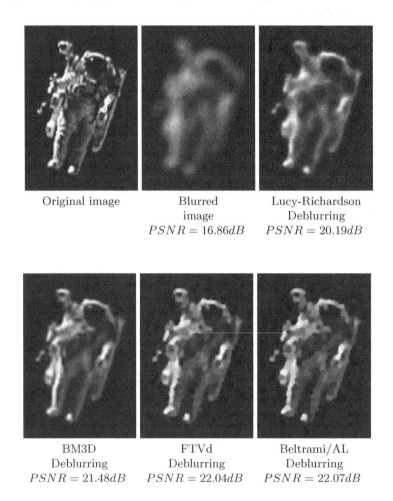

Original image	Blurred image $PSNR = 16.86dB$	Lucy-Richardson Deblurring $PSNR = 20.19dB$

BM3D Deblurring $PSNR = 21.48dB$	FTVd Deblurring $PSNR = 22.04dB$	Beltrami/AL Deblurring $PSNR = 22.07dB$

Fig. 4. Deblurring results with a disc blur filter of radius 5 and an Gaussian noise of $\sigma = 5$. Left to right, top to bottom: (a) The original image. (b) The blurred image. (c) Deblurring using the Lucy-Richardson algorithm (d) BM3D-based deblurring. (e) Deblurring using the FTVd method. (f) Deblurring using the Beltrami / augmented Lagrangian algorithm.

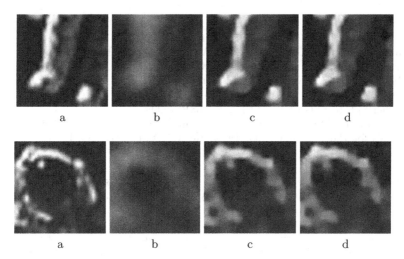

Fig. 5. Each row represents two regions zoomed-in from Figure 4. (a) The original image. (b) The corrupted image. (c) TV results. (d) Beltrami / AL restoration results.

5   Conclusions

We presented an extension of the augmented Lagrangian method for color image processing with Beltrami regularization. Unlike existing techniques, the method discretizes the functional itself, rather than the resulting optimality conditions or minimizing flow. We present numerical examples demonstrating its efficiency and accuracy compared to existing techniques for variational regularization, and its effectiveness in image deblurring. In future work we intend to add a robust fidelity term [36], and explore other possible applications for our framework.

References

1. Antoni Buades, B.C., Morel, J.-M.: A review of image denoising algorithms, with a new one. SIAM Interdisciplinary Journal 4, 490–530 (2005)
2. Bar, L., Brook, A., Sochen, N., Kiryati, N.: Deblurring of color images corrupted by impulsive noise. IEEE Trans. Image Process. 16(4), 1101–1111 (2007)
3. Barash, D.: A fundamental relationship between bilateral filtering, adaptive smoothing and the nonlinear diffusion equation. IEEE Trans. Pattern Anal. Mach. Intell. 24(6), 844–847 (2002)
4. Blomgren, P., Chan, T.F.: Color TV: Total variation methods for restoration of vector valued images. IEEE Trans. Image Processing 7, 304–309 (1996)
5. Bresson, X., Chan, T.: Fast dual minimization of the vectorial total variation norm and applications to color image processing. CAM-Report 07-25, UCLA (2007)
6. Bresson, X., Vandergheynst, P., Thiran, J.-P.: Multiscale active contours. Int. J. of Comp. Vision 70(3), 197–211 (2006)
7. Carter, J.L.: Dual methods for total variation-based image restoration. CAM-Report 02-13, UCLA (April 2002)

8. Chambolle, A.: An algorithm for total variation minimization and applications. J. Math. Imaging Vis. 20(1-2), 89–97 (2004)
9. Chan, T.F., Golub, G.H., Mulet, P.: A nonlinear primal-dual method for total variation-based image restoration. SIAM J. Sci. Comput. 20, 1964–1977 (1999)
10. Dabov, K., Foi, A., Katkovnik, V., Egiazarian, K.: Image restoration by sparse 3D transform-domain collaborative filtering. In: Astola, J.T., Egiazarian, K.O., Dougherty, E.R. (eds.) Proc. SPIE, vol. 6812 (2008)
11. Dascal, L., Rosman, G., Tai, X.-C., Kimmel, R.: On Semi-implicit Splitting Schemes for the Beltrami Color Flow. In: Tai, X.-C., Mørken, K., Lysaker, M., Lie, K.-A. (eds.) SSVM 2009. LNCS, vol. 5567, pp. 259–270. Springer, Heidelberg (2009)
12. do Carmo, M.P.: Riemannian Geometry. Birkhäuser Verlag, Boston (1992)
13. Elad, M.: On the bilateral filter and ways to improve it. IEEE Trans. Image Process. 11(10), 1141–1151 (2002)
14. Goldluecke, B., Cremers, D.: An approach to vectorial total variation based on geometric measure theory. In: Computer Vision and Pattern Recognition (2010)
15. Hesteness, M.R.: Multipliers and gradient methods. Journal of Optimization Theory and Applications 4, 303–320 (1969)
16. Kaftory, R., Sochen, N., Zeevi, Y.Y.: Variational blind deconvolution of multi-channel images. IJIST 15(1), 56–63 (2005)
17. Kimmel, R.: Numerical Geometry of Images: Theory, Algorithms, and Applications. Springer (2003)
18. Kimmel, R., Malladi, R., Sochen, N.: Images as embedding maps and minimal surfaces: Movies, color, texture, and volumetric medical images. Int. J. of Comp. Vision 39(2), 111–129 (2000)
19. Lü, T., Neittaanmääki, P., Tai, X.-C.: A parallel splitting up method and its application to Navier-Stokes equations. Applied Mathematics Letters 4(2), 25–29 (1991)
20. Osher, S., Burger, M., Goldfarb, D., Xu, J., Yin, W.: An iterative regularization method for total variation-based image restoration. Simul. 4, 460–489 (2005)
21. Paris, S., Durand, F.: A fast approximation of the bilateral filter using a signal processing approach. Int. J. of Comp. Vision 81(1), 24–52 (2009)
22. Polyakov, A.M.: Quantum geometry of bosonic strings. Physics Letters 103B(3), 207–210 (1981)
23. Powell, M.J.: Optimization. chapter A method for nonlinear constraints in minimization problems, pp. 283–298. Academic Press (1969)
24. Rosman, G., Dascal, L., Kimmel, R., Sidi, A.: Efficient beltrami image filtering via vector extrapolation methods. SIAM J. Imag. Sci. (3), 858–878 (2008)
25. Rosman, G., Tai, X.-C., Kimmel, R., Dascal, L.: Polyakov action minimization for efficient color image processing. Technical Report CIS-2010-04, Technion (2010)
26. Rudin, L.I., Osher, S., Fatemi, E.: Nonlinear total variation based noise removal algorithms. Physica D Letters 60, 259–268 (1992)
27. Sapiro, G., Ringach, D.L.: Anisotropic diffusion of multivalued images with applications to color filtering. IEEE Trans. Image Process. 5(11), 1582–1586 (1996)
28. Smith, S.M., Brady, J.: SUSAN – A new approach to low level image processing. Int. J. of Comp. Vision 23, 45–78 (1997)
29. Sochen, N., Kimmel, R., Bruckstein, A.M.: Diffusions and confusions in signal and image processing. J. of Math. in Imag. and Vis. 14(3), 195–209 (2001)
30. Sochen, N., Kimmel, R., Maladi, R.: A general framework for low level vision. IEEE Trans. Image Process. 7(3), 310–318 (1998)
31. Spira, A., Kimmel, R., Sochen, N.A.: A short-time Beltrami kernel for smoothing images and manifolds. IEEE Trans. Image Process. 16(6), 1628–1636 (2007)

32. Tai, X.-C., Wu, C.: Augmented Lagrangian method, dual methods and split Bregman iteration for ROF model. In: SSVM, pp. 502–513 (2009)
33. Tomasi, C., Manduchi, R.: Bilateral filtering for gray and color images. In: Int. Conf. on Comp. Vision, pp. 836–846 (1998)
34. Tschumperle, D., Deriche, R.: Vector-valued image regularization with pdes: A common framework for different applications. IEEE Transactions on Pattern Analysis and Machine Intelligence 27, 506–517 (2005)
35. Wang, Y., Yang, J., Yin, W., Zhang, Y.: A new alternating minimization algorithm for total variation image reconstruction. SIAM J. Imag. Sci. 1(3), 248–272 (2008)
36. Wu, C., Zhang, J., Tai, X.-C.: Augmented Lagrangian method for total variation restoration with non-quadratic fidelity. CAM Report 09-82, UCLA (December 2009)
37. Yaroslavsky, L.P.: Digital Picture Processing. Springer-Verlag New York, Inc., Secaucus (1985)
38. Yezzi, A.J.: Modified curvature motion for image smoothing and enhancement. IEEE Trans. Image Process. 7(3), 345–352 (1998)
39. Zenzo, S.D.: A note on the gradient of a multi-image. Computer Vision, Graphics, and Image Processing 33(1), 116–125 (1986)

Color Invariant SURF
in Discriminative Object Tracking

Dung Manh Chu and Arnold W.M. Smeulders

Intelligent Systems Lab Amsterdam (ISLA), University of Amsterdam
Science Park 107, 1098 XG, Amsterdam, The Netherlands
{Chu,A.W.M.Smeulders}@uva.nl

Abstract. Tracking can be seen as an online learning problem, where the focus is on discriminating object from background. From this point of view, features play a key role as the tracking accuracy depends on how well the feature distinguishes object and background. Current discriminative trackers use traditional features such as intensity, RGB and full body shape features. In this paper, we propose to use color invariant SURF features in the discriminative tracking. This set of invariant features has been shown to be of increased invariance and discriminative power. The resulting tracker inherits a good discrimination between object and background while keeping advantages of the discriminative tracking framework. Experiments on a dataset of 80 videos covering a wide range of tracking circumstances show that the tracker is robust to changes in object appearance, lighting conditions and able to track objects under cluttered scenes and partial occlusion.

Keywords: tracking, surf, color, invariant.

1 Introduction

In many visual object trackers [1–4], traditional features such as intensity, RGB and full body shape features are used. They reflect the state of the image directly and they are fast to compute. However, to cope with varying aspects of the object and the scene, features should be invariant to the undesired variations in the appearance of the object such as shadows, shadings and occlusions and discriminative enough to distinguish object from other objects and background. These above features are of limited invariance to such changes. The SIFT/SURF [5, 6] show increase in discriminative power [7, 8]. In particular Van de Sande et al. [9] show that the set of color and invariant SIFT obtains the best performance in the object recognition task. Moreover, the computations of SIFT and SURF are recently made fast enough for real-time application [10]. Inspired by these results, in this paper we aim to investigate invariant features in visual object tracking.

At large, trackers can be divided by three main mechanisms: background models [11, 12], foreground-based trackers [3, 4] and discriminative (foreground-background) trackers [2, 13, 14]. Many background-based trackers

K.N. Kutulakos (Ed.): ECCV 2010 Workshops, Part II, LNCS 6554, pp. 62–75, 2012.

and foreground-based trackers resort to assumptions that an aspect of the background or the foreground is constant (or at least predictable for the next image). They are designed to work well when disturbing scene-related circumstances develop slowly over time and place. Under that condition, the model of the background or the model of the foreground can be adapted. However, the assumption of slow development of the lighting and scene conditions is frequently violated in reality when there are abrupt changes in object appearance due to entering into shadow, abrupt albedo changes due to rotation, abrupt object motion changes, or abrupt silhouette changes due to occlusion. In many of such situations, discriminative trackers are in favor over the other two as they put in the center the distinction between foreground and background rather than modeling the foreground alone or background alone. Concentrating on discriminative trackers, invariant discriminative features are the natural ingredient to incorporate.

This paper proposes a novel tracking method using foreground/background discrimination. Unlike the above-mentioned methods, the proposed tracker uses color invariant SURF features for discrimination. The aim is to be robust to changes in object appearance and lighting conditions. And, the aim is to track objects under cluttered scenes and partial occlusions. An innovation of the research is the use of a broad dataset [15] developed to test the robustness of all sorts of tracking conditions as they occur in reality.

2   Related Work

Our work is based on two components: discriminative tracking and color invariant features. We hence review these two topics in this section.

2.1   Discriminative Trackers

The discriminative trackers in [16, 17] are focused on classifier selection. A set of weak classifiers is trained on object features and background features. Grabner et al. [16] use online boosting to establish a strong classifier. Avidan [17] combines the weak classifiers into a decision by AdaBoost. Although online boosting and AdaBoost help to select best results from the weak classifiers, they disregard the spatial relation between object features. They suffer from a large number of free parameters to estimate, making the tracking computationally expensive and unstable under varying conditions.

The discriminative trackers in [18, 19] are focused on feature selection. Grabner et al. [18] propose a semi-supervised online learning method to select features. Mahadevan and Vasconcelos [19] define saliency measure for features, which ranks features how well they discriminate. Since the features are not invariant with respect to varying tracking conditions, feature selection methods will select best features on the fly. This method however leaves many degrees of freedom.

In [2], linear discriminant analysis is applied to discriminative tracking. An analytical incremental solution is found for updating the classifier online. It enables fast updating scheme with a small number of free parameters. The tracker also retains a spatial relation between object features. This allows the tracker to overcome partial occlusions and compensate for global changes of illumination. Due to its computational simplicity and the small number of free parameters we follow this discrimination technique in our tracker.

2.2 Features in Object Trackers

Many trackers successfully replace grey features by color features (see an overview in [20]) and by SIFT/SURF features. He et al. [21] propose a SURF-based tracker where SURF-features are extracted from the object and its surrounding area using interest points. Object feature correspondence is estimated and then used to predict the object motion. Background features are only used to detect occlusions. The tracker imposes a smooth transition of the object appearance. Zhou et al. [22] apply original SIFT features into the mean shift tracking framework. Due to the discriminative power of SIFT, the resulting tracker outperforms the original version at the expense of considerably more computation. Tran and Davis [23] use SIFT in blob tracking, where objects are represented by a set of MSER regions. Object motion is estimated from the estimations of the blobs' motions. The tracker can track objects undergoing illumination changes due to the use of SIFT feature. These results show the potential of using SIFT/SURF in tracking.

The trackers in [24–26] successfully apply color features into the discriminative tracking framework. The tracker in Collins et al. [26] works on a pool of 49 linear combinations of R, G, B. For each feature, the log likelihood ratio between foreground and background feature histograms is computed, which is then used to rank the features. Similar mechanisms can also be found in [24] with multiple color spaces and color distribution models, or in [25] with 7 types of color histograms and gradient orientation histogram. These trackers demonstrate the usefulness of color features in discriminative tracking.

Our tracker is different from the above trackers. We use a different set of features in discriminative tracking. The features are the combinations of SURF with different color spaces and color invariants. These features are of enhanced discriminative and invariance power.

3 The Proposed Tracker

3.1 Discriminative Tracking Framework

Discriminative tracking treats tracking as a two-class instant classification problem between the object class and the background class. The object features are densely sampled in the object region and denoted by $\boldsymbol{f}_1^o, \ldots, \boldsymbol{f}_n^o$. The background features are also densely sampled in the neighbor background region and denoted by $\boldsymbol{f}_1^b, \ldots, \boldsymbol{f}_m^b$. As we aim to discriminate the object from background, with each object feature $\boldsymbol{f}_i^o$, a classifier g_i is trained to distinguish it from all the background features. The set of classifiers $\{g_1, \ldots, g_n\}$ constitutes the discrimination between the object and background. g_i should be fast to train in the incremental mode and have few free parameters to arrive at a robust solution on few samples. To this end, we follow [2] with the use a linear classifier:

$$g_i(\boldsymbol{x}) = \langle \boldsymbol{a}_i, \boldsymbol{x} \rangle + b_i, \tag{1}$$

where $\boldsymbol{a}_i \in \mathcal{R}^N$, $b_i \in \mathcal{R}$ and $\langle,\rangle$ denotes the inner product; N is the dimension of the used feature. The classifier g_i is trained such that

$$g_i(\boldsymbol{f}_i^o) > 0 \text{ and } g_i(\boldsymbol{f}_j^b) < 0 \text{ for all } \boldsymbol{f}_j^b. \tag{2}$$

When a new frame comes in, denote by θ the spatial transformation between the two frames and by $I(\boldsymbol{f}_i^o, \theta)$ the feature in the new frame that correspond to feature $\boldsymbol{f}_i^o$. The search for the object in the new frame is cast into the following maximization problem:

$$\hat{\theta} = \arg \max_{\theta} \sum_{i=1}^{n} g_i(I(\boldsymbol{f}_i^o, \theta)). \tag{3}$$

The maximization effectively pushes the object candidate as far away from the known background features as possible and pulls it close to the known object features. We notice that as $g_i(I(\boldsymbol{f}_i^o, \theta)) = \langle \boldsymbol{a}_i, I(\boldsymbol{f}_i^o, \theta) \rangle + b_i$ and b_i is independent from θ, we only need to compute $\boldsymbol{a}_i$.

Learning and Updating the Classifiers: given the object features $\boldsymbol{f}_1^o, \ldots, \boldsymbol{f}_n^o$ and the background features $\boldsymbol{f}_1^b, \ldots, \boldsymbol{f}_m^b$, we learn the classifiers g_i by solving the following optimization problem:

$$\min_{\boldsymbol{a}_i, b_i} \left[(\langle \boldsymbol{a}_i, \boldsymbol{f}_i^o \rangle + b_i - 1)^2 + \sum_{j=1}^{m} \alpha_j \left(\langle \boldsymbol{a}_i, \boldsymbol{f}_j^b \rangle + b_i + 1 \right)^2 + \frac{\lambda}{2} ||\boldsymbol{a}_i||^2 \right], \tag{4}$$

where α_j are the weighting coefficients of the background features, $\sum_{j=1}^{m} \alpha_j = 1$. The closed-form solution of (4) is given by ([2]):

$$\boldsymbol{a}_i = c_i \left(\lambda \boldsymbol{I} + \boldsymbol{B} \right)^{-1} \left(\boldsymbol{f}_i^o - \bar{\boldsymbol{f}}^b \right), \tag{5}$$

where $\boldsymbol{B}$ and $\bar{\boldsymbol{f}}^b$ are the weighted covariance and mean of the background features; $\boldsymbol{I}$ is the identity matrix:

$$\bar{\boldsymbol{f}}^b = \sum_{j=1}^{m} \alpha_j \boldsymbol{f}_j^b, \tag{6}$$

$$\boldsymbol{B} = \sum_{j=1}^{m} \alpha_j \left(\boldsymbol{f}_j^b - \bar{\boldsymbol{f}}^b \right) \left(\boldsymbol{f}_j^b - \bar{\boldsymbol{f}}^b \right)^T, \tag{7}$$

$$c_i = \frac{1}{1 + 0.5 \left(\boldsymbol{f}_i^o - \bar{\boldsymbol{f}}^b \right)^T \left(\lambda \boldsymbol{I} + \boldsymbol{B} \right)^{-1} \left(\boldsymbol{f}_i^o - \bar{\boldsymbol{f}}^b \right)}. \tag{8}$$

Equations (6), (7) and (8) allow a fast learning step for the classifiers. We notice that the background features are compactly represented by the weighted mean and the weighted covariance. It is hence not necessary to keep all the background features.

After each tracking step, we extract new object and background features. Suppose that $\hat{\theta}$ is the spatial transformation found by solving the optimization problem in Equation (3). Then $I(\boldsymbol{f}_1^o, \hat{\theta}), \ldots, I(\boldsymbol{f}_n^o, \hat{\theta})$ are the new object features. In order to allow the tracker to remember the past appearance of the object, we allow the old features to stay in the object representation with decreasing weights:

$$\boldsymbol{f}_i^{o(new)} = (1 - \gamma)\boldsymbol{f}_i^o + \gamma I(\boldsymbol{f}_i^o, \hat{\theta}), \tag{9}$$

where γ is a predefined decay coefficient.

Suppose that $\boldsymbol{f}_{m+1}^b, \ldots, \boldsymbol{f}_{m+k}^b$ are the new background features. We put total weight for the new background to be γ, while the weight of each old background feature is downscaled $(1 - \gamma)$. The updated background mean and covariance are given by:

$$\bar{\boldsymbol{f}}^{b(new)} = (1 - \gamma)\bar{\boldsymbol{f}}^b + \gamma \frac{1}{k} \sum_{j=m+1}^{m+k} \boldsymbol{f}_j^b, \tag{10}$$

$$\boldsymbol{B}^{(new)} = (1 - \gamma)\boldsymbol{B} + (1 - \gamma)\bar{\boldsymbol{f}}^b \bar{\boldsymbol{f}}^{bT} - \bar{\boldsymbol{f}}^{b(new)} \bar{\boldsymbol{f}}^{b(new)T} + \frac{\gamma}{k} \sum_{j=m+1}^{m+k} \boldsymbol{f}_j^b \boldsymbol{f}_j^{bT}. \tag{11}$$

The set of Equations (5), (8), (9), (10) and (11) allows the tracker to update the classifiers in the incremental mode efficiently.

3.2   Features

The use of SURF in visual tracking is rather limited in few foreground-based trackers [21–23]. One of the reasons is due to the expensive procedure to compute SURF descriptors at interest points. We overcome this problem by extracting features $\{\boldsymbol{f}_1^o, \ldots, \boldsymbol{f}_n^o; \boldsymbol{f}_1^b, \ldots, \boldsymbol{f}_m^b\}$ densely and using the fast algorithm to compute SURF descriptors recently proposed in [10].

The original intensity-based SURF features have been extended to different color spaces and color invariant spaces. They have not yet been explored in visual tracking. Among the color spaces, we choose the opponent space as the high decorrelation between the 3 channels. Opponent color space contains one intensity channel and two chromaticity channels. As the three channels are highly decorrelated they are likely to improve the discriminative power when used together:

$$\begin{pmatrix} O_1 \\ O_2 \\ O_3 \end{pmatrix} = \begin{pmatrix} \frac{R-G}{\sqrt{2}} \\ \frac{R+G-2B}{\sqrt{6}} \\ \frac{R+G+B}{\sqrt{3}} \end{pmatrix}. \tag{12}$$

With the color invariants, Geusebroek et al. [27] show an inclusion relationship: $H \subset C \subset W$, where H, C and W are three invariants derived from the Kubelka-Munk photometric model under different assumptions. The inclusion implies that H has highest invariance and essentially H flattens out all patterns in an image. This is not a desired property for tracking since we want to keep a certain level of discriminative power to distinguish the object from the scene and from other objects. On the other hand, W lacks invariance. It does not wipe out accidental changes from illumination. We did experiments with the 3 invariants separately and observed consistently degraded performance of the H and W versions over the C version (the differences are approximately 58% and 8% respectively. Further data is not shown here). We hence will focus on C-SURF. We also use the intensity SURF (I-SURF) as baseline.

The C invariant [27] is an object reflectance property independent of the viewpoint, surface orientation, illumination direction and illumination intensity. The C color space consists of one intensity channel and 2 channels $\{C_\lambda, C_{\lambda\lambda}\}$ computed as follows:

$$\begin{aligned} C_\lambda &= \frac{E_\lambda}{E} \\ C_{\lambda\lambda} &= \frac{E_{\lambda\lambda}}{E}, \end{aligned} \tag{13}$$

where $E(\lambda)$ is the energy distribution of the incident light over wavelength λ. $E, E_\lambda, E_{\lambda\lambda}$ are estimated from an RGB image as follows:

$$\begin{pmatrix} E \\ E_\lambda \\ E_{\lambda\lambda} \end{pmatrix} = \begin{pmatrix} 0.06 & 0.63 & 0.27 \\ 0.3 & 0.04 & -0.35 \\ 0.34 & -0.6 & 0.17 \end{pmatrix} \begin{pmatrix} R \\ G \\ B \end{pmatrix}. \tag{14}$$

4   Dataset and Evaluation Metric

As we aim to design a tracker robust to the wide variety of tracking circumstances, we use the dataset in [15] covering 12 most important tracking conditions: lighting condition, object albedo, object specularity, object transparency, object shape, motion smoothness of object, motion coherence of object, clutter, confusion, occlusion, moving camera and zooming camera (the reference gives more detail on the selection and creation of the dataset). This dataset enables evaluation of a tracker with respect to different tracking circumstances. The dataset contains 80 videos covering both realistic videos and in-lab videos. The distribution of the videos over the categories are uniform. The videos are manually annotated in every $5th$ frame. Some example videos from the dataset are depicted in Figures 3, 4 and 5.

To measure the trackers' performance, [15] proposes to use a category-level average tracking accuracy measure (CATA), which indicates how much a tracker covers the object in each frame in average. CATA ranges from 0 to 1. The higher CATA is, the more accurate the tracker is. A CATA value of 0.6, for example, implies that in average in each frame where the object is present, the tracker covers at least 60% of the object and at least 60% of the tracked box is covered by the object.

5   Results

We demonstrate the performance of the proposed tracker in this section. For comparison purpose, three other state-of-the-art trackers are considered: the foreground background tracker (FBT) in [2]; the incremental visual tracker (IVT) in [3] and the Kalman predictive tracker (KAT) in [4]. We reimplemented the FBT and KAT, while the IVT is publicly available online from the author website.

5.1   Quantitative Comparison between Features

This section shows comparison of the proposed discriminative tracking framework with different types of features. In [2], the intensity Gabor feature is used. We extended it to include rudimental color information, resulting in the RGB Gabor feature. We compute CATA values of the discriminative tracking framework for 5 different types of features: intensity Gabor, RGB Gabor, I-SURF, C-SURF and Opponent-SURF. The data is visualized in Figure 1. As can be seen from the figure, the SURF-based versions outperform the Gabor-based versions in 11 out of 12 cases. This is attributed to the high discriminativeness of the SURF-based features, which especially is suited for our discriminative tracking framework. Large differences between the SURF-based versions and the Gabor-based versions can be seen in the following categories: albedo, transparency, clutter, confusion and occlusion.

Among the SURF-based versions, Opponent-SURF and C-SURF show better performance than I-SURF. This is attributed to the high decorrelation between three channels in the opponent color space, which contains one intensity channel decorrelated from the two chromaticity channels. The discriminative power of C-SURF regardless accidental shadows and shadings makes it well suited in combination with the online classifier which is at the core of this tracker. C-SURF improves the classification accuracy in our tracker especially in the confusion and occlusion cases where the object shares similar patterns with other neighbor objects or the object loses part of its appearance in occlusion.

Table 1. The average performance of the discriminative tracking framework with the 5 features in the whole dataset. This is computed by averaging all the CATA values of the 12 categories.

	Intensity Gabor	RGB Gabor	I-SURF	C-SURF	Opponent-SURF
Average	0.43	0.51	0.58	0.61	0.60

To conclude, SURF-based features outperform Gabor-based features. Further, color-based features outperform intensity-based features. As can be seen in Table 1, I-SURF gains improvement of 0.15 (35%), while Opponent-SURF and C-SURF gain even 0.17 (40%) and 0.18 (42%) respectively with respect to the original tracker in [2].

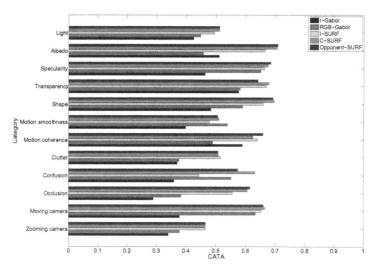

Fig. 1. Performance of the discriminative tracking framework with different types of features and different tracking circumstances. The x-axis indicates the CATA measure. The y-axis contains 12 different tracking categories in the dataset with total 80 videos.

5.2   Quantitative Comparison to Other Trackers

This section shows a quantitative comparison of the proposed tracker with the KAT and the IVT. We have integrated RGB, SURF, C-SURF and Opponent-SURF into the KAT and the IVT. However the SURF-based features do not improve the two trackers. The reason is that the numbers of free parameters in the IVT and the KAT are proportional to the feature's dimension. The use of the SURF-based features hence increases the number of free parameters to be estimated in the IVT and KAT with a limited number of samples. Hence the SURF-based features downgrade their performances. With IVT, we observe the best performance with the RGB feature, while the intensity feature is the best with KAT. The results of the proposed tracker with C-SURF, KAT with intensity and IVT with RGB are shown in Figure 2. As can be seen from the figure, the proposed tracker is more robust to changes in illumination conditions, object albedo and transparency. This is explained by the invariance of SURF to light intensity change and light intensity shift, which aids the tracker to overcome a certain level of illumination changes. The KAT gets affected most in the transparency case. The reason is that in such a case the object appearance reflects the color of the local background behind the object. Because of the inhomogeneous background, the object appearance changes abruptly, which violates the smooth assumption the KAT imposes on the object features.

Figure 2 also shows that the proposed tracker is more robust to confusion with the CATA value 63% while the scores for the IVT and the KAT are about 40%. The discriminative and invariance power of C-SURF enables the proposed tracker to distinguish the object from other nearby objects of similar

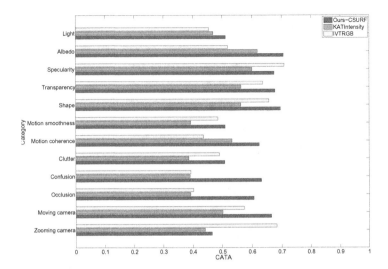

Fig. 2. Quantitative comparison between the proposed tracker with the IVT and the KAT. We select the best features: C-SURF for the proposed tracker, intensity for KAT and RGB for IVT. The x-axis indicates the CATA measure. The y-axis contains 12 different tracking categories in the dataset.

appearance. We notice that confusion downgrades the IVT and the KAT as the two trackers have no mechanism to isolate the object even though they keep good representations of the object. The proposed tracker also outperforms the IVT and the KAT in the occlusion category. We notice that the IVT is the best in the zooming camera case. This is attributed to the scaling handling mechanism enabling the tracker to cope with objects with changing size due to camera's zooming. Overall, as can be seen from Table 2, the proposed tracker gains improvement of 0.12 (24%) and 0.07 (13%) over the KAT and the IVT respectively.

Table 2. The average performance of each tracker in the whole dataset. This value is computed by averaging the CATA values of the 12 categories.

	IVT-RGB	KAT-Intensity	Proposed-CSURF
Average	0.54	0.49	0.61

5.3   Robustness to Changes of Illumination and Object Appearance

In this section we analyze the performance of the proposed tracker with changes in illumination and object appearance. We select the best feature for each tracker: RGB with FBT, intensity with KAT, RGB with IVT and C-SURF with the proposed tracker.

Fig. 3. The first row: a person undergoing foliage-like illumination. The second row: a person undergoing large changes in illumination intensity. Results of the 4 trackers are shown: yellow - IVT; red - FBT; blue - KAT; green - ours. Our tracker is able to track the targets despite abrupt changes of illumination over space and time.

In Figure 3, two targets undergoing different illumination conditions are being tracked. In the first row, the target is a person walking under dense foliage with abrupt changes in lighting over space and time. The FBT suffers small drift in each time step and eventually loses the object at frame 193 as the limited discriminative power of the feature and the presence of similar patterns in foreground and background. The KAT and IVT get small drifts at the end when the object turns left and the trackers are locked at an illuminated region in the background. The uneven illumination does not affect our tracker. Despite many false movements of the object, the results of tracker remain accurate.

In the second row of Figure 3, the target is a person moving from a dark area to a brighter area with the illumination intensity changing largely. The IVT gets difficulty at the beginning of the sequence since it confuses the face with the background. Due to lack of invariance of the features, the FBT and KAT drift away from the object at frame 170 and 380 respectively. Our tracker successfully tracks the object because of the invariance to light intensity changes of the SURF feature.

Figure 4 demonstrates the performance of our tracker with changes of object appearance. In the first row, a face undergoes translation and rotation movements. At frame 50, the other 3 trackers lose the object due to the rotation movement of the object. After that the KAT and the IVT accidentally recover the object. But only the KAT and the proposed tracker successfully follow the object till the end. This video shows the ability of our tracker in coping with new patterns when the object rotates in the vertical axis. The use of highly discriminative features enables the tracker to avoid the confusion of the black area of the head with the blackboard in the background. This is the reason why the FBT loses the object. In the second row of Figure 4, an experimental video is shown to demonstrate our tracker's robustness to changes in object appearance. The target is a rotating three-color ball. At frame 50 when the pink area occurs, the other 3 trackers drift away while our tracker still can follow the ball.

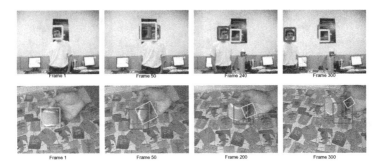

Fig. 4. The first row: A person with translation and rotation motion. The second row: a 3-color ball undergoing rotation. In both cases, the targets undergo large variations in appearance. Our tracker can adapt to new appearance patterns and successfully follow the targets.

5.4   Robustness to Confusion and Partial Occlusions

Figure 5 shows examples of tracking under clutter and confusion conditions. In the first row, a pupil in uniform runs in front of many other classmates. We notice that as all the pupils are in uniform, the object looks very similar to other nearby objects. This causes KAT and FBT to fail at the beginning and IVT to fail at frame 75. Our tracker succeeds in disregarding the confusion as the use of the discriminative feature, which allows it to focus on very distinct pattern of the object that discriminate it from the background patterns. A similar phenomenon can be seen in the second row and the third row of Figure 5, where our tracker successfully follows a person running in a marathon with similar objects in the vicinity and Waldo moving in front of a Where's Waldo picture.

The two videos in Figure 6 demonstrate the ability of the proposed tracker to cope with partial occlusion. Before the object enters the occlusion area, it enters a shadow area. As can be seen from the two videos, both IVT and KAT fail as the shadows change the object appearance abruptly. With the red ball video in the first row, the FBT overcomes the shadow area due to the distinct color of the object. It however fails to follow the toy car in the second row when it is occluded. Due the shadow invariance property of C-SURF, our tracker does not get affected by shadow and successfully follow the objects in both situations.

5.5   Failure Analysis

We search for failure cases of the proposed tracker. Figure 7 depicts 3 situations where the proposed tracker fails. In the first row, the target gets bigger as the camera is zooming in. The proposed tracker does not drift away from the target. However it cannot cope with the changing size of the object. The IVT however precisely follow the target. The reason is that the IVT considers scaling while

Fig. 5. Tracking under cluttered scene and confusion. The first row: a pupil running in front of other classmates in the same uniform. The second row: a person in a marathon. The third row: tracking Waldo. Our tracker successfully discriminates the targets from nearby objects with similar appearance and cluttered background due to the use of invariant feature.

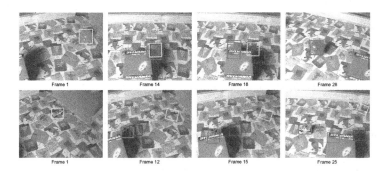

Fig. 6. Tracking under partial occlusion. The targets are the red ball and the toy car undergoing partial occlusion. Our tracker is able to follow the target accurately when they enter shadow and partial occlusion.

searching for the object. The proposed tracker, on the other hand, uses a fixed template window. In the second row, the target is a flock of birds. We notice that the dynamics of the flock shape makes it very difficult for the trackers to follow where many background patterns are present in the object region. In the third row, the changing light color is the challenge. At frame 13, the light becomes completely dark. We notice that the second and third rows represent two very extreme cases in visual tracking.

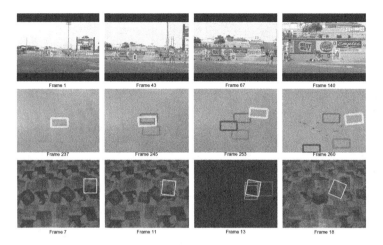

Fig. 7. Failure cases of the proposed tracker. The first row: tracking under zooming-in condition. The second row: tracking a flock of birds. The third row: tracking under changing light color.

6   Conclusion

We have presented a tracker that takes advantage of the discriminative tracking framework and highly discriminative power of SURF-based features. The resulting tracker is capable of tracking objects under changes in lighting conditions and object appearance and undergoing partial occlusion. The proposed tracker is also robust against confusion and cluttered scenes where there are similar objects in the vicinity of the tracked object.

The combination of SURF with the C invariant and the opponent color space are shown to be the best choice for the discriminative tracking framework. The conclusion goes along with the finding in Van de Sande et al. [9] in the object classification task. This makes an interesting link between object classification and discriminative tracking.

Acknowledgments. We thank Theo Gevers and Arjan Gijsenij for insightful comments and discussions.

References

1. Zivkovic, Z., Kröse, B.: An EM-like algorithm for color-histogram-based object tracking. In: CVPR (2004)
2. Nguyen, H., Smeulders, A.: Robust track using foreground-background texture discrimination. IJCV 68(3), 277–294 (2006)
3. Ross, D., Lim, J., Lin, R.S.: Incremental learning for robust visual tracking. IJCV 77, 125–141 (2008)
4. Nguyen, H., Smeulders, A.: Fast occluded object tracking by a robust appearance filter. PAMI 26, 1099–1104 (2004)

5. Lowe, D.G.: Distinctive image features from scale-invariant keypoints. IJCV 60, 91–110 (2004)
6. Bay, H., Ess, A., Tuytelaars, T., Van Gool, L.: Speeded-up robust features (surf). CVIU 110, 346–359 (2008)
7. Mikolajczyk, K., Schmid, C.: A performance evaluation of local descriptors. PAMI 27, 1615–1630 (2005)
8. Burghouts, G.J., Geusebroek, J.M.: Performance evaluation of local colour invariants. CVIU 113, 48–62 (2009)
9. Van de Sande, K.E.A., Gevers, T., Snoek, C.G.M.: Evaluating color descriptors for object and scene recognition. PAMI 32, 1582–1596 (2010)
10. Uijlings, J., Smeulders, A., Scha, R.: Real-time bag of words, approximately. In: CIVR (2009)
11. Alper Yimaz, O.J., Shah, M.: Object tracking: a survey. ACM Computing Surveys 38 (2006)
12. Sheikh, Y., Javed, O., Kanade, T.: Background subtraction for freely moving cameras. In: ICCV (2009)
13. Grabner, H., Grabner, M., Bischof, H.: Real-time tracking via on-line boosting. In: BMVC (2006)
14. Babenko, B., Yang, M.H., Belongie, S.: Visual tracking with online multiple instance learning. In: CVPR (2009)
15. Chu, D.M., Smeulders, A.W.M.: Thirteen hard cases in visual tracking. In: AVSS (2010)
16. Grabner, M., Grabner, H., Bischof, H.: Learning features for tracking. In: CVPR (2007)
17. Avidan, S.: Ensemble tracking. PAMI 29, 261–271 (2007)
18. Grabner, H., Leistner, C., Bischof, H.: Semi-supervised On-Line Boosting for Robust Tracking. In: Forsyth, D., Torr, P., Zisserman, A. (eds.) ECCV 2008, Part I. LNCS, vol. 5302, pp. 234–247. Springer, Heidelberg (2008)
19. Mahadevan, V., Vasconcelos, N.: Saliency-based discriminant tracking. In: CVPR (2009)
20. Tremeau, A., Tominaga, S., Plataniotis, K.N.: Color in image and video processing: most recent trends and future research directions. EURASIP Journal on Image and Video Processing 2008 (2008)
21. He, W., Yamashita, T., Lu, H., Lao, S.: Surf tracking. In: ICCV (2009)
22. Zhou, H., Yuan, Y., Shi, C.: Object tracking using sift features and mean shift. CVIU 113, 345–352 (2009)
23. Tran, S., Davis, L.: Robust object tracking with regional affine invariant features. In: ICCV (2007)
24. Stern, H., Efros, B.: Adaptive color space switching for tracking under varying illumination. IVC 23, 353–364 (2005)
25. Wang, J., Yagi, Y.: Integrating color and shape-texture features for adaptive real-time object tracking. TIP 17, 235–240 (2008)
26. Collins, R.T., Liu, Y., Leordeanu, M.: Online selection of discriminative tracking features. PAMI 27, 1631–1643 (2005)
27. Geusebroek, J.M., van den Boomgaard, R., Smeulders, A.W.M., Geerts, H.: Color invariance. PAMI 23, 1338–1350 (2001)

The Narrow-Band Assumption in Log-Chromaticity Space

Eva Eibenberger[1,2,3] and Elli Angelopoulou[1,3]

[1] Pattern Recognition Lab, University of Erlangen-Nuremberg, Germany
[2] International Max Planck Research School for Optics and Imaging
[3] Erlangen Graduate School in Advanced Optical Technologies (SAOT), Erlangen, Germany
{eva.eibenberger,elli.angelopoulou}@informatik.uni-erlangen.de

Abstract. Despite the strengths and popularity of the log-chromaticity space (LCS), there is still a significant amount of concern regarding its narrow-band assumption (NBA). Though not always necessary, this assumption is relatively common, as it leads to elegant formulations. We present a scheme for evaluating whether a deviation from the NBA will have an impact on the expected LCS values. We also introduce two metrics for measuring the divergence from the expected behavior under the NBA in LCS. Lastly, we empirically analyze how different types of reflectance spectra are affected in varying degrees by this assumption. For example, experiments with real and synthetic data show that the violation of the NBA typically has insignificant impact on bright unsaturated colors.

1 Introduction

Many applications in computer vision, like tracking, image retrieval, and object recognition are affected by variations in the illumination conditions. Therefore, a considerable amount of research has been focused on the development of illumination-invariant color spaces [1,2]. One such color space is the log-chromaticity space (LCS). The transformation of RGB values (I_R, I_G, I_B) to this space is done by first computing the 2D chromaticity values $\{I_R/I_G, I_B/I_G\}$ and then taking the logarithm of these color ratios. Two important properties are provided by this transformation: Firstly, a surface color seen under different illuminant colors tends to lie on a straight line in this space. Secondly, for a given camera, all these lines are parallel to each other for different surface colors. These two characteristics of LCS make it a very promising space for color and reflectance analysis. Hence, LCS is already quite widely used for applications like shadow removal [3,4,5,6,7], illumination estimation [8] and illumination invariant representations [1].

Many of these techniques make an additional assumption, the so-called *narrow-band assumption* (NBA) (e.g. [9,4,5,6,7]), which states that the sensor spectral sensitivities can be approximated by delta Dirac functions. Though this assumption leads to elegant and tractable mathematical formulations, most available

K.N. Kutulakos (Ed.): ECCV 2010 Workshops, Part II, LNCS 6554, pp. 76–89, 2012.

sensors exhibit non-narrow spectral sensitivities. Therefore, it is often argued that this assumption is too restrictive and not generally applicable [10,11,12].

In order to broaden the applicability of methodologies that assume narrow-spectral bands, *sensor sharpening* algorithms have been proposed [13,14,15]. Although, sensor sharpening enhances color constancy performance [16], its biggest limitation is the required camera calibration, which is can be tedious [16,5]. Furthermore, sharpening can only be performed if the sensor is available. Thus, it can not be applied on arbitrary images (like those found on the web), where the sensor is not available for calibration.

In this paper we evaluate the error in LCS values that is introduced by the violation of the NBA. We show that although deviations from the expected behavior in LCS can occur, it is often the case that for certain families of reflectivity (albedo) the violation of the Dirac delta assumption does not affect the LCS values. Due to the image formation process, it is difficult to separate the influences of the sensor characteristics, the illumination and the surface reflectance. In our efforts to address this challenge, we were influenced by previous evidence that for certain materials, like asphalt and skin, the violation of the NBA has minimal impact [11,17]. Therefore, we chose to focus our analysis on the suitability of the NBA for different surface reflectances. We introduce a new formulation which explicitly describes the deviation from the NBA. We then propose two error metrics for quantitative evaluation of the impact of the deviation. Our experiments on both synthetic and real data show that these error metrics can be used for determining whether a particular material is unaffected by possible violations of the NBA. Such an assessment can have a direct impact on broadening the applicability of LCS methods on arbitrary images.

2   Theory of the Log-Chromaticity Space

In order to systematically assess the impact of the NBA in the LCS one needs to first closely examine the image formation process as well as the influence of the incident illumination.

2.1   Planckian Illuminant

Empirical measurements of daylight spectra [18] have shown that outdoor light as well as indoor illuminants (CIE standard illuminants between $4000K$ and $13000K$) closely fit the corresponding black body radiators. The behavior of a black body radiator is in turn described by Planck's law. For the visible range $\exp(\frac{c_2}{\lambda T}) \gg 0$ and thus one can use Wien's approximation for describing the spectral distribution $E(\lambda, T)$ of such illuminants:

$$E(\lambda, T) \approx Ic_1\lambda^{-5} \exp\left(-\frac{c_2}{T\lambda}\right),   \tag{1}$$

where λ and T are the wavelength and illuminant temperature respectively, $c_1 = 2\pi h v^2$ and $c_2 = hv/k$ are constants containing the Planck constant h, the

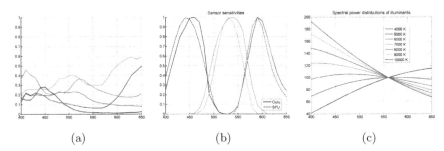

Fig. 1. Image formation. (a) Surface reflectance functions. (b) Sensor sensitivities. (c) Spectral power distributions of Planckian illuminants.

Boltzmann constant k, and the speed of light v in vacuum. As in Finlayson and Hordley [9], the intensity constant I is introduced to model the varying intensity power. Fig. 1(c) shows the emission spectra of different color temperatures.

2.2   Image Formation

An image captured by a typical color camera can be modeled as:

$$I_c(\mathbf{x}) = g \left(\int_\Omega q_c(\lambda) S(\mathbf{x}, \lambda) E(\mathbf{x}, \lambda) d\lambda \right)^{\frac{1}{\gamma}}, \quad c \in \{R, G, B\}. \tag{2}$$

This equation states that at a position $\mathbf{x}$ the sensor response for a certain color channel c is a combination of the sensor sensitivity q_c, the illumination E and the surface reflectance S. The integral is computed over the visible spectrum Ω. In order to incorporate further sensor characteristics we also consider the camera gain g and gamma γ. The image sharpening, which is also often built-in in modern digital cameras, is not considered in this context, as the proposed analysis is not based on spatial but rather only on color information. Fig. 1 shows the three components of image formation.

The *narrow-band assumption* (NBA) [9,6] directly affects the image formation model. This assumption states that the sensor sensitivities are considered to be Dirac delta functions, $q_c(\lambda) = k_c \delta(\lambda - \lambda_c)$, centered at wavelength λ_c. Assuming a constant illuminant color across the scene, Eq. 2 becomes:

$$I_c(\mathbf{x}) = g k_c^{\frac{1}{\gamma}} S(\mathbf{x}, \lambda_c)^{\frac{1}{\gamma}} E(\lambda_c)^{\frac{1}{\gamma}}. \tag{3}$$

2.3   The Log-Chromaticity Color Space

Among the different chromaticity spaces, we choose to use the ratios of the red and blue channel with respect to green (as in [9]). By combining Eq. 1 and Eq. 3 the chromaticity values become

$$\frac{I_c(\mathbf{x})}{I_G(\mathbf{x})} = \frac{k_c^{\frac{1}{\gamma}} S(\mathbf{x}, \lambda_c)^{\frac{1}{\gamma}} \left(\lambda_c^{-5} \exp\left(-\frac{c_2}{T\lambda_c} \right) \right)^{\frac{1}{\gamma}}}{k_G^{\frac{1}{\gamma}} S(\mathbf{x}, \lambda_G)^{\frac{1}{\gamma}} \left(\lambda_G^{-5} \exp\left(-\frac{c_2}{T\lambda_G} \right) \right)^{\frac{1}{\gamma}}} \quad c \in \{R, B\}. \tag{4}$$

In order to remove the γ-nonlinearity and the exponential function in Wien's approximation, we take the natural logarithm. Furthermore, we model the surface reflectance as diffuse reflectance $S(\mathbf{x}, \lambda) = w_d(\mathbf{x})\rho(\mathbf{x}, \lambda)$, which can be decomposed to a wavelength-independent geometric factor $w_d(\mathbf{x})$ and a material dependent albedo $\rho(\mathbf{x}, \lambda)$ at a certain position $\mathbf{x}$. Thus, the LCS value of a diffuse surface at a particular point $\mathbf{x}$ is:

$$r_{c,G} = \ln\left(\frac{I_c}{I_G}\right) = \frac{1}{\gamma}\ln\left(\frac{\rho_c}{\rho_G}\right) + \frac{1}{\gamma}\ln(k_c k_G^{-1}\lambda_c^{-5}\lambda_G^5) + \frac{1}{\gamma}\frac{1}{T}\left(\frac{c_2}{\lambda_G} - \frac{c_2}{\lambda_c}\right) . \quad (5)$$

$r_{R,G}$ and $r_{B,G}$ are then the LCS values of a particular pixel $\mathbf{x}$. This color space is also known as the log-ratio space and log-chromaticity differences [9]. Please note that for the remainder of the paper we omit writing that the log-chromaticity $\mathbf{r}$, the image value I, the geometry term w_d and the albedo ρ are functions on $\mathbf{x}$.

If we consider the LCS values of a pixel to be a point in the 2D vector space, the point coordinates are given by

$$\mathbf{r} = \begin{pmatrix} r_{R,G} \\ r_{B,G} \end{pmatrix} = \frac{1}{\gamma}\underbrace{\begin{pmatrix} \ln(\frac{\rho_R}{\rho_G}) \\ \ln(\frac{\rho_B}{\rho_G}) \end{pmatrix}}_{\mathbf{s}_\rho} + \frac{1}{\gamma}\underbrace{\begin{pmatrix} \ln(k_R k_G^{-1}\lambda_R^{-5}\lambda_G^5) \\ \ln(k_B k_G^{-1}\lambda_B^{-5}\lambda_G^5) \end{pmatrix}}_{\mathbf{b}} + \frac{1}{\gamma}\frac{1}{T}\underbrace{\begin{pmatrix} \frac{c_2}{\lambda_G} - \frac{c_2}{\lambda_R} \\ \frac{c_2}{\lambda_G} - \frac{c_2}{\lambda_B} \end{pmatrix}}_{\mathbf{d}} . \quad (6)$$

This equation illustrates that in the LCS all the color values of an albedo seen under different illuminants fall on a straight line. The line is defined by a point lying on $(\frac{1}{\gamma}\mathbf{s}_\rho + \frac{1}{\gamma}\mathbf{b})$ and the direction $\mathbf{d}$. The position of the line is dependent on the albedo ρ and the sensor characteristics (k_R, k_G, k_B, λ_R, λ_G and λ_B) The scaling factor $\frac{1}{T}$ denotes that depending on the illumination color (defined by the temperature T) the same material color ρ will fall on a different position of the same line. Note that the slope of the line $\mathbf{d}$ is independent of the material. As a consequence, different albedos will lie on different lines, as vector $\mathbf{s}_\rho$ changes. However, all these lines are parallel, since they share the same slope. The factor $1/\gamma$ only causes a constant scaling of the vectors. Thus, the LCS exhibits two key characteristics (see dotted lines in Fig. 2(b)): Firstly, **linearity** (As the illuminant color changes the LCS values of a surface fall on a straight line, pointing in the so-called invariant direction [1]) and secondly, **parallelism** (For a given camera, all such lines for different surface colors are parallel). Both properties are extremely helpful for illumination invariance, as a normalized image can be generated although the illuminant color is unknown or inhomogeneous across the image (like shadow regions). On the other hand, the violation of the NBA may disarrange the linearity and parallelism in LCS (see crosses in Fig. 2(b)).

3   Influence of the Narrow-Band Assumption

In order to analyze the influence of the NBA, we have to establish a scheme for estimating the introduced error. The sensor sensitivities can be better approximated by Gaussian functions with means $\mu = \lambda_c$ and standard deviation σ (see Fig. 1(b)). The standard deviation can be seen as the descriptor for the

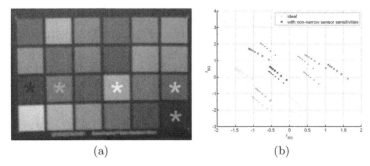

Fig. 2. (a) Sample reflectances. (b) LCS values of the different color patches. The ideal values form parallel straight lines.

narrowness of the sensitivities. Assuming for clarity of presentation $g = 1$, $\gamma = 1$, $k_c = 1$, Eq. 2 is then transformed to:

$$I_c(\mathbf{x}) = w_d(x)Ic_1\frac{1}{\sqrt{2\pi}\sigma}\int_\Omega \rho(\mathbf{x},\lambda)e^{-\frac{c_2}{T\lambda}}e^{-\frac{(\lambda-\lambda_c)^2}{2\sigma^2}}d\lambda, \tag{7}$$

In this formula we assume diffuse reflectance and a Planckian illuminant $E(\lambda, T)$ as in Eq. 1. As this equation shows, there are three factors influencing the deviation from the Dirac delta assumption: the albedo $\rho(\lambda)$ of the material, the standard deviation of the sensor sensitivities, and the color temperature T of the illuminant. Since, for arbitrary images the illuminant is typically unknown, we focus our error analysis on the influence of the albedo $\rho(\lambda)$ and the filter width σ. Such an analysis will then allow one to either safely use the Dirac assumption or avoid it depending on the scene materials.

By rearranging Eq. 7, we obtain:

$$I_c = w_d Ic_1\left(\underbrace{\rho(\lambda_c)e^{-\frac{c_2}{T\lambda_c}}}_{D_c} + \underbrace{\int_{\Omega\setminus\lambda_c}\rho(\lambda)e^{-\frac{c_2}{T\lambda}}\frac{1}{\sqrt{2\pi}\sigma}e^{-\frac{(\lambda-\lambda_c)^2}{2\sigma^2}}d\lambda}_{Q_c}\right), \tag{8}$$

Thus, the LCS values can then be expressed as:

$$r_{c,G} = \ln\left(\frac{I_c}{I_G}\right) = \ln\left(\frac{Q_c + D_c}{Q_G + D_G}\right), \tag{9}$$

where D_c corresponds to the ideal intensity assuming Dirac delta functions and Q_c corresponds to the error which is introduced when employing cameras with wider sensor sensitivities. Hence, in order to have an error as minimal as possible, the ratio inside the logarithm of Eq. 9 has to be as close as possible to the ideal ratio D_c/D_G. This is equivalent to requiring that

$$Q_B D_R = Q_R D_B \quad \text{or} \quad \frac{Q_B}{Q_R} = \frac{D_B}{D_R}, \tag{10}$$

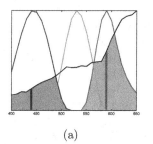
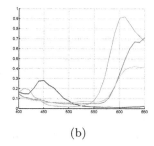

(a)   (b)

Fig. 3. Impact of the NBA. (a) The red and blue vertical lines are the sensor responses under the Dirac delta assumption. The shaded regions denote the error due to non-narrow sensor sensitivities. There is no impact on the LCS values if the ratio of the shaded regions is equal to the ratio of the corresponding vertical lines. (b) The diversity of the shape of the spectra makes the error analysis difficult.

which is obtained when $(Q_R+D_R)/(Q_G+D_G) = D_R/D_G$ and $(Q_B+D_B)/(Q_G+D_G) = D_B/D_G$. This means that the ratio of the errors in the red and blue channel has to be equal to the ratio of the Dirac responses. Fig. 3(a) illustrates this relation. This means that as long as the ratio in Eq. 10 is satisfied, one can use the NBA, even though $Q_c \neq 0$. On the other hand, if the combination of a sensor sensitivity with the spectrum of an albedo causes an inequality in this relation, the position of the resulting values and the ideal Dirac values will differ in LCS. It is important to note that this relation is dependent on the temperature of the illuminant. Furthermore, the diversity of the shape of real spectra makes this analysis difficult.

4   Experiments

Our goal is to systematically evaluate the impact of the deviation from the NBA on the LCS. Unfortunately, the non-separability of the different factors of image formation make the analytic estimation of Eq. 9 and Eq. 10 intractable for arbitrary images. We can however measure for specific surface spectra $\rho(\lambda)$ and for different filter widths σ how deviations from the NBA affect the position and orientation of the invariant lines in LCS.

We computed the product of different albedo curves with Planckian illuminants and different sensor sensitivities. The resulting RGB values were transformed in LCS and the resulting deviations were evaluated using three different error measures. We analyzed spectra of both synthetic and real data. We simulated different spectral sensitivities by using Gaussians of varying σ.

4.1   Data

For the evaluation of synthetic reflectance curves, 36 lines of different slopes and intensity levels have been generated (see Fig. 6). For analysis of real reflectances, we used about 160 different reflectance spectra which were extracted from the CAVE database [19]. In order to gain insight into the influence of their shape on the introduced error, the spectra have been categorized into 37 groups according to their shape. Examples for shape-categories are shown in Fig. 5. Furthermore, 357 skin reflectance curves (from 119 different persons) of the UOPB Face Database [20] have been analyzed in Sec. 4.6.

As examples of sensor sensitivities we took the spectral responses from two 3CCD cameras: a Sony DXC-755P [20] (denoted as "Oulu" in our plots) and a Sony DXC-930 [21] (denoted as "SFU"), see Fig. 1(b). There is a mismatch of the wavelength-range between the natural reflectance curves from the CAVE database ($\lambda \in [400\,nm, 700\,nm]$) and the sensor sensitivities. The sensors have a non-zero sensitivity at $\lambda < 400\,nm$, while the sensitivity at $\lambda > 700\,nm$ is zero. In order to avoid asymmetry in the resulting log-chromaticities due to this spectral cut off, we limited the spectral range to $\lambda \in [400\,nm, 650\,nm]$. For the evaluation we selected $T \in [4000\,K, 10000\,K]$ and the dominant wavelength of the dirac Delta functions as $\lambda_G = 450$, $\lambda_B = 530$ and $\lambda_R = 590$ with $k_B = k_G = k_R = 1$.

4.2   Error Measures

The error analysis is performed on the basis of three error measures: the *angular error* ϵ_{ang}, the *average distance* ϵ_{dist} and the *difference of ratios* ϵ_{rat}. The *angular error* $\epsilon_{ang} \in [0°, 90°]$ defines the angle between the invariant line l_{Dirac} obtained with the Dirac functions and the invariant line l_{sens} computed using non-Dirac sensor sensitivities. Not only the parallelism of the two lines is affected, but also a shift between line l_{sens} and l_{Dirac} can be observed. Thus, we define a second error metric, the *average distance* ϵ_{dist} between the LCS values of the sensor sensitivities r_{cG} and those of the Dirac function $\hat{r}_{cG}$ as:

$$\epsilon_{dist} = \sum_{T=4000}^{10000} \sqrt{(r_{RG}(T) - \hat{r}_{RG}(T))^2 + (r_{BG}(T) - \hat{r}_{BG}(T))^2}, \qquad (11)$$

Depending on the application ϵ_{dist} (clustering/segmentation in LCS) or ϵ_{ang} (illumination-invariant representation) is more important.

We also evaluated the deviation from Eq. 10 by computing the difference between the two ratios. We denote this error measure as *difference of ratios* ϵ_{rat} and compute it as:

$$\epsilon_{rat}(T) = (Q_B(T)/Q_R(T)) - (D_B(T)/D_R(T)). \qquad (12)$$

Note that both ϵ_{dist} and ϵ_{rat} are explicitly dependent on the temperature of the illuminant. In our analysis it turned out that the correlation of ϵ_{rat} and ϵ_{ang} was extremely high. In order to avoid redundancy we limited parts of our presentation to ϵ_{ang}.

4.3   Synthetic Surface Reflectances

In order to analyze the influence of a) the reflectance level and b) the general shape of the albedo on the accuracy of the LCS values, we generated linear reflectance spectra with different slopes and intercepts (see Fig. 6). Several important observations can be made:

1. The **slope** of the line: The slope of the line influences the average error ϵ_{dist}. The larger the slope of the line, the smaller ϵ_{dist} (see e.g. Fig. 6(i), 6(l)). In all the analyzed curves, ascending lines lead to a smaller ϵ_{dist} than descending lines (see Fig. 6(c), 6(f), 6(i), 6(l)). This observation can be explained by the shape of the sensor sensitivities. Consider a horizontal albedo. As the blue filter is often broader than the red one, the error in blue will be larger than in red ($Q_B > Q_R$) while for the ideal values they will be equal ($D_B = D_R$). In order to achieve a more balanced ratio of Eq. 10, the albedo needs to have a smaller level in the blue part of the spectrum.

2. The **level** of the reflectance curves: In most analyzed curves it was observable that the angular error ϵ_{ang} decreases with increasing level of intensity (see e.g. Fig. 6(c), 6(i), 6(l)). Again, let us consider two horizontal albedos of different reflectivity levels. As the blue filter is wider, the error in the blue channel is larger than in the red one. However, closer to the dominant wavelength, the difference between the red and blue curves is decreasing. Therefore, the higher the intensity level, the smaller the additional error in the blue channel and the better the error ratio.

Furthermore, it seems that the average distance ϵ_{dist} is affected more by variations in the shape of the albedo curves, while the angular error ϵ_{ang} is more sensitive to the overall level of reflectivity.

4.4 Real Surface Reflectances

Similar trends can also be observed for real reflectance data. However, due to the more complex structure of the albedo curves and the simultaneous variation in shape and level, the interpretation of the results is less intuitive than for the synthetic data.

1. **Balancing** of the red and blue part of the albedo: Similar to the synthetic data, Fig. 5(c) illustrates that albedos with slightly increasing slopes result in a low ϵ_{dist}, as the ratio of Eq. 10 is well balanced. This observation is also supported by the example in Fig. 5(f). If the error in the blue band is too high compared to the error in the red one (see Fig. 7(f)) or the other way around (see Fig. 7(c)) both errors, ϵ_{dist} and ϵ_{ang}, increase.

2. The **level** of the reflectance curves: Here again, it can be nicely observed that an increased reflectivity reduces the angular error ϵ_{ang}. This effect is illustrated in Fig. 5(i).

3. **Minimal level** of reflectivity: Closely related to the previous investigation is the observation that extremely small levels (e.g. $\rho(\lambda) < 0.03$) over some parts of the considered wavelengths result in an increased error. For instance, this is observable is Fig. 7(i), where the curve with the highest level in the range of $\lambda \in [400\,nm, 570\,nm]$ results in the lowest error.

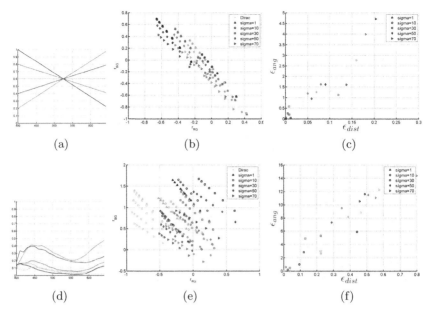

(a)   (b)   (c)

(d)   (e)   (f)

Fig. 4. Results of synthetic and natural albedo curves with changing narrowness of the sensor sensitivities. Left: Surface reflectances. Middle: LCS values; the values for $\sigma \in \{1, 10, 30\,nm\}$ almost fall on each other. Right: Error scatter plot.

4.5   Influence of Sensor Narrowness and Image Gamma

In order to analyze the influence of the narrowness on the errors, we also modeled sensor sensitivities as Gaussian curves with $\mu \in \{450, 530, 590\,nm\}$ and different widths, $\sigma \in \{1, 10, 30, 50, 70\,nm\}$. Examples for results on synthetic and natural reflectance curves are given in Fig.4. As expected decreasing bandwidth results in decreasing errors. This tendency could be observed in all the analyzed curves, independent of the shape of the surface spectra.

We also tested the effects of different gamma-values. A value of $\gamma > 1$ results in a compression of the LCS values. In almost 100% of the synthetic data and about 70% of the natural data $\gamma = 2.2$ resulted in an increased ϵ_{dist} and a reduced ϵ_{ang}. Sample plots are provided in the supplemental material.

4.6   Favorable Reflectance Spectra

Due to the observation that slightly increasing albedo curves (higher red and lower blue component) fit well to the NBA, we performed an additional evaluation on skin reflectance curves. Based on the melanin absorption, skin reflectance curves tend to have this advantageous shape (see Fig. 8(a)).

As expected, in LCS, the skin values cluster well (see Fig. 8(b)). Still, the performance of the more narrow SFU spectral sensitivities is better. This is also supported by the error scatter plot in Fig. 8(c). We want to emphasize

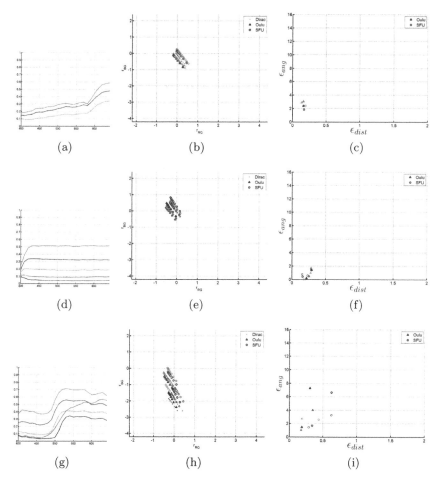

Fig. 5. Results for real reflectances (different shape categories). Left: Color-coded surface reflectances. Middle: LCS values. Right: Error scatter plot.

that reported errors are very good results compared to the average error of the arbitrary albedos of the CAVE database. Tab. 1 illustrates this, by showing the mean and standard deviation of the skin reflectance curves and the extracted spectra of the CAVE database.

Tab. 2 lists the best and worst measured errors for the CAVE database and Oulu sensor sensitivities. The corresponding spectra are shown in Fig. 3(b). The table reveals, how the performance is dependent on the sensor sensitivities (e.g. ϵ_{dist} for cyan). See supplemental material for further results.

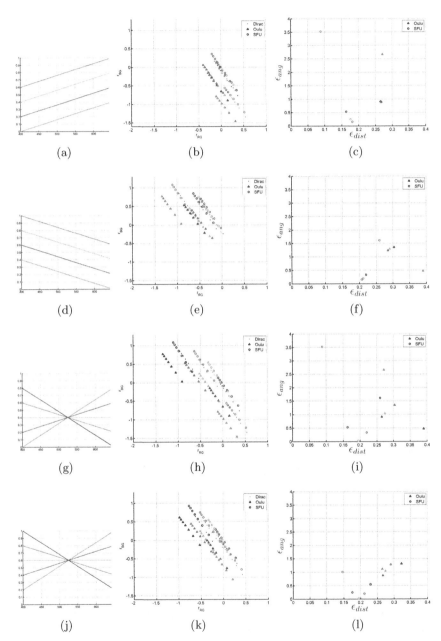

Fig. 6. Results for synthetic reflectances (different slopes and intensity levels). Left: surface reflectances. Middle: LCS values. Right: Error scatter plot.

Table 1. Mean and standard deviation for the average distance ϵ_{dist} and the angular error ϵ_{ang} computed for the CAVE database and the skin reflectances. Both analyzed sensor sensitivities are listed separately.

	Oulu		SFU	
	ϵ_{dist}	ϵ_{ang}	ϵ_{dist}	ϵ_{ang}
CAVE	0.398 ± 0.273	$5.128° \pm 3.913°$	0.449 ± 0.310	$3.718° \pm 2.864°$
Skin	0.192 ± 0.020	$3.924° \pm 0.848°$	0.146 ± 0.012	$3.226° \pm 0.716°$

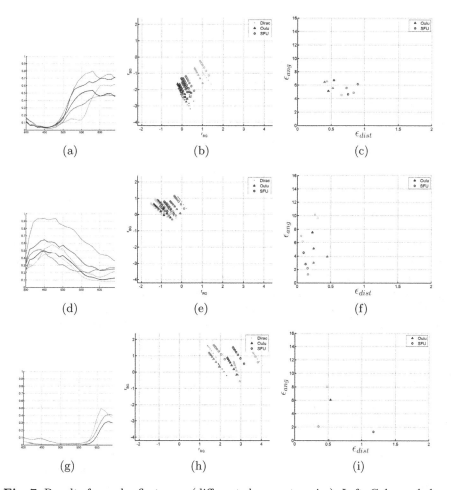

Fig. 7. Results for real reflectances (different shape categories). Left: Color-coded surface reflectances. Middle: LCS values. Right: Error scatter plot.

Table 2. Spectra with the minimal and maximal errors of the CAVE database and Oulu sensor sensitivities. The corresponding curves (see color) are shown in Fig. 3(b).

	Oulu		SFU	
	ϵ_{dist}	ϵ_{ang}	ϵ_{dist}	ϵ_{ang}
CAVE min(ϵ_{dist}) for Oulu (cyan)	**0.07**	0.01°	0.44	1.00°
CAVE max(ϵ_{dist}) for Oulu (blue)	**1.71**	16.37°	0.93	12.86°
CAVE min(ϵ_{ang}) for Oulu (magenta)	0.21	**0.01°**	0.37	1.67°
CAVE max(ϵ_{ang}) for Oulu (green)	1.03;	**16.72°**	0.59	11.38°

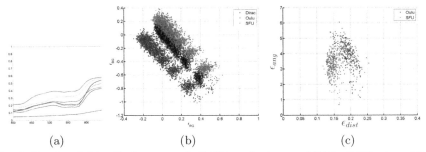

(a)   (b)   (c)

Fig. 8. Results of skin albedo curves. Left: Skin reflectances. Middle: LCS values. Right: Error scatter plot.

5   Conclusions

This paper addressed the influence of the violation of the NBA on the results in LCS are addressed. The introduced error depends on the the color temperature of the illuminant, the sensor sensitivities and the surface reflectance. Due to the image formation process, these three factors are not separable. In our evaluation we, therefore, concentrated on the color of the captured materials. Our theoretical formulation of the NBA-deviation showed that: when the ratio of the errors in the blue and red channels approximates the ratio of the respective Dirac delta values, the violation of the NBA leads to insignificantly small errors. Our analysis was based on two error metrics. These were designed so as to evaluate the suitability of reflectances for two groups of applications: illumination invariance and clustering/segmentation in LCS. In our analysis on synthetic and real surface reflectances it turned out that especially for bright and unsaturated colors, like skin color, the error in LCS is very small. Object colors with large errors, will benefit from spectral sharpening. Furthermore, due to Eq.10, the band which is less balanced with respect to the other two bands should be selected as the normalizing channel in Eq.4.

Acknowledgments. The authors gratefully acknowledge funding of the Erlangen Graduate School in Advanced Optical Technologies (SAOT) by the German National Science Foundation (DFG) in the framework of the excellence initiative. Eva Eibenberger is supported by the International Max Planck Research School for Optics and Imaging.

References

1. Finlayson, G., Drew, M., Lu, C.: Intrinsic Images by Entropy Minimization. In: Pajdla, T., Matas, J(G.) (eds.) ECCV 2004. LNCS, vol. 3023, pp. 582–595. Springer, Heidelberg (2004)
2. Tan, R., Nishino, K., Ikeuchi, K.: Color Constancy through Inverse-Intensity Chromaticity Space. Journal of the Optical Society of America A 21, 321–334 (2004)
3. Barnard, K., Finlayson, G.: Shadow Identification Using Colour Ratios. In: Color Imaging Conference, pp. 97–101 (2000)
4. Finlayson, G., Hordley, S., Lu, C., Drew, M.: On the Removal of Shadows from Images. IEEE Transactions on Pattern Analysis and Machine Intelligence 28, 59–68 (2006)
5. Álvarez, J., López, A., Baldrich, R.: Illuminant-Invariant Model-Based Road Segmentation. In: IEEE Intelligent Vehicles Symposium, pp. 1175–1180 (2008)
6. Finlayson, G.D., Drew, M.S., Lu, C.: Entropy Minimization for Shadow Removal. International Journal of Computer Vision 85, 35–57 (2009)
7. Tian, J., Sun, J., Tang, Y.: Tricolor Attenuation Model for Shadow Detection. IEEE Transactions on Image Processing 18, 2355–2363 (2009)
8. Finlayson, G., Fredembach, C., Drew, M.: Detecting illumination in images. In: IEEE International Conference on Computer Vision (2007)
9. Finlayson, G.D., Hordley, S.D.: Color Constancy at a Pixel. Journal of the Optical Society of America A 18, 253–264 (2001)
10. Xu, L., Qi, F., Jiang, R., Hao, Y., Wu, G., Xu, L., Qi, F., Jiang, R., Hao, Y., Wu, G.: Shadow Detection and Removal in Real Images: A Survey. Technical report, Shanghai Jiao Tong University (2006)
11. Álvarez, J., López, A., Baldrich, R.: Shadow Resistant Road Segmentation from a Mobile Monocular System. In: Martí, J., Benedí, J.M., Mendonça, A.M., Serrat, J. (eds.) IbPRIA 2007. LNCS, vol. 4478, pp. 9–16. Springer, Heidelberg (2007)
12. Zhang, G., Dong, Z., Jia, J., Wan, L., Wong, T., Bao, H.: Refilming with Depth-Inferred Videos. IEEE Transactions on Visualization and Computer Graphics 15, 828–840 (2009)
13. Drew, M., Finlayson, G.: Spectral Sharpening with Positivity. Journal of the Optical Society of America A 17, 1361–1370 (2000)
14. Barnard, K., Ciurea, F., Funt, B.: Sensor Sharpening for Computational Color Constancy. Journal of the Optical Society of America A 18, 2728–2743 (2001)
15. Drew, M., Joze, H.: Sharpening from Shadows: Sensor Transforms for Removing Shadows using a Single Image. In: Color Imaging Conference, pp. 267–271 (2009)
16. Barnard, K., Funt, B., Burnaby, B.: Experiments in Sensor Sharpening for Color Constancy. In: Color Imaging Conference, pp. 43–46 (1998)
17. Kawakami, R., Takamatsu, J., Ikeuchi, K.: Color Constancy from Blackbody Illumination. Journal of the Optical Society of America A 24, 1886–1893 (2007)
18. Henderon, S., Hodgkiss, D.: The Spectral Energy Distribution of Daylight. British Journal of Applied Physics 15, 947–952 (1964)
19. Yasuma, F., Mitsunaga, T., Iso, D., Nayar, S.: Generalized Assorted Pixel Camera: Post-Capture Control of Resolution, Dynamic Range and Spectrum, Technical Report CUCS-061-08, Department of Computer Science, Columbia University (2008)
20. Marszalec, E., Martinkauppi, B., Soriano, M., Pietikäinen, M.: Physics-based Face Database for Color Research. Journal of Electronic Imaging 9, 32–38 (2000)
21. Barnard, K., Martin, L., Funt, B., Coath, A.: A Data Set for Colour Research. Color Research and Application 27, 147–151 (2002)

Is Light Blue (*azzurro*) Color Name Universal in the Italian Language?

Giulia Paggetti and Gloria Menegaz

Department of Computer Science, University of Verona, Italy
{giulia.paggetti,gloria.menegaz}@univr.it

Abstract. In the study of 1969 Berlin and Kay have argued that there are a limited number of universal "basic color terms" which are the same for each culture [1]. They postulate the existence of 11 basic color terms, including a single blue term. After Berlin and Kay's work, several researcher have tried to confirm or refuse this theory. Those successive studies led to two principal theories: universalistic [2] (confirming the Berlin and Key theory) and relativistic (refusing the Berlin and Key hypothesis) theories [3–6]. This papers brings a new argument in favor of the relativistic theory and provides some evidence on the existence of a twelfth color class in the Italian language. In particular, results support the hypothesis of the existence of an additional monoleximic color name for the class corresponding to light blue (*azzurro* in Italian language). This hypothesis is proved by using the Stroop effect, introduced in 1953 by John Ridley Stroop [7]. The Stroop effect is based on the analysis of the reaction time in a given task. Our claim is that when the name of a color (e.g., "blue," "green," or "red") is printed in a color which is not denoted by the name (e.g., the word "red" printed in blue ink instead of red ink), naming the color of the word takes longer and is more prone to errors than when the color of the ink matches the name of the color. Accordingly, we investigated the reaction time of Italian mother language speakers performing a Stroop task with both dark blue and light blue color. Results show that the reaction time is statistically different when the light blue is associated to the monoleximic color name *azzurro* than to monoleximic color name blue (*blu* in Italian language).

Keywords: Color perception, Color categories, Italian color terms, Cultural influence.

1 Introduction

When Berlin and Kay introduced basic color terms in their 1969 book "Basic color terms, their universality and evolution", a new way of thinking about colors and color terms had begun [1]. The predominant view of linguistic relativity gave way to cross-cultural color universals that could be identified for all languages. Since then, many studies investigated this issue either to support the universalistic theory [2] or to refuse it in favor of the cultural relativistic one [3–6]. Nevertheless, no agreement has been reached so far. The cultural relativistic

K.N. Kutulakos (Ed.): ECCV 2010 Workshops, Part II, LNCS 6554, pp. 90–103, 2012.

view posits that color perception is greatly shaped by cultural specific language associations and perceptual learning. The universalist view is that panhuman shared color processing is the basis of color naming within and across cultures. The study of Berlin and Kay [1] rose the universal theory which claims that every culture would categorize all the colors in 11 classes (Red, Green, Blue, Yellow, Orange, Purple, Pink, Brown, Gray, Black and White). According to their definition, color terms are operationally defined as *basic* only if monolexemically named and psychologically salient for all speakers, but not if restricted to narrow classes of objects or included in the signification of other color terms. This theory received relevant support from subsequent studies [8, 2]. At the same time, the Berlin and Kay's theory received considerable criticism consequently to empirical evidence on the perceptual processing of color. This evidence includes the proof of considerable variation in color processing among individuals in the same culture, and new results on important cross-cultural differences in color naming and categorization [9]. Another relevant critique is the existence of single blue term in the universal theory. Some studies support the existence of two terms for blue in some culture. Greek, Russian and Turkish belong to this category [10–13].

Our claim is that Italian also have this feature. Previous results [14] have provided some evidence in support to the hypothesis that Italian subjects suffer the absence of the Italian color name for the light blue color (named *azzurro*). In this work, the subjects were constrained to use monolexemic color names from the eleven basic color categories identified by Berlin and Kay in a color naming task. In this way it was emphasized that for Italian subjects it is not spontaneous to classify the light blue color inside the blue color class. To get further evidence, another experiment based on the Stroop effect was designed and implemented, as described in what follows. Results show that the *azzurro* term holds has all the features of a basic color: it is monoleximic, it is used with high-frequency and it is agreed upon speakers of that language[1].

The paper is organized as follows. Section 1 summarizes the background, namely the Stroop effect. Section 2 describes the methodology and the details of the experiments that have been performed and introduces the results of each experiment. Section 4 derives conclusions.

2   Background

In 1935 Stroop [7] investigated color naming versus word reading, and hit upon the idea of a compound stimulus where the word was incongruent with the color. The two major questions were: (i) what effect each dimension of the compound stimulus would have on trying to name the other dimension? (ii) how would this affect the observed interference? Stroop developed two main experiments: in the first one the effect of incompatible colors on reading words aloud was investigate and in the second the task was switched to naming the colors aloud. This study proved that when the name of a color (e.g., "blue," "green," or "red") is printed in a color not corresponding to the name (e.g., the word "red" printed in blue ink instead of red ink), naming the color of the word takes longer and is more prone to errors than when the color of the ink matches the name of the color. This accounts for the fact that naming colors can be slower than reading words. Moreover, the Stroop study proved that there was no interference from incongruent colors in reading words but there was highly significant interference from incongruent words in naming colors [15]. After many years the Stroop effect is still in use for different purposed, mainly in the clinical field (e.g., [16–18]).

Our claim is that in the Italian language the light blue color do not fall inside the blue color class. Instead, it falls inside an additional universal color class named *azzurro*. Naming a color takes longer if it is printed or rendered on a monitor in association to a non congruent color word. Consequently, our hypothesis is that naming a light blue color should take longer than naming a dark blue color if both are associated to "blue" color word. To demonstrate it, five experiments were performed. Different colors, extract from the Munsell system, were shown in both congruent and not congruent conditions (e.g. ,red color-red color word and red color-yellow color word).

The basic idea is to prove that naming a dark blue color needs shorter time than naming the light blue color if both are associated to the "blue" color word (*blu*). Similarly, according to our hypothesis naming a light blue color would need shorter time if it is associated to light blue color word (*azzurro*) than if it is associated to blue color word. Results support the hypothesis that two blue colors with the same Hue but different Value belong to two different color classes.

3   Methodology and Results

Five experiment are carried out in order to prove the hypothesis of the existence in the Italian language of an additional monoleximic color name for the class corresponding to light blue.

In this section, the methodology and the results are presented in separate subsections, one for each experiment: Experiment 1 (Control Experiment), Experiment 2, Experiment 3, Experiment 4 (Control Experiment) and Experiment 5.

3.1   Experiment 1: Control Experiment

In this test the subjects were asked to name freely, without constraints, the name of the color displayed on the screen. The color was shown as a string of "x". This allows to collect the names used by the subjects and thus to highlight the spontaneous use of the term *azzurro*.

During this test the reaction times were collected. These can be considered as a benchmark of naming time for simple colornaming, namely in absence of the linguistic influence of the color word. The subjects were completely blind to the goal of the experiment.

Methods. The experiment were implemented in Matlab by means of the CRS toolbox (http://www.crsltd.com/catalog/vsgtoolbox/index.html). The stimuli were shown in a calibrated Mitsubishi Diamond Pro 320 display on a middle gray background in a completely silent dark room. Subjects answer were recorded using a microphone to automatically detect the onset of the speech.

The stimuli shown on the screen were of six different colors and were chosen from the Munsell color system. Specifically, the prototype for *azzurro* color was chosen at the same Hue of the dark blue color but at a different Value. The Munsell colors were converted in the RGB system to show them in the calibrated CRT screen. This set of colors included: red (*rosso*) [Munsell system: 7.5R 5/20], blue (*blu*) [Munsell system: 5PB 1/10] , yellow (*giallo*) [Munsell system: 5Y 9/12], purple (*viola*) [Munsell system: 2.5P 3/18] , pink (*rosa*) [Munsell system: 7.5RP 7/10] , and light blue (*azzurro*) [Munsell system: 5PB 6/14], in Italic the Italian color word.

These colors were chosen for two main reasons. First, except for the light blue color, all are universal basic colors. Second, a color was chosen for each step of the evolutionary pattern by Berlin and Kay [1], except for the achromatic colors which were not relevant to this experiment because of the chosen paradigm (it is very usual seeing names of colors wrote in black).

Our hypothesis is that light blue color is in Italian language a basic color. The idea consists in comparing different reaction times between dark and light blue with other different basic colors and color words based on the Stroop effect. The number of colors was bounded to six in order to limit the duration of the experiment.

A string of "x" was shown in one of the six different colors cited above. The use of a string of "x" was chosen because is perceptually similar to a string of letters composing a color word but do not have a semantic meaning. More in details, a string of characters composing the word "orange" have a semantic meaning while a string of "x" of the same length (e.g., "xxxxx") does not have any linguistic significance. A "xxxx" control was used also in past studies (e.g [19]). The number of characters composing the string was changed randomly at each trial to reproduce the changes in the number of characters of the words corresponding to Italian colors (e.g., 'xxxxx' to simulate the length of the name red in Italian language "rosso"). In this way we were able to perform another control experiment. This allowed us to check if the length of the string can influence the reaction time of the subjects in naming the color.

Subjects were asked to name the colors loud as quickly as possible. The subjects were free to use every color word. The stimulus was shown at the center of the screen subtending 10 degrees of visual angle. Data were collected in two sessions of 18 trials each. Six sessions were performed for each color. Between each stimulus, a middle gray image was displayed with a fixation point at the center of the screen. The rest time between the stimuli was set to 2 seconds, in order to avoid the post visual effect or effects of linguistic influence from the previous color or color word. Neill and Westherry ([20]) manipulated speed-accuracy instructions and inter-trial interval in Stroop experiment. The suppression effect was found to persist for at least one second; after 2 sec the effect was completely dissipated.

In this study, every time the subject gave an answer the researcher pressed a key on the keyboard to show the new stimulus. The answer was record by means of microphone and the time of the stimulus presentation was recorded. An acoustic bip at the start of the experiment was used to synchronize the two data flows for the audio and the reaction time recording respectively (WAVEform audio format and MAT-file). The reaction times are extract from the audio file automatically (http://www.fon.hum.uva.nl/praat/) which permits to detect when the subject is in silent and when the subject is speaking.

Subjects. Seventeen subjects (7 females and 10 males) aged between 21 and 31 participated in the experiment. All were blind to the goals of the experiments. The subjects had normal or corrected to normal vision and were tested for normal color vision (Ishihara test).

Results. The results of this experiment show that the average time required for naming a color on a string of "x" it is not significantly different for all the considered colors (ANOVA p-value<0.05). Noteworthy, the subjects used the term *azzurro* completely spontaneously for the light blue color. This could be an indication of the fact that this is a monolexic name and it is salient for all the subjects.

In figure 1 the median and the 25th and 75th percentiles of the reaction times are reported for all the colors.

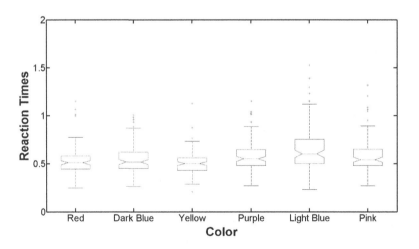

Fig. 1. The median and the 25th and 75th percentiles of the reaction times for each color of Experiment 1 are reported. The central mark represents the median, the edges of the box are the 25th and 75th percentiles; the whiskers extend to the most extreme datapoints not outliers, while the outliers are plotted individually.

3.2   Experiment 2

The second experiment was aimed at investigating whether reaction times are shorter for correlated color and color word (e.g., red color and red color word) than they otherwise (e.g, red color and blue color word). More specifically, the different reaction times between dark blue and light blue color on the color word blue (*blu* in Italian language) were tested.

Methods. The experimental set-up was the same as for Experiment 1 but the stimuli were different. In particular, the strings of "x" were replaced with real Italian color words. Four colors names were considered: red (*rosso*), blue (*blu*), purple (*viola*) and yellow (*giallo*), in Italic the Italian color word. The light blue (*azzurro*) and the pink (*rosa*) color words were not included. The first one was not included in order to avoid any influence on the subjects from the Italian color word *azzurro*. The pink color was not included to investigate if the reaction times for the light blue color could be due to consequence of the lack of the corresponding color word. In such case, the same effect would be observed for the pink color.

Data were collected in two sessions, totally six times for each couple of color and color word. The data were collect in two sessions to avoid the fatigue and practice and learning effects proved by Stroop [7]. For the same reason we preferred to collect data from more subjects without putting them under stress.

Subjects. Six subjects (2 females and 4 males) aged between 25 and 27 participated in the experiment. The same subjects were tested, first, for Experiment 1. All the subjects had normal or corrected to normal vision and were tested for normal color vision (Ishihara test).

Results. ANOVA test revealed that for all the colors, the mean of the reaction times are shorter when the name and the color are congruent. It could be useful to mention that the "corresponding" color words for the light blue and the pink color were not used in this experiment. For both of these colors (pink and light blue) the reaction times are not significantly different when they are associated to red, blue, yellow or purple color word. A difference could be observed for reaction times for both light blue and pink colors when associated to the blue word. However, but this was not statistically significant.

ANOVA test revealed that the mean reaction time of the these two colors (light blue and pink) when associated to all the considered color words are not statistically different. Instead, for the color that have the corresponding color word (e.g., red color and red color word) the difference is significant.

In figure 2 the median and the 25th and 75th percentiles of the reaction times are reported for the dark and the light blue colors when associated to any color words.

The t-student test showed that for each possible combination of stimuli (color and color word):

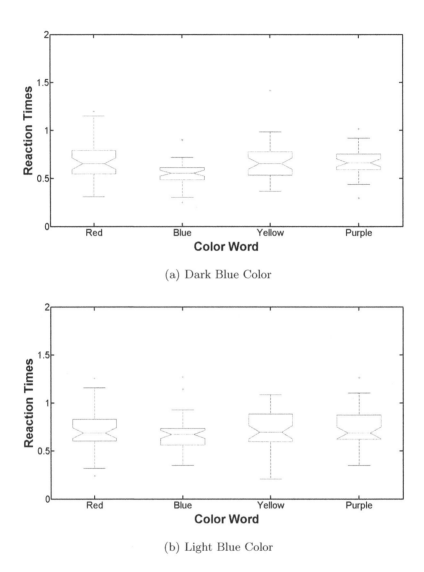

(a) Dark Blue Color

(b) Light Blue Color

Fig. 2. The median and the 25th and 75th percentiles of the reaction times for the dark and the light blue colors associated to any color words we used in Experiment 2 are reported. The central mark represents the median, the edges of the box are the 25th and 75th percentiles; the whiskers extend to the most extreme datapoints not outliers, while the outliers are plotted individually. The dark blue color have significantly shorter reaction time if associated to the blue color word than all the others color words (red, yellow and purple). No statistically significant differences are recorded for the light blue color in relating to the different colors words (red, blue, yellow and purple).

- the color word red have significantly shorter reaction time if associated to red color than for the other colors
- the color word blue have significantly shorter reaction time if associated to dark blue color than all the other colors (dark blue color: 0.556 sec; red color: 0.661 sec; yellow color: 0.669 sec; purple color: 0.745 sec; light blue color: 0.671 sec; pink color: 0.668 sec). This means that the subjects name more quickly the dark blue than the light blue color if both are associated to the blue color word
- the color word yellow have significantly shorter reaction time if associated to yellow color than all the other colors
- no statistically significant differences are recorded for the purple color word in relating to the different colors

The point here is that the blue color word corresponds to a mean reaction time that is shorter for dark blue color than for light blue color. The case of purple color word will be investigated in future work.

3.3   Experiment 3

In this experiment the color words for light blue (*azzurro*) and pink (*rosa*) were introduced. The main goal was to test the reaction times for the light blue color associated to the blue color word (*blu*) and to the light blue color word (*azzurro*), respectively. The same six colors and color words of the Experiment 1 were kept.

Methods. The experimental set-up was the same as for Experiment 2 except for the addition of the light blue and pink Italian color words. Six color words used were: red (*rosso*), blue (*blu*), purple (*viola*), yellow (*giallo*), light blue (*azzurro*) and pink (*rosa*). The colors and the color words were show in completely random order in two different sessions, six times for each couple (color and color word).

Subjects. The subjects that performed this experiment were naïve to the task. This was done in order to avoid practice and learning effects. Furthermore, this allows to avoid the biasing of the performance that could be reduced for the awareness of the use of the color word *azzurro* in previous tasks. 11 subjects aged between 21 and 31 participated in the experiment (5 females and 7 males). The same subjects were tested first for Experiment 1. All the subjects had normal or corrected to normal vision and were tested to prove their normal color vision (Ishihara test).

Results. ANOVA revealed that for all the colors, the mean of the reaction time is significantly shorter when the name and the color are congruent. Importantly, this also applies to the light blue color associated to the *azzurro* color word.

In figure 3 the median and the 25th and 75th percentiles of the reaction times are reported for the dark and the light blue color associated to all the color words.

By a t-student test for each possible combination of stimuli (color and color word) we found the same results as for Experiment 2 for the color word Red,

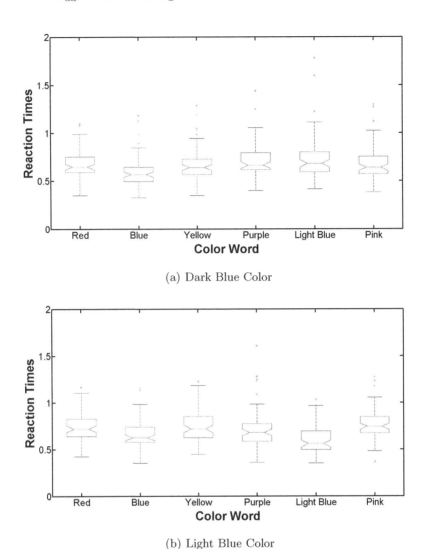

(a) Dark Blue Color

(b) Light Blue Color

Fig. 3. The median and the 25th and 75th percentiles of the reaction times for the dark and the light blue colors associated to any color words we used in Experiment 3 are reported. The central mark represents the median, the edges of the box are the 25th and 75th percentiles; the whiskers extend to the most extreme datapoints not outliers, while the outliers are plotted individually. The dark blue color have significantly shorter reaction time if associated to the blue color word than all the others color words (red, yellow, purple, light blue and pink). The light blue color have significantly shorter reaction time if associated to the light blue color word than all the others color words (red, blue, yellow, purple and pink).

Blue, Yellow and Purple. The new results are from the light blue (azzurro) and pink color words. In summary:

- the color word *azzurro* have significantly shorter reaction time if associated to light blue color than to all the other colors (light blue color: 0.601 sec; red color: 0.663 sec; dark blue color: 0.761; yellow color: 0.657 sec; purple color: 0.711 sec; pink color: 0.735 sec)
- the color word pink have significantly shorter reaction time if associated to pink color than all the other colors

In conclusion, our results show that naming a dark blue color needs shorter time than naming a light blue color if both are associated to the blue color word. Naming a light blue color needs significantly shorter time than naming a dark blue color if both are associated to the light blue color word (*azzurro*). Moreover, naming a light blue color associated to the light blue color word needs shorter time than associated at any other basic color word.

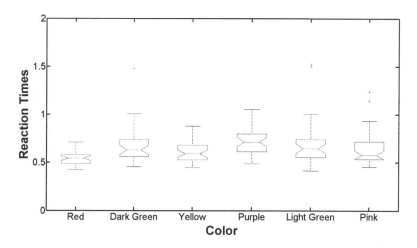

Fig. 4. The median and the 25th and 75th percentiles of the reaction times for each color of Experiment 4 are reported. The central mark represents the median, the edges of the box are the 25th and 75th percentiles; the whiskers extend to the most extreme datapoints not outliers, while the outliers are plotted individually.

3.4 Experiment 4: Control Experiment

Experiments 4 and 5 aim at investigating if the different reaction times between the dark blue and light blue color on the color word blue is a perceptual or a linguistic effect. To this end the dark and the light blue colors were replaced with dark and light green colors, respectively. Experiment 4 is a control test. The stimuli consisted of a string of "x", without any linguistic influence, colored with one of the six colors: red, dark green, yellow, purple, light green, pink.

Methods. The experimental set-up and the stimuli, as well as the number of trials, are the same as for Experiment 1. The only difference is in the colors. As mentioned above, both blue colors were replaced with two green colors. Both the blue colors have same Hue, but different Value in the Munsell color order system [dark blue, Munsell system: 5PB 1/10; light blue, Munsell system: 5PB 6/14;]. Similarly, both the green colors have the same Hue, but different Value [dark green, Munsell system: 10GY 1/10; light green, Munsell system: 10GY 6/14]. The difference in Value between dark and light blue colors is the same as between dark and light green colors. The task was to name freely, without constraints, the name of the colors on the screen.

Subjects. Six subjects (all males) aged between 21 and 29 performed the experiment. All the subjects had normal or corrected to normal vision and were tested for normal color vision (Ishihara test). As mentioned above a new group of subjects was selected to avoid the learning effect.

Results. This experiment shows that the mean reaction time to naming a color on a string of "x" it is not significantly different for all colors (ANOVA at a p-value<0.05). In this experiment both the blue colors were replaced with two green colors.

In figure 4 the median and the 25th and 75th percentiles of the reaction times are reported for all the colors.

3.5 Experiment 5

The objective of this experiment was to investigate if the results of previous experiments are driven by perceptual or linguistic effects. Our claim is that if the reaction time is the consequence of a perceptual effect then the same trend would be observed for both the blue and the green classes. Conversely, a different trend would support the linguistic hypothesis, since in this case the blue and the green classes would reveal a different underling mechanism ruling reaction time.

Methods. The set-up, the stimuli and number of trials of the last experiments were the same as for Experiment 2. The blue color word was replaced by the green color word. The two blue colors had the same Hue on the Munsell system but at two different Value. The green colors had the same Hue on the Munsell system and they are at the same difference of Value of the Blue colors.

Subjects. The same subjects that participated in Experiment 4 performed this experiment.

Results. Testing by ANOVA shows that for red, yellow and purple the reaction times are shorter, on average, when the name and the color word are congruent.

Noteworthy, this experiment also shows that the reaction time of the dark green and the light green are both shorter if associated to green color word than to all the other color words. For the pink color the reaction time are not

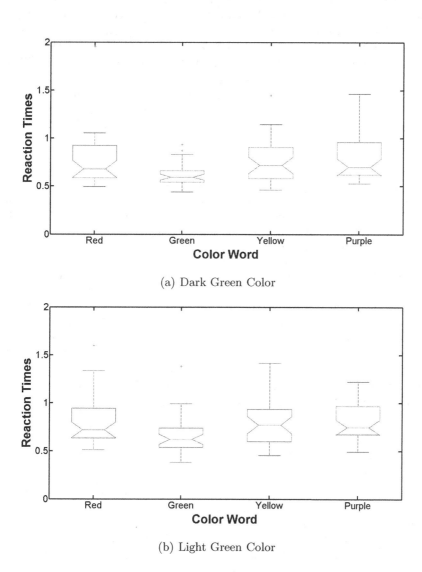

(a) Dark Green Color

(b) Light Green Color

Fig. 5. The median and the 25th and 75th percentiles of the reaction times for the dark and the light blue colors associated to any color words we used in Experiment 5 are reported. The central mark represents the median, the edges of the box are the 25th and 75th percentiles; the whiskers extend to the most extreme datapoints not outliers, while the outliers are plotted individually. The dark and the light green color have significantly shorter reaction time if associated to the green color word than all the others color words (red, yellow and purple).

significantly different if associated to color word red, green, purple or yellow. The color word pink was not included as in the Experiment 2.

In figure 5 the median and the 25th and 75th percentiles of the reaction times are reported for the dark and the light green colors associated to all color words.

In this experiment the subjects named *spontaneously* both the dark and the light green color with the color word green; only one subject used the modifiers "light" and "dark" with the color word green.

By a t-student test for each possible combination of stimuli (color and color word) the same results of Experiment 2 for the color word red, yellow and purple were obtained. The new results are from the green color word. In summary:

– the color word green have significantly shorter reaction time if associated to light and dark green colors than if associated to all the others colors (red color: 0.724 sec; dark green color: 0.621 sec; yellow color: 0.71 sec; purple color: 0.874 sec; light green color: 0.67 sec; pink color: 0.773 sec). Both the reaction times are not significatively different if the green color word is associated to light or dark green color.

These results support the hypothesis that the different reaction times for the dark and light blue color associated to the blue color word are the consequence of a linguistic influence. In fact, the reaction times were statistically different when the subjects named the dark and the light blue color associated to the blue color word, but they were not statistically different when the subjects were naming the dark and the light green color associated to the green color word. Both the blue and the green couple of colors were at the same Value distance and the subjects used freely two different colors names for dark and light blue color while they use the same color word for dark and light green color.

4   Conclusions

The observed reaction times show that naming a dark blue color needs statistically shorter time than naming a light blue color if both are associated to a blue color word. Moreover, this work demonstrates that the reaction times are statistically shorter if the light blue color is associated to the *azzurro* color word than to the *blu* color word. Differently, the reaction times in naming a dark green and a light green color associated to the green color word are not statistically different. Furthermore, the experiments revealed that the subjects were using the color word *azzurro* spontaneously.

All this results support the hypothesis of the existence of an additional class in the blue region in Italian language and that this could be a consequence of a linguistic, as opposed to a perceptual, effect. Further experiments are currently being performed in order to prove such theory.

References

1. Berlin, B., Kay, P.: Basic color terms. Univ. of California Press (1969)
2. Kay, P., Regier, T.: Resolving the question of color naming universals. Proceedings of the National Academy of Sciences of the United States of America 100, 9085 (2003)
3. Kay, P., Kempton, W.: What is the Sapir-Whorf hypothesis? American Anthropologist 86, 65–79 (1984)
4. Saunders, B., Van Brakel, J.: Are there nontrivial constraints on colour categorization? Behavioral and Brain Sciences 20, 167–179 (1997)
5. Roberson, D., Davies, I., Davidoff, J.: Color categories are not universal: Replications and new evidence from a stone-age culture. Journal of Experimental Psychology: General 129, 369–398 (2000)
6. Roberson, D.: Color categories are culturally diverse in cognition as well as in language. Cross-Cultural Research 39, 56 (2005)
7. Stroop, J.: Studies of interference in serial verbal reactions. Journal of Experimental Psychology 18, 643–662 (1935)
8. Kay, P.: Color categories are not arbitrary. Cross-Cultural Research 39, 39–55 (2005)
9. Jameson, K.: Culture and cognition: What is universal about the representation of color experience? International Journal of Clinical Monitoring and Computing 5, 293–347 (1988)
10. Paramei, G.: Singing the Russian blues: an argument for culturally basic color terms. Cross-Cultural Research 39, 10 (2005)
11. Winawer, J., Witthoft, N., Frank, M., Wu, L., Wade, A., Boroditsky, L.: Russian blues reveal effects of language on color discrimination. Proceedings of the National Academy of Sciences 104, 7780 (2007)
12. Androulaki, A., Gômez-Pestaña, N., Mitsakis, C., Jover, J., Coventry, K., Davies, I.: Basic colour terms in Modern Greek: Twelve terms including two blues. Journal of Greek Linguistics 7, 3–47 (2006)
13. Özgen, E., Davies, I.: Turkish color terms: Tests of Berlin and Kay's theory of color universals and linguistic relativity. Linguistics 36, 919–956 (1998)
14. Paggetti, G., Bartoli, G., Menegaz, G.: Shaping the universality hypothesis to the Italian language. Perception 38 ECVP Abstract Supplement, p. 39 (2009)
15. MacLeod, C.: Half a century of research on the Stroop effect: An integrative review. Psychological Bulletin 109, 163–203 (1991)
16. Casiglia, E., Schiff, S., Facco, E., Gabbana, A., Tikhonoff, V., Schiavon, L., Bascelli, A., Avdia, M., Tosello, M., Rossi, A., et al.: Neurophysiological correlates of post-hypnotic alexia: a controlled study with Stroop test. The American Journal of Clinical Hypnosis 52, 219 (2010)
17. Green, D., Grogan, A., Crinion, J., Ali, N., Sutton, C., Price, C.: Language control and parallel recovery of language in individuals with aphasia. Aphasiology
18. Rousseaux, M., Vérigneaux, C., Kozlowski, O.: An analysis of communication in conversation after severe traumatic brain injury. European Journal of Neurology
19. Dalrymple-Alford, E.: Associative facilitation and interference in the Stroop color-word task. Perception & Psychophysics 11, 274–276 (1972)
20. Neill, W., Westberry, R.: Selective attention and the suppression of cognitive noise. Journal of Experimental Psychology: Learning, Memory, and Cognition 13, 327–334 (1987)

Tone Correction with Dynamic Objects for Seamless Image Mosaic

Yong-Ho Shin[1], Min-Gyu Park[1], Young-Sun Jeon[2], Young-Su Moon[2], Shi-Hwa Lee[2], and Kuk-Jin Yoon[1]

[1] Gwangju Institute of Science and Technology
Cheomdan-gwagiro, Buk-gu, Gwangju, Republic of Korea
[2] Samsung Advanced Institute of Technology
Giheung-Gu, Yongin-Si, Gyeonggi-Do, Republic of Korea
{yongho,mpark,kjyoon}@gist.ac.kr,
{yong.jeon,mys66,hwa.lee}@samsung.com

Abstract. This paper presents a tone compensation method between images to make a seamless panoramic image. Different camera settings of input images, including white-balance, exposure time, and f-stops, affect the overall color tone of a resultant panoramic image. Although numerous methods have been proposed to deal with such color variations for seamless image stitching, most of them do not properly consider the dynamic scene in which different scene contents exist in input images. In this paper, we propose an efficient method that takes dynamic scene contents into account for compensating color tone difference. The proposed approach consists of three steps. First, we compensate the color tone difference by using the linear color transform with robust local features. Second, we filter out dynamic objects (i.e., dynamic scene contents) by measuring similarity between the linear transformed image and the reference image. Finally, we precisely correct the color variation with detected consistent regions only. The qualitative evaluation shows superior or competitive results compared to commercially available products.

Keywords: Panorama,Tone correction,Seamless image mosaic.

1 Introduction

Image stitching or panorama image mosaic has received substantial attention for decades. Since a resultant image provides wider field of view, it is well suited for some applications such as virtual tour guide and visual surveillance. Moreover, recent mobile phones and compact cameras have begun to embed panorama softwares to overcome their narrow field of view.

For the stitching, the registration of input images is essential that overlays multiple images of the same scene from the different view points at different time. The registration methods can be classified into two categories: direct methods and feature-based methods. Direct methods [1][2][3] use all the pixels in the overlapping area to register images. Although direct methods often require a

K.N. Kutulakos (Ed.): ECCV 2010 Workshops, Part II, LNCS 6554, pp. 104–117, 2012.
© Springer-Verlag Berlin Heidelberg 2012

Fig. 1. Image stitching result using images with large photometric variation

user input to determine ordering of images, these show accurate results through minimization of the error function which is defined for entire pixels. On the other hand, feature-based methods [4][5][6] stitch each image by identifying local features such as blobs or corner points. Such features are robust under particular variations which cause degenerative results. Furthermore, distinctiveness and repetitiveness of features ensure the correct alignment of an unordered set of input images. For that reason, feature-based approaches are recently esteemed as a standard method in commercial products.

The feature-based image registration usually consists of feature extraction, matching, outlier filtering, and bundle adjustment steps. However, the registration of images does not guarantee a plausible stitching result since the difference of color tones and the presence of dynamic objects cause unnatural heterogeneity at stitched boundary. Therefore, consequent steps such as blending and optimal seam algorithms, performed after the image registration, focus on eliminating these artifacts to make seamless panorama images. Blending has been widely used for seamless image mosaic. Burt and Adelson [7] introduced the multi-band blending method that controls the degree of blending according to image contents. Perez el al. [8] suggested Poisson blending which is developed for sophisticate merging. Instead of blending visual seam along the image boundary, an optimal seam method finds a path that passes through the overlapping area with minimum difference. Davis [9] used Dijkstra's algorithm with difference of intensity. Uyttendaele et al. [10] used a vertex cover algorithm and Mills and Dudek [11] proposed compound difference of intensities and magnitude of gradients.

Since any blending techniques can be applied after the optimal seam selection, the combination of two methods can handle geometric miss alignment error as well as dynamic objects. It works fairly nice, unless color tone variation is significant. Fig. 1 illustrates the result of applying the combination of two methods under large color tone variation. From the geometrical point of view, input images are well aligned. However, we can see the unnatural seam owing to the photometrical variation.

(a) input images with dynamic objects

(b) image stitching result

Fig. 2. Degenerative result due to different scene contents when using the linear color transform [14]

Several methods have been proposed to compensate color tones while making different assumptions on the scene. Some methods [12][13] used a histogram matching technique and Tian el al. [14] proposed a correction method based on the linear color transform. However, they assumed static scenes and, therefore, dynamic objects or scenes seriously degrade the quality of a stitching result (see Fig. 2). To cope with dynamic objects, Mills and Dudek [11] used a linear transform with the random sample consensus (RANSAC) technique to filter out moving objects. However, the linear color transform used in that method cannot handle complex color variation sufficiently. Goldman and Chen [15] tried to estimate the camera response function (CRF) and vignette coefficients from given correspondences, and then compensated the color tone with the calculated CRF. However, the performance of CRF-based correction totally depends on the given correspondence and, therefore, it requires very accurate feature matching results across images. Furthermore, if some assumptions made on the camera parameters (such as constant focal lengths and f-stops) are not satisfied, the CRF-based methods do not ensure plausible color tone correction results.

To resolve the problems in variety cases, we propose a new color tone compensation method. The proposed method consists of a few steps. Initially, the linear

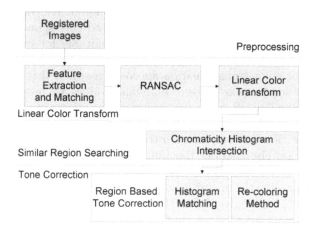

Fig. 3. Overall procedure of the proposed method

color transform is adopted to roughly compensate the different exposure and white balance under physically inconsistent situations. Then, geometrically consistent regions (corresponding to static scene contents) are computed by using the color histogram intersection method. Finally, globally adoptable tone correction methods such as histogram specification and re-coloring methods generate photometrically consistent panoramic images.

2   Proposed Color Tone Correction Method

As mentioned, the proposed algorithm consists of three main parts. The first part is the linear color transformation with robust local features. The second part is the color histogram based intersection to detect geometrically consistent regions. Finally, region based tone correction methods compensate the color variations of input images. Fig. 3 shows the overall procedure of the proposed method. Here, we assume that the input images are already well aligned geometrically in the preprocessing stage.

2.1   Linear Color Transform with Robust Features

The objective of this step is finding a linear color transform matrix as in [14] which compensates different camera settings such as white balances and exposures. To acquire a reliable color transform matrix, measurement data points should be physically consistent. Since the scene is not always static in practice, we need a methodology of finding reliable matches which correspond to the same physical scene points. For this, we use scale invariant feature transform (SIFT) [16] which is commonly used in many computer vision applications. SIFT features are invariant to rotation and scale changes, and it is also invariant to illumination variances. Because SIFT generates feature descriptors from the image gradients and normalizes the descriptor vectors, photometric variations merely affect the feature descriptors. Therefore, SIFT-based correspondence searching ensures physically consistent matches and it is suitable for calculating color transformation matrix as well.

Here, the linear color transformation approach assumes that optical sensors work fairly linear so that pixel color or luminance values are proportional to the amount of incoming light. Base on this assumption, a diagonal model [17] might be sufficient for the color tone correction. However, more accurate transform is required to deal with more complex color transition having non-linearity which is common in practice. For example, the auto white balance compensates different color temperatures non-linearly and the analog-digital converter for digital cameras does not guarantee the linearity, neither. Therefore, to solve these problems approximately as possible, we define the transformation matrix having twelve degrees of freedom as below,

$$
\mathbf{M} = \begin{pmatrix} a & b & c & d \\ e & f & g & h \\ i & j & k & l \end{pmatrix}, \mathbf{I_t} = \begin{pmatrix} R_t \\ G_t \\ B_t \\ 1 \end{pmatrix}, \mathbf{I_r} \begin{pmatrix} R_r \\ G_r \\ B_r \end{pmatrix}, \tag{1}
$$

where the subscript r and t indicate the reference image and the target image respectively. The reference is automatically set among overlapping images, which has the largest contrast of brightness. After that, the matrix representing linear transformation between the sets of pixels, can be calculated by

$$
\mathbf{MI_t} = \mathbf{I_r}. \tag{2}
$$

The matrix $\mathbf{M}$ can be computed in the least square sense. The linearly transformed image is shown in Fig. 4. It works well when corresponding features are obtained accurately.

2.2   Region Searching with Chromaticity Histogram Intersection

To apply region-based tone correction techniques, we first find geometrically consistent regions. Since the previous step is a feature-based technique, the transform uses insufficient color information from the overlapping area. The main concern of this step is that, although the feature-based linear tone correction has its own strengths, it does not guarantee plausible results if there are just a few correspondences. To deal with these problems, we introduce a consistent region searching method based on the chromaticity histogram, which examines geometrically consistent regions inside the overlapping area. Instead of using the direct comparison of RGB values, we transform the color space from RGB to chromaticity as

$$
c_r = \frac{R}{(R+G+B)}, c_b = \frac{B}{(R+G+B)}, \tag{3}
$$

(a) input images with dynamic objects

(b) image stitching result

Fig. 4. Image stitching result with the linearly transformed image

where R, G, B represent each RGB value and (c_r, c_b) represents the chromaticity. Since this conversion reduces the dimension of the color space, it reduces computational complexity while increasing the reliability of color matching under luminance changes.

Here, instead of using individual pixel values, we define the histogram and region based similarity measure to avoid the effect of geometrical misalignment as

$$\frac{\sum_{c_r} \sum_{c_b} min\left(h(c_r, c_b), g(c_r, c_b)\right)}{\sum_{c_r} \sum_{c_b} h(c_r, c_b)}, \tag{4}$$

where h and g represent the histogram of each image in the overlapping area. The denominator is a normalizing constant which counts the number of pixels in the overlapping area, and the numerator indicates summation of the intersected histogram. As the similarity ratio increases, the intersected histogram preserves an original shape of histogram. Therefore, it measures the region based similarity based on the color histogram which is not or merely affected by the geometrical misalignment errors.

Based on the color histogram intersection method, the proposed method finds reliable regions with the following procedure. First, we initialize a binary mask which represents the overlapping area and outside of the overlapping area (see Fig. 5). Each pixel serves as a label where white indicates inliers and black denotes outliers. Second, we compute the similarity ratio and compare it with the

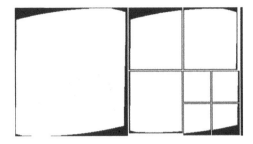

Fig. 5. A mask and the illustrative procedure of splitting

predefined threshold (we use 95 percent). If the similarity is less than the threshold, the region split into quad sub blocks as shown in Fig. 5. For each sub block, we repeat the same procedure until the size of a split block becomes smaller than the predefined size. The final result of the algorithm is the mask representing inliers (geometrically consistent scene contents) and outliers (geometrically inconsistent scene contents) as shown in Fig. 6. Based on this mask, region based tone compensation is performed in the next step.

Fig. 6. Two input images and the result of the consistent region examination

2.3 Region Based Tone Correction

Since the inlier mask represents geometrically consistent regions, the last stage of the proposed method is to create photometrically consistent results through region based tone correction methods such as the histogram specification and the re-coloring [18].

Histogram Based Tone Correction. The histogram based correction method performs histogram specification for each RGB channel. It finds an mapping function from the cumulative histogram H_2 of the target image to the reference histogram H_1 as follow,

$$z = H_1^{-1}(H_2(r)), \tag{5}$$

where r and z are continuous random variables representing input and output images, respectively. Although histogram specification is simple and quite conventional, it shows reasonable results. However, this method has a problem in cope with the tone correction when the cumulative histogram changes abruptly. For example, if one particular color is dominant and the distribution is narrow, numerous pixels are mapped to the dominant color.

Color Transfer Based Tone Correction. In this approach, we use a color transfer method instead of histogram specification. Color transfer or re-coloring [18] technique initially transforms the color space from RGB into $\ell\alpha\beta$, developed by Ruderman at al. [19], and corrects the color tone using mean and standard deviation of each image.

Since the $\ell\alpha\beta$ space has been developed to reduce correlation among channels assuming that the human visual system is ideally suitable for natural scenes. This color space shows the least correlation between each plane especially for natural scenes, thus, we do not need to change the value of pixel in a coherent way. Finally, by using characteristics of the each images in the $\ell\alpha\beta$ space, the re-colored image is obtained as below,

$$
\begin{aligned}
\ell' &= \frac{\sigma_r^\ell}{\sigma_t^\ell}(\ell - \mu_t^\ell) + \mu_r^\ell \\
\alpha' &= \frac{\sigma_r^\alpha}{\sigma_t^\alpha}(\alpha - \mu_t^\alpha) + \mu_r^\alpha \\
\beta' &= \frac{\sigma_r^\beta}{\sigma_t^\beta}(\beta - \mu_t^\beta) + \mu_r^\beta,
\end{aligned}
\tag{6}
$$

where σ and μ indicate standard deviation and mean, and r and t denote the reference and the target images. Fig. 7 shows the results by using the histogram based and re-coloring based methods, respectively.

3   Experiment

The experimental images are taken by differentiating white-balance, exposure time, ISO, and f-stops using a Cannon 1Ds camera with a manual focus Canon 24-70mm lens. Table 1 and 2 provide the camera settings for input images in Fig. 8 and Fig. 9. The experiment includes the results of the linear color transformation, the histogram matching, and the proposed method. In addition, three commercial products, PTGui [20], Hugin [21], and Autostitch [22], are compared for the performance evaluation.

Fig. 8 shows the result of each approach for the static scene and the same scene with a dynamic object. For the comparison, the second and the third rows illustrate the results from the static scene, (a) and (b), whereas the fifth and the sixth rows describe the results from the scene with the dynamic object, (i) and (j). First of all, the linear transformation [14] results, (c) and (k), are hazy because it cannot fully handle non-linear photometric variations. Moreover, (k) is also influenced by the dynamic object. Next, histogram matching deals with non-linearity and generates a reliable result, (d), for the static scene. However,

(a) histogram matching result

(b) $\ell\alpha\beta$ re-coloring result

Fig. 7. Results of histogram matching and $\ell\alpha\beta$ re-coloring

since histogram matching does not consider dynamic objects, it is dominated by the yellow artificial object as shown in (l). The proposed methods are shown to be robust in both cases, (e) and (m), regardless of inconsistence scene contents.

Table 1. Different camera settings for input images in Fig. 8

-	Input image 1	Input image 2
White-balance	Day light	Tungsten light
Exposure time	1/500 sec	1/320 sec
ISO	ISO-100	ISO-200
F-stops	f/3.5	f/4.5

Table 2. Different camera settings for input images in Fig. 9

-	Input image 1	Input image 2	Input image 3	Input image 4	Input image 5
White-balance	Day light	Cloudy	Day light	Tungsten light	Day light
Exposure time	1/200 sec	1/200 sec	1/100 sec	1/160 sec	1/320 sec
ISO	ISO-200	ISO-160	ISO-500	ISO-200	ISO-100
F-stops	f/8	f/6.3	f/8	f/11	f/5

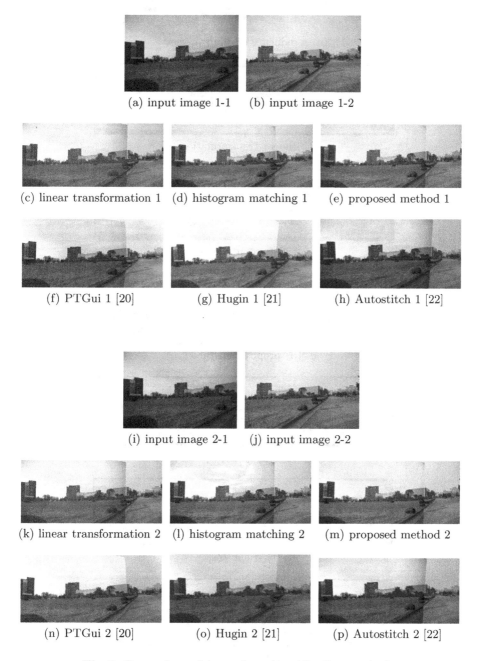

(a) input image 1-1   (b) input image 1-2

(c) linear transformation 1   (d) histogram matching 1   (e) proposed method 1

(f) PTGui 1 [20]   (g) Hugin 1 [21]   (h) Autostitch 1 [22]

(i) input image 2-1   (j) input image 2-2

(k) linear transformation 2   (l) histogram matching 2   (m) proposed method 2

(n) PTGui 2 [20]   (o) Hugin 2 [21]   (p) Autostitch 2 [22]

Fig. 8. Comparison of cropped results with other methods

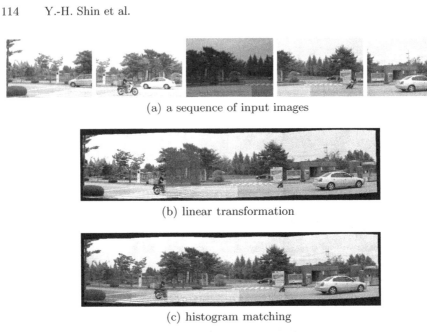

(a) a sequence of input images

(b) linear transformation

(c) histogram matching

(d) proposed method

(e) PTGui [20]

(f) Hugin [21]

(g) Autostitch [22]

Fig. 9. Comparison of results with other methods for dynamic scene contents

(a) image stitching result for input images in Fig. 2

(b) image stitching result for input images in Fig. 4

(c) image stitching result for input images in Fig. 8

(d) image stitching result for input images in Fig. 9

Fig. 10. Results of the proposed algorithm combined with the optimal seam selection and the multi-band blending

In addition, commercial products are evaluated for the comparison. CRF-based approaches, PTGui and Hugin, compute CRF based on local features, thus, they are not influenced by dynamic objects. However, variation of un-modeled camera parameters such as ISO and f-stops severely degrade quality of the results, (f),(g),(n),and (o). Autostitch which uses gain compensation method , adjusts global intensity for each channel. Thus, (h) and (p) looks better than the original images but it also has a problem with complex color variation, plus, (p) is dominated by the yellow artificial object.

Fig. 9 illustrates the results from a sequence of images having several dynamic objects and different camera settings. Similar to Fig. 8, dynamic objects degrade the results of (b), (c), and (g). Next, variation of un-modeled camera parameters spoil the results, (e) and (f). Lastly, complex color variation causes unsatisfactory results in (b) and (g). The proposed method can be combined the optimal seam and multi-band blending techniques to produce more natural and realistic results as shown in Fig. 10.

4   Conclusion

We have presented a new method which solves color tone correction problem for seamless image stitching, especially when the scene is not static and input images are taken with different settings. The proposed method redresses the photometric inconsistency through the linear color transform, chromaticity histogram inter-section, and region based compensation. The feature-based linear transform is robust under different camera settings and the existence of moving objects. How-ever, it is usually inadequate to solve entire color tone correction problem. To make up this limitation, chromaticity histogram intersection is adopted to find geometrically consistent regions. Afterwards, region based approaches compen-sate color tone difference more accurately with the consistent regions only. The overall procedure is designed to be used in the real environment where dynamic scene contents exist. The experimental results show that the proposed method is superior to the previous methods.

References

1. Szeliski, R.: Image mosaicing for tele-reality applications. In: IEEE Workshop on Applications of Computer Vision, pp. 44–53 (1994)
2. Szeliski, R., Corporation, M.: Video mosaics for virtual environments. IEEE Computer Graphics and Applications 16, 22–30 (1996)
3. Shum, H.Y., Szeliski, R.: Construction of panoramic mosaics with global and local alignment. International Journal of Computer Vision 36, 101–130 (2000)
4. Zoghlami, I., Faugeras, O., Deriche, R., Antipolis Cedex, F.S.: Using geometric corners to build a 2d mosaic from a set of images. In: CVPR 1997, pp. 420–425 (1997)
5. Mclauchlan, P.F., Jaenicke, A., Xh, G.G.: Image mosaicing using sequential bundle adjustment. In: Proc. BMVC, pp. 751–759 (2000)

6. Brown, M., Lowe, D.: Automatic panoramic image stitching using invariant features. International Journal of Computer Vision 74, 59–73 (2007)
7. Burt, J., Adelson, H.: A multiresolution spline with application to image mosaics. ACM Transactions on Graphics 2, 217–236 (1983)
8. Pérez, P., Gangnet, M., Blake, A.: Poisson image editing. ACM Trans. Graph. 22, 313–318 (2003)
9. Davis, J.: Mosaics of scenes with moving objects. In: CVPR 1998: Proceedings of the IEEE Computer Society Conference on Computer Vision and Pattern Recognition, p. 354. IEEE Computer Society, Washington, DC (1998)
10. Uyttendaele, M., Eden, A., Szeliski, R.: Eliminating ghosting and exposure artifacts in image mosaics. In: IEEE Computer Society Conference on Computer Vision and Pattern Recognition, vol. 2, p. 509 (2001)
11. Mills, A., Dudek, G.: Image stitching with dynamic elements. Image and Vision Computing 27, 1593–1602 (2009)
12. Zheng, L., Zhang, J., Luo, Y.: Color matching in colour remote sensing image. In: IMSCCS 2006: Proceedings of the First International Multi-Symposiums on Computer and Computational Sciences, vol. 1, pp. 303–306. IEEE Computer Society, Washington, DC (2006)
13. Azzari, P., Bevilacqua, A.: Joint Spatial and Tonal Mosaic Alignment for Motion Detection with PTZ Camera. In: Campilho, A., Kamel, M.S. (eds.) ICIAR 2006. LNCS, vol. 4142, pp. 764–775. Springer, Heidelberg (2006)
14. Tian, G.Y., Gledhill, D., Taylor, D., Clarke, D.: Colour correction for panoramic imaging. In: Proceedings of the Sixth International Conference on Information Visualisation, vol. 0, pp. 483–488. IEEE Computer Society, Los Alamitos (2002)
15. Goldman, D.B.: hung Chen, J.: Vignette and exposure calibration and compensation. In: ICCV 2005: Proceedings of the Tenth IEEE International Conference on Computer Vision, vol. 1, pp. 899–906. IEEE Computer Society (2005)
16. Lowe, D.G.: Distinctive image features from scale-invariant keypoints. International Journal of Computer Vision 60, 91 (2004)
17. Finlayson, G.D., Drew, M.S., Funt, B.V.: Color constancy: Generalized diagonal transforms suffice. J. Opt. Soc. Am. A 11, 3011–3020 (1994)
18. Reinhard, E., Ashikhmin, M., Gooch, B., Shirley, P.: Color transfer between images. IEEE Computer Graphics and Applications 21, 34–41 (2001)
19. Ruderman, L., Cronin, W., Chiao, C.C.: Statistics of cone responses to natural images: Implications for visual coding. Journal of the Optical Society of America A 15, 2036–2045 (1998)
20. PTGui, http://www.ptgui.com
21. Hugin, http://www.hugin.sourceforge.net
22. Autostitch, http://cvlab.epfl.ch/~brown/autostitch/autostitch.html

Saliency Maps of High Dynamic Range Images

Roland Brémond, Josselin Petit, and Jean-Philippe Tarel

Université Paris Est, LEPSiS, INRETS-LCPC
58 Bd Lefebvre, 75015 Paris, France
{bremond,petit,tarel}@lcpc.fr

Abstract. A number of computational models of visual attention have been proposed based on the concept of saliency map. Some of them have been validated as predictors of the visual scan-path of observers looking at images and videos, using oculometric data. They are widely used for Computer Graphics applications, mainly for image rendering, in order to avoid spending too much computing time on non salient areas, and in video coding, in order to keep a better image quality in salient areas. However, these algorithms were not used so far with High Dynamic Range (HDR) inputs. In this paper, we show that in the case of HDR images, the predictions using algorithms based on Itti, Koch and Niebur [1] are less accurate than with 8-bit images. To improve the saliency computation for HDR inputs, we propose a new algorithm derived from Itti and Koch [3]. From an eye tracking experiment with a HDR scene, we show that this algorithm leads to good results for the saliency map computation, with a better fit between the saliency map and the ocular fixation map than Itti, Koch and Niebur's algorithm. These results may impact image retargeting issues, for the display of HDR images on both LDR and HDR display devices.

Keywords: Saliency Map, High Dynamic Range, Eye Tracking.

1 Introduction

The concept of visual saliency was introduced in the Image community by the influential paper of Itti, Koch and Niebur [1]. The purpose of these algorithms is to compute, from an image, a Saliency Map, which models the image-driven part of visual attention (gaze orientation), for observers looking at the image. In the same last ten years, High Dynamic Range imaging emerged as a new field of research in image science, including computer graphics, image acquisition and image display [2]. Eight-bit images are not the only way to deal with digital images, since techniques have been proposed to capture, process and display HDR images.

In this paper, we show that a direct computation of the saliency map using algorithms derived from [1] leads to poor results in the case of HDR images. We propose a new algorithm derived from Itti and Koch [3], with a new definition of the visual features (intensity, colour and orientation), which leads to better

K.N. Kutulakos (Ed.): ECCV 2010 Workshops, Part II, LNCS 6554, pp. 118–130, 2012.
© Springer-Verlag Berlin Heidelberg 2012

results in the case of HDR images. The saliency maps computed with our algorithm and with [3] are compared to human Region of Interest (RoI), using an eye tracker experiment.

Previous work on visual saliency computation are reviewed in section 2. Evidence for the drawback of Itti and Koch's model for HDR images are given in section 3, as well as our alternative model. An eye tracker experiment is presented in section 4, allowing to compare the two computational models.The results are discussed in section 5.

2   Previous Work

Among theories of visual attention, the Feature Integration Theory (FIT) [4] was made popular by [1] because it leads to an efficient computational model of the bottom-up visual saliency. Other biologically plausible implementations of the saliency map have been proposed, and some authors include computational models of top-down biases (see [5] for a review).

Itti, Koch and Niebur's model [1], further refined in [3], tries to predict the bottom-up component of visual attention, which is the image-driven contribution to the gaze orientation selection. They implement the FIT using Koch and Ullman's hypothesis of a unique saliency map in the spatial attention process [6]. This model was tested against oculometric data, and proved to be better than random at predicting ocular fixations [3].

Itti and Koch's algorithm [3] is seen as the standard model for the computation of the saliency map in still images. It extracts three early visual features from an image (intensities, opponent colours and orientations), at several spatial scales. This computation is followed by center-surround differences (implemented as Gaussian Dyadic Pyramid) and a normalization step for each feature. Next, an across-scales combination and a new normalization step lead to the so-called conspicuity map for each feature. The normalizations are computed as follows: a conspicuity map is iteratively convolved by a Difference of Gaussian (DoG) filter, the original map is added to the result, and negative values are set to zero. Then, a constant (small) inhibitory term is added. Finally, the three conspicuity maps (Intensity, Colour and Orientation) are added into the saliency map (see [3] for implementation details). Other saliency algorithms, such as [7,8] use the same principles derived from [1]: selection of the visual features, center-surround differences, competition across features, and fusion of the conspicuity maps into the saliency map.

Saliency maps have been widely used in the recent years for Computer Graphics applications, mostly in order to save computing time in rendering algorithms [9,10]. Video coding applications have also emerged, keeping a better image quality in salient areas [11]. All these applications compute saliency maps using models derived from [1], with Low Dynamic Range (LDR) images. The present paper addresses the computation of saliency maps for HDR images, which has implications for both LDR and HDR display devices.

3   Saliency Maps of HDR Images

We have extended the Saliency Toolbox for Matlab [12] available online [13] to HDR input (`float` images). Alternative algorithms, such as [14] were not tested, so that our findings are restricted to Itti's computational strategy, which is the most popular in computer science, and led to the more convincing oculometric validations.

3.1   Drawback of the Standard Model

Focusing on biologically inspired algorithms derived from [1], it appears that a direct computation of the saliency map may lead to poor results for HDR images in terms of information: the saliency map selects the most salient item, loosing information about other salient items.

Fig. 1. *Space Needle* (left), *Memorial Church* (middle) and *Grace New* (right) HDR images. Top: LDR tone mapped images. Bottom: Saliency maps computed from the HDR images

Fig. 1 (bottom) gives three examples of saliency maps computed with [3] from 32-bit HDR images from Debevec's website [15]. As HDR images cannot be printed, they are displayed (Fig. 1, top) after being tone mapped into LDR images [16]. These examples suggest that a direct computation of the saliency map looses relevant information, as far as visual attention is concerned. In the

Grace New image, only windows and light sources are selected. The saliency map aims at predicting the visual behavior: one may doubt that observers would only look at light sources and windows in the HDR scene. This is even worst with the *Memorial Church* HDR image, where the saliency map only selects one window in the church. From these limited examples (more examples are available as supplementary material of the present paper), it seems that state-of-the art saliency map algorithms tend to select the most salient items in a HDR scene, the other salient items being either faded, or removed. These "poor" saliency maps of HDR images do not correspond to the actual visual behavior.

3.2   Contrast *vs.* Difference

A naive approach would be to compute the saliency maps after a tone mapping preprocessing (see section 3.3), however we were looking for a unified approach, which proved to give better result than the two-steps approach (see section 4.2). Looking carefully at the conspicuity maps of HDR images, we found that the color map seems to include more information than the two others. This observation suggested an hypothesis. When the feature maps are computed in [3], the Colour feature is normalized, at every pixel, with respect to intensity I, whereas the Intensity and Orientation features process differences (between spatial scales). Knowing that biological sensors are sensitive to contrasts rather than to absolute differences, we felt that the saliency map of HDR images would benefit from a computational model in terms of contrast on all three conspicuity maps (Intensity, Colour and Orientation). This normalization may be seen as a gain modulation, which is the physiological mechanism of visual adaptation.

Thus, we replace the Intensity channel in [3]. Instead of computing the intensity difference between scales c and s: $I(c, s) = |I(c) - I(s)|$, we compute an intensity contrast:

$$I'(c, s) = \frac{|I(c) - I(s)|}{I(s)} \tag{1}$$

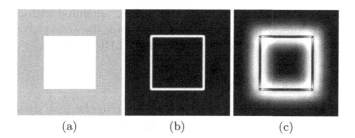

(a)   (b)   (c)

Fig. 2. Contour detection in (a) with (b) normalized Gabor filters (our proposal), and (c) differences of Gabor filters at successive scales, as in [3]

Then, we propose a modification of Itti, Koch and Niebur's definition of the Orientation features, so that the new feature is homogeneous to a contrast. In the original paper, orientation detectors were computed, for each orientation angle θ, as differences between Gabor filters at scales c and s: $O(c, s, \theta) = |O(c, \theta) - O(s, \theta)|$. This leads to orientation detectors where the borders themselves are not detected (see Fig. 2). Instead, we see a propagation across scales of what is actually detected: borders of borders. This observation, added to the fact that a Gabor filter is a derivative filter, led us to a new definition of the Orientation features:

$$O'(c, s, \theta) = \frac{O(c, \theta)}{I(s)} \tag{2}$$

with a normalization over the intensity channel, as for the two other features. Fig. 3 shows examples of saliency maps computed for HDR images with this new operator, denoted **CF** (for **C**ontrast **F**eatures) in the following, without the strong drawback of Fig. 1.

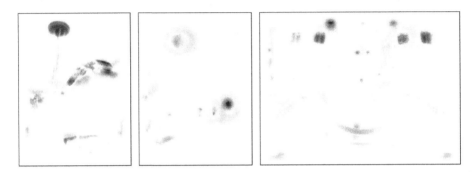

Fig. 3. Saliency maps of the *Space Needle*, *Memorial Church* and *Grace New* HDR images computed with the **CF** algorithm, with new definitions of the Intensity and Orientation features

In order to check the consistency of the **CF** algorithm for LDR images, we also compared the saliency map of the LDR images, computed with [3] and with the proposed algorithm. An example is given Fig. 4 for the *Lena* picture, showing that the saliency maps are close to each other for LDR inputs.

3.3   Tone Mapping Preprocessing

Usual sensors, either physical or biological, cope with the high dynamic range of input luminance by means of a non-linear sensitivity function, allowing to shrink the luminance dynamic into a LDR output dynamic: all sensors include a Tone Mapping Operator (TMO). Thus, one may argue that the apparent failure of [3] for HDR images comes from the HDR input data. One may expect that reproducing sensors properties and mapping HDR images to LDR images before computing a saliency map would lead to better results than without this preprocessing step.

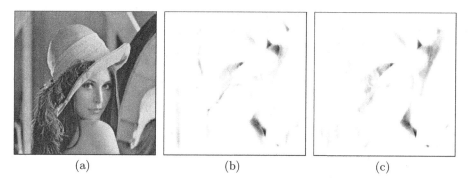

(a)   (b)   (c)

Fig. 4. Saliency maps of *Lena* (a), computed with (b) [3] and with (c) the **CF** algorithm

A number of TMO have been proposed so far in the Computer Graphics literature. Please note that in the following, we use TMO for a task which is not the usual rendering task. Instead of comparing the visual appearance of tone mapped images, we use them in order to compute accurate saliency maps. In section 4.2, we have compared our algorithm to six such operators from the literature, combined with a saliency map computed with [3]:

- Tumblin and Rushmeier [17] (denoted O_1), based on psychophysical data, tries to keep the apparent brightness in the images.
- Ward *et al.* [18] (denoted O_2) uses a histogram adjustment method (we did not consider the colour processing, nor the glare simulation of the operator), trying to keep the contrast visibility in the images.
- Pattanaik *et al.* [19] (denoted O_3) uses a colour appearance model (we used the static version of the operator).
- Reinhard *et al.* [16] (denoted O_4) uses a method inspired by photographic art (we use the global version of the operator).
- Reinhard and Delvin [20] (denoted O_5) is inspired by photobiology.
- Mantiuk *et al.* [21] (denoted O_6) optimizes tone mapping parameters in terms of visibility distortion, using Daly's Visual Difference Predictor (VDP) [22].

Given that these operators may be sensitive to the parameter tuning, we have used the default parameters as described in the cited publications.

4   Experiment

In order to test the relevance of a given saliency map computation for HDR images, a ground truth is needed. This was done on a limited scale in a psycho-visual experiment, with a HDR physical scene, collecting oculometric data.

In the general case, one may consider the saliency map as an input for the top-down biases in the attention process. However, we followed [3,23,11] and did not considered such top-down biases. Instead, we used the saliency map as a predictor of the gaze orientation, in an experiment where the visual task was chosen in order to avoid strong top-down biases. Thus, the fixation map could be compared to predictions from these saliency maps.

We have designed an eye tracking experiment to test our hypothesis about the visual behavior looking at HDR scenes. The ocular fixations of 17 observers looking at a physical HDR scene were recorded. Then, the scene was scanned with a camera with various exposures, in order to build a HDR image. This allowed to compute various saliency maps from the HDR image.

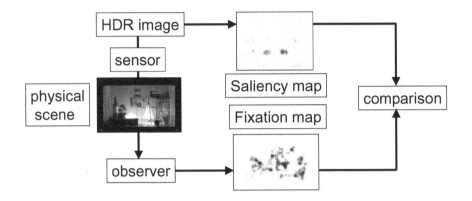

Fig. 5. Framework of the Saliency Map evaluation for HDR images

4.1   Material and Method

The experiment took place in a dark room (no windows, walls painted in black) under controlled photometry. The scene (Fig. 7, right) included dark (small box, yoghurt) and bright parts (lamps), leading to a luminance dynamic of 3,480,000:1 and very strong contrasts (the yoghurt and the open box are near the light sources). The scene was installed in a closed box (except for the front part, see Fig. 6).

Subjects were seated in an ergonomic automobile seat, allowing to adjust the eye height and to minimize head movements. The scene box angular size was 20°. Ocular fixations were recorded using a SMI X-RED distant eye tracker. Eight LEDs around the box served for the eye-tracker calibration, together with a central LED in the middle of the box, with a physical protection around, avoiding that any light would make the scene visible during the calibration. A video-projector displayed light on the back wall, avoiding possible glare due to the lamps in the scene box, however without light reflexion inside the box.

Seventeen subjects participated to the experiment (11 men, 6 women, mean age 29). Although some of them worked in the field of digital image, they were naive to the purpose of the experiment. They were asked to look freely at the scene during 30 s. We followed [23], telling them that they would be asked a very general question at the end of the experiment. Altogether, these instructions avoided strong task-dependent biases.

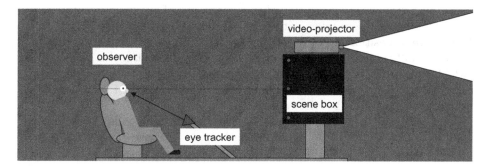

Fig. 6. Experimental setup

A black curtain hid the scene during the first part of the experiment (subjects entering the room, seating, seat adjustment in height, explanations about the experiment). Then, the light was turned off in the room, the curtain was opened, and the eye tracker was calibrated using the LEDs as reference fixation points. Finally, the LEDs were powered off, the scene box was lit, and the eye tracker record began. In the end, subjects were asked to mention the main objects they had noticed in the scene (these data are not analyzed here).

4.2   Results

We followed Le Meur *et al.* [11] and computed a Regions of Interest (RoI) map from the subject's fixations in the first 30 s. Fixations were defined as discs of 1° radius, where the gaze stayed for at least 100 ms. All fixation patterns (for the 17 subjects) were added together, providing a spatial distribution of human fixations. The RoI map is a probability distribution of the gaze direction, so its integral is normalized to 1. Fig. 7 (left) shows the RoI map obtained from individual fixations. Compared to the saliency maps of Fig. 8, the RoI map is smoother, which sets some limits to further comparisons.

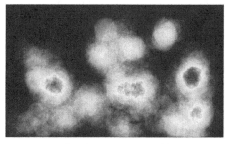 

Fig. 7. Left: Fixation map (RoI) recorded over the individual fixations of 17 observers, in false colours. Right: : LDR (JPEG) photograph of the HDR scene.

The next step was to compute saliency maps out of the experimental scene. First, photographs were taken with various integration times (bracketing) from the observer's position, in order to build a HDR image [24] close to what observers actually looked at. Saliency maps were computed out of this image, using both [3] and the **CF** algorithm. We also computed, for comparison, saliency maps using [3] after preprocessing with O_1 to O_6 (see section 3.3). Fig. 8 shows the resulting saliency maps in false colours.

Comparing the saliency maps suggests that some items which were missed by [3] were found by the **CF** algorithm, such as the yoghurt, the black box, the top right photograph, while the wine bottle is emphasized (see Tab. 1 for quantitative evidence). As expected, the direct saliency map computation with [3] only selects the two lamps and the colour chart (the colour feature is the only one to be normalized, see section 3.2).

An unexpected result is that some TMO fail in capturing more areas of interest than the direct saliency map computation with [3] (see O_5 for instance). Another interesting point is the strong difference between the saliency maps, depending on the TMO preprocessing. For instance, most TMO allow to capture the yoghurt (bottom right of the image) which is not detected by the direct computation, however O_2 and O_6 emphasize the left lamp, while O_2, O_4 and O_6 emphasize the wine bottle, O_5 captures the top right photograph, etc.

Table 1. Error indexes e and $\bar{s}$ comparing the RoI and the saliency maps, depending on the algorithm (rank in curly brackets)

Algo.	$10^4\, e$	rank	$\bar{s}$	rank
[3]	6.15	{6}	0.127	{6}
CF	4.63	{1}	0.161	{1}
$O_1 + $ [3]	4.65	{2}	0.158	{3}
$O_2 + $ [3]	5.47	{5}	0.131	{5}
$O_3 + $ [3]	7.67	{8}	0.093	{8}
$O_4 + $ [3]	4.89	{3}	0.160	{2}
$O_5 + $ [3]	6.22	{7}	0.126	{7}
$O_6 + $ [3]	5.36	{4}	0.145	{4}

The RoI only contains low spatial frequencies, partly due to accuracy issues in the eye tracking methodology. Thus, a direct quantitative comparison between the RoI and saliency maps is meaningless, as far as high frequencies are concerned. We took this limitation into account using the same 1° dilatation for the saliency maps as was previously done for the RoI, before any quantitative comparison. Then, we assumed that both the saliency maps and RoI map are probability distributions, and thus normalized in consequence.

Two criteria were used for the comparison. The first one is the square root e of the Mean Square Error (MSE) between the saliency and RoI distributions (see Tab. 1). However, as the MSE is a global criterion averaging on many pixels, we also used a finer comparison criterion based on level sets. For any probability value t between 0 and 1, saliency and RoI binary images can be

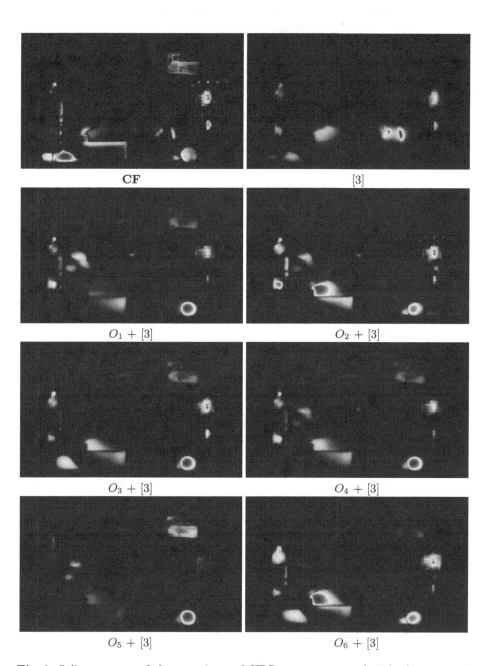

Fig. 8. Saliency maps of the experimental HDR scene computed with the proposed **CF** algorithm, and with [3] without and with preprocessing $O_1 - O_6$

built by thresholding the saliency and RoI distributions, and then compared. To compare two binary images, we used the Dice coefficient, which is relevant when the relative surface of the target is small:

$$s = \frac{2 \times TP}{2 \times TP + FP + FN} \tag{3}$$

where TP = True Positive, FP = False Positive and FN = False Negative pixels. The higher the Dice coefficient, the more similar the binary images. This leads to curves of the Dice coefficient s versus the threshold probability value t, as shown in Fig. 9. If the Dice curve obtained for one algorithm is always higher than the one obtained for another algorithm, the first one performs better.

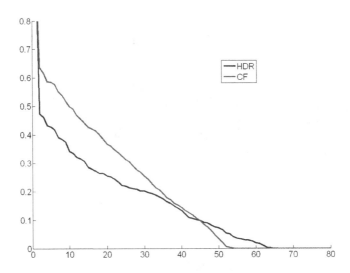

Fig. 9. Dice coefficient for the **CF** Saliency Map and [3] when compared to the RoI map, with threshold t as parameter

When comparing MSE values and mean Dice coefficients (see Tab. 1), the **CF** algorithms ranks first in both cases (the rank does not change much whether we use the MSE or the Dice). The square root of the MSE is improved by 33% compared to [3], while the mean Dice is improved by 27%. Besides, none of the TMO, used as preprocessing before [3], managed to perform better than the proposed **CF** algorithm in the tested situation. Furthermore, the tested TMO not always lead to a more predictive saliency maps than a direct saliency map computation without TMO, which is a counter-intuitive result. For instance, using O_3 and O_5 before [3] is worst than [3] alone.

5   Conclusion

We have focused on a drawback of the most popular computational models of the visual saliency when applied to HDR images. This can be put in terms of missing information: a direct saliency maps computation is poorly predictive of the gaze orientation. We have proposed a new algorithm, improving the saliency map quality on HDR images, that is, leading to a better fit with oculometric data. This **CF** algorithm was rated best in terms of the Dice coefficient and in terms of MSE, compared to [3]. In addition, it gives better results than 6 TMO from the literature (in order to compress the image dynamic) followed by [3]. This last result suggests that the drawback of Itti and Koch's standard model for HDR images is not due to the input image interpretation, but more probably to the feature's definition. Note that the standard feature definitions perform well on LDR images, and the need for modified features is limited to HDR images.

These results may benefit to HDR video coding and HDR display, as a number of compression and processing algorithms already use bottom-up saliency computations in order to optimize the computing time and compression rate. Thus, a more reliable computation of the bottom-up saliency of HDR input images should improve the quality of the displayed image.

Still, a predictive model of human fixations is beyond the possibility of such bottom-up saliency models [25]. This is emphasized by the fact that the Dice coefficients (Tab. 1 and Fig. 9) are quite low, whatever the method. This is partly due to the fact that visual attention is not only driven by the bottom-up visual saliency. In search for a more predictive model, alternative approaches may also compute the top-down component of visual attention, providing that a semantic description of the scene is available, which is often the case in Computer Graphic applications. For instance, in [26], the scene gist and *a priori* knowledge about the current task is used in order to bias the bottom-up saliency, in [27,28], a discriminant saliency linked to object recognition is computed.

References

1. Itti, L., Koch, C., Niebur, E.: A model of saliency-based visual attention for rapid scene analysis. IEEE Transactions on Pattern Analysis and Machine Intelligence 20, 1254–1259 (1998)
2. Reinhard, E., Ward, G., Pattanaik, S.N., Debevec, P.: High dynamic range imaging: acquisition, display, and image-based lighting. Morgan Kaufmann (2005)
3. Itti, L., Koch, C.: A saliency-based search mechanism for overt and covert shifts of visual attention. Vision Research 40, 1489–1506 (2000)
4. Treisman, A.M., Gelade, G.: A feature-integration theory of attention. Cognitive Psychology 12, 97–136 (1980)
5. Itti, L., Rees, G., Tsotsos, J.K. (eds.): Neurobiology of attention. Elsevier (2005)
6. Koch, C., Ullman, S.: Shifts in selective visual attention: towards the underlying neural circuitry. Human Neurobiology 4, 219–227 (1985)
7. Choi, S.B., Jung, B.S., Ban, S.W., Niitsuma, H., Lee, M.: Biologically motivated vergence control system using human-like selective attention model. Neurocomputing 69, 537–558 (2006)
8. Parkhurst, D., Law, K., Niebur, E.: Modeling the role of saliency in the allocation of overt visual attention. Vision Research 42, 107–123 (2007)
9. Reddy, M.: Perceptually optimized 3D graphics. IEEE Computer Graphics and Applications 22, 68–75 (2001)

10. Lee, C.H., Varshney, A., Jacobs, D.W.: Mesh saliency. ACM Transactions on Graphics 24, 659–666 (2005)
11. LeMeur, O., LeCallet, P., Barba, D., Thoreau, D.: A coherent computational approach to model bottom-up visual attention. IEEE Transactions on Pattern Analysis and Machine Intelligence 28, 802–817 (2006)
12. Walther, D., Koch, C.: Modeling attention to salient proto-objects. Neural Networks 19, 1395–1407 (2006)
13. Walther, D.: http://www.saliencytoolbox.net/ (2006)
14. Bruce, N., Tsotsos, J.K.: Saliency based on information maximization. Advances in Neural Information Processing Systems 18, 155–162 (2006)
15. Debevec, P.: http://gl.ict.usc.edu/Data/HighResProbes/ (2000)
16. Reinhard, E., Stark, M., Shirley, P., Ferwerda, J.: Photographic tone reproduction for digital images. In: Proceedings of SIGGRAPH (2002)
17. Tumblin, J., Rushmeier, H.: Tone reproduction for realistic images. IEEE Computer Graphics and Applications 13, 42–48 (1993)
18. Ward, G., Rushmeier, H., Piatko, C.: A visibility matching tone reproduction operator for high dynamic range scenes. IEEE Transactions on Visualization and Computer Graphics 3, 291–306 (1997)
19. Pattanaik, S.N., Tumblin, J., Yee, H., Greenberg, D.P.: Time-dependent visual adaptation for fast realistic image display. In: Proceedings of SIGGRAPH, pp. 47–54. ACM Press (2000)
20. Reinhard, E., Devlin, K.: Dynamic range reduction inspired by photoreceptor physiology. IEEE Transactions on Visualization and Computer Graphics 11 (2005)
21. Mantiuk, R., Daly, S., Kerofsky, L.: Display adaptive tone mapping. ACM Transactions on Graphics 27, article no. 68 (2008)
22. Daly, S.: The visible differences predictor: an algorithm for the assessment of image fidelity. In: Watson, A.B. (ed.) Digital Images and Human Vision, pp. 179–206. MIT Press, Cambridge (1993)
23. Itti, L.: Automatic foveation for video compression using a neurobiological model of visual attention. IEEE Transactions on Image Processing 13, 1304–1318 (2004)
24. Debevec, P., Malik, J.: Recovering high dynamic range radiance maps from photographs. In: Proceedings of ACM SIGGRAPH, pp. 369–378 (1997)
25. Knudsen, E.I.: Fundamental components of attention. Annual Review Neuroscience 30, 57–78 (2007)
26. Navalpakkam, V., Itti, L.: Modeling the influence of task on attention. Vision Research 45, 205–231 (2005)
27. Gao, D., Han, S., Vasconcelos, N.: Discriminant saliency, the detection of suspicious coincidences, and applications to visual recognition. IEEE Transactions on Pattern Analysis and Machine Intelligence 31, 989–1005 (2009)
28. Simon, L., Tarel, J.P., Brémond, R.: Alerting the drivers about road signs with poor visual saliency. In: Proceedings of IEEE Intelligent Vehicle Symposium (IV 2009), Xian, China, pp. 48–53 (2009), http://perso.lcpc.fr/tarel.jean-philippe/publis/iv09b.html

Visibility Maps for Improving Seam Carving

Alex Mansfield[1], Peter Gehler[1], Luc Van Gool[1,2], and Carsten Rother[3]

[1] Computer Vision Laboratory, ETH Zürich, Switzerland
[2] ESAT-PSI, KU Leuven, Belgium
[3] Microsoft Research Ltd, Cambridge, UK
{mansfield,pgehler,vangool}@vision.ee.ethz.ch,
carrot@microsoft.com

Abstract. In this paper, we present a new, improved seam carving algorithm. Seam carving efficiently removes pixels from an image to produce a retargeted image. It has proved popular with users and has been used as a component in many retargeting algorithms. We introduce the visibility map, a new framework for pixel removing image editing methods. This allows us to cast retargeting as a binary graph labelling problem. We derive a general algorithm which uses seam carving operations for efficient greedy optimization of a well defined energy, and compare this with forward energy seam carving and shift map image editing. We test this method with varying parameters on a large number of images, and present an improved seam carving algorithm which can demonstrably produce better results. We draw general conclusions about pixel removing methods for retargeting and motivate future directions of research.

1 Introduction

Image retargeting aims to generate effective visualizations of images from different sources on different displays. Given the increasing variation of sources and displays, from more traditional cameras and monitors to time-of-flight webcams and smartphones, there has been great interest in this application in recent years.

Seam carving [2, 15] is one of the most popular image retargeting methods. This simple algorithm removes a set of pixels from the input image to generate the output. Since its introduction by Avidan and Shamir in 2007, many seam carving implementations have become available, including in Adobe Photoshop[1], the Liquid Rescale plugin for GIMP[2] and online at rsizr.com. Seam carving has also been built on in many academic works [4, 6–8, 11, 16, 20]. However, most of this work uses seam carving as a complete algorithm, without modification.

The goal of this paper is to analyze, extend and improve seam carving itself. To this end we cast the problem in a new framework, the *visibility map*, illustrated in Fig. 1. This map provides a natural description of methods that remove pixels from the input image to generate the output, allowing us to describe retargeting as a binary graph labelling problem. We define an energy over a visibility map that can still be optimized using seam carving operations. We explore different

---

[1] See http://www.adobe.com/products/photoshop/photoshopextended/features/
[2] Available at http://liquidrescale.wikidot.com/

K.N. Kutulakos (Ed.): ECCV 2010 Workshops, Part II, LNCS 6554, pp. 131–144, 2012.
© Springer-Verlag Berlin Heidelberg 2012

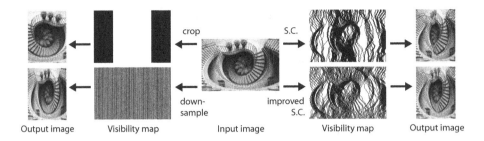

Output image   Visibility map   Input image   Visibility map   Output image

Fig. 1. The visibility map shows which pixels are visible in the output image after an image editing operation. Visible pixels are labelled 1 (shown in white), non-visible pixels labelled 0 (shown in black). As with all figures, best viewed in colour

versions of the visibility map energy and also optimization options that open up due to this new viewpoint. Results for numerous parameters are generated on a large set of images to determine an improved seam carving algorithm.

Our improved seam carving has a number of advantages. Most importantly, it optimizes an energy defined directly between the input and output images, unlike the commonly used forward energy seam carving of [15], as shown in Sect. 5.1. This allows a clearer understanding of our energy and allows direct comparison to results generated by other optimization methods. It also produces demonstrably better results on many images, e.g. see Fig. 1.

In summary, our key contributions are: (1) The definition of retargeting as a binary graph labelling problem. (2) An efficient optimization scheme using seam carving operations, given energy terms from a well defined general family. (3) An improved seam carving algorithm.

We next describe related work. In Sect. 3 we then define the visibility map, from which we derive the general form of our improved seam carving algorithm (Sect. 4). In Sect. 5 we compare this to related methods. In Sections 6 and 7 we describe various energy and optimization options. In Sect. 8 we show results, and present our improved seam carving algorithm. Finally, in Sect. 9 we conclude and discuss future directions.

2 Related Work

Scaling and cropping have been long used in image editing and retargeting. Automatic methods have been used to guide these simple processes [16, 17]. However, these operations have fundamental limitations. Scaling keeps uninteresting parts of the image, while distorting structured objects such as faces and man-made objects when the scaling is non-uniform. A good crop maintains only the interesting parts of the image, but not all may fit within the desired output image size.

Cropping has been generalized to more flexible pixel removal methods. These methods may remove areas of uninteresting content while being able to rearrange the image to better show all of the interesting parts.

Seam carving [2, 15] fits into this category. Using simple low level energy terms, this algorithm iteratively removes pixels. Retargeted images at a range of sizes can be quickly generated. Its simplicity, speed and effectiveness has led it to be used as component of many retargeting methods including [4, 6–8, 11, 16, 20]. Most use seam carving as a complete algorithm, with the exceptions of our previous work [11] where we extended seam carving to better protect objects during retargeting, and [7] which redefines seams for video retargeting to achieve improved results.

Other methods also operate by pixel removal. These include shift map image editing [12], which optimizes a mapping from pixels in the output image to pixels in the input image. For retargeting they add a label ordering constraint which maintains the ordering of pixels in the input image in the output image. In this case, the result can equivalently be generated by removing pixels.

Shift map image editing without this constraint, and other algorithms which generate outputs in terms of input pixels, e.g. [1, 5, 13, 14], also owe much of their effectiveness to pixel removal. However, allowing pixel re-arrangement and duplication gives greater flexibility, which must be appropriately constrained.

These methods have a number of drawbacks. When approximating scaling through downsampling, these methods suffer the same problem of causing non-uniform scaling of structured objects. Also, they may lead to discontinuities in lines and curves in the image, which can be very visually disturbing.

These issues have motivated other paradigms for retargeting. Non-linear warping/interpolation is used in [9, 10, 18, 19] among others to determine the output image. Pixel estimation is used in [3, 17] to minimize a patch-based bidirectional image similarity. The patch match algorithm [3] achieves interactive speeds, and allows very effective user interaction to be used to preserve lines and structured regions. However, these methods can be complex to implement, and usually require the optimization to be re-run from the beginning for each target size.

However, despite the drawbacks of seam carving, it is still popular in practice due to its simplicity, speed and effectiveness in a wide range of images. This motivates our aim to better understand and improve seam carving, which we do through the framework of the visibility map we introduce in the next section.

3 Visibility Map

In image editing and retargeting methods such as seam carving, the output image is created from the input image by simply removing pixels and squashing them together. This operation can be naturally defined through a binary graph labelling problem as follows. For each pixel (r, c) in the input image, there is one node that can take on one of two labels $X_{r,c} \in \{0, 1\}$. If the node label is 1 the corresponding pixel is visible in the output image; if 0, it is non-visible. In other words the output image is generated by only showing the pixels whose nodes are labelled with a 1. We refer to this graph as the visibility map over the image.

Example visibility maps for cropping, downsampling, seam carving and our improved seam carving of an image are shown in Fig. 1. Due to the simple relationship between the input image and output image via the visibility map, this representation provides an intuitive framework through which to view pixel-removal methods.

Regarding notation: throughout the paper we will denote row indices with r and column indices with c, in an image $R \times C$ in size.

4   Seam Carving Operations to Optimize a Visibility Map

The visibility map allows retargeting to be formulated as a binary labelling problem. However, the structure of the problem does not allow for a simple solution by standard binary labelling methods. For example, a fixed number of pixels must be removed from each row and column to maintain a rectangular output image. This constraint would take the form of higher order cliques in the graph which may make its solution intractable.

Instead, we determine a seam carving based approach for optimization. An important property of algorithms based on seam carving is their computational efficiency. At each iteration, the optimization is a dynamic program. We want to retain this efficiency, while extending the method to optimize a well-defined graph labelling problem. In this section, we show how this can be achieved.

4.1   Energy

We consider a general energy over a visibility map $\mathbf{X}$ for retargeting that allows for efficient optimization by seam carving operations, as described in the following section. Throughout, we assume that vertical seams are being removed, without less of generality. This energy takes the form

$$E(\mathbf{X}) = \sum_{r,c} \psi_{r,c}^{\mathrm{U}}(\mathbf{X}) + \sum_{r,c_{\mathrm{l}}<c_{\mathrm{r}}} \psi_{r,c_{\mathrm{l}},c_{\mathrm{r}}}^{\mathrm{H}}(\mathbf{X}) + \sum_{r>1,c_{\mathrm{u}},c_{\mathrm{d}}} \psi_{r,c_{\mathrm{u}},c_{\mathrm{d}}}^{\mathrm{V}}(\mathbf{X}) \ . \tag{1}$$

Unary Terms. $\forall r, c$

$$\psi_{r,c}^{\mathrm{U}}(X_{r,c}) = E_{r,c}^{\mathrm{U}}[X_{r,c} \neq 0] \ , \tag{2}$$

where $[.]$ is the indicator function.

Horizontal Contact Terms. These are potential functions over higher order cliques defined $\forall r, c_{\mathrm{l}} < c_{\mathrm{r}}$ as

$$a\psi_{r,c_{\mathrm{l}},c_{\mathrm{r}}}^{\mathrm{H}}(X_{r,c_{\mathrm{l}}}, \dots, X_{r,c_{\mathrm{r}}}) = \begin{cases} E_{r,c_{\mathrm{l}},c_{\mathrm{r}}}^{\mathrm{H}}, & X_{r,\{c_{\mathrm{l}},c_{\mathrm{r}}\}} = 1, X_{r,\{c_{\mathrm{l}}+1,\dots,c_{\mathrm{r}}-1\}} = 0 \\ 0, & \text{otherwise} \end{cases} \ . \tag{3}$$

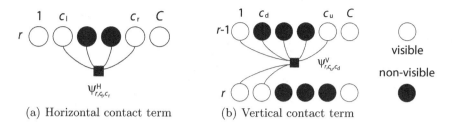

(a) Horizontal contact term   (b) Vertical contact term

Fig. 2. Contact term potentials over higher order cliques are turned on when certain pixels come into contact. Nodes are shaded to show example configurations which turn these potentials on.

Vertical Contact Terms. These are potential functions over higher order cliques defined $\forall r > 1, c_u, c_d$ as

$$\psi^V_{r,c_u,c_d}(X_{r-1,1}, \ldots, X_{r-1,c_u}, X_{r,1}, \ldots, X_{r,c_d}) =$$
$$\begin{cases} E^V_{r,c_u,c_d}, & X_{r-1,c_u} = 1, X_{r,c_d} = 1, \sum_{c=1}^{c_u-1} X_{r-1,c} = \sum_{c=1}^{c_d-1} X_{r,c} \\ 0, & \text{otherwise} \end{cases} \quad (4)$$

Note that the specific terms we use for E^*_* are defined later in Sect. 6.

The contact terms are so named because of their special sparsity properties. These potentials are only non-zero for configurations where certain pixels are brought into contact, e.g. for the horizontal terms only when nodes (r, c_l) and (r, c_r) are labelled 1 and all nodes in between are labelled 0. This is illustrated in Fig. 2. Although there are a huge number of these potentials, only a small number are "turned on" for each image configuration. This is the main reason why seam carving operations can be applied to minimize this energy.

We also place locality constraints on the non-zero values these potential functions can take. We enforce that the term E^H_{r,c_l,c_r} may not be a function of the properties of any pixels other than those on row r, and E^V_{r,c_u,c_d} of any pixels other than those on rows $r - 1$ and r.

4.2 Optimization

In this section we show how the form of energy described in the previous section may be optimized by seam carving operations.

Let us first recap the seam carving method. Seam carving greedily removes one seam per iteration, where a seam is defined as an 8-connected path across the image with one pixel per row. Dynamic programming is used to efficiently optimize for the seam with lowest energy, with order $O(RC + R)$. This process of optimizing for a seam to remove we refer to as a *seam carving operation*. We define these operations explicitly in order to distinguish them from seam carving *algorithms*, which also define the energy terms to be used.

In terms of the visibility map, seam carving can be understood as follows. From an initial all-ones labelling, each seam 'removed' encodes a label switch

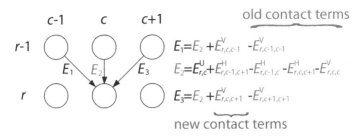

Fig. 3. Energy terms for seam carving operations. Green terms relate to new pixel contact, red terms to old pixel contact.

of nodes with label 1 to label 0. This process is iterated until the target size is acquired.

We now explain why our energy can be optimized using seam carving operations. During the forward pass of dynamic programming, as each pixel in the seam is chosen, the seam pixel in the row above is already known, conditioned on the current pixel being contained in the optimal seam. With this information, it is clearly possible to determine the correct non-zero energy terms as described in Sect. 4.1, which are subject to locality constraints.

It is also possible to determine which pixels are newly brought into contact, as used in [15]. Hence it is known which of the potential functions over higher order cliques are turned on and off, as these depend only on pixel contact.

It is therefore clear that, at each iteration, seam carving operations can find the seam to remove which results in the minimum energy visibility map. The energy terms defined in Sect. 4.1 are used in dynamic programming over the current image as shown in Fig. 3. The (red) old contact terms are paid negatively at the shown locations as an equivalent but simpler alternative to paying these terms positively everywhere *except* at the locations shown. This is because this distortion would remain for seams elsewhere in the image. Note that these old contact terms are only paid if they were previously paid as (green) new contact, i.e. if the pixels referenced were not neighbours in the input image.

5   Relationship to Other Methods

5.1   Forward Energy Seam Carving

Our new algorithm results in the generalized energy terms for the seam carving operations shown in Fig. 3. The terms of forward energy seam carving [15] are similar, but with a key difference: they pay only the new contact terms, and not the terms related to old contact. Sean carving can thus be thought of as "forgetting" the original image and only taking into account distortion introduced at that iteration.

This means that forward energy seam carving does not optimize for an energy defined over a visibility map, and therefore not for an energy defined simply between the input and output images. This can also be seen from the fact that

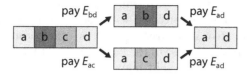

Fig. 4. Seam carving forward energy is dependent on the seam removal order

the energy is dependent on the order of seam removal, as illustrated in Fig. 4. Consider the four neighbouring pixels shown and their horizontal contact terms. Removing pixels b then c brings into contact a and c with cost E_{ac} in the first seam and then a and d with cost E_{ad} in the second seam. Removing pixels c then b incurs costs E_{bd} and then E_{ad}, which are different in general.

This makes the seam carving forward energy harder to understand. An energy defined between the input and output allows better energy modelling and also comparison to other methods which produce visibility maps.

5.2   Shift Map Image Editing

The visibility map framework also has close connections with the shift map framework described by Pritch et al. [12]. The shift map is a multi-label mapping over the output image, where the label describes the shift between the pixel in each position and its original position in the input image.

The shift map is related to the visibility map. When a label ordering constraint is enforced, a shift map result can be represented by a visibility map. This relationship is illustrated in Fig. 5. If the shift map is given by $M_{r,c}$, then then this relationship can be written formally as

$$X_{r,c} = \begin{cases} 1, \exists(u,v) \text{ such that } ((u,v) + M_{u,v}) = (r,c) \\ 0, \text{otherwise} \end{cases} \quad . \tag{5}$$

Comparing the two representations, while the shift map offers a clear description of the energy terms as shown in [12] and is not limited to maintaining pixel

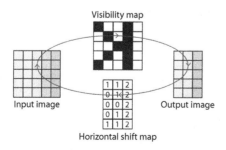

Fig. 5. The shift map is closely related to the visibility map. The corresponding entries for pixel (2,3) are highlighted.

ordering, it yields a multi-label problem. The visibility map is an alternative which poses a binary labelling problem with the pixel ordering being implicitly enforced. In the context of image retargeting, or other problems where a pixel ordering may be desirable, the use of the visibility map therefore yields a simpler formulation than the equivalent shift map.

6   Improved Seam Carving – Energy

We have shown in Sect. 4 that seam carving operations can be used to optimize for a well defined energy over a visibility map. This gives us the key advantage of greater intuition into the behaviour of the algorithm, given a defined energy. This intuition can be used in designing a good energy for the problem. With this in mind, we now consider a number of different options for the energy terms.

For the contact energy terms, we consider the general form

$$E_{r,c_l,c_r}^{H} = D_{r,c_l,c_r}^{H} + S_{r,c_l,c_r}^{H}$$
$$E_{r,c_u,c_d}^{V} = D_{r,c_u,c_d}^{V} + S_{r,c_u,c_d}^{V} \quad . \tag{6}$$

We now describe options for these terms.

6.1   Distortion Terms

These terms measure the distortion created in the output image. The following notation is used: D_{r,c_l,c_r}^{H} is the horizontal distortion term, and D_{r,c_u,c_d}^{V} the vertical distortion term, $\mathbf{I}$ is the input image, with magnitude $|\mathbf{I}|$. All terms have an order term n_D. In our experiments, we consider $n_D \in \{1, 2\}$.

Magnitude Distance

$$D_{r,c_l,c_r}^{H} = ||I|_{r,c_l} - |I|_{r,c_r}|^{n_D}$$
$$D_{r,c_u,c_d}^{V} = ||I|_{r-1,c_u} - |I|_{r,c_d}|^{n_D} \quad . \tag{7}$$

For $n_D = 1$, this is the contact energy used in forward energy seam carving [15].

RGB Distance

$$D_{r,c_l,c_r}^{H} = \sum_{x \in \{R,G,B\}} \left| I_{r,c_l}^{x} - I_{r,c_r}^{x} \right|^{n_D}$$
$$D_{r,c_u,c_d}^{V} = \sum_{x \in \{R,G,B\}} \left| I_{r-1,c_u}^{x} - I_{r,c_d}^{x} \right|^{n_D} \quad . \tag{8}$$

This energy is similar to the above, but makes use of differences in RGB colour rather than intensity magnitude.

Relative RGB Distance

$$D_{r,c_l,c_r}^{\mathrm{H}} = \sum_{x \in \{\mathrm{R,G,B}\}} \left| I_{r,c_l}^{x} - I_{r,c_r-1}^{x} \right|^{n_{\mathrm{D}}} + \left| I_{r,c_r}^{x} - I_{r,c_l+1}^{x} \right|^{n_{\mathrm{D}}}$$

$$D_{r,c_u,c_d}^{\mathrm{V}} = \sum_{x \in \{\mathrm{R,G,B}\}} \left| I_{r-1,c_u}^{x} - I_{r-1,c_d}^{x} \right|^{n_{\mathrm{D}}} + \left| I_{r,c_d}^{x} - I_{r,c_u}^{x} \right|^{n_{\mathrm{D}}} . \tag{9}$$

For $n_{\mathrm{D}} = 2$, this is part of the contact energy used in shift map image editing [12].

6.2   Seam Terms

We can regularize the spatial distribution of the seams and thus provide an explicit regularization against seam 'clumping'. Such clumping can occur when the distortion cost of removing a single clump of seams is lower than the cost of removing seams spread throughout the image, resulting in a visually disturbing seam of high distortion in the output image.

We consider two different possibilities. The following notation is used: $S_{r,c_l,c_r}^{\mathrm{H}}$ is the horizontal shift control term, and $S_{r,c_u,c_d}^{\mathrm{V}}$ the vertical shift control term.

Repeat Cost for Intermediate Seams

$$S_{r,c_l,c_r}^{\mathrm{H}} = (c_r - c_l - 1) D_{r,c_l,c_r}^{\mathrm{H}}$$

$$S_{r,c_u,c_d}^{\mathrm{V}} = (c_u - c_d - 1) D_{r,c_u,c_d}^{\mathrm{V}} . \tag{10}$$

This seam term ensures that the some cost is paid for each seam that has been removed, with that cost given by the energy of the currently visible seam.

Average Unary Cost for Intermediate Seams

$$S_{r,c_l,c_r}^{\mathrm{H}} = \frac{(c_r - 1) - (c_l + 1)}{(c_r - 1) - (c_l + 1) + 1} \sum_{c=c_l+1}^{c_r-1} E_{r,c}^{\mathrm{U}}$$

$$S_{r,c_u,c_d}^{\mathrm{V}} = (c_u - c_d - 1) D_{r,c_u,c_d}^{\mathrm{V}} . \tag{11}$$

This seam term leads to an approximation of the forward energy seam carving algorithm [15]. Consider removing a pixel with an already removed neighbour. Additional distortion energy and seam term energy $(\Delta D + \Delta S)$ is paid. The additional seam term energy, using this measure, approximates the previous distortion energy by the average unary term of the previously removed pixels $(\Delta S \approx D_{\mathrm{old}})$. The remaining energy is the new distortion energy $(\Delta D + \Delta S = D_{\mathrm{new}} - D_{\mathrm{old}} + \Delta S \approx D_{\mathrm{new}})$, which is what the forward energy seam carving algorithm optimizes for.

Note that a similar approximation for the vertical term is hard to define, so the repeating cost is again used.

6.3   Unary Energy Terms

By inspection of the form of the contact energies, it can be seen that they alone do not well model the problem of retargeting. Consider a retarget in which an area of interesting texture is completely removed, leaving only a homogeneous background. The contact energy terms will be low due to the low visible distortion, but clearly this is not the best way to retarget the image. In the terminology of [17], the contact terms provide a measure of *coherence* but not of *completeness*.

A unary term may be used to model this loss. We consider using the following as a simple saliency-based unary term, with a variable order given by n_U:

$$E_{r,c}^{U} = \left(\left| \left(\frac{\partial}{\partial x} \mathbf{I} \right)_{r,c} \right| + \left| \left(\frac{\partial}{\partial y} \mathbf{I} \right)_{r,c} \right| \right)^{n_U} . \tag{12}$$

For $n_U = 1$, this is the unary energy used in backward energy seam carving [2]. In our experiments, we consider $n_U \in \{1, 2\}$ and also consider not using the unary term.

7   Improved Seam Carving – Optimization

7.1   Refinement

A key advantage of having a well defined energy over a visibility map is that we can compare different optimization techniques and combine them to achieve a lower energy. We consider an optimization step based on the observation that we can not only remove seams, but also put them back in. We refer to this as visibility map refinement. Using refinement steps may allow a lower energy to be reached by allowing greater flexibility to explore the solution space.

At each refinement step, we run our improved seam carving algorithm in the visibility map for pixels labelled 0 (non-visible) in the visibility map, and relabel the pixels in the optimal seam to 1 (visible) as illustrated in Fig. 6. We run such a refinement step at each iteration after the seam removal step. We then run another removal step to maintain the current image size. If the energy is decreased, we keep this new labelling proposal. We repeat this until the overall energy is no longer decreased.

Note that by relabelling seams in the visibility map, the property of 8-connected seam removal in the current image is not preserved. However, we did not observe this as causing any lack of pixel consistency in our results.

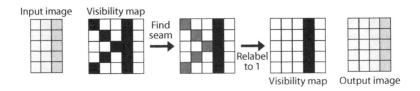

Fig. 6. Refinement by seam carving in the non-visible pixels of the visibility map

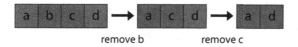

Fig. 7. Simple example of linear blending with $w = 0.25$

7.2 Blending

It is also possible to relax the visible/non-visible interpretation of the visibility map. We consider instead an interpretation of a label of 0 as indicating a low weight w in a blending operation. If pixel (r, c) is labelled 0, we use a linear interpolation to blend it into its horizontally neighbouring pixels $\forall x \in \{R, G, B\}$

$$I_{r,c-1}^x = wI_{r,c}^x + (1 - w)\, I_{r,c-1}^x$$
$$I_{r,c+1}^x = wI_{r,c}^x + (1 - w)\, I_{r,c+1}^x \; . \tag{13}$$

This is illustrated in Fig. 7.

Note that this simple blending operation can be taken into account before calculating the energy terms, and therefore can be optimized for directly. In our experiments where we use blending, we use $w = 0.25$.

8   Results

We have described a framework for visibility map optimization for retargeting using seam carving operations, and given a range of energy terms and optimization options. We collected a set of 100 images of different kinds of scenes from flickr.com and ran all 288 combinations of these options on them.[3]

We give a selection of the many results we generated in Fig. 8 to demonstrate our findings, and show a larger selection in the supplementary material[4].

To compare the results, we tried to rank them by average bidirectional similarity [16, 17]. However, we found a poor alignment with human judgement.

Overall Trends. We found that the use of distortion energy terms alone, without unary or seam terms, gave poor results. As can be seen from the results in the supplementary material, such an energy favours the creation of few high energy seams over distribution of the error over the image. This was found to be much improved by the use of a unary term. For good results, we found the use of seam terms to be necessary.

With regard to the different optimization options, we found that use of blending reduced the energy in 99.6% of our results, and refinement in 68.2%. Blending

---

[3] All code is available at www.vision.ee.ethz.ch/~mansfiea/improvingsc/ under the GNU General Public License

[4] Also available at www.vision.ee.ethz.ch/~mansfiea/improvingsc/

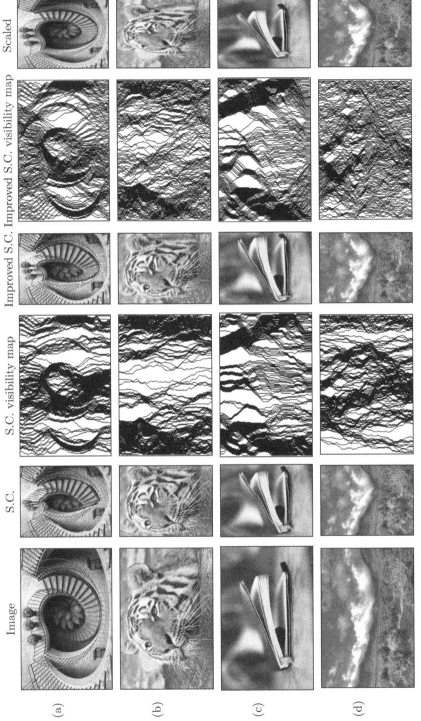

Fig. 8. Results comparing seam carving (S.C.), improved S.C. and scaling for halving image width

gave an average energy reduction of 19.3% but refinement an average energy increase of 2.3%. This is possible because the use of refinement only guarantees the energy is the same or lower at each iteration. This result shows that this greediness in some cases leads to an increased energy of the end result. However, for both of these techniques, we found that in practice their effect on the visual appearance of the images was limited.

Improved Seam Carving. From our results we chose the following parameters. We use the forward energy seam carving distortion energy (7) with $n_D = 1$, unary terms with $n_U = 1$ and the seam carving-approximating seam term (11). Refinement and blending had little visual effect on our results, so neither are used.

Representative Results. A small sample of results from our improved seam carving are shown, with the seam carving and scaling results, in Fig. 8. In these images, cropping would clip interesting areas out. Scaling shows the whole scene, but may include uninteresting areas at the cost of distortion due to non-uniform scaling (see (b)).

The results of seam carving show all the interesting areas, but may include line discontinuities and other distortion (see (a) and (c)). Our improved seam carving distributes seams more evenly in these areas and reduces these artefacts, while maintaining good performance in images where seam carving does well (see (b)). In non-structured images such as landscape seams, all methods perform well (see (d)).

9   Conclusions

In this work we introduced the visibility map, which can be used to define retargeting as a binary graph labelling problem. We described a general energy that can be efficiently optimized using seam carving operations. From tests on a large training database, we presented a new, improved seam carving algorithm.

Many works build upon seam carving as a complete algorithm. Our improved seam carving thus may also be used to improve these methods.

However, the improvements we are able to show are relatively minor and do not overcome the major problems of seam carving. Indeed, these problems clearly cannot be solved by simple low level pixel removal methods. Seam carving and related pixel removal methods fundamentally cannot retarget smooth curves to smooth curves. Methods making use of low level information do not know which areas of an image are structured such that non-uniform scaling would be distorting. The limits of such methods seem now to have been reached.

Alternatives do exist, as described in Sect. 2. These have problems of their own, typically in optimization. Nevertheless, it is clear that work using more general image synthesis frameworks, additional images (e.g. video, image databases, stereo cameras), intelligent use of user input and automated feature detection (e.g. lines, vanishing points, artificial structure) will strongly shape future methods in retargeting. Combining these sophisticated methods with the success of existing simple methods is also a promising direction.

Acknowledgements. We would like to thank the following users of Flickr for allowing us to use their work under the Creative Commons License: telmo32 for Fig. 8(a), Tambako the Jaguar for (b), Amir K. for (c) and Michal Osmenda for (d).

References

1. Agarwala, A., Dontcheva, M., Agrawala, M., Drucker, S., Colburn, A., Curless, B., Salesin, D., Cohen, M.: Interactive digital photomontage. In: SIGGRAPH (2004)
2. Avidan, S., Shamir, A.: Seam carving for content-aware image resizing. In: SIGGRAPH (2007)
3. Barnes, C., Shechtman, E., Finkelstein, A., Goldman, D.B.: PatchMatch: A randomized correspondence algorithm for structural image editing. In: SIGGRAPH (2009)
4. Chen, B., Sen, P.: Video carving. In: Eurographics Short Papers (2008)
5. Cho, T.S., Butman, M., Avidan, S., Freeman, W.: The patch transform and its applications to image editing. In: CVPR (2008)
6. Dong, W., Zhou, N., Paul, J.C., Zhang, X.: Optimized image resizing using seam carving and scaling. In: ACM SIGGRAPH (2009)
7. Grundmann, M., Kwatra, V., Han, M., Essa, I.: Discontinuous seam-carving for video retargeting. In: CVPR (2010)
8. Han, D., Wu, X., Sonka, M.: Optimal multiple surfaces searching for video/image resizing - a graph-theoretic approach. In: ICCV (2009)
9. Kim, J.S., Kim, J.H., Kim, C.S.: Adaptive image and video retargeting technique based on fourier analysis. In: CVPR (2009)
10. Krähenbühl, P., Lang, M., Hornung, A., Gross, M.: A system for retargeting of streaming video. In: SIGGRAPH (2009)
11. Mansfield, A., Gehler, P., Van Gool, L., Rother, C.: Scene Carving: Scene Consistent Image Retargeting. In: Daniilidis, K., Maragos, P., Paragios, N. (eds.) ECCV 2010, Part I. LNCS, vol. 6311, pp. 143–156. Springer, Heidelberg (2010)
12. Pritch, Y., Kav-Venaki, E., Peleg, S.: Shift-map image editing. In: ICCV (2009)
13. Rother, C., Bordeaux, L., Hamadi, Y., Blake, A.: AutoCollage. In: SIGGRAPH (2006)
14. Rother, C., Kumar, S., Kolmogorov, V., Blake, A.: Digital tapestry. In: CVPR (2005)
15. Rubinstein, M., Shamir, A., Avidan, S.: Improved seam carving for video retargeting. In: SIGGRAPH (2008)
16. Rubinstein, M., Shamir, A., Avidan, S.: Multi-operator media retargeting. In: SIGGRAPH (2009)
17. Simakov, D., Caspi, Y., Shechtman, E., Irani, M.: Summarizing visual data using bidirectional similarity. In: CVPR (2008)
18. Wang, Y.S., Tai, C.L., Sorkine, O., Lee, T.Y.: Optimized scale-and-stretch for image resizing. In: SIGGRAPH Asia (2008)
19. Wolf, L., Guttmann, M., Cohen-Or, D.: Non-homogeneous content-driven video-retargeting. In: ICCV (2007)
20. Zhang, X., Hua, G., Zhang, L., Shum, H.Y.: Interest seam image. In: CVPR (2010)

Feedback Retargeting

Eitam Kav-Venaki and Shmuel Peleg

School of Computer Science and Engineering
The Hebrew University of Jerusalem
91904 Jerusalem, Israel

Abstract. Feedback retargeting combines the benefits of two previous retargeting methods: Bidirectional similarity [1] and Shift-Map [2]. The first method may have blurry areas due to patch averaging and the latter can remove entire objects. Feedback retargeting has the sharpness of shift-map and the completeness of bidirectional similarity, avoiding the removal of salient objects.

In Shift-Map retargeting the output image is made from segments of the input image, and this minimizes the forward direction of bidirectional similarity. An iterative feedback procedure is developed to take care of the backward direction, assuring that the input image can be reconstructed from the output image. This is done by using Shift-Map backwards, reconstructing the input image back from the output image. Areas in the input image that are difficult to reconstruct from the output image get a feedback priority score. A second Shift-Map retargeting is then performed, adding this feedback priority to the data term. These regions now have a higher priority to be included in the output.

After a few iterations of forward retargeting and backward feedback the retargeted image includes all salient features from the input image. Computational efficiency and image sharpness remain as high as in ordinary Shift-Map.

1 Image Retargeting Background

Image retargeting algorithms [1–7] take an input image A and generate an output image B having new dimensions, mostly having a new aspect ratio (e.g. reducing image width by two). These algorithms attempt to preserve some of the image's important qualities and features, that may be lost or distorted when using simple scaling or cropping.

The most recognized method for image retargeting is seam-carving [4, 8]. In this approach continuous seams of pixels are removed from the image in an iterative greedy manner, selecting in each step a seam whose removal will minimize the error measured by image gradients. Seam-carving methods and also methods that apply non-homogeneous warping to the image [5, 6, 9] may induce noticeable distortions even if objects with high gradients are unchanged. Obviously, some texture or details in the image will have to change their aspect ratio.

Some retargeting approaches [1, 2, 10] are based on algorithms that were used in the fields of texture synthesis and image completion (see [11–13]). Paper

K.N. Kutulakos (Ed.): ECCV 2010 Workshops, Part II, LNCS 6554, pp. 145–155, 2012.

[1] introduces a bidirectional similarity formulation. Every patch in the output image B should have a similar patch in the input image A ("coherence") and vice versa: every patch in the input image A should have a similar patch in the output image B ("completeness"). Shift-Map retargeting [2] has a high coherence but does not guarantee completeness. An epitome [14] is an example for visual summarization that imposes no coherence.

The minimization of the bidirectional dissimilarity score in [1] assumes retargeting with a small scale change. To obtain any significant scale change, multiple iterations of small image scaling are performed. Feedback retargeting as proposed in this paper can perform any scale change, with no need for repetitive small changes.

Another bidirectional-similarity score was developed by [7]. They combine several resizing operators (seam-carving, cropping, and scaling), and find an optimal combination that minimizes that score. Their work was followed by the work of [15], which use a similar technique to minimize a similarity score based on the formulation in [1] and on dominant color descriptors.

2   Shift-Map

Following [2, 16, 17], we define the relationship between the pixels in the output image $R(u, v)$ to pixels in the source image $I(x, y)$ by a shift-map $M(u, v) = (t_x, t_y)$. The pixel $R(u, v)$ in the output image will be derived from the source pixel $I(u + t_x, v + t_y)$. The optimal shift-map is defined using graph labeling, where the nodes are the pixels of the output image, and each output pixel is labeled by a shift $t = (t_x, t_y)$. The optimal shift-map M minimizes the following cost function:

$$E(M) = \alpha \sum_{p \in R} E_d(p, M(p)) + \sum_{(p,q) \in N} E_s(p, q, M(p), M(q)). \qquad (1)$$

E_s is a smoothness term defined over neighboring pixels N in section 2.1. The data term E_d depends on whether the shift-map is forward or backward:

1. Forward direction, when retargeting the input image A to a smaller version B. In this direction we use $E_{d,ret}$ (Eq. 3 and Eq. 7). The role of α in that case, and the value that was used will be discussed in Sec. 4.
2. Backward feedback stage, when trying to reconstruct the input image A from the reduced image B. In this direction we use $E_{d,sim}$ (Eq. 4), and an α value of 1.

Once the graph is given, shift-map labeling is computed using the alpha-expansion algorithm [18–20]. As in [2] a hierarchical pyramid scheme is used to speed up the optimization.

Assignment of new locations to pixels using a similar energy minimization scheme was done in the texture-synthesis application of [11], and formulating image synthesis problems as a graph labeling problem was done by [2, 16, 17].

We follow [16] in using a heuristic adaptation of the alpha-expansion algorithm for smoothness costs where the triangle inequality is not guaranteed (Eq. 2). Video retargeting using shift-map is described in [21].

2.1 The Smoothness Term

The smoothness term E_s is identical to the one used in [2], and is based on the formulation in [22]. The smoothness term represents discontinuities added to the output image by discontinuities in the shift-map. The smoothness term should reflect, for each of the two neighboring output pixels, how different the value of its output neighbor is from the value of its input neighbor, as well as the difference of the output-neighbor gradient from the input-neighbor gradient. The smoothness term between two neighboring locations p and q in the output image R, having shift-maps $r = M(p)$ and $t = M(q)$, is defined as follows:

$$E_s(p, q, r, t) = \|I(p + r) - I(p + t)\|^2 + \|I(q + r) - I(q + t)\|^2 + \tag{2}$$
$$\beta_s(\|\triangledown I(p + r) - \triangledown I(p + t)\|^2 + \|\triangledown I(q + r) - \triangledown I(q + t)\|^2).$$

we used a value of $\beta_s = 2$, and as in [2] the squared norm is used over RGB values.

2.2 Image Retargeting

In horizontal image retargeting, horizontal monotonicity is often required. I.e., if $M(u, v) = (t_x, t_y)$ and $M(u + 1, v) = (t'_x, t'_y)$, than $t'_x \geq t_x$. This constraint assures that input objects are not duplicated in the output, and that the left-right relationship between objects will be maintained. In Shift-Map [2] this constraint is imposed through the smoothness term, giving a large penalty if $t'_x < t_x$.

The priority of input pixels to appear in the output image can be controlled using the data term as follows:

$$E_{d,ret}((u, v), (t_x, t_y)) = D(u + t_x, v + t_y), \tag{3}$$

where $D(x, y)$ is a value between 0 to 1 given to each input location (x, y). The higher the value of $D(x, y)$, the smaller are the chances to include the pixel at input location (x, y) in the output image.

2.3 A New Shift-Map Application: Similarity Guided Composition

Shift-Map can be used for the composition of an output image $R(x, y)$ from segments taken from a source image $I(x, y)$ while requiring that the resulting image $R(x, y)$ will be similar to a given target image $T(x, y)$. This is done by using the data term $E_{d,sim}$:

$$E_{d,sim}(p, t) = \|R(p) - T(p)\|^2 = \|I(p + t) - T(p)\|^2 \tag{4}$$

This data term is defined for every output pixel location $p = (u, v)$ and for every candidate shift-value $t = (t_x, t_y)$.

While similarity guided composition can be used to create very interesting visual effects, these will not be addressed here. In feedback retargeting only the following question is important: "how hard is it to reconstruct the target image T from pieces of an image I". The output image R itself is not used in retargeting. The next section will describe how to extract this information from the optimal shift-map.

3   Composition Score

After performing similarity guided composition and assigning shift-map labels to all output pixels, values of the data term (Eq. 4) and the smoothness term (Eq. 2) indicate how difficult it was to compose the target image T from pieces of the source image I. This indicates features in the target image that did not appear in the source image.

For an ordered pair of images $\langle T, I \rangle$, an optimal shift-map M will be computed to construct the target image T from the source image I. This will be done as described in Sec. 2 for similarity guided composition. Once the optimal shift-map has been computed, A composition score indicates for every image location $p \in T$ how hard it is to build its neighborhood from the source image I. This composition score is defined as follows:

$$E_{\langle T|I \rangle}(p) = \alpha E_d(p, M(p)) + E_{s,mean}(p, M), \tag{5}$$

where E_d is the data term as defined in Eq. 4, and $E_{s,mean}(p, M)$ is the average smoothness term E_s (Eq. 2) between a pixel p and its neighbors:

$$E_{s,mean}(p) = \frac{1}{4} \sum_{q \in N(p)} E_s(p, q, M(p), M(q)).$$

The composition-energy for the entire image is defined as

$$E(T|I) = \sum_{p \in T} E_{\langle T|I \rangle}(p), \tag{6}$$

and is equal to the value of $E(M)$ in Eq. 1.

It may be relevant to compare this score to the score used in [23], as both answer the abstract question: "How difficult is it to compose a signal S_1 from the signal S_2". The two algorithmic frameworks are designed for different tasks, and our score does not use SIFT descriptors nor an exhaustive search. In addition, our score is flexible enough to match patches of different sizes and shapes due to the use of similarity guided shift-map composition.

We get back to the retargeting of an input image A to a smaller output image B, and to the issue of similarity. Terms used in previous papers are also used here: "coherence" will indicate the ease of constructing the output B from the input A, and will be inversely proportional to the global composition energy $E(B|A)$.

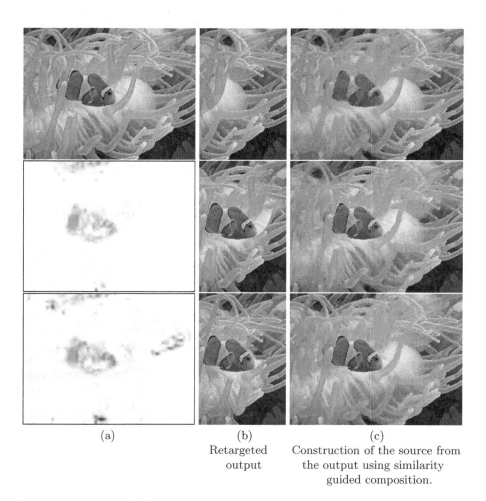

(a)

(b)

Retargeted
output

(c)

Construction of the source from
the output using similarity
guided composition.

Fig. 1. Iterations of feedback retargeting, reducing the width of an image by 2.
Top Row: (a) The source image A. (b) The initial output B_0 using Shift-Map retargeting, when data term is set to zero everywhere except the left and right columns. The fish disappeared. (c) Backward reconstruction of the input A from B_0 using similarity guided composition. The fish is poorly restored (best visible in color).
Middle Row: (a) The feedback score C_1 corresponding to regions in the input A that are poorly restored from B_0. High values are given to the fish area. (b) Shift-Map retargeting of the input A to B_1, this time using an updated data-term with the feedback values C_1. The fish returned! (c) Backward reconstruction of the input A from B_1 using similarity guided composition. This reconstruction is much better than the first attempt.
Bottom Row: The last iteration. (a) The cumulative feedback C_2 from the first two iterations. (b) Shift-Map retargeting to B_2 using the updated data-term. (c) The last and best Backward reconstruction of the input A from the retargeted image B_2.

"Completeness" will indicate the ease of constructing the input A from the output B, and will be inversely proportional to $E(A|B)$. Shift-Map retargeting [2] creates, by definition, a "coherent" output B.

In the bidirectional similarity work of [1], coherence and completeness are modeled slightly differently. In their work, the penalty for each rectangular patch (in different scales) equals to the SSD with its nearest neighbor in the other image. The global score adds up the scores of all patches. A similar formulation to [1] was used in [24] in the field of texture transfer.

In feedback retargeting we use Shift-Map [2] to reduce either the width or the height of the image. Shift-Map retargeting minimizes the value of $E(B|A)$ with respect to a constraint given by the data-term $E_{d,ret}$. In [2], the data term included maintaining the borders and perhaps a user-given saliency. Completeness, however, is not guaranteed by the original Shift-Map retargeting method. To improve completeness, feedback retargeting uses the data-term mechanism: input regions with lower value of $D(x,y)$ (Eq. 3) are more likely to appear in the output image. We propose to determine the value of $D(x,y)$ of an input pixel $p = (x,y)$ from the composition score for that pixel $E_{\langle A|B\rangle}(p)$.

4   Feedback Retargeting

Input regions with a high composition score $E_{\langle A|B\rangle}$ indicate that these input regions cannot be reconstructed accurately and easily from the output image B. If we decrease the value of $D(x,y)$ in Eq. 3 for pixels in these input regions, and recompute again the output B using Shift-Map, we increase the likelihood that components from these regions will appear in the output, increasing the completeness. The iterative feedback retargeting algorithm, creating a retargeted image having bidirectional similarity, is as follows:

In each iteration we use Shift-Map retargeting to compute the retargeting result B from the input image A using the updated data-term. In the first iteration $D(x,y)$ is set to zero for all input pixels, and it is possible that important features of the input image will disappear in the initial retargeted image. Given the retargeted image B, the composition score $E_{\langle A|B\rangle}$ is computed using similarity guided composition as described in sections 2.3 and 3.

The composition score computed during the similarity guided composition is used as a feedback to improve the data term in the following way:

$$D(x,y) = e^{-C(x,y)} \tag{7}$$

where $C(x,y)$ is a cumulative feedback, summing the feedback $E_{\langle A|B\rangle}(x,y)$ from all previous iterations. We do not know which weight to use when adding $E_{\langle A|B\rangle}(x,y)$ to the cumulative feedback $C(x,y)$ in a way that will maximize completeness. We therefore search through a decreasing sequence of weights as follows, until we reach the first weight which reduces the global composition energy $E(A|B)$ therefore improves completeness.

$$C_{temp}(x,y) = C(x,y) + \frac{E_{\langle A|B\rangle}(x,y)}{\gamma 2^k}. \tag{8}$$

Fig. 2. Reducing width by 50%: (a) Source image. (b) Initial Shift-Map retargeting. (c) Intermediate result does not reduce the composition energy $E(A|B)$. (d) Final result with lower composition energy.

We use $\gamma = 0.05$, and the value of k is determined by searching $k = 0, 1, 2, \ldots$. Each k gives a candidate feedback C_{temp} computed by Eq. 8.

As mentioned before, we increase k until we reach the first value of k which reduces the global composition energy $E(A|B)$ (Eq. 6). In order to compute that value, retargeting of A to B, and reconstruction of B from A, are performed for each step of the search. An example with intermediate results of this process is shown in Fig. 2. Once an improved composition energy $E(A|B)$ is obtained, we update the value of C to this of C_{temp}, and iterations continue. This is a common way to perform gradient descent: A step in the direction of the gradient is tested; If the value of function is decreased the step is taken, and minimization continues, otherwise the step is not taken and a smaller step is tested.

Convergence is obtained after 2-3 iterations, once the improvement in the composition score is smaller than a given threshold. In each iteration we start with an initial value of k that was used in the previous iteration so we have about 6 calls for each of the shift-map optimization routines (retargeting or composition). The algorithm is demonstrated in Fig. 1.

To accelerate performance, the composition score $E_{\langle A|B \rangle}$ can first be computed on a downscaled version of the images. Then the composition map can be either magnified to the original resolution using bilinear interpolation, or the

Fig. 3. Feedback retargeting without border constraints: For every test image we show (from left to right): The input image, the result of [2] and our final output image.

hierarchical scheme of [2] can be used. Fig. 4 shows the difference between the two schemes. The synthesis itself is fine in both schemes, as the retargeting step is left the same, but the sensitivity to unique fine details increases. A compromise can obviously be made between the two schemes by performing optimization only on some of the levels of the pyramid. As for the Shift-Map retargeting step, one or two pyramid levels were used when the images were large. Horizontal shift-map is inherently faster due to a smaller number of allowed shifts. This makes the total running time only a few minutes.

Even though the value of C determines the priority of input pixels, it should not be confused with "saliency" or "importance" of the regions of the input image A. When an important feature is not removed by Shift-Map retargeting, it can have a low value of C.

As in the original shift-map algorithm, an infinite penalty was added if either the left-most or right-most column were not mapped to the new border location. Feedback retargeting works well also without this border constraint. Now that the values of $D(x, y)$ are not uniform, removing this constraint will not result in an under-determined problem. Practically, this means that pixels can be

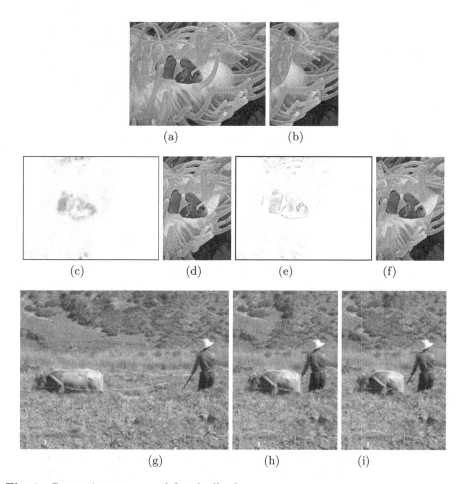

Fig. 4. Comparing coarse and fine feedbacks.
Fish: (a) Source image. (b) Initial retargeting (i.e., result of [2]). (c) Coarse Feedback. (d) Retargeted output using the coarse feedback (second iteration). (e) Feedback computed using the hierarchical scheme of [2]. (f) Retargeted output using this feedback. In this case a finer feedback does not improve the result.
Man and Cow: (g) Source image. (h) Final result using coarse feedback. (i) Final result using a finer feedback. The sensitivity to fine details is increased.

removed from the boundaries of the image as long as they does not increase the value of $E(A|B)$. But unlike the crop operator, we do not restrict pixels from the boundaries to be removed as entire columns. Fig. 3 shows results of this retargeting strategy. As it can be seen, in some cases most of the pixels removed were from the left and right boundaries, and in other cases most of the pixels removed were from the interior of the image.

The use of a negative exponent in Eq. 7 limits the data-term value to be between 0 and 1. This serves well our intentions, as we do not want the gradient

| Simakov et. al [1] | Shift-Map[2] | Feedback Retargeting |

Fig. 5. Comparison of Feedback retargeting with the Image-Summarization of [1]. Input image (same as in Fig. 4.g) and result of their method were taken from their article. Feedback retargeting does not suffer from blur caused by patch averaging.

descent technique to lead us to put too much weight on completeness. We also do not want to sacrifice coherence for completeness, but to make sure a certain amount of coherence will always be implied. The balance between the two can be controlled by the value of α in Eq. 1 in the forward retargeting stage. In our specific implementation we have used a value of $\alpha = 0.02$, and it worked well for most of our test images. But this value can be changed if the result should be more complete or coherent.

5   Comparison and Conclusion

Feedback retargeting combines the low level qualities of shift-map retargeting with the bidirectional similarity property [1]. As can be seen in Fig. 5, the result of [1] suffers from blurring caused by voting techniques, and possible distortions caused by repeated gradual resizing. Shift-Map retargeting does not capture the entire content of the input image. Feedback retargeting benefits from the best of both worlds, producing a good retargeting without blurring or distortions.

References

1. Simakov, D., Caspi, Y., Shechtman, E., Irani, M.: Summarizing visual data using bidirectional similarity. In: CVPR (2008)
2. Pritch, Y., Kav-Venaki, E., Peleg, S.: Shift-map image editing. In: ICCV, Kyoto (2009)
3. Setlur, V., Takagi, S., Raskar, R., Gleicher, M., Gooch, B.: Automatic image retargeting. In: Proceedings of the 4th International Conference on Mobile and Ubiquitous Multimedia (MUM 2005), pp. 59–68 (2005)
4. Avidan, S., Shamir, A.: Seam carving for content-aware image resizing. In: SIGGRAPH (2007)
5. Wolf, L., Guttmann, M., Cohen-Or, D.: Non-homogeneous content-driven video-retargeting. In: ICCV (2007)
6. Wang, Y., Tai, C., Sorkine, O., Lee, T.: Optimized scale-and-stretch for image resizing. In: SIGGRAPH (2008)

7. Rubinstein, M., Shamir, A., Avidan, S.: Multi-operator media retargeting. In: SIG-GRAPH (2009)
8. Rubinstein, M., Shamir, A., Avidan, S.: Improved seam carving for video retargeting. In: SIGGRAPH (2008)
9. Krähenbühl, P., Lang, M., Hornung, A., Gross, M.: A system for retargeting of streaming video. In: SIGGRAPH Asia (2009)
10. Barnes, C., Shechtman, E., Finkelstein, A., Goldman, D.B.: Patchmatch: a randomized correspondence algorithm for structural image editing. In: SIGGRAPH (2009)
11. Kwatra, V., Schodl, A., Essa, I., Turk, G., Bobick, A.: Graphcut textures: image and video synthesis using graph cuts. In: SIGGRAPH, pp. 277–286 (2003)
12. Wexler, Y., Shechtman, E., Irani, M.: Space-time video completion. In: CVPR, vol. 1, pp. 120–127 (2004)
13. Kwatra, V., Essa, I., Bobick, A., Kwatra, N.: Texture optimization for example-based synthesis. In: SIGGRAPH, pp. 795–802 (2005)
14. Jojic, N., Frey, B.J., Kannan, A.: Epitomic analysis of appearance and shape. In: ICCV, vol. 1 (2003)
15. Dong, W., Zhou, N., Paul, J.C., Zhang, X.: Optimized image resizing using seam carving and scaling. In: SIGGRAPH (2009)
16. Rother, C., Kumar, S., Kolmogorov, V., Blake, A.: Digital tapestry. In: CVPR, pp. 589–596 (2005)
17. Rother, C., Bordeaux, L., Hamadi, Y., Blake, A.: Autocollage. In: SIGGRAPH, pp. 847–852 (2006)
18. Boykov, Y., Veksler, O., Zabih, R.: Fast approximate energy minimization via graph cuts. IEEET-PAMI 23, 1222–1239 (2001)
19. Kolmogorov, V., Zabih, R.: What Energy Functions Can Be Minimized via Graph Cuts? In: Heyden, A., Sparr, G., Nielsen, M., Johansen, P. (eds.) ECCV 2002, Part III. LNCS, vol. 2352, pp. 65–81. Springer, Heidelberg (2002)
20. Boykov, Y., Kolmogorov, V.: An experimental comparison of min-cut/max-flow algorithms for energy minimization in vision. IEEET-PAMI 26, 1124–1137 (2004)
21. Hu, Y., Rajan, D.: Hybrid shift-map for video retargeting. In: CVPR (2010)
22. Agarwala, A., Dontcheva, M., Agrawala, M., Drucker, S., Colburn, A., Curless, B., Salesin, D., Cohen, M.: Interactive digital photomontage. In: SIGGRAPH, pp. 294–302 (2004)
23. Boiman, O., Irani, M.: Similarity by composition. In: Schölkopf, B., Platt, J., Hoffman, T. (eds.) Advances in Neural Information Processing Systems 19, pp. 177–184. MIT Press, Cambridge (2007)
24. Wei, L.Y., Han, J., Zhou, K., Bao, H., Guo, B., Shum, H.Y.: Inverse texture synthesis. In: SIGGRAPH (2008)

How to Measure the Relevance of a Retargeting Approach?

Christel Chamaret[1], Olivier Le Meur[2], Philippe Guillotel[1], and Jean-Claude Chevet[1]

[1] Technicolor R&I, France
{philippe.guillotel,christel.chamaret,jean-claude.chevet}@technicolor.com
[2] University of Rennes 1
olemeur@irisa.fr

Abstract. Most cell phones today can receive and display video content. Nonetheless, we are still significantly behind the point where premium *made for mobile* content is mainstream, largely available, and affordable. Significant issues must be overcome. The small screen size is one of them. Indeed, the direct transfer of conventional contents (*i.e.* not specifically shot for mobile devices) will provide a video in which the main characters or objects of interest may become indistinguishable from the rest of the scene. Therefore, it is required to retarget the content. Different solutions exist, either based on distortion of the image, on removal of redundant areas, or cropping. The most efficient ones are based on dynamic adaptation of the cropping window. They significantly improve the viewing experience by zooming in the regions of interest. Currently, there is no common agreement on how to compare different solutions. A retargeting metric is proposed in order to gauge its quality. Eye-tracking experiments, zooming effect through coverage ratio and temporal consistency are introduced and discussed.

1 Introduction

Due to the proliferation of new cell phones having the capacity to play video, new video viewing experiences on small screen devices are expected. To reach this goal, conventional contents have to be retargeted in order to guarantee an acceptable viewing comfort. Today it is generally done manually: an operator defines a cropping area with its size and its location and also controls the cropping window location temporally. Retargeting the video content is thus expensive and time consuming. Live events require short delays that manual operations cannot provide. As most of video contents are not produced with small-screen viewing in mind, the direct transfer of video contents would provide a video in which the main characters or other objects of interest may become indistinguishable from the rest of the image. An automated way, delivering a compromise between the time consumption and the retargeting relevancy, would be a high economic differentiator.

In the past, three basic video format conversion techniques have been used to cope with such problem, e.g. anamorphic distortion, letter/pillar box and

K.N. Kutulakos (Ed.): ECCV 2010 Workshops, Part II, LNCS 6554, pp. 156–168, 2012.
© Springer-Verlag Berlin Heidelberg 2012

centered cropping. The anamorphism consists in applying a non-linear filtering in one direction. Letter/pillar box technique adds black rows or columns to reach the target aspect ratio. Cropping a sequence consists in extracting a subarea of the picture. The centered cropping technique corresponds to the extraction of a centered sub-window assuming that the interesting areas are located at the center. All those techniques process all frames of the sequence in the same way. The drawback of these methods lies on the fact that they are not driven by the content. More recently, many new techniques have been published. A solution is to focus on the most visually interesting parts of the video. As simple as it appears, this solution brings a number of difficulties: the first concerns the detection (in an automatic manner) of the regions where an observer would look at (usually referred to region of interest or RoI). The principle of first studies [6,4,12] is based on the use of a visual attention model. This kind of model [7,9,8,2] is able to provide a map indicating the hot spots of a scene. Once the regions of interest have been identified, a cropping window enclosing the most visually interesting parts of the picture is computed. Rather than displaying the whole picture, the content of the cropping window is only displayed. One advantage of such approach is to keep the ratio of object as well as the distance between objects in the scene. One drawback concerns the loss of the context that can undermine the scene understanding. A different approach is the famous seam-carving approach [1]. Seam carving is a method for content-aware resizing that changes the size of an image according to its content. There exists a number of variant of such approach that deals with seam-carving's drawbacks. Indeed, the initial version selects the seam that has the lowest energy. Such seam can cross important contents. Since seam-carving approach removes seams having the lowest energy, significant distortions may occur on the shapes of object. To deal with this issue, Zhang et al. [20] added geometric constraints to preserve the original shape of the objects.

Concerning the video, existing methods are based on an extension of still images solutions. As there exist spatio-temporal models of visual attention indicating the positions of the salient areas of a video sequence, a natural extension of saliency-based retargeting approach has been proposed [11,19,17,5]. Those techniques can be classified into three categories depending on the strategy used to reframe the content: crop based, warp based or a mix. For the first category, Tao et al. [17] compute saliency clusters which are temporally tracked to estimate the position of the cropping window. Limitations are mainly due to wrong detections of RoIs. Wolf et al. [19] warp pixels from the original frame to the retargeted one depending on their visual importance. An extension of the seam-carving also exist [14]. They applied a graph cut technique to connect removed energy lines. These techniques have proved a high efficiency for some content, but still allows visual distortion which may be annoying. It is interesting to note that some works have mixed different techniques. Liu et al. [11] consider three different cases dealing with different kinds of content: a static cropping window, a horizontal pan and cutting the shot into two shots. The technique favors the original aspect ratio, but the selection is performed per shot which may be inadequate if scene content is changing over time. When facing a sparse content, Deselaers et al. [5] allow the alteration of the image by enlarging the original aspect ratio to potentially enclose more columns in the pan-scan window; one additional strategy is to zoom out by adding black stripes/pixels when RoI is spatially sparse. Some approaches [11,17] intentionally prefer preserving the aspect ratio without distortion of the original frame, although others [19,14,5] have based their algorithm on introducing local distortion of the frame for a better rendering of original content. How are these approaches assessed? How to gauge their quality? Up to now, subjective approaches [11,17,15,19,13] are the most used. Some authors [11,17] have assessed their own algorithm by giving their visual opinion. However, most of the time, a subjective comparison is performed between a new algorithm and a baseline algorithm (the seam-carving algorithm is the most used as the baseline). Another approach [5] goes further in the validation by using annotated ground truth. A hand labelling was used to identify relevant regions from unrelevant ones. The percentage of those important pixels present in the cropping window is then computed and compared to a state-of-the-art implementation. In the same vein, Chamaret and Le Meur [3] proposed to assess the quality of a retargeting algorithm by using eye tracking data. The idea was to check whether fixation points were present in the retargeted result.

In this paper, we propose a metric to assess quantitatively the quality of a retargeting approach. Section II first dresses a list of important points that a retargeting approach should obey. From these features, a quality metric is proposed. Section III presents a video retargeting method. Its performance is measured in Section IV. Finally, some conclusions are drawn.

2   What Is a Good Retargeting Algorithm and How to Measure Its Quality?

Before describing the features that a retargeting approach should follow, it is important to define the context in which we are. The context is the TV broadcast for cell phones. Two solutions to retarget the video content exist. First, the retargeting approach is performed by the cell phones. The final users can switch from the original to the retargeted video. This is the most convenient approach for a number of reasons. The first one is the right over video. As this is the final user that chooses between both versions, the video content can be modified without problem. Object's shapes, aspect ratio and distance between objects can be significantly different from the original sequence. Seam-carving, warped-based approach can be used. The second solution consists in retargeting the video sequence just before its encoding and its broadcasting over the network. In this case, this is the responsibility of the broadcasters to provide a good quality of retargeting.

In this context the retargeting algorithm must obey a number of constraints:

- the object's shapes must be kept;
- the distance between objects must be kept.

These constraints are important since they significantly influence the choice of the retargeting algorithm. For instance, the seam-carving does not respect the distance between objects. An example for a soccer game is given in figure 1. The soccer game is a good example since the distance between players is fundamental to understand the action and the game.

Fig. 1. Example of a retarget picture with the seam-carving approach. (a) Original picture; (b) retargeted picture.

The two constraints listed above are required in a broadcasting system. However, they do not reflect at all the quality of the final result. In order to assess the quality of a retargeted video in the context of TV broadcasting, three features are examined:

- The preservation of the visually important areas, called p_f: This first constraint of a retargeting algorithm is to keep in the final result the most visually important areas. This first property is obvious. However, it is difficult to assess automatically the extent to which a retargeting algorithm succeeds in keeping the regions of interest. In a similar vein of [3], an elegant solution would use data coming from an eye tracking experiment. From the spatial positions of visual fixations, it is easy to count the number of visual fixations that falls inside the retargeted sequence. The value p_f is the percent of visual fixation inside the cropping window (see figure 2). A database of video sequence, for which eye fixations would be available[1], might be proposed to the community.
- Temporal consistency of the cropping window center, called $c = (x, t)^T$:
  The previous constraint is necessary but not sufficient to draw a conclusion on the quality of the retargeted video sequence. Indeed, it is also required that the cropping window moves coherently along the sequence. A second fundamental rule would be that displacements of the cropping window should be as smooth as possible. In practice, it is not so easy to obtain due to the

---

[1] Such database already exist for still images (see for instance, http://www.irisa.fr/temics/staff/lemeur/visualAttention/ and http://www-sop.inria.fr/members/Neil.Bruce/)

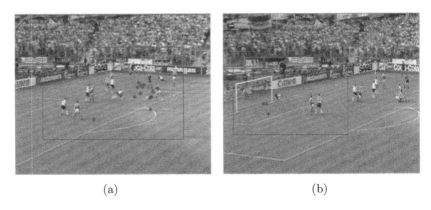

(a)   (b)

Fig. 2. Pictures extracted from the Sports clip. Red points correspond to visual fixations from eye-tracking experiments. Red boxes are the cropping windows.

high number of particular cases. For instance, on a still shot, it might be necessary to track a person walking. In other case, a close-up of a person moving his head does not necessary imply a displacement of the cropping window.

– Temporal consistency of the zoom, called z: In the context of this study, the retargeting approach aims at providing a better visual experience. The solution is to dynamically adapt the amount of zoom over the sequence. No matter how this zooming factor is computed, what is important is to first respect the first constraint (to keep the RoI) and to be coherent over time. However, the more the zooming factor, the more the visual experience might be. It does not mean that the zoom factor have to be high whatever the visual content. The zooming factor has to be content-dependent. This rule must be taken into account in the metric. We use the coverage ratio (CR) to measure the zoom. This is the ratio between the pixel number of the cropping window and the total number of pixel. A high coverage ratio means a low zoom in. The coverage ratio may stand for the quantity of lost data during the cropping process.

Based on these three constraints, the overall quality Q of a retargeted video sequence can be computed. The quality score is between 0 (lowest quality) and 100 (best quality). This is given by:

$$Q = f\left(p_f(t) \times \frac{100}{100 + coh_c(t)^\gamma} \times \frac{100}{100 + coh_z(t)^\beta} \times \frac{100}{100 + g(z(t), z_{opt}(t))^\alpha}\right) \tag{1}$$

where, N is the number of frames of the video sequence. $coh_c(t) = \left\|\frac{\partial}{\partial t}c(t)\right\|$ is the temporal coherency of the cropping center window. $coh_z(t) = \frac{\partial}{\partial t}z(t)$ is the temporal coherency of the coverage factor. $g()$ is a function that computes a distance between the current zoom factor and the optimal coverage factor $z_{opt}(t)$.

In our case, $g()$ is the absolute value function. The optimal coverage factor $z_{opt}(t)$ can be deduced from the eye tracking data or fixed to an average value. α and β are coefficients that could be used to favor one particular dimension. They are all set to 1, except γ. This coefficient is set to 3 in order to strengthen the weight of the temporal consistency of the cropping window. The function $f()$ is used to pool all the quality scores to an unique one. The most common is the average function. However, as it is performed to assess the quality of a video sequence, we can use a Minkowsky pooling or a percentile-based approach. In these last solutions, the lowest $t\%$ scores are used to compute the final score. Our hypothesis is that a bad retargeting even on few pictures can dominate the subjective perception.

3   Application to a Video Retargeting Algorithm

The video retargeting algorithm used in this study is an extension to the temporal dimension of the algorithm published in [10]. We briefly describe it since the scope of this paper is to present a method to assess the quality of a retargeting approach rather than to propose a new method. Figure 3 gives the synoptic of the proposed algorithm. The starting point of the proposed method is based on the computation of a saliency map. The model proposed in [8] is used. This is a purely bottom-up model based on luminance, color and motion information. These visual information are merged to create a final/global saliency map per frame. This spatio-temporal saliency map is the first step of the reframing process. Once regions of interest have been identified, a cropping window which encloses the most important parts of the frame is deduced. This step is composed of three sequential operations:

- Window extraction: the goal of this step is to define a bounding box that encloses the most conspicuous parts of the picture. Based on the results coming from the attention model, a Winner-Take-All algorithm is applied. This algorithm allows the detection of the first N most important locations (having the highest saliency values). When the kth maximum location is selected and memorized, this location as well as its neighborhood is inhibited. Due to the inhibition process, a new salience peak will dominate and will be selected at the next iteration. The selection process is influenced by the center of the picture. Indeed, the bias of scene center has an important role: observers tend to fixate near the center of scenes, even if the salience is null. This tendency is due to a number of reasons notably detailed in [18]. Finally, it is important to underline that the value N is chosen in order to predict most of the salience of the saliency map. However, upper and lower bounds, called CR_{max} and CR_{min} respectively are used to control the amount of zoom. Note that the term zoom and coverage ratio (CR) have here the same meaning. A CR of 1 indicates that there is no zoom.
- Temporal consistency: as mentioned before, the temporal stability is likely the most important issue of a video retargeting process. The temporal stabilization acts here both on the position and the size of the bounding box. Two

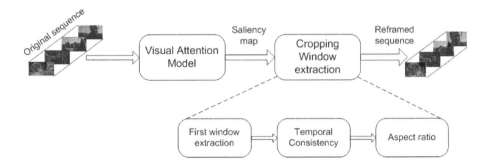

Fig. 3. General description of the proposed automatic retargeting process. Main operations are the visual attention model, the cropping window extraction and the temporal consistency.

filters are used. A Kalman filter is first applied in order to better predict the spatial and the size of the cropping window. However, in order to deal with small displacement, a temporal median filter is used to lock the position as well as the size of the cropping window;

– Aspect ratio: as the first step (window extraction) does not guarantee the good aspect ratio, it is required to adapt the size of the window. This adaptation is arranged by extending the window size. The extension is either performed on the width or the height to reach the targeted aspect ratio.

Figure 4 gives some results of the proposed algorithm.

4   Quality Assessment

4.1   Database of Eye Tracking

Sixteen subjects have participated in the experiments. All observers had normal or corrected to normal visual acuity and normal color perception. All were inexperienced observers and naive to the experiment. Before each trial, the subject's head was correctly positioned so that their chin pressed on the chin-rest and their forehead lean against the head-strap. The height of the chin-rest and head-strap system was adjusted so that the subject sat comfortable and their eye level with the center of the presentation display.

Eye movement recording has been performed with a dual-Purkinje eye tracker from Cambridge Research Corporation. The eye tracker is mounted on a rigid EyeLock headrest that incorporates an infrared camera, an infrared mirror and two infrared illumination sources. The camera recorded a close-up image of the eye. Video was processed in real-time to extract the spatial location of the eye position. Both Purkinje reflections are used to calculate the eye's location. The guaranteed sampling frequency is $50Hz$ and the accuracy is about 0.5 degree.

Four video sequences have been selected: *Movie*, *Cartoon1*, *Cartoon2* and *Sports*. The features of those clips are given in table 1.

Fig. 4. Visual comparison of still pictures for the seam carving and dynamic reframing schemes. Top row is the computed saliency heat maps (the reddish pixels are salient, the blue ones are not). Second row is the original picture with the cropping window in white. Third row is the resulting cropped picture.

Table 1. Features of the clips used during the eye-tracking experiments

Clip	Number of observers	Spatial resolution	Length (frames)	Type
Movie	16	720 × 480	1000	Trailer (action)
Cartoon1	16	720 × 480	1200	Trailer (cartoon)
Cartoon2	16	720 × 480	2000	Trailer (cartoon)
Sports	16	720 × 480	2000	basketball, soccer, cycling...

Each sequence was presented to subjects in a free-viewing task. Experiments were conducted in normalized conditions (ITU-R BT 500-10). The spatial resolution of video sequence is 720×480 with a frequency of $50Hz$ in a progressive mode. They are displayed at a viewing distance of four times the height of the picture ($66cm$). Subjects were instructed to look around the image. The objective is to encourage a visual bottom-up behavior and to lessen the top-down effects. Analysis of the eye movement record was carried out off-line after completion of the experiments. The raw eye data is segmented into saccades and fixations. The start- and end-points of each fixation were extracted as well as the spatial coordinates of visual fixation. A visual fixation must last at least $100ms$ with a maximum velocity of 25 degrees per second.

4.2   Preservation of the Visually Important Areas p_f

The loss of the region of interest is to be avoided, not only for the viewing experience but also in order to understand the content of the sequence. The idea is to compute the ratio of visual fixations that fall into the cropping window. A ratio of 1 would mean that all regions of interest are enclosed in the bounding box. As mentioned before, this is necessary but not sufficient.

Figure 5 gives the percentage of the human fixation points that fall into the cropping window for four video sequences. Two other information are given:

the minimum percentage as well as the average value of the lowest values (10% of the lowest values are taken into account). The former is about 20% for the *Movie* and *Sports* clips and greater than 60% for the other clips. These relatively low values are due to the temporal masking induced by a scene cut [8]. After a scene cut, the spatial coordinates of the visual fixation depend on the content displayed prior the cut. This temporal shifting is due to the inability of visual system to instantaneously adjust to changes. Previous studies demonstrated that the perception is reduced after a brutal changes and can last up to $100ms$ [16]. Therefore, just after a scene cut, the cropping window is well located whereas the position of the human's gaze is still locked on areas corresponding to the content prior the cut. Then, the use of the averaged 10% lowest value is more reliable that the raw value. Results are between 60% and 80% with an average value greater than 90%, suggesting that most important areas are preserved and that the accuracy of the proposed reframing solution is very high. The worst value (60%) is obtained by the *Sports* clip. It is not surprising since this kind of content contains numerous regions of interest and the consistency in visual fixation locations is not as high as those obtained by animated sequences or movie clips.

4.3   Temporal Consistency of the Cropping Window Center $c = (x, t)^T$

The third validation method deals with the temporal behavior of a reframing solution. The best solution is to observe the evolution of the cropping window, the more stable the position and size of the cropping window the better the subjective quality. Figure 6 (a) depicts this evolution for the position of the cropping window (horizontal only).

In order to highlight the role of the temporal filtering in the proposed re-targeting scheme, the location of the cropping box center is drawn in figure 6

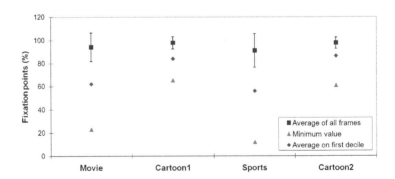

Fig. 5. Percentage of human fixation points in cropping window. Blue squares indicate the average values over time (the standard deviation is also given). The pink triangle and the purple diamond respectively correspond to the frame with the lowest percentage and the average of the 10% lowest values.

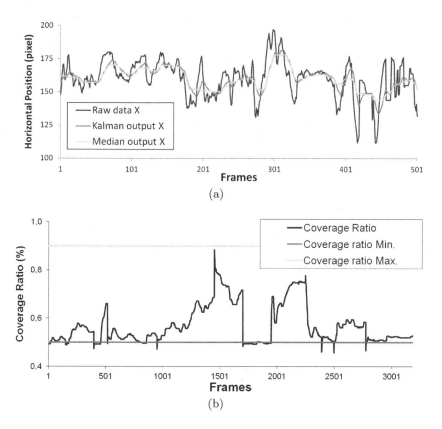

Fig. 6. Temporal evolution of the center of the cropping window (just the spatial coordinate X is presented) (a) and of the coverage value (b) for the *Sports* clip. Concerning the position of the cropping window, the temporal evolution is given after the cropping window extraction, the Kalman and the median filter.

(a) considering different processing steps. The dark blue, pink and light blue curves stand respectively for the raw data, the data after Kalman filtering and data after the median filtering. The curves clearly show the role of each filtering. The kalman filter attenuates the bound to the next sample and then creates smooth trajectories between strong gaps. However, when looking at the video, the cropping window location and size move still too much or too often compared to the few changes of content even if they are changing more smoothly. Too many changes of cropping window do not lead to a natural camera effect such as an operator would shoot. The median filter is used to cope with this issue. This filtering also fixes a visually disturbing problem: the backward and forward displacement of the window. Finally, the final curve of the cropping window location reaches the objective of both a smooth trajectory and a high adaptability to video content.

4.4   Temporal Consistency of the Zoom, z

The coverage ratio, called CR, is used to measure the amount of zoom. It may stand for the quantity of lost data during the cropping process. Figure 6 (b) depicts the coverage ratio over time for the *Sports* sequence. Upper and lower bounds are used to control the amount of zoom. It is interesting to note that the coverage value depends on the scene. For instance, a classical sky view is shot for a cycling race at the frame 1000. The coverage ratio has a low value because the region of interest (typically the cyclists) covers few pixels and is not spatially spread out.

The average, minimum and maximum coverage ratios per clip are presented in Table 2. All clips have the same tendency for average and minimum statistics. The CR average is low (close to the minimum boundary), while the CR minimum is a bit inferior to the minimum boundary. Regarding the CR maximum, results are different: although the *Sports* sequence reaches a maximum of 0.88, the *Cartoon1* sequence comes up to 0.66. This difference is clearly due to the sequence content.

Table 2. Coverage ratio data for different sequences

Clip	$Avg \pm std$	Minimum	Maximum
Movie	0.54 ±0.05	0.44	0.69
Cartoon1	0.54 ±0.052	0.49	0.66
Cartoon2	0.51 ±0.04	0.44	0.70
Sports	0.57 ±0.08	0.46	0.88

4.5   Final Quality

The formula 1 is used to compute the final quality score. The setting are: $f()$ is the average function, $g()$ is the absolute value function. α and β are set to 1 and γ is equal to 3. The optimal coverage is arbitrary set to 0.65 for the sequences *Cartoon1*, *Cartoon2* and *Sports*. The optimal coverage for the sequence *Movie* is set to a smaller value (0.5) due to the presence of black stripes.

Table 3 gives the average quality scores over these sequences. These scores are given after the different filters used in the proposed algorithm. Results indicate that the quality increases when the temporal filters are used. These results are consistent with our subjective perception. Table 4 gives the distribution of the quality scores per quartile. The quality scores of the final retargeted sequence are much more uniformly distributed than the two other distributions. This is again consistent with our own perception. However, there still exist a number of problem since the quality scores of the first quartile is dramatically weak. Several reasons can explain it: first, the performance is strongly tied to the ability of the computational model of visual attention to predict the RoI. Second, we did not handle the scene cut in the computation of the quality scores. Finally, the proposed metric does not handle a smooth and coherent displacement of the cropping window.

Table 3. Quality score for the sequences (average with the standard error of the mean. A value of 100 indicates the best quality.

Clip	Optimal Coverage	$Avg \pm sem$		
		Original data	Filtered data (Kalman)	Filtered data (Kalman+median)
Movie	0.5	50.31 ± 0.181	71.85 ± 0.157	81.7 ± 0.127
Cartoon1	0.65	59.99 ± 0.177	78.48 ± 0.139	84.64 ± 0.109
Cartoon2	0.65	50.34 ± 0.126	67.86 ± 0.102	73.25 ± 0.08
Sports	0.65	43.69 ± 0.135	73.96 ± 0.107	77.27 ± 0.101

Table 4. Distribution of the quality per quartile for the sequence *Sports*. The first quartile represents the lowest quality scores.

Clip	Original data	Filtered data (Kalman)	Filtered data (Kalman+median)
First	2.12×10^{-7}	4.92×10^{-5}	8.43×10^{-6}
Second	1.67	69.01	74.02
Third	42.32	82.95	86.16
Fourth	82.09	88.25	88.94

5   Conclusion and Future Work

This paper proposes a metric to assess the quality of a video retargeting algorithm. This metric is based on four fundamental factors: the capacity to keep the visually interesting areas in the retargeted sequence, the temporal coherence of the cropping window, the temporal coherence of its size and the ability to be close to an optimal zoom factor.

Such metric requires to collect the human visual fixations. At first sight, it might seem too complex and time-consuming. However, as it was done for the video/image quality assessment, we believe that such databases are necessary to benchmark the different retargeting algorithms. It will be required to make in a near future a comparison between the proposed metric and user studies. Indeed, it will be important to check whether the proposed metric match the user's preferences. Moreover, the different setting used here might be learned to reflect our perception.

In the future, we will endeavor to provide to the community such databases and to make a benchmark between different approaches by using the proposed quality metric.

Supplement materials are available at http://www.thlab.net/~guillotelp/.

References

1. Avidan, S., Shamir, A.: eam carving for content-aware image resizing. ACM Transactions on Graphics, SIGGRAPH 26 (2007)

2. Aziz, M.Z., Mertsching, B.: Fast and robust generation of feature maps for region-based visual attention. Image Processing 17(5), 633–644 (2008)
3. Chamaret, C., Le Meur, O.: Attention-based video reframing: validation using eye-tracking. In: ICPR (2008)
4. Chen, L., Xie, X., Fan, X., Ma, W., Zhang, H., Zhou, H.: A visual attention model for adapting images on small displays. ACM Multimedia Systems Journal 9(4) (2003)
5. Deselaers, T., Dreuw, P., Ney, H.: Pan, zoom, scan – time-coherent, trained automatic video cropping. In: IEEE Conference on Computer Vision and Pattern Recognition. IEEE (2008)
6. Fan, X., Xie, X., Ma, W., Zhang, H., Zhou, H.: Visual attention based image browsing on mobile devices. In: ICME 2003, vol. 1, pp. 53–56 (2003)
7. Itti, L., Koch, C.: Model of saliency-based visual attention for rapid scene analysis. IEEE Trans. on Pattern Analysis and Machine Intelligence 20(11), 1254–1259 (1998)
8. Le Meur, O., Le Callet, P., Barba, D.: Predicting visual fixations on video based on low-level visual features. Vision Research 47(19), 2483–2498 (2007)
9. Le Meur, O., Le Callet, P., Barba, D., Thoreau, D.: A coherent computational approach to model the bottom-up visual attention. IEEE Trans. on Pattern Analysis and Machine Intelligence 28(5), 802–817 (2006)
10. Le Meur, O., Castellan, X., Le Callet, P., Barba, D.: Efficient Saliency-Based Repurposing Method. In: IEEE International Conference on Image Processing, pp. 421–424 (2006)
11. Liu, F., Gleicher, M.: Video retargeting: automating pan and scan. In: MULTI-MEDIA 2006: Proceedings of the 14th Annual ACM International Conference on Multimedia, pp. 241–250. ACM Press, New York (2006)
12. Liu, H., Xie, X., Ma, W., Zhang, H.: Automatic browsing of large pictures on mobile devices. In: ACM Multimedia Conference, pp. 148–155 (2003)
13. Kraehenbuehl, P., Manuel Lang, A.H., Gross, M.: A system for retargeting of streaming video. In: ACM Transactions on Graphics (Proc. of SIGGRAPH Asia) (2009)
14. Rubinstein, M., Shamir, A., Avidan, S.: Improved seam carving for video retargeting. ACM Transactions on Graphics (SIGGRAPH) 27(3), 1–9 (2008)
15. Santella, A., Agrawala, M., Decarlo, D., Salesin, D., Cohen, M.: Gaze-based interaction for semi-automatic photo cropping. In: Proceedings of ACM's CHI 2006, pp. 771–780 (2006)
16. Seyler, A.J., Budrikis, Z.: Details perception after scene changes in television image presentations. IEEE Trans. Inform. Theory 11(1), 31–43 (1965)
17. Tao, C., Jia, J., Sun, H.: Active window oriented dynamic video retargeting. In: International Conference Computer Vision (2007)
18. Tatler, B.W., Baddeley, R.J., Gichrist, I.D.: Visual correlates of eye movements: Effects of scale and time. Vision Research 45(5), 643–659 (2005)
19. Wolf, L., Guttmann, M., Cohen-Or, D.: Non-homogeneous content-driven video-retargeting. In: IEEE 11th International Conference on Computer Vision, ICCV 2007, pp. 1–6 (October 2007)
20. Zhang, G., Cheng, M., Hu, S., Martin, R.R.: A shape-preserving approach to image resizing. Pacific Graphics 28 (2009)

3D Modelling of Static Environments
Using Multiple Spherical Stereo

Hansung Kim and Adrian Hilton

Centre for Vision, Speech and Signal Processing, University of Surrey
Guildford, GU2 7XH, Surrey, UK
{h.kim,a.hilton}@surrey.ac.uk

Abstract. We propose a 3D modelling method from multiple pairs of spherical stereo images. A static environment is captured as a vertical stereo pair with a rotating line scan camera at multiple locations and depth fields are extracted for each pair using spherical stereo geometry. We propose a new PDE-based stereo matching method which handles occlusion and over-segmentation problem in highly textured regions. In order to avoid cumbersome camera calibration steps, we extract a 3D rigid transform using feature matching between views and fuse all models into one complete mesh. A reliable surface selection algorithm for overlapped surfaces is proposed for merging multiple meshes in order to keep surface details while removing outliers. The performances of the proposed algorithms are evaluated against ground-truth from LIDAR scans.

Keywords: Environment modelling, Spherical stereo, PDE-based disparity estimation, Multiple stereo reconstruction.

1   Introduction

In recent years generating accurate graphical models of environments has been addressed through computer vision techniques. Approaches to the environment modelling can be classified into active methods using range sensors and passive methods using normal camera images. Light Detection and Ranging (LIDAR) is one of the most popular depth ranging techniques [1]. However, there are problems with respect to hardware cost, materials in the environment and temporal/spatial consistency with an imaging sensor. Therefore active sensing methods are used as reference for image-based modelling [2] or manual computer graphics modelling.

On the other hand, passive approaches require a simpler and less expensive setup. They are temporally and spatially consistent with images because they extract depth information from the captured images. There have been many researches into accurate outdoor scene reconstruction from multi-view images [3-5]. Strecha et al. created a benchmarking site for the quantitative evaluation of algorithms against ground-truth by LIDAR scanning [2]. However, the biggest problem of multi-view stereo is the fact that normal cameras provide only a partial description of the surrounding environment. Agarwal et al. reconstructed full 3D model of streets from 150,000 photos on internet using grid computing with 500 cores for 24 hours [6]. This is very

K.N. Kutulakos (Ed.): ECCV 2010 Workshops, Part II, LNCS 6554, pp. 169–183, 2012.
© Springer-Verlag Berlin Heidelberg 2012

impressive work but it requires higher costs for renting parallel compute resources and data transfer. The second problem is calibration of multiple cameras. Strecha et al. provided accurate calibration data calculated using attached markers on buildings and LIDAR scanning for the data sets [2], but it is sometimes hard to accurately calibrate all cameras in advance.

Instead of using fixed multiple cameras, structure from motion (SfM) uses video sequences from a moving camera [7][8]. The basic idea of the SfM is similar as the multi-view reconstruction but it reconstructs 3D positions and the cameras motions simultaneously by feature tracking. However, the limitation from narrow field of view (FOV) of normal cameras still remains. Pollefeys et al. used 3,000 frames to reconstruct one building and 170,000 frames for a small town [9].

Another way to capture the full 3D space is to use a catadioptric omnidirectional camera or fisheye lens [10, 11], These approaches only use one CCD to capture the full 3D space so that the resolution of partial images from the full view is too low to recover details of the environment. Instead of using original spherical images, Feldman and Weinshall [12] used a cross-slits projection with a rotating fisheye camera to generate a high quality spherical image. Kim and Hilton extended this to spherical stereo for reconstructing a 3D environment from a stereo pair of high resolution images [13].

There have been researches on combining active and passive sensors for outdoor environment modelling. Boström et al. reconstructed large urban environments using a wide angle laser range finder (LRF) and a calibrated colour CCD camera [14]. Asai et al. also reconstructed wide outdoor areas using an omnidirectional LRF and an omnidirectional multi-camera system which can capture high-resolution images [15].

In this paper, we propose a 3D environment modelling method from multiple pairs of spherical stereo images. We capture a static environment as a vertical stereo pair with a rotating line scan camera at multiple locations. Dense floating-point disparity fields are estimated using a novel PDE-based stereo method giving a 3D reconstruction of the scene for the surfaces visible from each stereo pair. A 3D rigid transform is calculated between views using SURF feature matching [16] and RANSAC algorithm to register the reconstructed models from multiple viewpoints. Finally a complete 3D model of the environment is generated as a single mesh by selecting the most reliable surfaces.

The main contributions of this paper are:

(1) We propose to use vertical stereo with a rotating line scan camera for scene modelling which does not require calibration steps for stereo reconstruction and model registration. (Section 2.1 and 3.1)

(2) We extend an existing stereo PDE formulation to handle the occlusion problem in stereo and over-segmentation problem in highly textured regions. (Section 2.2)

(3) We propose a simple and efficient approach to merge multiple stereo reconstructions into a single model based on selection of the best viewpoint for unoccluded surface regions by considering visibility, surface normal vectors and distance. (Section 3.2 and 3.3)

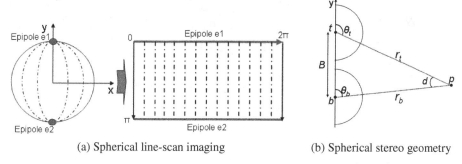

(a) Spherical line-scan imaging   (b) Spherical stereo geometry

Fig. 1. Spherical geometry

(4) We evaluate the accuracy of reconstruction against ground-truth model scanned by a LIDAR sensor. (Section 4)

2   Depth Reconstruction from Spherical Stereo

2.1   Capture System and Spherical Stereo Geometry

We use a line scan camera system which captures a full spherical view from a rotating lens around a vertical axis [13][17]. A spherical image is generated by mosaicing rays from a vertical slit at the centre of a rotating fisheye lens. The maximum resolution of the image is 12574x5658. The scene is captured with the camera at two different heights to recover depth information of the scene through stereo geometry. There are two advantages of using this line scan cameras for stereo imaging as well as acquiring high resolution images. First, the stereo matching can be simplified to a 1D search along the scan line if the two capture points are vertically aligned as shown in Fig. 1 (a), while normal spherical images require complex search along conic curves or rectification of images. Second, calibration for depth reconstruction only requires knowledge of the baseline distance between the stereo image pair. Radial distortion is rectified using a 1D table to evenly map pixels on the vertical central line to 0 ~ 180° range. Internal lens distortion parameters are fixed so it can be calculated for the lens in advance.

If we assume the angles of the projection of the point p onto the spherical image pair displaced along the y-axis are θ_t and θ_b, respectively, the angle disparity d of point p can be defined as the difference of the angles as $d = \theta_t - \theta_b$, and the distances of the point p from the two cameras are calculated as follows from the relationship between two cameras in Fig. 1 (b).

$$r_t = B / \left(\frac{\sin\theta_t}{\tan(\theta_t + d)} - \cos\theta_t \right) \tag{1}$$

$$r_b = B / \left(\cos\theta_b - \frac{\sin\theta_b}{\tan(\theta_b - d)} \right)$$

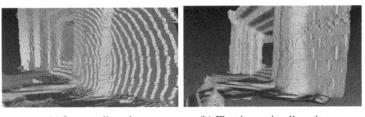

(a) Integer disparity   (b) Floating-point disparity

Fig. 2. Precision in surface reconstruction

2.2   PDE-Based Disparity Estimation

There have been a large number of algorithms proposed to solve the stereo correspondence problem over the last four decades. Scharstein and Szeliski present a test bed for the quantitative evaluation of stereo algorithms [18]. However, most disparity estimation algorithms including graph-cut (GC) and belief-propagation (BP) methods solve the correspondence problem on a discrete domain such as integer, half- or quarter-pixel levels which are not sufficient to recover a smooth surface. Spherical stereo image pairs have relatively small variations in disparity and serious radial distortion because of wide FOV of the fisheye lens. Figure 2 shows the difference in surface reconstructions from integer and floating-point disparity fields. We can see that all surface details have disappeared and it shows stepwise artefact in Fig. 2 (a).

A variational approach which theoretically works on a continuous domain can be a solution for accurate floating-point disparity estimation. In this approach, the disparity vector fields are extracted by minimizing an energy functional involving a fidelity term and a smoothing term such as:

$$E(d) = E_f(d) + E_s(d) = \int_\Omega (I_t(x) - I_b(x+d))^2 dx + \lambda \int_\Omega \psi(\nabla d, \nabla I_t) dx, \qquad (2)$$

where $x \in \Omega$ is an open bounded set of R^2 and d is a 2D disparity vector. The minimization problem can be solved by solving the associated partial differential equation (PDE) in Eq. (3) and (4) with Neumann boundary conditions [19][20].

$$-\nabla E(d) = \lambda div(g(\nabla I_t)\nabla d) + (I_t(x) - I_b(x+d))\frac{\partial I_b(x+d)}{\partial x} = 0 \qquad (3)$$

$$\frac{\partial d}{\partial t} = \lambda div(g(\nabla I_t)\nabla d(x)) + (I_t(x) - I_b(x+d))\frac{\partial I_b(x+d)}{\partial x} \qquad (4)$$

This method produces accurate depth fields across most regions, but it has several limitations related to stereo occlusion around depth discontinuities and over-segmentation in highly textured regions.

In Eq. (4), $g(\bullet)$ is a regularisation function which controls the direction and amount of smoothing of the disparity field. Traditional image-driven functions preserve sharp object boundaries but results in over-segmentation in highly textured regions [13][19]. Zimmer et al. proposed a disparity-driven method to avoid this problem [21], but this method tends to blur object boundaries. Sun et al. recently proposed joint image-/flow-driven optical flow based on steerable random fields to obtain sharp object boundaries without over-segmentation [22].

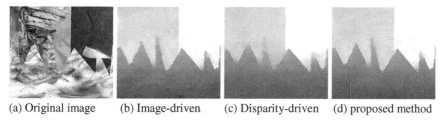

| (a) Original image | (b) Image-driven | (c) Disparity-driven | (d) proposed method |

Fig. 3. Disparity fields produced by various diffusivity functions

In terms of the occlusion problem, Ben-Ari and Sochen proposed an iterative method consisting of occlusion detection, disparity estimation and anisotropic filtering [23]. Alvarez et al. proposed a symmetrical dense optical flow energy functional which includes a bi-directional disparity checking term [24]. Ince and Konrad also proposed similar bi-directional disparity checking method, but they put it into the data term [25].

We propose a new PDE which handles occlusions and over-segmentation while preserving sharp object boundaries as follows.

$$\frac{\partial d_t}{\partial t} = \lambda_1 div\big(g(\nabla I_t, \nabla d_t)\nabla d_t(x, y)\big) + H(1 - O(x))(I_t - I_b(x + d_t))\frac{\partial I_b(x + d_t)}{\partial x} \quad (5)$$

$$g(\nabla I, \nabla d) = \frac{1}{(1 + s(\nabla I, \nabla d))^2} \cdot K_{2\sigma} * (\nabla I_\sigma \nabla I_\sigma^T) \quad (5\text{-}1)$$

$$s(\nabla I, \nabla d) = -\ln(0.35 + 0.65e^{-|\nabla d|}) \cdot |\nabla I|^2 \quad (5\text{-}2)$$

$$O(x) = |d_t(x) + d_b(x + d_t(x))| \quad (5\text{-}3)$$

In the above equations, $I_\sigma = K_\sigma * I$, K_σ denotes a Gaussian kernel with standard deviation σ, * is a convolution operator and $H(\bullet)$ is a unit step function.

The term $K_{2\sigma} * (\nabla I_\sigma \nabla I_\sigma^T)$ in Eq. (5-1) works as a structure tensor for anisotropic diffusion filtering [20] and the first term $-\ln(0.35 + 0.65e^{-|\nabla d|})$ in Eq. (5-2) is a monotonically increasing function and scales the diffusivity according to the gradient of the disparity field. As a result, the diffusivity function of Eq. (5-1) for regularisation is mainly controlled by image gradient but scaled by disparity gradient to avoid over-segmentation in highly textured region. This is simpler and more intuitive than Sun's method [22]. Figure 3 shows a comparison of diffusivity functions. The scene is composed of three slanted planes and the image-driven method cannot regularise the fields enough due to strong textures. The disparity-driven method produces smooth surfaces, but object boundaries are blurred because of diffusion of the field across discontinuities. Compared with the other two methods, the proposed method produces a very smooth field on each plane while keeping sharp object boundaries.

For occlusion handling, we take a compromise between Ben-Ari's work [23] and Ince's work [25]. Ince used a bi-directional disparity matching as a scaling factor for the data term in Eq. (4), but the data term still causes blurred and distorted fields in occluded regions because there is no correspondence for the regions. Ben-Ari detected occlusions by a level-set method and performed disparity estimation only for

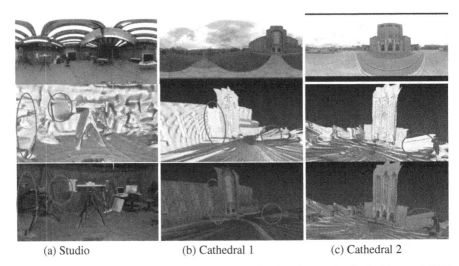

(a) Studio   (b) Cathedral 1   (c) Cathedral 2

Fig. 4. Reconstruction from single spherical stereo pair (Top Captured spherical image, Middle: Reconstructed mesh model, Bottom: Model with texture mapping

visible regions. They filled up the occlusions by anisotropic filtering as a separate step. This approach produces very good results but it is inefficient to run all steps iteratively. Therefore, we use the bidirectional matching as a switch to turn on/off the data term in Eq. (5). The normal balanced diffusion equation with data term is run to find the optimised solution in visible regions while only pure anisotropic diffusion filtering is performed to propagate correct depth information from visible regions to occluded regions.

Equation (5) can be solved explicitly or semi-implicitly with an iterative method by updating the timely discretised field [19][20]. One mathematical problem is the convergence of the proposed PDE. As the Ince's method could not guarantee the mathematical convergence of an iterative solver with the bi-directional disparity matching term, the switch $H(1-O(x))$ in Eq. (5) can make the solver stuck and resonant between visible and occlusion modes. We set a maximum number of iterations in the solver to avoid being trapped into an eternal loop. However, we have not found this problem in our experiments.

Another problem is a local minimum problem. Alvarez et al. used a scale-space approach [19] and Brox et al. used a warping method [26] to avoid the local minimum problem for large displacements. We also use a similar coarse-to-fine structure which starts from the lowest resolution images and recursively refines the result at higher levels. For expanding multi-resolution images, we utilize a pyramidal approach to construct the L-level hierarchical image structure, which involves low-pass filtering and down-sampling the image by a factor of 2. At each level, the input disparity field from a previous level is up-sampled and used as an initial field for calculating disparity field at that level. At the earliest level, initial disparity is calculated by block matching with a region-dividing technique [27]. This hierarchical approach has another merit of reducing computation time for large images.

3   3D Model Reconstruction

3.1   Single-View Reconstruction

The estimated dense disparity fields can be converted into depth information by camera geometry as described in Section 2.1. A mesh model of the scene is obtained by sampling vertices and triangulating adjacent vertices from the original texture and depth fields. The original images are described in spherical coordinates, so we convert them into the Cartesian coordinate system, and then project them to 3D space to generate a 3D mesh.

Figure 4 shows examples of reconstruction from a spherical stereo image pair. The results show a natural-looking environment around the captured location, but changes in viewpoints cause distortion because of self-occlusion from a spherical image as seen in the circled regions in Fig. 4. There is no way to get information about invisible regions behind any object from a single input image. This occlusion problem occurs not only between objects but even on the same object due to the wide FOV of the fisheye lens. The faces on occluded regions can be removed by thresholding with angles of their normal vectors, but it can damage other parts such as the ground or details on the surfaces. It produces noisy surface with small isolated faces. We found that it looks more natural to remain them as long as they do not conflict with other surfaces in multi-view reconstruction.

In order to overcome the occlusion problem, we need more information of the scene structure, shape and appearance from multiple viewpoints. Merging multiple stereo pairs into a common 3D scene structure is a possible solution.

3.2   Registration of Multiple Stereo Reconstructions

As listed on Strecha's multi-view benchmarking site [2] and the Middlebury benchmarking site [28], a number of multi-view reconstruction algorithms have been developed. However, most of them are not applicable for our data sets because they are focused on optimising surfaces with accurate calibration parameters of normal cameras, while we are using spherical line scan cameras with very simple calibration.

One way to get a complete model is to merge partial meshes into one complete mesh by registration. Iterative closest point (ICP) algorithm is widely used for mesh registration [29]. The ICP algorithm iteratively find the optimized transform matrix $A(R,t)$ minimizing the energy:

$$E(R,t) = \sum_{i}^{N_m} \sum_{j}^{N_d} w_{i,j} \left\| m_i - (Rp_j + t) \right\|^2 \tag{6}$$

where N_m and N_d are the number of points in the model set M and data set P, respectively, and $w_{i,j}$ are the weights for a point match.

In order to automate the registration, we use SURF feature matching [16] between views on captured images and used them as 3D matching references by projecting them into 3D space with the estimated depth field. However, these points are not reliable enough to be used for references of ICP algorithms because two possibilities of errors exist: one from SURF matching error between image pairs with radial distortion and the other from depth error (this is more serious because many features are extracted around depth discontinuity regions which induce stereo occlusions). Therefore we use a RANSAC algorithm to calculate an optimised 3D rigid transform between two meshes excluding outliers. If the SURF matching cannot extract enough features, we can still use the ICP algorithm with manual feature matches.

3.3   Reliable Surface Extraction

The final step is to merge registered meshes into one complete mesh structure with surface refinement because the registered meshes have many overlapped parts and false surfaces from self-occlusion. Poisson reconstruction [30] or range image merging algorithm [31] can be ways to produce single mesh structure from set of oriented points or multiple depth fields, but they may lose details on the original surface because the algorithms generate combined surface from overlapped surfaces. False surfaces from self-occlusion also induce errors in optimisation. Furukawa et al. proposed an optimized surface boundary extraction for self-occlusion using axis alignment for Manhattan-world scenes [32] but it also has limitations on keeping surface details. Therefore we propose a dominant surface selection algorithm to choose the most reliable surface among overlapped surfaces.

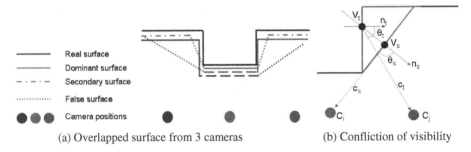

(a) Overlapped surface from 3 cameras   (b) Confliction of visibility

Fig. 5. Reliable surface extraction

Figure 5 (a) shows an illustration of real surface and overlapped surfaces reconstructed from three camera pairs. The overlapped surfaces include false surfaces from self-occlusion and less reliable (secondary) surfaces. We assume that the reconstructed surface is more reliable when the surface normal vector and camera viewing direction are aligned, and the distance to the camera is closer. Our purpose is to choose dominant surfaces from the set of false and secondary surfaces.

Figure 5 (b) shows notations used for evaluating reliabilities of conflicted surfaces. Let V_s is a vertex on a surface reconstructed from camera C_i. A projection vector c_s, a surface normal vector n_s and a facing angle θ_s are expressed as follows:

$$c_s = C_i - V_s \tag{7}$$

$$n_s = \frac{1}{N^2} \sum_{k \in N(s)} n_k \tag{8}$$

$$\theta_s = \arccos\left(\frac{c_s \cdot n_s}{|c_s\|n_s|}\right) \tag{9}$$

In Eq. (8), we use an average of normal vectors of neighbouring NxN vertices to calculate a global normal of the vertex. First, we remove all vertices whose facing angle θ_s is larger than an angle threshold Th_θ because they have high possibility to be a false surface. Then we search conflicted surface from the vertex V_s along the normal vector n_s in the range of Th_R. If confliction with other vertex V_t from camera C_j is detected, we calculate c_t, n_t, θ_t for the vertex V_t and camera C_j as Eq. (7)-(9), and also calculate unreliability $U(V)$ of each vertex based on the facing angle and the distance as Eq. (10). Finally the vertex with higher unreliability is removed.

$$U(V_s) = U_d(V_s) + \lambda_2 U_\theta(V_s) \tag{10}$$

$$U_d(V_s) = \begin{cases} |c_s|/d_{max}, & if\,|c_s| < d_{max} \\ 1, & else \end{cases} \tag{10-1}$$

$$U_\theta(V_s) = \left|\frac{\theta_s}{\pi/2}\right|, \quad \left(-\frac{\pi}{2} < \theta_s < \frac{\pi}{2}\right) \tag{10-2}$$

Application of the algorithm for all vertices simultaneously is time-consuming process and produces erroneous results with small isolated surfaces. For efficient computation we segment the surface into $N/2$x$N/2$ vertex patches and perform the merging in patches. In our experiment, we set the thresholds as: $N=10$, $Th_\theta=1.48$ (85°), $d_{max}=30$ and $Th_R=d_{max}/50$.

4   Experimental Results

4.1   Evaluation of Disparity Estimation

In order to evaluate the general performance of the proposed disparity estimation algorithm, we used the Middlebury stereo benchmarking test bed [28]. Figure 6 shows subjective comparison of estimated disparity maps with state-of-the-art algorithms which also include occlusion handling. The proposed method produces smoother maps with sharp object boundaries even in occlusion regions. However, the proposed algorithm is ranked at 47 in the Bad Pixel Percentage (BPP) test among 78 algorithms on the test bed, while the Cost-Aggr [33] and Semi-Global [34] algorithms are ranked at 27th and 33rd, respectively. The BPP test calculates only the ratio of erroneous pixels and ignores the magnitude of errors. PDE-based methods tend to spread errors into neighbouring pixels to suppress prominent errors, and it caused the low ranks in the BPP test despite good subjective performance. Therefore we changed measuring method and compared root mean square error (RMSE) to the ground truth.

Figure 7 shows the result with two additional methods. Adapting-BP [35] is a improved BP method which is ranked at the top in the BPP test and Graph-cut is an alpha-expansion method with occlusion handling [36] which is ranked at 42nd. All algorithms compared in this test are ranked higher than the proposed algorithm in the BPP test. Comparison of RMSE shows that the proposed PDE-based method gives comparable to the best error rate for state-of-the-art methods.

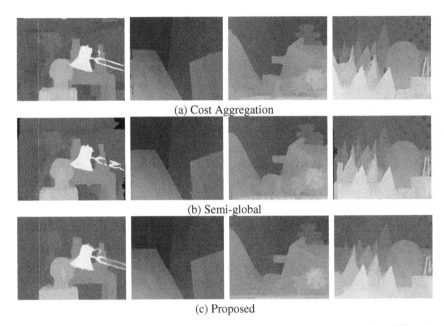

(a) Cost Aggregation

(b) Semi-global

(c) Proposed

Fig. 6. Estimated disparity maps (from left to right: Tsukuba, Venus, Teddy and Cones)

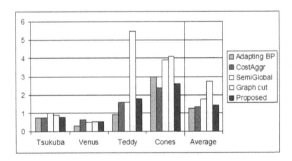

Fig. 7. Comparison of RMSE

However, good performance in these tests does not mean that it guarantees good surface reconstruction. The Semi-Global and Graph-cut algorithms produce discrete disparity maps which can cause stepwise artifact as discussed in section 2.2. The Adapting BP algorithm fits the disparity fields into segmented planes so it loses all surface details. The advantage of the proposed approach is to generate continuous depth map while preserving surface details.

4.2   Evaluation of Model Reconstruction

For objective evaluation of scene modelling, we chose two objects reconstructed from image pairs captured at three different locations and compared the models with ground-truth models scanned by a LIDAR sensor. Figure 8 shows the ground-truth models and the reconstructed models from single/multiple views by the proposed

(a) Gate

(b) Cupola

Fig. 8. Reconstructed models (Left: Ground-truth by LIDAR scan, Middle: Reconstruction from single pair, Right: Reconstruction from multiple pairs)

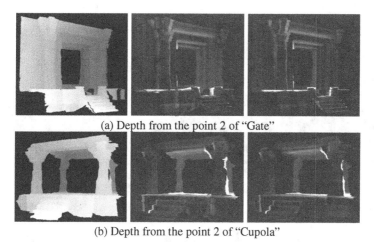

(a) Depth from the point 2 of "Gate"

(b) Depth from the point 2 of "Cupola"

Fig. 9. Depth errors (Left: Ground-truth depth in common regions, Middle: Depth error of single view reconstruction, Right: Depth error of multi view reconstruction)

algorithm. The "Gate" has width of 9m and height of 6m, and the "Cupola" has 6.2m x 3.8m. Both objects are around 6m apart from the central capture point and stereo pairs are captured with a baseline of 60cm. We can see that the reconstructed model shows very fine structure with details of the surface relief pattern. Especially the multi-view reconstruction recovers self-occluded regions while keeping surface details.

It is hard to compare the accuracy and completeness of reconstructed meshes because the reconstructed ranges and areas are different (even the model from the LIDAR scan does not have complete structure.). Therefore we produced depth maps from arbitrarily chosen viewpoints and measured an average depth error of common regions. Table 1 shows evaluation results from two different viewpoints for each model and Fig. 9 shows examples of errors mapped into gray scale. In Table 1, we can see that the multi-view reconstructions have slightly better results than single-view reconstruction. It is a bit more obvious in the slanted view (Viewpoints 2) than the frontal view (Viewpoints 1). However, the differences are not remarkable because most of the errors in Table 1 are from the vertical self-occlusions as seen in Fig. 9. The vertical self-occlusions could not be recovered in this experiment because the test models were captured from horizontally scattered locations. Another point to be considered is the fact that this comparison was performed only for commonly reconstructed regions. As seen in Fig. 8 (a), the multi-view reconstruction could recover the third lower walls that the single-view reconstruction could not.

Table 1. Depth error evaluation (unit: cm, a: mean, σ: standard deviation)

	Gate				Cupola			
	Point 1 (frontal)		Point 2 (Fig. 9)		Point 1 (frontal)		Point 2 (Fig. 9)	
	a	σ	a	σ	a	σ	a	σ
Single-view	5.68	15.29	1.83	22.24	3.84	19.65	5.64	28.85
Multi-view	4.59	16.68	1.05	20.13	3.37	17.10	4.58	24.19

Fig. 10. Full 3D scene rendering (Geometry and texture mapping)

Figure 10 shows the reconstructed full outdoor scene of Fig. 4 (c) from three spherical stereo pairs and results of texture mapping from the same viewpoints. The results show a natural-looking geometry and textures of the environment. Three hole-like regions on the ground show the capture points which could not be reconstructed because of the divergence of spherical stereo in Eq. (1). Free-viewpoint videos of the reconstructed models are included in the supplemental video file.

5   Conclusion

In this paper, a 3D environment modelling method using multiple pairs of spherical stereo images was proposed. The environment is captured by spherical cameras at multiple locations and 3D mesh models for each pair are reconstructed by spherical stereo geometry. The proposed PDE-based stereo method reconstructs continuous depth fields with sharp object boundaries even in occluded regions and highly textured regions. Instead of cumbersome camera calibration for all cameras, 3D rigid transforms between views are calculated by SURF feature matching. A RANSAC algorithm is introduced to fuse incomplete models including self-occlusions. Finally a complete 3D model of the environment is generated as a single mesh by selecting the most reliable surfaces among overlapped surfaces by considering visibility, surface nomals and distance. The biggest advantage of the proposed surface selection algorithm against other surface merging algorithms is to effectively eliminate outlier surfaces from occlusion. The performances of the proposed algorithms were evaluated against ground-truth from the stereo test bed and LIDAR scans. The final composite model can be rendered from any viewpoint with high quality textures.

Acknowledgments. This research was executed with the financial support of the EU IST FP7 project i3Dpost.

References

1. Lemmens, M.: Airborne LiDAR Sensor. GIM International 21 (2007)
2. Strecha, C., Hansen, W., Gool, L.V., Fua, P., Thoennessen, U.: On Benchmarking Camera Calibration and Multi-View Stereo for High Resolution Imagery. In: Proc. CVPR, pp. 1–8 (2008)
3. Furukawa, Y., Ponce, J.: Accurate, Dense, and Robust Multi-View Stereopsis. In: Proc. CVPR (2007)
4. Vu, H., Keriven, R., Labatut, P., Pons, J.P.: Towards high-resolution large-scale multi-view stereo. In: Proc. CVPR, pp. 1430–1437 (2009)
5. Salman, N., Yvinec, M.: Surface Reconstruction from Multi-View Stereo. In: Proc. ACCV (2009)
6. Agarwal, S., Snavely, N., Simon, I., Seitz, S.M., Szeliski, R.: Building Rome in a Day. In: Proc. ICCV (2009)
7. Pollefeys, M., Koch, R., Vergauwen, M., Gool, L.V.: Automated reconstruction of 3D scenes from sequences of images. ISPRS 55, 251–267 (2000)
8. Cornelis, N., Leibe, B., Cornelis, K., Gool, L.V.: 3D urban scene modeling integrating recognition and reconstruction. IJCV 78, 121–141 (2008)
9. Pollefeys, M., et al.: Detailed real-time urban 3D reconstruction from video. IJCV 78, 143–167 (2008)

10. Nayar, S.: Catadioptric Omnidirectional Camera. In: Proc. CVPR, pp. 482–488 (1997)
11. Li, S.: Full-View Spherical Image Camera. In: Proc. ICPR, pp. 386–390 (2006)
12. Feldman, D., Weinshall, D.: Realtime IBR with Omnidirectional Crossed-Slits Projection. In: Proc. ICCV, pp. 839–845 (2005)
13. Kim, H., Hilton, A.: 3D Environment Modelling Using Spherical Stereo Imaging. In: Proc. 3DIM Workshop in ICCV (2009)
14. Boström, G., Fiocco, M., Puig, D., Rossini, A., Gonçalves, J.G.M., Sequeira, V.: Acquisition, Modelling and Rendering of Very Large Urban Environments. In: Proc. 3DPVT, pp. 191–198 (2004)
15. Asai, T., Kanbara, M., Yokoya, N.: 3D Modeling of Outdoor Environments by Integrating Omnidirectional Range and Color Images. In: Proc. 3DIM, pp. 447–454 (2005)
16. Bay, H., Ess, A., Tuytelaars, T., Gool, L.V.: SURF: Speeded Up Robust Features. CVIU 110, 346–359 (2008)
17. Li, S., Fukumori, K.: Spherical Stereo for the Construction of Immersive VR Environment. In: Proc. IEEE VR, pp. 217–222 (2005)
18. Scharstein, D., Szeliski, R.: A Taxonomy and Evaluation of Dense Two-frame Stereo Correspondence Algorithms. IJCV 47, 7–42 (2002)
19. Alvarez, L., Deriche, R., Sánchez, J., Weickert, J.: Dense Disparity Map Estimation Respecting Image Discontinuities: A PDE and Scale-Space Based Approach. Journal of Visual Comm. and Image Repr. 13, 3–21 (2002)
20. Weickert, J.: A Review of Nonlinear Diffusion Filtering. In: ter Haar Romeny, B.M., Florack, L.M.J., Viergever, M.A. (eds.) Scale-Space 1997. LNCS, vol. 1252, pp. 3–28. Springer, Heidelberg (1997)
21. Zimmer, H., Bruhn, A., Valgaerts, L., Breuß, M., Weickert, J., Rosenhahn, B., Seidel, H.P.: PDE-based anisotropic disparity-driven stereo vision. In: Proc. VMV, pp. 263–272 (2008)
22. Sun, D., Roth, S., Lewis, J., Black, M.: Learning Optical Flow. In: Forsyth, D., Torr, P., Zisserman, A. (eds.) ECCV 2008, Part III. LNCS, vol. 5304, pp. 83–97. Springer, Heidelberg (2008)
23. Ben-Ari, R., Sochen, N.: Variational Stereo Vision with Sharp Discontinuities and Occlusion Handling. In: Proc. ICCV, pp. 1–7 (2007)
24. Alvarez, L., Deriche, R., Papadopoulo, T., Sánchez, J.: Symmetrical Dense Optical Flow Estimation with Occlusions Detection. In: Heyden, A., Sparr, G., Nielsen, M., Johansen, P. (eds.) ECCV 2002, Part I. LNCS, vol. 2350, pp. 721–735. Springer, Heidelberg (2002)
25. Ince, S., Konrad, J.: Occlusion-aware optical flow estimation. IEEE Trans. Image Proc. 17, 1443–1451 (2008)
26. Brox, T., Bruhn, A., Papenberg, N., Weickert, J.: High Accuracy Optical Flow Estimation Based on a Theory for Warping. In: Pajdla, T., Matas, J(G.) (eds.) ECCV 2004. LNCS, vol. 3024, pp. 25–36. Springer, Heidelberg (2004)
27. Kim, H., Sohn, K.: Hierarchical Depth Estimation for Image Synthesis in Mixed Reality. In: Proc. SPIE Electronic Imaging, pp. 544–553 (2003)
28. Middlebury stereo and multi-view benchmarking site, http://vision.middlebury.edu/
29. Besl, P., McKay, N.: A method for Registration of 3-D Shapes. IEEE Trans. PAMI 14, 239–256 (1992)
30. Kazhdan, M., et al.: Poisson Surface Reconstruction. In: Proc. SGP, pp. 61–70 (2006)
31. Curless, B., Levoy, M.: A volumetric method for building complex models from range images. In: Proc. SIGGRAPH, pp. 303–312 (1996)

32. Furukawa, Y., Curless, B., Seitz, S.M., Szeliski, R.: Reconstructing Building Interiors from Images. In: Proc. ICCV (2009)
33. Min, D., Sohn, K.: Cost aggregation and occlusion handling with WLS in stereo matching. IEEE Trans. Image Proc., 1431–1442 (2008)
34. Hirschmüller, H.: Accurate and efficient stereo processing by semi-global matching and mutual information. IEEE Trans. PAMI 30, 328–341 (2008)
35. Klaus, A., Sormann, M., Karner, K.: Segment-based stereo matching using belief propagation and a self-adapting dissimilarity measure. In: Proc. ICPR, pp. 15–18 (2006)
36. Kolmogorov, V., Zabih, R.: Computing visual correspondence with occlusions using graph cuts. In: Proc. ICCV (2001)

Hallucination-Free Multi-View Stereo

Michal Jancosek and Tomas Pajdla

Center for Machine Perception, Department of Cybernetics
Faculty of Elec. Eng., Czech Technical University in Prague
{jancom1,pajdla}@cmp.felk.cvut.cz

Abstract. We present a multi-view stereo method that avoids producing hallucinated surfaces which do not correspond to real surfaces. Our
approach to 3D reconstruction is based on the minimal s-t cut of the
graph derived from the Delaunay tetrahedralization of a dense 3D point
cloud, which produces water-tight meshes. This is often a desirable property but it hallucinates surfaces in complicated scenes with multiple objects and free open space. For example, a sequence of images obtained
from a moving vehicle often produces meshes where the sky is hallucinated because there are no images looking from the above to the ground
plane. We present a method for detecting and removing such surfaces.
The method is based on removing perturbation sensitive parts of the
reconstruction using multiple reconstructions of perturbed input data.
We demonstrate our method on several standard datasets often used to
benchmark multi-view stereo and show that it outperforms the state-of-
the-art techniques [1].

Keywords: multi-view stereo, stereo, 3D reconstruction.

1 Introduction

Promising approaches to Multi-View Stereo (MVS) reconstruction, which have
appeared recently [1–7], get the degree of accuracy and completeness comparable
to laser scans [8, 9]. Yet, producing complete reconstructions of outdoor and
complicated scenes is still an open problem.

In this work we extend previous work by presenting a method for hallucination-
free MVS reconstruction. By hallucinated surfaces we mean the surfaces which
are present in the reconstruction but do not correspond to real surfaces.

We build on the global approach to 3D reconstruction based on the minimal
s-t cut of the graph derived from the Delaunay tetrahedralization of a dense
3D point cloud [4, 10]. It solves the visibility task by accumulating energy in
free space between the surface and cameras, which is later used to solve the s-t
cut. The main advantages of this approach are robustness to noise in the 3D
point cloud and producing water-tight reconstructions. This approach is very
opportunistic and tends to produce complete meshes by using a strong visibility
prior to explain missing data by surfaces.

---

[1] The authors were supported by SGS10/186/OHK3/2T/13, FP7-SPACE-241523
PRoViScout and MSM6840770038.

K.N. Kutulakos (Ed.): ECCV 2010 Workshops, Part II, LNCS 6554, pp. 184–196, 2012.

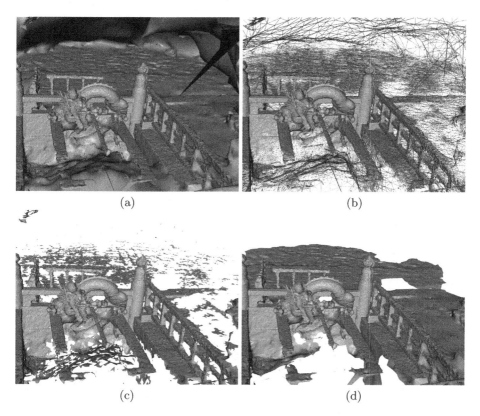

Fig. 1. Dragon-P114 data set: (a) 3D surface before removing hallucinations, (b) 3D surface wireframe before removing hallucinations, (c) 3D surface after removing hallucinations using approach proposed in [7], (d) 3D surface after removing hallucinations using our method.

In contrast to this, the alternative state-of-the art method [7] is focused on producing a noise free oriented point cloud to generate 3D mesh using [11]. This approach is rather conservative and tends to reconstruct surfaces which have strong support from the data. It leaves the space free where the support is not sufficient.

In many situations, the former method is preferable to the later one since it is difficult to fill in the holes in 3D reconstruction in later processing stages when the access to original images may not be available anymore. Recent work of Vu [1], which produces the initial mesh as in [10] and later refines it by using a variational method, demonstrates that this approach can be used to produce excellent results for closed objects and scenes sufficiently represented by images from all directions.

In this work, we focus on removing hallucinated surfaces which are often generated by the approach [10] when reconstructing complicated scenes with multiple objects and free open space. This happens, for instance, when reconstructing outdoor scenes where a hallucinated surface is generated in place of the sky to obtain a closed surface, Figures 1(a,b) and 2(a,b).

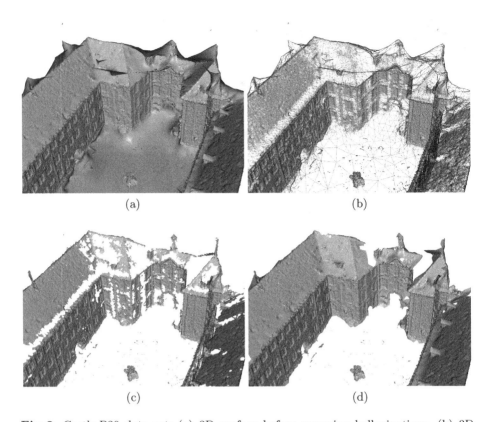

(a)   (b)

(c)   (d)

Fig. 2. Castle-P30 data set: (a) 3D surface before removing hallucinations, (b) 3D surface wireframe before removing hallucinations, (c) 3D surface after removing hallucinations using approach proposed in [7], (d) 3D surface after removing hallucinations using our method.

In [7] the problem is solved by removing large triangles, i.e. they discard the triangles whose average edge length is greater than six times the average edge length of the whole mesh. Here we show that there exist important situations when the large triangles are not hallucinations and are needed to produce complete meshes. Our approach can avoid discarding such triangles. On the other hand we show that sometimes we need to discard small triangles, too.

Our method can play an important role in a large-scale city modeling system. In such datasets top views are usually missing which, as we have mentioned above, often leads to hallucinations.

2   Motivation

The approach by using triangle (or related tetrahedron) property like average edge length [7], maximal edge length, triangle area, radius of circumscribed sphere of the related tetrahedron, and so on, can not be used to remove hallucinated surfaces well in general. The reason is that it is possible (and we demonstrate it in our experiments) that the reconstruction pipeline will produce the mesh where one can often find two subsets of triangles of the same average edge length of the mesh such that the first subset corresponds to a hallucination but the second one corresponds to a real surface. Therefore, it is in general not possible to find a threshold on these dimensional parameters which would separate hallucinated triangles, see Figure 5 .

The main idea behind our approach is motivated by the following observation. The surfaces which have strong support from the data are mostly not affected by small perturbations. By the strong support we mean that there are many reconstructed points near the real surface. On the other hand the surfaces, which are originally created due to false positive points, are usually strongly affected by perturbations because false positives are generated randomly and usually sparsely distributed far from true surfaces.

We assign a confidence value to each triangle based on the sensitivity to perturbations (see Section 6). We build the s-t graph [12] from the triangulation and the confidences and solve it by the implementation [13]. If a triangle is labelled as sink we deem the triangle as hallucinated.

One can argue that large triangles will be mostly created from false positive 3D points. That is often true but large triangles are also created in textureless parts of the scene (see Figure 2) and in parts which have very oblique viewing angles (see Figure 1). Such triangles are important because they make the reconstruction complete. The main contribution of our method is to keep such triangles in the reconstruction while removing the triangles that are hallucinated.

We have to point out that our method may keep unseen parts of the surface when they are a part of the visual hull of the scene (see Figure 6 with the roof region behind dormers is filled). We do not consider such parts as hallucinations.

3   Reconstruction Pipeline

Our MVS pipeline is similar to the pipeline proposed in [1]. First, we compute feasible camera pairs based on the epipolar geometry as in [14]. Next, we detect and match SIFT features [15] in the feasible camera pairs using [16]. We triangulate matches and create seeds. A seed is a 3D point with a set of cameras it was triangulated from. For each camera we compute the minimal and the maximal depth based on the related seeds. Then, we perform the plane-sweeping and filtering (see Section 4) at several scales. To remove hallucinated surfaces, we run a mesh computation k times from differently perturbed data. In each iteration we perturb (see Section 5) the point cloud generated by plane-sweeping and use it as the input to our implementation of the method proposed in [10]. We do not perform mesh refinement as in [1] but do mesh smoothing as in [10]. This gives us k meshes. We remove hallucinated surfaces from the first mesh using other meshes (see Section 6 and 7). This gives us the resulting mesh.

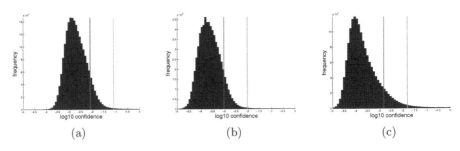

(a)   (b)   (c)

Fig. 3. Histogram of log_{10} of confidences for (a) Castle-P30 dataset, (b) Fountain-P11 dataset and (c) Dragon-P114 dataset with s (red) and t (green) values. (see text)

4   Plane-Sweeping and Filtering

Our plane-sweeping is slightly different from the state-of-the art [17–19]. We do plane sweeping for each reference camera with respect to the set of α nearest feasible target cameras (we use $\alpha = 4$ in all of our experiments). For each pixel p and for each depth d (corresponding to a plane parallel to the reference image plane) we compute the photo-consistency $f(p, d)$ of the depth as follows. For each pair of the reference r and target t cameras we compute photo-consistency value $c(p, d, r, t)$ as the NCC between 5×5 window centred in the pixel on the reference image and its projection to the target image. The projection is generated by the homography inducted by the plane and consistent with the epipolar geometry between the reference and target images. The NCC value is in the range $\langle -1, 1 \rangle$, where value -1 represents the worst photo-consistency and value 1 the best one. The photo-consistency $f(p, d)$ equals the maximum of $c(p, d, r, t)$ over all target cameras t and fixed r. The reconstructed depth $\gamma(p)$ of the pixel p is chosen as the depth d for which $f(p, d)$ is maximal and $f(p, d) > \delta$ (we use $\delta = 0.8$ in all of our experiments). If there does not exist such depth, then we set $\gamma(p)$ as unknown. This plane-sweeping strategy produces a lot of true positive 3D points, but a lot of false positive ones. Therefore, we perform a simple but fast and effective filtering after plane-sweeping. For each 3D point we search for other 3D points in its small neighbourhood. If there are at least β (we use $\beta = 2$ in Fountain dataset and $\beta = 3$ in all others) 3D points from β different cameras, then we accept the point. We consider all depths which were filtered out as unknown. We choose this approach because we have experimentally verified that this approach produces more true positives than for example [18, 19]. On the other hand it still (even after filtering) produces some false positives. But this is not critical because we are later using a strong tool [10] which can effectively deal with noise.

5   The Principle of the Removal of Hallucinated Surfaces

Method [10] tends to produce closed meshes and hence it generates false (hallucinated) surfaces in places which are not well captured by any camera. The hallucinated surfaces are often related to missing cameras which would otherwise lead to cleaning the space between the cameras and the real surface of the scene. When cameras are not present, method [10] hallucinates surfaces from sparsely distributed false positive points which are present in the point cloud. On the other hand, surfaces, which are strongly supported by the data, i.e. where the point cloud is dense near the real surface, or which are strongly supported by a visibility prior, and hence do not have to be strongly supported by the data, are not affected by the sparsely distributed false positive points. We build our approach on this observation. We introduce a small amount of false positive points into the original point cloud several times and filter out unstable hallucinated surfaces. We implement it by adding a small amount of noise into the depth maps constructed by plane-sweeping in each iteration. Consider a depth map and all the pixels with unknown depth in that map. We randomly choose γ (we use $\gamma = 0.1$ in all of our experiments) percent of the pixels with unknown depth and assign them depths randomly. The new depth is chosen randomly from the four times the depth range of the camera. The values were selected experimentally and were sufficient in all of our experiments.

6   Perturbation Based Triangle Confidence Computation

We assign a confidence value to each triangle of each of the k meshes. Let's assume the $i-th$ mesh and the $j-th$ triangle t. For each $k-th$ mesh $k \neq i$ we find the nearest triangle t_k to the triangle t. We measure the distance of triangles by the distance of the triangle centers (c_t, c_{t_k}). Now, for each pair (t, t_k) of triangles we compute $d(t, t_k) = \min\{d(c_t, t_k), d(c_{t_k}, t)\}$ over all pairs t_k, t (with fixed t) where $d(c_t, t_k)$ is the distance of the point c_t to the plane defined by triangle t_k. To compute the confidence of the triangle $\delta(t)$ we use Gaussian kernel voting to cluster values $d(t, t_k)$.

7   Graph-Cut Based Hallucinations Removing

To remove triangles with high confidence, we formulate a minimum s-t cut problem [12]. We create a graph from the mesh such that the nodes correspond to triangles. If two triangles are neighbouring, then we create the edge between the corresponding nodes. We compute $90th$ percentile s of all triangle confidences to find the threshold on the triangle confidence. The threshold at the $90th$ percentile is very conservative because majority of confidences are from small triangles which have usually similar confidences near zero, see Figure 3. We introduce value $t = 10\,s$. Value s should correspond to triangles which should be definitely in the final mesh, value t to triangles which should definitely be removed. We assign $(s - \delta(t))^2$ value to each s-edge and $(t - \delta(t))^2$ value to each t-edge. To each edge between nodes we assign value $s + (t - s)/4$. This value is established experimentally to remove isolated triangles. We use this value in all of our experiments. To solve the s-t cut problem we use the implementation described in [13]. The final mesh consists of the triangles represented by the s-nodes.

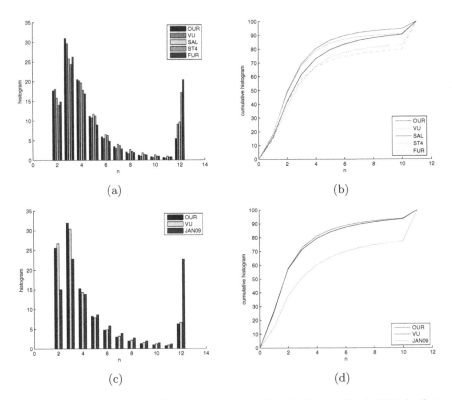

(a)

(b)

(c)

(d)

Fig. 4. Strecha's evaluation [9] for the Fountain-P11 (a,b) and Castle-P30 (c,d) data sets. OUR - this paper, VU [1], SAL [20], ST4 [21], FUR [7], JAN09 [14]. (a,c) histograms of the relative error with respect to $n\sigma$ for all views. The σ is determined from reference data by simulating the process of measurement and can vary across the surface and views. (b,d) relative error cumulated histograms.

8   Performance Discussion

In this section we provide the time performance discussion of our pipeline. We discuss how to make significant speedup, too.

The plane-sweeping was performed on the original scale and on two, three and four times sub-sampled images. The plane-sweeping is implemented on GPU. The computation time of one depth map varies from a few minutes on 3072×2048 resolution to a second on the smallest scale (768×512). The time complexity is cubic, because the number of depths scales with the image resolution. The computation time of the filtering step is approximately tens of seconds. We have to point out that the plane-sweeping and filtering is performed only once for each camera at each scale. The computation time of one perturbation iteration using our implementation of [10] is approximately tens of minutes. The time depends on the number of input points. In our experiments the number of points varies

(a)   (b)

Fig. 5. Dragon-P114 data set: (a) 3D surface before removing hallucinations colored by average edge length of the triangle, blue - smallest, red - 10-times average edge length of the whole mesh and more (using JET color model), (b) red - triangles with average edge length smaller than 3-times or larger than 6-times average edge length of the whole mesh, green - triangles with average edge length between 3-times and 6-times average edge length of the whole mesh, top ellipse - real surface, bottom ellipses - hallucination. Conclusion: average edge length does not separate real surface triangles from the hallucinated ones.

in the range of one to six millions. The computation time of consistencies and graph-cut based hallucinations removal is approximately minutes.

We have tested our method with $k = 10$. We think that $k = 3$ should be enough, too. The code can be later optimized with respect to that only small amount of 3D points are changing in each iteration. Therefore we would build the triangulation from original points and remember it. Later we would add perturbed points (0.1% of original points in all of our experiments) and update the weights to the triangulation in each iteration. This optimization would cause that the computation time of all iterations should be similar to the computation time of one iteration.

9   Results

Based on the experiments we observed that using the criterial function based on the triangle (or related tetrahedron) property like average edge length, maximal edge length, triangle area and so on, can not be used to remove hallucinated surfaces with sufficient quality. Figure 5 shows the input mesh (including hallucinations) colored by the average edge lengths using JET color model. Red color represents the triangles whose average edge lengths are greater or equal to 10-times average edge length of the whole mesh. Blue color represents the triangles which average edge lengths goes to zero. Areas marked by the ellipses show two different parts of the mesh. Both of them (see the distribution of colors) contain the triangles with the same average edge lengths. But, the top set

(a)   (b)

Fig. 6. Castle-P30 data set (top view): (a) 3D surface after removing hallucinations using approach proposed in [7], (b) 3D surface after removing hallucinations using our method.

(a)   (b)

Fig. 7. Fountain-P11 data set: (a) 3D surface removing hallucinations using approach proposed in [7], (b) 3D surface after removing hallucinations using our method

of triangles represents real object part and the bottom ones are hallucinated. This example demonstrates that it is impossible to find a threshold which would separate the hallucinated part from the real one in general. We carried out several experiments on this dataset using maximal edge length, triangle area and maximal radius of circumscribed sphere of the related tetrahedron, and all of them produced similar results.

To evaluate the quality of our reconstructions, we present results on data sets from the standard Strecha's [9] evaluation database. We show the result for three different outdoor datasets: Fountain-P11, Castle-P30, Dragon-P114. The first two datasets are Strecha's datasets [9] and the last one is the data set of a dragon's sculpture in Kyoto. Strecha's Fountain-P11 data set contains 11 3072×2048 images. Strecha's Castle-P30 data set contains 30 3072×2048 images. Dragon data set contains 114 1936×1296 images.

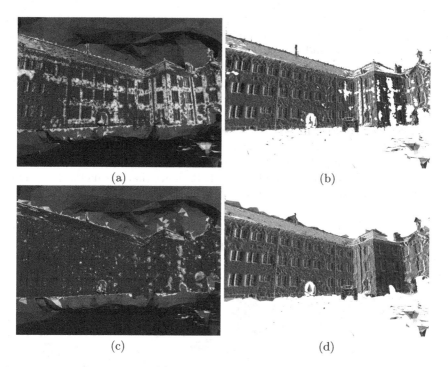

Fig. 8. Castle-P30 data set: (a) 3D surface before removing hallucinations colored by average edge length of the triangle, blue - smallest, red - 10-times average edge length of the whole mesh and more (using JET color model), (b) 3D surface after removing hallucinations using approach proposed in [7], (c) 3D surface before removing hallucinations colored by the perturbation based confidence (blue - smallest confidence, red - largest confidence), (d) 3D surface after removing hallucinations using our method.

Figure 4 shows the evaluation on the Strecha's Fountain-P11 as well as Castle-P30 data sets. See the Strecha's evaluation page for JAN10 results and their comparison. The histograms shows that our reconstructions are more or less on the same level at 2σ and 3σ as the method [1] which uses an additional mesh refinement step. The cumulative histograms shows that our method outperforms all other methods in completeness. In Figure 4 (a) and (b) we are comparing our results with four best methods [1, 7, 20, 21]. For complete results, we refer the reader to the challenge website [22]. This experiment demonstrates that methods based on the opportunistic approach [10] produces complete and accurate results and outperforms the other state-of-the-art methods, and it is therefore important to deal with its negatives which was the goal of this paper.

We made several experiments to demonstrate that our method produces better results than the state-of-the art approach proposed in [7], which solves this problem by removing large triangles, i.e. they discard the triangles which average edge length is greater than six times the average edge length of the whole mesh.

Figures 1 and 5 show the comparison of the results computed using the approach proposed in [7] with the results computed using our method on Dragon-P114 data set. Figures 6 (a) and (c) show that our method can better deal with larger triangles which are on the ground and which cover surfaces captured at oblique angles. Figures 6, 8 and 2 show the comparison of the results computed using the approach proposed in [7] with the results computed using our method on Castle-P30 data set. Figures 6 (a) and (c) show that our method can better preserve large triangles which are in between the windows where is a lack of the texture but which are not hallucinated. Figure 7 shows the comparison of the results computed using the approach proposed in [7] with the results computed using our method on Fountain-P11 data set. It shows that our method can avoid discarding important low-textured parts of the scene.

Figure 9 shows the detailed view of the dragon's head before and after removing hallucinations using our method (untextured and textured). We have used the nearest camera to texture each triangle without texture color unification.

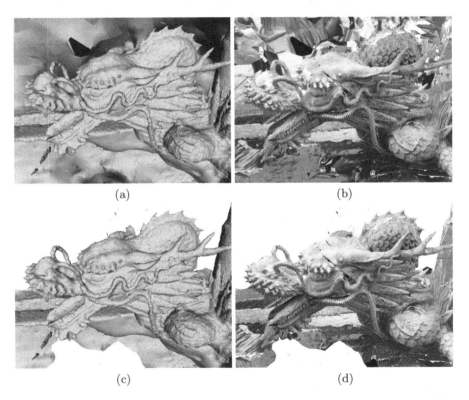

(a)   (b)

(c)   (d)

Fig. 9. Detailed view of the dragon's head. (a) 3D surface before removing hallucinations untextured, (b) 3D surface before removing hallucinations textured, (c) 3D surface after removing hallucinations using our method untextured, (d) 3D surface after removing hallucinations using our method textured.

10 Conclusion

In this work we proposed a hallucination-free multi-view stereo method. We demonstrated that the quality of our reconstructions is comparable to the best state-of-the art methods on several benchmark datasets. We have shown experimentally that our method produces more complete reconstructions while removing falsely generated surfaces.

References

1. Vu, H., Keriven, R., Labatut, P., Pons, J.P.: Towards high-resolution large-scale multi-view stereo. In: CVPR (2009)
2. Bradley, D., Boubekeur, T., Heidrich, W.: Accurate multi-view reconstruction using robust binocular stereo and surface meshing. In: CVPR, pp. 1–8 (2008)
3. Zaharescu, A., Boyer, E., Horaud, R.: TransforMesh: A Topology-Adaptive Mesh-Based Approach to Surface Evolution. In: Yagi, Y., Kang, S.B., Kweon, I.S., Zha, H. (eds.) ACCV 2007, Part II. LNCS, vol. 4844, pp. 166–175. Springer, Heidelberg (2007)
4. Labatut, P., Pons, J., Keriven, R.: Efficient multi-view reconstruction of large-scale scenes using interest points, delaunay triangulation and graph cuts. In: ICCV, pp. 1–8 (2007)
5. Campbell, N.D.F., Vogiatzis, G., Hernández, C., Cipolla, R.: Using Multiple Hypotheses to Improve Depth-Maps for Multi-View Stereo. In: Forsyth, D., Torr, P., Zisserman, A. (eds.) ECCV 2008, Part I. LNCS, vol. 5302, pp. 766–779. Springer, Heidelberg (2008)
6. Goesele, M., Snavely, N., Curless, B., Hoppe, H., Seitz, S.: Multi-view stereo for community photo collections. In: ICCV (2007)
7. Furukawa, Y., Ponce, J.: Accurate, dense, and robust multi-view stereopsis. In: CVPR, pp. 1–8 (2007)
8. Seitz, S.M., Curless, B., Diebel, J., Scharstein, D., Szeliski, R.: A comparison and evaluation of multi-view stereo reconstruction algorithms. In: CVPR, pp. 519–528 (2006)
9. Strecha, C., von Hansen, W., Van Gool, L., Fua, P., Thoennessen, U.: On benchmarking camera calibration and multi-view stereo for high resolution imagery. In: CVPR, pp. 1–8 (2008)
10. Labatut, P., Pons, J., Keriven, R.: Robust and efficient surface reconstruction from range data. In: Computer Graphics Forum (2009)
11. Kazhdan, M., Bolitho, M., Hoppe, H.: Poisson surface reconstruction. In: SGP 2006, pp. 61–70 (2006)
12. Ford, L.R., Fulkerson, D.R.: Flows in Networks. Princeton University Press (1962)
13. Boykov, Y., Kolmogorov, V.: An experimental comparison of min-cut/max-flow algorithms for energy minimization in vision. IEEE Transactions on Pattern Analysis and Machine Intelligence 26, 1124–1137 (2004)
14. Jancosek, M., Shekhovtsov, A., Pajdla, T.: Scalable multi-view stereo. In: 3DIM (2009)
15. Lowe, D.: Distinctive image features from scale-invariant keypoints. IJCV 60, 91–110 (2004)
16. Wu, C.: SiftGPU, http://cs.unc.edu/~ccwu/siftgpu

17. Gallup, D., Frahm, J., Mordohai, P., Yang, Q., Pollefeys, M.: Real-time plane-sweeping stereo with multiple sweeping directions. In: CVPR, pp. 1–8 (2007)
18. Yang, R., Pollefeys, M.: Multi-resolution real-time stereo on commodity graphics hardware. In: CVPR, pp. I: 211–I: 217 (2003)
19. Collins, R.: A space-sweep approach to true multi-image matching. Technical Report UM-CS-1995-101 (1995)
20. Salman, N., Yvinec, M.: Surface reconstruction from multi-view stereo. In: Modeling-3D (2009)
21. Strecha, C., Fransens, R., Van Gool, L.: Wide-baseline stereo from multiple views: a probabilistic account. In: CVPR (2004)
22. Strecha, C.: Evaluation page, http://cvlab.epfl.ch/~strecha/multiview/denseMVS.html

Removing the Example
from Example-Based Photometric Stereo

Jens Ackermann[1], Martin Ritz[2], André Stork[2], and Michael Goesele[1]

[1] TU Darmstadt
[2] Fraunhofer IGD

Abstract. We introduce an example-based photometric stereo approach that does not require explicit reference objects. Instead, we use a robust multi-view stereo technique to create a partial reconstruction of the scene which serves as scene-intrinsic reference geometry. Similar to the standard approach, we then transfer normals from reconstructed to unreconstructed regions based on robust photometric matching. In contrast to traditional reference objects, the scene-intrinsic reference geometry is neither noise free nor does it necessarily contain all possible normal directions for given materials. We therefore propose several modifications that allow us to reconstruct high quality normal maps. During integration, we combine both normal and positional information yielding high quality reconstructions. We show results on several datasets including an example based on data solely collected from the Internet.

1 Introduction

Passive large-scale geometry reconstruction of outdoor scenes has so far mostly relied on (multi-view) stereo techniques. In contrast, photometric stereo approaches have rarely been used on outdoor scenes—mostly due to the lack of control over the scene, illumination conditions, and capture setup (see Section 2 for details). In fact, we are not aware of any large scale photometric stereo approach. In this paper, we therefore take a step in this direction and propose a novel photometric stereo technique generalizing photometric stereo by example [1]. The approach is applicable to very general indoor and outdoor scenes and demonstrates strong improvements in terms of accuracy and completeness compared to standard multi-view stereo approaches.

Photometric stereo by example [1] is an elegant method to determine normal maps from a set of images with fixed viewpoint and varying, distant illumination. For each pixel, the vector of color values in all input images is matched to the closest vector of color values of pixels on one or more reference objects with known geometry. The corresponding normals are then transferred back yielding a complete normal map. Photometric stereo by example has two key advantages. First, lighting can be general and unknown and does not need to be reconstructed. Second, it works for objects with a broad range of reflectance properties as long as they are well approximated by the reference objects. Photometric stereo by example is therefore one of the most general photometric stereo techniques known today. There is, however, one disadvantage: Current techniques require explicit reference objects in the scene from which the normals are transferred. Scenes without reference object cannot be reconstructed.

K.N. Kutulakos (Ed.): ECCV 2010 Workshops, Part II, LNCS 6554, pp. 197–210, 2012.

a)   b)   c)   d)   e)

Fig. 1. *Tower* model. *a)* images captured by a static webcam for photometric stereo, *b)* images taken casually without special capturing setup for multi-view stereo, *c)* normal map of partially reconstructed geometry using multi-view stereo serving as scene-intrinsic reference geometry (SIRG), *d)* reconstructed normal map using photometric stereo with SIRG as reference object, *e)* final model rendered from novel viewpoint.

Our key observation is that many objects' geometry can at least be partially reconstructed using multi-view stereo as long as additional images are available that provide sufficient parallax (see, e.g., Figure 1). We propose to use this partial geometric scene model after suitable processing as *scene-intrinsic reference geometry* (SIRG) for a standard photometric stereo by example approach. This approach works if the reconstructed geometry (and therefore the normals) of the SIRG are sufficiently accurate and if the range of represented normals is wide enough to cover the normal directions represented in the scene. In addition, the reconstructed reference geometry should be a good representation of the reflectance properties in the scene, a condition that is often met since it is actually part of the scene.

Removing the need for explicit reference objects strongly extends the applicability of example-based photometric stereo at a comparably small acquisition cost (just a couple additional images for the multi-view stereo reconstruction). We demonstrate this with two examples where we base our reconstruction partially or completely on imagery available from Internet sources. The resulting normal maps and integrated geometry are nevertheless of high quality.

2   Related Work

Photometric stereo was introduced by Woodham [2] who assumed known distant point lighting and a known parametric reflectance model. Given three images of a diffuse surface from the same viewpoint, it is possible to determine the surface normal unless the illumination directions are coplanar. The basic theory of photometric stereo was then developed in the 1980s (see, e.g., Horn [3] for an overview) and research focused on generalizing it in various ways.

For example, Basri and Jacobs [4] introduced a system that simultaneously recovers unknown distant lighting. Illumination is estimated using a low degree spherical harmonics basis suitable for approximately diffuse objects [5]. Shen and Tan [6] extended this technique to images with varying viewpoints but determine normals only at sparse points matched between the images. They demonstrate their approach also on images downloaded from an online image collection. Joshi et al. [7] propose a combination of multi-view and photometric stereo. They first reconstruct a rough geometry model using multi-view stereo and refine it with a photometric stereo approach. Hernandez et al. [8] describe a multi-view photometric stereo approach that additionally takes silhouette information into account. A similar approach was shown to work for dynamic scenes by Vlasic et al. [9] using a highly controlled capture setup. Higo et al. [10] introduce a system that simultaneously optimizes photoconsistency, normals, and surface smoothness.

Goldman et al. [11] use known lighting directions and cluster the surface in different materials. For each cluster, they determine the parameters of an analytic BRDF. Alldrin et al. [12] follow a similar approach but use a data-driven reflectance model instead of the analytic BRDF model.

2.1 Example-Based Photometric Stereo

Based on Woodham's ideas, Silver [13] applied photometric stereo to objects with uniform but unknown surface reflectance. A matte white sphere serving as calibration object is captured under three different lighting conditions. Given its known geometry, one can construct a lookup table matching triples of intensity values with the sphere's surface gradient. For reconstruction, other matte white objects are captured under the same lighting conditions; corresponding surface gradients are determined using the lookup table.

Hertzmann and Seitz [1] generalized this approach using the orientation-consistency cue: Two points with the same surface orientation reflect the same light toward the viewer if they have the same BRDF, all light sources are distant, the camera is orthographic, and the points are not influenced by non-local lighting effects (e.g., shadows, interreflections). Their approach is very general and operates with arbitrary distant lighting on a very wide class of materials while still yielding high quality results. It requires, however, one or two reference objects in the captured scene that are used for normal transfer.

Koppal and Narasimhan [14] also exploit orientation-consistency to find clusters of iso-normals in a scene captured by a video camera. They do not require a reference object, but rely on a continuous, unstructured light source path and a dense sampling in the time domain. In an additional step, a classical photometric stereo approach can assign absolute normals to the clusters or other techniques can use the clusters as starting point for more detailed reconstructions.

In this work, we show that detailed normal maps can be reconstructed without the need for explicit reference objects or densely sampled video. We build on the standard photometric stereo by example approach [1] but replace the separate reference objects by the captured scene's own geometry which we partially and approximately reconstruct using a robust multi-view stereo technique.

3 Scene-Intrinsic Reference Geometry

Given a static scene, we capture multiple images $I^{PS} = \{I_1^{PS}, \ldots, I_n^{PS}\}$ from the same camera position under unknown, distant, varying illumination for photometric stereo. We make the standard assumption that the camera well approximates an orthographic camera. We additionally capture another set of images $I^{MVS} = \{I_1^{MVS}, \ldots, I_m^{MVS}\}$ from varying viewpoints for multi-view stereo. The latter images should provide sufficient parallax and lighting suitable for multi-view stereo reconstruction. The images I^{MVS} and one of the images for photometric stereo, without loss of generality I_1^{PS}, are registered using a robust structure from motion system [15]. Since the images I^{PS} were taken with identical intrinsic and extrinsic camera parameters, all images are now registered into a common coordinate system. Our goal is to first reconstruct a (partial) geometry model that serves as scene intrinsic reference geometry. Using the reference geometry, we then aim at creating a complete and accurate normal map. We finally reconstruct the scene geometry by integrating the resulting normal field while taking the reconstructed reference geometry into account.

There is a large body of existing work on multi-view stereo reconstruction (see Seitz et al. [16] and the accompanying web page) and our proposed technique can be based on any of them. Since we aim at handling very general input data, we selected the method of Goesele et al. [17] (see Section 6 for a comparison with a different algorithm) that is known to be robust and accurate even for very general input data. This method reconstructs individual, incomplete depth maps using a region-growing approach. We merge these depth maps into a combined triangular geometry model using volumetric range image processing (VRIP) [18]. This approach exploits redundancy in the input depth maps to reduce noise and remove outliers. It also assigns confidence values to vertices which we use to remove less reliable geometry from the reference geometry. Finally, we compute per-vertex normals for the reference geometry from surrounding face normals using area-weighted averaging. Using a variant of Laplacian smoothing, we iteratively smooth the computed normals according to

$$\mathbf{n}^k = \mathbf{n}^{k-1} + \lambda \sum_{i \in \mathcal{N}} \left(\frac{\mathbf{n}_i^{k-1} - \mathbf{n}^{k-1}}{|\mathcal{N}|} \right) \tag{1}$$

where $\mathcal{N}$ describes the neighborhood of $\mathbf{n}$. The resulting normal vector is normalized. In our standard matching, we perform 10 iterations with $\lambda = 0.05$.

4 Correspondence and Normal Transfer

In this section, we describe the details of our example-free photometric stereo by example approach. We first introduce the basic matching as in [1], restricted to a single reference object. In contrast to their approach, the scene intrinsic reference geometry is not a noise-free and complete reference object. We therefore introduce an orientation-consistency based averaging and an adapted normal transfer approach to achieve high quality reconstructions.

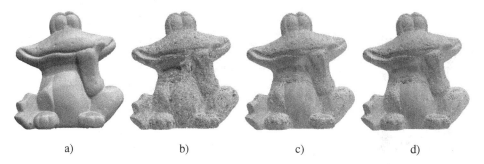

a)   b)   c)   d)

Fig. 2. Effect of best matches averaging. *a)* Ground-truth normal map, *b)* reconstructed normal map using only a single best match, *c)* average computed over 50 best matches, *d)* average computed over 100 best matches. Note that normals on the scene-intrinsic reference geometry (Figure 5b) remain unchanged.

4.1 Basic Matching

We first manually segment the target object in the images I^{PS} from the background and then project the reference geometry into I^{PS}. All pixels are classified into those covered by the scene-intrinsic reference geometry $\mathbf{Q}$ and those for which no reconstruction is available $\mathbf{P}$. Each pixel $q \in \mathbf{Q}$ is assigned a unique normal $\mathbf{n}(q)$ by projecting the reference geometry's vertices onto q. If multiple vertices are mapped to the same pixel, we choose the normal of the vertex with highest reconstruction confidence. We furthermore define the observation vector for each point in $\mathbf{P}$ and $\mathbf{Q}$ which is formed by all the color values for this particular pixel location in the image stack I^{PS}:

$$V_{p,c} = (I^{PS}_{1,p,c}, \ldots, I^{PS}_{n,p,c})^T, \quad V_{q,c} = (I^{PS}_{1,q,c}, \ldots, I^{PS}_{n,q,c})^T, \quad c \in \{R, G, B\}. \quad (2)$$

The core of geometry completion is the appropriate transfer of normals derived from the scene intrinsic reference geometry to positions where reconstruction is missing. We define the following metric for the similarity between two observation vectors that models differences of surface albedo using a per-color channel material coefficient $m_{p,c}$:

$$\Delta = \sum_{c \in \{R,G,B\}} \|m_{p,c}V_{q,c} - V_{p,c}\|_2^2 \quad (3)$$

For a given target point $p \in \mathbf{P}$, we first determine for each $q \in \mathbf{Q}$ optimal per-color channel material coefficients $m_{p,c}$:

$$m_{p,c}V_{q,c} = V_{p,c} \quad \Leftrightarrow \quad m_{p,c}V_{q,c}^T V_{q,c} = V_{q,c}^T V_{p,c} \quad \Leftrightarrow \quad m_{p,c} = \frac{V_{q,c}^T V_{p,c}}{V_{q,c}^T V_{q,c}}. \quad (4)$$

In order to find the best matching observation vector, we then select the q for which the residual error Δ in Equation 3 is minimal. We apply these steps for all points $p \in \mathbf{P}$ where reconstruction is missing.

Figure 2 (b) shows the resulting normal map for the *frog* example. Note that normals show strong artifacts in filled-in regions. This could be due to several reasons: First,

Algorithm Overview

1. Reconstruct SIRG using MVS.
2. For each pixel p in the object's mask, i.e. $\mathbf{P} \cup \mathbf{Q}$, do:
   - Compute $m_{p,c}$ for all $q \in \mathbf{Q}$.
   - Select the $s = 50$ matches $\{q_i\} \subset \mathbf{Q}$ that have minimal error

$$\sum_{c \in \{R,G,B\}} \|m_{p,c} V_{q,c} - V_{p,c}\|_2^2.$$

   - Average normals for $\{q_i\}$ and transfer result to p.
3. Integrate normals.

Fig. 3. *Left:* Distribution of normal directions for 500 best matches of two target points $p, \tilde{p}$ (boundaries manually drawn for clarity). *Right:* Summary of proposed photometric stereo algorithm.

some normal directions are not represented in the reference geometry (including some individual directions but also most of the downward pointing normals on the frog's neck area). Second, the material coefficient m_p can only model differences in albedo but is unable to adapt the specularity by mixing multiple observation vectors (as in [1]). Third, even if the matching according to the orientation-consistency cue is correct, the reference geometry can still contain erroneous normal information.

4.2 Averaging Multiple Matches

If we look at a plot of the normal directions corresponding to the s best matching observation vectors for a given p (Figure 3), we notice that these are spread out over a range of directions due to the various errors in our approximation. We can, however, also observe that those normals are clustered around an average direction.

We therefore propose to not only use the normal corresponding to the best-matching observation vector but to compute an average normal from the s best matches. This reduces the impact of wrong matches and erroneous normals and can interpolate missing normals. Note that it will not fix the case of normal directions outside the convex hull of normals observed in the scene intrinsic reference geometry but may at least assign a nearby normal direction inside the convex hull. Figure 2 shows the effect of averaging multiple matches for the frog model. Averaging the 50 best-matching normals yields a much smoother normal field. Increasing the number to 100 leads only to a small improvement. We therefore use in all cases shown in this paper $s = 50$.

4.3 Global Matching

So far, we only transferred normals from $\mathbf{Q}$ to $\mathbf{P}$. This assumes, however, that the scene intrinsic reference geometry is reconstructed with high quality which is typically not the case (see, e.g., Figure 4 showing an example of a bronze bust). Even after Laplacian smoothing, the scene-intrinsic reference geometry still contains very noisy normals.

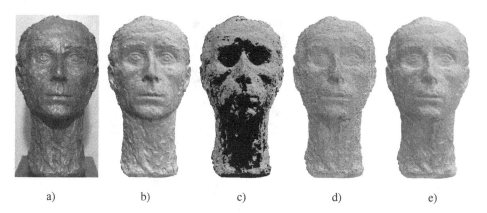

a)   b)   c)   d)   e)

Fig. 4. Effect of global matching. *a)* Example input image, *b)* ground-truth normal map, *c)* SIRG normal map, *d)* reconstructed normal map with best matches averaging only on **P**, *e)* reconstructed normal map with global matching.

We therefore apply the orientation-consistency based averaging described in Section 4.2 not only to unreconstructed regions but also to the scene-intrinsic reference geometry, thereby discarding the originally reconstructed normals. More formally, we adapt the matching in Section 4.1 to transfer normals from **Q** to both **P** *and* **Q**. In contrast to [1], Equation 3 is then minimized not only for $p \in \mathbf{P}$, but for $p \in \mathbf{P} \cup \mathbf{Q}$ with material coefficients computed for all pairs $(p, q) \in (\mathbf{P} \cup \mathbf{Q}) \times \mathbf{Q}$. This considerably improves the resulting normal map as can be seen in Figure 4 e).

5 Normal Field Integration

Several methods have been developed to integrate normal maps to recover a 3D surface (e.g. [19,20,21,22,23]). To constrain the possible solutions, some works propose to impose consistency with sparsely given control points from a laser scanner [24], with a visual hull [9], or with a complete depth map [25].

We follow a similar, optimization based approach as in [25] and [9]. Both operate in a perspective setting, i.e., optimize for surface points $R = (Z \cdot r_x, Z \cdot r_y, Z)$ determined by their depth Z along the ray $(r_x, r_y, 1)$. Instead of directly comparing the difference of optimized normals $\mathbf{n}_p$ to reconstructed normals $\bar{\mathbf{n}}_p$, they use the dot product between the tangent to the optimized surface and the given normal as an error metric.

Nehab et al. [25] additionally propose to introduce per pixel weights for positional and normal constraints. We use w_p as geometry weight ($w_p = \lambda$ for **Q**, $w_p = 0$ for **P**) and $u_p = v_p = 1$ as gradient weights respectively. The error function is then given as a sum over all N pixels $p \in I_1^{\mathrm{PS}}$:

$$E = \sum_p \left[u_p^2 \left\| \bar{\mathbf{n}}_p \cdot \frac{\partial Z}{\partial x} \right\|^2 + v_p^2 \left\| \bar{\mathbf{n}}_p \cdot \frac{\partial Z}{\partial y} \right\|^2 + w_p^2 \left\| \bar{Z}_p - Z_p \right\|^2 \right] \tag{5}$$

where $\bar{Z}_p$ is the depth of a reconstructed pixel. Approximating the partial derivatives with finite differences, the whole system can be written as a least squares problem with

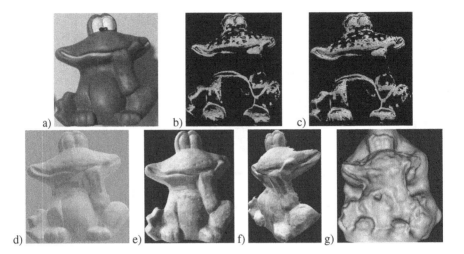

Fig. 5. *Frog* model. *a)* Example input image, *b)* partially reconstructed geometry using multi-view stereo serving as scene-intrinsic reference geometry (SIRG), *c)* SIRG normal map, *d)* reconstructed normal map using PSE with SIRG as reference object, *e)* final model after integration, *f)* final model rendered from a novel viewpoint, *g)* reconstruction with Furukawa's multi-view stereo [26] and poisson surface reconstruction [27].

a sparse $3N \times N$ matrix (see [25] for details). Because our weighting scheme does not exclude any gradients from the integration, the matrix has full rank and there exists a unique solution to the least squares problem.

6   Results

Since it is difficult to acquire ground truth data for large-scale objects, we first present a quantitative analysis on small objects that can be easily captured in a laboratory setting. We then give a qualitative evaluation for two large-scale datasets, reconstructed partially or completely from Internet images.

6.1   Lab-Based Datasets

We demonstrate results on three different datasets captured under lab conditions. The *frog* is a roughly 25 cm tall clay figure with a close to diffuse surface (see Figure 5). The scene-intrinsic reference geometry covers 34 % of the foreground region $\mathbf{P} \cup \mathbf{Q}$ in the normal maps. The *bunny* is a plastic figurine with shiny coating (about 20 cm tall, 47 % coverage, see Figure 6). The bronze *bust* (40 cm tall, 53 % coverage, see Figure 4 a)) exhibits complex surface structure and a difficult BRDF.

The datasets were all acquired using a 7 M pixel consumer camera. We captured 15-20 I^{PS} images from a fixed camera position while manually moving a simple light bulb around the object. We additionally captured ≈ 50 I^{MVS} images from various positions

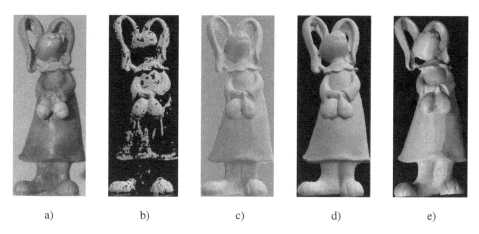

a)   b)   c)   d)   e)

Fig. 6. *Bunny* model. *a)* Example input image, *b)* normal map of partially reconstructed geometry using multi-view stereo serving as scene-intrinsic reference geometry (SIRG), *c)* reconstructed normal map, *d)* ground truth, *e)* final model rendered from a novel viewpoint.

facing the front side of the objects. Neither camera nor light source were calibrated. In order to evaluate our reconstructions quantitatively, we scanned the objects using a structured light scanner. From the merged and cleaned point model, we created ground-truth normal maps for comparison. Note that these ground-truth normal maps show holes in areas where scanning was difficult due to self-occlusion, e.g., the bunny's ear region in Figure 6.

Evaluation. Figures 5, 4, and 6 demonstrate clearly that our approach is able to reconstruct high quality normal maps without requiring special reference objects in the scene. Even small details such as the flowers on the bunny's dress are reconstructed. Normals outside the convex hull of captured normal directions such as the chin area in Figure 4 or areas with self shadowing around the bust's nose are reconstructed plausibly without introducing strong artifacts. The final integrated models are of high quality and avoid large scale distortions due to the inclusion of reference geometry in the integration routine.

Figure 7 shows for all lab datasets histograms over the deviation of reconstructed normals compared to normals computed from the scanned ground truth model. The graphs clearly show that normals obtained from multi-view stereo techniques are improved by our proposed normal transfer.

To demonstrate that our technique works also with more general lighting, we captured two additional datasets for the *bust* where we used a studio light with and without diffuser for illumination. The close-ups in Figure 8 demonstrate that the recovered normals change only marginally. Note that this is a key requirement for applying the technique to outdoor scenes as shown in the next section.

It does not matter to our approach in which manner the scene intrinsic reference geometry is obtained. We therefore additionally applied the multi-view stereo algorithm

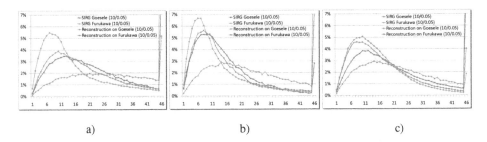

a)   b)   c)

Fig. 7. Normal deviation in degrees against ground truth for *a) frog*, *b) bunny*, and *c) bust*. The purple (green) line shows the deviation of the SIRG obtained by multi-view stereo of Goesele et al. (Furukawa et al.) after Laplacian smoothing. The orange (blue) line demonstrates the result of our complete pipeline on Goesele et al. (Furukawa et al.) multi-view stereo input data. Data point 46 represents deviations greater than $45°$. Values out of scale are: a) SIRG G. 9.4%, SIRG F. 29.5%, Rec. F. 9.8%; b) SIRG F. 15.9%, Rec. G. 7.1%, Rec. F. 7.2%; c) SIRG G. 8.9%, SIRG F. 14.2%.

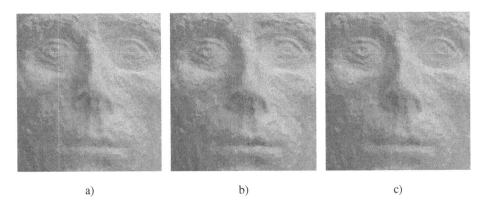

a)   b)   c)

Fig. 8. Reconstruction of *bust* for light situations *a)* diffuse spot, *b)* bright spot, and *c)* point light

of Furukawa and Ponce [26] to the *bunny* and *frog* datasets. The resulting point set was then used as input to our adapted photometric stereo by example technique. Figure 7 shows the deviation of the results from groundtruth. Like for the input from Goesele et al., we observe a significant improvement (blue lines) of the normals (green lines) through our matching scheme. Furthermore, the figure shows that input normals from Furukawa's method (green lines) are farther away from the groundtruth than those reconstructed by VRIP and Goesele's method (purple lines). Obviously, this leads to the differences in the resulting normal map's quality (comparing the orange and blue lines). We also attempted to reconstruct a triangle mesh from the point cloud created by Furukawa's method using Poisson surface reconstruction [27] but despite several trials with different parameter settings the Poisson reconstruction did not yield satisfying results (see Figure 5 g) for an example).

a)   b)

Fig. 9. *Cathedral* dataset. *Left:* Images captured by a static webcam used as I^{PS}. *Right:* Images downloaded from a community photo collection site used as I^{MVS}.

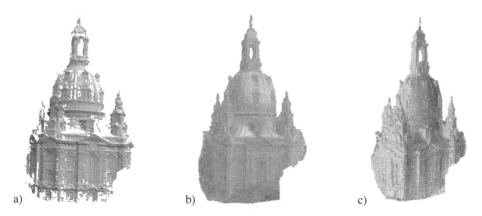

a)   b)   c)

Fig. 10. *Cathedral* model. *a)* Normal map of partially reconstructed geometry using multi-view stereo serving as scene-intrinsic reference geometry (SIRG), *b)* reconstructed normal map, *c)* final model rendered from novel viewpoint.

6.2 Outdoor Datasets

We discuss the performance on outdoor scenes using two large buildings (about 60 m and 90 m tall) with non-planar surfaces and interesting details. For each dataset, we retrieved an image of a public webcam every 20 min over the course of 3 months. The webcam images have VGA resolution.

We manually selected 11 suitable I^{PS} images for the *cathedral* dataset (all taken between 10 am and 5 pm) and 36 images for the *tower* dataset (taken between 9 am an 7 pm) on different days, see Figures 9 a), 1 a). For the *cathedral*, we furthermore downloaded 2000 I^{MVS} images from the community photo platform Flickr (see Figure 9 b)). The multi-view stereo step automatically selected a suitable subset of those for reconstruction of the scene intrinsic reference geometry achieving a completeness of 84 %. The SIRG for the *tower* was reconstructed from 324 images taken by a student with a consumer camera (see Figure 1 b)) and covers 58 % of the foreground.

Evaluation. Figure 10 demonstrates the results for the *cathedral* model. The fairly complete reference geometry is a good basis for reconstruction. The global matching softens the extremes in the normal map but strongly increases the available detail. Artifacts can be seen due to cast shadows on the object that violate the assumption of distant illumination and are not modeled by our approach (e.g., lower right corner of Figure 10 c)).

As a cylindrical object, the *tower* is well-suited for reconstruction. Parameterizing its surface by height $h \in [0, H]$ and angle φ, a normal at (h, φ) can be reconstructed quite accurately if some normal on the line $([0, H], \varphi)$ is contained in the reference geometry. This works so well that the bottom of the tower can be recovered up to fine details like individual stones (see Figure 1 d)). Even if the roof has a different albedo and only sparse coverage of normal directions pointing to the right, we are able to reconstruct it quite convincingly.

7   Discussion

Being able to reconstruct sufficient geometry for the SIRG is a key requirement of our algorithm. However for some scenes, it will most likely be impossible to reconstruct sufficient geometry with *any* multi-view stereo algorithm. Such scenes need to be treated differently. We argue, however, that this is a rare case and that the chosen multi-view stereo algorithm [17] (or another MVS approach) will for most scenes be able to reconstruct at least some geometry. We demonstrated that this geometry can be used as reference geometry, bootstrapping the photometric stereo by example approach. This yields the clear benefit that neither lighting nor scene reflectance need to be known or even controlled.

Another critical point is the reasoning in Section 4.2 why averaging multiple matches works. It is, e.g., clear that averaging multiple normal directions will not handle a mismatch in reflectance between a point and the scene intrinsic reference geometry as well as mixing the contributions of two reference objects in [1] would do. We found, however, that it is a procedure based on the available information that in practice yields surprisingly good results.

8   Conclusion and Future Work

Reconstructing accurate normals for large-scale objects with photometric stereo methods is a non-trivial task. As we cannot put whole buildings in a laboratory, many traditional photometric stereo methods cannot be easily applied. In this paper we presented a combination of multi-view stereo and photometric stereo that is able to cope with outdoor imagery and has minimal capturing requirements. Like standard photometric stereo by example, it neither requires known lighting or reflectance nor does it reconstruct either of them explicitly. By introducing the scene-intrinsic reference geometry, we are able to extend the applicability of photometric stereo by example to scenes for which it is undesired or even impossible to include reference objects.

The reference geometry can be seen as a set of noisy samples of the function f from observation vectors to normals. The current best matches averaging does not consider how close the individual matches actually are to the candidate and it does not model the noise in the input data. This could be remedied by interpolation methods like Kriging that estimates unknown values based on known values at nearby points. However, better understanding of the space of observation vectors and their distribution is needed and we will further explore this field. A starting point is already provided by Sato et al. [28] who investigate similarity measures for observation vectors and apply a dimension reduction technique to the space of observation vectors.

In the future, we would furthermore like to improve robustness against cast shadows and local influences. Finally, the reconstructed 3D geometry might benefit from better integration, e.g., by avoiding to integrate over depth discontinuities similar to Vlasic et al. [9] or Agrawal et al. [29].

Acknowledgments. This work was partially supported by the European project 3D-COFORM (FP7-ICT-2007.4.3-231809) and the DFG Emmy Noether fellowship GO 1752/3-1.

References

1. Hertzmann, A., Seitz, S.M.: Example-based photometric stereo: Shape reconstruction with general, varying BRDFs. PAMI 27, 1254–1264 (2005)
2. Woodham, R.J.: Photometric method for determining surface orientation from multiple images. Optical Engineering 19, 139–144 (1980)
3. Horn, B.: Robot Vision. MIT Press (1986)
4. Basri, R., Jacobs, D.: Photometric stereo with general, unknown lighting. In: Proc. ICCV (2001)
5. Ramamoorthi, R., Hanrahan, P.: A signal-processing framework for inverse rendering. In: Proc. SIGGRAPH, pp. 117–128 (2001)
6. Shen, L., Tan, P.: Photometric stereo and weather estimation using internet images. In: Proc. CVPR (2009)
7. Joshi, N., Kriegman, D.: Shape from varying illumination and viewpoint. In: Proc. CVPR (2007)
8. Hernandez, C., Vogiatzis, G., Cipolla, R.: Multi-view photometric stereo. PAMI (2008)
9. Vlasic, D., Peers, P., Baran, I., Debevec, P., Popovic, J., Rusinkiewicz, S., Matusik, W.: Dynamic shape capture using multi-view photometric stereo. ACM Trans. Graph. 28 (2009)
10. Higo, T., Matsushita, Y., Joshi, N., Ikeuchi, K.: A hand-held photometric stereo camera for 3-d modeling. In: Proc. ICCV (2009)
11. Goldman, D.B., Curless, B., Hertzmann, A., Seitz, S.M.: Shape and spatially varying BRDFs from photometric stereo. In: Proc. ICCV, pp. 341–348 (2005)
12. Aldrin, N., Zickler, T., Kriegman, D.: Photometric stereo with non-parametric spatially-varying reflectance. In: Proc. CVPR (2008)
13. Silver, W.M.: Determining shape and reflectance using multiple images. Master's thesis, Massachusetts Institute of Technology (1980)
14. Koppal, S.J., Narasimhan, S.G.: Clustering appearance for scene analysis. In: Proc. CVPR, pp. 1323–1330 (2006)
15. Snavely, N., Seitz, S.M., Szeliski, R.: Photo tourism: exploring photo collections in 3D. ACM Trans. Graph. 25, 835–846 (2006)

16. Seitz, S., Curless, B., Diebel, J., Scharstein, D., Szeliski, R.: A comparison and evaluation of multi-view stereo reconstruction algorithms. In: Proc. CVPR, pp. 519–526 (2006), `http://vision.middlebury.edu/mview/`
17. Goesele, M., Snavely, N., Curless, B., Hoppe, H., Seitz, S.M.: Multi-view stereo for community photo collections. In: Proc. ICCV (2007)
18. Curless, B., Levoy, M.: A volumetric method for building complex models from range images. In: Proc. SIGGRAPH, pp. 303–312 (1996)
19. Wu, Z., Li, L.: A line-integration based method for depth recovery from surface normals. Computer Vision, Graphics, and Image Processing 43, 53–66 (1988)
20. Klette, R., Schluens, K.: Height data from gradient fields. In: Proc. Machine Vision Applications, Architectures, and Systems Integration V, pp. 204–215 (1996)
21. Smith, W.A.P., Hancock, E.R.: Statistical methods for surface integration. In: Proc. IMA Conference on the Mathematics of Surfaces, pp. 427–441 (2007)
22. Ho, J., Lim, J., Yang, M.-H., Kriegman, D.: Integrating Surface Normal Vectors Using Fast Marching Method. In: Leonardis, A., Bischof, H., Pinz, A. (eds.) ECCV 2006. LNCS, vol. 3953, pp. 239–250. Springer, Heidelberg (2006)
23. Durou, J.D., Aujol, J.F., Courteille, F.: Integrating the normal field of a surface in the presence of discontinuities. In: Proc. EMM-CVPR, pp. 261–273 (2009)
24. Horovitz, I., Kiryati, N.: Depth from gradient fields and control points: Bias correction in photometric stereo. Image and Vision Computing 22, 681–694 (2004)
25. Nehab, D., Rusinkiewicz, S., Ramamoorthi, R.: Efficiently combining positions and normals for precise 3d geometry. ACM Trans. Graph. 24, 536–543 (2005)
26. Furukawa, Y., Ponce, J.: Accurate, dense, and robust multi-view stereopsis. PAMI 32 (2010)
27. Kazhdan, M., Bolitho, M., Hoppe, H.: Poisson surface reconstruction. In: Proc. SGP, pp. 61–70 (2006)
28. Sato, I., Okabe, T., Yu, Q., Sato, Y.: Shape reconstruction based on similarity in radiance changes under varying illumination. In: Proc. ICCV, pp. 1–8 (2007)
29. Agrawal, A., Raskar, R., Chellappa, R.: What Is the Range of Surface Reconstructions from a Gradient Field? In: Leonardis, A., Bischof, H., Pinz, A. (eds.) ECCV 2006. LNCS, vol. 3951, pp. 578–591. Springer, Heidelberg (2006)

iModel: Interactive Co-segmentation for Object of Interest 3D Modeling

Adarsh Kowdle[1], Dhruv Batra[2], Wen-Chao Chen[3], and Tsuhan Chen[1]

[1] Cornell University, Ithaca, NY, USA
[2] Carnegie Mellon University, Pittsburgh, PA, USA
[3] Industrial Technology Research Institute, Taiwan
apk64@cornell.edu, batradhruv@cmu.edu,
chaody@itri.org.tw, tsuhan@ece.cornell.edu

Abstract. We present an interactive system to create 3D models of objects of interest in their natural cluttered environments.

A typical setting for 3D modeling of an object of interest involves capturing images from multiple views in a multi-camera studio with a mono-color screen or structured lighting. This is a tedious process and cannot be applied to a variety of objects. Moreover, general scene reconstruction algorithms fail to focus on the object of interest to the user. In this paper, we use successful ideas from the object cut-out literature, and develop an interactive-cosegmentation-based algorithm that uses scribbles from the user indicating foreground (object to be modeled) and background (clutter) to extract silhouettes of the object of interest from multiple views. Using these silhouettes, and the camera parameters obtained from structure-from-motion, in conjunction with a shape-from-silhouette algorithm we generate a texture-mapped 3D model of the object of interest.

1 Introduction

If there is one thing the growing popularity of immersive virtual environments (like Second-Life® with 6.1 Million members) and gaming environments (like Project Natal®) has taught us – it is that people crave personalization. For example, gamers want to be able to "scan" and use their own gear (like skateboards) in a skateboarding game. While there exist some tools to enable this implanting of real-world objects in virtual environments, we believe this is an important problem, worth studying formally by computer vision researchers. This paper takes a first step towards enabling users to create 3D models of an object of interest, which may then be easily implanted in a virtual environment.

One approach to achieve this, would be to haul an expensive laser scanner to get precise depth estimates in a controlled setup, and reconstruct the object [1]. However, this might be not a feasible solution for average users. Another typical approach for this problem is to capture images of the object in a controlled environment like a multi-camera studio with mono-color screen and structured lighting, and use a shape-from-silhouette algorithm [2–5] to render the 3D model. Although these techniques have produced promising results in these constrained settings, this is a tedious process, and in some cases not an option (for example, immovable objects like a statue, historically

K.N. Kutulakos (Ed.): ECCV 2010 Workshops, Part II, LNCS 6554, pp. 211–224, 2012.

(a)   (b)   (c)   (d)

Fig. 1. Overview of system: (a) Stone dataset (24 images) - subset of images given to the system shown; (b) User interactions to indicate the object of interest (blue scribbles = object of interest, red scribbles = background); (c) Resulting silhouettes after co-segmentation (object of interest in cyan color) (d) Some sample novel views of the rendered 3D model (Best viewed in color)

or culturally-significant artifacts). However, in a world where we are surrounded by cellphone-cameras, a more accessible approach is to capture images of the object in its natural environment and directly estimate the 3D structure from these natural images. The images captured in this case would typically have cluttered backgrounds, which is known to be problematic for background subtraction algorithms.

Overview. In this work, we present an interactive system to create 3D models of objects of interest in their natural cluttered environments. Our approach builds on the success of recent works in interactive co-segmentation [6–9] that have shown that foreground and background statistics can be shared across images to jointly segment or *co*-segment the common foreground from multiple images. Our interactive algorithm, uses scribbles from the user indicating foreground and background to extract silhouettes of the object of interest from multiple views. Using these silhouettes, and camera parameters obtained from structure-from-motion [10], in conjunction with a octree-reconstruction-based shape-from-silhouette algorithm [2, 4] we generate a texture mapped 3D model of the object of interest. We demonstrate the effectiveness of our algorithm on a wide range of objects and show that this same approach extends to obtain 3D models of even monuments.

Contributions. The main contribution of this paper is a simple interactive system for 3D modeling of an *object of interest*. The approach obviates the need for a complicated, controlled studio environment and works for objects in their natural cluttered environments. To the best of our knowledge this is the first approach to use ideas from the interactive co-segmentation literature for object of interest 3D modeling.

Organization. The rest of this paper is organized as follows. Section 2 discusses related work. Section 3 describes our approach to co-segment the object of interest in all images using our interactive algorithm and then extract a 3D model of this object of interest using these silhouettes. Section 4 presents our modeling results on a wide range of objects. Finally, we conclude in Section 5 with discussions.

2   Related Work

Controlled Setups. Several works [11–16] use a multi-camera studio setup, with controlled lighting and a mono-color screen to capture images. This allows for easy background subtraction with chroma keying. A shape-from-silhouette algorithm can be applied to the silhouettes obtained after background subtraction [2–5]. Levoy et al. [1] construct Cyberware gantry, a laser scanner setup that is able to obtain extremely precise depth map of the object. Zhang et al. [17] perform spacetime analysis by sweeping multiple color stripes across the object to obtain the shape of the object. They also propose an approach of using a structured lighting to perform spacetime stereo by matching a pair of video streams which can help recover the shape of even dynamic objects [18]. Yezzi et al. [19] propose 'stereoscopic segmentation' to obtain the silhouettes of the object, which works well in a controlled setting of an object with a lambertian surface and constant albedo. Lee et al. [20] also propose a method to obtain silhouettes of the foreground object with the assumption that the background is homogeneous to some extent, and differs from foreground. We note that all these methods require a controlled setup and are not (directly) applicable to a wide range of objects that cannot be captured in such a controlled enviroment.

Multiview Stereo. When we move from images taken in controlled environments to images taken outdoors in cluttered scenes, background subtraction becomes a significantly harder task. In these cases, algorithms typically try to reconstruct the entire scene as a whole and do not focus on any object of interest. A popular work by Snavely et al. [21] relies on structure-from-motion to render sparse point clouds. However, this results in only a sparse reconstruction and not a complete 3D model of the object, which is the goal of this paper. Multiview stereo algorithms [22] like patch-based multi-view stereo introduced by Furukawa et al. [23] can generate reasonably dense models. Other notable dense-reconstruction algorithms include Van Gool et al. [24] which offers dense 3D reconstruction from user-supplied images via a publicly available web service. Goesele et al. [25] and Furukawa et al. [26] worked with internet-scale community photo collections. They used a multi-view stereo approach to get dense reconstructions of the geometry of objects like monuments and statues using many images. We note that our scenario is slightly different from these works – we focus on the 3D reconstruction of the object *of interest* alone and typically have access to a few consumer images (significantly fewer than community photo collections).

Interactive Algorithms. As discussed before, there have been a number of automatic algorithms to obtain the silhouettes of the object. However, the notion of an 'object of interest' clearly requires some form of user input. This is especially true when the natural surroundings of the object being modeled make it difficult to automatically extract the object from the background (see for example, the stone dataset in Figure 2a). Campbell et al. [27] tried to incorporate user interaction by assuming that the object of interest is at the center of attention. Thus, they used a seed at the center of the image to perform region growing to extract the foreground across images. This would work when the object has a fairly uniform color but, would fail if the object had multiple colors. Also, this approach does not allow the algorithm to recover from an incorrect labeling. We believe that our application requires a fully interactive algorithm. This was first explored in image segmentation by Boykov and Jolly [28] who posed interactive segmentation as a discrete optimization problem. Li et al. [29] and Rother et al. [6] presented simplified user interactions and other improvements to the basic framework.

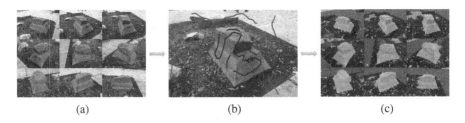

(a)   (b)   (c)

Fig. 2. Interactive Co-segmentation: (a) Group of images; (b) User interactions to indicate the object of interest (blue scribbles = object of interest, red scribbles = background); (c) Resulting silhouettes after co-segmentation (in cyan color). For this example, we only needed to scribble on a single image, but our system allows for scribbles on multiple images. Other groups in our dataset with more diverse appearances needed scribbles on multiple images. (Best viewed in color)

This idea has been extended to object modeling by Sormann et al. [30]. They start with a dense binary segmentation of one of the images using intelligent scrissors or grab-cut. The foreground and background color model are then learnt using this segmentation and this model is then tranfered to the other views. The problem with this approach is that the background of the image can change very rapidly and a segmentation on one image will not be representative of this. We use recent work by Batra et al. [9] which extends this interactive approach to co-segmentation of groups of images. This makes for a very simple interactive system and also allows the user to provide additional interactions if required.

Hengel et al. [31] and Sinha et al. [32] have proposed interactive 3D modeling systems that produce piecewise planar approximations. Our work differs from them, in that we make no such planar assumptions and can model even non-planar objects.

3   Approach

We now describe our approach. We are given multiple images of the object of interest taken in cluttered scenes. Our approach, involves two main parts: 1) an energy-minimization framework for interactive co-segmentation that extracts silhouettes of the object of interest and 2) a shape-from-silhouette approach to obtain the final texture-mapped 3D model. An overview of the system is shown in Fig. 1.

3.1   Interactive Co-segmentation

We create a simple interface to accept interactions from the user in the form of scribbles to indicate the object of interest (foreground) and background as shown in Fig. 2b. Our interactive co-segmentation approach is based on the work of Batra et al. [9], which we briefly describe here.

We cast our co-segmentation problem as a binary labeling energy-minimization problem solved via graph-cuts. We begin by over-segmenting each image. The task is to label each superpixel[1] in each image as foreground (object of interest) or background. For each image, we construct a graph over superpixels, where adjacent superpixels are joined by an edge. Associated with each graph is an energy which is a weighted combination of a data-term and an edge-term. We model the data-term as the negative log-likelihood of the features extracted at superpixels given the class model. Our features are average Luv colour features extracted over superpixels, and the class model is a Gaussian Mixture Model, which is learnt from *all* labeled superpixels (in all images). We consider a superpixel labeled if any pixel within it has been scribbled on. Our approach allows for scribbles on single or multiple images. The edge-term is a contrast sensitive Potts model. Finally, we use one graph-cut per image to compute the MAP labels for all superpixels, using the implementation provided by Bagon [34] and Boykov et al. [35, 36] and Kolmogorov [37]. This results in a co-segmentation of the object of interest across multiple images. More details about the performance of this co-segmentation algorithm may be found in Batra et al. [9].

3.2   Shape from Silhouette

We have now extracted the silhouettes of the object of interest from multiple views. We use the structure-from-motion implementation by Snavely et al. [10] called 'Bundler' to recover camera parameters for each image. We then use a shape-from-silhouette approach to extract a volumetric 3D reconstruction of this object. Specifically, we use an octree-reconstruction method [2, 4].

An octree is a tree-structured representation which is used to describe a set of binary-valued data (in this case indicating the presence or absence of cubes of voxels in the 3D model). The octree is constructed by recursively subdividing a cube to eight sub-cubes, starting with the root which represents the bounding volume in which the object of interest lies as shown in Fig. 3. This cube representation captures the high degree of coherence between adjacent voxels. Each sub-cube in an octree is projected onto the silhouette images and can be one of three colors. A *black* node indicates that the cube is totally occupied (i.e. it projects completely inside the silhouettes), and a *white* node indicates that it is totally empty (i.e. it projects completely outside the silhouettes). Both black cubes and white cubes are leaf nodes in the tree. A *gray* node indicates that the cube lies on the boundary of the object and is only partially filled. The gray cube is subdivided till each of the sub-cubes can be assigned a black or white color.

We use a variant of this algorithm which is optimized for speed [2, 4]. For more details the reader is referred to Szeliski et al. [2] and Chen et al. [4]. We note here that our system allows users to visually examine the 3D reconstruction and give more scribbles to improve silhouettes that would in turn lead to better 3D reconstruction. However, we do not perform multiple iterations for our experiments.

It is worth mentioning that shape-from-silhouette algorithms have well-understood limitations. Specifically, they are unable to model certain concavities in the structure (e.g. details on the surface of the structure). However, as we show through our

---

[1] We use mean-shift [33] to extract these superpixels, and typically break down 350×500 images into ~ 400 superpixels per image.

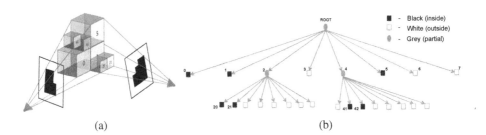

Fig. 3. Simple two-level octree: (a) Synthetic visualization to show octree reconstruction (Silhouettes of the object shown in black in two views); (b) Corresponding tree representation of the two-level octree (Best viewed in color)

results (Section 4), our approach might be a good first-approximation for consumer applications. Recently, Fabbri et al. [38] developed an algorithm which allows for reconstructing curves in the structure. Although not done here, this approach could provide cues to help tackle the problem of concavities in the structure.

4 Results and Discussions

We demonstrate the effectiveness of our algorithm on a number of datasets ranging from a simple collection taken in a controlled setup to a community photo collection and a video captured in cluttered scenes. In this section, we show the rendered 3D model for each dataset, captured from novel viewpoints. For all datasets except the dino dataset, we texture map the model by back-projecting the faces of the mesh onto a single image. We observed that in outdoor scenes texture mapping from multiple views can lead to some artifacts at the seams due to changes in illumination.

Dino Dataset. The first dataset we use is a standard dataset from the Oxford Visual Geometry Group[2], shown in Fig. 4a. One of the images in the dataset was chosen at random and the interactions were provided to indicate the dino as foreground and the blue screen as the background. The resulting silhouettes are shown in Fig. 4b. The 3D model obtained from the shape-from-silhouette algorithm. This dataset was captured in a controlled setup which allowed us to texture map the model using multiple views i.e. by projecting the faces onto the corresponding image where they are visible. Occlusion poses a significant problem for multiview texturing, we use the approach of Chen et al. [39] to overcome this by using the depth buffer (z-buffer) data from the graphics card.

This result simply serves as a proof of concept under a controlled setup, and it is encouraging to see that our approach is able to render a good reconstruction *without* any prior knowledge about this setup.

---

[2] Oxford Visual Geometry Group multiview dataset: http://www.robots.ox.ac.uk/~vgg/data/data-mview.html

(a)   (b)   (c)

Fig. 4. Dino dataset (36 images): (a) Subset of the collection of images given to the system where the dino was marked the object of interest; (b) Resulting silhouettes after co-segmentation (in cyan color); (c) Some sample novel views of the 3D model (Best viewed in color)

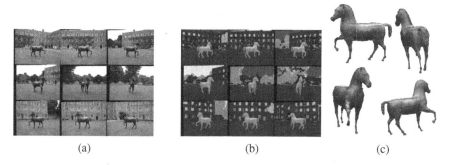

(a)   (b)   (c)

Fig. 5. Cambridge unicorn dataset (14 images): (a) Subset of the collection of images given to the system where the unicorn statue was marked as the object of interest; (b) Resulting silhouettes after co-segmentation (in cyan color); (c) Some sample novel views of the 3D model (Best viewed in color)

Cambridge Unicorn Dataset. We use the Cambridge unicorn dataset [40], shown in Fig. 5a. Using interactions to indicate the unicorn as the object of interest, we obtain the silhouettes as shown in Fig. 5b which results in the texture-mapped 3D model as shown in Fig. 5c.

Stone Dataset. This dataset demonstrates that our algorithm performs well even when the background becomes highly cluttered. The stone dataset is shown in Fig. 2a. Note that the stone is visually very similar to the ground surface. The silhouettes obtained after providing the interactions to indicate the stone as object of interest, are shown in Fig. 2c. It is worth mentioning that the noisy (incorrectly-labeled) superpixels in the segmentations can be removed by increasing the smoothness penalty in our energy-minimization framework. However, these sparse incorrectly-labeled superpixels do not affect the reconstruction, as they get filtered out in the shape-from-silhouette algorithm. The texture-mapped 3D model obtained from the shape-from-silhouette algorithm is shown in Fig. 1d.

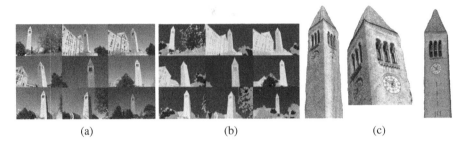

(a)   (b)   (c)

Fig. 6. Clock tower dataset (32 images): (a) Subset of the collection of images given to the system where the clock tower was marked as the object of interest; (b) Resulting silhouettes after co-segmentation (in cyan color); (c) Some sample novel views of the 3D model (Best viewed in color).

Clock Tower Dataset. We now try to reconstruct immovable objects that cannot be taken to a standard studio setup as shown in Fig. 6a. With interactions we obtain the silhouettes of our object of interest (clock tower), as shown in Fig. 6b which can be used to obtain texture mapped 3D model using the shape-from-silhouette algorithm as shown in Fig. 6c. We note that algorithms like structure-from-motion and patch based multi-view stereo would try to reconstruct the whole scene and result in an incomplete reconstruction in this case.

Statue Dataset. We now demonstrate the effectiveness of our algorithm on images where the background changes drastically as shown in Fig. 7a. The silhouettes of the object of interest (statue) obtained using our algorithm are shown in Fig. 7b. The texture mapped 3D model of the statue obtained using these silhouettes are shown in Fig. 7c. Note here that a part of the head of the statue gets clipped off in the generated model. The reason for this is a leak in the superpixels where a portion of the head became part of the sky superpixel. We can overcome this problem by working on pixels instead of superpixels i.e. set up the energy minimization over a graph of pixels instead of superpixels. This would increase the computational complexity but result in better silhouettes.

Video Dataset. Our work opens up the possibility of allowing users to render themselves as avatars in virtual worlds. We consider this scenario of reconstructing a person in 3D. We captured a video of the person to be modeled by walking around them. Selected frames this video are shown in Fig. 8a. With interactions, we obtain the silhouettes as shown in Fig. 8b which results in the texture mapped 3D model as shown in Fig. 8c. We can see that the reconstruction is fairly complete, however we observe a leak in the superpixel map here as well.

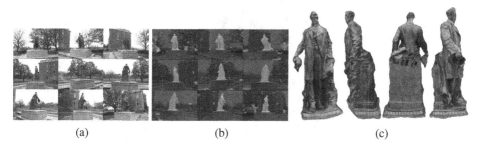

(a)   (b)   (c)

Fig. 7. Statue dataset (38 images): (a) Subset of the collection of images given to the system where the statue was marked as the object of interest; (b) Resulting silhouettes after co-segmentation (in cyan color); (c) Some sample novel views of the 3D model (Best viewed in color).

(a)   (b)   (c)

Fig. 8. Video dataset (17 images obtained by sampling the video): (a) Subset of the collection of images given to the system where the person was considered the object of interest; (b) Resulting silhouettes after co-segmentation; (c) Some sample novel views of the 3D model (Best viewed in color).

Community Photo Collection - Statue of Liberty Dataset. With millions of images available on the internet, we consider an application geared towards internet-scale reconstruction of objects where the user searches for an object of interest, in this case the *Statue of Liberty*. We start with a set of 1600 images of the Statue of Liberty collected by Snavely et al. from Flickr®. We use all the images to estimate the camera matrices using structure-from-motion [10]. For our algorithm, we sampled a subset of 15 images spanning a large field of view, as shown in Fig. 9a. The silhouettes are shown in Fig. 9b and the texture-mapped 3D model are shown in Fig. 9c. We note here that there are a few artifacts like the blue sky above the shoulder as well as the thinned arm. Some of these problems (like the superpixel leaks) may be corrected by working with pixels. However, some (like the lack of detail on the face of the Statue of Liberty) are a direct result of our reliance on a segmentation framework and may not be possible to fix. The

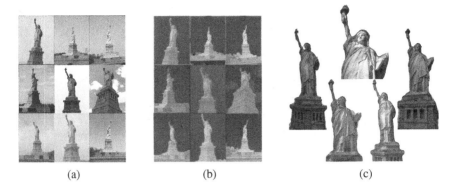

(a)   (b)   (c)

Fig. 9. Community photo collection - Statue of Liberty dataset: (a) Subset of the collection of images given to the system - for our co-segmentation algorithm we use a subset of 15 images spanning a large field of view from a collection of 1600 images; (b) Resulting silhouettes after co-segmentation (in cyan color); (c) Some sample novel views of the 3D model (Best viewed in color).

results on this dataset have also been reported by the multi-view stereo work of Goesele et al. [25], where they obtain a dense depth model for the statue. A comparison between the model we generate, the point cloud model from photo-tourism [10] and multi-view stereo model [25] is shown in Fig. 10.

It is worth mentioning that once we obtain the silhouettes of the object of interest, we can use any known shape-from-silhouette algorithm at this stage to obtain the 3D model (not necessarily the octree-based reconstruction approach we used here), for example, the approach by Wong et al [41]. In addition, we can use this co-segmentation algorithm with the popular multi-view stereo reconstruction approach, to focus the output of the multi-view stereo algorithm on the object of interest. As an illustration, we show the model generated using patch-based multi-view stereo (PMVS) [3] in Fig. 11 when constrained by the silhouettes extracted using our interactive co-segmentation algorithm. We used the statue dataset in Fig. 7a for this experiment. In Fig. 11a, we show the result of PMVS without any prior knowledge of the object of interest. In Fig. 11b we show the 3D model obtained from PMVS using our silhouettes. As we explained earlier, multi-view stereo algorithms would try to reconstruct the whole scene without giving importance to the object of interest. We can see that use of silhouettes helps obtain a more accurate 3D model of the object of interest. Another crucial advantage of using the silhouettes is to speed up the multi-view stereo algorithm with geometrically consistent reconstructions. In our experiment with PMVS, it took 3 hours to obtain the model in Fig. 11a, as opposed to 8 minutes using the silhouettes to render Fig. 11b. However, faster implementations may be available for PMVS.

---

[3] We use the PMVS implementation described in [23] available at `http://grail.cs.washington.edu/software/pmvs/pmvs-1/index.html`

(a)   (b)

(c)

Fig. 10. Statue of Liberty comparison: (a) Point cloud reconstruction by photo-tourism, using 1600 images; (b) Dense reconstruction using multi-view, using 72 images (figure from [25], used with permission). With a lot of images, multi-view stereo can give a good depth model; (c) Pleasing texture mapped reconstruction rendered using our interactive co-segmentation algorithm, using 15 images. (Best viewed in color).

(a)

(b)

Fig. 11. Patch-based multi-view stereo experiment using images in Fig. 7a where the statue is the object of interest: (a) When the silhouettes are not available PMVS tries to reconstruct the whole scene as shown; (b) Using the silhouettes produced by our co-segmentation algorithm, we can use PMVS to obtain the 3D model of the statue which was the object of interest (Best viewed in color).

5 Conclusions and Future Work

With the growing popularity of immersive virtual environments and large-scale reconstructions in mind, we present a simple interactive algorithm which enables the user to obtain a 3D model of an object of interest and render it as part of the reconstruction.

The interactive algorithm obviates the need for a complicated, controlled environment and works reasonably well in cluttered scenes. We demonstrate the effectiveness of the algorithm by modeling a wide range of objects captured in cluttered environments, *in the wild*. We also show that the same system extends well to community photo collections, thus taking a step towards building better large scale 3D environments.

We note that, in our work we only make use of camera parameters and *not* correspondences or 3D positions of feature points. As a future work, we want to incorporate this information which should help obtain better reconstructions. Moreover, in this work, co-segmentation and shape-from-silhouette steps were used purely in a "feedforward" manner. A possible future direction would be to place the 3D modeling and 2D image co-segmentation into an iterative loop where they aid each other. Geometric consistency constraints between different images would help achieve better co-segmentation and thereby help create better 3D models. In addition, improved techniques to use texture from multiple views while texture mapping objects in outdoor scenes would be useful and can be explored in the future.

References

1. Levoy, M., Pulli, K., Curless, B., Rusinkiewicz, S., Koller, D., Pereira, L., Ginzton, M., Anderson, S., Davis, J., Ginsberg, J., Shade, J., Fulk, D.: The digital michelangelo project: 3d scanning of large statues. In: Siggraph, pp. 131–144 (2000)
2. Szeliski, R.: Rapid octree construction from image sequences. CVGIP: Image Understanding 58, 23–32 (1993)
3. Fang, Y.H., Chou, H.L., Chen, Z.: 3d shape recovery of complex objects from multiple silhouette images. Pattern Recogn. Lett. 24, 1279–1293 (2003)
4. Chen, Z., Chou, H.L., Chen, W.C.: A performance controllable octree construction method. In: ICPR, pp. 1–4 (2008)
5. Forbes, K., Nicolls, F., de Jager, G., Voigt, A.: Shape-from-Silhouette with Two Mirrors and an Uncalibrated Camera. In: Leonardis, A., Bischof, H., Pinz, A. (eds.) ECCV 2006. LNCS, vol. 3952, pp. 165–178. Springer, Heidelberg (2006)
6. Rother, C., Kolmogorov, V., Blake, A.: "Grabcut": interactive foreground extraction using iterated graph cuts. In: SIGGRAPH (2004)
7. Hochbaum, D.S., Singh, V.: An efficient algorithm for co-segmentation. In: ICCV (2009)
8. Mukherjee, L., Singh, V., Dyer, C.R.: Half-integrality based algorithms for cosegmentation of images. In: CVPR (2009)
9. Batra, D., Kowdle, A., Parikh, D., Luo, J., Chen, T.: icoseg: Interactive co-segmentation with intelligent scribble guidance. In: CVPR (2010)
10. Snavely, N., Seitz, S., Szeliski, R.: Photo tourism: Exploring photo collections in 3d. In: SIGGRAPH, pp. 835–846 (2006)
11. Franco, J.S., Boyer, E.: Exact polyhedral visual hulls. In: BMVC, vol. 1, pp. 329–338 (2003)
12. Starck, J., Hilton, A.: Surface capture for performance-based animation. IEEE Computer Graphics and Applications 27, 21–31 (2007)
13. Vlasic, D., Baran, I., Matusik, W., Popović, J.: Articulated mesh animation from multi-view silhouettes. In: SIGGRAPH, pp. 1–9. ACM (2008)
14. Curless, B., Levoy, M.: A volumetric method for building complex models from range images. In: SIGGRAPH, pp. 303–312. ACM (1996)
15. Chen, Y., Medioni, G.: Object modelling by registration of multiple range images. Image Vision Comput. 10, 145–155 (1992)
16. Fitzgibbon, A.W., Cross, G., Zisserman, A.: Automatic 3D Model Construction for Turn-Table Sequences. In: Koch, R., Van Gool, L. (eds.) SMILE 1998. LNCS, vol. 1506, pp. 155–170. Springer, Heidelberg (1998)
17. Zhang, L., Curless, B., Seitz, S.M.: Rapid shape acquisition using color structured light and multi-pass dynamic programming. In: 3DPVT, vol. 24 (2002)
18. Zhang, L., Curless, B., Seitz, S.M.: Spacetime stereo: Shape recovery for dynamic scenes. In: CVPR, vol. 2, p. 367 (2003)

19. Yezzi, A., Soatto, S.: Stereoscopic segmentation. IJCV 53, 31–43 (2003)
20. Lee, W., Woo, W., Boyer, E.: Identifying Foreground from Multiple Images. In: Yagi, Y., Kang, S.B., Kweon, I.S., Zha, H. (eds.) ACCV 2007, Part II. LNCS, vol. 4844, pp. 580–589. Springer, Heidelberg (2007)
21. Snavely, N., Seitz, S.M., Szeliski, R.: Modeling the world from internet photo collections. IJCV 80, 189–210 (2008)
22. Seitz, S.M., Curless, B., Diebel, J., Scharstein, D., Szeliski, R.: A comparison and evaluation of multi-view stereo reconstruction algorithms. In: CVPR, vol. 1, pp. 519–528 (2006)
23. Furukawa, Y., Ponce, J.: Accurate, dense, and robust multi-view stereopsis. PAMI 32, 1362–1376 (2010)
24. Vergauwen, M., Van Gool, L.: Web-based 3d reconstruction service. Mach. Vision Appl. 17, 411–426 (2006)
25. Goesele, M., Snavely, N., Curless, B., Hoppe, H., Seitz, S.M.: Multi-view stereo for community photo collections. In: ICCV, pp. 265–270 (2007)
26. Furukawa, Y., Curless, B., Seitz, S.M., Szeliski, R.: Towards internet-scale multi-view stereo. In: CVPR (2010)
27. Campbell, N., Vogiatzis, G., Hernndez, C., Cipolla, R.: Automatic 3d object segmentation in multiple views using volumetric graph-cuts. In: BMVC (2007)
28. Boykov, Y., Jolly, M.P.: Interactive graph cuts for optimal boundary and region segmentation of objects in n-d images. In: ICCV (2001)
29. Li, Y., Sun, J., Tang, C.K., Shum, H.Y.: Lazy snapping. In: SIGGRAPH (2004)
30. Sormann, M., Zach, C., Bauer, J., Karner, K., Bischof, H.: Automatic Foreground Propagation in Image Sequences for 3D Reconstruction. In: Kropatsch, W.G., Sablatnig, R., Hanbury, A. (eds.) DAGM 2005. LNCS, vol. 3663, pp. 93–100. Springer, Heidelberg (2005)
31. Hengel, A., Dick, A.R., Thormhlen, T., Ward, B., Torr, P.H.S.: Videotrace: rapid interactive scene modelling from video. ACM Trans. Graph. 26, 86 (2007)
32. Sinha, S., Steedly, D., Szeliski, R., Agrawala, M., Pollefeys, M.: Interactive 3d architectural modeling from unordered photo collections. ACM Transactions on Graphics (Proceedings of SIGGRAPH Asia 2008) (2008)
33. Comaniciu, D., Meer, P.: Mean shift: a robust approach toward feature space analysis. PAMI 24, 603–619 (2002)
34. Bagon, S.: Matlab wrapper for graph cut (2006)
35. Boykov, Y., Kolmogorov, V.: An experimental comparison of min-cut/max-flow algorithms for energy minimization in vision. PAMI 26, 1124–1137 (2004)
36. Boykov, Y., Veksler, O., Zabih, R.: Efficient approximate energy minimization via graph cuts. PAMI 20, 1222–1239 (2001)
37. Kolmogorov, V., Zabih, R.: What energy functions can be minimized via graph cuts? PAMI 26, 147–159 (2004)
38. Fabbri, R., Kimia, B.B.: 3D curve sketch: Flexible curve-based stereo reconstruction and calibration. In: CVPR (2010)
39. Chen, W.C., Chou, H.L., Chen, Z.: A quality controllable multi-view object reconstruction method for 3d imaging systems. JVCIR 21, 427–441 (2010)
40. Wong, K.Y.K., Cipolla, R.: Reconstruction of sculpture from its profiles with unknown camera positions. IEEE Transactions on Image Processing 13, 381–389 (2004)
41. Wong, K.Y.K., Cipolla, R.: Structure and motion from silhouettes. In: ICCV (2001)

Automatic Registration of Large-Scale Multi-sensor Datasets

Quan Wang and Suya You

Computer Science Department, University of Southern California,
Los Angeles, California, U.S.A.
{quanwang,suyay}@graphics.usc.edu

Abstract. This paper proposes an automatic method for registering images from different sensors, particularly 2D optical sensors and 3D range sensors, without any assumption about initial alignment.

Many existing methods try to reconstruct 3D points from 2D image sequences, and then match 3D primitives from both sides. The availability of appropriate multiple images associated with 3D range data, the well-known challenge of inferring 3D from 2D and the difficulty of establishing correspondences among 3D primitives when there is no pre-knowledge about initial pose estimation, lead us to a different approach based on region matching between optical images and depth images projected from range data.

This paper details our interest region extraction method for optical images and also the efficient region matching component. Experiments using several cities' aerial images and LiDAR (Light Detection and Ranging) data illustrate the effectiveness of the proposed approach even when facing considerably geometric distortions.

Keywords: different sensors registration, 2D-3D matching, LiDAR data.

1 Introduction

Recent years, there has been an increasing awareness of the growing need for registering images from different sensors, especially the range and optical sensors. For example, the photorealistic modeling of urban scenes using range data from airborne or ground laser scanner requires the registration of those 3D range data onto aerial or ground 2D images for recognition and texture mapping purposes. In the medical image processing domain, there has a long standing concern about how to automatically align Computed Tomography or Magnetic Resonance images with optical camera images. Traditional texture-based image matching approaches such as [1] can not be directly adapted to above tasks, basically because unlike the optical sensors, range sensors capture no texture information.

In this paper, we propose an automatic registration method based on matching of local interest regions extracted from 2D images and depth images of 3D range data for urban environment. The regions we are interested in (ROI) are typically well separated regions of individual buildings. Global context information is implicitly

K.N. Kutulakos (Ed.): ECCV 2010 Workshops, Part II, LNCS 6554, pp. 225–238, 2012.

used for outlier removal and matching propagation (system overview in figure 1). Our approach can register images from different sensors with large initial location and scale errors. Although today there exist systematic ways to obtain initially well aligned 3D and 2D data at the same time for large scale scenes, possible applications of our work include data fusion from different sources and sensors, and updating existing GIS (Geographic Information System) with new content, when data from different sources may have non-unified calibration or no georeference at all, e.g. historic photos or photos from common users. Furthermore, the ROI extraction component proposed in this paper is an important prerequisite to a variety of recognition, understanding, and rendering tasks in urban environments.

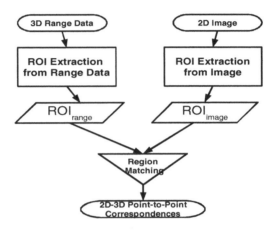

Fig. 1. Overview of the proposed 2D-3D registration system

Our two basic assumptions are: first the dominant contours of most interest regions are repeatable under both optical and range sensors. A similar assumption was used and verified in [8]. Second, focusing on different sensor problems, in this paper we assume both optical and depth images have similar viewing directions (nadir view in our experiments) though position, zoom level and in-plan rotations of capture devices can be different. Our idea for the whole system is to first handle different sensor problems in this stage, and then register nadir, oblique and even ground images all from optical sensors to handle 3D view point changes by using approaches such as [13] and [16]. In the end, oblique and ground images can be indirectly registered.

Intensive experiments have verified the effectiveness of the proposed approach in terms of scale, rotation and location invariance, significant geometric distortion and partially missing data due to occlusion or historic data. After the related works, section 3 details our interest region extraction method for optical images and section 4 presents the region matching component.

2   Related Works

To register images from different sensors, many recently developed methods reconstruct sparse or dense 3D point clouds from image sequence, then use high level features (e.g. 3D edges, intersection of perpendicular 3D lines) which are preserved and consistent on both 3D and 2D sides to establish correspondences.

Zhao, et al. [2] use motion stereo to recover dense 3D point clouds from continuous oblique video and ICP algorithm to register recovered 3D points with LiDAR data with initial alignment provided by positioning hardware such as GPS (Global Positioning System) and IMU (Inertial Measurement Unit). Ding, et al. detect 2D orthogonal corners (2DOC) and use them as primitives to match single oblique image with airborne LiDAR [3]. The proposed method achieves overall 61% accuracy and the processing time of each image is only several minutes in contrast to 20 hours of the previous work of [4].

Both [2] and [3] utilize positioning hardware for initial alignment. Our own visualization of similar datasets indicates the readings from the airplane-bonded GPS and IMU are accurate enough to significantly simplify the registration problem. However, for historic data or photos from common users, we can not assume such assistant hardware is always available for GIS data fusion and updating problems. Moreover, though accurate for large city scenes, the current accuracy of positioning hardware makes their application to small scenes (e.g. indoor environment and medical imaging settings) impractical. If initial orientation, scale and location errors are significant, ICP or local search of orthogonal corners could not be sufficient.

Multiview geometry methods are used in [2] and [6] to recover 3D point clouds from image sequences. The first limitation is appropriate multiple views of the interest object might not always be readily available. Second, as the first step of 3D reconstruction, correspondence among 2D images needs to be established. This is a challenge problem by its own especially for wide baseline cases. Simple Harris corners and correlation are used in [2] for continuous video frames, while in [6], SIFT is use. However, for non-planar 3D object and significant view point changes, even SIFT and its many variations can not be confidently counted for dense and stable correspondences. Last but not the least, even a number of perfect correspondences can be obtained , traditional stereo or structure from motion techniques still tend to produce inconsistent and noisy results.

3   ROI Extraction from Aerial Images

One important component of our 2D-3D registration method is ROI extraction from aerial images (major components in fig. 2), which can be viewed as a special case of general image segmentation problem. Related recent works include: Comaniciu and Meer's non parametric mean shift segmentation algorithm [9] and Felzenszwalb and Huttenlocher's efficient graph based segmentation methods [10].

The fractal geometry used in our method, originally introduced by Mandelbrot [11], has long been used for aerial image understanding tasks. Solka et al. use fractal measurement combined with classical statistical features such as the coefficient of variation to identify ROI for unmanned aerial vehicle imagery [12]. Recent work of Cao et al. [14] tries to minimize an energy function representing how well the current boundary contains the interest region using fractal error image and texture edge image generated by Discrete Cosine Transformation.

This section presents our ROI extraction algorithm for aerial photography. The proposed algorithm produces initial ROI through a region-growing process utilizing various image cues from low level features such as intensity and color preference to high level ones such as fractal errors and multiple assistant information maps (AIMs). The detected initial ROI could be further refined by a learning-based region regulation step. This component is to extract, from aerial images, buildings' most external contours repeated and consistent with those extracted from 3D range data.

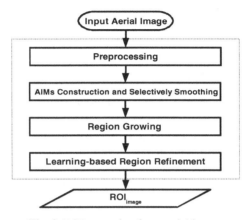

Fig. 2. ROI extraction from aerial images

3.1   AIMs Construction and Selectively Smoothing

There are three kinds of assistant information maps the region growing process frequently refers to: vege maps, shadow maps and edge maps. The aerial image is also selectively smoothed during the construction of three AIMs.

Vege-Map (M_{vege}): By utilizing color information in the aerial photograph, we identify pixels that are dominated by the green channel and possibly vegetations.

Shadow-Map (M_{shadow}): For each pixel, let I represent the intensity value and (C_r, C_g, C_b) represent its RGB color channels. A pixel is said be to a shadow pixel if:

$$I < T_{shadow1} \text{ and } \max\{C_r, C_g, C_b\} < T_{shadow2} \tag{1}$$

where $T_{shadow1}$ and $T_{shadow2}$ are thresholds specifying how low the intensity and color channel need to be for a shadow pixel. Because vegetations typically form low reflection regions, the shadow-map typically have many overlaps with the vege-map.

Edge-Map (M_{edge}): There are two kinds of edges in our edge-map, the true edges and the in-region edges. Among the initial edges returned by Canny operator, most are not actual boundaries of ROI (true edges) but rather edge responses within those regions (in-region edges) due to slope or textures of the roofs, items like air conditioners on the building's top, or even noises from image sensors.

The existence of in-region edges is one primary reason for over-segmentation. Moreover, since our ROI extraction process is a combination of region-driven and edge-driven, it is meaningful to distinguish those two kinds of edges from the very beginning. For urban scenes with regular buildings, an edge pixel is deemed as a part of true edges unless neighboring horizontal or vertical non-edge pixels have similar hues. HSV instead of RGB color space is used because neighboring pixels of either true or in-region edges tend to be affected by different lighting, and hue is generally more robust under such circumstance. The separation of in-region edges from true edges serves two purposes. First, while the true edges will become strict barrier during the region-growing process, those in-region pixels will not. The region-growing process is allowed to pass those in-region pixels with certain penalty to the confidence attribute. Second, we perform selectively smoothing based on the results of in-region edges. The color and intensity of each confirmed in-region edge pixel will be replaced by the average of its non-edge eight neighbors, helping us eliminate those in-region details which will otherwise compromise segmentation performance.

3.2   Region Growing

A uniform grid is placed on top of aerial images to determine seed locations. Each cell's center P is used as a tentative seed location and if it fails the seed conditions:

$$P \notin M_{vege} \text{ and } P \notin M_{shadow} \text{ and } P \notin M_{edge} \tag{2}$$

the cell is equally divided into four smaller cells and each center of those four sub-cells is tested again. It is possible that all five tests fail and the corresponding cell has no marker at all (e.g., when the cell is placed on trees).

During the region growing process, the current pixel ($p_{current}$) will be accepted and recursively expanded only if it meets the three expansion requirements:

1) The fractal error requirement: The theory is based on the properties of nature features to fit a fractional Brownian motion model. The definition of fractal error in image domain concerns two pixel locations (p_c and p_r). The measurement (e.g. intensity) difference of those two locations should be normally distributed with a mean of zero and a variance proportional to the 2H power of the Euclidean distance.

For intensity measurement, if the model fits, the average absolute intensity change across several pairs of pixels should follow exponential scaling:

$$E[|I(p_c) - I(p_r)|] = k | p_c - p_r |^H , \tag{3}$$

where E is the topological dimension (the number of independent variables) and in the image domain E = 2. k > 0 and 0 < H < 1 are two parameters. The parameter H is related to the fractal dimension D by: D = E + 1 - H.

The above equation can be linearized by logarithm:

$$\ln(E[I(p_c) - I(p_r)]) = \ln(k) + H \ln(| p_c - p_r |) . \tag{4}$$

With the linear equation, we can use machine learning technique to obtain the estimates of H and k. To obtain training data, a window operator is placed on one aerial image's non-building regions. After collecting pixel distances and their associated intensity changes in those regions, the least-squares linear regression is used to compute the optimized $\overline{H}$ and $\overline{k}$.

The individual fractal error for a pixel location p_c is calculated as the difference between the actual and estimated values from one of its neighboring pixel p_r:

$$F_{error}(p_c, p_r) = E[I(p_c) - I(p_r)] - \overline{k} \mid p_c - p_r \mid^{\overline{H}}.$$ (5)

Finally, the overall fractal error (OFE) for p_c is computed as the root mean square (RMS) of these individual errors using a local window centered at p_c:

$$OFE_{p_c} = \sqrt{\frac{1}{n}\sum_{p_r} F_{error}(p_c, p_r)},$$ (6)

where n is number of pixels considered in a local window.

A low OFE indicates that the center pixel's neighboring region is more likely to belong to a non-building region. Therefore, the center pixel will be excluded from the current growing region. A center pixel with sufficient high OFE will pass this expansion requirement. We never compute a fractal map for the entire aerial image because there are many regions in the aerial images that are never reached throughout the region-growing process due to one expansion requirement or another. Instead, we take the compute-on-demand-then-save way.

2) Requirements from AIMs: The current pixel will fail this requirement if $p_{current} \in M_{vege}$ or $p_{current} \in M_{shadow}$. The requirement for shadow-map can be relaxed in heavily urbanized scenes with long shadows overlapping buildings. If the current pixel belongs to an in-region edge, it will still pass this test though a penalty to this region's confidence needs to be taken. If the current pixel belongs to a true edge, it will be neither accepted nor further expanded.

3) The dynamic intensity range: Finally the current pixel's intensity must lie within the current dynamic intensity range, defined by two variables: the upper bound (U_{range}) and the lower bound (L_{range}). Both are initialized as the intensity of initial seed point. The range is expanded simultaneously with the region growing process with a limit for the range's length (*range_len*).

The current pixel will immediately pass the dynamic intensity range requirement without any update if:

$$L_{range} < I(p_{current}) < U_{range}$$ (7)

Otherwise, we introduce a tolerate threshold T_{range} as an expansion limit. The threshold is softened and fluctuated based on the current area to handle the case when the current point falls into a small distinct region contained in a large region we are interested in. The current pixel will still pass this requirement and update the range if: when the current area is smaller than the minimum acceptable area,

$$I(p_{current}) > L_{range} - (T_{range} + (-e^{(cur\_area - Area_{min})} + 1) \cdot Range_{max})$$

$$I(p_{current}) < U_{range} + (T_{range} + (-e^{(cur\_area - Area_{min})} + 1) \cdot Range_{max})$$ (8)

or when the current area is larger,

$$L_{range} - T_{range} < I(p_{current}) < U_{range} + T_{range},$$ (9)

where $Range_{max}$ is the maximum adjustable range for T_{range}.

Each pixel of the aerial image is associated with a 2-bit attribute called color preference. It is set to 1, 2 or 3 if the corresponding channel is dominant or 0 if no channel can obtain the dominate position. A region's color preference is set to be the color preference of the seed pixel. We use a more strict T_{range} value if the current expanding pixel has a color preference different from the growing region.

Those pixels that pass the above three expansion requirements will form the initial ROI. Regions with high confidence should be those clearly distinguished from surrounding background and consequently have small dynamic intensity range (*DIR*). Moreover, one region will have high uncertainty if it contains a large number of in-region edge pixels (*#IREP*). Therefore, we define a region *R*'s uncertainty as:

$$UCT(R) = (1 + \frac{DIR}{range\_len}) \cdot (\#IREP) \cdot \quad (10)$$

A larger region has higher chance to encounter in-region edge pixels. Avoiding this, we compute the uncertainty per pixel (*UPP*) as:

$$UPP(R) = \frac{UCT(R)}{R.area} \cdot \quad (11)$$

Initial segments with comparatively large *UPP* or small size / area will be discarded. The rest are called ROI candidates. *UPP* is also used in the region merging step and the final region matching component.

3.3   ROI Candidate Refinement

The actual number of buildings in the scene is typically less than half the number of ROI candidates because many candidates are false positives such as grounds and roads, and some buildings are over-segmented due to factors such as shadows. The candidate refinement consists of two steps handling the two problems respectively.

First, **learning-based region regulation** is to prune those ROI that are too irregular to become building regions or a part of such regions. For each ROI contour, we construct x and y histograms in the roation-relative frame and compute two attributes measuring their peak strength. Linear Discriminant Analysis is applied to the 5D augmented space to decide a linear boundary, which results a quadratic decision boundary in the original space. Around half of the ROI candidates are pruned by this step. Second, **region merging** is used to iteratively merge those regions that are spatially close to each other (especially when their color preferences are compatible) and form additional interest regions. Only ROI candidates with higher confidences (lower *UPP* attributes) will enter the region merging step because regions with high *UPP* already contain too many.

The outputs of our aerial image ROI extraction are interest regions (ROI$_{aerial}$) and their contour point lists. We also develop an efficient algorithm to extract ROI$_{range}$ from 3D LiDAR data (not covered in this paper).

4   Region Matching under Different Sensors

Given dominant and most-external ROI contours from both aerial images and 3D range data, we choose to use the shape context [15] as our contour descriptor because as a histogram-based approach, it is able to handle issues like pixel location error well. It can also tolerate various shape deformations (common situation in our case due to imperfect segmentation) while capturing the essence of similarity. Last, shape context generates one descriptor for each contour point, which enables us to establish point-to-point correspondences.

Each ROI's contour points are uniformly sampled to form a contour point list of fixed size (N_{CPL}). We ordered the list in a counter-clockwise manner starting from the point with the smallest y coordinate. Each CPL point j on ROI_i is described by its relative angle difference $\theta_{j,k}$ (to other points k of CPL and k≠j) and logarithm normalized distance $r_{j,k}$ using a log-polar histogram:

$$H_{i,j}(b_\theta, b_r) = \# of\{\theta_{j,k} \in bin(b_\theta) \text{ and } r_{j,k} \in bin(b_r) : 0 < k < N_{CPL_i}\} \qquad (12)$$

Scale invariance is achieved by distance normalization (we normalize distances using the size of ROI bounding boxes) and by placing shapes of different scales into histograms with a fixed number of r bins. For rotation invariance [7], tangent vectors are computed at each point and treated as x-axis so that the descriptors are based on a relative frame that automatically turns with tangent angles.

Despite many previous efforts in our ROI extraction stage, over-segmentation and segmentation-leaking can still be observed among ROI_a and ROI_r. Therefore it is still important to allow partial matching (fig. 5) in the region matching stage, achieved by forming partial descriptors in our algorithm. Continuous subsets of the original sampled contour points are used. We re-sample the partial contour and form new partial descriptors. Though imperfectly segmented regions will have better chance of matching through this, adding more descriptors will also enlarge the necessary searching space and raise the distinctiveness requirement. To better handle this trade-off, only those partial contours containing larger number of corners, consequently generating richer and more distinctive partial descriptors will be considered. To further restrict the total number of ROI descriptors, we generally compute partial descriptors only for ROI_r, which are relatively clean and more accurate than ROI_a.

Fig. 3. ROI partial matching

To search for optimal correspondences, for each ROI_r described as N_{CPL} histograms $H_r(j)$, all the $ROI_{a,i}$ ($0 \le i < num_a$) described as $H_{a,i}(j)$ are sequentially scanned. We efficiently measure the similarity of two ROI as the minimum average histogram distance (matching cost) of their corresponding CPL points.

$$\min_{0 \le i < num_a} \left\{ \frac{1}{N_{CPL}} \sum_{k=0}^{N_{CPL}} \sum_{j=0}^{N_{CPL}} \frac{H_r(j) - H_{a,i}((j+k)\%N_{CPL})}{H_r(j) + H_{a,i}((j+k)\%N_{CPL})} \right\} \tag{13}$$

The searching for minimum has a constant low computational cost of O(N_{CPL}) because CPL is organized as a counter-clock list of most-external contour points. Once one point's matching is determined, the rest points are automatically corresponded. There is no need to compute the solution for general bipartite matching problem.

After the searching process, each ROI_r is associated with its best and second best matched ROI_a. Among all those tentative correspondences, typically only 10%-40% are correct. The final task is to detect and correct the outliers.

We define "cost ratio" for each ROI_r as the matching cost ratio of its best matching over the second best matching. Lower cost ratio combined with lower *UPP* attributes for ROI indicates a higher matching confidence. For example, regular rectangle buildings are generally ambiguous and produce higher cost ratio because many buildings have similar shapes, while buildings of unique shapes will produce lower cost ratio and higher matching confidence.

For comparatively easy tests with a few distinguished buildings in the scene, correct initial matchings can be found by simply picking several ROI_r with the lowest cost ratio. Each selected ROI_r can contribute 10 uniformly sampled contour points providing a large set of point to point correspondences, based on which a global perspective transformation is estimated using least square method. The result is propagated to those unselected ROI_r using the recovered transformation and produces the final point to point correspondences across the entire scene.

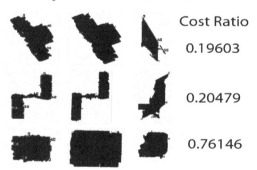

Cost Ratio

0.19603

0.20479

0.76146

Fig. 4. the 1st column is ROI contours extracted from range data, the 2nd and 3rd column are the best and second best matching from the input aerial image. Cost ratio for each row is given.

For challenging scenes, the correctness of initial matchings can not by solely decided by cost ratio. We propose a unified framework combining outlier removal and matching propagation together. We first construct a subset of matchings with relatively low cost ratio. This high-confidence subset of matchings serves as the foundation group of transformation estimation. For each iteration of the process, we randomly pick one pair of matchings from the subset and compute a global transformation using least square method. The remaining matchings are scanned to locate those consistent with the estimated transformation by comparing the point-to-point correspondences generated by region matching with the matching propagation results. The transformation matrix is updated every time the size of consistent set increases. We compare and evaluate the results of different iterations using two criteria: the number of propagated matching points that are within the spatial range of ROI_a, and the average *UPP* of the consistent set.

Throughout the process, global context is implicitly taken into consideration. The whole process runs iteratively until a global transformation meeting some predefined criteria is found, in which case matchings have already been propagated to all buildings across the scene, or when the list is exhausted, the system will claim that no correspondence could be established.

5   Experimental Results

The proposed registration method was tested using aerial images and LiDAR data of Atlanta, Baltimore, Denver and Los Angeles. Both real and synthesized data were tested. Though most LiDAR data we used are current and of high resolution, some (e.g. Los Angeles dataset) are captured years ago with very low resolution and some recently built buildings missing from the range data such as the two bottom left buildings in figure 7(c). As a local region based approach, our method can robustly handle such situation common for historic data.

Most aerial images we used are captured in early years with low resolution and from various sources (e.g. returned from online image search engine) and no georeference data can be tracked at all. Others are casually cropped from satellite images. Some testing areas are heavily urbanized with a large number of close buildings while others have sparsely distributed buildings but a lot of vegetations. To focus on different sensors problems in this work, the sides of buildings could be visible but should be comparatively small (Details about how our whole 2D-3D registration system registers images from nadir views to oblique, e.g. [16], are not covered in this paper.). Other than that, we made no assumption about the initial alignment. The images may have any in-plane rotation, even upside down. The scale difference from aerial image to depth image ranges from 0.3 to 3. Perspective and skew distortions could be applied. Concerning location errors, the corresponding building might lie on the opposite corner of the image. The inputs data may originally have no correspondence. Our method is robust enough to handle those factors challenging to general matching and registration system.

Last, the proposed method had been successfully integrated into two application systems for urban rendering and UAV localization respectively.

5.1   ROI Extraction Results

Figure 5 and 6 show the color-coded ROI extraction results from aerial and depth images, compared with results generated by classical segmentation algorithm [10]. Our ROI extraction result meets the particular need of our registration system considerably better than others. The returned segmented regions are more focused on interest buildings and can provide more accurate dominant external contours.

For setting parameters, we choose *UPP* and *OFE* in rather conservative ways only to remove those ROI that are clearly false positives. *T_range* is dynamically related to the current ROI size. We found changing of *range_len* have no significant impact on the segmentation results. Those ROI distinctive from background can robustly be obtained unless some unreasonable values are used, while we were not able to find a

Fig. 5. ROI extraction results (from aerial images)

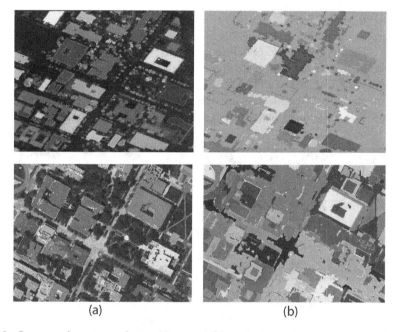

(a)   (b)

Fig. 6. Segmentation comparison. (a) our ROI extraction algorithm; (b) graph-based segmentation. 1st row for depth image, 2nd row for aerial image.

universal value that can possibly help all the rest ambiguous ones. An average of more than 80% buildings can be correctly extracted from 3D range data during our experiments, while the percentage for correct ROI extraction from aerial images is around 60%. Nonetheless, instead of asking for perfect image segmentation, which is still not feasible today, we also believe the important thing is "how to make the best use of imperfect segmentation results" [8]. In our case, how to establish correct matchings at least for parts of the scene and expand the partial results to the rest.

5.2   2D-3D Registration

First, for registration accuracy, the final average pixel registration error of our method is typically within 5 pixels even for propagated matchings. Methods using high-level features (better suitable for handling different sensors problem) such as curves and regions typically don't have an accuracy as high as pixel-based methods (e.g. SIFT has sub-pixel level accuracy). That's primarily because of the difficulty of locating exact pixel locations inside high-level features due to many challenging factors, e.g. in our case the influence of shadows, the segmentation leaking and breaking, etc.

Second, like other registration and matching systems, the successful registration of our system also relies on the existence and acquisition of proper matching primitives. In our case, three properly segmented ROI repeated in both 2D image and 3D range data sides are sufficient. This requirement could, sometimes, be difficult to meet either basically because the lack of such primitives in the scene, in which case even human found the registration difficult or impossible, or because such primitives can not be accurately acquired through segmentation technique although it "seems" obvious to human observers.

Our test set currently consists of 918 images, averaging over 200 images for urban areas of each city. Roughly 60% are real images from diverse sources. Large synthesized geometric distortions are applied to those real images to generate the rest. Overall, our method achieves around 56% of success rate for the four city's dataset. To the best of our knowledge, there is no existing registration method that can achieve similar performance without support from positioning hardware. The closest one is: the

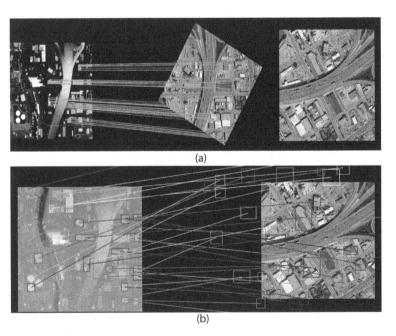

(a)

(b)

Fig. 7. Registration results of our proposed approach. (a) initial correspondences (left: normalized depth image; right: input aerial image; middle: aerial image wrapped by the recovered transformation); (b) the final results after matching propagation visualized by the bounding boxes and centers of all interest regions' point-to-point correspondences. (c) distorted and partially missing inputs due to historic data. (d) results registering oblique views.

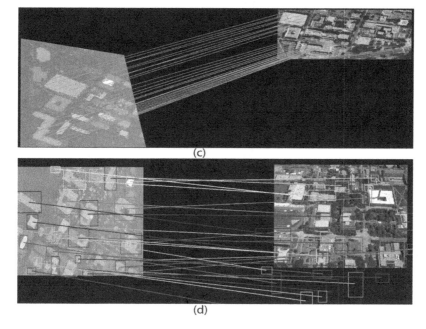

(c)

(d)

Fig. 7. (*continued*)

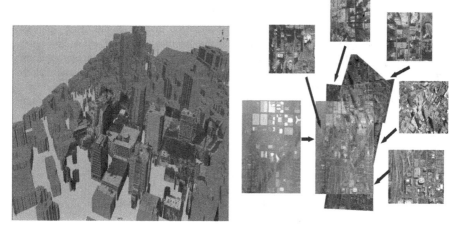

Fig. 8. Apply the proposed approach to urban rendering (left) and UAV localization (right)

system proposed in [5] can directly register 5 camera images out of a test set of 22 images to ground scanned range data. Both methods are working on 2D-3D registration problem without positioning hardware support.

Concerning efficiency, regardless of offline training our entire registration process of one single test for a scene containing around 30 buildings takes roughly one minute in a P4 3.4G PC with a peak memory occupation of 35M.

6   Conclusion

This paper presents our automatic 2D-3D registration method. We provide details for the aerial image ROI extraction component as well as the region matching. Future directions include the propagation of correct registrations to those aerial images that failed the initial registration by iteratively expansion and refinement.

References

1. Lowe, D.: Distinctive image features from scale-invariant keypoints. International Journal of Computer Vision (2004)
2. Zhao, W., Nister, D., Hsu, S.: Alignment of continuous video onto 3d point clouds. IEEE Transactions on Pattern Analysis and Machine Intelligence 27(8), 1305–1318 (2005)
3. Ding, M., Lyngbaek, K., Zakhor, A.: Automatic registration of aerial imagery with untextured 3D LiDAR models. In: Computer Vision and Pattern Recognition, pp. 1–8 (2008)
4. Fruh, C., Zakhor, A.: An automated method for large-scale, ground-based city model acquisition. International Journal of Computer Vision 60(1), 5–24 (2004)
5. Liu, L., Stamos, I.: Automatic 3D to 2D registration for the photorealistic rendering of urban scenes. In: Computer Vision and Pattern Recognition, pp. 137–143 (June 2005)
6. Liu, L., Yu, G., Wolberg, G., Zokai, S.: Multiview Geometry for Texture Mapping 2D Images Onto 3D Range Data. In: IEEE Conference on Computer Vision and Pattern Recognition, vol. 2, pp. 2293–2300 (2006)
7. Belongie, S., Malik, J., Puzicha, J.: Shape matching and object recognition using shape contexts. Technical Report UCB//CSD-00-1128, UC Berkeley (January 2001)
8. Comanicu, D., Meer, P.: Mean shift: A robust approach toward feature space analysis. IEEE Transactions on Pattern Analysis aind Machine Intelligence 24, 603–619 (2002)
9. Hedau, V., Arora, H., Ahuja, N.: Matching Images under Unstable Segmentation. In: Proceedings of IEEE Computer Society Conference on Computer Vision and Pattern Recognition, Anchorage, AL (2008)
10. Felzenszwalb, P.F., Huttenlocher, D.P.: Effie Graph-Based Image Segmentation. International Journal of Computer Vision 59(2) (2004)
11. Mandelbrot, B.B.: The Fractal Geometry of Nature. W.H. Freeman and Co., New York (1983) ISBN: 0716711869
12. Solka, J.L., Marchette, D.J., Wallet, B.C., Irwin, V.L., Rogers, G.W.: Identification of man-made regions in unmanned aerial vehicle imagery and videos. IEEE Transactions on Pattern Analysis and Machine Intelligence (1998)
13. Wang, Q., You, S.: Explore Multiple Clues for Urban Images Matching. In: International Conference on Image Processing (September 2010)
14. Cao, G., Yang, X., Mao, Z.: A two-stage level set evolution scheme for man-made objects detection in aerial images. In: IEEE Computer Society Conference on Computer Vision and Pattern Recognition, pp. 474–479 (June 2005)
15. Belongie, S., Malik, J., Puzicha, J.: Shape matching and object recognition using shape contexts. IEEE Transactions on Pattern Analysis and Machine Intelligence 24(4), 509–522 (2002)
16. Wang, Q., You, S.: A Vision-based 2D-3D Registration System. In: IEEE Winter Vision Meeting, WACV, Salt Lake City (December 2009)

Region Graphs for Organizing Image Collections

Alexander Ladikos[1], Edmond Boyer[2], Nassir Navab[1], and Slobodan Ilic[1]

[1] Chair for Computer Aided Medical Procedures, Technische Universität München
[2] Perception Team, INRIA Grenoble Rhône-Alpes

Abstract. In this paper we consider large image collections and their organization into meaningful data structures upon which applications can be build (e.g. navigation or reconstruction). In contrast to structures that only reflect local relationships between pairs of images we propose to account for the information an image brings to a collection with respect to all other images. Our approach builds on abstracting from image domains and focusing on image regions, thereby reducing the influence of outliers and background clutter. We introduce a graph structure based on these regions which encodes the overlap between them. The contribution of an image to a collection is then related to the amount of overlap of its regions with the other images in the collection. We demonstrate our graph based structure with several applications: image set reduction, canonical view selection and image-based navigation. The data sets used in our experiments range from small examples to large image collections with thousands of images.

1 Introduction

Dealing with large image collections has recently become a subject of interest in the vision community. It includes such diverse topics as 3D reconstruction [1,2], canonical view selection [3,4], image-based navigation [5] and image retrieval [6,7] among others. While applications in this domain can be very different, a key issue that all must address is how to efficiently organize and handle the available and often redundant data. In image retrieval, for instance, state-of-the-art approaches deal with image datasets containing up to one million images [6] and even in 3D reconstruction applications the sizes of the image sets grow rapidly, reaching up to 150,000 images [2]. Most approaches in this field organize images with graphs where edges relate images that share information and edge weights depend on the application. For instance [8] uses a graph where the edge weight is based on the covariance of the camera positions, while [4] weights the edges by the number of inlier matches between images. The resulting data structures reveal little on how informative an image is with respect to all other images. In this work, we take a different strategy and propose a data structure, region graphs, that encodes spatial relationships between an image and a collection of images. This provides a basis upon which various applications can be build, navigation or reconstruction for instance, where not all but only the most informative images are of interest.

K.N. Kutulakos (Ed.): ECCV 2010 Workshops, Part II, LNCS 6554, pp. 239–252, 2012.
© Springer-Verlag Berlin Heidelberg 2012

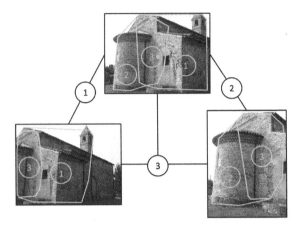

Fig. 1. Region graph for three images. Overlapping regions are denoted as 1, 2 and 3.

The central idea behind our approach is to use image regions and their redundancies over an image set to define a global hierarchy in the set. More precisely, we consider the overlap between images, where we consider the overlap to be the image regions which contain the same part of the scene. This is a natural criterion, based on objective evidence, that does not require any information about the 3D structure of the scene. It also adapts to the sampling of the scene given by the images. The overlapping regions are then used to build a graph relating all images spatially. The graph contains two kinds of nodes, one representing images and the other representing overlapping regions. Each region is connected with an edge to the images it is contained in. This means that region and image nodes are alternating on any given path through the graph. Using this graph we can efficiently represent the spatial relationship between the regions and images and identify redundancies over regions. This allows us to model the importance of regions shared by many images and to identify less important regions shared only by few or even no images. These less important regions are often small and not very essential to the scene. They typically contain background or other irrelevant information.

Figure 1 shows an exemplary region graph constructed from a three image data set. There are three image nodes and three region nodes in the graph, representing the images and the distinct overlapping regions, i.e. regions visible in a set of images. Using the region graphs as a basis we build applications for image set reduction, canonical view selection and image-based navigation. We tested our method on several real data sets ranging from a few dozen to thousands of images. The results obtained show that the data structure we propose reveals intrinsic properties of an image set that are useful for various applications.

In the remainder of the paper we first discuss the related work in section 2. We then proceed to describe the construction of the region graphs in section 3 and show some exemplary applications built on them in section 4. We present results in section 5 and conclude with section 6.

2   Related Work

In the last few years many papers dealing with the issue of large image collections have been published. Most of them focus on specific applications, for instance image retrieval [6,7,9] or 3D reconstruction [1,4,2]. In the 3D reconstruction literature one of the first major works on this topic was the Photo Tourism project [1]. In that paper a large set of images taken from Internet photo collections is used for performing a point-based 3D reconstruction of the scene. An exhaustive pairwise matching followed by an incremental bundle adjustment phase have been used both for the reduction of the image set and for 3D reconstruction. Follow-up work focused on navigating through large image collections [5], summarizing the scene by selecting canonical views [3] and speeding up the initial reconstruction process by building skeletal graphs over the image set [8]. While an image graph was used for instance in [8] it was designed for the goal of finding a better subset of images for the initial reconstruction. Li *et al.* [4] presented an application for performing reconstructing and recognition on large image sets. They construct a so called iconic scene graph which relates canonical views of the scene and use it for 3D reconstruction. The edge weights used are the number of inlier matches. Recently Farenzena *et al.* [10] proposed a hierarchical image organization method based on the overlap between images. The overlap is used as an image similarity measure used to assemble the images into a dendrogramm. The hierarchy given by the dendrogramm is then used for a hierarchical bundle adjustment phase. In this regard that work is interesting, because it also considers a global criterion. However, it is focused on Structure from Motion and not on defining global representations of image collections. Schaffalitzky [11] *et al.* also present some work dealing with handling large unordered data sets. They focus on the task of performing a 3D reconstruction from unordered image sets and only briefly mention image navigation, which they base on homographies.

Contribution. Most existing work organizes images with respect to the application, which is often 3D reconstruction. We follow a different strategy and organize images with respect to the regions they share. This allows us to score images according to the information they bring and without 3D reconstruction. Subsequent applications can then easily build on the region graph structure, even navigation as shown later in section 4. We are not aware of any attempt to build such an intermediate structure based on 2D cues only. We think that these structures will become a key component when dealing with large and highly redundant image datasets.

3   Building Region Graphs

In this section we describe how to construct region graphs. The most important construction principle is to identify overlapping regions in the images. Overlapping regions are regions in different images showing the same part of the scene. Figure 2 gives an example. For instance region 1 is an overlapping region shared by images A, B and E. To identify this overlapping region, the intersection of the overlap between image A and E and the overlap between image B and E has to be computed. Each overlapping region is represented as a *region node* in the graph. The images are represented in the graph as *image nodes*. Each region node is connected to the images in which it is detected. In the example of Figure 2 this means that node 1 representing region 1 is connected to the nodes of images A, B and E. In the following sections the graph construction process is described in more detail. The construction process is summarized in algorithm 1.

3.1   Identifying Overlap between Images

The first step in the graph construction is to identify the overlap between the images. This is accomplished in a multi-step process. First we extract features using a scale-invariant interest-point detector on all input images [12]. We then match the features among the images. Since we are dealing with very large image sets, performing an exhaustive pairwise matching is computationally infeasible. Therefore we use vocabulary trees [13] to perform a preselection among the images (in our experiments we use the implementation provided by [14]). For every image we retrieve the k (we use $k = 10$ in all our experiments) most similar images using the vocabulary tree.

This preprocessing step significantly reduces the size of the set of image pairs which have to be matched. The matching is performed using the standard SIFT distance ratio on the descriptors and the resulting putative matches are pruned using epipolar constraints in a RANSAC framework. Given the feature correspondences between two images we compute the convex hull spanned by the matched features in each image. This is illustrated in Figure 3. The area enclosed by the convex hull in each image is the overlap between the two images.

3.2   Identifying Overlapping Regions

After performing the matching, we generally obtain several different convex hulls per image, one per matched image. In general these convex hulls will overlap with

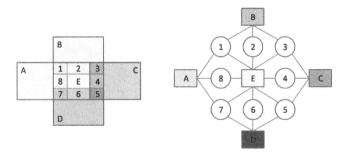

Fig. 2. Graph construction for a synthetic example containing five images (A to E) which create 8 different overlap regions

each other. We want to identify each overlapping region created by the intersection of these convex hulls. In the following let CH_i^j be the convex hull spanned in image i by the features matching image j. To determine unique overlapping regions we assign each CH_i^j a label (i, j) to indicate that this region is shared by images i and j. When two regions CH_i^k and CH_i^l overlap, the common region will receive the label $L = (i, k, l)$. After performing this labeling for all convex hulls every intersection will have an associated label L. The image is then subdivided into regions sharing the same label. While it is possible to perform these computations directly on the image by discretizing the convex hulls, we chose to perform the computations purely geometrically by representing the convex hulls as polygons and using CGAL to perform the intersection operations. This has the advantage of being image resolution independent and does not require to allocate a discretization space for every image, which would be very memory intensive for large image data sets. Finally every identified region is merged into a region list storing its label and the images in which it was detected.

3.3 Constructing the Region Graph

After all overlapping regions have been identified, the region list contains all the information needed to build the region graph. It is constructed by inserting one image node per image and one region node for every entry in the region list. The region nodes are subsequently connected to the image nodes specified in the region list. The weight of the edges connecting the region nodes to the image nodes is application specific. One generic choice is to assign the normalized size of the region, defined as the size of the overlapping region divided by the image size, as an edge weight. This is the edge weight which is used in most of our experiments.

4 Using Region Graphs

In this section we discuss several applications based on the proposed region graphs. The first application is image-based navigation which allows the user to

Fig. 3. The convex hull of the set of matched features between two images defines the regions considered during graph construction

---

Algorithm 1. Graph Construction

1: Extract feature points on all images I
2: Use a vocabulary tree to select the k most similar images for each image
3: Perform robust matching
4: **for** each image i in I **do**
5:    **for** each image j matched to i **do**
6:       Compute the convex hull CH_i^j and assign it the label (i, j)
7:    **end for**
8:    Intersect the convex hulls in image i to obtain the overlapping regions
9:    Add overlapping regions into region list
10: **end for**
11: **for** each image i in I **do**
12:    Create an image node in the graph
13: **end for**
14: **for** each region entry l in the region list **do**
15:    Create a region node and connect it to the image nodes of the images in which it was detected
16:    Set the weight of the outgoing edges according to the application criteria, e.g. the normalized size of the region
17: **end for**

---

traverse the image set in a spatially consistent way. The second application is image set reduction. Its goal is to reduce the size of the data set while retaining as much information as possible. The final application we are considering is canonical view selection. In this application we want to find a small orthogonal subset of images which summarizes the whole image set.

4.1   Image Set Reduction

The goal of image set reduction is to remove redundant and non-contributing images from the data set. In [8] for instance a subset of an image set is selected for performing a 3D reconstruction. However, the graph structure and edge-measure were application specific and based on the covariance of the camera positions. We would like to define a more general measure for the information content of an image. Intuitively an image which contains many regions shared with other images is more important for the data set than an image having little overlap with the other images in the data set. We therefore formalize an information criterion for an image i and its associated image node v_i in the region graph as

$$\rho(v_i) = \sum_{r \in N(v_i)} \sum_{e \in E(r)} w(e) \tag{1}$$

where $N(v_i)$ is the set of neighboring region nodes of image node v_i, $E(r)$ is the set of edges in the region graph connected to node r and $w(e)$ is the weight of edge e. The intuition behind this information criterion is that an image which contains many regions which are also present in many other images is more

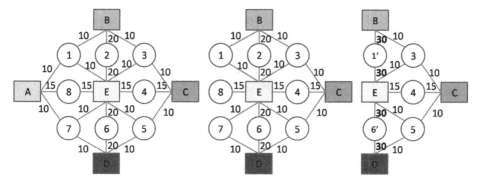

Fig. 4. Removal process on the synthetic example given in Figure 2. The image with the least score among all images is removed first (left). Leaf nodes created by the removal of the image are removed (middle). Newly created duplicate paths are joined. (right).

important than an image which only contains few regions shared with few other images. The choice of which images to remove is directly related to this criterion. At each step of the removal process the image with the smallest image score is removed. In Figure 4 we give an example of the image removal process in the graph. Once the image to be removed has been identified, its corresponding node and all incident edges are removed from the graph. The resulting graph might then contain leaf nodes (node 8 in the example) which are also removed. Due to the removal of an image it can also happen that two previously distinct regions collapse into one. This can be seen in the graph through the existence of several identical paths between two image nodes (paths $E \to 1 \to B$ and $E \to 2 \to B$ in Figure 4 (middle)). These paths are joined and their edge weights summed up to obtain a region node representing the new region. All these computations can purely be based on the graph. No recomputations are needed. This is due to the explicit representation of regions in the graph. If only images were represented in the graph it would have to be recomputed after every image removal.

4.2   Canonical Views

Canonical views are views which are of high importance in a given image set. They show parts of the scene which are captured in many images (e.g. because they are considered to be very important). We want to automatically find these important parts of the scene and select one representative view, i.e. the canonical view, for each of them. Some previous work on this subject was done in [3]. In that work the criterion for selecting a canonical view was based on the visibility of the points in the scene. A canonical view was defined to be an image which is very different from all other canonical views in terms of the scene points it observes. This criterion was optimized by a greedy approach. We have a similar definition of canonical views. However, we do not assume any explicit visibility

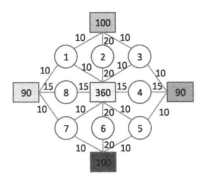

Fig. 5. Canonical view selection on the synthetic example given in Figure 2. The numbers inside the image nodes indicate the image score computed according to equation 1. The central image has a maximum score in its neighborhood and is therefore selected as the canonical view.

information to be available. We also do not perform a greedy optimization, but instead deduce the canonical views directly from the region graphs.

Intuitively the images having the highest amount of overlap with the image set should be selected as canonical views. However, we would like to avoid selecting multiple images of the same part of the scene. One natural way of including this constraint is to find maxima over the graph. Each image node v_i is assigned a weight using the score function given in equation 1. Only the nodes which have a score bigger than all their neighboring image nodes are selected. These nodes then constitute the canonical views. The neighboring image nodes are defined to be all the image nodes which are only separated by a region node, i.e. two images are considered to be neighbors in the graph when they share a common region. Figure 5 gives an example.

4.3 Image-Based Navigation

The goal of image-based navigation is to allow the user to traverse the image set in a spatially consistent order. For instance the user can choose to view the image to the right or to the left of the current image. In order to allow such a navigation the spatial relationship among the images has to be determined. While some prior work [5] assumes the availability of a 3D scene reconstruction we base the navigation purely on the images. This is achieved by considering the spatial positions of matching regions in the images. To represent this information in the graph we augment the edges with information about the spatial relationship of the associated nodes. In practice we assign each edge in the region graph a three-dimensional vector $(x\,y\,z)^\top$ which describes the relative position and scale of the region within the image. The position inside the image is specified with respect to the image center and normalized to the range $[-1; 1] \times [-1; 1]$. The first two components of the vector describe the horizontal and vertical position, while the third one represents the scale. They are computed by considering the

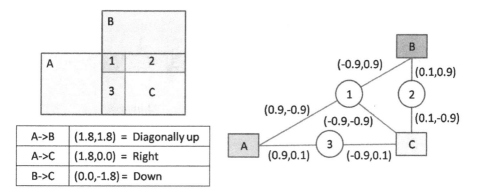

A->B	(1.8,1.8) = Diagonally up
A->C	(1.8,0.0) = Right
B->C	(0.0,-1.8) = Down

Fig. 6. Illustration of the image navigation. The region graph is augmented with the computed relative positions of the regions within the image. For determining the relative motion between two images all shared regions are considered and their relative motions are averaged. The resulting relative motions between the images are shown in the table. Note that for clarity scale is not considered in this example.

position of the center of gravity of the convex hull in the image. Let $\mathbf{g}_i = (g_i^x\, g_i^y)^\top$ represent the center of gravity of the region in image i and let w_i and h_i be the size of the image in pixels. Then the relative position of the convex hull inside the image is given by

$$\mathbf{p}_i = \begin{pmatrix} \frac{2g_i^x - w_i}{w_i} \\ \frac{2g_i^y - h_i}{h_i} \end{pmatrix} \qquad (2)$$

To represent the scale we consider the relative area of the region with respect to the image area. This makes us independent of the image resolution. Let A_i be the number of pixels in the convex hull and I_i the total number of pixels in image i. Then the scale is given by

$$s_i = \frac{A_i}{I_i} \qquad (3)$$

The region movement (position and scale) for a region shared by images i and j is computed as

$$x_{i->j} = -(p_j^x - p_i^x) \qquad (4)$$
$$y_{i->j} = p_j^y - p_i^y \qquad (5)$$
$$z_{i->j} = s_j - s_i \qquad (6)$$

To navigate the user specifies a spatial movement in the image plane (two dimensions) and a zoom-in/zoom-out movement (one dimension). This results in the desired movement vector. To find the next image to move to, the movement between the current and all neighboring images is computed. Given two images the relative movement is given by the average of the region movement of the regions shared by the images. The image whose region movement agrees most

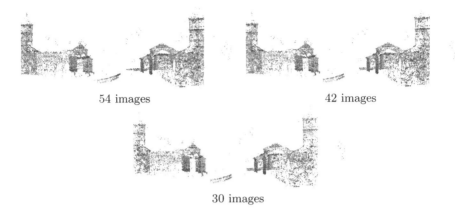

54 images   42 images

30 images

Fig. 7. Image set reduction for the *pozzoveggiani* data set. The first row shows the full reconstruction, while the second and third row show the results after removing 12 and 24 of the 54 images respectively.

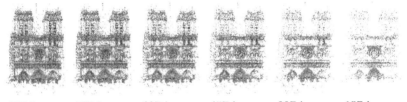

157 images   757 images   607 images   457 images   307 images   157 images

Fig. 8. Image set reduction for the *Notre Dame* data set. The first image shows the full reconstruction (907 images). Each following image shows the result after 150 images were removed from the previous reconstruction.

with the user motion (in the sense of the dot-product) is then displayed to the user. Figure 6 gives an example of how the relative movement between images is computed using the shared regions. Since we explicitly represent the regions in our graph it is also possible for the user to select a specific region of interest inside the image and to perform the navigation with respect to this region instead of the whole image.

5   Experimental Results

To validate our approach we performed experiments on several data sets of different sizes. In the following we will first briefly describe each data set used and then show results for the different applications we are proposing. The first two data sets we used were provided by [10]. The *pozzoveggiani* data set contains 54 images of a church and the *piazzaerbe* data set contains 259 images of a big town square. The other data set we used was the *Notre Dame* data set provided

Fig. 9. Canonical views for the *pozzoveggiani* data set. One image was selected for each side of the church.

Fig. 10. Canonical views for the *pozzoveggiani* data set as produced by [3]. The parameters for obtaining this result had to be manually adjusted until a reasonable result was obtained.

by [4]. It contains 6248 images of the Notre Dame cathedral in Paris collected from Flickr.

The first step common to all application is the construction of the region graph. The construction times (excluding feature extraction and matching) were 1 minute for *pozzoveggiani*, 3 minutes for *piazzaerbe* and 38 minutes for *Notre Dame* on a 2.66 GHz Intel QuadCore CPU (only one core was used). Most of the time was spent on intersecting the convex hulls.

5.1 Image Set Reduction

To show the validity of the reduction we first perform a 3D reconstruction with the full data set and then compare it to a reconstruction on the reduced data set. Figure 7 shows the results for the *pozzoveggiani* data set. The first row shows two views of the reconstruction obtained on the full data set, while the next two rows show the results obtained after removing 12 and 24 images respectively. While the point cloud does get sparser the whole structure is still present.

Figure 8 shows the results we obtained on the *Notre Dame* data set. We computed the connected components of the region graph and used the biggest

Fig. 11. Canonical views for the *piazzaerbe* data set

Fig. 12. Image-based navigation on the *pozzoveggiani* data set. Starting from the top left image the user always moves to the right, thereby circling the church once.

one (907 images). The first image shows the full reconstruction. Each of the following reconstructions was obtained by removing 150 images from the previous one. Again the point cloud gets sparser, but the overall structure of the scene is retained.

5.2   Canonical Views

The results of the canonical view selection on the *pozzoveggiani* data set are shown in Figure 9. One view is selected for each side of the church. To compare to previous work we implemented the canonical view selection method described by Simon *et al.* [3]. The results of their method are shown in Figure 10. They are comparable to ours. The first four canonical views are virtually identical, while the last two are not very essential to the scene. Since Simon's method uses two tuning parameters, it was necessary to manually adjust them until a reasonable result was obtained. Their method also requires the availability of

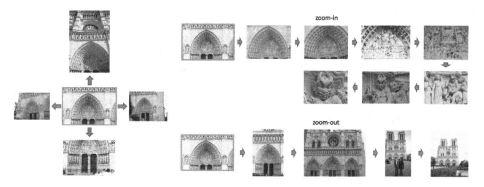

Fig. 13. Image-based navigation on the *Notre Dame* data set. The user starts with the highlighted image and then performs several navigation operations resulting in the shown images. The images on the left show the results of a spatial navigation (left, right, up and down) while the images on the right show the results of zooming in and out respectively.

visibility information for each scene point, which is not always easy to obtain. Our method on the other hand is parameter free.

The results of the canonical view selection on the *piazzaerbe* data set are shown in Figure 11. The selected images are very distinct from each other. Only the fountain and the pagoda are seen twice in the images. However, they are pictured from approximately opposite sides and have a completely different background.

Since we initially only use a sparse set of matches (i.e. we do not match every image to every other image), the region graph is also only sparsely connected. This means that similar images might not be connected in the region graph. The effect of this is that similar images might be selected as canonical views. Therefore we apply the canonical view selection twice. Once on the initial sparse graph and then on the obtained canonical views after performing an exhaustive pairwise matching on them. This is generally not very computationally expensive, since the number of canonical views is comparatively small compared to the size of the original data set. Optionally a vocabulary tree could be used to speed up the matching.

5.3   Image-Based Navigation

Figure 12 shows the results for image-based navigation obtained on the *pozzoveggiani* data set. The user starts with the top left image and then continues to move to the right, circling the church once.

Figure 13 shows the results of an image-based navigation on the *Notre Dame* data set. On the left the user starts with the highlighted image and then navigates in the direction of the arrows (left, right, up and down). On the right the user performs a zoom-in and a zoom-out movement respectively. Note the number of scale levels traversed during the zoom-in and zoom-out operation.

6   Conclusion

We presented a novel framework for organizing large spatially related image collections. Our approach is based on the overlapping regions between multiple images. We represent these regions and the images in a graph and use this graph as a foundation for several different applications related to organizing large image collections, such as image-based navigation, image set reduction and canonical view selection. Using these applications we presented results on several image sets of different sizes, showing the validity of our image organization approach.

References

1. Snavely, N., Seitz, S.M., Szeliski, R.: Modeling the world from internet photo collections. International Journal of Computer Vision 80, 189–210 (2008)
2. Agarwal, S., Snavely, N., Simon, I., Seitz, S.M., Szeliski, R.: Building Rome in a day. In: International Conference on Computer Vision (2009)
3. Simon, I., Snavely, N., Seitz, S.M.: Scene summarization for online image collections. In: International Conference on Computer Vision (2007)
4. Li, X., Wu, C., Zach, C., Lazebnik, S., Frahm, J.-M.: Modeling and Recognition of Landmark Image Collections Using Iconic Scene Graphs. In: Forsyth, D., Torr, P., Zisserman, A. (eds.) ECCV 2008, Part I. LNCS, vol. 5302, pp. 427–440. Springer, Heidelberg (2008)
5. Snavely, N., Garg, R., Seitz, S.M., Szeliski, R.: Finding paths through the world's photos. ACM Transactions on Graphics (Proceedings of SIGGRAPH 2008) 27, 11–21 (2008)
6. Jegou, H., Douze, M., Schmid, C.: Hamming Embedding and Weak Geometric Consistency for Large Scale Image Search. In: Forsyth, D., Torr, P., Zisserman, A. (eds.) ECCV 2008, Part I. LNCS, vol. 5302, pp. 304–317. Springer, Heidelberg (2008)
7. Philbin, J., Chum, O., Isard, M., Sivic, J., Zisserman, A.: Lost in quantization: Improving particular object retrieval in large scale image databases. In: IEEE Conference on Computer Vision and Pattern Recognition (2008)
8. Snavely, N., Seitz, S.M., Szeliski, R.: Skeletal graphs for efficient structure from motion. In: IEEE Conference on Computer Vision and Pattern Recognition (2008)
9. Whyte, O., Sivic, J., Zisserman, A.: Get out of my picture! internet-based inpainting. In: British Machine Vision Conference (2009)
10. Farenzena, M., Fusiello, A., Gherardi, R.: Structure-and-motion piepline on a hierarchical cluster tree. In: IEEE International Workshop on 3-D Digital Imaging and Modeling (2009)
11. Schaffalitzky, F., Zisserman, A.: Multi-view Matching for Unordered Image Sets, or How Do I Organize My Holiday Snaps? In: Heyden, A., Sparr, G., Nielsen, M., Johansen, P. (eds.) ECCV 2002, Part I. LNCS, vol. 2350, pp. 414–431. Springer, Heidelberg (2002)
12. Lowe, D.: Distinctive image features from scale-invariant keypoints. International Journal of Computer Vision 60, 91–110 (2004)
13. Nister, D., Stewenius, H.: Scalable recognition with a vocabulary tree. In: IEEE Conference on Computer Vision and Pattern Recognition (2006)
14. Fraundorfer, F., Wu, C., Frahm, J.-M., Pollefeys, M.: Visual word based location recognition in 3D models using distance augmented weighting. In: Fourth International Symposium on 3D Data Processing, Visualization and Transmission (2008)

Automatic Registration of Oblique Aerial Images with Cadastral Maps

Martin Habbecke and Leif Kobbelt

Computer Graphics Group, RWTH Aachen University, Germany
http://www.graphics.rwth-aachen.de

Abstract. In recent years, oblique aerial images of urban regions have become increasingly popular for 3D city modeling, texturing, and various cadastral applications. In contrast to images taken vertically to the ground, they provide information on building heights, appearance of facades, and terrain elevation. Despite their widespread availability for many cities, the processing pipeline for oblique images is not fully automatic yet. Especially the process of precisely registering oblique images with map vector data can be a tedious manual process. We address this problem with a registration approach for oblique aerial images that is fully automatic and robust against discrepancies between map and image data. As input, it merely requires a cadastral map and an arbitrary number of oblique images. Besides rough initial registrations usually available from GPS/INS measurements, no further information is required, in particular no information about the terrain elevation.

1 Introduction

Aerial images of urban regions have been in wide-spread use for various applications for more than a century, with a strong focus on images taken vertically to the ground (i.e. nadir images). In contrast to vertical images, aerial images taken at an oblique angle with respect to the ground have the important advantage of providing information on building heights, appearance of facades, and terrain elevation. Thus, they are not only more intuitive for untrained viewers [1] but enable new kinds of applications like 3D city modeling [2–4], texturing [5–7], dense stereo matching [8], or photo augmentation [9], which are not possible in this form with vertical images. In recent years oblique aerial images have been created in large-scale projects even for medium-sized cities [1] and have become widely available e.g. as "bird's-eye view" in Microsoft's internet map service [10]. The combination of oblique images with cadastral maps is of special interest since it not only simplifies standard cadastral applications [1] but has the potential of strongly improving 3D city reconstruction techniques [2–4] in terms of automation and speed. However, the established standard tools for vertical aerial images cannot easily be applied to oblique imagery due to the varying scale of pixels across an image caused by perspective foreshortening, the strongly changing appearance between different views, and the inevitable (self-)occlusion of buildings. While the registration of oblique aerial images with

K.N. Kutulakos (Ed.): ECCV 2010 Workshops, Part II, LNCS 6554, pp. 253–266, 2012.
© Springer-Verlag Berlin Heidelberg 2012

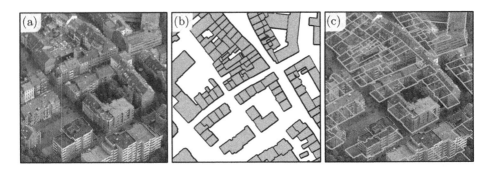

Fig. 1. Problem statement: Given a set of oblique aerial images (a) and a cadastral map (b), we compute the registration of the images with the map as shown in (c). Besides rough initial registrations, no further information is required. In particular, the cadastral map does not contain terrain elevation or building height information.

vertical images [11] and with LiDAR data [6, 7] has been studied before, the precise registration with cadastral maps and the process of *conflation* [12] (i.e., the removal of misalignment between images and map vector data) is still a challenging problem for oblique aerial images that has not been automated yet [13]. This problem is amplified by the fact that, instead of a single vertical image, at least four oblique views from different directions are required to fully cover individual objects. Thus, there is a strong need for a fully automated processing pipeline that includes a robust and precise geo-registration.

In this paper, we address the problem of registering oblique aerial images (cf. Fig. 1a) with digital cadastral maps containing the footprints of buildings (cf. Fig. 1b). The set of images is assumed to be sparse with the viewing directions being just the four cardinal directions since images of this kind are widely available. To allow for a robust registration, neighboring images are required to overlap by about 30-40%. While the resulting registrations (cf. Fig. 1c) can be used for various purposes, our main target application is the reconstruction and texturing of 3D city models.

We assume that rough initial estimates of the per-image registrations are known, as they can usually be acquired using in-flight GPS and orientation measurements. No further information is required, in particular no information about the terrain elevation. In contrast to previous approaches, our system is fully automatic without the need for user interaction. For each input image, the registration is recovered as parameters of a perspective projection that aligns the map with the image. If the intrinsic calibration of the input images is not known, it is recovered during the registration process in addition to the extrinsic calibration. While the recovery of radial distortion parameters could seamlessly be integrated as well, this has not been necessary for the images used in our experiments. Due to different creation times and measurement errors during map generation, a certain level of discrepancy between the digital map and the input images is inevitable. We employ robust sampling techniques to cope with such cases.

1.1 Method Overview

The registration process performs the following steps. Similarly to [6], for each individual image our algorithm first detects the vanishing point that corresponds to the vertical scene direction (cf. Section 2.1). This vanishing point reduces the degrees of freedom of the extrinsic calibration from 6 to 4, thereby effectively simplifying the later search for camera parameters. For each image, the algorithm then detects line segments that correspond to vertical scene edges, i.e., line segments that pass through the respective vanishing point.

In the second step, our method estimates the extrinsic and, if not provided, intrinsic calibration of each image (cf. Section 2.2). This process is based on corresponding pairs of map corner vertices and image line segments detected in the previous step. Since these correspondences are unknown, we generate a large set of candidates and employ the RANSAC [14] approach to find a valid subset. Distance measurements using the Mahalanobis distance and an integrated approximation of the per-image terrain elevation yield a robust procedure. This step already results in very good alignments of the oblique images with the map.

Due to the usage of vertex-to-line constraints, however, there is still an unknown height offset between pairs of images left. Furthermore, due to slight inaccuracies in the detected vanishing points, the offset usually is not constant for an image but varies according to an unknown linear height function. To compensate for both effects, in a final step, we detect horizontal (in scene space) edges on building facades, robustly match them across pairs of images, and solve a bundle-adjustment-like global optimization problem over all camera parameters (cf. Section 2.3). This results in precise and compatible registrations of all oblique images with the cadastral map.

The paper continues with a discussion of related work. The steps of our processing pipeline are presented in detail in Section 2. Results are presented in Section 3 and we conclude with a discussion of our method in Section 4. Please see the accompanying video for an extended overview of our approach.

1.2 Related Work

Geo-registration, the alignment of overlapping images, and conflation are well-understood problems for vertical aerial images and a variety of established techniques exists [15, 16]. While these processes can often be automated for vertical images, the same approaches cannot easily be transferred to oblique images due to perspective foreshortening, occlusion of ground points and buildings, and the strongly varying appearance of e.g. facades for different vantage points. Gerke and Nyaruhuma [17] explicitly address the calibration of the extrinsic and intrinsic parameters of oblique aerial images. They present a method based on manually specified points, horizontal or vertical lines, and right angles, and compare their approach to several commercial products. It was shown that for the case of oblique images, commercially available solutions are still inferior compared to an approach tailored to the specific properties of these images. Frueh et al. [5] present a system that automatically registers oblique aerial images with a 3D city model with the goal of texture generation. With the same goal, Ding et al. [6]

and Wang and Neumann [7] register 3D LiDAR models with oblique aerial images. All three approaches are based on matching line segments between the 3D model and the images. [5] matches lines directly, [6] and [7] combine individual line segments to more complex descriptors for improved matching robustness. While these methods yield very good registration results, they cannot easily be transferred to our setting since cadastral maps do not provide a sufficient number of edge candidates for matching. Furthermore, cadastral maps do not provide information about building heights, roof shapes, and terrain elevation, all of which is contained in LiDAR / 3D model data and which is crucial for the above methods to work. The lack of this information makes the problem of registration with cadastral maps more challenging.

Läbe and Förstner [18] have demonstrated the feasibility of a general structure-from-motion approach for the recovery of camera parameters of oblique images. However, since structure from motion requires a sufficiently large set of features matched across the images, this approach only works for densely sampled image sequences. Due to the strong appearance changes in sparse sets of oblique images as we use them, automatic feature matching is not feasible. Sheikh et al. [11] present a technique to register perspective oblique images to a geo-referenced orthographic vertical image mapped onto a digital elevation model (DEM). While this works well for images taken at high altitudes such that the DEM can be considered to be a smooth surface, it cannot be applied to images taken at lower altitudes where buildings result in considerable relative height differences. Mishra et al. [13] detect inconsistencies in vector data, especially street data, by projection into oblique images. Their approach is able to detect errors in the vector data as well as in the calibration. It is, however, not able to correct the calibration.

An alternative to the traditional approach of geo-registration in a post-process (i.e., off-line) is the *direct geo-registration*. Here the position and orientation of the camera is measured during flight. To achieve a sufficient level of registration precision, this approach requires specialized, expensive GPS/INS equipment and a large manual calibration effort to compensate for the different poses of the measurement devices and the camera. Such systems have been shown to achieve registration precisions of below 1m for vertical [19] and for oblique aerial images [20]. However, in the same work Grenzdörfer et al. [20] also report that the fully automatic texturing of an existing 3D model has not been possible due to too large registration errors of about 1-3 meters. Similarly, the texturing efforts by Stilla et al. [21], the evaluation of oblique aerial images for cadastral applications by Lemmens et al. [1], and the texturing approaches [6, 7] have shown that the precision of direct geo-registration solutions is often not sufficient without further processing. Furthermore, as discussed by Gerke and Nyaruhuma in [17], the traditional approach of off-line determination of camera poses cannot be replaced by direct geo-registration for several reasons: this technology is not applicable to unmanned airborn vehicles (UAVs) with limited loading weight, it has a high burden of precise calibration that has to be redone every time the system is modified, and the registration information might not be available at all depending on the source of the images. We hence believe that a combination of direct and automated off-line geo-referencing is the simplest, most robust, and most effective approach.

2   Image Registration Pipeline

As outlined in the introduction, our registration approach consists of three main steps. These steps will now be discussed in detail.

2.1   Vanishing Point and Vertical Edge Detection

Vanishing points corresponding to the scene's vertical direction are among the few entities that can easily be computed in oblique aerial images without further scene knowledge. Even for images with strong occlusion caused by tall buildings, usually a large number of vertical building edges is visible. Furthermore, although oblique images are most often captured with long focal distances, there is still enough variation in the orientation of projected vertical edges to allow for a stable detection of this particular vanishing point. Following [6], we exploit these points to fix two degrees of freedom of the extrinsic camera orientation, thereby stabilizing the estimation of initial registrations in the next step.

The detection of vanishing points is accomplished by a very simple yet effective procedure. We compute edge-pixels using the Canny-operator [22] and then extract straight line segments by least-squares line fitting. We then employ a simple RANSAC-based procedure that randomly picks two line segments, computes their intersection as hypothesis of the vanishing point, and evaluates its support using the remaining segments. By exploiting a-priori knowledge about the position of the vanishing point, this approach has proven to be extremely robust in our experiments: Since we can safely assume that the vertical vanishing point lies way below the image, only hypotheses with a y-coordinate of at least two times the image height are considered for further evaluation. The winning hypothesis is refined by an MLE procedure [23] with all inlying line segments.

The camera parameter optimizations in the second and third step are based on correspondences between map corner vertices and image line segments that agree with the vanishing points. While the inlying line segments of the previous step could well be used for this purpose, we found that additional segments

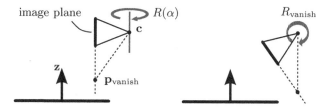

Fig. 2. Parameterization of the extrinsic camera calibration. $\mathbf{z}$ denotes the scene's vertical direction and $\mathbf{p}_{\text{vanish}}$ denotes the vanishing point in image space. $R(\alpha)$ rotates around $\mathbf{z}$, R_{vanish} aligns the vanishing direction induced by $\mathbf{p}_{\text{vanish}}$ with $\mathbf{z}$.

can be detected by a slightly modified second detection pass. For each pixel, we compute the derivative along the direction perpendicular to the line connecting the vanishing point and the pixel's position. Applying the Canny-operator (non-maximum suppression and thresholding) to the directional derivatives effectively suppresses pixels with strong but wrongly oriented gradients. A low threshold then yields many small connected components that can easily be discarded, but also preserves line segments distorted by noise or with smaller gradient magnitude. The final line segments are again obtained as ML estimates constrained to pass through the vanishing point.

2.2   Estimation of Initial Registrations

The central goal of this step is the recovery of good estimates of the registration parameters for each individual image in the form of perspective pin-hole projections [24] with 6 extrinsic (rotation and camera center) and 5 intrinsic parameters, respectively. Due to the known vanishing points, we need to recover 4 extrinsic parameters only: the vertical vanishing point of an image determines the orientation of the camera relative to the scene's vertical direction. We therefore only need to recover a single orientation parameter α, yielding an extrinsic orientation parameterized as

$$T(\alpha, \mathbf{c}) := R_{\text{vanish}} R(\alpha)(I \mid -\mathbf{c}) \ \in \mathbb{R}^{3 \times 4} \tag{1}$$

where $\mathbf{c}$ is the camera center, $R(\alpha) \in \mathbb{R}^{3 \times 3}$ is a rotation around the scene's vertical axis, and $R_{\text{vanish}} \in \mathbb{R}^{3 \times 3}$ aligns this axis with the vanishing direction induced by the vanishing point (cf. Fig. 2). In contrast to [6] and [7], we do not assume a fixed camera center $\mathbf{c}$ in this step to be able to handle cases where the initial registrations are not provided by GPS measurements and are hence less precise. We assume that a rough estimate of the focal distance is known at this point and set the remaining intrinsic parameters to their canonical values (aspect ratio 1, zero skew, principal point in the image center). A full optimization of all intrinsic parameters is done in the last step (cf. Section 2.3).

The parameter computation is based on correspondences between line segments $\mathbf{l}$ in image space as detected in the previous step and corner vertices $\mathbf{v}$ of the given map. For a set of corresponding lines and map vertices $M := \{(\mathbf{l}_i, \mathbf{v}_i)\}$, we find the optimal projection parameters by minimizing

$$E(\alpha, \mathbf{c}) := \sum_i \text{dist}_2(\mathbf{l}_i, KT(\alpha, \mathbf{c})\mathbf{v}_i)^2 \tag{2}$$

with respect to α, $\mathbf{c}$. Here $K \in \mathbb{R}^{3 \times 3}$ is the intrinsic calibration matrix, $KT\mathbf{v}$ denotes the perspective projection of a map corner vertex $\mathbf{v}$ into image space and $\text{dist}_2(\cdot, \cdot)$ denotes the Euclidean distance between a 2D point and the supporting line of an image space line segment. The varying parameters are optimized using the Levenberg-Marquardt method. Notice that, if only lines $\mathbf{l}$ passing through the vanishing point are used in (2) as assumed so far, the solution would degenerate to a state where the projections of all map vertices collapse into the vanishing point. In other words, the recovered camera would be moved up extremely high above the

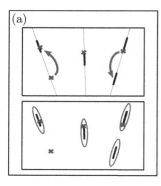 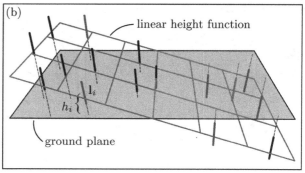

Fig. 3. (a) Inlier determination with Euclidean distance to the supporting line (top) and with Mahalanobis distance (bottom). The latter case effectively prevents false positive inliers denoted by arrows in the top figure. (b) Illustration of a linear height function computed for a random set of vertical lines l_i (shown in red) in the RANSAC procedure that finds initial per-image registration parameters. This approach relaxes the assumption of a horizontally flat terrain to a planar but arbitrarily oriented terrain.

map. To prevent this, we construct an additional line constraint perpendicular to the first line. More precisely, for the first constraint (l_0, v_0) we add a constraint $(\tilde{l}_0, v_0)$ with $\tilde{l}_0$ being perpendicular to l_0 and passing through l_0's center.

Since it is not known which are the valid correspondences, we employ RANSAC to find them. If a rough estimate of the focal distance is known, the size of each sampling set is 3 to determine the 4 unknown extrinsic parameters, due to the additional constraint for the first correspondence. Candidate correspondences are constructed by first determining a set of visible (from the initially provided rough camera perspective) map vertices v, projecting them into image space, and finding all nearby line segments l. The search radius in image space has to be chosen according to the discrepancy between the initially provided registration and the correct solution. That is, the search space has to be large enough such that the correct matches are contained in the set of candidate correspondences, and as small as possible to speed up the RANSAC process. In our experiments, we have found that usually a search radius of 80 to 130 pixels (i.e., about 12 to 20 meters in world space) is sufficient even for only rough initial registrations. The RANSAC procedure then works in the usual way by picking random correspondences, solving for optimal parameters by minimizing (2), and counting all inlying correspondences.

Depending on the radius of the candidate search space, the number of false positive inliers can become very large. Here false positives are map vertices v that project close to the supporting line of a segment l, but do not actually belong to the respective segment (cf. Fig. 3a). To counter this problem, the Euclidean distance to a segment's supporting line is replaced by an elliptical Mahalanobis distance during inlier determination. As a consequence, by keeping the stretch of the ellipses along the line segment directions small, it is implicitly assumed that the underlying terrain is horizontally flat, since only line segments slightly

Fig. 4. Result of the initial registration process. Starting from a rough estimate of the registration parameters (left), our system automatically recovers good initial registrations for each individual image (right). Vertical line constraints are shown in green.

above or below the projection of the map yield a sufficiently small Mahalanobis distance. We relax this assumption by approximating the fraction of the terrain visible in a single image by a plane with arbitrary slope. This is implemented by computing a linear height field for each random set of matching candidates. More precisely, after the optimization of (2), a height value h_i is computed for each random match $(\mathbf{l}_i, \mathbf{v}_i)$. The least-squares plane of all height values then yields the linear height function (cf. Fig. 3b). During the determination of inlying correspondences, all map vertices $\mathbf{v}$ are shifted up or down according to the height function before projection into the image. In our experiments we have found that both the Mahalanobis distance and the linear height functions introduce little extra computational effort, but effectively reduce the number of false positive inliers. Fig. 4 shows an example of the alignment before and after the initial registration process.

2.3   Global Optimization

Up to now, we have considered the separate registration of individual images only. Due to the additional, arbitrarily chosen height constraints $(\tilde{\mathbf{l}}_0, \mathbf{v}_0)$ introduced in the previous step, the registration is not yet globally consistent across all images. In an ideal setting, the only step missing for a consistent registration of all images would be a height adjustment of each image with respect to a common reference, i.e., a translation of all but one cameras along the scene's vertical direction. Unfortunately, as shown in Fig. 5, this is not sufficient most of the time, since the necessary height offset to align pairs of images is not constant but rather varies over the images.

An analysis of this problem shows that the offset variations are caused by slight inaccuracies in the detected vanishing points: For a fixed focal distance, the orientation of the ground plane with respect to the camera is determined by the vanishing point only. While the vanishing points detected in Section 2.1 yield plausible alignments for each individual image, comparing the ground plane orientations for overlapping pairs of images as done in Fig. 5 reveals slightly incompatible orientations. Due to limited image quality and resolution, we cannot

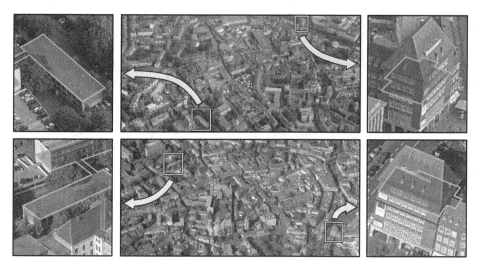

Fig. 5. Visualization of height differences between pairs of images. The map is projected to compatible positions for a certain region of the map (left). Due to slightly inaccurate vanishing points, the orientations of the cameras are slightly tilted. This yields incompatible map projections in other map regions. The expected map position is marked with a red line on the facade (right). We solve this problem by optimizing the parameters of all cameras including the vanishing points in the final step of the registration pipeline.

expect to improve the precision of the vanishing point detection to a sufficient level. We therefore decided to integrate the vanishing points as varying parameters into the final global optimization and thereby recover compatible orientations of all images with respect to the ground plane.

To be able to do so, we need to define constraints that act as coupling forces between different images and that are able to capture the orientation differences we want to remove. A viable approach is to detect horizontal (in scene space) edges on building facades and match them across two or more images. While the systematic detection of horizontal facade edges is difficult without scene knowledge, it becomes feasible due to the individual registrations of each image with the map: For each image, we can now determine visible map edges, restrict the search for facade line segments to narrow vertical bands (cf. Fig. 6a), and discard facade lines with false orientations. To match facade line segments between images, we need to take the unknown ground plane orientation differences into account. From the above analysis follows that the orientation difference between two images can be compensated for by a bivariate linear height function, i.e., by a planar offset. We thus determine an appropriate height function for each (but one) aerial image using a RANSAC procedure. The size of the sampling set is 3, the set of candidates consists of all possible pairs of line segments on the same facade in both images which additionally have the same gradient orientation. All pairs of facade edges that agree with the winning hypothesis are used as constraints in the subsequent

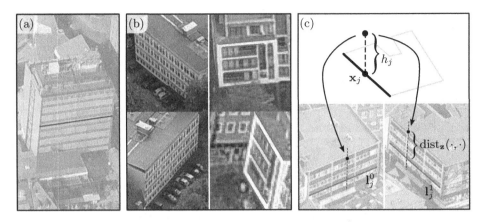

Fig. 6. (a) Search area for horizontal facade edges defined by the projection of a map edge. The height of the search area is defined by the expected height of buildings. We use 20m above and below each edge in all our experiments. (b) Examples of matching facade edges in two different views. (c) Construction of facade edge constraints. The unknown height values h_j are part of the optimization as varying parameters.

global optimization. Notice that for a single facade several pairs of edges can agree with the winning hypothesis as depicted in Fig. 6b.

The global optimization is solely based on constraints measuring the distance between projections of 3D vertices to 2D lines. We reuse the correspondences between map corner vertices and vertical image lines and add horizontal line constraints for facade edges visible in two or more images. Hence, in addition to the correspondences $(\mathbf{l}_i^k, \mathbf{v}_i)$ from Section 2.2 (with an additional index k counting images), we construct correspondences of the form $(\mathbf{L}_j, \mathbf{x}_j)$ with $\mathbf{L}_j$ being a set of horizontal lines in two or more images corresponding to the same map edge, and $\mathbf{x}_j$ being the 3D center point of this edge. See Fig. 6c for an illustration for the case of two images. The objective function of the global optimization over all cameras is

$$E(\{P_k\}, \{h_j\}) := \sum_{(\mathbf{l}_i^k, \mathbf{v}_i)} \text{dist}_2\left(\mathbf{l}_i^k, P_k \mathbf{v}_i\right)^2 + \sum_{(\mathbf{L}_j, \mathbf{x}_j)} \sum_{\mathbf{l}_j^k \in \mathbf{L}_j} \text{dist}_\mathbf{z}\left(\mathbf{l}_j^k, P_k(\mathbf{x}_j + h_j \mathbf{z})\right)^2.$$

(3)

Since the per-constraint height values h_j above the map's supporting plane are unknown, they are part of the optimization as varying parameters. $\mathbf{z}$ denotes the scene's vertical direction. Notice that for facade edge terms we do not compute the minimal Euclidean distance but rather the correct distance along the projection of $\mathbf{z}$, denoted by $\text{dist}_\mathbf{z}$ (cf. Fig. 6c). In this procedure there is no need for artificial height constraints anymore. To prevent the solution from collapsing, we simply fix the first height value to $h_0 := 0$. The parameters are again optimized using the Levenberg-Marquardt algorithm. We now perform a full optimization of all 6 extrinsic and, if required, also of the intrinsic parameters of all cameras simultaneously. Please notice that the employed optimization strategy is prone

Fig. 7. Left: Registration result for one out of 36 images (3 × 3 for each cardinal direction) of an urban area. Right: Projection of a 3D building model into 4 images (out of 11 in which it is visible) to verify the precision of the automatically obtained registrations. The projections of the model are aligned with the images with only minor deviations of at most 1-2 pixels, which translates into a maximal positional imprecision of 15-30cm in scene space.

to converge to a local minimum if not initialized properly. Due to the good initial per-image registrations obtained in Section 2.2, we have, however, never encountered a case where the optimization converged to a local minimum.

3   Results

In the first experiment, we have applied our algorithm to a set of 36 oblique images (i.e., 3 × 3 for each of the four cardinal directions) of an urban region. The images, which have been downloaded from [10], have a resolution of 4008×2672. Neighboring images of the same cardinal direction have an overlap of about 30-40%. The per-image processing steps (detection of vanishing point and vertical lines, computation of initial registration, detection of horizontal facade lines and height offset estimation) take about 20 seconds for each image on an Intel Core i7 920 CPU. The subsequent full Levenberg-Marquardt optimization of all parameters for 36 images took 80 seconds with $7 \times 36 = 252$ varying camera parameters and 16,340 varying height values, as well as 9,617 vertical and 46,915 horizontal line constraints. The resulting RMSE of (3) is 0.863 pixels per 3D vertex to 2D image line projection. Vertical vanishing points move by 150 pixels on average during the optimization. This translates into an orientation change of the ground plane by 0.8 degrees.

To validate the accuracy of the recovered registration, we have constructed several 3D building models and projected them into various different views. The footprint of the highest building in Fig. 7 has dimensions 30m×12m. Visual inspection (due to the lack of ground truth registrations) shows a precise alignment of the 3D scene with the images within 1-2 pixels. This translates into an accuracy in scene space of below 15-30cm.

Fig. 8. Left: Result of 5 minutes of modeling with a prototype system which is based on the automatically computed registrations and the cadastral map. Right: Application of our approach to a sub-urban region. Even though less vertical and horizontal edges are available in such images, our system is able to recover precise registrations.

With the registration in place, the generation of a correct terrain height map and the adjustment of building heights both become simple one-dimensional problems. In particular, a valid height map can be generated by means of linearly interpolating very few constraints. To further validate the quality of our registrations, we have implemented a simple interactive modeling system similar to those of [3, 4] to rapidly create 3D buildings. The precise registration enables a modeling approach that overlays the current state of the model on top of the aerial images, thereby allowing for the easy reconstruction of correct building shapes and dimensions. Fig. 8(left) shows the result of just about 5 minutes of manual modeling using the automatically generated registration and the cadastral map as a basis.

In a second experiment we have applied the automatic registration approach to a sub-urban region, cf. Fig. 8(right). Even though much less vertical and horizontal lines have been detected, our system still works as expected and generates a precise registration. For more result please see the supplemental video.

4   Discussion

The main sources of information exploited in our work are horizontal and vertical lines in the input images. Thus, our method only works correctly if a sufficient number of lines is available. During this project we have found, however, that a large number of both kinds of lines can safely be assumed to be present in images of urban regions: Vertical edges frequently appear at the corners of buildings or due to the different appearances of neighboring facades; horizontal edges are induced by the rims of roofs, by balconies, or by windows. We have never encountered a case where the system failed due to too few available lines. For the detection of vertical vanishing points (cf. Section 2.1), more sophisticated methods like, e.g., [25] are available. However, we use a simpler approach that exploits a-priori knowledge about the position of the vanishing points since it has turned out to be extremely robust, and since perfect precision that renders the adjustment of the vanishing points unnecessary during the global optimization (cf. Section 2.3) cannot be expected for any alternative method.

Our system has a few intuitive parameters that need to be specified by the user. Foremost, a threshold is required to distinguish inliers from outliers during the search for 3D vertex to 2D line correspondences (cf. Section 2.2) and for matching horizontal facade lines (cf. Section 2.3). For both cases a distance threshold of 2.0 pixels has worked well in all our experiments. In the search for vertex-to-line correspondences to determine per-image registrations, we have found that we usually have to deal with an inlier ratio of only 6-7%. For a sampling set size of 3 correspondence we therefore require about 20k RANSAC iterations for a confidence of 99% to find an inlier-only subset at least once. The RANSAC process in Section 2.3 is less problematic since the inlier ratio usually is larger than 13%. Thus, for 3 random correspondences in each iteration, 2.1k iterations are sufficient.

If no information about the position and orientation of the input images is known (as it may be the case for images from the internet), our approach enables a simple interface to specify rough initial registrations: Due to the recovered vanishing points, the user needs to only specify a one-dimensional orientation α (cf. Fig. 2) and the rough translation $\mathbf{c}$ of the camera. Both operations can be mapped to simple interactions in an interface that overlays the input images with the cadastral map. After a precise estimate of the first image's registration parameters has been computed (cf. Section 2.2), these parameters are used as starting values for neighboring views, thereby turning the process of providing rough initial registrations into a matter of seconds per image.

From the constraints used in the global optimization, a rough estimate of the terrain's height map can be derived. Vertical line segments provide height information by their lower endpoint, for horizontal line segments height values h_j have been explicitly computed (cf. Section 2.3). Thus, a height map can be constructed by collecting the minimal height value for each building footprint and by propagating height information to buildings without constraints by linear interpolation. While this construction yields only a very rough approximation, it is able to compensate for large-scale variations of the terrain elevation.

Acknowledgment. This project was funded by the DFG Cluster of Excellence *UMIC* (DFG EXC 89), and the Aachen Institute for Advanced Study in Computational Engineering Science (AICES).

References

1. Lemmens, M., Lemmen, C., Wubbe, M.: Pictometry: Potentials for land administration. In: Proc. of the 6th FIG reg. Conf., Int'l Fed. of Surveyers (2007)
2. Vanegas, C.A., Aliaga, D.G., Benes, B.: Building reconstruction using manhattan-world grammars. In: Proc. of CVPR (2010)
3. Google Building Maker: A 3d city modeling approach based on oblique aerial images (2010), http://sketchup.google.com/3dwh/buildingmaker.html

4. Gülch, E.: Extraction of 3d objects from aerial photographs. In: Proc. COST UCE ACTION C4 Workshop (1996)
5. Frueh, C., Sammon, R., Zakhor, A.: Automated texture mapping of 3d city models with oblique aerial imagery. In: Proc. of 3DPVT, pp. 396–403 (2004)
6. Ding, M., Lyngbaek, K., Zakhor, A.: Automatic registration of aerial imagery with untextured 3d lidar models. In: Proc. of CVPR (2008)
7. Wang, L., Neumann, U.: A robust approach for automatic registration of aerial images with untextured aerial lidar data. In: Proc. of CVPR (2009)
8. Gerke, M.: Dense matching in high resolution oblique airborne images. In: CMRT 2009, pp. 77–82 (2009)
9. Kopf, J., Neubert, B., Chen, B., Cohen, M., Cohen-Or, D., Deussen, O., Uyttendaele, M., Lischinski, D.: Deep photo: Model-based photograph enhancement and viewing. In: Proc. of SIGGRAPH Asia (2008)
10. Microsoft Corp.: Bing maps (2010), http://www.bing.com/maps
11. Sheikh, Y., Khan, S., Shah, M., Cannata, R.: Geodetic alignment of aerial video frames. In: Video Registration. Video Computing Series (2003)
12. Wu, X., Carceroni, R., Fang, H., Zelinka, S., Kirmse, A.: Automatic alignment of large-scale aerial rasters to road-maps. In: Proc. of ACM GIS. (2007)
13. Mishra, P., Ofek, E., Kimchi, G.: Validation of vector data using oblique images. In: Proc. of ACM GIS (2008)
14. Fischler, M.A., Bolles, R.C.: Random sample consensus: a paradigm for model fitting with applications to image analysis and automated cartography. Communications of the ACM 24, 381–395 (1981)
15. Fogel, D.N., Tinney, L.R.: Image registration using multiquadric functions, the finite element method, bivariate mapping polynomials and thin plate spline. Technical Report 96-1, National Center for Geographic Information and Analysis (1996)
16. Mena, J.B.: State of the art on automatic road extraction for gis update: a novel classification. Pattern Recogn. Lett. 24, 3037–3058 (2003)
17. Gerke, M., Nyaruhuma, A.: Incorporating scene constraints into the triangulation of airborne oblique images. In: ISPRS, vol. XXXVIII 1-4-7/WS (2009)
18. Läbe, T., Förstner, W.: Automatic relative orientation of images. In: Proc. of the 5th Turkish-German Joint Geodetic Days (2006)
19. Cramer, M., Stallmann, D.: System calibration for direct georeferencing. In: IAPRS, vol. XXXIV, Com. III, Part A (2002) 79–84
20. Grenzdörffer, G.J., Guretzki, M., Friedlander, I.: Photogrammetric image acquisition and image analysis of oblique imagery. The Photogrammetric Record 23, 372–386 (2008)
21. Stilla, U., Kolecki, J., Hoegner, L.: Texture mapping of 3d building models with oblique direct geo-referenced airborne IR image sequences. In: ISPRS Workshop: High-Resolution Earth Imaging for Geospatial Information (2009)
22. Canny, J.: A computational approach to edge detection. IEEE Trans. Pattern Analysis and Machine Intelligence 8, 679–714 (1986)
23. Liebowitz, D., Zisserman, A.: Metric rectification for perspective images of planes. In: Proc. of CVPR, pp. 482–488 (1998)
24. Hartley, R., Zisserman, A.: Multiple View Geometry in Computer Vision, 2nd edn. Cambridge University Press (2003)
25. Almansa, A., Desolneux, A., Vamech, S.: Vanishing point detection without any a priori information. IEEE PAMI 25, 502–507 (2003)

A Multi-stage Linear Approach
to Structure from Motion

Sudipta N. Sinha[1], Drew Steedly[2], and Richard Szeliski[1]

[1] Microsoft Research, Redmond, USA
[2] Microsoft, Redmond, USA
{sudipsin,steedly,szeliskli}@microsoft.com

Abstract. We present a new structure from motion (Sfm) technique based on point and vanishing point (VP) matches in images. First, all global camera rotations are computed from VP matches as well as relative rotation estimates obtained from pairwise image matches. A new multi-staged linear technique is then used to estimate all camera translations and 3D points simultaneously. The proposed method involves first performing pairwise reconstructions, then robustly aligning these in pairs, and finally aligning all of them globally by simultaneously estimating their unknown relative scales and translations. In doing so, measurements inconsistent in three views are efficiently removed. Unlike sequential Sfm, the proposed method treats all images equally, is easy to parallelize and does not require intermediate bundle adjustments. There is also a reduction of drift and significant speedups up to two order of magnitude over sequential Sfm. We compare our method with a standard Sfm pipeline [1] and demonstrate that our linear estimates are accurate on a variety of datasets, and can serve as good initializations for final bundle adjustment. Because we exploit VPs when available, our approach is particularly well-suited to the reconstruction of man-made scenes.

1 Introduction

The problem of simultaneously estimating scene structure and camera motion from multiple images of a scene, referred to as *structure from motion* (Sfm), has received considerable attention in the computer vision community. Recently proposed Sfm systems [2–5] have enabled significant progress in image-based modeling [3] and rendering [4, 5]. Most Sfm systems [2–6] are either sequential, starting with a small reconstruction and then incrementally adding in new cameras by pose estimation and 3D points by triangulation, or hierarchical [7, 8] where smaller reconstructions are progressively merged. Both approaches require intermediate bundle adjustment [9] and multiple rounds of outlier removal to minimize error propagation as the reconstruction grows. This can be computationally expensive for large datasets.

This paper investigates ways to compute a direct initialization (estimates for *all* cameras and structure) in an efficient and robust manner, without any intermediate bundle adjustment. We propose a new multi-stage linear approach for the *structure and translation* problem, a variant of Sfm where camera rotations are already known. A robust approach for first recovering all the global camera

K.N. Kutulakos (Ed.): ECCV 2010 Workshops, Part II, LNCS 6554, pp. 267–281, 2012.

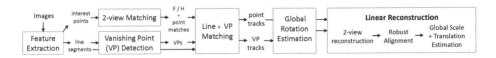

Fig. 1. Overview: First, all camera rotations are estimated. All structure and translation parameters are then directly estimated using a new multi-stage linear approach.

rotations based on vanishing points (VPs) and pairwise point matches is also described. Because we exploit VPs when available, our approach is particularly well-suited for man-made scenes, a topic that has received a lot of recent attention [5, 10–13]. When VPs are absent, the rotations can be computed from only pairwise point matches using one of the methods described in [14–16].

Approaches for such direct initialization of cameras and structure have been explored in the past. Factorization based approaches, such as [17], usually require all points to be visible in all views, or do not scale to large scenes with large amounts of missing data [18]. Linear *reference-plane* based techniques [11], can handle missing data, but minimize an algebraic error. This can cause points close to infinity to bias the reconstruction, unless the measurements are correctly weighted, which in turn requires a good initialization.

Direct linear methods [11, 19] also cannot cope with outliers, which are more common when matching features in unordered image datasets, as compared to tracking features in video. Outliers are also common in architectural scenes due to frequently repeating structures. Such outliers are caused by mismatches that survive pairwise epipolar geometry estimation and get merged with good matches in other views to form long, erroneous tracks.

Recently, the L_∞ framework for solving multi-view geometry problems, where the maximum reprojection error of the measurements is minimized rather than the sum of squared errors, was shown to be applicable to the problem of structure and translation estimation, where camera rotations are known apriori [16, 20–22]. Although a global minimum can be computed using convex optimization techniques, L_∞ problems become computationally expensive for a large number of variables [21], and are also not robust to outliers. The known outlier removal strategies for L_∞ norm, such as [20], do not scale to large problems [16, 21].

Instead of directly solving a linear system as in [11, 19], we first perform pairwise reconstructions, and then robustly align pairs of such reconstructions, thereby detecting matches consistent over three views. In a subsequent linear step, these reconstructions are jointly aligned by estimating their unknown relative scales and translations. Once approximate depths are available, a direct, linear method can be used to jointly re-estimate the camera and point locations. A final bundle adjustment step refines all camera parameters (including rotations) and structure parameters. Our proposed approach is fast, treats all images equally, and is easy to parallelize. Our technique could also be extended to incorporate linear constraints for 3D lines with known directions, and coplanarity constraints on 3D points and lines, as described in [11, 23].

For estimating rotations, we show the benefit of exploiting parallel scene lines, which are assumed to be either vertical, or orthogonal to the vertical direction.

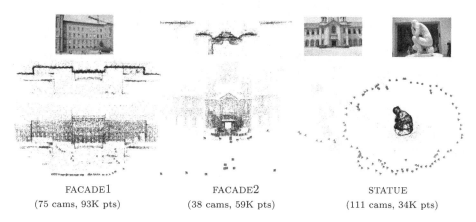

| FACADE1 | FACADE2 | STATUE |
| (75 cams, 93K pts) | (38 cams, 59K pts) | (111 cams, 34K pts) |

Fig. 2. The proposed method generates accurate reconstructions and is significantly faster than a standard sequential Sfm pipeline [1] (see Table 2)

This is more general than Manhattan-world assumptions and is common in a variety of man-made scenes [13]. Currently, we assume known focal lengths (using values present in EXIF tags) but these could also be estimated from orthogonal VPs [24]. Our method builds upon known techniques for estimating global rotations from VP matches [10, 15, 24], and pairwise relative rotation estimates [14–16]. However, unlike [10, 15] where omni-directional images with small baselines were used, we perform VP matching on unordered regular images, which is a more difficult case. We show that when VPs can be accurately detected and matched in images, the global rotation estimates can be very accurate. Figure 2 shows some accurate reconstructions obtained using our proposed method.

2   Proposed Approach

Figure 1 provides an overview of the three stages of our Sfm pipeline. First, points, line segments, and vanishing points are extracted and matched in all images. Next, camera rotations are estimated using vanishing points whenever possible, but also using relative rotation estimates obtained from pairwise point matches. Finally, all cameras and 3D points are directly estimated using a linear method, followed by a final bundle adjustment.

Notation and Preliminaries: In our Sfm formulation, a set of 3D points $\mathbf{X}_j$ are observed by a set of cameras with projection matrices P_i. The i-th camera has focal length f_i and has a center of projection $\mathbf{C}_i$. We assume camera intrinsics of the form $\mathsf{K}_i = \text{diag}(f_i, f_i, 1)$, and denote camera pose (rotation, translation) by $(\mathsf{R}_i, \mathbf{t}_i)$ respectively, with $\mathsf{P}_i = \mathsf{K}_i[\mathsf{R}_i \ \mathbf{t}_i]$, and $\mathbf{t}_i = -\mathsf{R}_i\mathbf{C}_i$. The j-th point is observed in the i-th camera at the point $\mathbf{x}_{ij}$. A point at infinity in the direction $\mathbf{d}_m$, is observed at a VP $\mathbf{v}_{im}$ in the i-th camera.

Match and Image-pair Graphs: From pairwise point matches, we form a *pruned match graph* G_m, consisting of nodes for each image and edges between images with good matches. We first compute a full match graph G by exhaustively matching all image pairs, and using the match inlier counts as the corresponding edge weights. The graph G_m is initialized to the maximum spanning tree of G. We then iterate through the set of remaining edges, sorted by decreasing edge weights, and insert edges into G_m, as long as the maximum degree of a node in G_m does not exceed k (set to 6 by default). We also build G_r, the edge dual graph of G_m, referred to as the *image-pair graph* by [6]. Every node in G_r corresponds to an edge in G_m and represents image pairs with a sufficient number of matches. Two nodes in G_r are connected by an edge if and only if the corresponding image pairs share a camera and 3D points in common.

3   Feature Extraction and Matching

Interest Points: We extract point features using a state of the art feature detector [25], and perform kd-tree based pairwise matching as proposed in [26] to obtain the initial two-view matches based on photometric similarity. These are then filtered through a standard RANSAC-based geometric verification step [27], which robustly computes pairwise relations – a fundamental matrix F, or a homography H (in the case of pure rotation or dominant planes) between cameras.

Line Segments and Vanishing Points: We also recover 2d line segments in the images through edge detection, followed by connected component analysis on the edgels. A local segment growing step with successive rounds of RANSAC then recovers connected sets of collinear edgels. Finally, orthogonal regression is used to fit straight line segments to these. Quantized color histogram-based two-sided descriptors [28] are computed for each segment and are used later for appearance-based matching. Vanishing point (VP) estimation in each image also uses RANSAC to repeatedly search for subsets of concurrent line segments. Once a VP has been detected along with a set of supporting lines, the process is repeated on the remaining lines. In each image, we heuristically determine which VP (if any) corresponds to the vertical direction in the scene, by assuming that most images were captured upright (with negligible camera roll). The line segments are labeled with the VPs they support. Although, the repeated use of RANSAC is known to be a sub-optimal strategy for finding multiple structures, in our case, it usually detects the dominant VPs with high accuracy.

VP and Line Segment Matching: First, VPs are matched in every image pair represented in the pruned match graph G_m for which a pairwise rotation estimate can be computed. We allow for some errors in this estimate, and retain multiple VP match hypotheses that are plausible under this rotation up to a conservative threshold. We verify these hypotheses by subsequently matching line segments, and accept a VP match that unambiguously supports enough segment matches. Line segments are matched using appearance [28] as well as guided matching (correct line matches typically have interest point matches nearby). Note that VP matching has an ambiguity in polarity, as the true VP can be confused with its antipode, especially when they are close to infinity in the image. The orientation of line segments, matched using two-sided descriptors, is used to resolve this ambiguity. VP matches are linked into multi-view tracks by finding connected components, in the same way as is done for point matches, while also ensuring that the polarity of the VP observations are in agreement. Note that VP tracks are often disconnected, but different tracks that correspond to the same 3D direction may subsequently get merged, as described next.

4 Computing Rotations

Given three orthogonal scene directions, $\mathbf{d}_1 = [1,0,0]^\mathsf{T}$, $\mathbf{d}_2 = [0,1,0]^\mathsf{T}$ and $\mathbf{d}_3 = [0,0,1]^\mathsf{T}$, the global camera rotation in a coordinate system aligned with the $\mathbf{d}_i$'s, can be computed from the VPs corresponding to these directions.

$$\mathbf{v}_{im} = \mathrm{diag}(f_i, f_i, 1)\mathsf{R}_i\mathbf{d}_m \tag{1}$$

For each m, the mth column of R_i can be computed. In fact, two VPs are sufficient, since the third column can be computed from the other two.

4.1 Rotations from VP Matches

The rotation estimation method just described assumes that the directions $\{\mathbf{d}_m\}$, are known. Our goal however, is to recover all camera rotations given M VP tracks, each of which corresponds to an unknown 3D direction. As some of the VPs were labeled as vertical in the images, we know which tracks to associate with the unique *up* direction in the scene. Now, pairwise angles between all M directions are computed. Every image where at least two VPs were detected contributes a measurement. We rank the M directions with decreasing weights, where each weight is computed by counting the number of supporting line segments over all images where a corresponding VP was detected. Next, we find the most salient orthogonal triplet of directions such that at least one track corresponding to the vertical direction is included.

For all images where at least two of these directions are observed, camera rotations can now be computed using (1). If some of the remaining (M-3) directions were observed in any one of these cameras, those can now be computed as well. This step is repeated until no more cameras or directions can be added. This produces the first *camera set*—a subset of cameras with known rotations, consistent with a set of 3D directions. We repeat the process and obtain a partition of the cameras into mutually exclusive camera sets, some of which may potentially share a common direction (typically this is the up direction). A camera that sees fewer than two matched VPs generates a set with a single element.

4.2 Global Rotations

If a single camera set is found, we are done. Otherwise, the K camera sets must be rotationally aligned to obtain the global camera rotations. A unique solution can be found by fixing the rotation of one of the camera sets to identity. Note that we have an estimate of the relative rotation between camera pairs in the match graph. Let us denote this rotation involving the i-th and j-th cameras, chosen from camera sets a and b respectively, by the quaternion $\mathbf{q}_{ij}$. Each estimate of $\mathbf{q}_{ij}$ provides a non-linear constraint relating the unknown rotations of the two camera sets denoted by $\mathbf{q}^a$ and $\mathbf{q}^b$ respectively.

$$\mathbf{q}^a = (\mathbf{q}_i^a \cdot \mathbf{q}_{ij} \cdot (\mathbf{q}_j^b)^{-1})\mathbf{q}^b \tag{2}$$

where $\mathbf{q}_i^a$ and $\mathbf{q}_i^b$ denotes the known rotations of the i-th and j-th camera in their own camera sets. As proposed by [16], by ignoring the orthonormality constraints on the quaternions, we linearly estimate the set $\{\mathbf{q}^k\}$. When the vertical VPs are detected in a rotation set, the corresponding quaternion represents an unknown 1-dof rotation in the horizontal plane, as the vertical direction is assumed to be unique. We solve the full 4-dof system (2), and snap the near vertical rotations (within 5° degrees of each other) to be vertical. The scene directions within 5° of each other are also snapped together, and all the rotations are re-estimated under these additional constraints. This is useful in scenarios such as identifying parallel lines on opposite sides of a building, which are never seen together.

In the absence of VPs, rotations can be recovered via the essential matrices obtained from pairwise point matches for image pairs with an adequate number of matches. In [15], relative rotations were chained over a sequence followed by a non-linear optimization of the global rotations. We perform the chaining on a maximum spanning tree of the match graph G_m and then use its nontree edges in the non-linear optimization step. The rotations could also have been initialized using linear least squares (by ignoring the orthonormality constraint of rotation matrices) [16], or by averaging on the Lie group of 3D rotations [14].

5   Linear Reconstruction

When the intrinsics K_i and rotations R_i are known, every 2D image point $\mathbf{x}_{ij}$ can be normalized into a unit vector, $\hat{\mathbf{x}}_{ij} = (\mathsf{K}_i\mathsf{R}_i)^{-1}\mathbf{x}_{ij}$, which is related to the j-th 3D point $\mathbf{X}_j$ (in non-homogenous coordinates) as,

$$\hat{\mathbf{x}}_{ij} = d_{ij}^{-1}(\mathbf{X}_j - \mathbf{C}_i), \tag{3}$$

where d_{ij} is the distance from $\mathbf{X}_j$ to the camera center $\mathbf{C}_i$. Note that (3) is written with d_{ij} on the right side to ensure that measurements are weighted by inverse depth. Hereafter, $\hat{\mathbf{x}}_{ij}$ is simply denoted as $\mathbf{x}_{ij}$. By substituting approximate values of d_{ij}, if known, (3) can be treated as a linear equation in $\mathbf{X}_j$ and $\mathbf{C}_i$. All measurements together form a sparse, non-homogeneous, linear system, which can be solved to estimate the cameras and points all at once. These can be further refined by iteratively updating d_{ij} and solving (3). Notice that if we multiply the above equation by the rotation and calibration matrices and divide by z_{ij}, where z_{ij} is the distance between $\mathbf{X}_j$ and $\mathbf{C}_i$ projected along the camera axis (the last row of R_i), we get the usual pixel matching error. Therefore, if the focal lengths for all the cameras are similar, minimizing (3) is similar to the usual bundle adjustment equations (when the depths are approximately known, and ignoring any robust cost function).

An alternative approach [11] is to eliminate d_{ij} from (3), since $d_{ij}\mathbf{x}_{ij} \times (\mathbf{X}_j - \mathbf{C}_i) = \mathbf{0}$. All cameras and points can be directly computed by solving a sparse, homogeneous system, using SVD (or a sparse eigensolver), and fixing one of the cameras at the origin to remove the translational ambiguity. The points at infinity must be detected and removed before this method can be used. Since this method minimizes a purely algebraic cost function, if the linear equations are not weighted correctly, points farther away from the camera may bias the linear system, resulting in large reconstruction errors. Neither of these methods can handle outliers in the 2D observations, which are inevitable in many cases.

In this paper, instead of directly solving (3) for *all* cameras and points at once, we propose to independently compute two-view reconstructions for camera pairs that share points in common. Various approaches for computing two-view reconstructions are known and the situation is even simpler for a pair of cameras differing by a pure translation. Next, pairs of such reconstructions, sharing a camera and 3D points in common, are robustly aligned by estimating their relative scales and translations. This key step allows us to retain matches found to be consistent in the three views. Finally, once a sufficient number of two-view reconstructions have been pairwise aligned, we can linearly estimate the unknown scale and translation of each individual reconstruction, which roughly brings all of them into global alignment. An approximate estimate of depth d_{ij} can now be computed and substituted into (3), and the linear system can be solved with the outlier-free tracks obtained by merging three-view consistent observations. We now describe these steps in more detail.

5.1   Two-View Reconstruction

A pairwise reconstruction for cameras (a,b), treated as a translating pair, is denoted as $\mathcal{R}^{ab} = \{\mathbf{C}_a^{ab}, \mathbf{C}_b^{ab}, \{\mathbf{X}_j^{ab}\}\}$ where the superscript denotes a local coordinate system. Under pure translation, it is known that the epipoles in the two images coincide, and all points in the two views $\mathbf{x}_{aj}$ and $\mathbf{x}_{bj}$ are collinear with the common epipole $\mathbf{e}$, also known as the *focus of expansion* (FOE), i.e. $\mathbf{x}_{aj}^\top [\mathbf{e}]_\times \mathbf{x}_{bj} = 0$. The epipole $\mathbf{e}$ is a vector that points along the baseline for the translating camera pair. We compute $\mathbf{e}$ by finding the smallest eigenvector of a 3×3 matrix produced by summing the outer product of all 2D lines $\mathbf{l} = \mathbf{x}_{aj} \times \mathbf{x}_{bj}$, and then choose $\mathbf{C}_a^{ab} = \mathbf{0}$ and $\mathbf{C}_b^{ab} = \hat{\mathbf{e}}$, corresponding to a unit baseline. Each point $\mathbf{X}_j^{ab}$ is then triangulated using the linear method.

$$\mathbf{x}_{kj} \times (\mathbf{X}_j^{ab} - \mathbf{C}_k^{ab}) = \mathbf{0}, \quad \text{for } k \in \{a, b\}. \tag{4}$$

Finally, we remove all points reconstructed behind both cameras and the ones with small triangulation angles $(< 1°)$.

5.2   Robust Alignment

Each pairwise reconstruction $\mathcal{R}^{ab}$ involving cameras (a,b) differs from a global reconstruction by 4-*dofs*, i.e. an unknown scale s^{ab} and translation $\mathbf{t}^{ab}$, unique up to an arbitrary global scale and translation. Suppose, $\mathcal{R}^{bc}$ and $\mathcal{R}^{ab}$ share camera

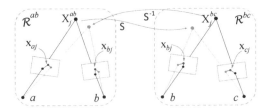

Fig. 3. The symmetric transfer error of the 3D similarity (scale and translation) transformation S from $\mathcal{R}^{ab}$ to $\mathcal{R}^{bc}$ is the sum of distances between the observed points $\mathbf{x}_{aj}$, $\mathbf{x}_{bj}$, $\mathbf{x}_{cj}$ and the projected points shown in grey.

b and some common 3D points. Using MLESAC [29], we robustly align $\mathcal{R}^{ab}$ to $\mathcal{R}^{bc}$ by computing a 4-*dof* 3D similarity S_{bc}^{ab} (parameterized by relative scale s_{bc}^{ab} and translation $\mathbf{t}_{bc}^{ab}$). A hypothesis is generated from two 3D points common to both reconstructions. These are chosen by randomly sampling two common 3D points, or only one common point when the camera center of b is chosen as the second point. Assuming exact correspondence for one of the two points in $\mathcal{R}^{bc}$ and $\mathcal{R}^{ab}$ gives a translation hypothesis $\mathbf{t}$. A scale hypothesis s is computed by minimizing the image distance between the observed and reprojected points for the second 3D point. This can be computed in closed form as the reprojected point traces out a 2D line in the image as the scale varies. The hypothesis $(s, \mathbf{t})$ is then scored using the total symmetric transfer error for all common 3D points in all three images. As illustrated in Figure 3, this error for each $\mathbf{X}_j$ is equal to

$$\sum_k d\big(\mathbf{x}_{kj}, f_k^{ab}(S^{-1}\mathbf{X}_j^{bc})\big) + \sum_k d\big(\mathbf{x}_{kj}, f_k^{bc}(S\mathbf{X}_j^{ab})\big) \tag{5}$$

Here, function f_k^{ab} projects a 3D point into each of the two cameras of $\mathcal{R}^{ab}$ where $k \in \{a, b\}$, f_k^{bc} is defined similarly for $\mathcal{R}^{bc}$, and d robustly measures the distance of the projected points from the original 2D observations $\mathbf{x}_{kj}$, where $k \in \{a, b, c\}$.

5.3   Global Scale and Translation Estimation

Once a sufficient number of transformations $(s_{bc}^{ab}, \mathbf{t}_{bc}^{ab})$ between reconstructions $\mathcal{R}^{ab}$ and $\mathcal{R}^{bc}$ are known, their absolute scale and translations, denoted by $(s^{ab}, \mathbf{t}^{ab})$ and $(s^{bc}, \mathbf{t}^{bc})$, can be estimated using the relation,

$$s^{bc}\mathbf{X} + \mathbf{t}^{bc} = s_{ab}^{bc}(s^{ab}\mathbf{X} + \mathbf{t}^{ab}) + \mathbf{t}_{ab}^{bc}, \tag{6}$$

where $\mathbf{X}$ is an arbitrary 3D point in global coordinates. Eliminating $\mathbf{X}$, gives us four equations in eight unknowns:

$$w_{ab}^{bc}(s^{bc} - s_{ab}^{bc}s^{ab}) = 0,$$
$$w_{ab}^{bc}(s^{bc}\mathbf{t}^{bc}) = w_{ab}^{bc}(s_{ab}^{bc}\mathbf{t}^{ab} + \mathbf{t}_{ab}^{bc}). \tag{7}$$

Here, the weight w_{ab}^{bc} is set to the number of three-view consistent points found common to $\mathcal{R}^{ab}$ and $\mathcal{R}^{bc}$. The scale of any one reconstruction is set to unity and its translation set to zero to remove the global scale and translational ambiguity.

The size of the linear system (7), depends on the number of edges in the *image-pair graph* G_r, (defined in Section 2), whose construction is described below. Any spanning tree of G_r will result in a linear system with an exact solution, but a better strategy is to use the maximum spanning tree, computed using w_{ab}^{bc} as the edge weight between nodes corresponding to $\mathcal{R}^{ab}$ and $\mathcal{R}^{bc}$. Solving an over-determined linear system using additional edges of G_r is usually even more reliable. Note that even when the match graph G_m is fully connected, G_r may be disconnected. This can happen if a particular pairwise reconstruction did not share any 3D points in common with any other pair. However, to obtain a reconstruction of all the cameras in a common coordinate system, all we need is a connected sub-graph of G_r, which covers all the cameras. We denote this connected subgraph by G' and compute it as follows.

To construct G_r, for each camera we first form a list of pairwise reconstructions the camera belongs to. We sort these reconstructions in increasing order of some accuracy measure (we use the number of reconstructed points with less than 0.6 pixel residual error). We iterate through the sorted list of reconstructions, labeling the ones that contain fewer than τ accurately reconstructed points ($\tau = 20$ by default), provided it is not the only reconstruction a particular camera is part of. Next, we remove all the nodes corresponding to labeled reconstructions from G_r, along with the edges incident on these nodes. The maximum spanning tree of the largest connected component of G_r, denoted by G', is then computed. Finally, we sort the remaining edges in G_r in decreasing order of weights, and iterate through them, adding an edge to G', as long as the maximum vertex degree in G' does not exceed k' ($k' = 10$ by default). With n cameras, our pruned match graph G_m with maximum vertex degree k has at most $O(kn)$ edges. Hence, G_r has $O(kn)$ nodes as well. Every node in G_m with degree d, gives rise to $\binom{d}{2}$ edges in G_r. Therefore, G_r has $O(nk^2)$ edges. Thus, both the number of pairwise reconstructions as well as the number of pairwise alignment problems are linear in the number of cameras. Moreover, each of the pairwise reconstructions and subsequent alignment problems can be easily solved in parallel.

6   Results

We have tested our approach on nine datasets (three sequences and six unordered sets), many of which are representative of common man-made scenes. Radial distortion was removed in advance using PTLENS [30]. Our linear estimates had low mean reprojection error in the range of 0.7–3.8 pixels, as shown in Column e_1 in Table 1, prior to bundle adjustment (BA) and without further optimization of the rotations or intrinsics. A subsequent full BA on all cameras and points, initialized with these estimates, converged in only 4–10 iterations, with mean reprojection errors of 0.3–0.5 pixels for most of the datasets (Column e_2).

The linear estimates were more accurate when VPs were used for recovering rotations (column e_1 v.s. e_3 in Table 1). In some of our datasets, multiple groups of parallel lines were present and reliable VPs could be matched in most images (see columns V–D in Table 1). In some of these cases, up to five rotation sets had to be aligned based on point matches, using the approach described in

Table 1. Statistics for the six unordered sets (U) and three sequences (S) used in our experiments. #images (I), #images with at least two VPs (V), #3D vanishing directions (D), #2D observations, #3D points, #pairs (P) and #triplets (T) in G_r. Columns (e_1) and (e_2) show the mean reprojection errors *before* and *after* bundle adjustment for VP-based rotation estimates. Columns (e_3) and (e_4) show the errors *before* and *after* bundle adjustment when using point-based rotations.

Name	C	I	V	D	#2D obs.	#3D pts	P	T	e_1	e_2	e_3	e_4
JESU-P25	U	25	25	3	118,977	49,314	75	383	0.71	0.29	0.86	0.29
CASTLEP30	U	30	28	3	104,496	42,045	90	445	2.22	0.32	2.34	0.32
FACADE1	U	75	72	3	254,981	72,539	192	958	1.75	0.49	8.89	1.31
FACADE2	U	38	34	3	148,585	59,413	114	572	1.94	0.43	11.5	0.55
BUILDING1	S	63	60	3	201,803	77,270	186	907	2.31	0.35	2.91	0.39
BUILDING2	U	63	63	3	185,542	52,388	173	764	1.82	0.35	1.09	0.39
STREET	S	64	64	3	182,208	51,750	184	855	1.24	0.34	0.52	0.34
HALLWAY2	S	184	181	3	140,118	27,253	435	1982	3.85	1.01	6.33	1.89
STATUE	U	111	0	0	137,104	34,409	350	1802	–	–	3.07	0.46

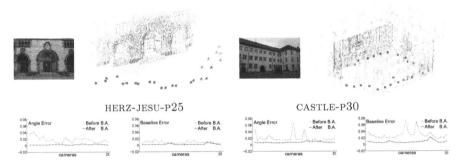

HERZ-JESU-P25   CASTLE-P30

Fig. 4. [HERZ-JESU-P25, CASTLE-P30]: Ground truth camera pose evaluation [31] (see text). The mean reprojection errors were 0.29 and 0.32 pixels after bundle adjustment.

Section 4.2. For the STATUE dataset where VPs were absent, all rotations were computed from essential matrices. They were initialized by chaining pairwise rotations on a spanning tree, and then refined using non-linear optimization, as described in [15]. Incorporating the covariance of the pairwise rotations [6], or using the method from [14] could lead to higher accuracy in the rotations, and also our linear estimates. Nevertheless, the STATUE reconstruction was still quite accurate (see Figure 2).

To test the need for robustness, during the pairwise alignment (Section 5.2) we disabled MLESAC, and computed relative scale and translations by registering all common 3D points shared by reconstruction pairs. This produced large errors up to 50 pixels in the linear estimates, and with these as initialization, BA was never able to compute an accurate reconstruction.

The reconstructions from the FACADE1 and FACADE2 unordered datasets are shown in Figure 2. Although highly textured, these scenes also contain frequent repeated patterns, resulting in more outliers, and some *false* epipolar geometries

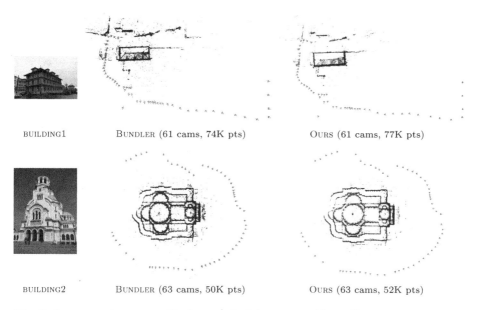

Fig. 5. [BUILDING1,BUILDING2]: Our method is comparable to BUNDLER in terms of accuracy, but is two orders of magnitude faster (see Table 2 for details).

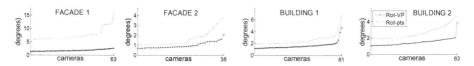

Fig. 6. Accuracy test of global rotations estimates (VP-based v.s. pure point-based) compared to the final rotations after bundle adjustment (better seen in color).

(this is also noted by [16]). The reconstructions from our linear method showed no drift, and were visually accurate even without BA. In comparison, the reference plane based linear method [11] only worked on small selected subsets of the input, and failed on most of the other datasets too, mainly due to its inability to handle points at infinity and its lack of robustness.

We evaluated our method on two ground truth datasets from Strecha et. al. [31] – HERZJESU-P25 and CASTLE-P30. Our reconstructions, shown in Figure 4, are quite accurate. We compared our camera pose estimates (before and after BA) with ground truth, using camera centers for registration and then comparing errors in baseline lengths and angles between camera optical axes. Figure 4 shows the average error for each camera over all possible baselines. For HERZJESU-P25, most cameras had less than 2% errors (baseline as well as angle) while the worst had 4% angle and 2% baseline error. These reduced to less than 1% after BA. The worst two out of 30 cameras in CASTLE-P30 initially had 7% error (due to small inaccuracies in rotation estimates), but the angle and baseline error in all cameras went below 1% and 2% respectively, after BA.

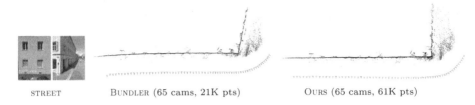

STREET   BUNDLER (65 cams, 21K pts)   OURS (65 cams, 61K pts)

Fig. 7. STREET (65 images): Using vanishing points for rotation estimation eliminates drift in our method. The linear estimate obtained by our method is shown on the right.

Where ground truth was absent, we compared the VP-based and point-based rotation estimates to the final bundle adjusted rotation estimates. Figure 6 shows the mean angle error per camera for four datasets. Point-based rotation estimates for FACADE1 were inaccurate due to the presence of a few false epipolar geometries. The VP-based rotation estimates were consistently better and produced higher accuracy in the linear method (columns e_1 v.s e_3 in Table 1).

Table 2. The #cameras, #3D points and timings (excluding feature extraction and matching) for BUNDLER [1] and our method. A breakup of our timings is shown– for estimating rotations (T_{rots}), pair reconstructions (T_{pairs}), triplet and global alignment ($T_{triplets}$) and bundle adjustment (T_{bundle}). The significant differences between BUNDLER and our method are highlighted in bold.

DATASET	#IMGS	BUNDLER		OURS					
		#CAMS/#PTS	TIME	#CAMS/#PTS	T_{rots}	T_{pairs}	$T_{triplets}$	T_{bundle}	TOTAL
JESU-P25	25	**25/11583**	**1m 24s**	**25/49314**	0.7s	3.6s	6.7s	1.1s	**13s**
CASTLEP30	30	**30/17274**	**3m 51s**	**30/42045**	0.8s	3.7s	4.1s	1.5s	**11s**
FACADE1	63	**63/71964**	**31m 28s**	63/72539	2.7s	6.2s	9.1s	7.6s	**26s**
FACADE2	38	**38/70098**	**23m 15s**	38/59413	1.0s	4.4s	6.4s	3.6s	**16s**
BUILDING1	61	**61/74469**	**57m 40s**	61/77270	2.6s	7.6s	9.6s	4.4s	**25s**
BUILDING2	63	**63/50381**	**39m 50s**	63/52388	1.1s	4.3s	4.8s	4.3s	**15s**
STREET	65	**65/20727**	**8m 47s**	**65/51750**	1.5s	4.0s	4.8s	7.3s	**18s**
HALLWAY	184	**139/13381**	**38m 05s**	**184/27253**	1.9s	5.2s	6.8s	12.6	**28s**
STATUE	111	**109/9588**	**7m 17s**	**111/34409**	3.6s	2.6s	3.7s	6.9s	**17s**

For seven out of nine datasets, the accuracy of our reconstructions is comparable to that of BUNDLER [1], a standard pipeline based on sequential Sfm, as shown in Figure 5 for the BUILDING1 and BUILDING2 sequences. However, our approach is up to two orders of magnitude faster even when more 3D points are present in our reconstructions (see Table 2). Our reconstructions are more accurate on the remaining two datasets – STREET and HALLWAY. The STREET sequence (Figure 7) captured from a driving car with a camera facing sideways, demonstrates the advantage of using vanishing points for rotation estimation. Virtually no drift is present in our linear estimate, whereas Bundler [1], produced some drift at the corner as well as in the straight section of the road. The HALLWAY sequence is an open-loop sequence, with narrow fields of view, poorly textured surfaces, and predominantly forward motion. Our reconstruction shown

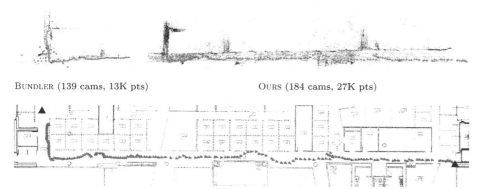

Bundler (139 cams, 13K pts)   Ours (184 cams, 27K pts)

Fig. 8. HALLWAY (184 images): Unlike BUNDLER, our method reconstructs the full hallway. (c) The camera path from our reconstruction overlaid on the floor plan.

in Figure 8, is qualitatively accurate with no rotational drift, although some drift in scale can be noticed with the camera path overlaid on the floor plan. In comparison, BUNDLER produced an incomplete reconstruction of the hallway where only 139 out of the 184 cameras were reconstructed.

7   Conclusions

We have developed a complete Sfm approach, which uses vanishing points when possible, and point matches to first recover all camera rotations, and then simultaneously estimates *all* cameras positions and points using a multi-stage linear approach. Our method is fast, easy to parallelize, treats all images equally, efficiently copes with substantial outliers, and removes the need for frequent bundle adjustments on sub-problems. Its accuracy and efficiency is demonstrated on a variety of datasets. In the future, we plan to extend bundle adjustment to incorporate constraints on camera rotations based on vanishing points and 2D line correspondences. We also plan to make our approach robust to the presence of false epipolar geometries [16] and test it on large Internet photo collections [6].

References

1. Snavely, N.: Bundler (2007), http://phototour.cs.washington.edu/bundler/
2. Schaffalitzky, F., Zisserman, A.: Multi-view Matching for Unordered Image Sets, or How Do I Organize My Holiday Snaps? In: Heyden, A., Sparr, G., Nielsen, M., Johansen, P. (eds.) ECCV 2002, Part I. LNCS, vol. 2350, pp. 414–431. Springer, Heidelberg (2002)
3. Pollefeys, M., Van Gool, L.J., Vergauwen, M., Verbiest, F., Cornelis, K., Tops, J., Koch, R.: Visual modeling with a hand-held camera. IJCV 59, 207–232 (2004)
4. Snavely, N., Seitz, S.M., Szeliski, R.: Photo Tourism: exploring photo collections in 3d. ACM Trans. Graph 25, 835–846 (2006)

5. Agarwal, S., Snavely, N., Simon, I., Seitz, S.M., Szeliski, R.: Building Rome in a Day. In: ICCV (2009)
6. Snavely, N., Seitz, S.M., Szeliski, R.: Skeletal graphs for efficient structure from motion. In: CVPR, pp. 1–8 (2008)
7. Fitzgibbon, A.W., Zisserman, A.: Automatic Camera Recovery for Closed or Open Image Sequences. In: Burkhardt, H.-J., Neumann, B. (eds.) ECCV 1998. LNCS, vol. 1406, pp. 311–326. Springer, Heidelberg (1998)
8. Gherardi, R., Farenzena, M., Fusiello, A.: Improving the efficiency of hierarchical structure-and-motion. In: CVPR (2010)
9. Triggs, B., McLauchlan, P.F., Hartley, R.I., Fitzgibbon, A.W.: Bundle Adjustment – A Modern Synthesis. In: Triggs, B., Zisserman, A., Szeliski, R. (eds.) ICCV-WS 1999. LNCS, vol. 1883, pp. 298–372. Springer, Heidelberg (2000)
10. Antone, M., Teller, S.: Scalable extrinsic calibration of omnidirectional image networks. IJCV 49, 143–174 (2002)
11. Rother, C.: Linear multi-view reconstruction of points, lines, planes and cameras using a reference plane. In: ICCV, pp. 1210–1217 (2003)
12. Brand, M., Antone, M., Teller, S.: Spectral Solution of Large-Scale Extrinsic Camera Calibration as a Graph Embedding Problem. In: Pajdla, T., Matas, J(G.) (eds.) ECCV 2004. LNCS, vol. 3022, pp. 262–273. Springer, Heidelberg (2004)
13. Schindler, G., Krishnamurthy, P., Dellaert, F.: Line-based structure from motion for urban environments. In: 3DPVT, pp. 846–853 (2006)
14. Govindu, V.M.: Lie-algebraic averaging for globally consistent motion estimation. In: CVPR, vol. 1, pp. 684–691 (2004)
15. Uyttendaele, M., Criminisi, A., Kang, S.B., Winder, S.A.J., Szeliski, R., Hartley, R.I.: Image-based interactive exploration of real-world environments. IEEE Computer Graphics and Applications 24, 52–63 (2004)
16. Martinec, D., Padjla, T.: Robust rotation and translation estimation in multiview reconstruction. In: CVPR (2007)
17. Sturm, P., Triggs, B.: A Factorization Based Algorithm for Multi-Image Projective Structure and Motion. In: Buxton, B.F., Cipolla, R. (eds.) ECCV 1996. LNCS, vol. 1065, pp. 709–720. Springer, Heidelberg (1996)
18. Tardif, J.-P., Bartoli, A., Trudeau, M., Guilbert, N., Roy, S.: Algorithms for batch matrix factorization with application to structure-from-motion. In: CVPR (2007)
19. Hartley, R.I., Kaucic, R., Dano, N.Y.: Plane-based projective reconstruction. In: ICCV (2001)
20. Sim, K., Hartley, R.: Removing outliers using the l_{inf} norm. In: CVPR (2006)
21. Agarwal, S., Snavely, N., Seitz, S.M.: Fast algorithms for L_∞ problems in multiview geometry. In: CVPR (2008)
22. Kahl, F., Hartley, R.I.: Multiple-view geometry under the L_∞-Norm. PAMI 30, 1603–1617 (2008)
23. Bartoli, A., Sturm, P.F.: Constrained structure and motion from multiple uncalibrated views of a piecewise planar scene. IJCV 52, 45–64 (2003)
24. Caprile, B., Torre, V.: Using vanishing points for camera calibration. IJCV 4, 127–140 (1990)
25. Winder, S., Hua, G., Brown, M.: Picking the best DAISY. In: CVPR (2009)
26. Lowe, D.G.: Distinctive image features from scale-invariant keypoints. IJCV 60, 91–110 (2004)

27. Fischler, M.A., Bolles, R.C.: Random sample consensus: A paradigm for model fitting with applications to image analysis and automated cartography. Communications of the ACM 24, 381–395 (1981)

28. Bay, H., Ferrari, V., Gool, L.V.: Wide-baseline stereo matching with line segments. In: CVPR, vol. 1, pp. 329–336 (2005)

29. Torr, P.H.S., Zisserman, A.: MLESAC: a new robust estimator with application to estimating image geometry. In: CVIU, vol. 78, pp. 138–156 (2000)

30. Niemann, T.: PTLens (2009), http://epaperpress.com/ptlens

31. Strecha, C., von Hansen, W., Gool, L.V., Fua, P., Thoennessen, U.: On benchmarking camera calibration and multi-view stereo. In: CVPR (2008)

32. Havlena, M., Torii, A., Knopp, J., Pajdla, T.: Randomized structure from motion based on atomic 3d models from camera triplets. In: CVPR, pp. 2874–2881 (2009)

Relative Bundle Adjustment Based on Trifocal Constraints

Richard Steffen[1], Jan-Michael Frahm[1], and Wolfgang Förstner[2]

[1] Department of Computer Science, The University of North Carolina at Chapel Hill
{rsteffen,jmf}@cs.unc.edu
[2] Department of Photogrammetry, University of Bonn
wf@ipb.uni-bonn.de

Abstract. In this paper we propose a novel approach to bundle adjustment for large-scale camera configurations. The method does not need to include the 3D points in the optimization as parameters. Additionally, we model the parameters of a camera only relative to a nearby camera to achieve a stable estimation of all cameras. This guarantees to yield a normal equation system with a numerical condition, which practically is independent of the number of images. Secondly, instead of using the classical perspective relation between object point, camera and image point, we use epipolar and trifocal constraints to implicitly establish the relations between the cameras via the object structure. This avoids the explicit reference to 3D points thereby handling points far from the camera in a numerically stable fashion. We demonstrate the resulting stability and high convergence rates using synthetic and real data.

1 Introduction

Motivation. Bundle adjustment has become the workhorse of structure from motion estimation, triggered by the review by Triggs et al. [1] and the first public domain software by Lourakis and Argyros [2] and more recently made fully aware by the software *bundler* [3]. The generality of the concept and the optimality of the achieved solution cause bundle adjustment to serve as a reference and to be of broad interest.

Despite these advantages, some problems still exist: The stability of large systems is sensitive to the arrangement of images as in classical photogrammetric mapping applications, tend to show instabilities. These instabilities are difficult to identify, and to date, there are still no tools for giving recommendations how to cure the situation by deliberately taking additional images, a precondition to make bundle adjustment usable by non-specialists. In real time applications, identifying and resolving so-called loop closures, where after long image strips one reaches positions visited in the past, requires careful storage management for fast access and proper representation of the geometry taken up to that point.

This paper proposes a novel model for bundle adjustment, especially useful for dealing with weak configurations due either to long motion sequences or due to the existence of points far from the cameras. First of all, long image sequences accumulate drift leading to a random walk, which decreases the accuracy

K.N. Kutulakos (Ed.): ECCV 2010 Workshops, Part II, LNCS 6554, pp. 282–295, 2012.

and increases the numerical condition number. The condition number increases super-linear with time. Secondly, points far from the cameras cause problems when determining approximate values, especially in the case where the camera positions are not yet determined with enough stability. This can happen for example, when the parallactic angle between two viewing rays is too small to reliably identify the depth of a point.

The proposed concept integrates two remedies: (1) camera parameters are not represented w. r. t. a common world system, but relative to a well chosen set of cameras distributed over the complete set of all cameras. This leads to a tree type structure with kinematic chains linking the cameras with the reference cameras. This increases the numerical stability of the bundle adjustment, increases the speed of convergence and the robustness with respect to bad initial values. (2) The object structure is not represented explicitly but using pairs and triplets of geometric constraints between cameras. This avoids the handling of 3D points far off the cameras, which in turn avoids any problem with determining approximate values. On the contrary, points far away from the cameras can be used advantageously to stabilize the rotation information. The cost for using this advantage is the slightly increased complexity of the Jacobians.

Related work. There is a lot of work on hierarchically representing large sets of images, in order to partition the bundle estimation into smaller better conditioned subsystems, for example partitioning an image sequence hierarchically [4], applying a spectral decomposition of the connection graph [5], [6] or building a tree based on the overlap of pairs of images [7], building a hierachical map during simultaneous localisation and mapping [8] and performing an effcient, close to optimal estimation. These approaches may also be coupled with our setup. The most closely related work is the setup in [9], where camera parameters are related to reference views which are related to a world system. However, the individual parts are connected in a second step, which altogether does not lead to a statistically optimal solution. Similarly, non-Euclidian object point representation like the inverse depth representation proposed by [10] can be applied to bundle adjustment to model points at infinity. In contrast to our proposed method, [10] still has to include the points as parameter.

Using trifocal constraints has been proposed to avoid the explicit representation of 3D points within the estimation of an image triplet [11]. To use trifocal constraints within bundle adjustment already has been proposed in [4], however, only for chaining within an image sequence and deriving approximate values. Trifocal constraints have been used within an extended Kalman filter approach in [12]. No approach is known to the authors that (1) only uses constraints between the image observations and the cameras; (2) uses a relative representation of the camera positions for improving the numerical condition; (3) performs a statistically optimal estimation equivalent to classical bundle adjustment.

The paper is structured the following way: we first describe the estimation procedure base on epipolar and trifocal constraints, give an insight into the modelling of the relative camera poses and then demonstrate the strengths of the approach with synthetic and real data.

2   Model for Relative Bundle-Adjustment with Image Triplet Constraints

This section describes the approach in more detail, first contrasting the classical bundle adjustment model using direct observations equations with the estimation procedure with implicit constraints, then deriving the constraints and their use in the bundle adjustment and finally introducing the representation with relative camera poses.

2.1   Classical Bundle Adjustment

Classical bundle adjustment simultaneously estimates the 3D structure of the environment and the camera parameters by minimizing the reprojection error in a weighted least square manner. The co-linearity constraint relates the parameters q describing the object, usually being a set of 3D points, the parameters z describing the 2D image observations, usually the image points, and the extrinsic, possibly also the intrinsic camera parameters p using an explicit observation model $z = f(p, q)$, often called a non-linear Gauss-Markov model. Additional constraints $h(p, q) = 0$ on the object or camera parameters may be used to fix the gauge and to enforce certain properties of the object to be recovered. Assuming the image measurements have a covariance that is denoted in matrix form as C_{zz}, the classical approach [1] minimizes the reprojection errors or residuals $v(p, q) = f(p, q) - z$ weighted with the inverse covariance matrix under the given constraints leading to the energy function

$$E(p, q, \mu) = v^\mathsf{T}(p, q) \, C_{zz}^{-1} \, v(p, q) + \mu^\mathsf{T} h(p, q) \tag{1}$$

to be minimized, where μ are the corresponding Lagrangian parameters for the constraints. The iterative solution typically exploits the sparsity of the structure of the normal equation system and is optimized by a marginalization to the usually much smaller number of camera parameters p using the *Schur complement*.

A novel model for bundle adjustment to gain efficiency and numeric stability by first deploying implicit constraints between the observations and the camera parameters to eliminate the object points as estimated parameters and second, by instead of referring the camera parameters p to a common world system representing the camera poses by the relative poses p_{rs} between neighbouring cameras p_r and p_s is presented.

2.2   Estimation with Implicit Constraints

We replace the classical reprojection model using the epipolar and trifocal constraints, well known from the two and three view epipolar geometry [13]. The epiolar and trifocal constrains are implicit functions of both the camera parameters and the observations, and do not allow to express the observations as a function of the parameters. Thus, instead of using the explicit observation functions $z = f(p, q)$, we use constraints $g(p, z)$ between the camera parameters p and the observed image observations z. Constraint optimization is known in the classical least square estimation technique as the Gauss-Helmert model and can be solved by minimizing

$$E(\boldsymbol{p}, \boldsymbol{v}, \boldsymbol{\lambda}, \boldsymbol{\mu}) = \boldsymbol{v}^\mathsf{T} C_{zz}^{-1} \boldsymbol{v} + \boldsymbol{\lambda}^\mathsf{T} \boldsymbol{g}(\boldsymbol{p}, \boldsymbol{z} + \boldsymbol{v}) + \boldsymbol{\mu}^\mathsf{T} \boldsymbol{h}(\boldsymbol{p}) \tag{2}$$

w. r. t. the parameters $\boldsymbol{p}$, the residuals $\boldsymbol{v}$ and the Lagrangian parameters $\boldsymbol{\lambda}$ and $\boldsymbol{\mu}$. The optimal estimates $\widehat{\boldsymbol{p}}$ for the parameters and the fitted observations $\widehat{\boldsymbol{z}}$ should fulfill the model constraints $\boldsymbol{g}(\widehat{\boldsymbol{p}}, \widehat{\boldsymbol{z}}) = \boldsymbol{0}$ and $\boldsymbol{h}(\widehat{\boldsymbol{p}}) = \boldsymbol{0}$. Minimizing the energy function (2) can be iteratively achieved by determining the corrections $\widehat{\Delta \boldsymbol{p}}$ from the linear equation system

$$\begin{bmatrix} J_p^\mathsf{T}(J_z^\mathsf{T} C_{zz} J_z)^{-1} J_p & H \\ H^\mathsf{T} & 0 \end{bmatrix} \begin{bmatrix} \Delta \boldsymbol{p} \\ \boldsymbol{\lambda} \end{bmatrix} = \begin{bmatrix} J_p^\mathsf{T}(J_z^\mathsf{T} C_{zz} J_z)^{-1} \boldsymbol{c}_g \\ \boldsymbol{c}_h \end{bmatrix}, \tag{3}$$

with

$$\boldsymbol{c}_g = -\boldsymbol{g}(\widehat{\boldsymbol{p}}, \widehat{\boldsymbol{z}}) + J_z^\mathsf{T}(\widehat{\boldsymbol{z}} - \boldsymbol{z}) \quad \text{and} \quad \boldsymbol{c}_h = -\boldsymbol{h}(\widehat{\boldsymbol{p}}), \tag{4}$$

starting at approximate values $\widehat{\boldsymbol{p}}^{(\nu)}$ for the estimated parameters and the fitted observations $\widehat{\boldsymbol{z}}$. The matrices J_p and J_z^T are the Jacobian of the constraints $\boldsymbol{g}$ with respect to the parameter vector $\boldsymbol{p}$ and the observations $\boldsymbol{z}$ and H^T is the Jacobian of $\boldsymbol{h}$ with respect to the parameters evaluated at the approximate values. The residuals can be determined from $\boldsymbol{v}^{(\nu)} = -C_{zz} J_z (J_z^\mathsf{T} C_{zz} J_z)^{-1} (\boldsymbol{c}_g - J_p \Delta \boldsymbol{p})$. We iteratively find new approximate values for the estimated parameters $\widehat{\boldsymbol{p}}^{(\nu+1)} = \widehat{\boldsymbol{p}}^{(\nu)} + \Delta \boldsymbol{p}$ and the fitted observations $\widehat{\boldsymbol{z}}^{(\nu+1)} = \boldsymbol{z} + \boldsymbol{v}^{(\nu)}$. This will be very useful to reconstruct the structure of the environment in our approach simply by intersecting two estimated projection rays, as the rays derived from the fitted observations $\widehat{\boldsymbol{z}}$ intersect and no optimization needs to be performed anymore.

Conceptionally, the explicit estimation and the implicit estimation model both minimize the residuals $\boldsymbol{v}$. It has been shown in [14,15], that the implicit model is a generalization of the least square estimation framework. Our proposed implicit model minimizes the backprojection errors (residuals) in a least square manner, using the constraint that the projection rays intersect in a single point as the explicit model does. The used epipolar and trifocal constraints can be derived from the explicit reprojection model by eliminating the object point [16]. Therefore, the results of the classical formulation and our proposed formulation are equal w.r.t the solution and its precision. Additionally, robustification can be achieved by reweighting the residuals as used in the classical model as a standard enhancement.

2.3   Epipolar and Trifocal Constraint Bundle

In all cases we rely on the classical partitioning of the projection $\mathbf{x}_t = \mathsf{P}_t \mathbf{X}$ of a 3D point with homogeneous coordinates $\mathbf{X}$ into the t-th camera and the partitioning of the projection matrix P_t into its internal part, containing the intrinsic parameters in K and its external part, containing its motion M_t w. r. t. to a reference system

$$\mathsf{P}_t = \mathsf{P}_{0t} \mathsf{M}_t \quad \text{with} \quad \mathsf{P}_{0t} = [\mathsf{K}_t \mid \mathbf{0}] \quad \text{and} \quad \mathsf{M}_t = \begin{bmatrix} R_t & \boldsymbol{T}_t \\ \mathbf{0}^\mathsf{T} & 1 \end{bmatrix} \tag{5}$$

This decomposition will be deployed in the next section for introducing the kinematic chains.

We now propose to replace the classical projection model by using the epipolar and trifocal constraints in order to achieve two goals: (1) avoid the provision of approximate values for the 3D object points, which in case of bad approximate values, may be far off the true values and hinder the estimation process to converge and (2) to allow for points which are very far from the cameras or even at infinity. The epipolar constraint for two cameras, r and s, can be written as

$$0 = g_E(\boldsymbol{p}, \boldsymbol{z}) = \mathbf{x}_r^\mathsf{T} \mathsf{K}_r^{-\mathsf{T}} R_r S(\boldsymbol{B}_{r,s}) R_s^\mathsf{T} \mathsf{K}_s^{-1} \mathbf{x}_s \tag{6}$$

with $S(\cdot)$ indicating the skew matrix of the base line vector $\boldsymbol{B}_{r,s} = \boldsymbol{T}_s - \boldsymbol{T}_r$ between the two projection centres of camera r and s. For calibrated cameras the observed homogeneous image coordinates $\mathbf{x}$ can be normalized by applying K. Equation (6) constrains the parameters of the two cameras, which themselves will in general depend on all relative motions which connect the two cameras indexed with r and s. The trifocal constraint can be interpreted as the intersection of 4 planes in a single point. As for instance outlined in [17], it can be written as

$$0 = g_T(\boldsymbol{p}, \boldsymbol{z}) = \det\left[\mathbf{A}_{r,i_a}, \mathbf{A}_{r,i_b}, \mathbf{A}_{s,i}, \mathbf{A}_{t,i}\right] \tag{7}$$

with the projection plane

$$\mathbf{A}_i = \mathsf{P}^\mathsf{T} \mathbf{l}_i \tag{8}$$

for the line $\mathbf{l}_i$ in camera t. The 2d line in each image has to intersect the observed image point $\mathbf{x}_i$. Our method ensures this by choosing an arbitrary direction α and computing the line by

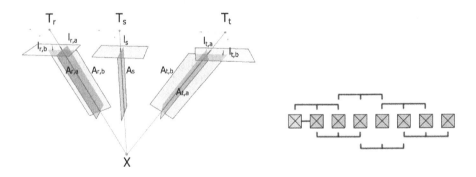

Fig. 1. Left: Scheme of the trifocal constraint. Four planes have to intersect in a single object point. The planes are inverse projections of 2D lines intersecting the observed image points. Right: Chaining the trifocal constraint using consecutive images. An epipolar constraint is introduced between the first (blue) and second image. Two trifocal constraints are introduced for every new image the point is observed

$$\mathbf{l}_i = \begin{bmatrix} \sin(\alpha) \\ -\cos(\alpha) \\ \cos(\alpha)y_i - \sin(\alpha)x_i \end{bmatrix}. \tag{9}$$

After introducing the basic constraints (6) and (7) used by our method we will now detail the constraint selection for each observation of an observed image point $\mathbf{x}_i$.

Assume an object point i is observed in a set of cameras $t_1...t_k$. A point observed for the first time provides no constraint. A point observed in two cameras delivers one epipolar constraint (6). The observation of a point in more than two cameras provides two constraints based on the trifocal tensor. We introduce two trifocal constraints in the following manner. We randomly select two lines $l_{1,a}$ and $l_{1,b}$, one line $l_{2,a}$ and two lines $l_{k,a}$ and $l_{k,b}$ (a and b are the indices of two lines in the image), which have different directions and hence provide two constraints through Equation 1, c. f. Figure 1.

The scheme for chaining trifocal constraints for consecutive images is outlined in Figure 6. When using the epipolar and trifocal constraints in the bundle adjustment, we do not need 3D object point coordinates, which have to be optimized. Instead, the object points are encoded implicitly in the trifocal constraints. Furthermore, the trifocal constraints are accountable for the transition of the scale through the chain of images ensuring a reconstruction with a consistent scale.

The choice of the lines for the trifocal constraint in Equation (8) directly influences the numerical stability of the system. We use this to our advantage by determining a proper combination of five lines that leads to the smallest condition of $J_z^{\mathsf{T}} J_z$ for the camera triplets in concern. This enhances the numerical stability of our bundle adjustment. The choice has five degrees of freedom, corresponding to the rotations of the planes A around the projection rays. Obtaining the best configuration is a non-trival optimization problem in itself.

For efficiency we opted for a simple random sampling strategy to obtain an acceptable set of lines. First, we choose random line directions and then we evaluate the condition number for our particular choice of lines. In case the condition number is too high to obtain a numerically stable solution, we randomize again. We empirically found that the space of acceptable configurations in order to achieve numerical stability is significantly larger than the space of the weak configurations. We leave a formal proof of this fact to future work.

2.4   Relative Camera Representation with Kinematic Chains

Modeling camera poses. One of the main problems of traditional bundle adjustment is that the condition of the information matrix (normal equation matrix) for large scale environments becomes huge leading to numerical instabilities of the linear solvers used. This is one of the reasons why hierarchical representations of large sets of images and the relative representation of camera positions are used. The camera orientations are represented locally, depending on an arbitrary local coordinate system.

The idea of [9] we are following here is to choose some reference cameras, say with pose M_t and model the pose of its k-th neighbour M_{t+k} using the relative pose $M_{t,k} = M_{t+k}M_{t+k-1}^{-1}$ and estimate the rotation and translation parameters of this relative motion $M_{t,k}$. This leads to the recursive relation

$$M_{t+k} = M_{t,k}M_{t+k-1} \tag{10}$$

or when modeling the complete kinematic chain from t to $t + k$

$$M_{t+k} = M_{t,k}M_{t,k-1}\cdot...\cdot M_{t,1}M_t. \tag{11}$$

The projection matrix P_{t+k} thus refers to the reference camera using

$$P_{t+k} = P_{0,t+k}M_{t+k} = P_{0,t+k}M_{t,k}M_{t,k-1}\cdot...\cdot M_{t,1}M_t \tag{12}$$

In case one has a constraint between two or three cameras, one needs to identify the path between these two via the reference cameras. Obviously, the sparseness of the Jacobian J_p now depends on the length of these chains of cameras observing the same individual object point.

Sparsity of the normal equation system. We now analyze, how our representation influences the structure of the linear solver and propose a strategy to increase the sparseness given an image sequence containing large loops. We are aware of the fact that this method may not always achieve optimal sparsity for example for image collections. Here we demonstrate that the sparsification is an important property to solve the unknown parameters more efficiently. While there are structural differences between the classical formulation of bundle adjustment and our method we will demonstrate how to take advantage of the same set of methods to improve the computational performance. We start with an example of a simulated environment illustrated on the left hand of Figure 2 and consisting of two loops. The simulated sequence contains of 71 images and approximately 170 object points on the planar surface. The structures of the normal equation matrices are shown in Fig. 3. The classical structure leads to the sparsest structure. A naive choice of the relative motions between cameras would follow the numbering of the cameras. Here, it leads to a nearly full normal equation matrix, as the first loop is the one from image 1 to image 41, and the second one is the large loop, containing all images except 1 to 16, resulting in the overlay of two square blocks. Therefore, one needs to analyze the effect of a certain numbering onto the structure of the normal equation matrix for the new type of representation

The matrix $J_z^T C_{zz} J_z$ is a block-diagonal matrix. Every block represents the set of constraints involving an observed object point. The determination of $(J_z^T C_{zz} J_z)^{-1} J_p$ in (3) then can be done block-wise by solving a linear equation system, exploiting the sparsity of $J_z^T C_{zz} J_z$. For structure from motion scenes, where an object point is only visible in a small subset of all cameras used, this is usually not computationally expensive. The resulting information matrix has the size of the number of the camera parameters plus the number of constraints

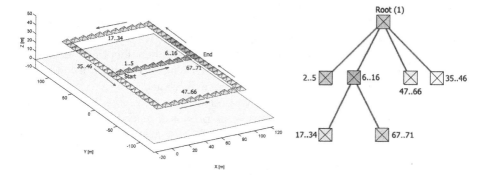

Fig. 2. Simulated example of a kinematic chain and spanning tree. The simulated sequence contains 71 images and 170 object points on a planar surface. Left: A camera trajectory at a birds eye view. Right: Simplified graph shown as a tree. The computed six subtrees are colored in a different manner.

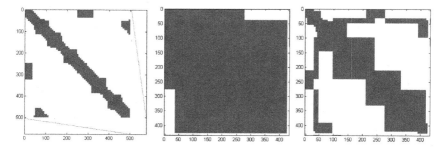

Fig. 3. Structure of the normal equation system. Left: Classical absolute representation. Middle: relative representation, naively taking all images in the order of appearance. Right: relative representation using our algorithm.

for the gauge only. As we can see in our example in Figure 3 the resulting information matrix is sparse too and therefore the equation system can be solved efficiently. The sparseness of the information matrix varies with the choice of the reference cameras, and thus the choice of the relative representations. We therefore need to select a representation which is optimal in some sense. This leads to a trade off between the condition of the information matrix and the sparseness and therefore the computational cost of the solution of the linear solver, taking the fill-in into account. In addition an optimal solver has to resort the information matrix to reduce the computational costs.

We have developed a scheme which aims at finding a good compromise. We can represent the whole set of relative cameras using a connection graph. As a camera has a unique reference system, we have to choose one of the possible spanning trees of the graph. For example, this can be easily achieved by enumerating all cameras in an arbitrary order. For image sequences an ordering by acquisition time is reasonable. We first sort the cameras in an ascending order. Then we obtain the connection graph for all connected cameras observing a common object point represented by an adjacency matrix. Next we search the subgraph that connects any camera to the camera with the smallest identifier. In a final step we merge the branches of the resulting tree to achieve a number of connected cameras larger than a threshold ($G_N = 5$) in each branch.

Figure 2 illustrates the simulated environment with two loops and the corresponding connection graph computed by our proposed method. The computed six sub-branches are colored differently in Figure 2. Images 1 and 6 are connected as they observing at least one common object point. Therefore our approach connects image *6* to the root node. In case a loop closing is detected, in our example in image *35*, a new branch is generated that connects it to the root node in the graph. This can be done for all used cameras incrementally.

3   Experimental Results

After the detailed description of the algorithm and the structure of the solution, we will verify its feasibility on synthetic and real datasets. The implementation has been done in Matlab^{TM}.

3.1   Simulation Results

We use two synthetic datasets to demonstrate the usefulness and practicality of our novel approach. The first dataset is a long linear camera motion, for instance acquired by an aerial vehicle or a mobile camera for urban scenes of facades. Using this dataset we will analyze the behaviour of the condition number of the linear solver and the demonstrate the benefit of including points at infinity. The second dataset has already been shown in Figure 2. This dataset is used to show the convergence behaviour and the applicability of our approach for datasets with loop closure.

Both datasets are generated using a synthetic camera setup with an image resolution of 800×600 pixel, a principal point in the middle of the image and a focal length of 400 pixel. In both datasets the distance between consecutive frames is $b = 10$ m and the distance of the camera centers to the plane of the observed object points is $h_g = 30$ m. The average number of observed object points per image is approximately $N \approx 20$.

In the first experiment we compare the the condition number of the information matrix between the classical and the novel approach. This issue will be noteworthy to solve the task of structure from motion in the presence of large-scale loops. On the left hand side of Figure 4 the simulated trajectory is outlined. We varied the length of the linear path in the experiment from 100 m to a maximal length of 1000 m. We assumed Gaussian noise of 1 pixel for the observations. The right hand side of Figure 4 shows the computed logarithmic condition numbers of the information matrix for the classical bundle adjustment and the newly proposed approach. We can observe that the condition number for the classical approach steadily increases. This increase is proportional to the increase of the uncertainty of the camera parameters toward the end of the strip. Due to the relative representation, the condition number is practically independent of the length of the trajectory in our approach. The peak at a strip length of 200 m is caused by a badly chosen direction to generate the trifocal constraint (see Section 2.3). Another important evaluation is the usefulness of incorporating points at infinity. In this experiment we added just three additional points at infinity. In Figure 5 the expected standard deviations of the camera parameter in the global coordinate system with and without the points at infinity are shown. The uncertainty is computed throughout all cameras by variance propagation. We can observe that the points at infinity have a significant influence on the determination of the rotation as well as the translation due to the correlation to the rotation parameters. As our approach can deal with points at infinity,

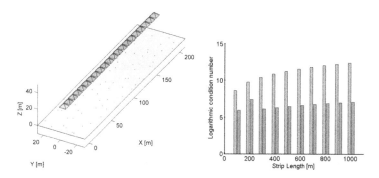

Fig. 4. Left: Long strip of consecutive cameras. The gauge is fixed to the first camera. The scale is introduced by the known true base length to the second camera. Right: Condition number of the linear equation system (Information-Matrix) for a long strip. Classical bundle adjustment (red), new method (blue). Observe, that the condition number of the experiment with a strip length of 1000 m differ by a factor of $\approx 10^5$.

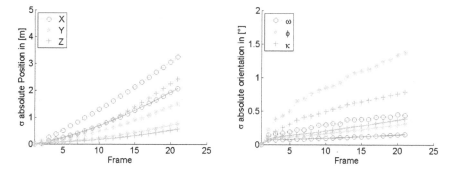

Fig. 5. Expected accuracy of the camera position (left) and rotation (right) without (dotted) and with (solid line) 3 additional points at infinity. The shown absolute uncertainty is computed by error propagation through the chain of relative representations.

the solution of a bundle will be significantly improved if points at infinity are available using the novel method.

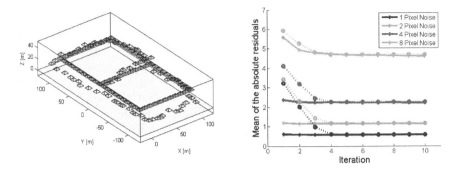

Fig. 6. Left: Simulated example with two loops. The approximated values are computed using a random walk with $3m$ Gaussian noise for the translation components and 0.5 degree for the rotation parameter, Right: Mean of the absolute sum of the residuals for 11 iterations. The dashed lines are the mean residuals for the classical bundle adjustment, the solid line for our approach.

In the last experiment using synthetic data our method is able to perform loop closures and it is robust to corrupted approximate values and large uncertainty of the observations. Approximate values for the exterior camera parameters are obtained in general computing a robust estimation of the essential matrix [13]. The rotation parameter can be usually determined very accurately, however the baseline vector can not be. Therefore, for image sequences the approximate values are chained, which leads to a random walk. In our example presented in Figure 6 (left), we generated approximate values chaining relative orientations with a randomized accuracy of 3 m for the translation parameters and 0.5 degree for the rotation parameters. On the right side of Figure 6 the mean of the absolute sum of the residuals for 11 iterations are presented. The dashed lines are the results using the classical model, the solid lines are the results of our approach. For the classical model the object points were initialized at the first projection ray with the known distance. Both simulations are run with the same observations and initial values. We can observe that in presence of small noise the residuals become significantly smaller in the first iterations in our method compared to the classical approach, since the object points act in the classical approach as anchor. Our proposed method does not show this disadvantageous behavior. The convergence behavior has to be examined in more detail in the future, when integration robustification methods is completed.

3.2   Real Data

We also tested our method on a real datasets. The first dataset consists of an image sequence of 624 images of the left camera of a stereo system. A feature

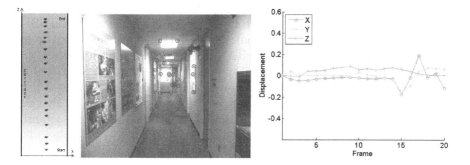

Fig. 7. Left: Birds-eye view of the corridor and estimated as well as reference camera position and orientation. Middle: Single frame extracted from an image sequence with tracked features. Right: Differences between reference camera and estimated camera parameter, X, Y, Z.

detection and flow computation system does tracking using a graphics processing unit implementation. Additionally SIFT features are extracted and descriptor matching is performed [18]. A keyframe dataset of the whole sequence using 20 images and 55 randomly selected feature tracks has been taken. A reference trajectory was computed using the stereo tracking system of [19] including a huge number of observations. In Figure 7 sample keyframe with detected image features is shown. To the left a schematic birds-eye view of the estimated camera trajectory derived by error propagation is presented. To the right the differences of the estimated camera position to the high accuracy reference trajectory is shown. We remark, that the present implementation is not robustified and optimized for speed yet.

The second dataset consists of an image collection of the *Brandenburger Tor* containing 100 images with 1600 3d-points and roughly 24000 trifocal constraints taken from a photo-sharing website like *Flickr.com*. The focal length initally is taken from the image header and the principal point is fixed to the image

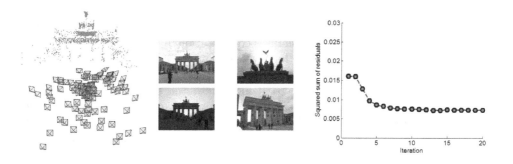

Fig. 8. Left: 3d-view of estimated camera parameters and reconstructed object points using the novel method. Middle: Example images of an image collection. Right: Absolute sum of the residuals for 20 iterations.

center. An existing robust classical bundle adjustment incorporating intrinsic parameters as unknowns determined intrisic parameter as references. Again SIFT features are extracted and descriptor matching is performed, then pairwise relative orientations are computed using a RANSAC based scheme and outliers are rejected. To the left of Figure 8 the estimated camera orientations, as well as the reconstructed 3d object points determined by intersection 2 estimated projection rays are shown. To the right the absolute sum of the residuals thought 20 iterations are presented. The novel method decrease the residuals constantly and seems to have converged for this real dataset.

4   Conclusions

This paper introduced a new approach to circumvent the limitations of classical bundle adjustment by changing the observation model and the camera representation of the least square solution. The results of the classical bundle and the novel approach are equal as proved in [14,15]. We focus in the paper on the structural differences of the normal equation system and proved the usefulness of the proposed concept on simulated data and real data. The main advantages can be summarized as follows:

- No approximate values for the object points are necessary any more. The new algorithm is therefore able to handle points at infinity. This can improve the solution of a structure from motion task significantly. In addition the pre-filtering of the observations can be neglected and there is no need of the reduction of the normal equation system using the Schur-Complement.
- Due to the relative representation the condition number of the information matrix seems to be independent of the length of a camera trajectory. This is very useful for structure from motion tasks on mobile platforms.
- We observed a faster convergence and robustness in present of corrupted approximate values in our experiments compared to a classical bundle adjustment. We are aware that this fact should be investigated in more detail in future experiments.

Although our algorithm shows significant positive properties, the computation of the Jacobians using kinematic chains is computationally more complex compared to the classical formulation. We have yet to examine how this interacts with the speed up due to faster convergence.

We leave it to future work to demonstrate the performance of the new method using large image sets along with applying robustification techniques to the parameter estimation. While not demonstarted the approach can be extended to a more general approach to accomodate uncalibrated cameras. We also plan to implement an online version, where images can be incrementally added.

References

1. Triggs, B., McLauchlan, P.F., Hartley, R.I., Fitzgibbon, A.W.: Bundle Adjustment – A Modern Synthesis. In: Triggs, B., Zisserman, A., Szeliski, R. (eds.) ICCV-WS 1999. LNCS, vol. 1883, pp. 298–372. Springer, Heidelberg (2000)
2. Lourakis, M.I.A., Argyros, A.A.: SBA: A Software Package for Generic Sparse Bundle Adjustment. ACM Trans. Math. Software 36, 1–30 (2009)
3. Agarwal, S., Snavely, N., Simon, I., Seitz, S.M., Szeliski, R.: Building Rome in a Day. In: Proc. ICCV. IEEE (2009)
4. Fitzgibbon, A., Zisserman, A.: Automatic camera recovery for closed or open image sequences, pp. 311–326 (1998)
5. Steedly, D., Essa, I., Delleart, F.: Spectral partitioning for structure from motion. In: ICCV 2003: Proceedings of the Ninth IEEE International Conference on Computer Vision, p. 996. IEEE Computer Society, Washington, DC (2003)
6. Ni, K., Steedly, D., Dellaert, F.: Out-of-core bundle adjustment for large-scale 3d reconstruction. In: ICCV 2007 (2007)
7. Farenzena, M., Fusiello, A., Gherardi, R.: Stucture-and-motion pipeline on a hierarchical cluster tree. In: Proceedings of the IEEE Internation Workshop on 3-D Digital Imaging and Modeling, pp. 1489–1496 (2009)
8. Estrada, C., Neira, J., Tardos, J.D.: Hierarchical SLAM: real-time accurate mapping of large environments. IEEE Transactions on Robotics, 588–596 (2005)
9. Sibley, G., Mei, C., Reid, I., Newman, P.: Adaptive relative bundle adjustment. In: Proceedings of Robotics: Science and Systems, Seattle, USA (2009)
10. Montiel, J., Civera, J., Davison, A.: Unified inverse depth parametrization for monocular slam. In: Proceedings of Robotics: Science and Systems, Philadelphia, USA (2006)
11. Hartley, R.I.: Lines and points in three views and the trifocal tensor. IJCV 22, 125–140 (1997)
12. Pagel, F.: Robust monocular egomotion estimation based on an iekf. In: CRV 2009: Proceedings of the 2009 Canadian Conference on Computer and Robot Vision, pp. 213–220. IEEE Computer Society, Washington, DC (2009)
13. Hartley, R.I., Zisserman, A.: Multiple View Geometry in Computer Vision, 2nd edn. Cambridge University Press (2004) ISBN: 0521540518
14. Koch, K.R.: Parameter estimation and hypothesis testing in linear models. Springer (1988)
15. Mikhail, E.M., Ackermann, F.: Observations and Least Squares. University Press of America (1976)
16. Faugeras, O.D., Mourrain, B.: On the geometry and algebra of the point and line correspondences between n images. In: ICCV, pp. 951–956 (1995)
17. Heuel, S.: Uncertain Projective Geometry. LNCS, vol. 3008. Springer, Heidelberg (2004)
18. Lowe, D.G.: Distinctive Image Features from Scale-Invariant Keypoints. International Journal of Computer Vision 60, 91–110 (2004)
19. Clipp, B., Zach, C., Frahm, J.M., Pollefeys, M.: A New Minimal Solution to the Relative Pose of a Calibrated Stereo Camera with Small Field of View Overlap (2009)

Accurate Single Image Multi-modal Camera Pose Estimation

Christoph Bodensteiner, Marcus Hebel, and Michael Arens

Fraunhofer IOSB,
Gutleuthausstraße 1, 76275 Ettlingen, Germany
{christoph.bodensteiner,marcus.hebel,michael.arens}@iosb.fraunhofer.de
http://www.iosb.fraunhofer.de

Abstract. A well known problem in photogrammetry and computer vision is the precise and robust determination of camera poses with respect to a given 3D model. In this work we propose a novel multi-modal method for single image camera pose estimation with respect to 3D models with intensity information (e.g., LiDAR data with reflectance information).

We utilize a direct point based rendering approach to generate synthetic 2D views from 3D datasets in order to bridge the dimensionality gap. The proposed method then establishes 2D/2D point and local region correspondences based on a novel self-similarity distance measure. Correct correspondences are robustly identified by searching for small regions with a similar geometric relationship of local self-similarities using a Generalized Hough Transform. After backprojection of the generated features into 3D a standard Perspective-n-Points problem is solved to yield an initial camera pose. The pose is then accurately refined using an intensity based 2D/3D registration approach.

An evaluation on Vis/IR 2D and airborne and terrestrial 3D datasets shows that the proposed method is applicable to a wide range of different sensor types. In addition, the approach outperforms standard global multi-modal 2D/3D registration approaches based on Mutual Information with respect to robustness and speed.

Potential applications are widespread and include for instance multi-spectral texturing of 3D models, SLAM applications, sensor data fusion and multi-spectral camera calibration and super-resolution applications.

Keywords: Multi-Modal Registration, Pose Estimation, Multi-Modal 2D/3D Correspondences, Self-Similarity Distance Measure.

1 Introduction

A fundamental issue in computer vision and photogrammetry is the precise determination of camera poses with respect to a given 3D model. It has many applications, e.g., augmented reality, image based localization or robot navigation. The involved registration task is mostly formulated as the determination of a geometric transformation[1] which maps corresponding features onto each other

---

[1] In case of camera pose estimation the geometric transformation is known as the external calibration matrix or extrinsic parameters of the camera.

K.N. Kutulakos (Ed.): ECCV 2010 Workshops, Part II, LNCS 6554, pp. 296–309, 2012.
© Springer-Verlag Berlin Heidelberg 2012

by minimizing a proper distance measure. In general there are two solution approaches for matching 2D/3D image data. Either one computes 3D information from 2 or more 2D images and performs the similarity comparison in 3D, or 2D data is simulated from the 3D dataset and compared in a two-dimensional space. We focus on the latter, since we assume only one available 2D image and a pre-recorded 3D dataset with intensity information as described in Sec.2. This paper considers 2D/3D camera pose estimation for multi-modal data, i.e., estimating the external camera $R, \mathbf{t}$ parameters when the internal camera parameters K are known and the involved datasets stem from different image modalities. The projection of 3D world points $\mathbf{M_i}$ to corresponding 2D image points $\mathbf{m_i}$ is modeled by a standard pinhole camera model. The intrinsic parameters K with the parameters skew s, focal length f, aspect ratio α and principal point $\mathbf{u} = [u_0 \ v_0]^T$ are assumed to be known.

$$\mathbf{m_i} = P\mathbf{M_i}, P = K\left[R|\mathbf{t}\right], K = \begin{bmatrix} f & s & u_0 \\ 0 & \alpha f & v_0 \\ 0 & 0 & 1 \end{bmatrix}. \tag{1}$$

1.1 Related Work and Contribution

2D/3D camera pose estimation received much attention in the last decades [1,2,3,4]. Existing methods can be roughly divided by the spatial extent/type of the used features/structures:

Pose from 2D/3D Point Correspondences: Pose estimation is basically solvable from 3 2D/3D point correspondences and is widely known as the *P3P* problem. A common approach is to determine the 3D point positions $\mathbf{M_i^C}$ in the camera coordinate frame C. This leads to a root finding problem for a polynomial of degree 8 with only even terms. To disambiguate the 4 solutions in the general case an additional point is often used. However, the computed pose from 4 point correspondences is usually not accurate and therefore it is advisable to simultaneously use $n >> 4$ point correspondences. This leads to the well known *PnP* (perspective n points) problem [3]. Often RANSAC type algorithms [5] or robust cost functions [3] are used to handle outliers in the correspondence set. A non-linear least squares optimization of the reprojection error with all inlying feature correspondences increases accuracy further:

$$\text{minimize}_{R,\mathbf{t}} \sum_i \|K(R\mathbf{M_i} + \mathbf{t}) - \mathbf{m_i}\|_2^2. \tag{2}$$

Modern algorithms [1,4] efficiently solve this problem under real-time constraints even on modest computing hardware [4].

Pose from Planar Structures: By observing a corresponding planar structure in both datasets one can extract the pose parameters directly from the homography H [6,7] which maps the structures onto each other. In this case the projection equation of model $\mathbf{M_i}$ and 2D image points $\mathbf{m_i}$ simplifies without loss of generality to:

$$s \begin{bmatrix} u \\ v \\ 1 \end{bmatrix} = K \begin{bmatrix} \mathbf{r_1} & \mathbf{r_2} & \mathbf{r_3} & \mathbf{t} \end{bmatrix} \begin{bmatrix} X \\ Y \\ 0 \\ 1 \end{bmatrix} = K \begin{bmatrix} \mathbf{r_1} & \mathbf{r_2} & \mathbf{t} \end{bmatrix} \begin{bmatrix} X \\ Y \\ 1 \end{bmatrix}, \qquad (3)$$

where $\mathbf{r_i}$ denotes the *i.th* column of the matrix R. Therefore the model points $\mathbf{M_i}$ and image points $\mathbf{m_i}$ are related by a homography H (defined up to a scale factor λ):

$$H = \begin{bmatrix} \mathbf{h_1} & \mathbf{h_2} & \mathbf{h_3} \end{bmatrix} = \lambda K \begin{bmatrix} \mathbf{r_1} & \mathbf{r_2} & \mathbf{t} \end{bmatrix}. \qquad (4)$$

Based on the assumption that K is known, the camera pose is given by:

$$\begin{aligned} \mathbf{q_1} &= \lambda K^{-1} \mathbf{h_1} \\ \mathbf{q_2} &= \lambda K^{-1} \mathbf{h_2} \\ \mathbf{q_3} &= \mathbf{r_1} \times \mathbf{r_2} \\ \mathbf{t} &= \lambda K^{-1} \mathbf{h_3} \end{aligned} \qquad (5)$$

Due to data noise the computed matrix $Q = \begin{bmatrix} \mathbf{q_1} & \mathbf{q_2} & \mathbf{q_3} \end{bmatrix}$ usually does not satisfy the ortho-normality constraint of a rotation matrix $R, R^T R = I$. Therefore R is computed to minimize$_R \| R - Q \|_F^2$ s.t. $R^T R = I$ in a Frobenius norm sense. This can be efficiently achieved [6] by a singular value decomposition of $Q = U\,S\,V^T$ and setting R to $U\,V^T$.

Pose from Intensity Based Distance Minimization: A standard approach for pose determination in the field of medical image computing (e.g., X-Ray/CT-computed tomography, X-Ray/MR-magnetic resonance imaging) is to simulate pose parametrized 2D views $V_{sim}(R, \mathbf{t})$ from the 3D dataset which minimize/maximize an intensity based distance/similarity measure $D_{(Typ)}, D : \mathbb{R}^N \times \mathbb{R}^N \rightarrow \mathbb{R}$ between the acquired reference image I_R and a simulated view over the support of the image region A.

$$\text{minimize}_{R,\mathbf{t}} \int_A D_{(Typ)}(V_{sim}(R, \mathbf{t}), I_R). \qquad (6)$$

We refer to [8,9] for a comparison of common intensity based 2D/3D distance measures e.g., Normalized Cross Correlation (NCC), Spearman Rank Order Correlation (SPROCC), Gradient Correlation (GC), Correlation Ratio (CR) and Mutual Information (MI).

Generally, intensity based similarity optimization allows for accurate registration results but is computationally expensive. Additionally, these methods often rely on a very good initialization to avoid local optima. Local feature methods are more advantageous when significant changes of the underlying scenery hamper global intensity based similarity computations. However, a common difficulty of the outlined approaches is the determination of 2D/3D feature/planar region correspondences, respectively a sufficiently close starting point for an intensity based similarity computation. Local feature based correspondence methods [10,11] work very well if the image data stems from the same image modality. An excellent review can be found in [12]. Local feature approaches mostly match common image features based on gradient information. The registration task becomes challenging if the image data is multi-modal, e.g., the image intensity data stems from different sensors with, e.g., different image acquisition techniques, spectral sensitivities or passive/active illumination. The problem of finding accurate local feature correspondences across different image modalities is less understood. Successful multi-modal matching applications mostly stem from medical image registration, e.g., the fusion of MR/CT or CT/PET (positron emission tomography) images by maximization of the information theoretic similarity measure MI. We focus on the determination of point and region correspondences using local multi-modal features. The main difficulty is the inherent trade off between feature correspondence discrimination and multi-modal matching capabilities. We adapt the approach of Shechtman and Irani [13] who proposed self-similarity descriptors for sketch based object and video detection and extend it with ideas from the work of Leibe et. al. [14] to determine multi-modal point and region correspondences. To the best of our knowledge there is no literature about accurate multi-modal pose determination with local correspondences based on self-similarity. We additionally propose to refine the pose optimization by minimizing locally a densely computed self-similarity distance to accurately align local image regions where standard multi-modal similarity measures like MI or CR have major difficulties. The fusion of 2D images with LiDAR data is still an active research field [15,16,17]. The closest work [18] with respect to our application uses MI to register optical images with LiDAR data. However, we claim that our method is more robust w.r.t. to pose initialization and cluttered image data.

The outline of the paper is as follows: first we give a short overview for laser based acquisition of 3D data. Then we describe the key parts of the approach and discuss specific details which enable the robust local correspondence search in the multi-modal case. We evaluate the method on different image datasets with a focus on IR/Vis in combination with airborne (ALS) and terrestrial laser scanning (TLS) datasets. In the end, we discuss the results and give further research directions.

2 Laser-Based 3D Data Acquisition

Remote sensing of 3D structures in the far-field is commonly approached with multi-view image analysis as well as active illumination techniques. In this context, LiDAR (light detection and ranging) is a comparatively new method that enables direct acquisition of 3D information [19]. LiDAR sensors emit laser radiation and detect its reflection in order to determine the precise distance between sensor and illuminated object. Currently available laser scanners are capable of performing hundreds of thousands of range measurements per second, thus allowing a complete 3D scenery to be captured in a reasonably short time interval. Two main types of laser scanners can be distinguished that follow different concepts of range determination: phase shift and time-of flight laser scanners. In case of phase-shift scanners, a continuous laser beam is emitted with sinusoidally modulated optical power. The distance to the reflecting object is estimated based on the phase shift between received and emitted signal. Phase-shift scanners are well suited for static terrestrial laser scanning. When operating the scanning head on a rigid tripod, ranging accuracies of few millimeters at distances up to hundred meters can be achieved. Mobile methods like airborne laser scanning usually combine a time-of-flight LiDAR device with high-precision navigational sensors mounted on a common sensor platform. The ranging accuracy of such a system is typically limited to few centimeters, while maximum distances up to one kilometer can be measured.

Currently available time-of-flight laser scanners are capable of acquiring the full waveform of reflected pulses, thus enabling new methods of data analysis [20]. The portion of the reflected energy can be considered in relation to the emitted radiation and the measured distance. This ratio reveals the local reflectivity at the specific laser wavelength, which typically lies in the near infrared due to eye-safety reasons. High-speed scanning and exploitation of reflectivity information results in highly detailed textured 3D point clouds. However, unlike ambient background light, the reflection of directed laser radiation is significantly affected by the incidence angle and the surface characteristics of the illuminated objects.

3   Method

The multi-modal 2D/3D registration procedure can be summarized as follows: first we utilize a point based rendering approach to generate a synthetic 2D View from the 3D dataset to enable the correspondence search. Then we establish 2D/2D point and local region correspondences based on local features. Correct correspondences are robustly identified by searching for small regions with a similar geometric relationship of local features by employing a Generalized Hough Transform. The 3D positions for the synthetically generated 2D features can easily be determined using the depth buffer information from the rendering procedure. The registration is then carried out by solving a PnP based pose determination. The calculated pose is finally refined with an intensity based registration. This refinement step is intended for applications with very high accuracy requirements, e.g., multi-spectral texturing of 3D models, multi-modal camera calibration or multi-modal super-resolution. Summarizing, the method can be divided (cf., Fig.1) as follows:

1. Synthetic 2D View Generation
2. Feature Extraction
3. Feature Correspondence Search and Constraint Filtering
4. Feature Correspondence Based Pose Determination
5. Intensity Based Multi-Modal Registration

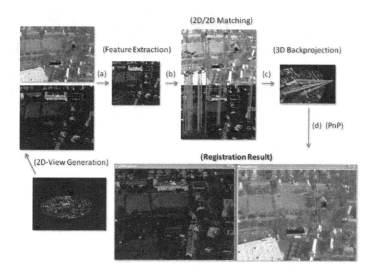

Fig. 1. Registration algorithm overview: (a) extracted local image regions, (b) feature matching by searching geometrically consistent feature matches and fundamental matrix filtering, (c) 3D backprojection of 2D feature matches, (d) pose determination. The registration result (bottom image) shows a superposition (red cross) of the airborne IR image and the textured LiDAR view from the left side.

Synthetic 2D View Generation: We propose a direct point based rendering approach [21] for synthetic view generation. The automated generation of texture mapped models (e.g., Fig. 4i) is still error prone and a time consuming process. To this end we use a simple rendering of the 3D point cloud data based on small spheres with adaptive sizes. In this work we selected the initial pose for the view generation manually. However, the proposed feature based method shows a wide convergence range.

Feature Extraction: We extract local features over different scales and use standard descriptors for an initial correspondence search. To this date we evaluated SIFT [10], SURF [11] and recently proposed self-similarity descriptors [13].

Feature Correspondence Search and Constraint Filtering: To enable a robust local feature based 2D/3D registration approach for multi-modal data we utilize the concept of simultaneously matching local features inside small image regions. The selection of these image regions serves as a starting point for the correspondence search. Each region defines a local coordinate frame, where the geometric layout of contained features is determined. Our experiments show that it is favorable to use image regions with strongly distinct features in order to increase the number of correct region matches. In this work we used constant region sizes (60x60px) and a simple heuristic based on Harris corners,

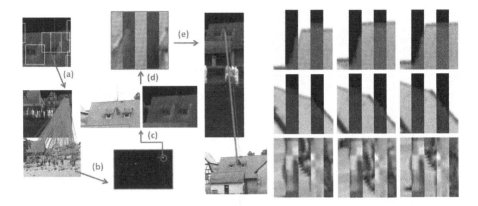

Fig. 2. Local feature correspondence search algorithm (IR/Vis example): (a) extracted local image regions (Harris/Foerstner), (b) feature matching by searching geometrically consistent feature matches, (c) best hypothesis supporting feature matches, (d) intensity based local image region alignment, (e) final point correspondences for one local image region. The right columns shows local patch alignments (Init/MI/Self-Sim).

which serve as the origin. We employ a Generalized Hough Transform similar to the one used in [14]. We also use a technique called soft-matching [14] for local feature matching which incorporates the k (e.g., 2-4) nearest neighbors in descriptor space as potential matches. Due to fundamentally different object appearances, many initial local feature matches are not correct and would lead to an enormous amount of wrong point correspondences (see Fig. 2a left). Therefore each local feature casts a vote for a corresponding region center according to the geometric layout in its reference coordinate system [14]. Under the assumption that wrong correspondences spread their votes randomly, we determine the corresponding image region center with a simple maximum search. The final 2D/2D point correspondences are feature matches which contributed a vote near to the maximum in voting space. We refer to Leibe et. al. [14] for a detailed description of the voting principle. However, the voting space maximum in multi-modal image pairs does not always correspond to a correct region match. We use point correspondences that contributed a vote near the maximum in voting space (backprojection of best hypothesis supporting feature matches) to estimate (RANSAC) a local affine transformation T_a of the corresponding image patch (e.g., 60x60px). We then discard matches with a high self-similarity distance (eqn. 12) based on an empirical determined threshold.

Intensity Based Optimization of Local Planar Patches: Due to small errors in the determined feature correspondences we also applied a local intensity based multi-modal distance optimization to find local region correspondences (cf., Fig.2right). Formally, we search for a set of optimal transformation parameters $\hat{\theta}$ which minimize a multi-modal distance measure $D : \mathbb{R}^N \to \mathbb{R}$ over the support of a local image region A_i around the determined point correspondences:

$$\hat{\theta} = argmin_\theta \; D(\theta), \tag{7}$$

$$D(\theta) = \int_{A_i} D_{(\cdot)}(I_{T_\theta}, I_R). \tag{8}$$

To this end we use parametric (projective) transformations T_θ with 8 degrees of freedom for distance minimization. The local image region A_i should be as small as possible for projective transformations since they inherently imply planarity. The affine transformation T_a serves as a starting point for the image alignment optimization. The nonlinear optimization is based on a specific pattern search method which does not rely on gradient information. Basically, we approximate the distance function $D(\theta)$ with a multi-variate polynomial of degree 2 and recenter/rescale a search pattern at the optimum of the surrogate polynomial. Given a proper initialization, the method needs only a few distance function evaluations to converge to a local optimum and is especially designed for computationally expensive distance functions. We plan to directly compute an accurate pose from the local projective transformations T_θ as described in Sec. 1.1. However, to this end we use this computationlly expensive step only for an optional point correspondence optimization, when we omit a global intensity based similarity optimization.

Feature Correspondence Based Pose Determination: The corresponding 3D feature positions from the 2D rendering are efficiently backprojected into 3D by using the depth buffer information from the rendering process[2]. Given the 2D/3D correspondences we calculate the pose using a standard PnP algorithm. We used the recently proposed EPnP [4] algorithm, which expresses the n 3D feature positions as a weighted sum of four virtual control points. This algorithm proved to be superior w.r.t. speed and accuracy compared to the popular POSIT algorithm [22]. To robustly detect outliers in the 2D/3D correspondence set we employed a RANSAC approach. We used $n = 8$ subset sizes and a $5px$ reprojection error (cf. eqn. 2) threshold for the inlier set. The computed pose was additionally refined by a non-linear Gauss-Newton minimization of the reprojection error (eqn. 2) w.r.t. the inlier set.

Intensity Based Multi-Modal Registration: To accurately align the multi-modal data sets we additionally minimize/maximize an intensity based distance/similarity measure. The convergence range of intensity based multi-modal 2D/3D methods is usually very small. However, the local feature based pose computation usually provides a sufficiently close starting point. An important design choice is the selection of an appropriate distance measure. Mutual Information [9] is considered the gold standard similarity measure for multi-modal matching. It measures the mutual dependence of the underlying image intensity distributions:

---

[2] It's important to transform the data into an adequate coordinate system to reduce inaccuracies caused by a limited Z-Buffer resolution.

$$D_{(MI)}(I_R, I_{T_\theta}) = H(I_R) + H(I_{T_\theta}) - H(I_R, I_{T_\theta}) \tag{9}$$

where $H(I_R)$ and $H(I_{T_\theta})$ are the marginal entropies and

$$H(I_R, I_{T_\theta}) = \sum_{X \in I_{T_\theta}} \sum_{Y \in I_R} p(X, Y) log(\frac{p(X, Y)}{p(X)p(Y)}) \tag{10}$$

is the joint entropy. $p(X, Y)$ denotes the joint probability distribution function of the image intensities X, Y in I_R and I_{T_θ}, and $p(X)$ and $p(Y)$ are the marginal probability distribution functions. However, MI is very difficult to estimate (e.g.,see Fig. 3) for small image regions and does not cope well with spatially-varying intensity fluctuations (eqn. (10)). Therefore we propose to minimize a self-similarity distance of corresponding image regions in I_R and I_{T_θ}. To compute the self-similarity description for an image patch point we compare a small image patch with a larger surrounding image region centered at $q \in R_i$ using simple sum of squared differences (SSD) between image intensities normalized by the image patch intensity variance and noise $c(I)_{noise,variance}$:

$$S_q(x, y) = \exp\left(-\frac{SSD_q(x, y)}{c(I)_{noise,variance}}\right) \tag{11}$$

This correlation image $S_q(x, y)$ is then transformed into a log polar coordinate system and partitioned into bins (e.g., 20 angles, 4 radial intervals) where the maximal correlation value in each bin is used as an entry for the self-similarity dimension description of the vector $S_q^{I(\cdot)}(x, y)$ located at the image position $(x, y) \in A_i$. Each vector is then linearly normalized to $[0, 1]$. The distance measure now simply computes the sum of squared distances of the self-similarity description vectors $S_q^{I(\cdot)}$ computed at the region A_i:

$$D_{(SSim)}(I_{T_\theta}, I_R) = \sum_{(x,y) \in A_i} \|S_q^{I_R}(x, y) - S_q^{I_{T_\theta}}(x, y)\|^2. \tag{12}$$

In multiple experiments we plotted the values of the optimization function while varying function parameters as shown in Fig. 3f,g. The plots of this distance measure show unique maxima and relatively smooth and monotonically increasing function shapes especially for small local image regions.

3.1   Implementation Details and Runtime Information

The implemented point based rendering and intensity based 2D/2D and 2D/3D registration software is based on the OpenCV and VTK [23] C/C++ libraries. We used the SiftGPU [24] and OpenSURF [11] implementation for the local descriptor computation. Since the voting based correspondence approach requires many feature correspondence searches, it is important to use fast search structures [25] for nearest neighbor determination in descriptor space (L_2 norm).

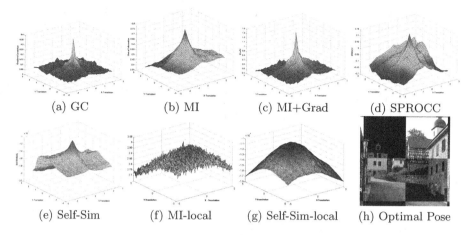

(a) GC   (b) MI   (c) MI+Grad   (d) SPROCC

(e) Self-Sim   (f) MI-local   (g) Self-Sim-local   (h) Optimal Pose

Fig. 3. Plots of global distance/similarity values (a-e) for deviations from the found value by the optimization algorithm (camera translation in x and y direction (± 2.5m)). Comparison of local MI and Self-Sim values (f,g) for a small image patch (60x60px) (image translation in x and y direction) from the found value by the optimization algorithm. The optimal value for the pose (h) is shown at where all parameters are zero.

Since our implementation is not runtime-optimized, the reported time measurements provide only a rough estimate for the actual overall algorithm runtime. The determination of 500 region correspondences ranges from 60-200s on an Intel Q9550 System. An intensity based local image patch refinement (60x60px) needs 10-15s (single core) for one image patch optimization (Self-Similarity features and distance measure).

4   Results

We evaluated the voting based feature correspondence method (Sec.3) by counting point correspondences w.r.t. a robustly estimated fundamental matrix (8-pt algorithm, RANSAC, 1.25px inlier threshold). When possible, e.g., in case of IR/Vis aerial images we estimated a global homography (RANSAC, 2.5px inlier threshold) to evaluate correct correspondences. In total we used 10 Vis/IR, 50 Vis/IR aerial and 2 LiDAR/IR/Vis image pairs. Our experiments show (Tab. 1, Fig. 4) that this method enables a robust determination of multi-modal feature correspondences. The self-similarity descriptors proved to be well suited for this task compared to well established local feature approaches like SIFT [10] or SURF [11] (see Fig. 4). A visualization comparing SIFT, SURF and Self-Similarity features for TLS/Vis image data is shown in Fig.4. This effect especially holds for ALS based renderings from close view points where rendering holes drastically affect gradient histogram based descriptors (e.g., Fig.4h).

Table 1. Averaged rounded (found/correct) point correspondences. The correctness of point correspondences was additionally checked by visual inspection in case of fundamental matrix constraint filtering.

Features	IR/Vis (2D/2D)	IR/Vis (Aerial 2D/2D)	ALS/IR
SIFT	0 / 0	63 / 85%	0 / 0
SURF	0 / 0	35 / 91%	0 / 0
Self-Sim	3706 / 49%	2185 / 64%	4881 / 23%

Given high quality synthetic renderings and high point densities local feature methods based on gradient information can still work. Fig.4(a-f) shows correspondences and PnP based pose computations for SIFT, SURF and Self-Sim features. However, the number and distribution of correct correspondences was considerably higher for Self-Sim features. In case of IR/ALS (cf., Fig.4h) data we were not able to compute correct correspondences using standard local features like SIFT and SURF. To evaluate the pose determination accuracy from the found point correspondences we calculated ground truth pose information by jointly matching small sets of 3-5 images in order to calculate accurate extrinsic and intrinsic parameters. Then we artificially perturbed the camera positions from T_{World}^{Cam} to $T_{World}^{pertCam}$. The translation parameters were randomly perturbed by maximally ± 5 m and the rotation parameters were perturbed by maximally ± 3 deg. After registration we calculated the Euler angle representation of the deviation matrix T_{dev} using the calculated registration matrix T_{regCam}^{World}.

$$T_{dev} = T_{regCam}^{World} T_{World}^{Cam}. \tag{13}$$

The average point based pose estimation accuracy for 20 TLS/Vis views showed rotational deviations of 0.95 (x), 1.12 (y) and 0.74 (z) degree and an average translational deviation of 0.93 (x), 0.72 (y), 0.69 (z) m for voting based SURF feature correspondences. Self-Similarity feature correspondences led to rotational deviations of 0.89 (x), 1.02 (y) and 0.97 (z) degree and an average translational deviation of 0.89 (x), 0.93 (y), 0.67 (z) m. For the intensity based multi-modal registration, we evaluated various intensity based distance measures like MI, CR, GC, SPROCC, linear combinations of MI+GC and the proposed densely computed Self-Similarity. First we evaluated intensity based registration performance for local patches by visual inspection with respect to MI, Spearman Rank Correlation Coefficient and Self-Similarity. We evaluated the number of (correct/false) alignments for a representative set of 113 local image patches. SPROCC led to 34% correct alignments, MI to 31%, and Self-Sim to 94% correct alignments (e.g., Fig.2right). By using the global intensity based 2D/3D camera pose estimation step we finally achieved very accurate visual registration results (cf., Fig. 5).

Fig. 4. Voting based correspondences using (a) SIFT, (b) SURF and (c) Self-Similarity features for identical Vis/TLS images. The second row (d-f) shows resulting poses using the PnP approach. The last row depicts Self-Similarity feature correspondences for TLS/Vis (g), IR/ALS (h) and TLS(Texture Mapped)/Vis (i) data. All correspondences are fundamental matrix constraint (RANSAC, 2.25px) filtered.

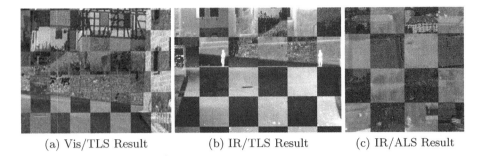

| (a) Vis/TLS Result | (b) IR/TLS Result | (c) IR/ALS Result |

Fig. 5. Intensity based camera pose estimation results for Vis/TLS-LiDAR (a), IR/TLS-LiDAR (b) and IR/ALS-LiDAR (c) image pairs

5   Conclusion and Future Work

In this work we proposed and implemented a robust method to determine accurate local multi-modal 2D/3D correspondences. The method is based on simultaneously matching geometrically consistent feature correspondences. Very accurate multi-modal 2D/3D alignments can be achieved in combination with local intensity based optimization which allows for a precise multi-spectral texturing of 3D models, sensor data fusion and multi-spectral camera calibration.

The registration of multi-modal 2D/3D datasets is inherently difficult due to fundamental differing object appearances. Multi-modal distance measures are usually application dependent and the suitability of self-similarity as a general multi-modal distance measure remains open. However, experiments show a clear dominance of the proposed self-similarity distance measure for IR/Vis and ALS/TLS/IR/Vis image pairs in case of small region sizes (see Fig.2right). In addition, we find the approach of locally matching self-similar structures [13] very intriguing since it does not assume a global functional relationship like correlation ratio or clusters in the joint intensity distribution like MI [9]. Most importantly Self-Sim copes well with spatially varying intensity fluctuations. Future research directions are manifold. The fast computation of self-similarity descriptors and distances is crucial for the practicability of the method. Moreover, we work on an extension of the voting procedure to enable wide baseline scenarios. We also plan to extend the method to allow a robust and accurate multi-modal 2D/3D registration starting from a sparsely sampled set of 2D renderings of large scale 3D models without any knowledge of extrinsic and intrinsic camera parameters.

References

1. Lu, C.P., Hager, G.D., Mjolsness, E.: Fast and globally convergent pose estimation from video images. IEEE Transactions on Pattern Analysis and Machine Intelligence 22, 610–622 (2000)

2. David, P., DeMenthon, D., Duraiswami, R., Samet, H.: Softposit: Simultaneous pose and correspondence determination. International Journal of Computer Vision 59, 259–284 (2004)
3. Hartley, R., Zisserman, A.: Multiple View Geometry in Computer Vision, 2nd edn. Cambridge University Press (2004) ISBN: 0521540518
4. Lepetit, V., Moreno-Noguer, F., Fua, P.: Epnp: An accurate o(n) solution to the pnp problem. International Journal of Computer Vision 81, 155–166 (2009)
5. Raguram, R., Frahm, J.-M., Pollefeys, M.: A Comparative Analysis of RANSAC Techniques Leading to Adaptive Real-Time Random Sample Consensus. In: Forsyth, D., Torr, P., Zisserman, A. (eds.) ECCV 2008, Part II. LNCS, vol. 5303, pp. 500–513. Springer, Heidelberg (2008)
6. Zhang, Z.: A flexible new technique for camera calibration. Technical report, Microsoft Research (1998)
7. Benhimane, S., Malis, E.: Homography-based 2d visual tracking and servoing. The International Journal of Robotics Research 26, 661–667 (2007)
8. Penney, G., Weese, J., Little, J.A., Desmedt, P., Hill, D.L., Hawkes, D.J.: A comparison of similarity measures for use in 2-d-3-d medical image registration. IEEE Transactions on Medical Imaging 17, 586–595 (1998)
9. Viola, P., Wells, W.: Alignment by maximization of mutual information. International Journal of Computer Vision 24, 137–154 (1997)
10. Lowe, D.G.: Distinctive image features from scale-invariant keypoints. International Journal of Computer Vision 60, 91–110 (2004)
11. Bay, H., Ess, A., Tuytelaars, T., Gool, L.V.: Speeded-up robust features (surf). Computer Vision and Image Understanding 110, 346–359 (2008)
12. Mikolajczyk, K., Schmid, C.: A performance evaluation of local descriptors. IEEE Transactions on Pattern Analysis and Machine Intelligence 27, 1615–1630 (2005)
13. Shechtman, E., Irani, M.: Matching local self-similarities across images and videos. In: CVPR (2007)
14. Leibe, B., Leonardis, A., Schiele, B.: Robust object detection with interleaved categorization and segmentation. International Journal of Computer Vision 77, 259–289 (2008)
15. Vasile, A., Waugh, F.R., Greisokh, D., Heinrichs, R.M.: Automatic alignment of color imagery onto 3d laser radar data. In: AIPR (2006)
16. Ding, M., Lyngbaek, K., Zakhor, A.: Automatic registration of aerial imagery with untextured 3d lidar models. In: CVPR (2008)
17. Wang, L., Neumann, U.: A robust approach for automatic registration of aerial images with untextured aerial lidar data. In: CVPR (2009)
18. Mastin, A., Kepner, J., Fisher, J.: Automatic registration of lidar and optical images of urban scenes. In: CVPR (2009)
19. Vosselman, G., Maas, H.G.: Airborne and Terrestrial Laser Scanning. Whittles Publishing, Dunbeath (2010)
20. Wagner, W., Ullrich, A., Ducic, V., Melzer, T., Studnicka, N.: Gaussian decomposition and calibration of a novel small-footprint full-waveform digitising airborne laser scanner. ISPRS Journal of Photogrammetry and Remote Sensing 60 (2006)
21. Gross, M., Pfister, H.: Point-Based Graphics. Morgan Kaufmann (2007)
22. DeMenthon, D.F., Davis, L.S.: Model-based object pose in 25 lines of code. International Journal of Computer Vision 15, 123–141 (1995)
23. Schroeder, W., Martin, K., Lorensen, B.: The Visualization Toolkit: An Object-Oriented Approach to 3-D Graphics. Kitware (2003)
24. Wu, C.: SiftGPU: A GPU implementation of scale invariant feature transform (SIFT). Technical report, University of North Carolina at Chapel Hill (2007)
25. Muja, M., Lowe, D.G.: Fast approximate nearest neighbors with automatic algorithm configuration. In: VISAPP (2009)

An Evaluation of Two Automatic Landmark Building Discovery Algorithms for City Reconstruction

Tobias Weyand, Jan Hosang, and Bastian Leibe

UMIC Research Centre, RWTH Aachen University
{weyand,hosang,leibe}@umic.rwth-aachen.de
http://www.mmp.rwth-aachen.de

Abstract. An important part of large-scale city reconstruction systems is an image clustering algorithm that divides a set of images into groups that should cover only one building each. Those groups then serve as input for structure from motion systems. A variety of approaches for this mining step have been proposed recently, but there is a lack of comparative evaluations and realistic benchmarks. In this work, we want to fill this gap by comparing two state-of-the-art landmark mining algorithms: spectral clustering and min-hash. Furthermore, we introduce a new large-scale dataset for the evaluation of landmark mining algorithms consisting of 500k images from the inner city of Paris. We evaluate both algorithms on the well-known Oxford dataset and our Paris dataset and give a detailed comparison of the clustering quality and computation time of the algorithms.

1 Introduction

Recently, significant advances in large-scale city reconstruction have been made. Structure from motion (SfM) is used as a basic tool for reconstructing environments as point clouds [1–3], dense 3D representations [4, 5], or for photo browsing applications [6]. A prerequisite for SfM is a high-quality set of photos of the object to be reconstructed. A simple and cheap approach for obtaining such image sets is to collect them from community photo sharing sites However, this typically results in unordered photos of several different buildings with a significant fraction of unrelated photos. Therefore, there is a need for efficient image mining algorithms that group photos on a building or view level and remove photos that do not show buildings. Such photo clustering approaches are also a prerequisite for other interesting applications such as photo auto-annotation [7, 8], landmark recognition [2] or automatic landmark detection [9, 10].

Despite their importance, there is not yet a suitable benchmark for evaluating and comparing large-scale landmark mining algorithms. In this paper we take a first step in this direction by performing an evaluation of two state-of-the-art approaches: The first [11] is a top-down method that builds the complete pairwise matching graph of the image collection and segments it using *spectral clustering*. The second [12, 13] is a fast and approximate bottom-up approach that finds *cluster seeds* using the *(geometric) min-hash* image hashing algorithm. The seeds are then grown to clusters using query expansion [14].

In their original publications, both clustering approaches were evaluated on the Oxford buildings dataset which was originally created for evaluating image retrieval [15].

K.N. Kutulakos (Ed.): ECCV 2010 Workshops, Part II, LNCS 6554, pp. 310–323, 2012.

The dataset was constructed by collecting images of touristic sites by querying Flickr with the site labels. This results in a clear segmentation into groups that show a particular building, making the clustering task very simple. We use this dataset in our evaluation for consistency, but show that due to its structure the results are not very meaningful.

An important question not fully answered in the original publications [11, 13] is how the performance of these approaches translates to a more unconstrained setting, *i.e.* unstructured photos of an entire city. In this paper, we investigate this question by applying spectral clustering and geometric min-hash to a dataset of 500k geotagged images from the inner city of Paris. We furthermore present a ground truth for the evaluation of landmark mining systems on this dataset[1]. We closely examine the performance tradeoff between the two methods and propose a combination of them that can help eliminate the shortcomings of each approach. The tradeoff between computation time and clustering recall can then be adjusted using a single parameter.

Related Work. In the following, we describe the most closely related approaches from the literature in more detail. Agarwal *et al.* [1] present a large-scale SfM system with a highly distributed clustering pipeline. Effectively, the major landmarks of Rome are discovered and reconstructed from 150,000 images in 21 hours (using 495 compute nodes) of which 13 hours are spent in the image matching stage. For the clustering, a full $tf \cdot idf$ matching is performed and the top 10 matches for each image are verified using epipolar geometry. The resulting clusters are then merged and extended using query expansion to produce the largest possible connected components. Opposed to this, Strecha *et al.* [16] propose to reconstruct cities at a building level and to then join the partial reconstructions into a city-scale model using meta data. A prerequisite for this is a clustering on the building level. Gammeter *et al.* [7] build a system for automatic tagging of landmarks in touristic photos. Retrieval is performed by overlaying a square grid of 200×200 m cells over entire cities. By performing matching only within these cells, scalable and distributed preprocessing is possible. Meta information such as tags are used as a cue to cluster photos and to distinguish between photos of events and photos of landmark buildings. An object-driven pruning of the inverted index is performed in order to speed up the retrieval process. Finally, the discovered clusters are associated with Wikipedia articles, which serves as an additional verification. Zhang *et al.* [17] build a web-scale image-based landmark search engine by compiling a list of landmarks from geotagged photos and online travel guides and then collecting images of these landmarks from community photo collections and image search engines. In settings where meta information is not available, approaches based only on image information are necessary. Philbin *et al.* [11] present an exhaustive method for landmark detection. A full pairwise matching graph is constructed and segmented using spectral clustering. The approach is discussed in detail in Section 2. Because this approach requires a complete pairwise matching including spatial verification of the image collection it does not scale well to larger datasets. Chum *et al.* [13] present a faster but approximate approach using a randomized hashing scheme that allows for constant-time discovery of near duplicates in web-scale databases. The authors propose to use the hash collisions as "cluster seeds" from which to start a graph discovery using query expansion [14].

---

[1] Both the dataset and the ground truth are available from
http://www.mmp.rwth-aachen.de/data/paris-dataset.

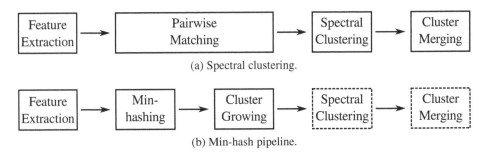

(a) Spectral clustering.

(b) Min-hash pipeline.

Fig. 1. The two different landmark discovery pipelines. The dashed lines denote the spectral clustering add-on that we propose for improving clustering precision.

2   Spectral Clustering on the Matching Graph

This section outlines the steps for clustering an image collection using spectral clustering, as proposed in [11]. Fig. 1a gives an overview of the pipeline.

Image Representation. A local feature representation of the images is built by first extracting scale-invariant Hessian affine regions [18] and SIFT descriptors [19]. The collected SIFT features are quantized into a codebook of 1M entries using k-means. To make this step computationally feasible, an approximate nearest neighbor (NN) search based on randomized kd-trees [15] is employed. The visual vocabulary is constructed on a smaller subset of the data with low-precision but a fast NN search. A higher precision NN search is used when matching features against the visual vocabulary.

Efficient Image Matching. The final image representation comprises the bag of visual words, feature positions, and the affine regions from the detector. Image retrieval is conducted in a similar fashion as text retrieval: query matches are retrieved using an inverted file structure that maps every visual word to all images it occurs in. The results are ranked using the cosine distance of their *"term frequency · inverse document frequency"* ($tf \cdot idf$) vectors. This results in a shortlist of k candidate matches, which are then geometrically verified by fitting a homography using SCRAMSAC [20]. The images for which the estimated homographies have sufficient support, are re-ranked above all other images [15] by adding 1.0 to the $tf \cdot idf$ score. This yields the final ranking score. The matching graph is constructed efficiently by querying the inverted file and inserting an edge for each match that exceeds a certain matching score threshold.

Spectral Clustering. In general, the connected components of the resulting matching graph correspond to a rough under-segmentation of the landmarks. Following [11] we first over-segment the connected components to get basic image clusters which can then be merged again with sufficient spatial verification. To this end, we use the spectral clustering algorithm of [21]. For each connected component, the optimal number of clusters is found by optimizing the Newman Q measure [22].

Re-merging Clusters. Philbin *et al.* [11] employ a heuristic to determine which spectral clusters show the same building and should therefore be merged: Each cluster is represented by its member image with the highest valence in the matching graph. The image boundaries are then projected using the homographies of the edges along the shortest paths between the representative images. This yields the length of the shortest paths and the size of the overlapping area between representative images. Thresholds for the path length and overlap influence precision and recall as we will show in Sec. 5.2.

3   Min-hash Cluster Discovery

Min-hash [12, 13, 23] is a technique from text retrieval [24] used for efficiently discovering pairs of similar images in large image collections. The special property of min-hash is that the probability of an image pair being discovered increases with its similarity. This makes min-hash suitable as a near-duplicate image detector [25]. Chum *et al.* [12] demonstrate that the discovered image pairs can also serve as *seeds* for image clustering. Clusters are discovered in a growing step starting with the cluster seeds. This way, instead of building a complete matching graph, the min-hash approach reduces computational time by only exploring certain connected components. An overview of the pipeline is given in Fig. 1b. The stages in dashed boxes are an extension that we propose later in this section.

Hashing Images.   A min-hash is a pseudo-random number generated from the visual words of an image. Let V be a visual word codebook. Given a random permutation of the numbers $\{1, \ldots, |V|\}$, the min-hash of an image is the first of the image's visual words occurring in the permutation. Typically, about 500-1000 random permutations are pre-generated and used for computing a set of min-hashes for each image. The probability of two images having the same min-hash equals the set overlap of their visual words [25]. To decrease the number of random collisions, several min-hashes are summarized into s-tuples called *sketches* ($s = 3, \ldots, 5$). An image pair is said to cause a *collision* if all min-hashes in a sketch are identical.

Detecting Collisions.   To efficiently find min-hash collisions, hash-tables are created, storing for each min-hash the list of images with this hash. Then, sketch collisions are the intersections of the s sets of colliding images. This hashing procedure enables constant-time collision detection [12]. The price to pay for this efficiency is a very low recall, particularly for less similar, but still relevant, image matches.

Geometric Min-Hash.   In geometric min-hash [13], sketches are created from features in a spatial neighborhood. This is done by selecting the first min-hash in a sketch randomly and then restricting the search for the remaining min-hashes to the affine region around the first feature. With this extension, a sketch collisions means that the colliding images not only have the colliding visual words in common, but also that the corresponding features come from the same image region. Because of this more distinctive definition of a sketch, Chum *et al.* report [13] an increase in precision and recall over standard min-hash even with the sketch size reduced to $s = 2$ and the number of min-hashes per image reduced to $k = 60$. Therefore, we only use geometric min-hash in our evaluation.

Cluster Growing.   Given a set of cluster seeds, clusters are *grown* by recursively applying query expansion [14]. For each cluster seed discovered by min-hash, codebook-based image retrieval is performed (Sec. 2). For each match above a ranking score

Table 1. Statistics of the datasets, their corresponding ground truths and matching graphs

(a) Statistics of Oxford and Paris datasets. GT denotes ground truth.

	Oxford	Paris
# Images	5,063	501,356
# Features	16,334,970	1,564,381,034
# GT Images	568	94,303
# GT Clusters	11	79

(b) Statistics of the complete matching graphs.

	Oxford	Paris
# Nodes	5052	501,356
# Edges	11,957	11,356,090
avg. valence	4.7	45.3
max valence	83	4,100

threshold, a recursive retrieval is performed until no new images are found. This process can be thought of as finding connected components in the matching graph.

Extension: Spectral clustering. The cluster growing process aims at maximizing recall by growing single-link components in the matching graph. Multiple landmarks can thus potentially end up in the same cluster (see Fig. 2b). We thus propose to segment the grown components with spectral clustering and subsequent merging (Sec. 2).

4   Experimental Setup

Datasets. We use two different datasets in our evaluation (Table 1a). The well-known Oxford Buildings dataset consists of selected photos depicting eleven distinct landmark buildings in Oxford that were retrieved from Flickr using keyword searches. With 5,063 images and well-separated objects, it is however quite limited. We use the dataset for the sake of comparison but show that the results are not very expressive. Following the approach of Philbin *et al.* [11], we build a clustering ground truth from the provided image retrieval ground truth by combining the sets of "good" and "ok" relevant images for each query.

Due to the lack of a large-scale landmark mining database with a "natural" distribution of tourist photos, we built a larger corpus of photos downloaded from Flickr. We deliberately neither queried particular landmarks nor filtered the query results, so the resulting dataset is closer to real-world conditions. We downloaded all geotagged photos from a bounding box around the inner city of Paris from Flickr and Panoramio and rescaled them to 1024×768 pixels. The Paris corpus therefore contains noise like heavily post-processed images, images of parties, pets, etc. that do not depict landmarks as well as many duplicates and near-duplicates, which we filtered out in order not to bias our evaluation. To establish a ground truth we first over-segmented the complete matching graph using spectral clustering on the connected components (Sec. 2). Inspection showed that the resulting clusters had a high purity with only a negligibly low number of outliers. We then manually joined clusters which showed the same buildings from the same view. The ground truth consists of 79 clustering covering 94k images (Tab. 1a).

Evaluation Measures. We adopt the measures *precision* and *recall* from classification evaluations. Let G denote the ground truth and C a clustering. Then N_C and N_G denote

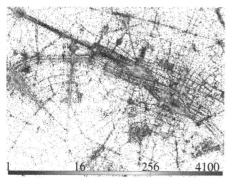
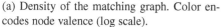

(a) Density of the matching graph. Color encodes node valence (log scale).

(b) Connected components of the matching graph larger than 20.

Fig. 2. Distribution of downloaded photos in Paris

the total number of images covered by C and G, respectively. To measure how well an algorithm groups similar photos, we use the well-known concept of purity:

$$P = \frac{1}{N_C} \sum_{c \in C} \max_{g \in G} \{|c \cap g|\} \tag{1}$$

Note that this formulation allows more than one cluster in C to be "assigned" to the same ground truth cluster. This measure is insensitive with respect to over-segmentation and missing borderline cases.

We define recall similar to [12]: For each ground-truth cluster g, we find its best representative c in the clustering C and sum up the fraction of member images actually represented by c.

$$R = \frac{1}{N_G} \sum_{g \in G} \max_{c \in C} \{|c \cap g|\} \tag{2}$$

The *Mean Cluster Recall* allows multiple ground-truth clusters to be assigned to the same cluster c, so assigning all photos to the same cluster would optimize recall. Thus, recall is insensitive with respect to under-segmentation and including borderline cases.

5   Results

We now evaluate spectral clustering and min-hash on the Oxford Buildings and Paris datasets. In particular, we show what level of performance spectral clustering can achieve and how the performance of min-hash compares to this. Finally, we give a detailed analysis of the computation time of both algorithms.

5.1   Matching Graph

The first step of the spectral clustering pipeline is to build a matching graph (Section 2). Table 1b shows statistics of the graphs for the two datasets. Interestingly, the average valence of the Paris dataset is an order of magnitude higher than the average valence

Table 2. Statistics of the connected components. The first column gives the number of connected components with a particular size, and the second column gives the total number of images in these components. Connected components of size 1 are images for which no match was found.

(a) Oxford				(b) Paris		
	CCs	images			CCs	images
total	3,297	5,052		total	303,522	501,356
= 1	2,917	2,917		= 1	277,490	277,490
≥ 2	380	2,135		≥ 2	26,032	223,866
≥ 20	11	929		≥ 20	397	150,367
≥ 100	2	518		≥ 100	63	138,122
≥ 500	0	0		≥ 500	19	129,961

of the Oxford dataset. This is due to the extreme density of tourist photos at the most popular public places. The photo with the highest valence (4,100) is a frontal shot of the facade of Notre Dame. Fig. 2a shows the distribution of valences in the matching graph of Paris and Figure 2b shows the connected components. The largest connected component (blue, 58,652 images) spans an area ranging from Notre Dame to the Louvre. This shows that connected components can give a good initial grouping [11], but further segmentation is required for a building-level clustering. In contrast, the largest connected component on the Oxford dataset is All Souls College (406 images). Table 2 gives statistics of the connected component sizes.

5.2 Spectral Clustering

For each connected component we perform a spectral clustering as described in Section 2. This results in 3,881 clusters for the Paris dataset and 410 clusters for the Oxford dataset. Since spectral clustering results in an over-segmentation (images of the same building are split up into several clusters), a subsequent homography-based merging step is performed [11]. We found that this step requires some tuning to produce the desired results, since the error in the estimated homographies increases when accumulating the transformations along long paths. Limiting the path length is an effective way to restrict this effect. Furthermore, it is necessary to define a lower bound on the overlap between the two cluster centers. A too low value results in different views being merged. A too high value limits the permitted degree of viewpoint change too much. Fig. 3 shows the effect of both parameters on precision and recall. On the Oxford dataset, when increasing the overlap threshold, we see an increase in recall while maintaining 100% precision, which means that only correct join operations are performed. From a certain point on, only wrong merges are performed, resulting in a decrease of precision without any change in recall. Due to the simplicity of the Oxford task we cannot draw any conclusions regarding the merging parameters. On the Paris dataset, the tradeoff is more clearly visible: A larger path length leads to a loss in precision, since clusters are incorrectly joined. Too short paths cause us to miss cluster pairs that should be joined, resulting in low recall. The best tradeoff is a path length of 5. Similarly, a too high

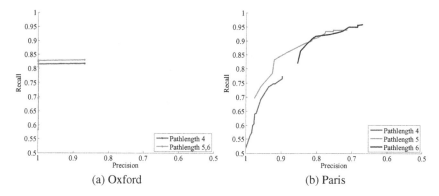

(a) Oxford   (b) Paris

Fig. 3. Cluster merging performance when varying the overlap parameter from 0% to 100%. The colored lines show results for different path length settings.

overlap threshold will cut off paths between valid matches, while a too low threshold will allow paths between barely overlapping images.

The merging step can still perform false merges in some problematic cases typical for internet photo collections: For example, time-stamps in photos or embedded signatures of the photographer can create false-positive edges in the matching graph that serve as "tunnels" between normally unconnected landmarks. Here, further heuristics would be necessary to discard such matches, which is not done here.

5.3   Geometric Min-Hash

Using spectral clustering as a baseline, we now evaluate the performance of min-hash. Min-hash generates suitable *cluster seeds i.e.* entry points into the image collection [12]. The reason is that many similar images are made at popular places, and thus the probability for a seed is high at landmark buildings. To show this, we compare the clusters discovered starting from min-hash seeds to clusters discovered starting from randomly drawn images. We then apply the spectral clustering and merging steps [11] to break down the connected components to building-level clusters and evaluate the resulting clustering.

Seed Generation. The parameters of the seed generation procedure are the sketch size s and the number of sketches k. Fig. 4 shows the influence of these parameters (dashed lines). The more sketches are used, the more collisions occur and the more seeds are generated. For larger sketch sizes the algorithm becomes more selective and returns only very similar images, which significantly decreases the number of seeds.

Duplicate Removal. Since by design, the probability for min-hash collisions is proportional to the similarity (visual word set overlap) of the colliding images, duplicate images are returned first and introduce arbitrary seeds which have a lower probability of belonging to a landmark cluster. Therefore, it is necessary to filter the duplicates from the seeds. Chum *et al.* [12] manually removed duplicates for their experiments. We chose to perform duplicate detection using the $tf \cdot idf$ distance of a seed image pair. By visual inspection of min-hash seeds, we determined a $tf \cdot idf$ threshold of 0.3. Seeds with a higher $tf \cdot idf$ score are considered duplicates and are removed. Figure 4 (solid

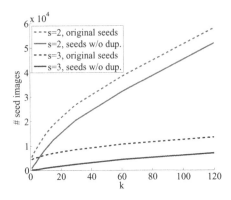
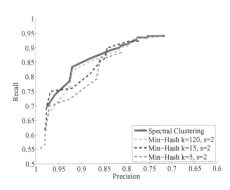

Fig. 4. Number of cluster seed images for the Paris dataset for different sketch counts k and sketch sizes s.

Fig. 5. Min-hash and spectral clustering recall and precision for varying overlap threshold. The path length is set to 5.

Fig. 6. Distribution of min-hash seeds (drawn as yellow dots) for k=60 and s=2 (left) and the distribution when drawing the same number images (31,946) randomly (right).

lines) shows the effect on the number of seeds for different settings of s. For $s = 3$, most of the returned seeds are duplicates, and the number of seeds detected increases only very slowly. We thus use a setting of $s = 2$ for our following experiments.

Min-Hash vs. Random. Fig. 6 (left) shows the distribution of the min-hash seeds for $k = 60$ and $s = 2$ (31,946 images), and Fig. 6 (right) shows the distribution when the same number of images is selected randomly. The random images are much more scattered over the city while the images selected by min-hash concentrate around the landmarks, which is the desired behaviour for a seed selection algorithm.

For a quantitative comparison, we use the following procedure: For each setting of s, we consider the number of seed images N_s that min-hash produces and randomly draw N_s images from the dataset. This is done 10 times, for each value of s. In our evaluation, we give the average results for the 10 sets of images. We only perform this comparison on the Paris dataset.

Cluster Growing. Starting from the seeds, we grow clusters by query expansion (Sec. 3). Each resulting cluster corresponds to a connected component of the matching graph. Table 3 shows the results of the cluster growing process. The number of discovered clusters

Table 3. Results of the cluster growing process starting from min-hash seeds and random images. On the Paris dataset, the ground truth consists of the 79 largest landmark clusters. CC and GT denote connected component and ground truth respectively. The sketch size is $s = 2$.

(a) Oxford

k	# seeds	# clusters	# images covered	GT covered
1	8	3	4	38.98%
2	12	4	40	52.56%
3	16	6	43	66.31%
5	36	8	54	66.31%
10	55	13	71	75.84%
30	167	26	108	80.07%
120	422	63	367	84.48%

(b) Paris

		min-hash			random (avg. of 10)		
k	# seeds	# CCs	avg. CC size	GT covered	# CCs	avg. CC size	GT covered
1	784	58	2,158.2	81.87%	590.0	222.6	87.11%
2	1,883	102	1,268.9	90.39%	1,407.5	97.6	94.53%
3	2,570	141	941.1	93.38%	1,887.9	74.5	96.70%
5	4,437	220	620.5	94.53%	3,236.1	44.9	98.63%
10	8,753	360	389.3	97.56%	6,292.2	24.5	99.60%
30	20,453	915	161.6	99.56%	14,463.7	11.8	99.98%
120	51,855	3,022	52.8	100.00%	35,607.5	5.7	100.00%

is roughly proportional to the number of seeds. However, we find less new images when increasing the number of sketches k, because the largest clusters have the highest probability of being found [12]. On the Paris dataset, the 79 largest clusters in the dataset (which make up the ground truth) are almost fully discovered already for $k = 10$.

Comparing min-hash to a random selection of seed images shows that roughly ten times the number of connected components are found, but their average size is roughly ten times smaller. This shows that randomly selected images more likely belong to small connected components than images selected using min-hash.

Spectral Clustering of Discovered Connected Components. Even very low settings of k produce impressive recall but the clustering lacks precision, because the clusters discovered using query expansion become too large and thus cover multiple landmarks. To break up the clusters to a building level, we apply spectral clustering and homography-based cluster merging (Sec. 2) on top of the min-hash pipeline [12]. Table 4 shows the effect of this additional step on the results. Since the results vary only slightly for different min-hash sketch counts, we only give mean and standard deviation values computed using settings of k from the range $[1, 120]$. The additional steps strongly improve the clustering precision while only slightly decreasing recall. Fig. 5 shows a comparison of the precision-recall curves of the two approaches when varying the minimum overlap parameter of the merging step. The recall of min-hash increases with a growing number of sketches and almost reaches the recall of spectral clustering at 120 sketches. Note that the precision of min-hash does not change much when varying the number of sketches.

Table 4. Summary of precision/recall of min-hash and subsequent cluster growing before and after spectral clustering on the Paris dataset. Tolerance values are given in standard deviation.

	Precision	Recall
w/o spectral clustering	50.1% ± 0.04	97.0% ± 0.07
w/ spectral clustering	85.7% ± 7.4	83.9% ± 9.9

To summarize, the extended min-hash pipeline achieves performance comparable to the spectral clustering pipeline for high values of k. However, the largest landmark clusters are already discovered for low settings of k. Reducing the number of sketches k trades off recall for computational speed. In the following section, we will investigate this tradeoff more closely.

5.4   Runtime Analysis

Pairwise Matching. The first step of the spectral clustering pipeline the pairwise image matching (Sec. 2). The runtime of this step consists of the inverted-file matching and the RANSAC verification of the top k matches. Performing inverted file lookup for such a database size has an effective runtime that is quadratic in the number of images[2]:

$$T_{if} = (N \cdot (N - 1))/2 \cdot c_m \ . \tag{3}$$

Here, N is the number of database images and c_m is a constant for the matching time of one image pair. In our measurements, $c_m \approx 5.75 \cdot 10^{-6}$ seconds. The time complexity of the RANSAC verification is linear in the number of images and depends on the number l of matches that we verify for a query.

$$T_v = N \cdot l \cdot c_v \tag{4}$$

Here, c_v denotes the time required for the spatial verification of one image pair. It can approximately be considered a constant. We measured the verification time to be on average $c_v = 0.0005$ seconds. The number of top l matches trades off missing potential matches for computational time. Following [15], we choose $k = 800$ for the Oxford dataset. For the Paris dataset we use $l = 15,000$ following considerations of worst-case match counts. Table 5a gives the number of operations and an approximate computation time for both databases using our implementation.

Cluster Growing. Cluster growing (Sec. 3) is performed using query expansion, *i.e.* by querying the inverted index with the seed image and using each verified result as another query. This process is iterated until no new results are found and the whole connected component is explored. Thus, the number N_c of queries for exploring a connected component corresponds to its size. The runtime for this can be written as:

$$T_g(c) = N_c \cdot (N \cdot c_m + l \cdot c_v) \ . \tag{5}$$

---

[2] Assuming N images, f matching features per image and a codebook with C entries, the expected number of inverted file entries processed per query is (without stop word removal) $\frac{N \cdot f^2}{C}$.

Table 5. (a) Number of matching operations and runtime estimates of the pairwise matching for both datasets. (b) Approximate runtime of cluster growing for different min-hash settings. For all results, a sketch size of 2 was used.

(a)

	Oxford		Paris	
	Ops	t	Ops	t
p/w matching	$1.2 \cdot 10^7$	73 s	$1.3 \cdot 10^{11}$	201 h
verification	$4.0 \cdot 10^6$	34 m	$7.5 \cdot 10^9$	44 d
Σ		35 m		52 d

(b)

	Oxford		Paris	
k	# imgs	t	# images	t
5	54	23 s	102,865	12.4 d
10	71	30 s	108,982	13.1 d
15	80	34 s	113,328	13.6 d
30	108	46 s	120,760	14.5 d
60	246	106 s	126,814	15.2 d
120	367	157 s	134,884	16.2 d

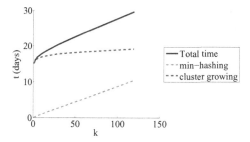

Fig. 7. Computation time of the min-hash pipeline for varying k

Table 5b gives a comparison of the computation times for different sketch counts. Since most of the large clusters are already discovered using very few sketches, the sketch count does not affect the computation time of the cluster growing step much.

Min-Hashing. An appealing property of min-hash is that its time complexity is (in practice) linear in the number of images [12]. The computation of the hashes itself takes up the major part of the processing time. Insertion into the hash table and finding collisions is comparably fast. Computation time increases linearly in both the number of sketches s and the sketch size k. In our implementation, the computation of a geometric min-hash took on average 0.015 seconds per image and sketch for $s = 2$, and 0.016 seconds per image and sketch for $s = 3$. Hashing and finding collisions took 0.0008 seconds per image and sketch. So, for $k = 5$ and $s = 2$, the total time for computing min-hash seed candidates for the Paris dataset is 10.4 hours, whereas for $k = 120$ computation would take 10.4 days. Additionally, a spatial verification of the candidate seeds is performed, but the computation time for this is negligible in comparison.

Spectral Clustering. Spectral clustering involves three basic steps. First, it is necessary to compute a singular value decomposition on a modified matching graph ($N \times N$) into k singular values, where k is the number of clusters we want to obtain for every connected component. Then we need to find k out of N vectors of dimension k which are orthogonal to each other to initialize k-means clustering in order to obtain stable results. Finally, we need one run of k-means with k centroids, N points, and k dimensions. This procedure has to be repeated for different k, to find the appropriate number of clusters for each connected component.

Experiments showed that runtime of one spectral clustering run is approximately linear in the number of photos, but quartic in the number of clusters k. For large connected components we also need larger values for k, in order to discover cluster on a building level. Therefore, runtime is dominated by the few largest connected components: Clustering the largest four connected components takes about 2 weeks, whereas clustering all other connected components (smaller than 5,000 images) only takes 2 hours in total. Since all methods explore the four largest connected components, we can approximate the runtime for spectral clustering with 2 weeks in each case.

Summary. We now summarize the computation times of both approaches for the Paris dataset. We will not cover feature extraction time, because this step is necessary for both approaches. The total computation time of the spectral clustering pipeline includes pairwise matching (47 days), spectral clustering (14 days) and cluster merging (12 hours). The total computation time of the spectral clustering pipeline on the Paris dataset is thus 61.5 days. (Computation was performed on a cluster of PCs.)

The computation time of min-hash is influenced by the sketch count k. This parameter directly affects the time for computing the min-hashes and it indirectly affects the cluster growing time through the number of discovered clusters. Fig. 7 gives an overview of the computation time of the min-hash pipeline for different settings of k. For a choice of $k = 5$, the total runtime is 16 days, and for $k = 120$, the runtime is 30 days. Depending on the parameter settings, min-hash is thus two to four times faster.

6   Conclusion and Outlook

We evaluated two approaches for landmark mining in large-scale image collections. We presented a new dataset and ground truth for the evaluation of such approaches. Our results show that spectral clustering is capable of clustering the pairwise image matching graph into building-level clusters, however at high computational cost.

Min-hash focuses the cluster growing step on promising entry points, and thus trades off speed for recall. However, it is necessary to implement duplicate removal to suppress low-quality seeds. We also showed that using the connected components directly as clusters, as proposed by Chum *et al.* [14], results in low precision, which can be improved by spectral clustering the connected components. The resulting approach was shown to be a good tradeoff between computation time and clustering quality, but is relatively complex. In particular, it seems overkill to first over-segment the image collection and to then again join clusters of the same building.

An ideal approach would find seed images with a high probability if they are good representatives for their neighbors. The growing step should avoid under-segmentation, so that it becomes unnecessary to run a costly re-segmentation process. That is, the seed growing step should stop as soon as a single building is covered. Achieving these goals will require deeper investigation, which is ongoing research.

Acknowledgements. This project has been funded by the cluster of excellence UMIC (DFG EXC 89). We thank O. Chum and J. Philbin for their help and for interesting discussions.

References

1. Agarwal, S., Snavely, N., Simon, I., Seitz, S., Szeliski, R.: Building Rome in a Day. In: ICCV 2009 (2009)
2. Li, X., Wu, C., Zach, C., Lazebnik, S., Frahm, J.-M.: Modeling and Recognition of Landmark Image Collections Using Iconic Scene Graphs. In: Forsyth, D., Torr, P., Zisserman, A. (eds.) ECCV 2008, Part I. LNCS, vol. 5302, pp. 427–440. Springer, Heidelberg (2008)
3. Snavely, N., Seitz, S., Szeliski, R.: Modeling the World from Internet Photo Collections. IJCV 80, 189–210 (2008)
4. Goesele, M., Snavely, N., Curless, B., Hoppe, H., Seitz, S.: Multi-View Stereo for Community Photo Collections. In: ICCV 2007 (2007)
5. Furukawa, Y., Curless, B., Seitz, S.M., Szeliski, R.: Manhattan-world stereo. In: CVPR 2009, IEEE (2009)
6. Snavely, N., Seitz, S., Szeliski, R.: Photo Tourism: Exploring Photo Collections in 3D. In: SIGGRAPH 2006 (2006)
7. Gammeter, S., Quack, T., Van Gool, L.: I Know What You Did Last Summer: Object-Level Auto-Annotation of Holiday Snaps. In: ICCV 2009 (2009)
8. Simon, I., Seitz, S.M.: Scene Segmentation Using the Wisdom of Crowds. In: Forsyth, D., Torr, P., Zisserman, A. (eds.) ECCV 2008, Part II. LNCS, vol. 5303, pp. 541–553. Springer, Heidelberg (2008)
9. Simon, I., Snavely, N., Seitz, S.: Scene Summarization for Online Image Collections. In: ICCV 2007 (2007)
10. Quack, T., Leibe, B., Van Gool, L.: World-Scale Mining of Objects and Events from Community Photo Collections. In: CIVR 2008 (2008)
11. Philbin, J., Zisserman, A.: Object Mining using a Matching Graph on Very Large Image Collections. In: ICCVGIP 2008 (2008)
12. Chum, O., Matas, J.: Large-scale discovery of spatially related images. In: PAMI (2010)
13. Chum, O., Perdoch, M., Matas, J.: Geometric min-Hashing: Finding a (Thick) Needle in a Haystack. In: ICCV 2007 (2007)
14. Chum, O., Philbin, J., Sivic, J., Zisserman, A.: Total Recall: Automatic Query Expansion with a Generative Feature Model for Object Retrieval. In: ICCV 2007 (2007)
15. Philbin, J., Chum, O., Isard, M., Sivic, J., Zisserman, A.: Object Retrieval with Large Vocabularies and Fast Spatial Matching. In: CVPR 2007 (2007)
16. Strecha, C., Pylvanainen, T., Fua, P.: Dynamic and Scalable Large Scale Image Reconstruction. In: CVPR 2010 (2010)
17. Zheng, Y.T., Zhao, M., Song, Y., Adam, H., Buddemeier, U., Bissacco, A., Brucher, F., Chua, T.S., Neven, H.: Tour the world: Building a web-scale landmark recognition engine. In: CVPR 2009 (2009)
18. Mikolajczyk, K., Schmid, C.: Scale and affine invariant interest point detectors. IJCV 60, 63–86 (2004)
19. Lowe, D.: Distinctive Image Features from Scale-Invariant Keypoints. IJCV 60 (2004)
20. Sattler, T., Leibe, B., Kobbelt, L.: SCRAMSAC: Improving RANSAC's Efficiency with a Spatial Consistency Filter. In: ICCV 2009 (2009)
21. Ng, A.Y., Jordan, M.I., Weiss, Y.: On spectral clustering: Analysis and an algorithm. In: NIPS 2001. MIT Press (2001)
22. Newman, M.E.J., Girvan, M.: Finding and evaluating community structure in networks. Physical Review E 69 (2004)
23. Chum, O., Philbin, J., Zisserman, A.: Near Duplicate Image Detection: min-Hash and tf-idf Weighting. In: BMVC 2008 (2008)
24. Broder, A.: On the resemblance and containment of documents. In: SEQS 1997 (1997)
25. Chum, O., Philbin, J., Isard, M., Zisserman, A.: Scalable near identical image and shot detection. In: CIVR 2007 (2007)

Vanishing Point Detection by Segment Clustering on the Projective Space

Fernanda A. Andaló[1], Gabriel Taubin[2], and Siome Goldenstein[1]

[1] Institute of Computing, University of Campinas (Unicamp), CEP 13083-852,
Campinas, SP, Brazil
{feandalo,siome}@ic.unicamp.br
[2] Division of Engineering, Brown University, Providence, RI 02912 USA
taubin@brown.edu

Abstract. The analysis of vanishing points on digital images provides strong cues for inferring the 3D structure of the depicted scene and can be exploited in a variety of computer vision applications. In this paper, we propose a method for estimating vanishing points in images of architectural environments that can be used for camera calibration and pose estimation, important tasks in large-scale 3D reconstruction. Our method performs automatic segment clustering in projective space – a direct transformation from the image space – instead of the traditional bounded accumulator space. Since it works in projective space, it handles finite and infinite vanishing points, without any special condition or threshold tuning. Experiments on real images show the effectiveness of the proposed method. We identify three orthogonal vanishing points and compute the estimation error based on their relation with the Image of the Absolute Conic (IAC) and based on the computation of the camera focal length.

Keywords: Vanishing point detection, Segment clustering, 3D reconstruction.

1 Introduction

Large-scale three-dimensional (3D) reconstruction is a challenging task in computer vision and has received considerable attention recently due to the usefulness of the recovered 3D model for a variety of applications, such as city planning, cartography, architectural design, fly-through simulations, and forensic science.

The key task in large-scale 3D reconstruction is to recover high-quality and detailed 3D scene models from two or more unordered and wide-baseline images [1], which may be taken from widely separated viewpoints.

Due to the complexity of the scenes, conventional modeling techniques are very time-consuming and recreating detailed geometry become very laborious. In order to overcome these difficulties, some works have been inclined towards image-based modeling techniques [2], using images to drive the 3D reconstruction [3, 4]. However, in many image-based modeling techniques, the scenes are

K.N. Kutulakos (Ed.): ECCV 2010 Workshops, Part II, LNCS 6554, pp. 324–337, 2012.
© Springer-Verlag Berlin Heidelberg 2012

reconstructed using camera calibrated images or, when this is not the case, it is nontrivial to establish correspondences between different images.

Recent works have focused on using scene constraints to optimize the reconstruction, especially the geometric ones found in almost man-made environments, such as parallelism and orthogonality [5, 6]. Vanishing points are an important geometric constraint widely found in images of man-made objects, that can be used to calibrate the camera [6, 7] and to find the relative pose.

A **vanishing point** is defined as the convergence point of a set of lines in the image plane that is produced by the projection of parallel lines in real space, under the assumption of perspective projection, e.g. with a pin-hole camera. The analysis of such vanishing points provides strong cues to make inferences about the 3D structures of a scene, such as depth and object dimension, because they are invariant features.

Each vanishing point corresponds to an orientation in the 3D scene and when the camera geometry is known, these orientations can be recovered. Even without this information, vanishing points can be used to group segments on the image with the same 3D orientation.

Because of its important role in 3D reconstruction, the detection of the vanishing points in a scene has to be effective, especially when no human intervention is required. This work proposes a novel and automated method based on a geometrical approach, in which all finite and infinite vanishing points are estimated in an image of a man-made environment. It does not rely on calibration parameters or thresholds. Our solution is based on the clustering of line segments that are detected in the image, representing points and segments on the projective space. The advantages of our method with respect to previous methods are:

- **Translational and rotational invariance.** Preserves the original distances among points and lines, because it does not operate on a bounded space, such as the Gaussian sphere or the Hough space.
- **Unlimited location accuracy.** It does not use accumulator-space techniques.
- **Unified handling of vanishing points.** It uses projective geometry.
- **Estimates all vanishing points.** It includes orthogonal and non-orthogonal vanishing points.
- **No need for camera calibration.** All camera parameters are unknown.

Figure 1 shows the stages of this method including detection of image line segments, determination of seeds based on a computed quality value for each segment, grouping of the line segments based on the distance among the intersection points of the corresponding lines in projective space (and not relying on any orthogonality assumption). The two later stages iteratively run until convergence to find the vanishing points. Experimental results on real images show that the proposed method can effectively detect all finite and infinite vanishing points. We also compute the estimation error based on the relation of the detected vanishing points with the Image of the Absolute Conic (IAC).

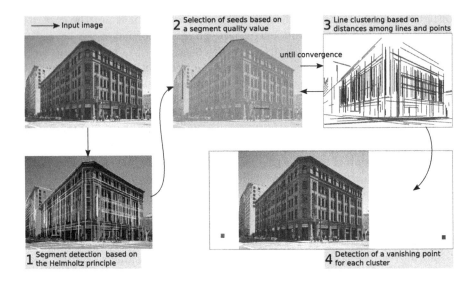

Fig. 1. Flowchart of the proposed vanishing point detection method

2   Related Work

In recent years, a lot of effort has been devoted to finding vanishing points out of 2D perspective projections and practical methods consider this task as a line intersection detection problem. Due to quantization and error on the detection of segments, the segments corresponding to a specific vanishing point do not intersect at a single point, but they intersect inside an area called **vanishing region**. To address this problem, methods often break the task into three steps:

1. Extraction of line segments on the image plane.
2. Clustering of line segments to groups of lines converging to the same vanishing point.
3. Vanishing point estimation for the extracted line clusters.

The first step is often implemented using a zero-crossing technique to extract edges that are subsequently grouped to form straight segments, e.g. Canny operator [8] followed by Hough transform [9]. For the second and third steps, the methods can be roughly divided in two categories: the ones that use accumulator spaces [10–14] and the ones that perform the clustering directly on the image plane [15, 16].

In the seminal technique due to Barnard [10], a Gaussian sphere is used to represent the orientation space. In this approach, lines from image space are projected onto a sphere that is tangent to the image plane at the center of the image. The projection of lines are circles and the sphere is discretized to compose an accumulator space for these circles; maxima on the sphere represents orientations shared by several line segments, and can be hypothesized as vanishing points for the image.

Since Bernard's work, however, methods for vanishing points detection in digital images have been based on some variation of the Hough transform in a conveniently quantized Gaussian sphere, for mapping the parameters of the line segments into a bounded Hough space [11]. One problem that arises in such methods is categorized as noise: artifacts of digital image geometry and textural effects can combine to produce spurious maxima on the Gaussian Sphere [12]. To address this problem, Almansa et al. [13] use the Helmholtz principle to partition the image plane into Meaningful vanishing regions and use Minimum Description Length to reject spurious vanishing points. Unfortunately, bounded spaces are not translational and rotational invariant (do not preserve distances between lines and points).

In [14], the image plane itself is chosen as the accumulator space and although it is not straight-forward to treat in the same way finite and infinite vanishing points, this method addresses the problem. But since determining local maxima is difficult and expensive, this method imposes an orthogonal criterion – the vanishing points must correspond to the three mutual orthogonal directions of the scene.

The second category of methods use the image plane itself for the clustering process, without the use of any accumulator technique [15, 16]. Generally, the clustering process depends on computations, such as distance among points and lines, that are performed on image space. Such methods have the advantage of not limiting the location accuracy and of preserving distances. It can be difficult, however, to handle infinite vanishing points without additional criterion.

Against this background, this work provides a method for vanishing point estimation that uses the projective space – a direct transformation from the image space – to perform the clustering of segments and to handle all vanishing points without special criterion, despite the fact that the space is unbounded.

3   Large-Scale 3D Reconstruction from Vanishing Points

Under perspective projection, a 3D point $x \in \mathbb{R}^3$ is projected to an image point $m \in \mathbb{R}^2$ via a projection matrix $\mathsf{P} \in \mathbb{R}^{3 \times 4}$ as

$$\tilde{m} = \mathsf{P}\tilde{x} = \mathsf{K}[\mathsf{R}|\mathsf{T}]\tilde{x} \, , \tag{1}$$

where $\tilde{m}$ and $\tilde{x}$ are the homogeneous form of points m and x, respectively; R is the rotation matrix, T is the translation vector from the world system to the camera system, and K is the camera intrinsic matrix. Matrix K is defined as

$$\mathsf{K} = \begin{bmatrix} f/m_x & \varsigma & p_x \\ 0 & f/m_y & p_y \\ 0 & 0 & 1 \end{bmatrix} , \tag{2}$$

where f is the focal length, (m_x, m_y) is the camera pixel dimension, (p_x, p_y) is the camera principal point, and ς refers to the skew factor. For a three-parameter camera, we have to assume square pixels, i.e., $\varsigma = 0$ and $m_x = m_y$; known principal point and known aspect ratio $\gamma = m_x/m_y$.

3.1   Recovering Camera Matrices

In [7], Wang et al. show that camera parameters can be learned from three orthogonal vanishing points, assuming some restrictions. More specifically, they prove that the camera projection matrix can be uniquely determined from three orthogonal vanishing points, assuming a three-parameter camera. Furthermore, they prove that the global consistent projection matrices can be recovered if an arbitrary reference point in space is observed across multiple views.

To calibrate the camera, we have to recover the image of the absolute conic [7]. The absolute conic $C_\infty = I_3$ is a conic on the plane at infinity composed of purely imaginary points. Under perspective projection, the image of the absolute conic (IAC) is defined as

$$\omega = K^{-T}K^{-1} . \tag{3}$$

It is know that two orthogonal vanishing points v and v^T satisfies

$$v^T \omega v = 0 . \tag{4}$$

Consequently, a set of three orthogonal vanishing points can provide three linearly independent constraints to ω and a three-parameter camera can be calibrated.

The projection matrix P is defined as $P = [s_x \tilde{v}_x, s_y \tilde{v}_y, s_z \tilde{v}_z, s_o \tilde{v}_o]$, where $\tilde{v}_x, \tilde{v}_y, \tilde{v}_z$ are the homogeneous form of the three orthogonal vanishing points, $\tilde{v}_o$ is the world origin; and s_x, s_y, s_z, s_o are unknown scalars.

Given a set of three orthogonal vanishing points v_x, v_y and v_z, the scalars s_x, s_y and s_z can be uniquely determined if the camera is assumed to have three-parameter and if $s_o \tilde{v}_o$ is known [7].

For large-scale 3D reconstruction, when we have multiple views of the scene, the scalars corresponding to the projection matrices of these views must be consistent. Given an arbitrary point in space which can be observed across multiple views, the consistent scalars associated with the translation terms of the projection matrices of these views can be uniquely determined [7].

In [2], the authors solved the inconsistency among the multiple views using digital compass information associated with each view, instead of using a key point in multiple views.

3.2   3D Reconstruction

A possible outline for large-scale 3D reconstruction based on vanishing point detection from uncalibrated images is presented in [7]:

(i) For each view:
   (a) Compute three orthogonal vanishing points;
   (b) Compute three scalars s_x, s_y and s_z for a specified world origin.
(ii) Determine the consistent scalars of the projection matrices:
   (a) Select a reference point in the first image and determine its correspondence in other views;

(b) Compute the scalars pair-wisely;

(c) Compute the consistence projection matrices for each view weighted by the scalars;

(iii) Detect and match key features across the images;

(iv) Recover the 3D structure of these key features via triangulations;

(v) Perform global optimization.

4   Effective Vanishing Point Detection

As presented in Figure 1, our method has four main steps. The first step, detection of line segments, is discussed in Section 4.1. The second and the third, that together characterize the clustering process are presented in Section 4.2. The last step is presented in Section 4.3.

4.1   Line Segment Detection

The line segments are used as primitives of our vanishing point estimator and to detected them, we use a method based on the Helmholtz Principle [17]. The usefulness of this specific method is beyond the task of segment detection. It also provides an important value – the number of false alarms for a segment – that is useful in the next steps to compute a quality value for the segment.

The Helmholtz principle states that if the expectation in the image of an observed configuration is very small, then the grouping of the objects is a Gestalt:

Definition 1 (ϵ-meaningful event). *An event is ϵ-meaningful, if the expectation of the number of occurrences of this event in an image is less than ϵ.*

Let f be an image of size $N \times N$ and $x_1, \ldots, x_l$ a set of l independents pixels of a line segment A. At each x_i, a random variable X_i equals 1 if the angle between the image gradient $\nabla f(x_i)$ and the normal to the segment A is less than $p\pi$, where p is the precision level (usually $p \approx 1/16$); and $X_i = 0$ otherwise, assuming a uniform distribution of the gradient orientations.

The random variable that represents the number of points having the same direction as the line is $S_l = X_1 + X_2 + \ldots + X_l$, which has a binomial distribution of parameters p and l.

The method considers a segment of length l_0 to be meaningful when its expected number of occurrences in the image is low (lower than ϵ).

Definition 2 (ϵ-meaningful segment). *A segment of length l is ϵ-meaningful in a $N \times N$ image if it contains at least $k(l, \epsilon)$ points having their direction aligned with that of the segment, where $k(l, \epsilon)$ is given by*

$$k(l, \epsilon) = min \left\{ k \in \mathbb{N}, P[S_l \geq k] \leq \frac{\epsilon}{N^4} \right\} . \tag{5}$$

Let l_i be the length of the i-th segment and e_i the event "the i-th segment is ϵ-meaningful". Let χ_{e_i} denote the characteristic function of the event e_i, so that

$$P[\chi_{e_i} = 1] = P[S_{l_i} \geq k(l_i, \epsilon)] = \sum_{k=k(l_i,\epsilon)}^{l_i} \binom{l_i}{k} p^k (1 - p)^{l_i - k} . \qquad (6)$$

Then the variable representing the number of ϵ-meaningful segments is $R = \chi_{e_1}, \chi_{e_2}, \ldots, \chi_{e_{N^4}}$, and its expectation $E(R)$ gives the expected number of false alarms.

Definition 3 (number of false alarms). *Given a segment of length l_0 in a $N \times N$ image containing k_0 points aligned with the direction of the segment, the number of false alarms for this segment is*

$$NF(k_0, l_0) = N^4 P[S_{l_0} \geq k_0] . \qquad (7)$$

To avoid spurious responses, the method considers a subset of the ϵ-meaningful segments that are maximal.

The described method depends on two parameters. The meaningful threshold ϵ is necessary and it is not critical. The standard setting $\epsilon = 1$ works well for all images. However, the precision parameters p is not really necessary. Even though $p = 1/16$ works well for most images, a finer p might do better in edges with highly precise gradient orientations [13].

4.2   Line Segment Clustering

The input of our method is a set $\mathcal{S} = \{s_1, \ldots, s_{|\mathcal{S}|}\}$ of detected image segments on Euclidean space $\mathbb{R}^2$, and the number M of clusters. The output is a classification $cluster(s_i)$ for each segment, representing its assignment to a cluster.

For the segment clustering process, the method constructs three sets: set $\mathcal{L}$ of lines on the real projective space $\mathbb{RP}^2$, corresponding to each segment in $\mathcal{S}$; set $\mathcal{W}$ of the intersection points for each pair of lines in $\mathcal{L}$, where $w_{(a,b)} \in \mathcal{W}$ corresponds to the intersection point between lines a and b; and set $\mathcal{Q}$ of quality values for each segment. For a segment s_i with the number of false alarms NF_i, the quality value q_i is

$$q_i = \left| \frac{NF_i - (max(NF_j) + min(NF_j))}{max(NF_j)} \right|, s_j \in \mathcal{S} . \qquad (8)$$

The goal of the line segment clustering is to assign a cluster for each one of the segments in $\mathcal{S}$. We denote C_j the j-th cluster. In addition, the following properties corresponds to C_j: a **seed** (d_{1_j}, d_{2_j}), where d_{1_j} and d_{2_j} are lines in $\mathcal{L}$; and a **pseudo-centroid** $t_j = w_{(d_{1_j}, d_{2_j})} \in \mathcal{W}$ that is the intersection point between lines d_{1_j} and d_{2_j}.

The clustering process is divided in three steps: selection of the first seeds, assignment step, and update step. The algorithm aims to minimize an objective function

$$\sum_{j=1}^{M} \sum_{s_i \in C_j} D_{LP}(l_i, t_j) , \tag{9}$$

where the function D_{LP} gives the distance between a line and a point. This function is defined in $\mathbb{RP}^2$ and is given by

$$D_{LP}(k, h) = \frac{|k \cdot h|}{\| k \| \| h \|} . \tag{10}$$

An important property is that the distance between two points in $\mathbb{RP}^n$ is the angle between the corresponding lines in $\mathbb{RP}^{n+1}$ [18]. Using this information, the function D_{LP} gives a value that is relative to the angle between the corresponding line and plane in $\mathbb{RP}^3$. This distance is symmetric, but it is not a full metric – it does not satisfy triangle inequality. However, it is a robust way to measure the amount of symmetry between lines and points.

First Seeds. For a number M of vanishing points, we select as seeds $2M$ lines based on the quality of the corresponding segments. More precisely, we select the $2M$ lines with highest corresponding segment quality and distribute these pairs of lines randomly across the clusters.

Assignment Step. At this step, the algorithm assigns each segment $s \in S$ to the cluster C that has the closest pseudo-centroid t. The "closest" concept is determined by the distance function D_{LP}. Formally,

$$cluster(s_i) = C \mid t = \underset{t_j, j \in [1,M]}{\operatorname{argmin}} D_{LP}(l_i, t_j) . \tag{11}$$

Update Step. When all segments in S have been assigned to a cluster, we need to recalculate the positions of the pseudo-centroids. To accomplish this task, the method selects a new seed for each cluster. For the cluster C_j, the new seed is (d_{1_j}, d_{2_j}).

The choice of the lines d_{1_j} and d_{2_j} is so that they minimize the error to the lines that would pass through the real corresponding vanishing point, i.e., line d_{1_j} minimizes the distance to the mean line of cluster C_j and d_{2_j} is chosen so that the new pseudo-centroid t_j minimizes the distance to some key intersection points.

The line d_{1_j} is the one that the corresponding segment is assigned to the cluster C_j and that minimizes the angular distance to the weighted mean orientation of the cluster. The angular distance is the smallest angle between two orientations. The weighted mean orientation $\bar{\theta}_j$ for the cluster C_j, considering the quality values as the weight, is computed as [19]

$$\bar{\theta}_j = arctan \left(\frac{\sum\limits_{s_i \in C_j} q_i * \sin(2\theta_i)}{\sum\limits_{s_i \in C_j} q_i * \cos(2\theta_i)} \right) , \tag{12}$$

where θ_i is the orientation of the line corresponding to the i-th segment assigned to the cluster.

The line d_{2_j} is the one that the corresponding segment is assigned to the cluster C_j and which intersection point with the line d_{1_j}, $w_{(d_{1_j}, d_{2_j})}$, minimizes the sum of the distances to all other intersection points $w_{(d_{1_j}, i)}$, where s_i is assigned to C_j.

The process of determining d_{1_j} and d_{2_j} on cluster C_j is illustrated on Figure 2. First, the mean orientation of segments assigned to C_j (corresponding to non-dotted lines) is computed. Line d_{1_j} is the one with closest orientation to the mean. Line d_{2_j} is the one that, together with d_{1_j}, forms the intersection point closest to all other intersection points of d_{1_j} (only considering the ones formed by lines corresponding to segments assigned to cluster C_j).

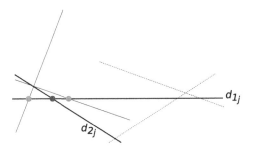

Fig. 2. Determination of the seed (d_{1_j}, d_{2_j}) of the cluster C_j. Non-dotted lines correspond to segments assigned to cluster C_j.

The relative distance between two intersection points in $\mathbb{RP}^2$ is given by the angle between the corresponding lines in $\mathbb{RP}^3$. Figure 3 illustrates the distance on the spherical model of $\mathbb{RP}^2$ between a finite point a and a infinite points b.

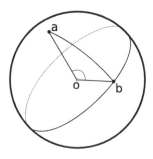

Fig. 3. Relative distance between a finite point a and a infinite points b, on a spherical model of $\mathbb{RP}^2$

The new pseudo-centroid t_j of cluster C_j is $w_{(d_{1_j}, d_{2_j})}$ – the intersection point between lines d_{1_j} and d_{2_j}.

The two last steps – assignment and update – must be computed until convergence is achieved, i.e. until the pseudo-centroids no longer change.

4.3 Vanishing Point Estimation

The final step is the estimation of the vanishing points location. For each detected cluster C_j, the method selects, as the corresponding vanishing point, the intersection point v_j that is the closest one to all lines in the cluster, according to D_{LP}:

$$v_j = \underset{p}{\operatorname{argmin}} \sum_{s_i \in C_j} D_{LP}(l_i, p) . \tag{13}$$

5 Experiments and Results

We implemented our algorithm in C++ and we conducted the experiments using the York Urban Database [20]. It consists of 102 indoor or outdoor images of man-made environments. Figure 4 illustrates a few obtained results. The first column shows input images with the detected segments. The second row shows the line clustering results and the location of the finite vanishing points. For experimental purposes, the parameter M was set for each image. For real purposes, the parameter M does not need to be tuned. If $M = 3$, the method will actually detect three vanishing points.

Our first experiment to test the effectiveness of the estimated vanishing points was to compute the error associated with their relation with the Image of Absolute Conic (IAC).

The York Urban Database provides the camera intrinsic parameters and therefore it is simple to construct the camera intrinsic matrix K (Equation 2). Given K, the IAC ω is given by Equation 3.

Let $v_i, i = 1, \ldots, M$ be the estimated vanishing points. Our goal is to find the triplet that is more orthogonal, i.e, we want to minimize

$$e_{i,j,w} = (v_i \omega v_j)^2 + (v_j \omega v_w)^2 + (v_w \omega v_i)^2 . \tag{14}$$

For all vanishing points estimated by our method, we select the triplet that minimizes Equation 14, the orthogonality error, as the three orthogonal vanishing points. A triplet (v_i, v_j, v_w) of orthogonal vanishing points leads to a zero $e_{i,j,w}$ (Equation 14), the error associated with our estimation procedure. Figure 5 shows the cumulative orthogonality error histogram for our method and for the method provided in York Urban database (hand detected segments and vanishing points detection on the Gaussian sphere), called here as Ground Truth.

The second experiment was to estimate the focal length with the vanishing point triplet that minimized Equation 14 and to compute the focal length error compared to the real focal length provided in the York Urban database.

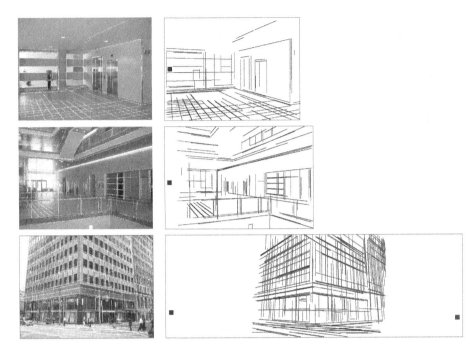

Fig. 4. The first column shows the input image and all detected segments. The second column shows the line clustering result and the estimated finite vanishing points. Each input image has exactly three vanishing points. Parallel lines with the same color represent lines associated with a vanishing point at infinity; the other lines are associated with finite vanishing points.

To compute the focal length, we recovered the camera intrinsic matrix K by decomposing the IAC matrix with unknown focal length.

Our method is compared with three other vanishing point detectors, summarized in Table 1. The method Almansa 2003 detects vanishing regions instead of vanishing points. For comparison purposes, we have selected the center of the detected regions as the vanishing points location. We called this extension as Almansa 2003 + vpe.

Figure 6 shows the cumulative focal length error histogram for our method and for the others methods (Table1) in the York Urban database. We can see that for the critical part of the histogram, where the focal length error is low, our method provides significant superior results.

Table 1. Vanishing point detectors used for comparison

Method	Line detection	VP estimation
Ground Truth [20]	by hand	Gaussian sphere
Tardif 2009 [16]	Canny detector+flood fill	J-Linkage
Almansa 2003 [13]	Helmholtz Principle	Helmholtz Principle

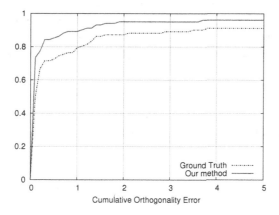

Fig. 5. Cumulative histogram for the estimated errors on York Urban Database. A point (x, y) represents the fraction y of images in the database that have error $e < x$.

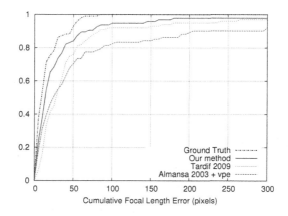

Fig. 6. Cumulative histogram for the focal length errors on York Urban Database. A point (x, y) represents the fraction y of images in the database that have focal length error less than x.

6   Conclusion

This work has examined the problem of estimating vanishing points on an image, a useful tool in large-scale 3D reconstruction, since vanishing points can be used for camera calibration and pose estimation.

We presented a new automated method to detect finite and infinite vanishing point, without any prior camera calibration or threshold tuning. Since the method is performed on an unbounded space – the projective plane – all vanishing points can be accurately estimated with no loss of geometrical information from the original image, as illustrated on the experimental results.

The method is effective when applied to images of architectural environments, where there is a predominance of straight lines corresponding to different 3D orientations. This is characterized as a strong perspective. However, if we go to ICCV 2011 in Barcelona, Spain, for example, our pictures will not be good inputs for the method. Most of the buildings in Barcelona have no straight lines, an important characteristic to achieve the detection of the vanishing points.

The results show visually the effectiveness of the vanishing points estimation. The method is also effective when relating the orthogonal vanishing points with the Image of Absolute Conic and for focal length estimation.

Acknowledgments. The authors are grateful to Professor Jorge Stolfi for the valuable discussions on projective space properties, to Jean-Philippe Tardif for providing the source code for his method, and to Patrick Denis for releasing the York Urban database. This work is primarily supported by CNPq (grant 141248/2009-2), with additional funding from NSF (grants CNS-0729126, CNS-0721703, IIS-0808718, and CCF-0915661), FAPESP and CAPES.

References

1. Zeng, X., Wang, Q., Xu, J.: MAP Model for Large-scale 3D Reconstruction and Coarse Matching for Unordered Wide-baseline Photos. In: British Machine Vision Conference (2008)
2. Jang, K.H., Jung, S.K.: Practical modeling technique for large-scale 3D building models from ground images. Pattern Recognition Letters 30(10), 861–869 (2009)
3. Lee, S.C., Jung, S.K., Nevatia, R.: Automatic Integration of Facade Textures into 3D Building Models with a Projective Geometry Based Line Clustering. In: USC Computer Vision (2002)
4. Teller, S., Antone, M., Bodnar, Z., Bosse, M., Coorg, S., Jethwa, M., Master, N.: Calibrated, Registered Images of an Extended Urban Area. International Journal of Computer Vision 53(1), 93–107 (2003)
5. Wilczkowiak, M., Sturm, P., Boyer, E.: Using Geometric Constraints through Parallelepipeds for Calibration and 3D Modeling. IEEE Transactions on Pattern Analysis and Machine Intelligence 27(2), 194–207 (2005)
6. Wang, G., Tsui, H.-T., Hu, Z., Wu, F.: Camera calibration and 3D reconstruction from a single view based on scene constraints. Image and Vision Computing 23(3), 311–323 (2005)
7. Wang, G., Tsu, H.-T., Wu, Q.M.J.: What can we learn about the scene structure from three orthogonal vanishing points in images. Pattern Recognition Letters 30(3), 192–202 (2009)
8. Canny, J.: A computational approach to edge detection. IEEE Transactions on Pattern Analysis and Machine Intelligence 8(6), 679–698 (1986)
9. Duda, R.O., Hart, P.E.: Use of the Hough transformation to detect lines and curves in pictures. Communications of the ACM 15(1), 11–15 (1972)
10. Barnard, S.T.: Interpreting perspective images. Artificial Intelligence 21(4), 435–462 (1983)
11. Tuytelaars, T., Van Gool, L.J., Proesmans, M., Moons, T.: A Cascaded Hough Transform as an Aid in Aerial Image Interpretation. In: International Conference on Computer Vision, pp. 67–72 (1998)

12. Shufelt, J.A.: Performance Evaluation and Analysis of Vanishing Point Detection Techniques. IEEE Transactions on Pattern Analysis and Machine Intelligence 21(3), 282–288 (1999)
13. Almansa, A., Desolneux, A., Vamech, S.: Vanishing Point Detection without Any A Priori Information. IEEE Transactions on Pattern Analysis and Machine Intelligence 25(4), 502–507 (2003)
14. Rother, C.: A New Approach for Vanishing Point Detection in Architectural Environments. In: British Machine Vision Conference (2000)
15. McLean, G.F., Kotturi, D.: Vanishing Point Detection by Line Clustering. IEEE Transactions on Pattern Analysis and Machine Intelligence 17(11), 1090–1095 (1995)
16. Tardif, J.-P.: Non-Iterative Approach for Fast and Accurate Vanishing Point Detection. In: International Conference on Computer Vision, pp. 1250–1257 (2009)
17. Desolneux, A., Moisan, L., Morel, J.-M.: Edge Detection by Helmholtz Principle. Journal of Mathematical Imaging and Vision 14(3), 271–284 (2001)
18. Stolfi, J.: Oriented Projective Geometry: A Framework for Geometric Computations. Academic Press (1991)
19. Mardia, K.V., Jupp, P.E.: Directional statistics. John Wiley and Sons (1999)
20. Denis, P., Elder, J.H., Estrada, F.J.: Efficient Edge-Based Methods for Estimating Manhattan Frames in Urban Imagery. In: Forsyth, D., Torr, P., Zisserman, A. (eds.) ECCV 2008, Part II. LNCS, vol. 5303, pp. 197–210. Springer, Heidelberg (2008)

Effective and Efficient Image Copy Detection Based on GPU

Hongtao Xie[1,2], Ke Gao[1], Yongdong Zhang[1], Jintao Li[1], Yizhi Liu[1], and Huamin Ren[1]

[1] Institute of Computing Technology, Chinese Academy of Sciences, Beijing, 100190, China
[2] Institute of Information Engineering, Chinese Academy of Sciences, Beijing, 100093, China
{xiehongtao,kegao,zhyd,jtl,liuyizhi,renhuamin}@ict.ac.cn

Abstract. To improve the accuracy and efficiency of image copy detection, a novel system is proposed based on Graphics Processing Units (GPU). We combine two complementary local features, Harris-Laplace and SURF, to provide a compact representation of an image. By using complementary features, the image is better covered and the detection accuracy becomes less dependent on the actual image content. Moreover, ordinal measure (OM) is applied as semilocal spatial coherent verification. To improve time performance, the process of local features generation and OM calculating are implemented on the GPU through NVIDIA CUDA. Experiments show that our system achieves a 15% precision improvement over the baseline Hamming embedding approach. Compared to the CPU-based method, the GPU realization reaches up to a 30-40x speedup, having real-time performance.

Keywords: image copy detection, CUDA, GPU, local feature, semilocal spatial coherent verification.

1 Introduction

The goal of image copy detection, given a query copy image, is to locate its original image in the database. The copy image is obtained by editing the original image through photometric and geometric changes. It is useful in many applications, such as copyright protection and redundant image filtering.

State-of-the-art image copy detection systems [1, 2, 3, 4] are based on a bag-of-features (BOF). BOF image retrieval systems first extract a set of local descriptors for each image, such as the popular SIFT descriptor [5]. Combined with effective region detectors [6, 7], these descriptors are invariant to local deformations [8]. Then, the detection systems quantize the descriptors into visual words and apply textual indexing and retrieval methods. The commonly used quantizer is k-means clustering. By adopting an inverted file index of visual words the retrieval systems avoid storing and comparing high-dimensional descriptors sequentially.

While critical for scalability, quantization has two major shortcomings. First, quantization reduces the discriminative capacity of local descriptors, since different descriptors quantized to the same visual word are considered to match with each other. Second, it is sensitive to transformations. The slight modifications to an image patch

K.N. Kutulakos (Ed.): ECCV 2010 Workshops, Part II, LNCS 6554, pp. 338–349, 2012.

can lead to its descriptor being quantized to different visual words. Soft-quantization [4] has been proposed to solve these two problems by quantizing a descriptor to several neighboring visual words, but it increases the index file size and still ignores the spatial information of feature points. Global spatial coherent verification [1, 2, 3] has been proposed as post-processing to reject mismatches, but it is computationally expensive. Besides, the extracting of local regions and descriptors is so time-consuming that most of the existing systems only apply one kind of local feature [1, 3, 4]. As different local features contain different characteristics of an image, adopting one kind of local feature cannot represent an image comprehensively [8].

In the past few years, the progress of GPU is tremendous. The computational capability of GPU today is much higher than that of the CPU. Due to its powerful computing capability, the GPU nowadays serves not only for graphics display, but also for general-purpose computation [9], such as molecular dynamics and image processing. To promote the use of GPU in the field of parallel computing, NVIDIA announced a powerful GPU architecture called "Compute Unified Device Architecture" (CUDA) [6]. CUDA provides two main modifications to effectively improve the programmability of GPU: unified shaders and shared memory. CUDA is basically a single instruction and multiple data architecture and can let programmers efficiently map a computing problem onto the GPU [11, 12, 13].

In this paper we propose a novel scheme which combines two local features, Harris-Laplace (with SIFT descriptor) [5, 6] and SURF [7], to design an effective and efficient image copy detection system. These two local features are complementary to each other and can provide highly compact representation of an image. We also employ OM [14, 15] to represent the spatial configuration around the interest point, supplying semilocal spatial coherent verification. OM is easy to calculate and has great distinguishability. Furthermore, the processes of interest point extraction, descriptor generation and OM computing are all accomplished on GPU, which improve the time performance significantly. Experiments show that our scheme achieves a 15% improvement over the baseline approach [1] and has real- time performance.

The paper is organized as follows. Section 2 describes the new image indexing strategy. Section 3 presents the details of GPU implementation. Finally, section 4 shows the experiment results and section 5 concludes the paper.

2   Image Indexing Strategy

In this section, we propose a novel image copy detection system. Instead of using a single local feature, we make use of two local features, which represent different parts of an image, to increase the detection accuracy of our system. Meanwhile, to avoid the complex global spatial coherent verification, we adopt OM [14] as semilocal spatial coherent verification. Then an effective image copy detection system is proposed.

2.1   Combination of Local Features

Local features have been widely used in image copy detection and other applications [1 - 8]. But the existing systems [1 - 4] usually adopt only one kind of local feature.

As a local feature just represents partial information of an image, such as corner, blob and region, it is not representative to distinguish an image in a large corpus of images [8]. Among all the local features, we pay special attention to Harris-Laplace [6] and SURF [7].

Fig. 1. Left: Interest points detected by Harris-Laplace. Right: Interest points detected by SURF. The red circles represent the detected features.

The Harris-Laplace detector [6] is based on the second moment matrix. The second moment matrix is also called the auto-correlation matrix, which is often used for feature detection and describing local image structures. This matrix describes the gradient distribution in a local neighborhood of a point.

$$M = \sigma_D^2 g(\sigma_I) * \begin{bmatrix} I_x^2(X,\sigma_D) & I_x I_y(X,\sigma_D) \\ I_x I_y(X,\sigma_D) & I_y^2(X,\sigma_D) \end{bmatrix} . \tag{1}$$

Where σ_I is the integration scale, σ_D is the differentiation scale; I_x and I_y are the derivatives computed in the x and y direction. The eigenvalues of matrix M represent two principal signal changes in the neighborhood of point X. This property enables the extraction of points, for which both curvatures are significant, that is the signal change is significant in the orthogonal directions i.e. corners, junctions etc [6], as the left image of Fig.1 shows.

The SURF detector is based on Hessian matrix [7], which can also be applied to describe the properties of local image structures. The Hessian matrix of an image is built with second order derivatives.

$$H(X,\sigma_D) = \begin{bmatrix} I_{xx}(X,\sigma_D) & I_{xy}(X,\sigma_D) \\ I_{xy}(X,\sigma_D) & I_{yy}(X,\sigma_D) \end{bmatrix} . \tag{2}$$

Where σ_D is the differentiation scale; I_{xx}, I_{yy} and I_{xy} are the second order derivatives. These derivatives encode the shape information by providing the description of how the normal to an isosurface changes, that is the signal change is conspicuous in all the directions around the point X. Based on this property, blob-like structures can be found in the image [7], as the right image of Fig.1 shows.

The theoretical analysis of Harris-Laplace and SURF shows that SURF is in a sense complementary to Harris-Laplace [8]. As an example shown in Fig.1, for an image of sunflower field, Harris-Laplace [6] detects "corner" like structures and the detected points are near object boundaries. For the same image, SURF [7] detects "blob" like structures and the detected points are localized in the object plane than corners. By using them together, the image is better covered and the detection performance becomes less dependent on the actual image content. In this motivation, we combine these two detectors to realize effective image copy detection.

2.2   Semilocal Spatial Coherent Verification

To improve the discriminative power of local features, global spatial coherent verification has been introduced to image copy detection [1-5]. By estimating the affine transformation between the query image and the candidate images, it can filter out images that do not arise from valid 2D geometric transforms of the query image. Global spatial coherent verification is effective, but it has a high degree of computational complexity. Local spatial consistency from k ($k = 15$) nearest neighbors, a weaker but computationally more feasible geometric constraint, is proposed in [2] to filter false matches. However it is sensitive to image transformations.

So far, little attention has been paid to using the information of the interest point's spatial neighborhood to improve its distinguishability [15]. In this paper, instead of using global spatial coherent verification, we adopt OM [14] to represent the semilocal spatial relation of the neighborhood around the detected interest point, providing semilocal spatial coherent verification. As shown in Fig.2, the red dot is the interest point p ; suppose the characteristic scale of p is σ, the side length of the local region and the spatial neighborhood are $k_1\sigma$ and $k_2\sigma$ respectively. In experiment, k_1 is 10 and k_2 equals to 20. We extract the descriptor of p from its local region and the OM of p from the spatial neighborhood.

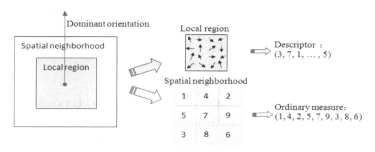

Fig. 2. Feature generation areas and corresponding features

Let $om_x = (x_1, x_2, \ldots, x_9)$ and $om_y = (y_1, y_2, \ldots, y_9)$ are the two OMs of interest points X and Y, the similarity of om_x and om_y is defined by:

$$S(om_x, om_y) = \sum_{i=1}^{9} d(x_i, y_i) , \qquad (3)$$

where $d(.)$ is the L_1 distance.

2.3   Image Copy Detection Strategy

Our image copy detection system is illustrated in Fig.3. To improve the detection accuracy, we apply approximate nearest neighbors (ANN) indexing structure [16] for feature storage and search.

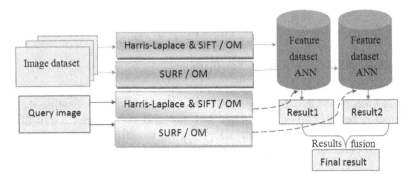

Fig. 3. The image copy detection system

The system consists of the following three steps:

1. Construct feature datasets: For each image in the image database we extract its local features, Harris-Laplace (with SIFT descriptor) [5, 6] and SURF [7]. The OMs are computed for all the interest points. Then the ANN algorithm [16] builds feature datasets to store and index the features, one dataset for a kind of feature. The OMs are stored in the document.

2. Query and filter: As we apply two kinds of features, there are twice query processes for a query image Q. For each interest point q of Q, we use approximate k ($k = 10$) near neighbor search to query the corresponding feature dataset, getting the initial candidate point set S'. Then we filter out the point p in S', if $S(om_q, om_p) < 5$. The score of the candidate image P is calculated by:

$$score(P) = \frac{match(Q,P)}{min(Q,P)} \quad . \tag{4}$$

Where $match(Q,P)$ is the number of matched points between image Q and P, and $min(Q,P)$ is the minimum point number of the two images. So Q have two result lists and P may appear in both lists and have two scores, $score_1(P)$ and $score_2(P)$.

3. Results fusion: We fuse the result lists returned by the queries of each kind of feature. For each candidate image in "Result 1" and "Result 2", the fusion is defined by:

$$final\ score(P) = max(score_1(P), score_2(P)) \quad . \tag{5}$$

It means to take its maximum score. The final returned images are sorted according to their scores, and the top-ranked images are the copy images of the query.

3   Implementation on the GPU

This section presents the implementation of our image copy detection system on the GPU. Limited to the architecture of GPU [10] and the characteristics of the algorithms, we cannot transplant the whole system to the GPU. So far, we can only realize interest point extraction, descriptor generation and OM computing on the GPU, while the rest of the system is still carried out on the CPU. The CPU and GPU co-working model of our system is illustrated in Fig.4.

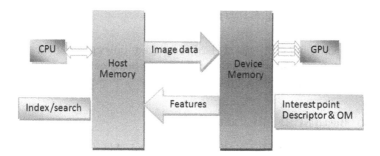

Fig. 4. The CPU and GPU co-working model

3.1   GPU- Based Harris-Laplace

Harris-Laplace algorithm only involves convolution and derivation operations, which have the inherent nature of parallelism. So, we partition the image data equally into data blocks and distribute them among the thread blocks, as shown in Fig.5. In the implementation, there are 16×16 threads in a thread block and the total number of thread block is:

$$Block\_num = \frac{image\_width}{16} \times \frac{image\_height}{16} \quad . \tag{6}$$

Each thread is responsible for the processing of a pixel, and the intermediate results are stored in the shared memory to reduce the time consuming caused by data transition. Furthermore, to speed up convolution operation, we approximate Gaussian with box filters, which is beneficial to GPU acceleration too. As box filters are constant, we put them in the constant memory when the program starts.

During the convolution calculation, the problem of "boundary cases" will be confronted. As shown in Fig.5, when calculating convolution for data blocks 1 and 6, the required data are represented by the red and blue dashed box. If we set "conditional check" for each pixel, speedup gain will be reduced [10]. So we copy image data to texture memory, which handles the "boundary cases" automatically.

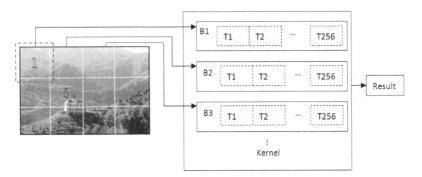

Fig. 5. Data partition and distribution

The data layout of our GPU-based Harris-Laplace follows the method of [11]. Four scales, which are four Gaussian filtered versions, are being calculated simultaneously. The scale-level parallelism can get further speedup.

3.2   GPU- Based SURF, SIFT and OM

We implement SURF and SIFT on GPU as [12] and [11] do, except for histogram computation, which can also be applied for OM calculation. As a commonly used analysis tool, histogram is quite difficult to compute efficiently on the GPU [10]. CUDA SDK takes advantages of atomic shared memory operations and designs an efficient histogram calculation method [13]. But atomic functions operating on shared memory are only available for devices of compute capability 1.2 and above.

Based on the compute capability of our device (NVIDIA GeForce 9800GTX+, 1.1), we use shared memory to calculate histogram step by step, as illustrated in Fig.6. To calculate the histogram of a 8×8 pixel block, we divide it into four 4×4 pixel blocks; then, four threads compute the four histograms of these blocks, one for each; the intermediate results are stored in the shared memory; finally, one thread combines the four histograms into one, getting the final result.

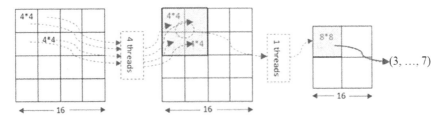

Fig. 6. Parallel histogram computation

4 Experiments

4.1 Experiment Data and Environment

We take the INRIA Copydays dataset as evaluation dataset[1].The dataset contains 157 original images. To represent typical transformations performed on images in a copy detection application, each image of the dataset has been transformed with three kinds of transformations:

- Image resizing (by a factor of 4 in dimension and 16 in total surface), followed by JPEG compression ranging from JPEG3 (low quality) to JPEG75 (high quality).
- Cropping ranging from 5% to 80% of the image surface.
- Strong transformations: print and scan, perspective effect, blur, paint, contrast change, etc.

The transformed images are illustrated in Fig.7. The goal of this dataset is to evaluate the behavior of indexing algorithms for most common image copies.

We also have 100 thousand images as "distracting images", which are crawled from Flickr[2]. The distracters include nature scenes, people, buildings and cartoons. Their size ranges from 256×364 to 1024×1024.

| Original | jpeg_3 | jpeg_8 | crops_30 | crops_80 | strong |

Fig. 7. Sample images from INRIA Copydays and corresponding transformed images

In the evaluation, we use the 157 original images as queries. Following the standard evaluation measure [1, 3], we use mean average precision (mAP) as our

---

[1] http://lear.inrialpes.fr/people/jegou/data.php
[2] http://www.flickr.com/

evaluation metric. For each query image we calculate its precision-recall curve, from which we obtain its average precision and then take the mean value over all queries.

The experiment environment is: Intel Core E8400 3.0GHz with 2048MB memory, NVIDIA GeForce 9800GTX+ with 512MB DRAM, Microsoft Windows XP sp2, CUDA Toolkit 2.1 and CUDA Driver (181.20).

4.2   Time Performance Analysis

Fig.8 and Fig.9 show the time used by CPU and GPU to extract Harris_Laplace, SIFT, SURF and OM for images of different size. From these tables, we observe that local feature extraction speed can get significant improvement with GPU. It only takes 67.4 ms to compute a 600×600 image, and the speedup for high resolution images is much more salient. This saves time for feature querying process and is the basis for real-time image copy detection.

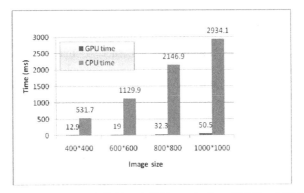

Fig. 8. Time cost of CPU and GPU to calculate SURF and OM

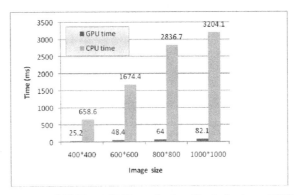

Fig. 9. Time cost of CPU and GPU to calculate Harris-Laplace, SIFT and OM

Table 1 illustrates the time used by the different parts of our system for detecting a 640×480 image. The matching process is implemented on CPU, so the time cost is identical. Compared to the CPU-based method, the GPU realization achieves up to a 30-40x speedup. With the powerful parallel computing capability of GPU, our system has real-time performance.

Table 1. Time (ms) used by the different parts of our system for detecting a 640×480 image

	Feature extraction	Matching	Total	Speedup
GPU	52.4		69.9	
		17.5		37.4
CPU	2602.5		2620	

4.3 Accuracy Performance Analysis

To prove the effectiveness of semilocal spatial coherent verification played by OM, we do queries with and without OM and compare the corresponding mAP values, as illustrated in Fig.10 (a) and (b). "Harris_Laplace_no_OM" means we only use Harris_Laplace, without applying OM. "Harris_Laplace_OM" means we not only use Harris_Laplace, but also adopt OM for semilocal spatial coherent verification. The same hold for "SURF_no_OM" and "SURF_OM".

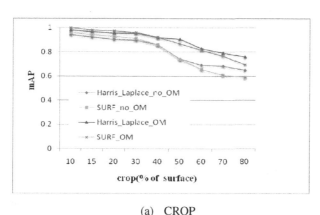

(a) CROP

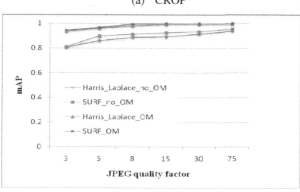

(b) SCALE (1/16) +JPEG

Fig. 10. The performance verification of OM as spatial coherent verification

From Fig.10, we can see that using OM as semilocal spatial coherent verification can obviously improve detection accuracy. The mAP values are increased by 10 – 20% for CROP and SCALE + JPEG attacks; the effect is more obvious when the attacks getting stronger. This is because that using the spatial neighborhood information can improve the distinguish ability of local features, and reduce mismatches.

To evaluate the detection accuracy of our system, we take Hamming embedding (HE) [1] as the "baseline" approach, which is one of the best methods in state-of-the-art [1, 3]. The vocabulary has 2000 visual words, which gives best performance when we experiment with different sizes. As our system has excellent performance in dealing with JPEG attack, we only show the comparison of handling cropping attack, as illustrated in Fig.11. "FUSE" is fusing the result lists returned by "Harris_Laplace_OM" and "SURF_OM", as described in 2.3.

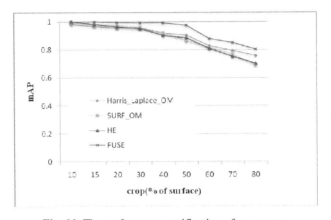

Fig. 11. The performance verification of our system

From Fig.11, we can draw two major observations. First, result fusion improves the mAP value remarkably, as can be seen by comparing the results for "FUSE" to "Harris_Laplace_OM" and "SURF_OM". This shows the benefit of using complementary features. As complementary local features has a much more compact representation of an image, and can deal with images of different content. Second, compared to HE [1], the mAP of "FUSE" gets significant improvement. When cropping rate is 50%, the mAP is increased from 0.83 to 0.96, about 15% improvement. It demonstrates the effectiveness of our system.

5   Conclusions

We have introduced an effective and efficient image copy detection system based on GPU. We combine two complementary local features together and use OM as semilocal spatial coherent verification. To speed up detection, the process of local features generation and OM computing are implemented on the GPU. The combination of complementary local features can represent the information of an image comprehensively. OM makes the features more discriminative and reduces mismatches. Experiments show that our system outperforms the current state-of-the-art and has excellent time performance.

Features combination and using GPU are two general and powerful frameworks. Our future work is to combine features in an advanced way and port the other parts of copy detection, such as indexing and matching on the GPU.

Acknowledgements. This work is supported by the National Basic Research Program of China (973 Program, 2007CB311100); National Nature Science Foundation of China (60873165 60802028); Beijing New Star Project on Science & Technology (2007B071); Co-building Program of Beijing Municipal Education Commission.

References

1. Jegou, H., Douze, M., Schmid, C.: Hamming Embedding and Weak Geometric Consistency for Large Scale Image Search. In: Forsyth, D., Torr, P., Zisserman, A. (eds.) ECCV 2008, Part I. LNCS, vol. 5302, pp. 304–317. Springer, Heidelberg (2008)
2. Sivic, J.: Video Google: A text retrieval approach to object matching in videos. In: ICCV (2003)
3. Perd'och, M., Chum, O., Matas, J.: Efficient Representation of Local Geometry for Large Scale Object Retrieval. In: CVPR (2009)
4. Philbin, J., Chum, O., Isard, M., Sivic, J., Zisserman, A.: Lost in quantization: Improving particular object retrieval in large scale image databases. In: CVPR (2008)
5. Lowe, D.: Distinctive Image Features from Scale In-variant Keypoints. IJCV, 91–110 (2004)
6. Mikolajczyk, K., Schmid, C.: Scale and affine invariant interest point detectors. IJCV, 63–86 (2004)
7. Bay, H., Tuytelaars, T., Van Gool, L.: SURF: Speeded Up Robust Features. In: Leonardis, A., Bischof, H., Pinz, A. (eds.) ECCV 2006. LNCS, vol. 3951, pp. 404–417. Springer, Heidelberg (2006)
8. Tuytelaars, T., Mikolajczyk, K.: A survey on local invariant features. In: FTCGV, pp. 177–280 (2008)
9. Owens, J.D., Houston, M.: GPU computing. Proceedings of the IEEE 96(5) (May 2008)
10. NVIDIA. NVIDIA CUDA Programming Guide version2.0, http://www.nvidia.com/object/cuda_get.html
11. Cornelis, N., Van Gool, L.: Fast scale invariant feature detection and matching on programmable graphics hardware. In: CVPR (2008)
12. Wu, C.C.: SiftGPU: A GPU Implementation of Scale Invariant Feature Transform, http://www.cs.unc.edu/
13. Podlozhnyuk, V.: Histogram calculation in CUDA, http://www.nvidia.com/object/cuda_get.html
14. Bhat, D.N., Nayar, S.K.: Ordinal measures for image correspondence. IEEE Transactions on Pattern Analysis and Machine Intelligence 20(4), 415–423 (1998)
15. Zhang, Y.D.: Content-Based Copy Detection by MCG-ICT-CAS. In: TRECVID Workshop (2008)
16. Lin, K.I.: The ANN-Tree: An Index for Efficient Approximate Nearest-Neighbor Search. In: CDSAA (2001)

Really Quick Shift: Image Segmentation on a GPU

Brian Fulkerson and Stefano Soatto

Department of Computer Science,
University of California, Los Angeles
{bfulkers,soatto}@cs.ucla.edu
http://vision.ucla.edu/

Abstract. The paper presents an exact GPU implementation of the quick shift image segmentation algorithm. Variants of the implementation which use global memory and texture caching are presented, and the paper shows that a method backed by texture caching can produce a 10-50X speedup for practical images, making computation of super-pixels possible at 5-10Hz on modest sized (256x256) images.

Keywords: super-pixels, segmentation, CUDA, GPU programming.

1 Introduction

Segmentation algorithms have played an important role in computer vision research, both as an end goal [1–3] and more recently as a preprocessing step for other domains, including stereo [4] and category-level scene parsing [5, 6]. Breaking the image into smaller components, often called super-pixels, allows algorithms to consider the image in meaningful chunks, rather than at the lowest common denominator (pixels).

Unfortunately, algorithms developed for segmentation are often quite costly in both memory usage and computation. This bottleneck limits the scale of the applications and data that they can be applied to.

In this work, we show that a GPU implementation of quick shift [3] can improve the performance of an already (relatively) fast segmentation algorithm by 10X-50X, opening up a host of potential new applications such as scene understanding in videos, and improved real time video abstraction [7].

2 Related Work

Most related work involving GPUs for segmentation is in the medical imaging domain, where the extra dimension of data (a volume instead of an image) has made speed a requirement rather than an option [8–11]. One notable exception found outside of medical imaging is that of Catanzaro *et al.* [12] who adapt a boundary detection technique (gPb [13]) to the GPU. While gPb can be used

K.N. Kutulakos (Ed.): ECCV 2010 Workshops, Part II, LNCS 6554, pp. 350–358, 2012.

for segmentation [14], our exact implementation of quick shift is over ten times faster on similar hardware.

In recognition, GPU based feature detectors and trackers [15, 16] have been proposed, as have learning components such as support vector machines [17] and k-nearest neighbors [18]. Recently, Wojek et al. [19] even proposed a GPU accelerated sliding window categorization scheme.

Other recent successes in using GPUs for vision include general purpose libraries such as OpenVIDIA [20], and specific applications which are often centered around video such as motion detection [21] or particle filtering [22].

Carreira et al. [23] have done work on approximating Gaussian Mean Shift (GMS) by decreasing the number of iterations required by the algorithm and the cost per iteration (by approximating the density). We effectively circumvent the need to optimize the number of iterations because quick shift only requires one iteration. Instead of approximating the density, we simply exploit the parallelism of the density computation to achieve a speedup by using hardware suited for the task (a GPU). We note that we could also approximate the density as in [23], and that would result in further speedups.

3   Quick Shift Algorithm

Quick shift is a kernelized version of a mode seeking algorithm similar in concept to mean shift [2, 24] or medoid shift [25]. Given N data points $x_1, \ldots, x_N$, it computes a Parzen density estimate around each point using, for example, an isotropic Gaussian window:

$$P(x) = \frac{1}{2\pi\sigma^2 N} \sum_{i=1}^{N} e^{\frac{-\|x - x_i\|^2}{2\sigma^2}}$$

Once the density estimate $P(x)$ has been computed, quick shift connects each point to the nearest point in the feature space which has a higher density estimate. Each connection has a distance d_x associated with it, and the set of connections for all pixels forms a tree, where the root of the tree is the point with the highest density estimate.

Quick shift may be used for any feature space, but for the purpose of this paper we restrict it to one we can use for image segmentation: the raw RGB values augmented with the (x, y) position in the image. So, the feature space is five dimensional: (r, g, b, x, y). To adjust the trade-off between the importance of the color and spatial components of the feature space, we simply pre-scale the (r, g, b) values by a parameter λ, which for these experiments we fix at $\lambda = 0.5$.

To obtain a segmentation from a tree of links formed by quick shift, we choose a threshold τ and break all links in the tree with $d_x > \tau$. The pixels which are a member of each resulting disconnected tree form each segment.

3.1   Segmentation Specific Optimizations

In the case where our feature space is restricted to contain components which are defined on the image plane, and our set of data points are the set of pixels, we can immediately put some useful bounds on both the density computation and the neighbor linking process.

First, when computing the energy we can restrict the domain of pixels we consider to a window which is less than 3σ pixels away, because beyond this the contribution to the density is guaranteed to be small. Second, when linking the neighbors, there is also a natural bound for the search window, because pixels which are further than τ away in the image plane must be at least that far away in the feature space. Conceptually we will talk about the density computation and linking process as separate components of the algorithm, because one (the density computation) must precede the other, and they operate on different domains of data. A pseudo-code implementation is shown in Figure 2, and some segmentations with various parameters are shown in Figure 1.

4   Quick Shift on a GPU

Because quick shift operates on each pixel of an image, and the computation which takes place at each pixel is independent of its distant surroundings, it is a good candidate for implementation on a parallel architecture.

We use CUDA 3.0 to develop a first implementation which simply copies the image to the device and breaks the computation of the density and the neighbors into blocks for the GPU to process.

Although this is faster than the CPU version, the bottleneck is clearly memory latency. Global memory on GPUs is slow, requiring hundreds of cycles to access, and for each pixel quick shift needs to access $\text{ceil}((6 * \sigma)^2)$ neighbors.

To address this, one option is to load an *apron* of pixels surrounding the block being computed into shared memory, so that when an element of the block computes its similarity with a pixel outside of the block, the memory access is cached. However, because this operation is not easily separable, the shared memory requirement scales quadratically with sigma. Even modest values of sigma will quickly exhaust the 16000 bytes of shared memory available on modern GPUs.

So, we instead map the image and the estimate of the density to a 3D and 2D texture, respectively. We have good locality of access because each thread accesses a block of pixels around it. The results based of this texture cached approach are labeled with a "Tex" suffix in the next section.

5   Evaluation

There are two aspects of the algorithm to evaluate: the correctness and the time required. To confirm the correctness of the GPU implementation, we compare

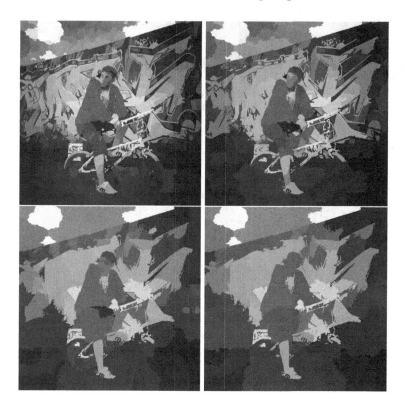

Fig. 1. Sample quick shift results. Increasing σ smoothes the underlying estimate of the density, providing fewer modes. Increasing τ increases the average size of a region as well as the error in the distance estimate. The top row of images have $\sigma = 2$, the bottom row $\sigma = 10$. The left column has $\tau = 10$ and the right $\tau = 20$.

```
function computeDensity()
for x in all pixels
  P[x] = 0
  for n in all pixels less than 3*sigma away
    P[x] += exp(-(f[x]-f[n])^2 / (2*sigma*sigma))

function linkNeighbors()
for x in all pixels
  for n in all pixels less than tau away
    if P[n] > P[x] and distance(x,n) is smallest among all n
      d[x] = distance(x,n)
      parent[x] = n
```

Fig. 2. Quick shift image segmentation in pseudo-code. The algorithm proceeds in two steps. First it iterates over the image creating a Parzen estimate of the density at each pixel. Then, it links each pixel to the nearest pixel (in the feature space) which increases the estimate of the density.

Fig. 3. Evaluation images. Four images from PASCAL-2007 used to evaluate the speed of the proposed algorithm.

the energy and segmentation to the one returned by the publicly available implementation of quick shift in VLFeat [26].

To measure the speed of the algorithm, we pick a few random images from the PASCAL-2007 dataset (shown in Figure 3). The images are cropped and up-sampled to 1024x1024. All reported performance numbers are obtained by averaging the results from all of the images.

We explore the effect of each parameter which changes the runtime of the algorithm. First, in Figure 4 we show the performance of the algorithms as the resolution of the image is increased while keeping σ and τ fixed. Next, in Figure 5 we keep the resolution fixed at 512x512, fix τ, and adjust σ, showing how it affects the runtime of just the density computation part of the algorithm. Finally, Figure 6 keeps both the resolution and σ fixed and instead adjusts τ, showing the time required to link the neighbors.

Hardware. The CPU ground truth version is evaluated on a 2.4Ghz Core 2 Duo. We show results for two GPUs: a laptop board (GeForce 8600M GT), and a mid-range desktop card (GeForce 9800 GT). The 8600M GT has 4 multiprocessors, 32 cores, and a core clock speed of 475MHz. The 9800 GT has 14 multiprocessors,

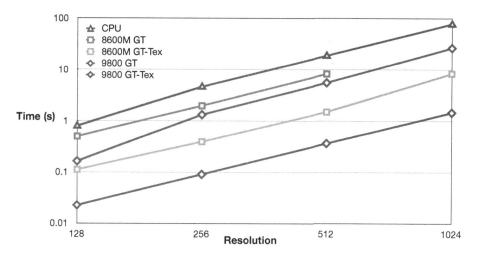

Fig. 4. Quick shift CPU vs GPU. The graph shows the amount of time required on two different GPUs as the resolution of the image is increased. Results are averaged over the four images from PASCAL-2007 shown in Figure 3. For this data, $\sigma = 6$ and $\tau = 10$. At 1024x1024, the speedup compared to the CPU version is 54X.

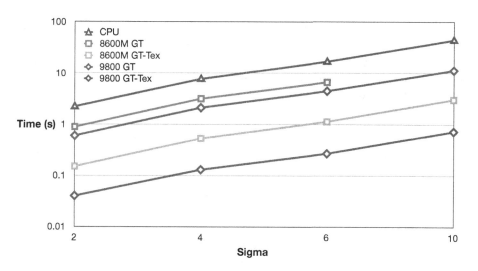

Fig. 5. Effect of σ on density computation time. As in Figure 4, we show that as σ is increased, processing time is increased and the texture memory-backed GPU version remains the most efficient option. Here we fix $\tau = 10$ and the image resolution to 512x512. Results are averaged over the same four images as before.

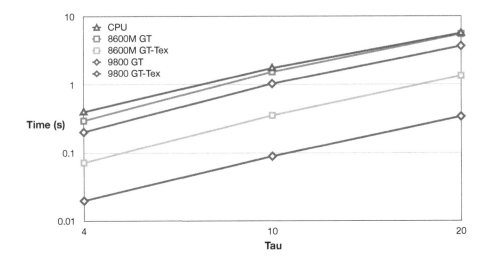

Fig. 6. Effect of τ on neighbor linking time. We show that as τ is increased, the amount of time required for finding the nearest neighbor which increases the density estimate is naturally increased. Here we fix $\sigma = 6$ and the image resolution to 512x512. Results are averaged over the same four images as before.

112 cores, a 550MHz core clock speed. Due to limits on the runtime of CUDA kernels on the 8600M, in Figures 5 and 6 results are not reported for the slowest running case because the kernel was stopped before completion. We note that while newer hardware (such as cards based on the recently released FERMI architecture) would undoubtedly be faster, we want to show what is possible with only limited hardware investment.

For both GPUs evaluated we use a block size of 16x16, even though it has been shown that tuning the block size for a particular GPU can provide a boost in performance.

Our complete source code as well as precompiled binaries for major architectures are available on our website at `http://vision.ucla.edu/~brian/qsgpu`.

6   Conclusion

We have shown a GPU implementation of quick shift which provides a 10 to 50 times speedup over the CPU implementation, resulting in a super-pixelization algorithm which can run at 10Hz on 256x256 images. The implementation is an exact copy of quick shift, and could be further speeded up by approximating the density, via subsampling or other methods. It is likely that the implementation would also present similar speedups for exact mean shift.

Acknowledgements.   This   research   was   supported   by   ONR   67F-1080868/N00014-08-1-0414, ARO56765-CI and AFOSR FA9550-09-1-0427.

References

1. Shi, J., Malik, J.: Normalized cuts and image segmentation. PAMI 22, 888 (2000)
2. Comaniciu, D., Meer, P.: Mean shift: A robust approach toward feature space analysis. PAMI 24 (2002)
3. Vedaldi, A., Soatto, S.: Quick Shift and Kernel Methods for Mode Seeking. In: Forsyth, D., Torr, P., Zisserman, A. (eds.) ECCV 2008, Part IV. LNCS, vol. 5305, pp. 705–718. Springer, Heidelberg (2008)
4. Lei, C., Selzer, J., Yang, Y.: Region-tree based stereo using dynamic programming optimization. In: Proc. CVPR (2006)
5. Fulkerson, B., Vedaldi, A., Soatto, S.: Class segmentation and object localization with superpixel neighborhoods. In: Proc. ICCV (2009)
6. Gould, S., Rodgers, J., Cohen, D., Elidan, G., Koller, D.: Multi-class segmentation with relative location prior. In: IJCV (2008)
7. Winnemoller, H., Olsen, S., Gooch, B.: Real-time video abstraction. ACM Transactions on Graphics (TOG) 25, 1226 (2006)
8. Sherbondy, A., Houston, M., Napel, S.: Fast volume segmentation with simultaneous visualization using programmable graphics hardware. In: Proceedings of the 14th IEEE Visualization 2003 (VIS 2003), p. 23. IEEE Computer Society (2003)
9. Cates, J., Lefohn, A., Whitaker, R.: GIST: an interactive, GPU-based level set segmentation tool for 3D medical images. Medical Image Analysis 8, 217–231 (2004)
10. Lefohn, A.E., Cates, J.E., Whitaker, R.T.: Interactive, GPU-Based Level Sets for 3D Segmentation. In: Ellis, R.E., Peters, T.M. (eds.) MICCAI 2003. LNCS, vol. 2878, pp. 564–572. Springer, Heidelberg (2003)
11. Lin, Y., Medioni, G.: Mutual information computation and maximization using gpu. In: Workshop on Computer Vision Using GPUs (2008)
12. Catanzaro, B., Su, B., Sundaram, N., Lee, Y., Murphy, M., Keutzer, K.: Efficient, high-quality image contour detection. In: Proc. ICCV (2009)
13. Maire, M., Arbelaez, P., Fowlkes, C., Malik, J.: Using contours to detect and localize junctions in natural images. In: Proc. CVPR (2008)
14. Arbeláez, P., Maire, M., Fowlkes, C., Malik, J.: From contours to regions: An empirical evaluation. In: Proc. CVPR (2009)
15. Sinha, S., Frahm, J., Pollefeys, M., Genc, Y.: GPU-based video feature tracking and matching. In: EDGE, Workshop on Edge Computing Using New Commodity Architectures, vol. 278, Citeseer (2006)
16. Heymann, S., Maller, K., Smolic, A., Froehlich, B., Wiegand, T.: SIFT implementation and optimization for general-purpose GPU. In: Proc. WSCG (2007)
17. Catanzaro, B., Sundaram, N., Keutzer, K.: Fast support vector machine training and classification on graphics processors. In: Proceedings of the 25th International Conference on Machine Learning, pp. 104–111. ACM (2008)
18. Garcia, V., Debreuve, E., Barlaud, M.: Fast k nearest neighbor search using gpu. In: Workshop on Computer Vision Using GPUs (2008)
19. Wojek, C., Dorkó, G., Schulz, A., Schiele, B.: Sliding-windows for rapid object class localization: A parallel technique. Pattern Recognition, 71–81 (2008)
20. Fung, J., Mann, S.: OpenVIDIA: parallel GPU computer vision. In: Proceedings of the 13th Annual ACM International Conference on Multimedia, p. 852 (2005)
21. Yu, Q., Medioni, G.: A gpu-based implementation of motion detection from a moving platform. In: Workshop on Computer Vision Using GPUs (2008)
22. Murphy-Chutorian, E., Trivedi, M.M.: Particle filtering with rendered models: A two pass approach to multi-object 3d tracking with the gpu. In: Workshop on Computer Vision Using GPUs (2008)

23. Carreira-Perpinán, M.: Acceleration strategies for Gaussian mean-shift image segmentation. In: Proc. CVPR (2006)
24. Fukunaga, K., Hostler, L.D.: The estimation of the gradient of a density function, with applications in pattern recognition. IEEE Trans. on Information Theory 21 (1975)
25. Sheikh, Y.A., Khan, E.A., Kanade, T.: Mode-seeking by medoidshifts. In: Proc. CVPR (2007)
26. Vedaldi, A., Fulkerson, B.: VLFeat - an open and portable library of computer vision algorithms. In: Proceedings of the 18th Annual ACM International Conference on Multimedia. (2010)

GPU Accelerated Likelihoods for Stereo-Based Articulated Tracking

Rune Møllegaard Friborg, Søren Hauberg, and Kenny Erleben

The eScience Centre, Dept. of Computer Science, University of Copenhagen
{runef,hauberg,kenny}@diku.dk

Abstract. For many years articulated tracking has been an active research topic in the computer vision community. While working solutions have been suggested, computational time is still problematic. We present a GPU implementation of a ray-casting based likelihood model that is orders of magnitude faster than a traditional CPU implementation. We explain the non-intuitive steps required to attain an optimized GPU implementation, where the dominant part is to hide the memory latency effectively. Benchmarks show that computations which previously required several minutes, are now performed in few seconds.

Keywords: CUDA · GPU Computing · Articulated Tracking · Particle Filtering.

1 The Computational Problem of Articulated Tracking

Three dimensional articulated human motion tracking is the process of estimating the configuration of body parts over time from sensor input [1]. One approach to this estimation is to use motion capture equipment where e.g. electromagnetic markers are attached to the body and then tracked in three dimensions. While this approach gives accurate results, it is intrusive and cannot be used outside laboratory settings. Alternatively, computer vision systems can be used for non-intrusive analysis such as the one shown in Figure 1. One standard approach

Fig. 1. The type of articulated tracking for which we achieve a speed up factor of up to 600 when using a GPU optimization. The images show stereo points with a super imposed illustration of the skin model.

K.N. Kutulakos (Ed.): ECCV 2010 Workshops, Part II, LNCS 6554, pp. 359–371, 2012.
© Springer-Verlag Berlin Heidelberg 2012

is to use a particle filter [2] for finding a sequence of poses that match the observed data well. From a practical point of view this means making many random guesses of the current pose and comparing these to the observed data. In terms of performance, the critical part is comparing each guess to the data. In this paper, we present a GPU-based solution to this problem and show a substantial increase in performance compared to a CPU-based implementation. Such performance increases are essential in allowing us to build proper generative likelihood models, that otherwise would be impractical.

Before dwelling into the details of this work, we briefly describe in Section 2 the general particle filter based framework for articulated tracking that forms the foundation for this work. Next we consider related work in Section 3 and in Section 4 we describe the likelihood model for our work. We focus on using the GPU in Section 5 and results can be found in Section 6 before we conclude in Section 7.

2   Particle Filtering for Articulated Tracking

The objective of articulated human tracking is to estimate the position and orientation of each limb in the human body. This, as such, requires a representation of the human body. The most common choice [1] is the *kinematic skeleton* which is a collection of rigid bones organised in a tree structure (see Fig. 2(a)). Each bone can be rotated at the point of connection between the bone and its parent. We will refer to such a connection point as a *joint*.

(a)   (b)

Fig. 2. (a) A rendering of the kinematic skeleton. Each bone position is computed by a rotation and a translation relative to its parent. The joints are drawn as circles. (b) A rendering of the skin model.

We model the bones as having known constant length (i.e. rigid), so the direction of each bone constitute the only degrees of freedom in the kinematic skeleton. The direction in each joint can be parametrised with a vector of angles, noticing that different joints may have different number of degrees of freedom. We may collect all joint angle vectors into one large vector θ_t representing all joint angles in the model. The objective of the tracking system then becomes to estimate this vector at each time step.

At the heart of our articulated tracker is the well-known particle filter [2], which we will briefly describe here. The particle filter is, in general, concerned with estimating an unobserved state of a system from observations. In terms of articulated tracking it is concerned with estimating the pose $\boldsymbol{\theta}_t$ at each frame in a video sequence. In terms of statistics, we seek $p(\boldsymbol{\theta}_t|\mathcal{X}_{1:t})$, where the subscript denotes time and $\mathcal{X}_{1:t} = \{\mathcal{X}_1, \ldots, \mathcal{X}_t\}$ denotes all observations seen at time t. This distribution is crudely represented as a set of samples that are propagated through time by sampling from $p(\boldsymbol{\theta}_t|\boldsymbol{\theta}_{t-1})$. Each sample $\boldsymbol{\theta}_t^{(j)}$ is assigned a weight according to its likelihood $p(\mathcal{X}_t|\boldsymbol{\theta}_t^{(j)})$. Thus, at each time step t we compute

for $j = 1$ to J **do**
    Sample $\boldsymbol{\theta}_t^{(j)}$ from $p(\boldsymbol{\theta}_t|\boldsymbol{\theta}_{t-1}^{(j)})$;
    $w_j \leftarrow p(\mathcal{X}_t|\boldsymbol{\theta}_t^{(j)})$;
end for

Usually it is computationally cheap to sample from $p(\boldsymbol{\theta}_t|\boldsymbol{\theta}_{t-1}^{(j)})$, whereas it is expensive to evaluate the likelihood $p(\mathcal{X}_t|\boldsymbol{\theta}_t^{(j)})$. It is worth noting that the loop can be executed in parallel as each sample is treated completely independent.

Once we have drawn new samples and assigned them weights, we can estimate the current pose as the mean value of $p(\boldsymbol{\theta}_t|\mathcal{X}_{1:t})$. This can be approximated as

$$\bar{\boldsymbol{\theta}}_t \approx \sum_{j=1}^{J} \frac{w_j}{\sum_{l=1}^{J} w_l} \boldsymbol{\theta}_t^{(j)} \; . \tag{1}$$

3   Related Work on Computational Tracking

Most work in the articulated tracking literature falls in two categories. Either the focus is on improving the image likelihoods or on improving the predictions. Due to space constraints, we forgo a review of various predictive models as this paper is focused on computational efficient likelihoods. For an overview of predictive models, see the review paper by Poppe [1].

Most publications on likelihood models for articulated tracking are concerned with finding descriptive image features. Sminchisescu and Triggs [3] showed successful tracking using a combination of edge strength and horizontal flow in a monocular setup. This approach is, however, bound to have difficulties due to only having one viewpoint. One solution is to use multiple calibrated cameras as, amongst others, was done by Deutscher et. al. [4] who used a combination of edge strength and background subtraction. Due to the difficulties of calibration, such approaches are, however, hard to use in non-laboratory settings. A possible compromise is to use a pre-calibrated stereo camera as was done by Hauberg et. al. [5]. Their solution did, however, not cope with limbs occluding each other.

While much work has gone into developing functional likelihood models, not much has been published on efficient implementations on GPU hardware. Exceptions include the work of Bandouch et. al. [6] that use a simple colour based appearance model in a multiple camera setup. By representing pixel colours as bitmasks they are able to make likelihood evaluations using only bitwise operations that can be efficiently implemented on the GPU. Cabido et. al. [7] use a combination of background subtraction along with binary template matching for a planar low-dimensional articulated model. They rephrase the entire optimisation as an application of textures on the GPU and as such get very high frame rates.

4   Our Likelihood Model

In this section we define the likelihood model $p(\mathcal{X}_t|\boldsymbol{\theta}_t)$ used in this paper. We use an off-the-shelf consumer stereo camera[1], which provides us with a set of points in 3D at each time step. We, thus, have $\mathcal{X}_t = \{\boldsymbol{x}_{1,t}, \ldots, \boldsymbol{x}_{I,t}\}$, where I denotes the number of points and each $\boldsymbol{x}_{i,t} \in \mathbb{R}^3$.

We will assume that each point generated by the stereo camera is independent and is normally distributed around the skin of the pose. Thus, we have

$$p(\mathcal{X}_t|\boldsymbol{\theta}_t^{(j)}) \propto \prod_{i=1}^{I} \exp\left(-\frac{d_i^2(\boldsymbol{\theta}_t^{(j)})}{2\sigma^2}\right) , \tag{2}$$

where $d_i^2(\boldsymbol{\theta}_t^{(j)})$ denotes the square Euclidean distance between the ith stereo point and the skin of the pose parametrised by $\boldsymbol{\theta}_t^{(j)}$. For numerical stability [2] we implement the particle filter on a logarithmic scale and as such only need to compute

$$\log p(\mathcal{X}_t|\boldsymbol{\theta}_t^{(j)}) = -\frac{1}{2\sigma^2} \sum_{i=1}^{I} d_i^2(\boldsymbol{\theta}_t^{(j)}) + \text{constant} , \tag{3}$$

where the constant term can be ignored. For this definition to be complete, we need a definition of the skin model and a suitable metric.

For the skin of the jth sample we will use a collection of capsules $\mathcal{C}^j = \{c_1^j, \ldots, c_K^j\}$. Specifically, we assign a capsule to each bone in the kinematic skeleton, such that the capsule is aligned with the bone. The radius of the capsule depends on the bone. We then define the skin of the skeleton as the union of these capsules. This gives us skins such as the one in Fig. 2(b). This model is very similar to the common model (see e.g. [8,9]) where a cylinder is assigned to each bone. Here, we use capsules for mathematical convenience.

To compute the distance between a point and the skin, we compute the distance from the point to each capsule and pick the smallest, i.e.

$$d_i^2(\boldsymbol{\theta}_t^{(j)}) = \min_k d^2(\boldsymbol{x}_{i,t}, c_k^j) , \tag{4}$$

where $d^2(\boldsymbol{x}_{i,t}, c_k^j)$ denotes the square distance from the ith stereo point to the kth capsule of the jth sample. We will define this distance in terms of ray casting in

---

[1] http://www.ptgrey.com/products/bumblebee2/

the following. To avoid notational clutter, we will omit the time subscript from our notation in the rest of the paper.

Let the capsule c_k^j be defined by the two bone end points $\boldsymbol{a} \in \mathbb{R}^3$ and $\boldsymbol{b} \in \mathbb{R}^3$ and the radius $r \in \mathbb{R}_+$. Consider the stereo point $\boldsymbol{x}_i$. This is a point seen by the camera. Thus, $\boldsymbol{x}_i$ must lie on a ray starting at the camera origin $\boldsymbol{p} \in \mathbb{R}^3$ and casting in the direction of $\boldsymbol{v} = \frac{\boldsymbol{x}_i - \boldsymbol{p}}{\|\boldsymbol{x}_i - \boldsymbol{p}\|}$. We can therefore think of $\boldsymbol{x}_i$ as a function of the ray length parameter Δ. That is, we have the ray definition

$$\boldsymbol{x}_i(\Delta) = \boldsymbol{p} + \boldsymbol{v}\Delta \qquad \forall \Delta \geq 0 \ . \tag{5}$$

From this definition we may define a measure indicating how well a given stereo point $\boldsymbol{x}_i$ fits with a given capsule. Let Δ be the ray length of the stereo point and let $\Delta_{\min}$ be the shortest ray length corresponding to an intersection point between the ray and the capsules then intuitively a distance measure may be taken as $|\Delta - \Delta_{\min}|$. This corresponds to rendering a depth map of the capsules, and computing the absolute difference between this and the depth map from the stereo camera.

Since stereo data contains outliers, both from other objects appearing in the scene and from false matches, we need a robust metric. Here we simply truncate the distance if it exceeds a given threshold

$$\mathbf{d}(\boldsymbol{x}_i, c_k^j) = \begin{cases} |\Delta_{\min} - \Delta| & \text{if } \Delta_{\min} \text{ exists and } |\Delta_{\min} - \Delta| \leq \tau. \\ \tau & \text{otherwise.} \end{cases} \tag{6}$$

For this metric to be computable, we need to be able to determine if a given ray intersects the capsules and if so compute the distance $\Delta_{\min}$. The details of ray capsule intersection can be found in Appendix A. It is worth noting that the basic model works for all skin models, though ray casting details will have to be adapted.

5   Optimizing for the GPU

The algorithm presented in this paper achieves a major speedup when implemented on the GPU. However, it requires careful planning in designing for the massive parallelism in the GPU architecture. The first problem to be addressed is how to block data and computations most efficiently with respect to performance. The task is to minimize data communication and maximize the amount of computations done by one block of threads. Our targeted GPU architectures are the CUDA enabled Nvidia GPUs with compute capability from 1.1 to 1.3.

For our current applications we typically use in the order of $I \approx 50000$ stereo points, $K \approx 40$ capsules and $J \approx 2000$ samples. One simple approach would be to create a 3D float array of dimension $J \times K \times I$ where entry (j, k, i) would hold the value of $\mathbf{d}(\boldsymbol{x}_i, c_k^j)$. This would result in a naive data parallel computation where each thread would compute a single distance measurement. However, such an array would require $2000 \times 40 \times 50000 \times 4$ bytes ≈ 16 Gigabytes of memory.

This clearly exceeds the maximum available device memory, so some tiling must be applied to our problem.

Thus, we create a grid of thread blocks in such a way that each thread block corresponds to one sample and one tile of stereo points and we launch a measure kernel on this grid. During execution the measure kernel will loop over samples in consecutive launches to avoid kernel time-outs. Additionally, support for multiple GPU devices is performed by dividing the samples into one chunk for each GPU. If multiple GPUs are available the same number of CPU worker threads is created and then given a GPU to control. The overhead of launching CPU threads is small and the effect will only be visible for small problem sizes which are not the target for this paper. This orchestration results in the grid setup illustrated in Figure 3. Using this approach we will have an intermediate 2D result array $\mathcal{A}$ consisting of $J \times$ POINTS_TILES computed measurements, where POINT_TILES is set to $\frac{I}{POINTS\_PER\_BLOCK}$. The number of threads in each block is identical to POINTS_PER_BLOCK, thus this value is tuned to achieve the best occupancy for a given GPU.

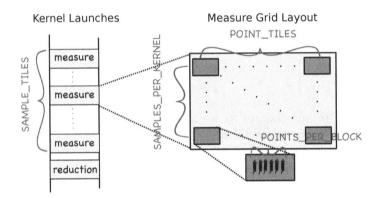

Fig. 3. Illustration of the grid layout and kernel launches for a single GPU. A sequence of measure kernel launches is executed: one for each tile of samples where SAMPLE_TILES = SAMPLES_PER_GPU/SAMPLES_PER_KERNEL. Only a single reduction kernel is launched prior to returning to the CPU thread handling the GPU.

Subsequently we will launch a partial sum reduction kernel. We execute the reduction kernel on a grid where each thread block corresponds with one sample. The kernel performs partial sum reduction on the result array $\mathcal{A}$ to produce the final measurement set $\mathcal{M}$. The jth component in set $\mathcal{M}$ holds the final measurement value of the jth sample. Observe that partial sum reduction is a well studied problem on the GPU and we will therefore not treat it further in this paper. The NVIDIA CUDA SDK version 3.0 contains a sample with code [10] and the next release of CUDPP will also contain sum reduction [11].

To perform the entire computation on the GPU we need to transfer the stereo points $\mathcal{X}$ and the capsules $\{\mathcal{C}^j\}_{j=1}^{J}$ to the GPU device and then read back the set $\mathcal{M}$ from the GPU device. We also need to setup the intermediate storage $\mathcal{A}$. Since each capsule takes 7 floats to store and each stereo point 3 floats the total memory requirements on device memory is for our typical use: $7JK + 3I + J\,\text{POINT\_TILES} + I \approx 3$ Megabytes. This is far from our upper bound on global memory of 256 Megabytes and means that we can keep all points, capsules and measurements in device memory during execution.

The problem that we have specified is memory bound, since it traverses the set of capsules $\{\mathcal{C}^j\}_{j=1}^{J}$ for every stereo point in $\mathcal{X}$ while the computation does not outweigh the latency of the memory. It is essential that we hide this memory latency. The GPU is perfect for doing exactly this, if enough thread blocks are active and the memory operations are handled with care. For optimal performance it will be necessary to keep data aligned in host memory and ensure coalesced access to host memory by using the 16 Kb shared memory available in each SM (streaming multiprocessor)[2]. Seven threads are used to fetch the data of one capsule (7 floats). In Figure 4 and Listing 1.1 we show how the stereo point data, consisting of the coordinates x, y, and z for a single point, are handled in a similar manner, where every set of three threads is working together to fetch one stereo point (3 floats).

```
/* blockDim.x = POINTS_PER_BLOCK */
__shared__ float Xds[3][blockDim.x];
size_t i = threadIdx.x;
size_t total = blockDim.x*3u;
size_t offset = blockDim.x*blockIdx.y*3u;
for (size_t ii = i; ii < total; ii += blockDim.x)
  Xds[ii%3][ii/3] = Xd[offset+ii];
```

Listing 1.1. All threads in a warp of 32 threads will request data from aligned neighboring addresses in device memory, Xd. This results in two coalesced memory requests of maximum size (64 bytes). The data is then copied to shared memory and organized as illustrated in Figure 4, to avoid bank conflicts.

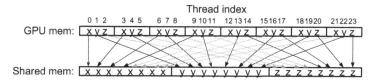

Fig. 4. Ensuring coalesced memory transfers when transferring stereo points from GPU device memory to shared memory. Data is fetched in blocks of 16 and thus aligned in host memory.

---

[2] The Nvidia Fermi architecture has 64 Kb of cache / shared memory reserved for each SM.

The reason for orchestrating the arrays coordinate-wise in shared memory is to avoid bank conflicts [12]. The GPU is a SIMT (single instruction, multiple thread) architecture and executes in an SM one instruction for a warp of 32 threads. When the 32 threads access a shared memory address, it is crucial that they balance the requests onto all 16 banks. Since the shared memory is organized in a round-robin fashion to the 16 banks, we can make sure that we access neighbouring addresses.

When the GPU executes branch instructions all threads in a warp (32 threads) follow the same branch. This means that if some threads in a warp follow one branch and others follow another branch, all threads must visit both branches and the instruction count goes up. With this in mind we have worked to minimize the number of divergent branches, and where we knew there would be divergent branches, conditional expressions were preferred instead, since both expressions would be evaluated anyway.

The resulting measure kernel uses 24 registers, which means that we can run up to 320 threads on devices with compute capability 1.1 or 1.2 (8192 registers) and 640 threads on devices with compute capability 1.3 (16384 registers). 24 registers is not low enough to completely hide the memory latency, but to go lower would require to split the measure kernel into multiple kernels which could each use less registers. This task would require a huge temporary data set in device memory and thus we concluded that 24 registers is the best we can do. The block size used for the benchmarks in Section 6 is chosen so that the maximum number of active blocks is 8 and can go to either 320 or 640 active threads.

6   Two Orders of Magnitude Speedup

To benchmark the implementation, it was run on the three systems listed in Table 1. For every benchmark, a sequential CPU implementation was also executed and the result values compared for correctness. We varied the number of stereo points and the number of samples to see how well the solution scales for up to 43000 stereo points and 3500 samples. The number of capsules was constant at 48. The current GPU implementation is only limited by the maximum grid sizes and the shared memory, thus it actually supports up to 4.194.240 stereo points and 65535 samples of 64 capsules, which can all fit inside 256Mb device memory.

Table 1. Benchmark systems

System 1	System 2	System 3
Intel Core 2 Quad @ 2.4Ghz	Intel Core 2 Duo @ 2.33Ghz	Intel Core 2 Duo @ 2.4Ghz
4Gb DDR2 800Mhz	4Gb DDR2 800Mhz	2Gb DDR2 667Mhz
Nvidia C1060 Tesla 4Gb	2 * Nvidia 9800GX2 1Gb	Nvidia 8600M GT 256Mb
Compute cap. 1.3	Compute cap. 1.1	Compute cap. 1.1
240 cores @ 1.30Ghz	512 cores @ 1.50Ghz	32 cores @ 0.94Ghz

When comparing the performance of the two 9800GX2 with the C1060, notice that one 9800GX2 actually consists of 2 GPUs with hardware similar to a 8800GTX. This means that we are comparing a system with a total of 4 GPUs with a system with 1 GPU, which gives a disadvantage to the system with 4 GPUs, since the benchmark results include the overhead of handling 4 threads. The plots in Figure 5 clearly shows that the GPU implementation scales linearly with an increasing number of stereo points or samples for both systems. The effect of handling the extra threads can be seen for the smaller problems and we expect that the C1060 will be fastest for small problems. For the largest problem the two 9800GX2 are 2.1 times faster than the C1060, but theoretically two 9800GX2 can actually execute 2.46 times more FLOPS than one C1060. The two 9800GX2 are also more capable at hiding the memory latency, since they can have 4 times 320 active threads, while the C1060 is limited to 512 active threads for our implementation. System 3 was not included in these plots, since the benchmark results was around 20 times slower.

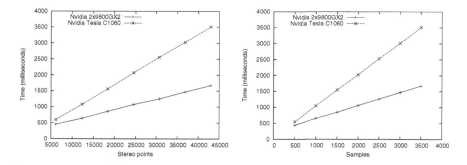

Fig. 5. Plots showing linear scaling for increasing number of stereo points or samples. The number of capsules is kept constant at 48.

The speedup plot in Figure 6 is created using the CPU implementation in Listing 1.2 as the reference. We have used the same input data set for the CPU and the GPU benchmarks. The measurement function used in the CPU implementation (Listing 1.2) is identical to the measurement function used in the GPU implementation (Listing 1.3), but the invocation of the measurement function in listing 1.2 is purely sequential and thus only utilize one core. Since the problem is memory bound, the one thread will have to wait on memory. We expect that an optimized CPU implementation could execute twice as fast, compared to the reference CPU implementation. On the GPU the memory latency has been successfully hidden, which becomes apparent when looking at the speedup numbers in Figure 6.

```
for(size_t j = 0; j < J; ++j)
{
  M[j] = 0.0f;
  for(size_t i = 0; i < I; ++i)
  {
    size_t const ii = i*3u;
    float3 const x_i = make_float3(X[ii],X[ii+1],X[ii+2] );
    float value = MAX_DISTANCE;
    for(size_t k = 0u; k < K; ++k)
    {
      size_t const kk = (j*K + k)*7u;
      float3 const a = make_float3(C[kk],  C[kk+1], C[kk+2] )
      ;
      float3 const b = make_float3(C[kk+4],C[kk+5], C[kk+6] )
      ;
      float  const r = C[kk+3];
      value = min( measurement(  x_i, r, a, b ), value );
    }
    M[j] += value;
  }
}
```

Listing 1.2. The CPU implementation used for benchmarking. This code is executed in a single thread for the CPU.

```
/* Extracted from the body of the measurement_kernel */
float3 const x_i=make_float3(Xds[0][i], Xds[1][i], Xds[2][i])
;
float value = Ads[i];
for(size_t k = 0u; k<K; ++k)
{
  float3 const a = make_float3(Cds[0][k],Cds[1][k],Cds[2][k])
  ;
  float3 const b = make_float3(Cds[4][k],Cds[5][k],Cds[6][k])
  ;
  float  const r = Cds[3][ k ];
  value = min( value,  measurement( x_i, r, a, b ) );
}
Ads[i] = value;
```

Listing 1.3. The GPU implementation, which computes results identical (apart from rounding differences) to the CPU implementation in Listing 1.2. This code is executed in $J * I$ threads for the GPU.

The 8600M GT achieves a stable speedup of ≈ 20, while the others increase in speedup until reaching their maximum stage. The increase in speedup is explained by the overhead of running many kernels. For these benchmarks a kernel

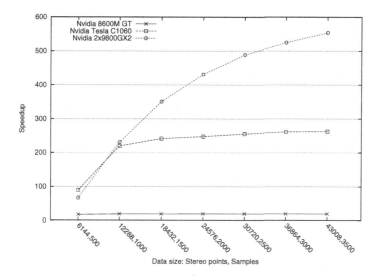

Fig. 6. The speedup achieved when computing a data set of the specified size on a GPU vs. the CPU. The number of capsules is kept constant at 48.

was called for every 8 samples, thus the overhead of calling a kernel takes up a larger proportion when the problem size is small and the GPUs are fast.

The fact that we see a correlation in Figure 6 between the speedup of the GPUs and with the GPU hardware specifications, means that we can conclude that the GPU implementation has succeeded to utilize the GPUs efficiently.

7 Conclusions and Future Work

In this work we have presented a tiling approach that results in a very efficient GPU acceleration of the measurement process for articulated tracking with a particle filter. The main causes to our two orders of magnitude speedup factor lies in careful hiding memory latencies from device memory and avoiding memory bank conflicts in the shared memory. We not only gain from the raw processing power of the GPU, but also from its alternative memory layout.

Our future work involves benchmarking on small scale GPU clusters as this may further interactive markerless computer vision based articulated tracking. Besides this, the sampling process of the particle filter is currently implemented in a naive consumer-producer scheme using a single CPU thread for each sample. This appears to be the next performance bottleneck that we will investigate.

References

1. Poppe, R.: Vision-based human motion analysis: An overview. Computer Vision and Image Understanding 108, 4–18 (2007)

2. Cappé, O., Godsill, S.J., Moulines, E.: An overview of existing methods and recent advances in sequential Monte Carlo. Proceedings of the IEEE 95, 899–924 (2007)
3. Sminchisescu, C., Triggs, B.: Kinematic Jump Processes for Monocular 3D Human Tracking. In: IEEE International Conference on Computer Vision and Pattern Recognition, pp. 69–76 (2003)
4. Deutscher, J., Blake, A., Reid, I.: Articulated body motion capture by annealed particle filtering. In: CVPR, p. 2126. IEEE Computer Society (2000)
5. Hauberg, S., Sommer, S., Pedersen, K.S.: Gaussian-Like Spatial Priors for Articulated Tracking. In: Daniilidis, K., Maragos, P., Paragios, N. (eds.) ECCV 2010, Part I. LNCS, vol. 6311, pp. 425–437. Springer, Heidelberg (2010)
6. Bandouch, J., Beetz, M.: Tracking Humans Interacting with the Environment Using Efficient Hierarchical Sampling and Layered Observation Models. In: IEEE Int. Workshop on Human-Computer Interaction (HCI) (2009)
7. Cabido, R., Concha, D., Pantrigo, J.J., Montemayor, A.S.: High Speed Articulated Object Tracking Using GPUs: A Particle Filter Approach. In: 2009 10th International Symposium on Pervasive Systems, Algorithms, and Networks, pp. 757–762. IEEE (2009)
8. Rohr, K.: Towards model-based recognition of human movements in image sequences. CVGIP-Image Understanding 59, 94–115 (1994)
9. Sidenbladh, H., Black, M.J., Fleet, D.J.: Stochastic Tracking of 3D Human Figures Using 2D Image Motion. In: Vernon, D. (ed.) ECCV 2000. LNCS, vol. 1843, pp. 702–718. Springer, Heidelberg (2000)
10. Sengupta, S., Harris, M., Zhang, Y., Owens, J.D.: Scan primitives for gpu computing. In: Proceedings of the 22nd ACM SIGGRAPH/EUROGRAPHICS Symposium on Graphics Hardware, Aire-la-Ville, Switzerland, pp. 97–106. Eurographics Association (2007)
11. CUDPP: Cuda data parallel primitives library, http://code.google.com/p/cudpp/ (accessed Online April 2010)
12. NVIDIA Corporation: NVIDIA CUDA Best Practices Guide. version 3.0 (2010)

A   Computing the Ray–Capsule Intersection Point

To find the intersection between the ray and the capsule we first consider the situation with an infinitely long capsule. Here we can find the point of intersection by first finding the point y_i on the line through a and b that is closest to the ray $x_i(\Delta)$. By orthogonal projection we find this as

$$y_i = a + \left((x_i(\Delta) - a)^T c \right) c \tag{7}$$

where we have defined $c = \frac{b-a}{\|b-a\|}$.

At the point of intersection between the ray and the infinite capsule we must have

$$\| x_i(\Delta) - y_i \|^2 = r^2 . \tag{8}$$

Inserting the ray definition from Eq. 5 gives us

$$r^2 = \| p + v\Delta - y_i \|^2 = \| v_\perp \Delta + p_\perp \|^2 , \tag{9}$$

where $\mathbf{P} = \left(\mathbf{I} - \mathbf{cc}^T\right)$ and $\boldsymbol{v}_\perp = \mathbf{P}\boldsymbol{v}$ and $\boldsymbol{p}_\perp = \mathbf{P}\left(\boldsymbol{p} - \boldsymbol{a}\right)$. This is readily identified as a second order polynomial in Δ

$$P_c(\Delta) = \boldsymbol{v}_\perp^T \boldsymbol{v}_\perp \Delta^2 + 2\boldsymbol{v}_\perp^T \boldsymbol{p}_\perp \Delta + \boldsymbol{p}_\perp^T \boldsymbol{p}_\perp - r^2 = 0 \ . \tag{10}$$

If no roots to this polynomial exist then the ray does not intersect the infinite long capsule. Otherwise we solve for the minimum positive root Δ_{cap} which will give us the intersection point on the infinite long capsule.

In practice, the skeleton model does not have infinite long limbs and as such we do not have infinite long capsules. The above approach thus needs to be modified to cope with finite capsules. In the case where $0 \leq \boldsymbol{c}^T \left(\boldsymbol{y} - \boldsymbol{a}\right) \leq 1$ the above analysis still holds. In all other cases we only need to see if the ray intersects with the spheres of radius r centred in $\boldsymbol{a}$ and $\boldsymbol{b}$. If the ray intersects the sphere centred in $\boldsymbol{a}$, we must have

$$\| \, \boldsymbol{x}_i(\Delta) - \boldsymbol{a} \, \|^2 = r^2 \ . \tag{11}$$

Once again, this gives as a second order polynomial

$$P_a(\Delta) = \boldsymbol{v}^T \boldsymbol{v} \Delta^2 + 2\boldsymbol{v}^T \left(\boldsymbol{p} - \boldsymbol{a}\right) \Delta + \left(\boldsymbol{p} - \boldsymbol{a}\right)^T \left(\boldsymbol{p} - \boldsymbol{a}\right) - r^2 = 0 \ . \tag{12}$$

If this polynomial has no roots then the ray does not intersect the sphere centred in $\boldsymbol{a}$. If it does have roots, we find the intersection from the smallest positive root. A similar treatment can be given to the sphere centred in $\boldsymbol{b}$.

Thus, the ray intersection algorithm will solve three second order polynomials $P_a(\Delta)$, $P_b(\Delta)$, and $P_c(\Delta)$ and use some **if**-statements that will determine select the proper smallest positive root as the ray intersection length.

A Highly Efficient GPU Implementation for Variational Optic Flow Based on the Euler-Lagrange Framework

Pascal Gwosdek[1], Henning Zimmer[1], Sven Grewenig[1],
Andrés Bruhn[2], and Joachim Weickert[1]

[1] Mathematical Image Analysis Group,
Faculty of Mathematics and Computer Science, Bldg. E1.1,
Saarland University, 66041 Saarbrücken, Germany
{gwosdek,zimmer,grewenig,weickert}@mia.uni-saarland.de
[2] Vision and Image Processing Group,
Cluster of Excellence Multimodal Computing and Interaction,
Saarland University, Campus E 1.1, 66123 Saarbrücken, Germany
bruhn@mmci.uni-saarland.de

Abstract. The Euler-Lagrange (EL) framework is the most widely-used strategy for solving variational optic flow methods. We present the first approach that solves the EL equations of state-of-the-art methods on sequences with 640×480 pixels in near-realtime on GPUs. This performance is achieved by combining two ideas: *(i)* We extend the recently proposed Fast Explicit Diffusion (FED) scheme to optic flow, and additionally embed it into a coarse-to-fine strategy. *(ii)* We parallelise our complete algorithm on a GPU, where a careful optimisation of global memory operations and an efficient use of on-chip memory guarantee a good performance. Applying our approach to the variational 'Complementary Optic Flow' method (Zimmer *et al.* (2009)), we obtain highly accurate flow fields in less than a second. This currently constitutes the fastest method in the top 10 of the widely used Middlebury benchmark.

1 Introduction

A fundamental task in computer vision is the estimation of the optic flow, which describes the apparent motion of brightness patterns between two frames of an image sequence. As witnessed by the Middlebury benchmark [1] [1], the accuracy of optic flow methods has increased tremendously over the last years. This trend was enabled by the recent developments in energy-based methods (e.g. [2,3,5,6,7,8,9,10,11]) that find the flow field by minimising an energy, usually consisting of a data and a smoothness term. While the data term models constancy assumptions on image features like the brightness, the smoothness term (regulariser) penalises fluctuations in the flow field.

To achieve state-of-the-art results, a careful design of the energy is mandatory. In the *data term*, robust subquadratic penaliser functions reduce the influence of outliers [5,7,11,10], higher-order constancy assumptions [7,10] help to deal with illumination changes, and a normalisation [4,10] prevents an overweighting at large image gradients. In the *smoothness term*, subquadratic penalisers yield a discontinuity-preserving

---

[1] Available at http://vision.middlebury.edu/flow/eval/

K.N. Kutulakos (Ed.): ECCV 2010 Workshops, Part II, LNCS 6554, pp. 372–383, 2012.

isotropic smoothing behaviour [5,7,11]. Anisotropic strategies [3,6,8,9,10] additionally allow to steer the smoothing direction, which in [10] yields an optimal complementarity between data and smoothness term.

A major problem of recent sophisticated methods is that their energies are highly nonconvex and nonlinear, rendering the minimisation a challenging task. Modern multi-grid methods are well-known for their good performance on CPUs [12,13], but still do not achieve even near-realtime performance on larger image sequences. Multigrid methods on GPUs do achieve realtime performance, but due to their complicated implementation, they were only realised for basic models so far [14].

Another class of efficient algorithms that can easily be parallelised for GPUs and additionally support modern models are primal-dual approaches; see e.g. [11,9]. These methods typically introduce an auxiliary variable to decouple the minimisation w.r.t. the data and smoothness term. For the data term, one ends up with a thresholding that can be efficiently implemented on the GPU. For the smoothness term, a projected gradient descent algorithm similar to [15] is used. Problems of primal-dual approaches are *(i)* the rather limited number of data terms that can be efficiently implemented and *(ii)* the required adaptation of the gradient descent algorithm to the smoothness term. The latter is especially challenging for anisotropic regularisers, see [9].

The most popular minimisation strategy for continuous energy-based (variational) approaches is the Euler-Lagrange (EL) framework, e.g. [2,3,7,10,16]. Following the calculus of variations, one derives a system of coupled partial differential equations that constitute a necessary condition for a minimiser. The benefits of this framework are: *(i) Flexibility:* The EL equations can be derived in a straightforward manner for a large variety of different models. Even non-differentiable penaliser functions like the TV penaliser [17] can be handled by introducing a small regularisation parameter. *(ii) Generality:* The EL equations are of diffusion-reaction type. This does not only allow to use the same solution strategy for different models, but also permits to adapt solvers known from the solution of diffusion problems. However, one persistent issue of the EL framework is an efficient solution. As mentioned above, multigrid strategies are either restricted to basic models [14] or do not give realtime performance for modern test sequences [12].

Our Contribution. In the present paper, we present the first method that achieves near-realtime performance on a GPU for solving the EL equations. To this end, we adapt the recent *Fast Explicit Diffusion* (FED) scheme [18] to the EL framework. FED is an explicit solver with varying time step sizes, where some time steps can significantly exceed the stability limit of classical explicit schemes. If a series of time step sizes is carefully chosen, the approach can be shown to be unconditionally stable. The already high performance is further boosted by a coarse-to-fine strategy. Finally, our whole approach is parallelised on a GPU using the NVidia CUDA architecture [19]. By doing so, we introduce FED for massively parallel computing, where it unifies algorithmic simplicity with state-of-the-art performance. To obtain high performance despite the large amounts of data involved in the computation, we pay particular attention to an efficient use of on-chip memory to reduce transfers from and to global memory.

To prove the merits of our approach, we apply it within the recent variational optic flow method of Zimmer *et al.* [10], which gives qualitatively good results. Moreover, due to its anisotropic regulariser, it can easily be specialised to less complicated smoothness terms. Experiments with our GPU-based algorithm show speedups by more than one order of magnitude over CPU implementations of both a multigrid solver and an FED scheme. Compared to the anisotropic primal-dual method of Werlberger *et al.* [9], we obtain better results in an equivalent runtime. In the Middlebury benchmark, we rank among the top 10 methods, and can report the smallest runtime among them.

Paper Organisation. In Sec. 2 we review the optic flow model of Zimmer *et al.* [10]. We then adapt the FED framework in Sec. 3, and present details on the GPU implementation in Sec. 4. Experiments demonstrating the efficiency and accuracy of our method are shown in Sec. 5, followed by a summary in Sec. 6.

2   Variational Optic Flow

Let $f(x) = (f^1(x), f^2(x), f^3(x))^\top$ denote an image sequence where f^i represents the i-th RGB colour channel, $x := (x, y, t)^\top$, with $(x, y)^\top \in \Omega$ describing the location within a rectangular image domain $\Omega \subset \mathbb{R}^2$ and $t \geq 0$ denotes time. We further assume that f has been presmoothed by a Gaussian convolution of standard deviation σ. The sought optic flow field $w := (u, v, 1)^\top$ that describes the displacements from time t to $t+1$ is then found by minimising a global energy functional of the general form

$$E(u, v) = \int_\Omega [M(u, v) + \alpha \, V(\nabla u, \nabla v)] \, dx \, dy \ , \tag{1}$$

where $\nabla := (\partial_x, \partial_y)^\top$ denotes the spatial gradient operator, and $\alpha > 0$ is a smoothness weight.

2.1   Complementary Optic Flow

The model we will use to exemplify our approach is the recent method of Zimmer *et al.* [10], because it gives favourable results at the Middlebury benchmark and uses a general anisotropic smoothness term.

Data Term. For simplicity, we use a standard RGB colour representation instead of the HSV model from the original paper. Our data term is given by

$$M(u, v) := \Psi_M \left(\sum_{i=1}^3 \theta_0^i \left(f^i(x+w) - f^i(x) \right)^2 \right) \tag{2}$$

$$+ \gamma \, \Psi_M \left(\sum_{i=1}^3 \left(\theta_x^i \left(f_x^i(x+w) - f_x^i(x) \right)^2 + \theta_y^i \left(f_y^i(x+w) - f_y^i(x) \right)^2 \right) \right) \ ,$$

where subscripts denote partial derivatives. The first line in (2) models the brightness constancy assumption [2], stating that image intensities remain constant under the displacement, i.e. $f(x + w) = f(x)$. To prevent an overweighting of the data term at large image gradients, a normalisation in the spirit of [4] is performed. To this end, one uses a normalisation factor $\theta_0^i := (|\nabla f^i|^2 + \zeta^2)^{-1}$, where the small parameter $\zeta > 0$

avoids division by zero. Finally, to reduce the influence of outliers caused by noise or occlusions, a robust subquadratic penaliser function $\Psi_M(s^2) := \sqrt{s^2+\varepsilon^2}$ with a small parameter $\varepsilon > 0$ is used [7].

Weighted by $\gamma > 0$, the second line in (2) models the gradient constancy assumption $\nabla f(x+w) = \nabla f(x)$ that renders the approach robust under additive illumination changes [7]. The corresponding normalisation factors are defined as $\theta^i_{\{x,y\}} := (|\nabla f^i_{\{x,y\}}|^2 + \zeta^2)^{-1}$. As proposed in [12] a separate penalisation of the brightness and the gradient constancy assumption is performed, which is advantageous if one assumption produces an outlier.

Smoothness Term. The data term only constraints the flow vectors in one direction, the *data constraint direction*. In the orthogonal direction, the data term gives no information (aperture problem). Thus, it makes sense to use a smoothness term that works *complementary* to the data term: In data constraint direction, a reduced smoothing should be performed to avoid interference with the data term, whereas a strong smoothing is desirable in the orthogonal direction to obtain a filling-in of missing information.

To realise this strategy, one needs to determine the data constraint direction. This can be achieved by considering the largest eigenvector of the regularisation tensor

$$R_\rho := \sum_{i=1}^{3} K_\rho * \left[\theta^i_0 \nabla f^i \left(\nabla f^i\right)^\top + \gamma \left(\theta^i_x \nabla f^i_x \left(\nabla f^i_x\right)^\top + \theta^i_y \nabla f^i_y \left(\nabla f^i_y\right)^\top \right) \right] , \quad (3)$$

where K_ρ is a Gaussian of standard deviation ρ, and $*$ denotes the convolution operator. Apart from this convolution, the regularisation tensor is a spatial version of the motion tensor that occurs in a linearised data term. For more details, see [10].

Let $r_1 \geq r_2$ denote the two orthonormal eigenvectors of R_ρ, i.e. r_1 is the data constraint direction. Then, the complementary regulariser is given by

$$V(\nabla u, \nabla v) = \Psi_V\left(\left(r_1^\top \nabla u\right)^2 + \left(r_1^\top \nabla v\right)^2 \right) + \left(r_2^\top \nabla u\right)^2 + \left(r_2^\top \nabla v\right)^2 . \quad (4)$$

To reduce the smoothing in data constraint direction, we use the subquadratic Perona-Malik penaliser (Lorentzian) [5,20] given by $\Psi_V(s^2) := \lambda^2 \ln(1 + (s^2/\lambda^2))$ with a contrast parameter $\lambda > 0$. In the orthogonal direction, a strong quadratic penalisation allows to fill in missing information.

2.2 Energy Minimisation via the Euler-Lagrange Framework

According to the calculus of variations, a minimiser (u,v) of the proposed energy (1) necessarily has to fulfil the associated Euler-Lagrange equations

$$\partial_u M - \alpha \operatorname{div}\left(D\left(r_1, r_2, \nabla u, \nabla v\right) \nabla u\right) = 0 , \quad (5)$$

$$\partial_v M - \alpha \operatorname{div}\left(D\left(r_1, r_2, \nabla u, \nabla v\right) \nabla v\right) = 0 , \quad (6)$$

with reflecting boundary conditions. These equations are of diffusion-reaction type, where the reaction part ($\partial_u M$ and $\partial_v M$) stems from the data term, and the diffusion part (written in divergence form) stems from the smoothness term.

To write down the reaction part of the EL equations, we use the abbreviations $f^i_{**} := \partial_{**}f^i(\boldsymbol{x}+\boldsymbol{w})$, $f^i_z := f^i(\boldsymbol{x}+\boldsymbol{w}) - f^i(\boldsymbol{x})$ and $f^i_{*z} := \partial_* f^i(\boldsymbol{x}+\boldsymbol{w}) - \partial_* f^i(\boldsymbol{x})$, where $** \in \{x, y, xx, xy, yy\}$ and $* \in \{x, y\}$. With their help, we obtain

$$\partial_u M = \quad \Psi'_M \left(\sum_{i=1}^{3} \theta_0^i \left(f_z^i\right)^2 \right) \cdot \left(\sum_{i=1}^{3} \theta_0^i f_z^i f_x^i \right) \tag{7}$$

$$+ \gamma \, \Psi'_M \left(\sum_{i=1}^{3} \left(\theta_x^i \left(f_{xz}^i\right)^2 + \theta_y^i \left(f_{yz}^i\right)^2 \right) \right) \cdot \left(\sum_{i=1}^{3} \left(\theta_x^i f_{xz}^i f_{xx}^i + \theta_y^i f_{yz}^i f_{xy}^i \right) \right) ,$$

$$\partial_v M = \quad \Psi'_M \left(\sum_{i=1}^{3} \theta_0^i \left(f_z^i\right)^2 \right) \cdot \left(\sum_{i=1}^{3} \theta_0^i f_z^i f_y^i \right) \tag{8}$$

$$+ \gamma \, \Psi'_M \left(\sum_{i=1}^{3} \left(\theta_x^i \left(f_{xz}^i\right)^2 + \theta_y^i \left(f_{yz}^i\right)^2 \right) \right) \cdot \left(\sum_{i=1}^{3} \left(\theta_x^i f_{xz}^i f_{xy}^i + \theta_y^i f_{yz}^i f_{yy}^i \right) \right) .$$

The joint diffusion tensor $D\left(\boldsymbol{r}_1, \boldsymbol{r}_2, \boldsymbol{\nabla}u, \boldsymbol{\nabla}v\right)$ is given by

$$D\left(\boldsymbol{r}_1, \boldsymbol{r}_2, \boldsymbol{\nabla}u, \boldsymbol{\nabla}v\right) := \Psi'_V\left(\left(\boldsymbol{r}_1^\top \boldsymbol{\nabla}u\right)^2 + \left(\boldsymbol{r}_1^\top \boldsymbol{\nabla}v\right)^2 \right) \boldsymbol{r}_1 \boldsymbol{r}_1^\top + \boldsymbol{r}_2 \boldsymbol{r}_2^\top . \tag{9}$$

Analysing the diffusion tensor, one realises that the resulting smoothing process is not only complementary to the data term, but can also be characterised as joint image- and flow driven: The smoothing direction is adapted to the direction of *image* structures, encoded in $\boldsymbol{r}_1$ and $\boldsymbol{r}_2$. The smoothing strength depends on the *flow* contrast given by the expression $(\boldsymbol{r}_1^\top \boldsymbol{\nabla}u)^2 + (\boldsymbol{r}_1^\top \boldsymbol{\nabla}v)^2$. As a result, one obtains the same sharp flow edges as image-driven methods, but does not suffer from their oversegmentation problems.

Solution of the Euler-Lagrange Equations. The preceding EL equations are difficult to solve because the unknown $\boldsymbol{w}$ implicitly appears in the argument of the expressions $f^i(\boldsymbol{x}+\boldsymbol{w})$. A common strategy to resolve this problem is to embed the solution into a coarse-to-fine multiscale warping approach [7]. To obtain a coarse representation of the problem, the images are downsampled by a factor of $\eta \in [0.5, 1)$. At each warping level k, the flow field is split up into $\boldsymbol{w}^k + d\boldsymbol{w}^k =: \boldsymbol{w}^{k+1}$, where $\boldsymbol{w}^k = (u^k, v^k, 1)^\top$ is the already computed solution from coarser levels and $d\boldsymbol{w}^k = (du^k, dv^k, 0)^\top$ is a small flow increment that is computed by a linearised approach.

Let us derive this linearised approach. To ease presentation, we omit the gradient constancy part, i.e. set $\gamma = 0$, and restrict ourselves to the first EL equation (5). The extension to the full model works straightforward in accordance to [7]. A first step is to perform a Taylor linearisation

$$f_z^{i,k+1} := f^i(\boldsymbol{x}+\boldsymbol{w}^{k+1}) - f^i(\boldsymbol{x}) \approx f_z^{i,k} + f_x^{i,k} du^k + f_y^{i,k} dv^k , \tag{10}$$

where in expressions of the form $f^{i,k}$ the flow $\boldsymbol{w}^k$ is used. Replacing all occurrences of f_z^i by this linearisation and using the information from level k for all other constituents, one obtains the linearised first EL equation (with $\gamma = 0$)

$$\Psi'_M \left(\sum_{i=1}^{3} \theta_0^{i,k} \left(f_z^{i,k} + f_x^{i,k} du^k + f_y^{i,k} dv^k\right)^2 \right) \cdot \sum_{i=1}^{3} \theta_0^{i,k} \left(f_z^{i,k} + f_x^{i,k} du^k + f_y^{i,k} dv^k\right) f_x^{i,k}$$

$$- \alpha \, \mathrm{div}\left(D\left(\boldsymbol{r}_1^k, \boldsymbol{r}_2^k, \boldsymbol{\nabla}\left(u^k + du^k\right), \boldsymbol{\nabla}\left(v^k + dv^k\right)\right) \boldsymbol{\nabla}\left(u^k + du^k\right) \right) = 0 . \tag{11}$$

At this point, it is feasible to use a solver for nonlinear systems of equations. However, we use a second coarse-to-fine strategy per warping level for an even faster convergence. Here the prolongated solution from a coarse level serves as initialisation for the next finer level.

3 Fast Explicit Diffusion Solver

A classical approach to solve elliptic problems such as the linearised EL equation (11) are semi-implicit schemes: They are unconstrained in their time step sizes, but require to solve large linear systems of equations in each step. In contrast, explicit schemes are much easier to implement and have a low complexity per step, but are typically restricted to very small step sizes to guarantee stability. In this paper, we use a new time discretisation that combines the advantages of both worlds [18]: *Fast Explicit Diffusion (FED)* schemes are as simple as classical explicit frameworks, but use some extremely large time steps to ensure a fast convergence. Still, the combination of large (unstable) and small (stable) time steps within one *cycle* guarantees the unconditional stability of the complete approach. Hence, FED schemes outperform semi-implicit schemes in terms of efficiency and are additionally much simpler to implement, especially on massively parallel architectures.

Let us first derive a *stabilised* explicit scheme [16] for solving the linearised EL equation (11) w.r.t. the unknown du^k. To this end, we introduce the iteration variable l:

$$\frac{du^{k,l+1} - du^{k,l}}{\tau_l} = \mathrm{div}\left(D\left(r_1^k, r_2^k, \nabla\left(u^k + du^{k,l}\right), \nabla\left(v^k + dv^{k,l}\right)\right)\nabla\left(u^k + du^{k,l}\right)\right)$$

$$-\frac{1}{\alpha}\left(\psi_M'^{k,l}(..)\cdot\sum_{i=1}^{3}\theta_0^{i,k}\left(f_z^{i,k} + f_x^{i,k}du^{k,l+1} + f_y^{i,k}dv^{k,l}\right)f_x^{i,k}\right), \quad (12)$$

where τ_l denotes the FED time step size at iteration $0 \leqslant l < n$ which is computed as [18]

$$\tau_l = \frac{1}{8}\cdot\left(\cos^2\left(\pi\frac{2l+1}{4n+2}\right)\right)^{-1}. \quad (13)$$

In (12), the term $\psi_M'^{k,l}(..)$ is an abbreviation for the expression $\Psi_M'(..)$ in the first line of (11), where we additionally replace du^k by $du^{k,l}$ and dv^k by $dv^{k,l}$. Finally, note that our scheme is stabilised by using $du^{k,l+1}$ from the next iteration in the last row.

In our next step we discretise the expression $\mathrm{div}(D(..)\nabla(u^k + du^{k,l}))$ in matrix-vector notation by $A(u^k + du^{k,l}, v^k + dv^{k,l})(u^k + du^{k,l}) =: A^{k+1,l}u^{k+1,l}$. This enables us to rewrite (12) as

$$du^{k,l+1} = \left[du^{k,l} + \tau_l A^{k+1,l}u^{k+1,l} - \frac{\tau_l}{\alpha}\left(\psi_M'^{k,l}(..)\cdot\sum_{i=1}^{3}\theta_0^{i,k}\left(f_z^{i,k} + f_y^{i,k}dv^{k,l}\right)f_x^{i,k}\right)\right]$$

$$\cdot\left(1 + \frac{\tau_l}{\alpha}\cdot\psi_M'^{k,l}(..)\cdot\sum_{i=1}^{3}\theta_0^{i,k}\left(f_x^{i,k}\right)^2\right)^{-1}. \quad (14)$$

Remarks. The number of individual time steps n in a cycle is given by $\min\{n \in \mathbb{N}^+ \mid (n^2 + n)/12 \geqslant T\}$, where T denotes the desired stopping time of the cycle. For $n \geqslant 3$, one can show that an FED cycle reaches this stopping time T faster than any other explicit scheme with n stable time step sizes.

Moreover, the ordering of steps within one FED cycle is irrelevant from a theoretical point of view, but can in practice affect the influence of rounding errors to the result. However, it is possible to find permutations of the set $\{\tau_l \mid 0 \leqslant l < n\}$ that are more robust w.r.t. floating-point inaccuracies than others. Given the next larger prime number p to n and $\kappa < p$, a series $\{\tau_{\tilde{l}} \mid \tilde{l} = ((l+1) \cdot \kappa) \bmod p, \tilde{l} < n\}$ is known to give good results [18,21]. In order to find a suitable value for the parameter κ, we analysed a simple 1-D problem and choose the one κ that minimises the error between the FED output and the analytic reference solution. These values were once computed for all practical choices of n to set up a lookup table which is used throughout our implementation.

4   Implementation on the GPU

Since our algorithm is hierarchic and uses different data configurations and cache patterns for the operations it performs, we split it up into single GPU kernels of homogeneous structure. This concept allows to have a recursive program flow on the CPU, while the data is kept in GPU memory throughout the process.

FED Solver. Our stabilised fast explicit scheme forms the heart of our algorithm. It is also the most expensive GPU kernel in our framework: Due to its low arithmetic complexity, it is strictly memory bound and requires significant amounts of data. For the smoothness term, we reduce the memory complexity by exploiting the symmetry of the non-diagonal matrix A from (14), which comes down to store the four upper off-diagonals. The remaining entries can be computed in shared memory. Where offset data loads are necessary for this strategy, they can be efficiently realised by texture lookups.

Derivatives. Spatial image and flow derivatives are discretised via central finite differences with consistency order 2 and 4, respectively [12]. For the motion tensor, these derivatives are averaged from the two frames $f(x, y, t)$ and $f(x, y, t + 1)$, whereas for the regularisation tensor, they are solely computed at the first frame. Where required, we compute both the first order and second order derivatives in the same GPU kernel which saves a large number of loads from global memory. Thanks to the texture cache, the slightly larger neighbourhood that is needed in this context does again not significantly affect the runtime.

Diffusion Tensor. In order to set up the diffusion tensor D for the smoothness term, we apply the diffusivity function to the eigenvalues of the structure tensor and use these new eigenvalues to assemble a new tensor. Both the derivative computation and the principal axis transforms that are used in this context are fully data parallel. Note that we do not store the tensor entries to global memory, but directly compute the weights that are later to be used in the solver. By this, we save again a significant number of global loads and stores. Due to our nonlinear model, we update the diffusion tensor after every cycle.

Gaussian Convolution. Our GPU-based Gaussian convolution algorithm is tailored to the small standard deviations σ that typically occur in the context of optic flow: We exploit the operation's separability and cut off the discretised kernel at a precision of 3σ. This allows our 'sliding window' approach to keep a full neighbourhood in shared memory, and thus to reduce global memory operations to one read and write per pixel. Along the main direction of the 2-D data in memory, we apply loop unrolling over data-independent rows and keep three consecutive sub-planes of the source image in a ring buffer. Across this direction, we cut our domain in sufficiently large chunks, and maintain a ring buffer of chunk-wide rows that cover the entire neighbourhood of the computed row.

Resampling. Key ingredients for hierarchic coarse-to-fine algorithms are prolongation and restriction operators. Several examples for such operators are known in the literature, but they are either quite expensive on GPUs due to their 'inhomogeneous' algorithmic structure, or do not possess necessary properties such as grey value preservation, aliasing artefact prevention, and flexibility with respect to the choice of the resampling factor [22,23]. As a remedy, we propose a fast but versatile technique that approximates the desired behaviour well enough to satisfy the quality requirements for optic flow. It has a uniform algorithmic structure for all target cells and uses the texturing mechanism of CUDA cards to obtain a high performance.

Textures can be queried at any point in a continuous domain, and in particular in between grid points. The resulting value is then computed in hardware by means of a bilinear interpolation. These properties alone yield an efficient prolongation algorithm: For any target cell of the result, we use the value at the corresponding point of the source texture. Note that this strategy does not guarantee grey value preservation from a theoretical point of view, but experimentally yields favourable results.

As it turns out, we must not apply the same algorithm for restriction purposes: Typical choices of restriction factors close to two cause undersampling and lead to aliasing artefacts. To overcome this problem, we use four sampling points instead of one: Let r_x, r_y be the restriction factors in $x-$ and $y-$direction, respectively, and assume textures to be defined on the domain $[0, n_x - 1) \times [0, n_y - 1)$. For any target point $(x, y)^\top$, we then average over the texture values at locations

$$\left(\frac{1}{r_x} \cdot \left(x \pm \frac{1}{4} \right), \frac{1}{r_y} \cdot \left(y \pm \frac{1}{4} \right) \right)^\top . \tag{15}$$

This modification allows us to choose arbitrary factors in the interval $[\frac{1}{2}, 1)$ which suffices for our purposes. Moreover, since nearby sampling points are likely to be in the 2-D texture cache at the same time, this strategy is almost as fast as prolongation.

Warping. In order to access images at warped positions, i.e. to evaluate expressions of type $f^i(\boldsymbol{x}+\boldsymbol{w}^k)$, we use the texturing mechanism of graphics cards: We store the image channel i that is to be warped in a texture, compute the target location by adding flow field and pixel coordinates, and fetch the texture at the respective point. Albeit incoherent memory access is often considered a major performance problem on massively parallel hardware, this operation turns out to be highly efficient: Optic flow is often piecewise laminar and sufficiently smooth, such that the missing data locality is largely compensated by the 2-D texture cache.

5 Experiments

Quality. We first consider a qualitative evaluation of our results. To this end, we chose 4 sequences with known ground truth from the Middlebury database, and computed the optic flow fields using our algorithm and an individual choice of parameters. A visualisation of the results is shown in Fig. 1. Like in the original CPU implementation of Zimmer *et al.* [10], the flow fields are accurate and without visual artefacts.

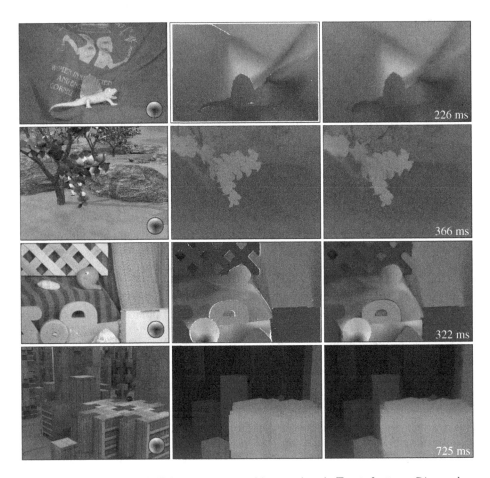

Fig. 1. Our results for 4 Middlebury sequences with ground truth. **Top to bottom:** *Dimetrodon, Grove2, RubberWhale, Urban2*. **Left to right:** First frame with flow key, ground truth, result with runtime. We use optimised parameter sets $(\alpha, \gamma, \zeta, \lambda)$ for the individual sequences (*D*: (400, 8, 1.0, 0.05), *G*: (50, 1, 1.0, 0.05), *R*: (1000, 20, 1.0, 0.05), *U*: (1500, 25, 0.01, 0.1)). Fixed parameters for all cases: $\eta = 0.91, \sigma = 0.3, \rho = 1.3$, 1 cascadic FED step with 1 nonlinear update and $T = 150$ per warp level.

Table 1. Error measures for 4 Middlebury sequences with known ground truth using the optimal parameter sets from Fig. 1, and a fixed parameter set (300, 20, 0.01, 0.1).

Sequence		Dimetrodon	Grove2	RubberWhale	Urban2
Optimised	AEE	0.08	0.16	0.09	0.29
	AAE	1.49	2.32	2.93	2.75
Fixed	AEE	0.11	0.19	0.11	0.36
	AAE	2.20	2.69	3.76	3.56

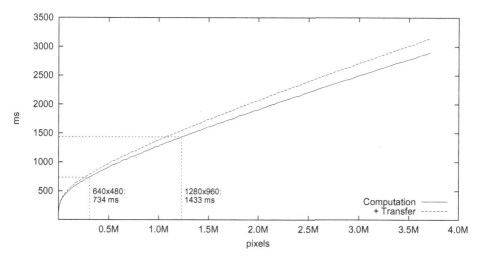

Fig. 2. Runtimes (with and without device transfer) on images with size ratio 4:3

We also evaluated our results to the ground truth by computing the Average Endpoint Error (AEE), as well as the Average Angular Error (AAE). In order to be better comparable to the results of other state-of-the-art methods, we additionally performed the same experiment on a fixed parameter set for all sequences, as it is required for the Middlebury benchmark. From Tab. 1, we see that if we use fixed parameters, we obtain results comparable to those of Werlberger *et al.* [9], which has been the top-ranked anisotropic GPU-based method in the Middlebury benchmark so far. Using individually tuned parameters as in Fig. 1, the obtained quality can be further enhanced.

The high quality of our algorithm is also reflected in the position in the Middlebury benchmark. In August 2010, it ranks seventh out of 35 both w.r.t. AAE and AEE.

Runtime. Finally, we evaluate the efficiency of our approach on image sequences of varying sizes. To this end, we benchmark the runtimes on an NVidia GeForce GTX 480 graphics card. Since runtimes are affected by the size ratio of the image sequence and the parameter set, we used a ratio of 4:3 and the fixed parameter set from Tab. 1. This is depicted in Fig. 2. On *Urban2* (640×480), our algorithm takes 734 ms. Compared to hand-optimised Multigrid (FAS) [12] and FED schemes with equivalent results on one core of an 2.33 GHz Intel Core2 Quad CPU, this performance results in speedups of 15 and 17, respectively. Thanks to a better GPU occupancy, these factors are even higher the larger the frame size, e.g. 23 and 28 for frames of 1024×768 pixels. Moreover, our algorithm has comparable runtimes to the approach of Werlberger *et al.* [9], despite yielding more accurate results, as seen in the Middlebury benchmark. Concerning the latter, our method currently is the fastest among the top 10 approaches, outperforming the competitors by one to three orders of magnitude.

6   Conclusions and Outlook

We have presented a highly efficient method for minimising variational optic flow approaches by solving the corresponding Euler-Lagrange (EL) equations. The core of our approach is the recently proposed Fast Explicit Diffusion (FED) scheme [18], which can be adapted to optic flow due to the diffusion-reaction character of the EL equations. Additionally, we apply a coarse-to-fine strategy, and parallelise our complete algorithm on a GPU, thereby introducing the first parallel FED implementation.

In our experiments, we used the proposed approach to minimise the optic flow model of Zimmer *et al.* [10], resulting in highly accurate flow fields that are computed in less than one second for sequences of size 640×480. This gives a speedup by more than one order of magnitude compared to a CPU implementation of *(i)* a multigrid solver and *(ii)* an FED solver. In the Middlebury benchmark, we rank among the top 10 and achieve the smallest runtime there.

Since most variational optic flow algorithms are based on solving the EL equations, we hope that our approach can also help to tangibly speedup other optic flow methods based on the EL framework. Note that we used an anisotropic regulariser, which results in the most general form of the diffusion part. Applying our approach with other popular smoothness terms, like TV regularisation, thus works straightforward by simply replacing the diffusion tensor by a scalar-valued diffusivity.

Our future research will be concerned with further reducing the runtimes to meet an ultimate goal: Realtime performance for state-of-the-art optic flow approaches on high resolution (maybe high-definition) image sequences.

Acknowledgements. We gratefully acknowledge partial funding by the cluster of excellence 'Multimodal Computing and Interaction', by the International Max Planck Research School, and by the Deutsche Forschungsgemeinschaft (project We2602/7-1).

References

1. Baker, S., Roth, S., Scharstein, D., Black, M.J., Lewis, J.P., Szeliski, R.: A database and evaluation methodology for optical flow. In: Proc. 2007 IEEE International Conference on Computer Vision. IEEE Computer Society Press, Rio de Janeiro (2007)
2. Horn, B., Schunck, B.: Determining optical flow. Artificial Intelligence 17, 185–203 (1981)
3. Nagel, H.H., Enkelmann, W.: An investigation of smoothness constraints for the estimation of displacement vector fields from image sequences. IEEE Transactions on Pattern Analysis and Machine Intelligence 8, 565–593 (1986)
4. Simoncelli, E.P., Adelson, E.H., Heeger, D.J.: Probability distributions of optical flow. In: Proc. 1991 IEEE Computer Society Conference on Computer Vision and Pattern Recognition, pp. 310–315. IEEE Computer Society Press, Maui (1991)

5. Black, M.J., Anandan, P.: The robust estimation of multiple motions: parametric and piecewise smooth flow fields. Computer Vision and Image Understanding 63, 75–104 (1996)
6. Weickert, J., Schnörr, C.: A theoretical framework for convex regularizers in PDE-based computation of image motion. International Journal of Computer Vision 45, 245–264 (2001)
7. Brox, T., Bruhn, A., Papenberg, N., Weickert, J.: High Accuracy Optical Flow Estimation Based on a Theory for Warping. In: Pajdla, T., Matas, J. (eds.) ECCV 2004. LNCS, vol. 3024, pp. 25–36. Springer, Heidelberg (2004)
8. Sun, D., Roth, S., Lewis, J.P., Black, M.J.: Learning Optical Flow. In: Forsyth, D., Torr, P., Zisserman, A. (eds.) ECCV 2008, Part III. LNCS, vol. 5304, pp. 83–97. Springer, Heidelberg (2008)
9. Werlberger, M., Trobin, W., Pock, T., Wedel, A., Cremers, D., Bischof, H.: Anisotropic Huber-L^1 optical flow. In: Proc. 20th British Machine Vision Conference. British Machine Vision Association, London (2009)
10. Zimmer, H., Bruhn, A., Weickert, J., Valgaerts, L., Salgado, A., Rosenhahn, B., Seidel, H.-P.: Complementary Optic Flow. In: Cremers, D., Boykov, Y., Blake, A., Schmidt, F.R. (eds.) EMMCVPR 2009. LNCS, vol. 5681, pp. 207–220. Springer, Heidelberg (2009)
11. Zach, C., Pock, T., Bischof, H.: A Duality Based Approach for Realtime TV- L^1 Optical Flow. In: Hamprecht, F.A., Schnörr, C., Jähne, B. (eds.) DAGM 2007. LNCS, vol. 4713, pp. 214–223. Springer, Heidelberg (2007)
12. Bruhn, A., Weickert, J.: Towards ultimate motion estimation: Combining highest accuracy with real-time performance. In: Proc. of the Tenth International Conference on Computer Vision, vol. 1, pp. 749–755. IEEE Computer Society Press, Beijing (2005)
13. El Kalmoun, M., Köstler, H., Rüde, U.: 3D optical flow computation using a parallel variational multigrid scheme with application to cardiac C-arm CT motion. Image and Vision Computing 25, 1482–1494 (2007)
14. Grossauer, H., Thoman, P.: GPU-Based Multigrid: Real-Time Performance in High Resolution Nonlinear Image Processing. In: Gasteratos, A., Vincze, M., Tsotsos, J.K. (eds.) ICVS 2008. LNCS, vol. 5008, pp. 141–150. Springer, Heidelberg (2008)
15. Chambolle, A.: An algorithm for total variation minimization and applications. Journal of Mathematical Imaging and Vision 20, 89–97 (2004)
16. Weickert, J., Schnörr, C.: Variational optic flow computation with a spatio-temporal smoothness constraint. Journal of Mathematical Imaging and Vision 14, 245–255 (2001)
17. Rudin, L.I., Osher, S., Fatemi, E.: Nonlinear total variation based noise removal algorithms. Physica D 60, 259–268 (1992)
18. Grewenig, S., Weickert, J., Bruhn, A.: From Box Filtering to Fast Explicit Diffusion. In: Goesele, M., Roth, S., Kuijper, A., Schiele, B., Schindler, K. (eds.) DAGM 2010. LNCS, vol. 6376, pp. 533–542. Springer, Heidelberg (2010)
19. NVIDIA Corporation: NVIDIA CUDA Programming Guide. 3rd edn.(2010), http://developer.download.nvidia.com/compute/cuda/3_0/toolkit/docs/NVIDIA_CUDA_ProgrammingGuide.pdf (retrieved June 10, 2009)
20. Perona, P., Malik, J.: Scale space and edge detection using anisotropic diffusion. IEEE Transactions on Pattern Analysis and Machine Intelligence 12, 629–639 (1990)
21. Gentzsch, W., Schlüter, A.: Über ein Einschrittverfahren mit zyklischer Schrittweitenänderung zur Lösung parabolischer Differentialgleichungen. Zeitschrift für angewandte Mathematik und Mechanik 58, T415–T416 (1978)
22. Trottenberg, U., Oosterlee, C., Schüller, A.: Multigrid. Academic Press, San Diego (2001)
23. Bruhn, A., Weickert, J., Feddern, C., Kohlberger, T., Schnörr, C.: Variational optical flow computation in real-time. IEEE Transactions on Image Processing 14, 608–615 (2005)

From Multiple Views to Textured 3D Meshes: A GPU-Powered Approach

K. Tzevanidis, X. Zabulis, T. Sarmis, P. Koutlemanis,
N. Kyriazis, and A. Argyros

Institute of Computer Science (ICS)
Foundation for Research and Technology - Hellas (Forth)
N. Plastira 100, Vassilika Vouton, GR 700 13
Heraklion, Crete, Greece
{ktzevani,zabulis,sarmis,koutle,kyriazis,argyros}@ics.forth.gr

Abstract. We present work on exploiting modern graphics hardware towards the real-time production of a textured 3D mesh representation of a scene observed by a multicamera system. The employed computational infrastructure consists of a network of four PC workstations each of which is connected to a pair of cameras. One of the PCs is equipped with a GPU that is used for parallel computations. The result of the processing is a list of texture mapped triangles representing the reconstructed surfaces. In contrast to previous works, the entire processing pipeline (foreground segmentation, 3D reconstruction, 3D mesh computation, 3D mesh smoothing and texture mapping) has been implemented on the GPU. Experimental results demonstrate that an accurate, high resolution, texture-mapped 3D reconstruction of a scene observed by eight cameras is achievable in real time.

1   Introduction

The goal of this work is the design and the implementation of a multicamera system that captures 4D videos of human grasping and manipulation activities performed on a desktop environment. Thus, the intended output of the target system is a temporal sequence of texture mapped, accurate 3D mesh representations of the observed scene. This constitutes rich perceptual input that may feed higher level modules responsible for scene understanding and human activity interpretation.

From the advent of GPU programmable pipeline, researchers have made great efforts to exploit the computational power provided by the graphics hardware (i.e. GPGPUs). The evolution of GPUs led to the introduction of flexible computing models such as shader model 4.0 and CUDA that support general purpose computations. Various GPU implementations of shape-from-silhouette reconstruction have been presented in the recent literature [1,2]. Moreover, following past attempts on real-time reconstruction and rendering (e.g. [3,4]), some recent works introduce full 3D reconstruction systems [5,6] that incorporate modern

K.N. Kutulakos (Ed.): ECCV 2010 Workshops, Part II, LNCS 6554, pp. 384–397, 2012.
© Springer-Verlag Berlin Heidelberg 2012

graphics hardware for their calculations. The later implementations take as input segmented object silhouettes and produce as output voxel scene representations. In contrast to these systems, the one proposed in this paper parallelizes the whole processing pipeline that consists of foreground object segmentation, visual hull computation and smoothing, 3D mesh calculation and texture mapping. The algorithms implementing this processing chain are inherently parallel. We capitalize on the enormous computational power of modern GPU hardware through NVIDIA's CUDA framework, in order to exploit this fact and to achieve realtime performance.

The remainder of this paper is organized as follows. Section 2 introduces the system architecture both at hardware and software level. Section 3 details the GPU-based parallel implementation of the 3D reconstruction process. Experiments and performance measurements are presented in Sec. 4. Finally, Sec. 5 provides conclusions and suggestions for future enhancements of the proposed system.

2   Infrastructure

2.1   Hardware Configuration

The developed multicamera system is installed around a $2 \times 1m^2$ bench and consists of 8 *Flea2* PointGrey cameras. Each camera has a maximum framerate of 30 *fps* at highest (i.e. 1280×960) image resolution. The system employs four computers with quad-core Intel i7 920 CPUs and 6 GBs RAM each, connected by an 1 Gbit ethernet link. Figure 1 shows the overall architecture along with a picture of the developed multicamera system infrastructure.

In our *switched-star* network topology, one of the four computers is declared as the *central workstation* and the remaining three as the *satellite workstations*. The central workstation's configuration, includes also a Nvidia GTX 295 dual GPU with 894 *GFlops* processing power and 896 MBs memory per GPU core. Currently, the developed system utilizes a single GPU core.

Each workstation is connected to a camera pair. Cameras are synchronized by a timestamp-based software that utilizes a dedicated *FireWire 2* interface (800 $MBits/sec$) which guarantees a maximum of 125 μsec temporal discrepancy in images with the same timestamp. Eight images sharing the same timestamp constitute a *multiframe*.

2.2   Processing Pipeline

Cameras are extrinsically and intrinsically calibrated based on the method and tools reported in [7]. The processing pipeline consists of the CPU workflow, responsible for image acquisition and communication management and the GPU workflow, where the 3D reconstruction pipeline has been implemented. Both processes are detailed in the following.

CPU Workflow and Networking
Each workstation holds in its RAM a buffer of fixed size for every camera that is connected to it. Each buffer stores the captured frames after they have been

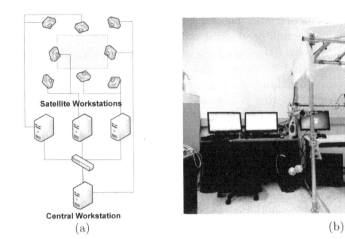

Satellite Workstations

Central Workstation

(a)   (b)

Fig. 1. The developed platform (a) schematic diagram (b) actual configuration

converted from Bayer Tile to RGB format. Moreover, prior to storing in buffer, each image is transformed so that geometric distortions are cancelled out based on the available calibration information. The rate of storing images into buffers matches the camera's acquisition frame rate. Image data are stored together with their associated timestamps. To avoid buffer overflow as newer frames arrive, older frames are removed.

Each time a new image enters a buffer in a satellite workstation, its timestamp is broadcasted to the central workstation. This way, at every time step the central workstation is aware of which frames are stored in the satellite buffers. The same is also true for central's local buffers. During the creation of a multiframe, the central workstation selects the appropriate timestamps for each buffer, local or remote. Then, it broadcasts timestamp queries to the satellite workstations and acquires as response the queried frames, while for local buffers it just fetches the frames from its main memory. The frame set that is created in this way constitutes the multiframe for the corresponding time step. The process is shown schematically in Fig. 2.

GPU Workflow

After a multiframe has been assembled, it is uploaded on the GPU for further processing. Initially, a pixel-wise parallelized foreground detection procedure is applied to the synchronized frames. The algorithm labels each pixel either as background or foreground, providing binary silhouette images as output. The produced silhouette set is given as input to a shape-from-silhouette 3D reconstruction process which, in turn, outputs voxel occupancy information. The occupancy data are then send to an instance of a parallel marching cubes algorithm for computing the surfaces of reconstructed objects. Optionally, prior to mesh calculation, the voxel representation is convolved with a 3D mean filter kernel to produce a smoothed output. Then, the texture of the original images is mapped onto the triangles of the resulted mesh. During this step multiple texture

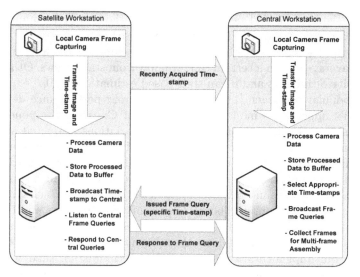

Fig. 2. Multiframe acquisition process

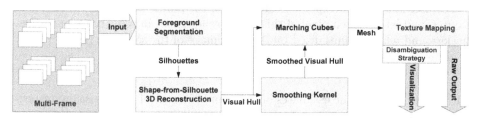

Fig. 3. GPU workflow

coordinate pairs are computed for each triangle. Each pair, projects the triangle's vertices at each view the triangle's front face is visible from. A disambiguation strategy is later incorporated to resolve the multi-texturing conflicts. Finally, results are formatted into appropriate data structures and returned to the CPU host program for further processing. In case the execution is intended for visualization, the process keeps the data on the GPU and returns to the host process handles to DirectX or OpenGL data structures (i.e. vertex and texture buffers). These are consequently used with proper graphics API manipulation for onscreen rendering. The overall procedure is presented schematically in Fig. 3.

3 GPU Implementation

In this section, the algorithms implemented on the GPU are presented in detail.

3.1 Foreground Segmentation

The terms *foreground segmentation* and *background subtraction* refer to methods that detect and segment moving objects in images captured by static cameras.

Due to the significance and necessity of such methods a great number of approaches have been proposed. The majority of these approaches define pixel-wise operations [8]. The most straightforward of those subtract the average, median or running average within a certain time window from static views. Others utilize kernel density estimators and mean-shift based estimation [9,10].

A very popular approach [11] that achieves great performance defines each image pixel's appearance model as a mixture of Gaussian components. This method is able to model complex background variations. Targeted at systems operating in relatively controlled environments (i.e., indoor environments with controlled lighting conditions) this work is based on the parallelization of the background modeling and foreground detection work of [12] which considers the appearance of a background pixel to be modeled by a single Gaussian distribution. This reduces substantially both the memory requirements and the overall computational complexity of the resulting process. Moreover, the assumption that pixels are independent, indicates the inherent parallelism of this algorithm. In addition, our implementation incorporates a technique for shadow detection that is also used in [13] and described thoroughly in [14]. Detected shadows are always labeled as background.

Formally, let $I^{(t)}$ correspond to an image of the multiframe acquired at timestamp t, and let $x^{(t)}$ be a pixel of this image represented in some colorspace. The background model is initialized by the first image of the sequence (i.e. $I^{(0)}$) and is given by

$$\hat{p}(x|x^{(0)}, BG) = N(x; \hat{\mu}, \hat{\sigma}^2 I), \tag{1}$$

with $\hat{\mu}$ and $\hat{\sigma}^2$ being the estimates of mean and variance of the Gaussian, respectively. In order to compensate for gradual global light variation, the estimations of μ and σ are updated at every time step through the following equations:

$$\hat{\mu}^{(t+1)} \leftarrow \hat{\mu}^{(t)} + o^{(t)} \alpha_\mu \delta_\mu{}^{(t)} \tag{2}$$

$$\sigma^{(t+1)} \leftarrow \sigma^{(t)} + o^{(t)} \alpha_\sigma \delta_\sigma{}^{(t)}, \tag{3}$$

where $\delta_\mu = x^{(t)} - \mu^{(t)}$, $\delta_\sigma = |\mu^{(t)} - x^{(t)}|^2 - \sigma^{(t)}$ and a_μ, a_σ are the update factors for mean and standard deviation, respectively, and

$$o^{(t)} = \begin{cases} 1 & if \ x^{(t)} \in BG \\ 0 & if \ x^{(t)} \in FG. \end{cases} \tag{4}$$

A newly arrived sample is considered as background if the sample's distance to the background mode is less than four standard deviations. If this does not hold, an additional condition is examined to determine whether the sample belongs to the foreground or it is a shadow on the background:

$$T_1 \le \frac{\mu \cdot x^{(t)}}{|\mu|^2} \le 1 \quad and \quad \left| \left(\frac{\mu \cdot x^{(t)}}{|\mu|^2} \right) \mu - x \right|^2 < \sigma^2 T_2 \left(\frac{\mu \cdot x^{(t)}}{|\mu|^2} \right)^2, \tag{5}$$

where T_1, T_2, are empirically defined thresholds that are set to $T_1 = 0.25$, $T_2 = 150.0$.

The above described foreground detection method has been parallelized in a per pixel basis. In addition, because there is a need to preserve the background model for each view, this is stored and updated on GPU during the entire lifetime of the reconstruction process. In order to keep the memory requirements low and to meet the GPU alignment constrains, the background model of each pixel is stored in a 4-byte structure. This representation leads to a reduction of precision. Nevertheless, it has been verified experimentally that this does not affect noticeably the quality of the produced silhouettes.

3.2   Visual Hull Computation

The idea of *volume intersection* for the computation of a volumetric object description was introduced in the early 80's [15] and has been revisited in several subsequent works [16,17,18]. The term *visual hull*, is defined as the maximal shape that projects to the same silhouettes as the observed object on all views that lay outside the convex hull of the object [19].

To compute the visual hull, every silhouette image acquired from a given multiframe, is back-projected and intersected into the common 3D space along with all others, resulting to the *inferred visual hull*, i.e. a voxel representation containing occupancy information. In this 3D space, a fixed size volume is defined and sampled to produce a 3D grid, $G = \{G^0, G^1, \ldots, G^n\}$ where $G^c = (X_c, Y_c, Z_c)$. Let C_i be the calibration matrix of camera i and R_i, T_i the corresponding rotation matrix and translation vector respectively, in relation to the global world-centered coordinate system. The general perspective projection of a point G expressed in homogeneous coordinates (i.e. $(X_c, Y_c, Z_c, 1)$) to the ith view plane is described through the following equation

$$(x_c, y_c, f_c)^T = C_i \left[R_i | T_i\right] (X_c, Y_c, Z_c, 1)^T , \tag{6}$$

where $P_i = C_i \left[R_i | T_i\right]$ is the projection matrix of the corresponding view. Each point can be considered to be the mass center of some voxel on the defined 3D volume. We also define two additional functions. The first, labels projections falling inside the FOV of camera i as

$$L_i(x, y) = \begin{cases} 1 & 1 \leq x \leq w_i \ \wedge 1 \leq y \leq h_i \\ 0 & otherwise, \end{cases} \tag{7}$$

where w_i and h_i denote the width and height of the corresponding view plane, respectively. The second function measures the occupancy scores of each voxel via its projected center of mass, as

$$O(X_k, Y_k, Z_k) = \begin{cases} 1 & s = l > \frac{|C|}{2} \\ 0 & otherwise \end{cases}, \quad \forall k \in [0, n], \tag{8}$$

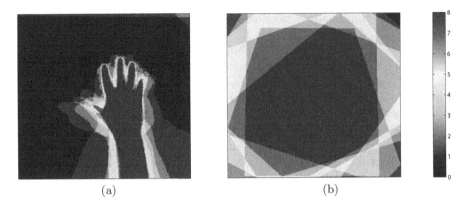

(a)   (b)

Fig. 4. Each figure presents a xy plane slice of the voxel space. (a) The intersection of the projected silhouettes in slice $Z_{slice} = 90cm$. (b) The voxel space defined in this example is much larger than the previous, visibility factor variations are shown with different colors. Dark red denotes an area visible by all views.

where $|C|$ is the number of views. l is the *visibility factor*, s the *intersection factor* and are defined as

$$l = \sum_{i \in C} L_i \left(\frac{x_k^i}{f_k^i}, \frac{y_k^i}{f_k^i} \right), \quad s = \sum_{i \in C} S_i \left(\frac{x_k^i}{f_k^i}, \frac{y_k^i}{f_k^i} \right), \tag{9}$$

with $\left(x_k^i / f_k^i, y_k^i / f_k^i \right)$ be the projection of (X_k, Y_k, Z_k) at view i and $S_i(x, y)$ is the function that takes value 1 if at view i the pixel (x, y) is a foreground pixel and 0 otherwise (i.e. background pixel). Figure 4 illustrates graphically the notion of l and s.

The output of the above process is the set $O(X_k, Y_k, Z_k)$ of occupancy values that represent the visual hull of the reconstructed objects. It can also be conceived as the estimation of a 3D density function. Optionally, the visual hull can be convolved with a 3D mean filter to smooth out the result. Due to its high computational requirements, this method targets the offline mode of 3D reconstruction.

The above described 3D reconstruction process has been parallelized on a per 3D point basis. More specifically, each grid point is assigned to a single GPU thread responsible for executing the above mentioned calculations. To speed up the process, shared memory is utilized for storing the static per thread block calibration information, silhouette images are preserved in GPU texture memory in a compact bit-per-pixel format and occupancy scores are mapped to single bytes.

3.3 Marching Cubes

Marching cubes [20,21] is a popular algorithm for calculating isosurface descriptions out of density function estimates. Due to its inherent and massive

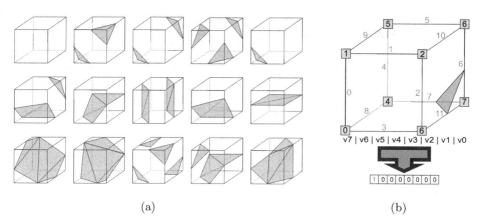

(a)   (b)

Fig. 5. (a) Marching Cubes fundamental states. (b) Byte representation and indexing.

data parallelism it is ideal for GPU implementation. Over the last few years, a lot of isosurface calculation variates that utilize GPUs have been proposed [22,23,24,25,26]. In this work we employ a slightly modified version of the marching cubes implementation found at [27] due to its simplicity and speed. More specifically, the occupancy grid resulting from 3D visual hull estimation is mapped into a CUDA 3D texture. Each voxel is assigned to a GPU thread. During calculations, each thread samples the density function (i.e. CUDA 3D texture) at the vertices of it's corresponding voxel. The normalized (in the range $[0,1]$), bilinearly interpolated, single precision values returned by this step, represent whether the voxel vertices are located inside or outside a certain volume. We consider the isosurface level to be at 0.5. Values between 0 and 1, also show how close a voxel vertex is to the isosurface level. Using this information, a voxel can be described by a single byte, where each bit corresponds to a vertex and is set to 1 or to 0 if this vertex lays inside or outside a volume, respectively. There are 256 discrete generic states in which a voxel can be intersected by an isosurface fragment, produced from the 15 fundamental cases illustrated in Fig. 5a.

Parallel marching cubes uses two constant lookup tables for its operation. The first lookup table is indexed by the voxel byte representation and is utilized for determining the number of triangles the intersecting surface consists of. The second table is a 2D array, where its first dimension is indexed by the byte descriptor and the second by an additional index $trI \in [0, 3N_{iso} - 1]$ where N_{iso} is the number of triangles returned by the first lookup. Given a byte index, sequential triplets accessed through successive trI values, contain the indices of voxel vertices intersected by a single surface triangle. An example of how the voxel byte descriptor is formed is shown in Fig. 5b. This figure also presents the vertex and edge indexing along with an example of an intersecting isosurface fragment that consists of a single triangle.

To avoid applying this process to all voxels, our implementation determines the voxels that are intersected by the iso-surface and then, using the CUDA data parallel primitives library [28], applies stream compaction through the exclusive

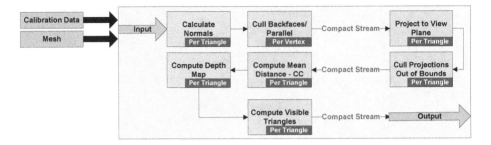

Fig. 6. Computation of texture coordinates

sum-scan algorithm [29] to produce the minimal voxel set containing only intersected voxels. Finally, lookup tables are mapped to texture memory for fast access.

3.4   Texture Mapping

Due to the fact that the employed camera setup provides multiple texture sources, texture mapping of a single triangle can be seen as a three step procedure: a) determine the views from which the triangle is visible, b) compute the corresponding texture coordinates and c) apply a policy for resolving multitexturing ambiguities (i.e. texture selection). The current implementation carries out the first two steps in a per view manner i.e.: a) determines the subset of triangles that are visible by a certain view and b) computes their projections on view plane. The third step is applied either on a per pixel basis through a pixel shader during the visualization stage, or is explicitly computed by the consumer of the offline dataset.

Specifically, given the calibration data for a view and the reconstructed mesh, a first step is the calculation of the triangle normals. Then, the direction of each camera's principal axis vector is used to cull triangles back-facing the camera or having an orientation (near-)parallel to the camera's view plane. The triangle stream is compacted excluding culled polygons and the process continues by computing the view plane projections of the remaining triangles. Projections falling outside the plane's bounds are also removed through culling and stream compaction. Subsequently, the mean vertex distance from the camera center is computed for each remaining triangle and a depth testing procedure (Z-buffering) is applied to determine the final triangle set. The procedure is shown schematically in Fig. 6. This figure also shows the granularity of the decomposition in independent GPU threads. During depth testing, CUDA atomics are used for issuing writes on the depth map. The reason for the multiple culling iterations prior to depth testing is for keeping the thread execution queues length minimal during serialization of depth map writes.

There is a number of approaches that one can use to resolve multitexturing conflicts. Two different strategies have been implemented in this work. The first assigns to each triangle the texture source at which the projection area is

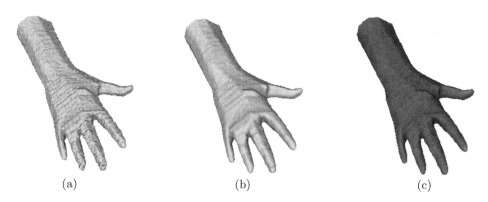

Fig. 7. 3D reconstruction of a single multiframe: (a) no smoothing, (b) smoothed reconstruction and (c) smoothed and textured output

maximal among all projections. The second blends all textures according to a weighting factor, proportional to the size of the projected area. A special case is the one where all weights are equal. This last approach is used during online experiments to avoid the additional overhead of computing and comparing the projection areas, while the others are used in offline mode for producing better quality results. In online mode the process is applied through a pixel shader implemented using HLSL and shader model 3.0. Visualizations of a resulted mesh are shown in Fig. 7. The supplemental material attached to this paper shows representative videos obtained from both online and offline experiments.

4 Performance

Given a fixed number of cameras, the overall performance is determined by the network bandwidth, the size of transferred data, the GPU execution time and the quality of the reconstruction. In online experiments, camera images are preprocessed, transferred through network and finally collected at the central workstation to construct a synchronized multiframe. This is performed at a rate of 30 multiframes per second (mfps). To achieve this performance, original images (i.e. 1280×960) are resized during the CPU preprocessing stage to a size of 320×240. Further reduction of image resolution increases the framerate beyond real-time (i.e. $\geq 30\,mfps$) at the cost of reducing the 3D reconstruction quality. Table 1 shows the achieved multiframe acquisition speed.

Table 1 also shows that, as expected, foreground segmentation speed is linearly proportional to image size. These last reported measurements do not include CPU/GPU memory transfers.

The number of voxels that constitute the voxel space is the primary factor that affects the quality of the reconstruction and overall performance. Given a bounded voxel space (i.e., observed volume), smaller voxel sizes, produce more accurate estimates of the 3D density function leading to a reconstruction output of higher accuracy. Moreover, higher voxel space resolutions issue greater

Table 1. Performance of acquisition and segmentation for various image resolutions

Image resolution	Multiframe acquisition	Foreground segmentation
320×240	30 *mfps*	22.566, 3 *fps* / 2.820, 8 *mfps*
640×480	13 *mfps*	6.773, 9 *fps* / 846, 4 *mfps*
800×600	9 *mfps*	4.282, 6 *fps* / 535, 3 *mfps*
1280×960	3, 3 *mfps*	1.809, 9 *fps* / 226, 2 *mfps*

numbers of GPU threads and produce more triangles for the isosurface that, in turn, leads to an increased overhead during texture mapping. The performance graph of Fig. 8a shows the overall performance impact of voxel space resolution increment in the cases of a) no smoothing of the visual hull, b) smoothed hull utilizing a 3^3 kernel and c) smoothed hull utilizing a 5^3 kernel. The graph in Fig. 8b presents computational performance as a function of smoothing kernel size. In both graphs, multiframe processing rate corresponds at the processing rate of the entire GPU pipeline including the CPU/GPU memory transfer times. It is worth mentioning that although image resolution affects the quality of the reconstruction and introduces additional computational costs due to the increased memory transfer and foreground segmentation overheads, it does not have a significant impact on the performance of the rest of the GPU reconstruction pipeline.

Table 2 presents quantitative performance results obtained from executed experiments. In the 3rd and 4th columns, the performance of 3D reconstruction and texture mapping are shown independently. The 3D reconstruction column corresponds to the processes of computing the visual hull, smoothing the occupancy volume and creating the mesh, while texture mapping column corresponds to the performance of the process depicted in Fig. 6. Finally, in the output column, as in the previous experiments, the performance of the entire reconstruction pipeline is measured including foreground segmentation and memory transfers. It can be seen that keeping the voxel space resolution at a fixed size, the multiframe processing rate of 3D reconstruction drops significantly when the smoothing process is activated. On the contrary, texture mapping is actually accelerated due to the fact that the smoothed surface is described by less triangles than the original

Table 2. Quantitative performance results obtained from representative experiments. Image resolution is set to 320×240 for online and 1280×960 for offline experiments.

Voxels	Smoothing	3D reconst.	Text. mapping	Output
Online Experiments				
$120 \times 140 \times 70$	No	136, 8 *mfps*	178, 0 *mfps*	64, 0 *mfps*
$100 \times 116 \times 58$	No	220, 5 *mfps*	209, 9 *mfps*	84, 5 *mfps*
Offline Experiments				
$277 \times 244 \times 222$	Kernel: 3^3	7, 7 *mfps*	27, 5 *mfps*	5, 0 *mfps*
$277 \times 244 \times 222$	Kernel : 5^3	4, 7 *mfps*	28, 9 *mfps*	3, 5 *mfps*
$277 \times 244 \times 222$	No	11, 4 *mfps*	25, 3 *mfps*	6, 2 *mfps*

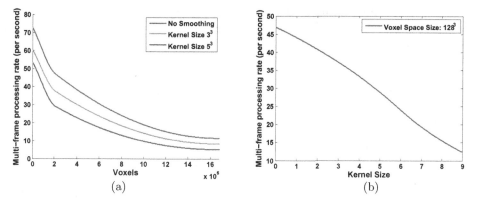

Fig. 8. Performance graphs. Image resolution is set to 640 × 480 in all experiments. (a) Performance impact of voxel space descretization resolution. (b) The performance effect of 3D smoothing kernel size.

one. Online experiments present clearly the effect of the voxel space resolution in overall performance.

5   Conclusions - Future Work

In this paper, we presented the design and implementation of an integrated, GPU-powered, multicamera vision system that is capable of performing foreground image segmentation, silhouette-based 3D reconstruction, 3D mesh computation and texture mapping in real-time. In online mode, the developed system can support higher level processes that are responsible for activity monitoring and interpretation. In offline mode, it enables the acquisition of high quality 3D datasets. Experimental results provide a quantitative assessment of the system's performance. Additionally, the supplementary material provides qualitative evidence regarding the quality of the obtained results.

The current implementation utilizes a single GPU. A future work direction is the incorporation of more GPUs either on central or satellite workstations, to increase the system's overall raw computational power in terms of GFlops. In this case, an intelligent method for distributing the computations over the entire GPU set must be adopted, while various difficult concurrency and synchronization issues that this approach raises must be addressed. Furthermore, performance gains could be achieved by transferring the image post-acquisition CPU processes of Bayer Tile-to-RGB conversion and distortion correction to GPUs as they also encompass a high degree of parallelism. Finally, mesh deformation techniques instead of density function smoothing and advanced texture source disambiguation/blending strategies that incorporate additional information (e.g. edges) can be utilized in order to further augment the quality of the results.

Acknowledgments. This work was partially supported by the IST-FP7-IP-215821 project GRASP and by the FORTH-ICS internal RTD Programme "Ambient Intelligence and Smart Environments".

References

1. Kim, H., Sakamoto, R., Kitahara, I., Toriyama, T., Kogure, K.: Compensated Visual Hull with GPU-Based Optimization. In: Huang, Y.-M.R., Xu, C., Cheng, K.-S., Yang, J.-F.K., Swamy, M.N.S., Li, S., Ding, J.-W. (eds.) PCM 2008. LNCS, vol. 5353, pp. 573–582. Springer, Heidelberg (2008)
2. Schick, A., Stiefelhagen, R.: Real-Time GPU-Based Voxel Carving with Systematic Occlusion Handling. In: Denzler, J., Notni, G., Süße, H. (eds.) DAGM 2009. LNCS, vol. 5748, pp. 372–381. Springer, Heidelberg (2009)
3. Matusik, W., Buehler, C., Raskar, R., Gortler, S.J., McMillan, L.: Image-based visual hulls. In: SIGGRAPH 2000: Proceedings of the 27th Annual Conference on Computer Graphics and Interactive Techniques, pp. 369–374. ACM Press/Addison-Wesley Publishing Co., New York, USA (2000)
4. Matsuyama, T., Wu, X., Takai, T., Nobuhara, S.: Real-time 3D shape reconstruction, dynamic 3D mesh deformation, and high fidelity visualization for 3D video. Computer Vision and Image Understanding 96(3), 393–434 (2004)
5. Ladikos, A., Benhimane, S., Navab, N.: Efficient visual hull computation for real-time 3D reconstruction using cuda. In: IEEE Conference on Computer Vision and Pattern Recognition, Workshops 2008, pp. 1–8 (2008)
6. Waizenegger, W., Feldmann, I., Eisert, P., Kauff, P.: Parallel high resolution real-time visual hull on gpu. In: IEEE International Conference on Image Processing, pp. 4301–4304 (2009)
7. Sarmis, T., Zabulis, X., Argyros, A.A.: A checkerboard detection utility for intrinsic and extrinsic camera cluster calibration. Technical Report TR-397, FORTH-ICS (2009)
8. Piccardi, M.: Background subtraction techniques: a review. In: IEEE International Conference on Systems, Man and Cybernetics, vol. 4, pp. 3099–3104 (2004)
9. Elgammal, A., Harwod, D., Davis, L.: Non-parametric model for background subtraction. In: IEEE International Conference on Computer Vision, Frame-rate Workshop (1999)
10. Han, B., Comaniciu, D., Davis, L.: Sequential kernel density approximation through mode propagation: applications to background modeling. In: Asian Conference on Computer Vision (2004)
11. Stauffer, C., Grimson, W.: Adaptive background mixture models for real-time tracking. In: IEEE Conference on Computer Vision and Pattern Recognition, pp. 246–252 (1999)
12. Wren, C., Azarbayejani, A., Darrell, T., Pentland, A.: Pfinder: Real-time tracking of the human body. IEEE Transactions on Pattern Analysis and Machine Intelligence 19, 780–785 (1997)
13. Zivkovic, Z.: Improved adaptive gaussian mixture model for background subtraction. In: International Conference on Pattern Recognition (2004)
14. Prati, A., Mikic, I., Trivedi, M.M., Cucchiara, R.: Detecting moving shadows: Algorithms and evaluation. IEEE Transactions on Pattern Analysis and Machine Intelligence 25, 918–923 (2003)

15. Martin, W., Aggrawal, J.: Volumetric descriptions of objects from multiple views. IEEE Transactions on Pattern Analysis and Machine Intelligence (1983)
16. Srinivasan, P., Liang, P., Hackwood, S.: Computational geometric methods in volumetric intersection for 3D reconstruction. Pattern Recognition 23, 843–857 (1990)
17. Greg, F.P., Slabaugh, G., Culbertson, B., Schafer, R., Malzbender, T.: A survey of methods for volumetric scene reconstruction. In: International Workshop on Volume Graphics (2001)
18. Potmesil, M.: Generating octree models of 3D objects from their silhouettes in a sequence of images. Computer Vision, Graphics, and Image Processing 40, 1–29 (1987)
19. Laurentini, A.: The visual hull concept for silhouette-based image understanding. IEEE Transactions on Pattern Analysis and Machine Intelligence 16, 150–162 (1994)
20. Lorensen, W.E., Cline, H.E.: Marching cubes: A high resolution 3D surface construction algorithm. Computer Graphics 21, 163–169 (1987)
21. Newman, T.S., Yi, H.: A survey of the marching cubes algorithm. Computers and Graphics 30, 854–879 (2006)
22. Klein, T., Stegmaier, S., Ertl, T.: Hardware-accelerated reconstruction of polygonal isosurface representations on unstructured grids. In: PG 2004: Proceedings of the Computer Graphics and Applications, 12th Pacific Conference, pp. 186–195. IEEE Computer Society, Washington, DC (2004)
23. Pascucci, V.: Isosurface computation made simple: Hardware acceleration, adaptive refinement and tetrahedral stripping. In: Joint Eurographics - IEEE TVCG Symposium on Visualization (VisSym.), pp. 293–300 (2004)
24. Reck, F., Dachsbacher, C., Grosso, R., Greiner, G., Stamminger, M.: Realtime isosurface extraction with graphics hardware. In: Proceedings of Eurographics (2004)
25. Goetz, F., Junklewitz, T., Domik, G.: Real-time marching cubes on the vertex shader. In: Proceedings of Eurographics (2005)
26. Johansson, G., Carr, H.: Accelerating marching cubes with graphics hardware. In: CASCON 2006: Proceedings of the 2006 Conference of the Center for Advanced Studies on Collaborative Research, p. 378. ACM Press (2006)
27. NVIDIA. GPU Computing SDK (2009), http://developer.nvidia.com/object/gpucomputing.html
28. Harris, M., Sengupta, S., Owens, J.: CUDA Data Parallel Primitives Library (2007), http://code.google.com/p/cudpp/
29. Sengupta, S., Harris, M., Zhang, Y., Owens, J.D.: Scan primitives for gpu computing. In: Graphics Hardware 2007, pp. 97–106. ACM (2007)

Comparison of Dense Stereo Using CUDA

Ke Zhu[1], Matthias Butenuth[2], and Pablo d'Angelo[3]

[1] Technische Universität München, Remote Sensing Technology, Germany
`ke.zhu@bv.tum.de`
[2] IAV GmbH, Active Safety and Driver Assistance, Germany
`matthias.butenuth@iav.de`
[3] German Aerospace Center (DLR), Remote Sensing Technology Institute, Germany
`pablo.angelo@dlr.de`

Abstract. In this paper, a local and a global dense stereo matching method, implemented using Compute Unified Device Architecture (CUDA), are presented, analyzed and compared. The purposed work shows the general strategy of the parallelization of matching methods on GPUs and the tradeoff between accuracy and run-time on current GPU hardware. Two representative and widely-used methods, the Sum of Absolute Differences (SAD) method and the Semi-Global Matching (SGM) method, are used and their results are compared using the Middlebury test sets.

1 Introduction

In this paper, two representative and widely-used dense matching methods of stereo processing for near real-time 3D reconstruction using Compute Unified Device Architecture (CUDA) on programmable GPUs are described and evaluated. Real-time stereo reconstruction is a very active research topic in computer vision and is required for many applications such as remote sensing tasks and close range applications. Compared with feature-based methods, the dense matching methods are less sensitive with application scenarios and can be used more diffusely for both video sequences in robotics and large observation images from airborne system [1]. Generally, the taxonomy divides dense stereo matching methods in local (block-based) and global methods. Global stereo methods show the best performance on the Middlebury online evaluation [2] than the simpler local methods without special postprocessing steps.

The Semi-Global Matching (SGM) method is selected, because it is a high performance global stereo method, but retains a complexity that is linear to the reconstructed volume. It is realized for many practical applications like in automobiles on FPGAs and the earth observation tasks on CPU [3]. The local methods are favorited by real-time applications because of their simple and fast implementations. Their mechanisms are similar and can be rephrased or extended from the Sum of Absolute Differences (SAD) method [4].

In 2007, the G80 series graphics card of NVIDIA was introduced based on the CUDA Architecture that enables the General-Purpose Computation on Graphics Hardware (GPGPU) in a familiar C programming language [5]. Compared to the

K.N. Kutulakos (Ed.): ECCV 2010 Workshops, Part II, LNCS 6554, pp. 398–410, 2012.
© Springer-Verlag Berlin Heidelberg 2012

earlier GPGPU programming paradigm, CUDA does not need the reformulation of the algorithms into a computer graphics rendering framework. This eases the implementation and allows more flexible use of the GPU hardware.

The novel core of our approach is to find a combination between the methods and the hardware, to demonstrate the general parallelization strategy of matching methods on GPUs and compare two different dense stereo matching algorithms. The presented work consists of three parts: the next section includes the basic algorithms and introduction to CUDA, section 3 the implementation of them on GPU and section 4 an evaluation using the Middlebury stereo images.

2   Basics

2.1   The Dense Matching Methods

A taxonomy of existing stereo algorithms is provided in [6]. Generally, the stereo algorithms perform four steps: matching cost computation, cost aggregation, disparity optimization and selection and disparity refinement. The taxonomic branch appears in the disparity optimization step: local methods perform a block-based "winner-take-all" optimization at each pixel in the aggregation step. In contrast, global methods skip it and are formulated in an energy-minimization frame work.

Generally, the disparity computation of local algorithms depends only on the intensities within a finite window. The Sum of Absolute Differences (SAD) algorithm is selected as an example, as it can be easily parallelized due to its simple structure. It can be described in the following steps: the cost of pixel $p(r,c)$ is the absolute difference of intensity values at the given disparity d. The cost aggregation is done by summing of matching costs over the window. Disparity is selected with the minimal aggregated value:

$$S(p(r,c),d) = \frac{1}{4 \times n \times m} \times \sum_{m}^{-m} \sum_{n}^{-n} |I_1(r+i,c+j) - I_2(r+i,c+j+d)|. \quad (1)$$

In contrast, global algorithms perform almost all of their work in the disparity optimization step. The Semi-Global Matching (SGM) method is chosen, because of its accuracy and computational complexity as $O(width \times height \times DisparityRange)$ like local methods [7]. Its methodical realization has a regular structure and maps to the Single Instruction Multiple Data (SIMD) mechanism of GPUs.

The matching cost for two pixels can be derived from different methods. The absolute differences between pixel intensities are used as correspondence cost. For larger baselines other cost functions, such as Mutual Information, result in a better performance [8], but are not evaluated here:

$$C(p,d) = L(p) - R(p+d), \quad (2)$$

where $C(p,d)$ is the cost of pixel p at the disparity d. $L(p)$ and $R(p,d)$ denote the intensities in the left and right image respectively.

The SGM method approximates the minimization of the global energy $E(D)$:

$$E(D) = \sum_p (C(p, D_p) + \sum_{q \in N_p} P_1 [|D_p - D_q| = 1] + \sum_{q \in N_p} P_2 [|D_p - D_q| > 1]). \quad (3)$$

The first term sums the costs of all pixels in the image with their particular disparities D_p. The next two terms penalize the discontinuities with penalty factors P_1 and P_2, which differ in small or large disparity differences within a neighbourhood q of the pixel p. This minimization approximation is realized by aggregating $S(p, d)$ of path wise costs into a cost volume:

$$S(p, d) = \sum_r L_r(p, d). \quad (4)$$

$L_r(p, d)$ in (4) represents the cost of a pixel p with disparity d along one direction r. It is described as following:

$$L_r(p, d) = C(p, d) + min(L_r(p - r, d), L_r(p - r, d - 1) + P_1,$$
$$L_r(p - r, d + 1) + P_1, \min_i L_r(p - r, i) + P_2) - \min_i L_r(p - r, i). \quad (5)$$

This regularization term function favors planar and sloped surfaces, but still allows larger height jumps in the direction of cost aggregation. The disparity at each pixel is selected as the index of the minimum cost from the cost cube.

2.2   Compute Unified Device Architecture (CUDA)

The computational design for Semi-Global Matching concerns not only the parallelization mechanism but also the limitations of the hardware. Hence, in this subsection the basic concepts of CUDA programming as well as the method-involved physical features are introduced.

CUDA divides the computation units into hosts, such as a CPU and device, normally such as a GPU. Massively parallel processing runs on the device during the *kernel*-functions. The kernels specify the code to generate a large number of threads to exploit data parallelism. They are organized in blocks and refer via the thread indices in 1D, 2D or 3D. A Warp is defined as a group of 32 threads, which is the minimum data processing size in a SM (Streaming Multiprocessor). All of these threads within a block execute the same code as well-known Single-Program, Multiple-Data (SPMD) parallel programming style [5]. Threads in the same block share data and synchronize while doing their share of the work. Figure 1 left shows CUDA thread organization. Each SM in graphics cards with compute capability 1.3 can take up to 8 blocks and allows maximal 1024 threads [9].

CUDA enabled devices have separate memory spaces with different characters. Figure 1 right shows an overview of the device memory model. Global and constant memories are used for data transfer between host and device. The constant memory allows read-only access and allows quick caching using a broadcast mechanism. The shared memory is the key for hidding memory access latency to avoid bandwidth saturation. Its latency is roughly 100 times faster than global memory latency [10]. The profitable strategy for performing computation on GPUs using this advantage is to partition data in subsets, copying them from global memory to shared memory using multiple threads, achieving them from shared memory locally in threads and copying the results back to global memory. The amount of shared memory per SM is 16 KB [9] and must be noticed by design for data tiling.

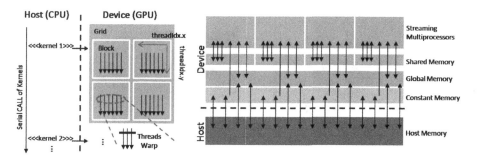

Fig. 1. Overview of the CUDA threads (left) and memory model (right)

3   GPU Implementations Using CUDA

3.1   Strategy for Real-Time Stereo Processing

The preprocessing for unconstrained stereo rigs to simplify the correspondence searching is the rectification of images using a compact algorithm of [11] on GPU. The pixel coordinates are mapped with the combination of the block ID and thread ID. The new pixel coordinates in the epipolar images are generated using locally defined transformation matrices in the kernel. The resulted epipolar images enable a linear correspondence searching. The remaining stereo processing stays in GPU until copying the results back.

The SAD and SGM method use the same GPU implementation by the cost calculation step: the absolute differences for each pixel along an epipolar line are calculated synchronously using the line-by-line tiled data in the shared memory. Like that, the SAD method uses the similar way to parallelize its cost aggregation on GPU. The disparities are selected directly after the aggregation. Differently, by the cost optimization of SGM method each data element in the 3D cost cube maps a thread in GPU and is path wise aggregated into the optimized cost cube in global memory. As disparity refinement, an additional median filter is implemented. The left-right check can be executed using the same processing with exchanged data sequence.

3.2 Matching Cost Calculation

In the cost computation step, each pixel in the left image is compared with all reference pixels in the disparity range of the right image. The accordant matching costs are read from the cost table using their intensities as indices. In fact, a pixel from the left image is related with all pixels between minimum and maximum disparity in the right image. The values in the image are partitioned line-by-line and tiled into the shared memory to reduce the memory accesses on global memory and increase the data utilization rate, because each pixel from the right image can be used $(DisparityRange - 1)$ times. The ground design idea is visualized in Figure 2.

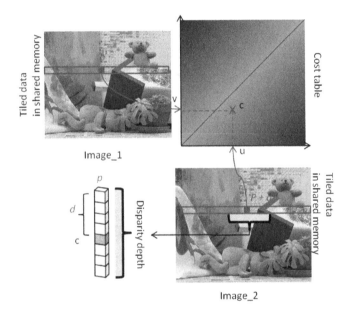

Fig. 2. Generation of cost cube from tiled data using lookup table: u is the intensity of pixel p in the first image, v is the intensity of his corresponded pixel in the second image along the epipolar line, c is the cost reading from the cost table

The block dimension is designed in 2D, because the maximum size of the x-, y-, and z-dimension of a thread block is limited for all GPUs up to the compute capability 1.3 at 512, 512, and 64, respectively [9]. One dimension block for large images exceeds the hardware competence. In the kernel function a barrier synchronization call ensures that all required data for the next step is already updated to the shared memory before their individual calculations. Consequently, each thread in a block answers to a pixel in the image line. A threads block generates a part of the complete cost cube. The excerpt of the CostCal reports the CUDA kernel code:

```
__global__ void CostCal(...){
    __shared__ float1 sData_l[IMG_LENGTH],
                      sData_r[IMG_LENGTH];

    for (int l = 0; l<imgH; l++){//over complete image
      //Update intensities from texture
      sData_l[ix] = tex2D(l_texImg, threadIdx.x, l);
      sData_r[ix] = tex2D(r_texImg, threadIdx.x, l);
      __syncthreads();

      for(int DStep = 0; DStep<DDepth; DStep++){
            //Cost Calculation
            cost = tex2D(ct_texImg, threadIdx.x, blockIdx.x);
            d_ccube[DStep*imgW*imgH + imgW*l + threadIdx.x]
              = cTable(sData_l[ix].x,sData_r[threadIdx.x].x);
      }
    }
}
```

This separate cost computation step is only required for the SGM method.

3.3   Cost Aggregation

In the local SAD method, the disparity is computed for all pixels independently. In this case, the cost computation, cost aggregation and disparity selection steps can be computed in parallel, without requiring additional storage space. The main CUDA kernel for the local SAD method is shown below:

```
for (int di = 0; di < Depth; di++){
    sad = 0;
    //Aggregation in windows
    for (int wj = 0; wj < w_width; wj++){
        for (int wi = 0; wi <w_height; wi ++){
            sad = sad + abs(tData[...].x - mData[...)].x);
        }
    }
    if (di == 0) tempM = sad; selI = 0;
    if (sad < tempM) tempM = sad; selI = di;
}
d_disp[imgW*iy + ix] = make_color1(selI);
```

Thus, each pixel is mapped to a thread. In a thread, the cost aggregation is iteratively executed d times. The block size is dependent on the window size. A rectangular window is selected to use the already stored data in shared memory repeatedly along the epipolar line shown in Figure 3.

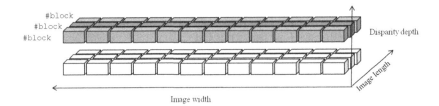

Fig. 3. Block tiling for the cost aggregation of the SAD method

In contrast, the semi-global cost aggregation is typically a serial computation from different paths. The cost optimization for each pixel in one direction requires the storage of both the computed cost values and the aggregated costs from the previously visited pixel. A pixel in the image contains *DisparityRange* data elements in the cost cube, in which each concerned element of them maps to a thread. The block size is depended on the disparity range and the number of pixels inside each block is shown in the following kernel configuration:

```
dim3 ca_threads(PixelAmount, DisparityRange, 1);
dim3 ca_grid(ImageWidth/PixelAmount,1,1);
CostAggr<<<ca_grid, ca_threads>>>(CostCube, TempL, ...);
```

A further challenge is that pixels are no more independently with each other by the path wise aggregation. The optimized results backwards along a path are used for the actual optimization. The results must be rewritten into the global memory for the aggregation with other paths. Thus, the massive data accessing on global memory is not avoided completely. The ground idea for the parallelization is visualized in Figure 4. In this example, one image line is tiled in *ImageWidth*/4 segments. In a block there are $4 \times DisparityRange$ threads. The computation is then executed *ImageLength* times iteratively in each block over the complete image.

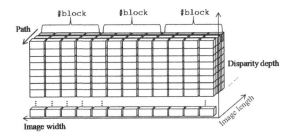

Fig. 4. Block tiling for the cost aggregation of the SGM method

Traditionally, the sweeping is executed more times for e.g. eight directions SGM. The fast implementation achieves the cost optimization in six directions with two passes through the images. Cost aggregation can be extended for more directions, if the sweepings start from the other sides of the image. The incline optimizations e.g. path 1 requires the communication with other blocks. Hence, the optimized costs must be stored in the global memory. A distinct problem for large images is that CUDA features no block synchronization. This hardware inherency barrages the block communication on boundaries. The visibilities of the aggregations from oblique paths are depended on the amount of SMs. The quick approach and its problem is shown in Figure 5.

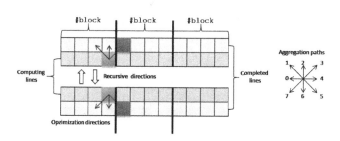

Fig. 5. Fast aggregation processing in three directions within one sweeping

The meanwhile optimized cost walls in the direction 0, 2, 4 and 6 are written to global memory, but not eliminated from shared memory, because they can be used for the next line. This finesse avoids reading the optimized cost from the global memory and economizes the expensive memory accessing for each block.

4   Results

The experimental results are computed on a NVIDIA GeForce GTX 295 graphics card. One of the both GT200 graphic processor is used for the calculation. This device core has 30 SMs on-chip and supports 1.3 CUDA compute capability [9]. The GPU implementations use the Middlebury Stereo Datasets [2] as well as aerial photos from the DLR's 3K system [1], which are additionally rectified on the GPU. Two comparisons are presented in this section: the run-time improvement of the GPU implementation with the CPU implementation and the accuracy and run-time differences between the SGM method and the SAD method.

Figure 6 shows the results of the Middlebury Teddy and Cones datasets using our SGM GPU implementation with an image size of 450 × 375 pixels. In addition, Figure 7 shows the results of the comparison between CPU and GPU implementation of an aerial image pair, which has an image size of 1000 × 1000 pixels with a disparity range of 80. Generally, they take similar results, but the disparities on the church roof on the GPU result are better than CPU execution, caused by the left to right and right to left cost aggregations on GPU use a different parameter with other aggregation paths. The compared CPU implementation runs on an Intel Core2 Q9450 CPU with 6 MB L2 Cache. The CPU implementation needs about 5200 ms to finish the stereo processing including rectification. In contrast, the CUDA improvement requires 722ms for six aggregation directions and 1120 ms for eight aggregations totally. A comparison of the execution time between CPU and GPU implementations with the above referred example are presented step by step in Table 1. The GPU implementation is roughly 5 times faster than the CPU implementation written in C.

Fig. 6. Results of SGM GPU implementation using the Middlebury Stereo Datasets: the left images are related input images, the middle images are the ground truth depths and the right images are the GPU results

Table 1. Run-time comparison between CPU and GPU SGM implementation

	CPU run-time (8x)	GPU run-time (8x)
Rectification	432ms	96ms
Cost computation	200ms	9ms
Cost aggregation	4215ms	481ms($6\times$)/879ms($8\times$)
Disparity selection	362ms	136ms
Total	5209ms	722ms($6\times$)/1120($8\times$)ms

Figure 8 shows the run-times of the different steps of the SGM method for different image sizes. The run-time on small images with 384×288 pixels and a disparity range of 64 reaches 13 *fps*. Even though the results are promising, a potential improvement could be reached with a more adaptive data tiling strategy. The experiment with large images of 1000×1000 pixels exhibits a slowdown due to bandwidth latency. The path-wise cost aggregation is the key for the better performance of SGM, but results in an algorithm that cannot be parallelized as effectively as the local SAD method, as the temporarily aggregated

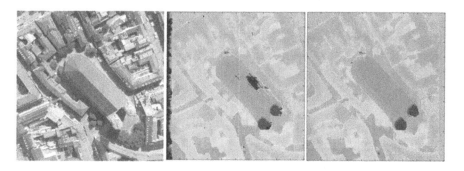

Fig. 7. Result comparison between CPU (middle) and GPU (right) SGM implementation. The left image is one of the related input images.

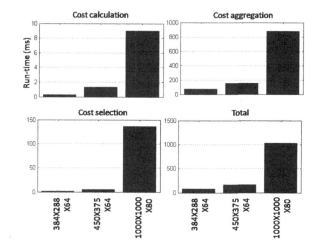

Fig. 8. The SGM GPU run-times on different image sizes

costs must be rewritten to the global memory in order to be used for aggregations with other directions.

The results of the SAD method with different window-sizes are compared with the SGM result and ground-truth in Figure 9. The SGM method achieves a less noisy result with more details. The results of SAD with a small window show many errors. The SAD with a larger window leads to a similar result as SGM, but it is still less precise. This comparison shows the improved reconstruction archived with the semi-global matching method.

With increasing window size, the local SAD method loses its runtime advantage with respect to SGM. Figure 10 shows strange spikes in the run-time graph with the window sizes in one dimension. The spikes at size 12 and 13 appear always using different test data and probably caused by hitting a cache limitation. After these impulses the factor of linear run-time increasing goes up and remains almost constantly.

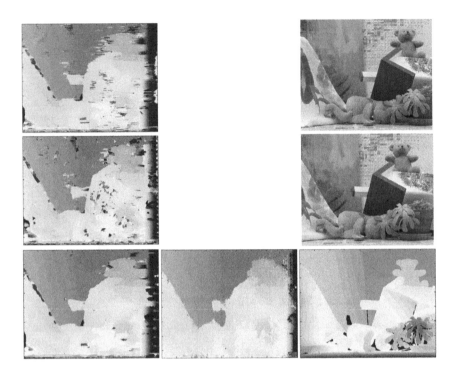

Fig. 9. The results compared between the SAD method with different window-sizes and the SGM result: the left part lists the SAD results with 3×31, 7×13 and 9×31 window size, respectively. In the middle is the SGM result shown. The input image pair and the disparity ground-truth are given on the right.

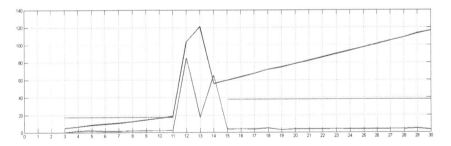

Fig. 10. The run-time analysis of a $3 \times x$ window of the SAD method: the blue line shows the processing time during the growing of window size in one direction. The red line demonstrates the run-time differences. The green line confirms the constantly run-time increasing before and after the impulse.

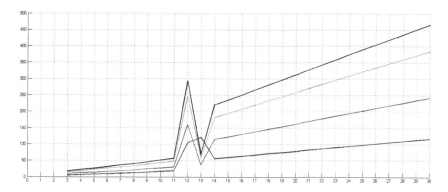

Fig. 11. The run-time analysis of the SAD method with different fixed window sizes in x direction: $3 \times x$ in blue , $5 \times x$ in red, $7 \times x$ in green and $9 \times x$ in black

In addition, the changes with different fixed window sizes in x direction are observed in Table 2 and shown in Figure 11. The comparison shows by the implementation of dense matching method on GPU, that the global methods keep their accuracy advantage and the cost/performance ratio of local matching methods is not beneficial for a fast processing on GPUs. The reason for inefficiencies of the local methods with large aggregation window sizes is that the computational win via the repeatedly employing of the updated data from the shared memory can not cover the memory accessing latency. Thus, the discret approached global methods like the SGM perform a better and more efficient result.

Table 2. Run-time increasing with fixed window sizes in x-direction and changed sizes in y-direction

	3x	5x	7x	9x	11x	13x	15x	17x	19x	21x	23x	25x	27x	29x
3x	4.9	8.4	10.0	14.3	18.6	121.0	59.5	67.1	74.7	82.2	89.9	97.3	104.9	113.2
5x	9.5	13.8	18.1	24.6	30.1	37.3	122.5	138.4	154.3	170.2	186.6	201.9	217.8	234.6
7x	14.6	22.7	29.3	38.3	48.1	59.5	194.6	220.0	245.2	270.6	295.9	322.0	346.6	371.9
9x	17.3	26.2	35.9	45.6	56.9	69.7	235.4	266.3	296.9	327.7	358.4	389.9	419.9	451.4

5   Conclusions

The proposed work demonstrates the general strategy for parallelization of dense matching methods on GPUs to show the potential capability of common graphics cards for general computation and to compare the implementations between local and global methods with the example of SAD and SGM method. The main architectural difference between CPU and GPU is the small amount of fast shared memory and massive parallel computation power. This makes them suitable for simple problems without many dependencies between the data to be processed.

In contrast, the CPUs have large L2 Cache, which is enough to store the locally relevant cost cube. In future work, the dense matching methods will be optimized in CPU-implementation and compared with their GPU-optimized visions. The combination and adaptation between the current methods and modern hardware is not suitable. A parallel design of new method will be researched.

Thus, the SGM implementation on the GPU cannot use the full computation power of the graphics card. Future work will include the design of a (semi) global matching algorithm with a structure adapted to the constraints of the GPU hardware architecture.

References

1. Butenuth, M., Reinartz, P., Lenhart, D., Rosenbaum, D., Hinz, S.: Analysis of image sequences for the detection and monitoring of moving traffic. Photogrammetrie Fernerkundung Geoinformation 5, 421–430 (2009)
2. Middlebury Stereo Website (May 2010), http://vision.middlebury.edu/stereo/
3. Gehrig, S.K., Eberli, F., Meyer, T.: A Real-Time Low-Power Stereo Vision Engine Using Semi-Global Matching. In: Fritz, M., Schiele, B., Piater, J.H. (eds.) ICVS 2009. LNCS, vol. 5815, pp. 134–143. Springer, Heidelberg (2009)
4. Banks, J., Bennamoun, M., Corke, P.: Non-parametric techniques for fast and robust stereo matching (1997)
5. Krik, D.B., Hwa, W.W.: Programming Massively Parallel Processors: A Hands-on Approach (2010)
6. Scharstein, D., Szeliski, R.: A taxonomy and evaluation of dense two-frame stereo correspondence algorithms. International Journal of Computer Vision 47, 7–42 (2002)
7. Hirschmüller, H.: Stereo processing by semi-global matching and mutual information. IEEE Transactions on Pattern Analysis and Machine Intelligence 30, 328–341 (2008)
8. Hirschmüller, H., Scharstein, D.: Evaluation of stereo matching costs on image with radiometric differences. IEEE Transactions on Pattern Analysis and Machine Intelligence 31, 1582–1599 (2009)
9. NVIDIA. CUDA Programming Guide Version 3.0 (2010)
10. NVIDIA. OpenCL Best Practices Guide Version 1.0 (2009)
11. Fusiello, A., Trucco, E., Verri, A.: A compact algorithm for rectification of stereo pairs. Machine Vision and Applications 12, 16–22 (2002)

Energy-Aware Real-Time Face Recognition System on Mobile CPU-GPU Platform

Yi-Chu Wang, Bryan Donyanavard, and Kwang-Ting (Tim) Cheng

Dept. of Electrical and Computer Engineering
University of California, Santa Barbara, CA 93106, USA
yichuwang@umaill.ucsb.edu, bryandony@gmail.com, timcheng@ece.ucsb.edu

Abstract. The Graphics Processor Unit (GPU) has expanded its role from an accelerator for rendering graphics into an efficient parallel processor for general purpose computing. The GPU, an indispensable component in desktop and server-class computers as well as game consoles, has also become an integrated component in handheld devices, such as smartphones. Since the handheld devices are mostly powered by battery, the mobile GPU is usually designed with an emphasis on low-power rather than on performance. In addition, the memory bus architecture of mobile devices is also quite different from those of desktops, servers, and game consoles. In this paper, we try to provide answers to the following two questions: (1) Can a mobile GPU be used as a powerful accelerator in the mobile platform for general purpose computing, similar to its role in the desktop and server platforms? (2) What is the role of a mobile GPU in energy-optimized real-time mobile applications? We use face recognition as an application driver which is a compute-intensive task and is a core process for several mobile applications. The experiments of our investigation were performed on an Nvidia Tegra development board which consists of a dual-core ARM Cortex A9 CPU and a Nvidia mobile GPU integrated in a SoC. The experiment results show that, utilizing the mobile GPU can achieve a 4.25x speedup in performance and 3.98x reduction in energy consumption, in comparison with a CPU-only implementation on the same platform.

1 Introduction

It has been an active research subject to explore the use of Graphics Processor Unit (GPU), an indispensable component in desktop computers, as a general purpose coprocessor to accelerate the compute-intensive part of an algorithm. The research directions include (1) to identify algorithms' parallelism or redesign algorithms to be suitable running on a GPU, and (2) to extend the fixed graphics pipeline into programmable pipelines with a more flexible memory manipulation by high-level APIs, such as CUDA[1]. Depending on the algorithms' inherent parallelism, the number of cores, and the available memory bandwidth of the GPU hardware, a speedup of tens to hundreds has been reported in the literatures for various applications. Computer vision is one of the areas for which

K.N. Kutulakos (Ed.): ECCV 2010 Workshops, Part II, LNCS 6554, pp. 411–422, 2012.
© Springer-Verlag Berlin Heidelberg 2012

the GPU has demonstrated significant performance improvement, such as image registration [2] and feature tracking [3].

The programmable GPU is now moving its way from desktop and server computers into handheld devices, such as smartphones and portable game consoles. While the GPUs inside mobile devices and desktop computers have similar high-level functionality, there are many differences under the hood. For example, a GPU inside a smartphone is usually integrated in a single chip with CPU, DSP, and other application-specific accelerators (e.g. [4]). Instead of having its own graphics memory, an embedded GPU shares the system bus with other computing components to access the external memory and therefore has much less available bus bandwidth than those of laptop and high-performance desktop systems [5]. Also, the only available APIs for current mobile GPUs are OpenGL ES [6], which is a graphics API and does not provide some essential components of GPGPU, such as "scatter" (i.e. write to an arbitrary memory location) and thread-level synchronization. As most existing CPU-GPU optimizations are based on, and optimized for, desktop and server platforms, it is highly desirable to characterize the mobile CPU-GPU platform and revisit the GPGPU strategies in order to better utilize the computational power of a mobile GPU. A study of comparing the use of a mobile CPU (ARM) and a mobile GPU (PowerVR SGX) for executing an image processing pipeline (adjusting geometry, Gaussian blur, and adjusting color) reports that the mobile GPU achieves 3.58x speedup (8.6 seconds per frame for CPU and 2.4 seconds per frame for GPU) [7]. Their investigation is conducted with an emulated version of OpenCL embedded profile [8], which is not available on current commodity smartphones and development boards. Also, the target task of their study is low-level image processing, not high-level vision tasks.

Power and energy efficiency is another critical design considerations when design applications on a battery-powered mobile platform. A mobile handheld device is typically limited by a power ceiling of less than 1 watt, while the power ceilings for the desktop processors alone range from 30 to 150 Watts. In addition to explore the utilization of mobile GPU to speedup time-consuming tasks, it is also important to characterize the power consumption of the mobile GPU and CPU. The overall objective of developing an application on a mobile platform should be to optimize the total energy consumption while meeting the real-time constraint.

In this paper, we investigate the computational capability and energy efficiency of current mobile CPU-GPU system for an exemplar computer vision application, automatic face annotation. We use Nvidia's Tegra SoC/platform [9], which is specifically designed for smartphones and tablets, as the target platform in our study. Running the face recognition algorithm on Tegra's CPU, on average, takes 8.5 seconds to detect and recognize a face. When utilizing Tegra's GPU by OpenGL ES 2.0 to offload the most compute-intensive task, face feature extraction, in the face recognition pipeline, the execution time as well as the total energy consumption can be significantly reduced. This paper is organized as follow: In Section 2 we first review the recent research of mobile computer vision and energy efficiency of desktop CPU-GPU systems. Section 3 provides an overview of the face annotation system and its runtime profile. Then in Section 4, we show the experimental setup of our study. The experimental results are presented in Section 5. Finally we conclude our study and the future exploration directions.

2   Related Works

While state-of-the-art face recognition algorithms can achieve a high accuracy to support automatic face annotation, their implementations on an embedded platform cannot achieve real-time performance due to the demanding computational requirement. Applications targeted for mobile platforms usually remove the compute-expensive operations, or rely on the clouds to do most of the computation. For example, a real-time face annotation system on PDA was demonstrated in [10]. Although it achieves real-time performance, the intensity-comparison based method is not sufficiently robust to handle the luminance variation or pose changes. Hence it could not achieve the level of accuracy needed for real-life applications.

As a sophisticated hardware component with massive parallelism, running tasks on a GPU consumes significant power. The Nvidia 8800GTS graphics card is measured consuming 210W before the kernel launches, and 310W while the kernel is running [12]. On the other hand, the CPU employs several advanced low-power design techniques and power management strategies, thus making it more power efficient. The measured standby power and active power of Intel i7 is 33.03W and 102.2W (for one core) respectively [12]. For applications where the GPU can finish the task in a significantly shorter period of time, in comparison with its CPU counterpart, the performance gain results in energy savings as well, making the GPU a preferred choice from both performance and energy points of view. However, when the GPU speedup is not as pronounced, the choice becomes less obvious. The cost/performance investigation of an Intel Core 2 Duo CPU and a Nvidia CUDA enabled GPU in [11] shows, despite an increase in total system power, using a GPU is more energy efficient when the performance improvement is 5x or greater.

3   Face Recognition System

Face recognition enables easy sharing and better management of digital photos and videos. Fig. 1 shows an exemplar face annotation application on smartphones. Given a newly taken photo, or one from the photo gallery in a smartphone, the face regions are identified, recognized and tagged with names automatically. The tagged face(s) could be added to the face database, linked to the user's address book, and/or uploaded the annotated photo to a photo-sharing or social networking websites such as Picasa or Facebook in real-time using the smartphone's Wi-Fi or 3G network connectivity. The face recognition process can be divided into four steps: (1) Face detection, which scans the whole image to identify face regions. (2) Face landmark localization, which identifies the face landmark locations such as eyes, nose and mouth within a detected face region, and then resize and register the face region accordingly. (3) Face feature extraction, which represents a face region by its features that are invariant or robust to the variations of illumination, pose, expression, and occlusion. (4) Face feature classification, which compares the face feature to the training face set and assigns a name of the most similar identity to the query face.

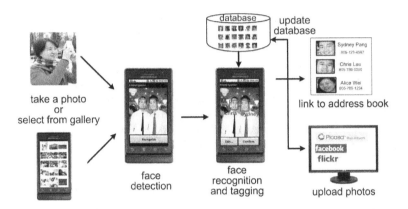

Fig. 1. A face annotation system on smartphones

3.1   Gabor-Based Face Feature Extraction

The Gabor-based feature descriptor [13] has been demonstrated as one of the most suitable local representation for face recognition. The Gabor wavelet representation of an image is the convolution of the image with a family of Gabor kernels as defined in the following:

$$\Psi_{\mu,v}(z) = \frac{||k_{\mu,v}||}{\sigma^2} e^{(-||k_{\mu,v}||^2||z||^2/2\sigma^2)} [e^{ik_{\mu,v}z} - e^{-\sigma^2/2}] \tag{1}$$

Where μ and v define the orientation and scale of the Gabor filters, $z = (x, y)$, $||.||$ denotes the norm operator, and the wave vector $k_{\mu,v} = k_v e^{i\phi_\mu}$, where $k_v = k_{max}/f^v$ gives the frequency, $\phi_\mu = \mu\pi/8$ gives the orientation. This representation captures the local structure corresponding to spatial frequency (scale), spatial localization, and orientation selectivity. As a result, it is robust to illumination and facial expression variations. A typical Gabor-based face descriptor uses 40 different Gabor kernels which include 5 different scales and 8 different orientations. After that, it is further processed by Principle Component Analysis (PCA) and Linear Discriminant Analysis (LDA) to reduce its dimensionality and forms the final face feature descriptor. The use of Gabor feature combined with the PCA-LDA method is reported to achieve 93.83% accuracy on the traditional face recognition dataset FERET [14] and 71.69% on a more challenging photo dataset LFW [15].

3.2   System Profiling

In order to understand the complexity of the face recognition system and the performance of such application on modern smartphones, we have implemented a Gabor-based face recognition system on an Android-powered [16] smartphone platform. The details of this platform are revealed in the next section. In our system, we use Android facedetector API [17] to identify face regions in a given photo, and an AdaBoost-based eye localization method to identify the landmark regions. Face feature classification is performed by the K-Nearest-Neighbor method. All the tasks, except the face detection (which is an Android API and the implementation details are not easy to obtained), are implemented in C and compiled using the tool chain provided by Android Native Development Kit r3 (NDK).

Table 1 shows the execution time breakdown of face recognition system running on a 1GHz ARM Cortex A9 CPU. The picture size in this study is 480x1000. The total number of training images is 15. The identified face region is aligned and scaled to 64x80 before extract face feature. The profiling results show that, feature extraction is the most time-consuming part. It takes 6.1 seconds to process one face, which is about 71.8% of the total computing time. Without any optimization, the overall execution time of the face recognition too long to be considered as a real-time mobile applications.

Table 1. Execution time breakdown of face recognition system running on Tegra platform's CPU

Task	Time (sec)	%
Face detection	1.5	17.6
Landmark detection	0.7	8.2
Feature extraction: Gabor wavelet	5.1	60.0
Feature extraction: PCA-LDA	1.0	11.8
Feature classification	0.2	2.4
Total	8.5	100

Since the Gabor wavelet in the face feature extraction is the most dominant component, optimization of this aspect will result in the most improvement. In the following, we examine using the mobile GPU to accelerate this part. The experimental setup is first described in Section 4, and then we discuss the implementation details and the experimental results in Section 5.

4   Experimental Setup

Our experiments were performed on a Nvidia Tegra SoC platform with the following specifications: a 1GHz dual-core ARM Cortex A9 CPU, 1GB of RAM, a Nvidia GeForce GPU, and 512MB of Flash memory. This chip is one of the representative heterogeneous processors designed for handheld devices such as smartphones and tablets. A Nvidia Tegra developer kit [9] is available for developing software running on the Tegra chip. Fig. 2 shows our experimental setting: the Tegra board is connected to a VGA monitor and a keyboard and a mouse are also connected. The operating system running on this platform is Android.

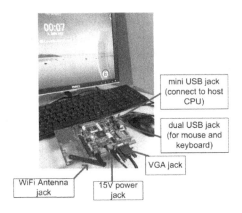

Fig. 2. Tegra development board and the experimental setup

The Tegra board is powered by a 15V DC input which is then converted into 3.3V, 5V, 1.8V and 1.05V for various components on the board by a regulator. It is difficult to precisely measure the power consumption because it requires isolating the traces on the board that provide power to the Tegra chip and measuring the current values. Also, because the CPU and the GPU respectively are integrated in a single chip, it's hard to measure exactly the current drawn by each individual component in the chip. Therefore, we approximate the current used by the CPU and the GPU by measuring the current consumed by the entire board. The average idle current is about 0.2A which is considered as the offset current.

The Tegra GPU has fully programmable unified vertex and fragment shaders. The shaders are programed through OpenGL ES 2.0 [6] which is the primary graphics library for handheld and embedded devices with a programmable GPU. The commonly used high-level API for a desktop environment, such as CUDA or OpenCL, is not supported in this, and any other embedded, platform yet.

5   Execution Efficiency and Energy Efficiency Study

Gabor wavelet can be implemented by convolution or the Fast Fourier Transform (FFT). The GPU implementation of the convolution method is suitable only for small-size kernels due to the memory limitation. However, a small-size kernel is not realistic for object and pattern recognition [18]. Therefore, our GPU-based Gabor face feature extraction is based on the FFT method: first transforming both face image and the Gabor kernel into the Fourier space, multiplying them together, and then inverse-transforming the result back to the space domain. In our study, we first take FFT as a benchmark program to investigate the computational and energy efficiency of mobile GPU, and then extend the result to the Gabor face feature extraction processing.

5.1 FFT Benchmark on Mobile CPU and GPU

Fig. 3 shows the pseudo code of our FFT benchmark program. The CPU implementation is written in C. In the GPU implementation, the GPU shaders, which are launched by the host CPU, perform FFT and IFFT computation. The data needs to first transfer from the CPU domain to the GPU domain and then transfer back after the GPU finishes its computation. The shader program is compiled on the Tegra GPU. After the execution is completed, the resulting image is displayed on the screen.

CPU-implementation	GPU-implementation
1. Allocate memory 2. Generate N*N sample 3. Repeat T times 4. { 5. FFT 6. IFFT 7. } 8. Display result on screen	1. Compile shader program 2. CPU allocate memory 3. CPU generate N*N sample 4. CPU copy data to GPU 5. Repeat T times 6. { 7. FFT 8. IFFT 9. } 10. CPU read data from GPU 11. Display result on screen

Fig. 3. FFT benchmark used in our study

A GPU-acceleration method in [21] is used in our study. Although some other GPU-accelerated FFT methods have been proposed [19][20][22], they were proposed for dedicated hardware and could not be applied to an embedded GPU which has significantly less resources due to the power constraint. The approach used in our study relies on the fragment shader to do the per-pixel (i.e. each sample of the 2D array) computation. The input index and weighting factor which are used for the calculation of the each sample are pre-computed and stored in the texture memory.

We ran a FFT benchmark program, which performs FFT and IFFT 50 times, on Tegra's CPU and GPU respectively for comparison. The measured power consumption results are shown in Figure 5. Both CPU and GPU start running roughly at reference time 0.6 second. After CPU starts running, it takes about 0.4 second for the CPU to initialize the GPU and to transfer data from the CPU to the GPU before the GPU runs at its full capacity. After the FFT and the IFFT computations are completed, the application program is still running (but does nothing). Therefore, the power consumption level is still higher than the level of the idle stage before the application was launched.

The measurement results show that, for this FFT benchmark, the GPU is 3x faster and consumes 8% more power than the CPU (1 second vs. 3.1 seconds, and 4.0 watts vs. 3.7 watts). The slightly higher power when using GPU is because the CPU is not idle when the GPU is running and is standing by for the completion of GPU. As a result, the ratio of the total energy consumption of the CPU version vs. the GPU version for this FFT benchmark is 2.86 to 1.

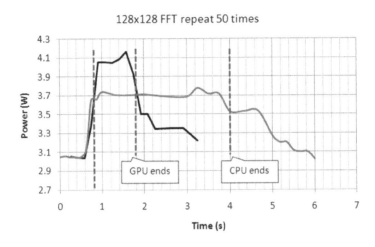

Fig. 4. Power consumption of our FFT benchmark on mobile CPU and GPU

5.2   GPU Accelerated Gabor-Based Face Feature Extraction

The FFT benchmark result demonstrates that using a mobile GPU is not only more computationally efficient but also more energy efficient. We then extend the GPU-accelerated FFT and IFFT to compute the Gabor-based face feature extraction, and compare the results with the CPU implementation. The left side of Fig. 5 shows the pseudo code of the Gabor-based face feature extraction. In the GPU implementation, the FFT and IFFT are the same shader program with different input arguments in order to perform either forward or inverse transform, and the MULTIPLY is a separate shader program. In other words, different shader programs have to be swapped back and forth repeatedly to complete the task. The execution time of both CPU and GPU implementation are shown in the first two rows of Table 2. The GPU implementation runs 4.25x faster than the CPU implementation (1.2 seconds vs. 5.1 seconds) while consuming slightly more power (3.75 Watt vs. 3.52 Watt).

Since the computation of convolving 40 different Gabor kernels with a face image can be computed concurrently and independently, processing multiple Gabor kernels in a batch mode may further improve the performance by reducing overall time spent on swapping shader programs. Three different configurations are examined in our study: The first configuration (Fig. 6(a)) is the original method which performs 40 Gabor wavelets with 40 different kernels. The second configuration (Fig. 6 (b)) combines four kernels in a batch, and the shader program is configured to draw a 256x256 quad but performs four 128x128 FFTs while each FFT tile has a different texture access address. This could be easily performed by loading another texture to lookup the index. The third configuration (Fig. 6 (c)), similar to the second one, combines nine Gabor kernels in a batch and performs nine 128x128 FFTs at a time.

Single mode	Batch mode
1. FFT (face)	1. FFT (N tile face) // same face in each tile
2. for i = 1~40	2. for i = 1~ceil(40/N)
3. {	3. {
4. FFT (kernel i)	4. FFT (N tilt kernel) // different kernel in each tile
5. MULTIPLY ()	5. MULTIPLY()
6. IFFT()	6. IFFT()
7. Read results back to CPU	7. Read results back to CPU
8. }	8. }

Fig. 5. Doing 40 Gabor filter in the single mode and batch mode

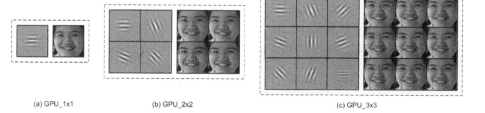

(a) GPU_1x1   (b) GPU_2x2   (c) GPU_3x3

Fig. 6. Combine various number of Gabor kernels to perform larger size FFT together. (a) Perform a 128x128 FFT for one kernel at a time. (b) Perform four 128x128 FFTs for four kernels at a time. (c) Perform nine 128x128 FFT for nine kernels at a time.

The measurement results show that, however, the batch mode does not reduce the computation time as we expected. As shown in Table 2, GPU_1x1, GPU_2x2, and GPU_3x3 take 1.2, 1.4, and 1.5 seconds respectively to complete the assigned tasks. This could be explained that a larger amount of data is required for the computation when running a larger number of concurrent tasks. If the GPU cache size is not large enough, it takes more time to store and load data from the main memory.

Table 2. The execution time and energy consumption of different implementation configurations

configuration	# of batch	Time (sec)	Power (Watt)	Energy (J)
CPU (1x1)	40	5.1	3.52	17.95
GPU (1x1)	40	1.2	3.75	4.50
GPU (2x2)	10	1.4	3.59	5.02
GPU (3x3)	5	1.5	3.63	5.44

5.3 Overall Performance

Computing Gabor representation of a face image is the most time consuming part of the whole face recognition system. It takes about 5.1 seconds for a 1 GHz ARM processor to complete this task. The mobile GPU takes only 1.2 seconds to complete the same task, which represents a 4.25x speedup. As shown in Fig. 7, with the GPU successfully offloading the computational burden from CPU, the overall computation time for recognizing a person on a smartphone is reduced from 8.5 seconds to 4.6 seconds. As for the total energy consumption, the mobile CPU-GPU implementation consumes 16.3 J while the CPU only implementation consumes 29.8 J. After the Gabor wavelet is accelerated by the GPU, the face detection and face feature dimension reduction by PCA-LDA become the most time-critical parts. We will further explore in the future the opportunity of utilizing mobile GPU to remove these new computational bottlenecks to achieve better performance and energy consumption level.

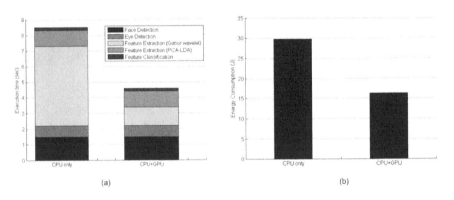

Fig. 7. Comparison of face recognition system running on Tegra's CPU and CPU+GPU. (a) Execution time (b) Total energy consumption.

6   Conclusion and Future Works

In this paper, we investigate the computing power and energy consumption of a mobile CPU-GPU platform for mobile computer vision applications. Compared to a CPU-only implementation, our preliminary GPU-accelerated Gabor face feature extraction, the most compute-intensive task in a face annotation system can achieve a 4.25x speedup and 3.94x reduction in energy consumption. This experimental investigation confirms that a mobile GPU, although is designed primarily for low-power rather than maximum performance, can provide significant performance speedup for vision tasks on a mobile platform, similar to the role of its high-performance counterparts in the desktop and server systems. Therefore, the performance improvement achieved by GPU-based computing also results in overall energy reduction, which is a tremendous benefit for mobile devices.

Due to the lack of a higher level programming environment, such as CUDA, for mobile GPUs, it is difficult to port existing GPU-optimized algorithms to the mobile SoCs, even for those already designed for generic GPU architectures. It is worthwhile to further explore low-power architectures and extend them toward a more programmable, general-purpose architecture. While increasing the programmability may somewhat compromise the execution efficiency or increase the power consumption, exploring the tradeoffs between energy efficiency and the programmability and identifying a solution for easier programming without costing too much degradation in performance and energy consumption are necessary steps for improving the productivity for programming for mobile GPUs.

References

1. Nvidia CUDA Compute Unified Device Architecture Programming Guide; Version 2.0, Nvidia Corporation (2008), www.nvidia.com
2. Samant, S.S., Xia, J., Muyan-Ozcelik, P., Owens, J.D.: High performance computing for deformable image registration: Towards a new paradigm in adaptive radiotherapy. Medical Phisics (2008)
3. Kim, J.-S., Hwangbo, M., Kanade, T.: Realtime Affine-photometric KLT Feature Tracker on GPU in CUDA Framework. In: IEEE Workshop of Embedded Computer Vision (2009)
4. OMAP3 family of multimedia application processors, Texas Instruments Inc. (2007), http://focus.ti.com
5. Akenine-Moller, T., Strom, J.: Graphics Processing Units for Handhelds. Proceedings of the IEEE 96(5), 779–789 (2008)
6. Munshi, A., Ginsburg, D., Shreiner, D.: OpenGL ES 2.0 Programming Guide. Addison-Wesley, USA (2008)
7. Leskela, J., Nikula, J., Salmela, M.: OpenCL embedded profile prototype in mobile device. In: IEEE Workshop on Signal Processing Systems (SiPS 2009), pp. 279–284 (2009)
8. Munshi, A., (ed.) Khronos OpenCL Working Group, The OpenCL Specification, Version 1.0, Rev. 43, Khronos Group, USA (May 2009)
9. Nvidia Corporation, http://tegradeveloper.nvidia.com/tegra/
10. Chu, S-W., Yeh, M-C., Cheng, K-T.: A real-time, embedded face-annotation system. ACM MM Technical Demonstrations (2008)
11. Rofouei, M., Stathopoulos, T., Ryffel, S., Kaiser, W., Sarrafzadeh, M.: Energy-Aware High Performance Computing with Graphic Processing Units. In: Workshop on Power Aware Computing and Systems (HotPower 2008), San Diego, December 8-10 (2008)

12. Ren, D.Q., Suda, R.: Power Efficient Large Matrices Multiplication by Load Scheduling on Multi-core and GPU Platform with CUDA. In: International Conference on Computational Science and Engineering, CSE 2009 (2009)
13. Su, Y., Shan, S., Chen, X., Gao, W.: Hierarchical Ensemble of Global and Local Classifiers for Face Recognition. IEEE Transactions on Image Processing 18(8), 1885–1896 (2009)
14. Phillips, P.J., Moon, H., Rizvi, S.A., Rauss, P.J.: The FERET evaluation methodology for face-recognition algorithms. PAMI 22(10), 1090–1104 (2000)
15. Huang, G.B., Ramesh, M., Berg, T., Learned-Miller, E.: Labeled faces in the wild: a database for studying face recognition in unconstrained environments. University of Massachusetts, Amherst,Technical Report 07-49 (2007)
16. http://developer.android.com/index.html
17. http://developer.android.com/reference/android/media/FaceDetector.html
18. Fialka, O., Cadik, M.: FFT and Convolution Performance in Image Filtering on GPU. In: Tenth International Conference on Information Visualization (2006)
19. Nvidia Corp., CUDA CUFFT Library
20. Mitchell, J.L., Ansari, M.Y., Hart, E.: Advanced image processing with DirectX 9 pixel shaders. In: Engel, W. (ed.) ShaderX2: Shader Programming Tips and Tricks with DirectX9.0. Wordware Publishing, Inc. (2003)
21. Sumanaweera, T., Liu, D.: Medical image reconstruction with the FFT in GPU Gems 2. In: Pharr, M. (ed.), pp. 765–784. Addison-Wesley (2005)
22. Brandon, L.D., Boyd, C., Govindaraju, N.: Fast computation of general Fourier Transforms on GPUS. In: IEEE International Conference on Multimedia and Expo. (ICME 2008), pp. 5–8 (2008)

Practical Time Bundle Adjustment
for 3D Reconstruction on the GPU

Siddharth Choudhary, Shubham Gupta, and P.J. Narayanan

Center for Visual Information Technology
International Institute of Information Technology
Hyderabad, India
{siddharth.choudhary@research.,shubham@students.,pjn@}iiit.ac.in

Abstract. Large-scale 3D reconstruction has received a lot of attention recently. Bundle adjustment is a key component of the reconstruction pipeline and often its slowest and most computational resource intensive. It hasn't been parallelized effectively so far. In this paper, we present a hybrid implementation of sparse bundle adjustment on the GPU using CUDA, with the CPU working in parallel. The algorithm is decomposed into smaller steps, each of which is scheduled on the GPU or the CPU. We develop efficient kernels for the steps and make use of existing libraries for several steps. Our implementation outperforms the CPU implementation significantly, achieving a speedup of 30-40 times over the standard CPU implementation for datasets with upto 500 images on an Nvidia Tesla C2050 GPU.

1 Introduction

Large scale sparse 3D reconstruction from community photo collections using the structure from motion (SfM) pipeline is an active research area today. The SfM pipeline has several steps. The joint optimization of camera positions and point coordinates using Bundle Adjustment (BA) is the last step. Bundle adjustment is an iterative step, typically performed using the Levenberg-Marquardt (LM) non-linear optimization scheme. Bundle adjustment is the primary bottleneck of the SfM, consuming about half the total computation time. For example, reconstruction of a set of 715 images of Notre Dame data set took around two weeks of running time [1], dominated by iterative bundle adjustment. The BA step is still performed on a single core, though most other steps are performed on a cluster of processors [2]. Speeding up of BA by parallelizing it can have a significant impact on large scale SfM efforts.

The rapid increase in the performance has made the graphics processor unig (GPU) a viable candidate for many compute intensive tasks. GPUs are being used for many computer vision applications [3], such as Graph Cuts [4], tracking [5] and large scale 3D reconstruction [6]. No work has been done to implement bundle adjustment on the GPUs or other multicore or manycore architectures.

In this paper, we present a hybrid implementation of sparse bundle adjustment with the GPU and the CPU working together. The computation requirements

K.N. Kutulakos (Ed.): ECCV 2010 Workshops, Part II, LNCS 6554, pp. 423–435, 2012.

of BA grows rapidly with the number of images. However, the visibility aspects of points on cameras places a natural limit on how many images need to be processed together. The current approach is to identify clusters of images and points to be processed together [7]. Large data sets are decomposed into mildly overlapping sets of manageable sizes. An ability to perform bundle adjustment on about 500 images quickly will suffice to process even data sets of arbitrarily large number of images as a result. We focus on exactly this problem in this paper.

Our goal is to develop a practical time implementation by exploiting the computing resources of the CPU and the GPU. We decompose the LM algorithm into multiple steps, each of which is performed using a kernel on the GPU or a function on the CPU. Our implementation efficiently schedules the steps on CPU and GPU to minimize the overall computation time. The concerted work of the CPU and the GPU is critical to the overall performance gain. The executions of the CPU and GPU are fully overlapped in our implementation, with no idle time on the GPU. We achieve a speedup of 30-40 times on an Nvidia Tesla C2050 GPU on a dataset of about 500 images.

2   Related Work

Brown and Lowe presented the SfM pipeline for unordered data sets [8]. Phototourism is an application of 3D reconstruction for interactively browsing and exploring large collection of unstructured photographs [1]. The problem of large scale 3D reconstruction takes advantage of the redundancy available in the large collection of unordered dataset of images and maximizes the parallelization available in the SFM pipeline [2,7]. Bundle Adjustment was originally conceived in photogrammetry [9], and has been adapted for large scale reconstructions. Ni et al. solve the problem by dividing it into several submaps which can be optimized in parallel [10]. In general, a sparse variant of Levenberg-Marquardt minimization algorithm [11] is the most widely used choice for BA. A public implementation is available [9]. Byröd and Äström solve the problem using preconditioned conjugate gradients, utilizing the underlying geometric layout [12]. Cao et al. parallelize the dense LM algorithm, but their method is not suited for sparse data [13]. Agarwal et al. design a system to maximize parallelization at each stage in the pipeline, using a cluster of 500 cores for rest of the computations but a single core for bundle adjustment [2]. Frahm et al. uses GPUs to reconstruct 3 million images of Rome in less than 24 hours [6]. They don't use the GPUs for the BA step. No prior work has been reported that parallelizes BA or the LM algorithm.

3   Sparse Bundle Adjustment on the GPU

Bundle adjustment refers to the optimal adjustment of bundles of rays that leave 3D feature points onto each camera centres with respect to both camera positions and point coordinates. It produces jointly optimal 3D structure and viewing parameters by minimizing the cost function for a model fitting error [9,14]. The re-projection error between the observed and the predicted image points, which is expressed for m images and n points as,

$$\min_{P,X} \sum_{i=1}^{n} \sum_{j=1}^{m} d(Q(P_j, X_i), x_{ij})^2 \tag{1}$$

where $Q(P_j, X_i)$ is the predicted projection of point i on image j and $d(x, y)$ the Euclidean distance between the inhomogeneous image points represented by x and y. Bundle Adjustment is carried out using the Levenberg-Marquardt algorithm [11,15] because of its effective damping strategy to converge quickly from a wide range of initial guesses. Given the parameter vector $\mathbf{p}$, the functional relation f, and measured vector $\mathbf{x}$, it is required to find δ_p to minimize the quantity $\|x - f(\mathbf{p} + \delta_p)\|$. Assuming the function to be linear in the neighborhood of p, this leads to the equation

$$(\mathbf{J^T J} + \mu \mathbf{I})\delta_p = \mathbf{J^T} \epsilon \tag{2}$$

where J is the Jacobian matrix $J = \frac{\partial \mathbf{x}}{\partial \mathbf{p}}$. LM Algorithm performs iterative minimization by adjusting the damping term μ[16], which assure a reduction in the error ϵ.

BA can be cast as non-linear minimization problem as follows. A parameter vector $\mathbf{P} \in \mathbf{R}^M$ is defined by the m projection matrices and the n 3D points, as

$$\mathbf{P} = (\mathbf{a}_1^T, \ldots, \mathbf{a}_m^T, \mathbf{b}_1^T, \ldots, \mathbf{b}_n^T)^T, \tag{3}$$

where $\mathbf{a}_j$ is the jth camera parameters and $\mathbf{b}_i$ is the ith 3D point coordinates. A measurement vector $\mathbf{X}$ is the measured image coordinates in all cameras:

$$\mathbf{X} = (\mathbf{x}_{11}^T, \ldots, \mathbf{x}_{1m}^T, \mathbf{x}_{21}^T, \ldots, \mathbf{x}_{2m}^T, \ldots, \mathbf{x}_{n1}^T, \ldots, \mathbf{x}_{nm}^T)^T. \tag{4}$$

The estimated measurement vector $\hat{\mathbf{X}}$ using a functional relation $\hat{\mathbf{X}} = f(\mathbf{P})$ is given by

$$\hat{\mathbf{X}} = (\hat{\mathbf{x}}_{11}^T, \ldots, \hat{\mathbf{x}}_{1m}^T, \hat{\mathbf{x}}_{21}^T, \ldots, \hat{\mathbf{x}}_{2m}^T, \ldots, \hat{\mathbf{x}}_{n1}^T, \ldots, \hat{\mathbf{x}}_{nm}^T)^T, \tag{5}$$

with $\hat{\mathbf{x}}_{ij} = \mathbf{Q}(\mathbf{a}_j, \mathbf{b}_i)$. BA minimizes the squared Mahalanobis distance $\epsilon^T \Sigma_x^{-1} \epsilon$, where $\epsilon = \mathbf{X} - \hat{\mathbf{X}}$, over $\mathbf{P}$. Using LM Algorithm, we get the normal equation as

$$(\mathbf{J^T \Sigma_X^{-1} J} + \mu \mathbf{I})\delta = \mathbf{J^T \Sigma_X^{-1}} \epsilon. \tag{6}$$

Apart from the notations above, mnp denotes the number of measurement parameters, cnp the number of camera parameters and pnp the number of point parameters. The total number of projections onto cameras is denoted by nnz, which is the length of vector $\mathbf{X}$.

The solution to Equation 6 has a cubic time complexity in the number of parameters and is not practical when the number of cameras and points are high. The Jacobian matrix for BA, however has a sparse block structure. Sparse

BA uses a sparse variant of the LM Algorithm [9]. It takes as input the parameter vector $\mathbf{P}$, a function $\mathbf{Q}$ used to compute the predicted projections $\hat{x}_{ij}$, the observed projections x_{ij} from i^{th} point on the jth image and damping term μ for LM and returns as an output the solution δ to the normal equation as given in Equation 6. Algorithm 1 outlines the SBA and indicates the steps that are mapped onto the GPU. All the computations are performed using double precision arithmetic to gain accuracy.

Algorithm 1. SBA $(\mathbf{P}, \mathbf{Q}, x, \mu)$

1: Compute the Predicted Projections $\hat{x}_{ij}$ using $\mathbf{P}$ and $\mathbf{Q}$.   ▷ *Computed on GPU*

2: Compute the error vectors $\epsilon_{ij} \leftarrow x_{ij} - \hat{x}_{ij}$ ▷ *Computed on GPU*

3: Assign $\mathbf{J} \leftarrow \frac{\partial \mathbf{X}}{\partial \mathbf{P}}$ (Jacobian Matrix) where

$\mathbf{A}ij \leftarrow \frac{\partial \hat{x}_{ij}}{\partial a_j} = \frac{\partial \mathbf{Q}(a_j, b_i)}{\partial a_j}$ $(\frac{\partial \hat{x}_{ij}}{\partial a_k} = 0 \; \forall i \neq k)$ and

$\mathbf{B}ij \leftarrow \frac{\partial \hat{x}_{ij}}{\partial b_i} = \frac{\partial \mathbf{Q}(a_j, b_i)}{\partial b_i}$ $(\frac{\partial \hat{x}_{ij}}{\partial b_k} = 0 \; \forall j \neq k)$ ▷ *Computed on GPU*

4: Assign $\mathbf{J}^T \Sigma_\mathbf{X}^{-1} \mathbf{J} \leftarrow \begin{pmatrix} \mathbf{U} & \mathbf{W} \\ \mathbf{W}^T & \mathbf{V} \end{pmatrix}$ where U,V,W is given as

$\mathbf{U}_j \leftarrow \sum_i \mathbf{A}_{ij}^T \Sigma_{x_{ij}}^{-1} \mathbf{A}_{ij}$, $\mathbf{V}_i \leftarrow \sum_j \mathbf{B}_{ij}^T \Sigma_{x_{ij}}^{-1} \mathbf{B}_{ij}$ and

$\mathbf{W}_{ij} \leftarrow \mathbf{A}_{ij}^T \Sigma_{x_{ij}}^{-1} \mathbf{B}_{ij}$ ▷ *Computed on GPU*

5: Compute $\mathbf{J}^T \Sigma_\mathbf{X}^{-1} \epsilon$ as $\epsilon_{a_j} \leftarrow \sum_i \mathbf{A}_{ij}^T \Sigma_{x_{ij}}^{-1} \epsilon_{ij}$,

$\epsilon_{b_i} \leftarrow \sum_j \mathbf{B}_{ij}^T \Sigma_{x_{ij}}^{-1} \epsilon_{ij}$ ▷ *Computed on CPU*

6: Augment $\mathbf{U}_j$ and $\mathbf{V}_i$ by adding μ to diagonals to yield

$\mathbf{U}_j^*$ and $\mathbf{V}_i^*$ ▷ *Computed on GPU*

7: Normal Equation: $\begin{pmatrix} \mathbf{U}^* & \mathbf{W} \\ \mathbf{W}^T & \mathbf{V}^* \end{pmatrix} \begin{pmatrix} \delta_a \\ \delta_b \end{pmatrix} = \begin{pmatrix} \epsilon_a \\ \epsilon_b \end{pmatrix}$ ▷ Using Equation (6)

8: $\begin{pmatrix} \underbrace{\mathbf{U}^* - \mathbf{W}\mathbf{V}^{*-1}\mathbf{W}^T}_{\mathbf{S}} & 0 \\ \mathbf{W}^T & \mathbf{V}^* \end{pmatrix} \begin{pmatrix} \delta_a \\ \delta_b \end{pmatrix} = \begin{pmatrix} \underbrace{\epsilon_a - \mathbf{W}\mathbf{V}^{*-1}\epsilon_b}_{e} \\ \epsilon_b \end{pmatrix}$ ▷ Using Schur Complement

9: Compute $\mathbf{Y}_{ij} \leftarrow \mathbf{W}_{ij} \mathbf{V}_i^{*-1}$ ▷ *Computed on GPU*

10: Compute $\mathbf{S}_{jk} \leftarrow \mathbf{U}_j^* - \sum_i \mathbf{Y}_{ij} \mathbf{W}_{ik}^T$ ▷ *Computed on GPU*

11: Compute $e_j \leftarrow \epsilon_{a_j} - \sum_i \mathbf{Y}_{ij} \epsilon_{b_i}$ ▷ *Computed on CPU*

12: Compute δ_a as $(\delta_{a_1}^T, \ldots, \delta_{a_m}^T)^T = \mathbf{S}^{-1}(e_1^T, \ldots, e_m^T)^T$ ▷ *Computed on GPU*

13: Compute $\delta_{b_i} \leftarrow \mathbf{V}_i^{*-1}(\epsilon_{b_i} - \sum_j \mathbf{W}_{ij}^T \delta_{a_j})$ ▷ *Computed on GPU*

14: Form δ as $(\delta_a^T, \delta_b^T)^T$

3.1 Data Structure for the Sparse Bundle Adjustment

Since most of the 3D points are not visible in all cameras, we need a visibility mask to represent the visibility of points onto cameras. Visibility mask is a boolean mask built such that the $(i, j)^{th}$ location is true if i^{th} point is visible in the jth image. We propose to divide the reconstruction consisting of cameras and 3D points into camera tiles or sets of 3D points visible in a camera. Since

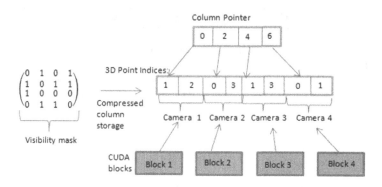

Fig. 1. An example of the compressed column storage of visibility mask having 4 cameras and 4 3D Points. Each CUDA Block processes one set of 3D points.

the number of cameras is less than number of 3D points and bundle of light rays projecting on a camera can be processed independent of other cameras, this division can be easily mapped into blocks and threads on fine grained parallel machines like GPU. The visibility mask is sparse in nature since 3D points are visible in nearby cameras only and not all. We compress the visibility mask using Compressed Column Storage (CCS) [17]. Figure 1 shows a visibility mask for 4 cameras and 4 points and its Compressed Column Storage. We do not store the *val* array as in standard CCS [17] as it is same as the array index in 3D point indices array. The space required to store this is $(nnz + m) \times 4$ bytes whereas to store the whole visibility matrix is $m \times n$ bytes. Since the projections $\hat{\mathbf{x}}_{ij}, \mathbf{x}_{ij}$ and the Jacobian $\mathbf{A}_{ij}, \mathbf{B}_{ij}$ is non zero only when the ith 3D point is visible in the jth camera, it is also sparse in nature and thereby stored in contiguous locations using CCS which is indexed through the visibility mask.

3.2   Computation of the Initial Projection and Error Vector

Given $\mathbf{P}$ and $\mathbf{Q}$ as input, the initial projection is calculated as $\hat{\mathbf{X}} = \mathbf{Q}(\mathbf{P})$ (Algorithm 1,line 1) where $\hat{\mathbf{X}}$ is the estimated measurement vector and $\hat{\mathbf{x}}_{ij} = \mathbf{Q}(\mathbf{a_j}, \mathbf{b_i})$ is the projection of point b_i on the camera a_j using the function $\mathbf{Q}$. The error vector is calculated as $\epsilon_{ij} = \mathbf{x}_{ij} - \hat{\mathbf{x}}_{ij}$ where $\mathbf{x}_{ij}$ and $\hat{\mathbf{x}}_{ij}$ are the measured and estimated projections. The estimated projections and error vectors consumes memory space of $nnz \times mnp$ each. Our implementation consists of m thread blocks running in parallel, with each thread of block j computing a projection to the camera j. The number of threads per block is limited by the total number of registers available per block and a maximum limit of number of threads per block. Since the typical number of points seen by a camera is of the order of thousands (more than the limit on threads) we loop over all the 3D points visible by a camera in order to compute projections. The GPU kernel to calculate the initial projection and error vector is shown in Algorithm 2.

Algorithm 2. CUDA_INITPROJ_KERNEL $(\mathbf{P}, \mathbf{Q}, \mathbf{X})$

1: CameraID ← BlockID
2: Load the camera parameters into shared memory
3: **repeat**
4:      Load the 3D point parameters (given ThreadID and CameraID)
5:      Calculate the Projection $\hat{x}_{ij}$ given 3D Point i and Camera j
6:      Calculate the Error Vector using $\epsilon_{ij} = \mathbf{x}_{ij} - \hat{\mathbf{x}}_{ij}$
7:      Store the Projections and Error Vector back into global memory
8: **until** all the projections are calculated

3.3   Computation of the Jacobian Matrix (J)

The Jacobian matrix is calculated as $\mathbf{J} = \frac{\partial \mathbf{X}}{\partial \mathbf{P}}$ (Algorithm 1, line 3). For $\hat{\mathbf{X}} = (\hat{\mathbf{x}}_{11}^T, \ldots, \hat{\mathbf{x}}_{n1}^T, \hat{\mathbf{x}}_{12}^T, \ldots, \hat{\mathbf{x}}_{n2}^T, \ldots, \hat{\mathbf{x}}_{1m}^T, \ldots, \hat{\mathbf{x}}_{nm}^T)^T$, the Jacobian would be $(\frac{\partial \hat{\mathbf{x}}_{11}}{\partial \mathbf{P}}^T, \ldots, \frac{\partial \hat{\mathbf{x}}_{n1}}{\partial \mathbf{P}}^T, \frac{\partial \hat{\mathbf{x}}_{12}}{\partial \mathbf{P}}^T, \ldots, \frac{\partial \hat{\mathbf{x}}_{n2}}{\partial \mathbf{P}}^T, \ldots, \frac{\partial \hat{\mathbf{x}}_{1m}}{\partial \mathbf{P}}^T, \ldots, \frac{\partial \hat{\mathbf{x}}_{nm}}{\partial \mathbf{P}}^T)$. Since $\frac{\partial \hat{x}_{ij}}{\partial a_k} = 0$ $\forall i \neq k$ and $\frac{\partial \hat{x}_{ij}}{\partial b_k} = 0$ $\forall j \neq k$, the matrix is sparse in nature.

For the example, shown in Figure 1, the Jacobian matrix would be

$$
J = \begin{pmatrix}
A_{10} & 0 & 0 & 0 & 0 & B_{10} & 0 & 0 \\
A_{20} & 0 & 0 & 0 & 0 & 0 & B_{20} & 0 \\
0 & A_{01} & 0 & 0 & B_{01} & 0 & 0 & 0 \\
0 & A_{31} & 0 & 0 & 0 & 0 & 0 & B_{31} \\
0 & 0 & A_{12} & 0 & 0 & B_{12} & 0 & 0 \\
0 & 0 & A_{32} & 0 & 0 & 0 & 0 & B_{32} \\
0 & 0 & 0 & A_{03} & B_{03} & 0 & 0 & 0 \\
0 & 0 & 0 & A_{13} & 0 & B_{13} & 0 & 0
\end{pmatrix}, \tag{7}
$$

where, $\mathbf{A}ij = \frac{\partial \hat{x}_{ij}}{\partial a_j} = \frac{\partial \mathbf{Q}(a_j, b_i)}{\partial a_j}$ and $\mathbf{B}ij = \frac{\partial \hat{x}_{ij}}{\partial b_i} = \frac{\partial \mathbf{Q}(a_j, b_i)}{\partial b_i}$. The matrix when stored in compressed format would be $\mathbf{J} = (A_{10}, B_{10}, A_{20}, B_{20}, A_{01}, B_{01}, A_{31}, B_{31}, A_{12}, B_{12}, A_{32}, B_{32}, A_{03}, B_{03}, A_{13}, B_{13})$ The memory required is $(cnp + pnp) \times mnp \times nnz \times 4$ bytes. The CUDA grid structure used in Jacobian computation is similar to initial projection computation. Block j processes the A_{ij} and B_{ij}, corresponding to the jth camera. The kernel to calculate the Jacobian Matrix is shown in Algorithm 3.

Algorithm 3. CUDA_JACOBIAN_KERNEL $(\mathbf{P}, \mathbf{Q})$

1: CameraID ← BlockID
2: **repeat**
3:      Load the 3D point parameters and Camera parameters (given ThreadID and CameraID) into thread memory.
4:      Calculate B_{ij} followed by A_{ij} using scalable finite differentiation
5:      Store the A_{ij} and B_{ij} into global memory at contiguous locations.
6: **until** all the projections are calculated

3.4   Computation of $J^T \Sigma_X^{-1} J$

$J^T \Sigma_X^{-1} J$ is given as $\begin{pmatrix} \mathbf{U} & \mathbf{W} \\ \mathbf{W}^T & \mathbf{V} \end{pmatrix}$ where $\mathbf{U}_j = \sum_i \mathbf{A}_{ij}^T \Sigma_{x_{ij}}^{-1} \mathbf{A}_{ij}$, $\mathbf{V}_i = \sum_j \mathbf{B}_{ij}^T \Sigma_{x_{ij}}^{-1}$ $\mathbf{B}_{ij}$ and $\mathbf{W}_{ij} = \mathbf{A}_{ij}^T \Sigma_{x_{ij}}^{-1} \mathbf{B}_{ij}$. For the example in Figure 1, $J^T \Sigma_X^{-1} J$ is given as:

$$
J^T \Sigma_X^{-1} J = \begin{pmatrix}
U_0 & 0 & 0 & 0 & 0 & W_{10} & W_{20} & 0 \\
0 & U_1 & 0 & 0 & W_{01} & 0 & 0 & W_{31} \\
0 & 0 & U_2 & 0 & 0 & W_{12} & 0 & W_{32} \\
0 & 0 & 0 & U_3 & W_{03} & W_{13} & 0 & 0 \\
0 & W_{01}^T & 0 & W_{03}^T & V_0 & 0 & 0 & 0 \\
W_{10}^T & 0 & W_{12}^T & W_{13}^T & 0 & V_1 & 0 & 0 \\
W_{20}^T & 0 & 0 & 0 & 0 & 0 & V_2 & 0 \\
0 & W_{31}^T & W_{32}^T & 0 & 0 & 0 & 0 & V_3
\end{pmatrix} \tag{8}
$$

Computation of U: The CUDA grid structure consists m blocks, such that each block processes U_j where j is the BlockID. Thread i in block j processes $\mathbf{A}_{ij}^T \Sigma_{x_{ij}}^{-1} \mathbf{A}_{ij}$, which is stored in the appropriate segment. The summation is faster when using a segmented scan[18] on Tesla S1070 whereas a shared memory reduction is faster on the Fermi GPU. The memory space required to store $\mathbf{U}$ is $cnp \times cnp \times m \times 4$ bytes. The computation of $\mathbf{U}$ is done as described in Algorithm 4.

Algorithm 4. CUDA_U_KERNEL (A)

1: CameraID $\leftarrow$ BlockID
2: **repeat**
3:     Load A_{ij} where $j =$ CameraID (for a given thread)
4:     Calculate $A_{ij} \times A_{ij}^T$ and store into appropriate global memory segment
5: **until** all the A_{ij} are calculated for the j_{th} camera
6: Perform a shared memory reduction to get final sum on Fermi. Write to global memory and perform a segmented scan on Tesla S1070.

Computation of V: The CUDA grid structure and computation of V is similar to the computation of U. The basic difference between the two is that $\mathbf{B}_{ij}^T \Sigma_{x_{ij}}^{-1} \mathbf{B}_{ij}$ is stored in the segment for point i for reduction using segmented scan on Tesla S1070 where as a shared memory reduction is done on Fermi. The memory space required to store $\mathbf{V}$ is $pnp \times pnp \times n \times 4$ bytes.

Computation of W: The computation of each W_{ij} is independent of all other W_{ij} as there is no summation involved as in $\mathbf{U}$ and $\mathbf{V}$. Therefore the computation load is equally divided among all blocks in GPU. $\lceil \frac{nnz}{10} \rceil$ thread blocks are launched with each block processing 10 W matrices. This block configuration gave us the maximum CUDA occupancy. The memory space required to store $\mathbf{W}$ is $pnp \times cnp \times nnz \times 4$ bytes. The computation of $\mathbf{W}$ is done as described in Algorithm 5.

Algorithm 5. CUDA_W_KERNEL $(\mathbf{A}, \mathbf{B})$

1: Load A_{ij} and B_{ij} for each warp of threads.
2: Calculate $A_{ij} \times B_{ij}^T$
3: Store W_{ij} back into global memory at appropriate location.

3.5   Computation of $\mathbf{S} = \mathbf{U}^* - \mathbf{W}\mathbf{V}^{*-1}\mathbf{W}^T$

The computation of S is the most demanding step of all the modules (Algorithm 1, line 10). Table 1 shows the split up of computation time among all components. After calculating U,V and W, augmentation of U,V is done by calling a simple kernel, with m, n blocks with each block adding μ to the respective diagonal elements. Since V^* is a block diagonal matrix, it's inverse can be easily calculated through a kernel with n blocks, with each block calculating the inverse of V^* submatrix (of size $pnp \times pnp$).

Computation of $\mathbf{Y} = \mathbf{W}\mathbf{V}^{*-1}$: Computation of $\mathbf{Y}$ is similar to the computation of $\mathbf{W}$. $\left\lceil \frac{nnz}{10} \right\rceil$ thread blocks are launched with each block processing 10 Y matrices and each warp of thread computing $W_{ij} \times V_i^{*-1}$.

Computation of $\mathbf{U}^* - \mathbf{Y}\mathbf{W}^T$: $\mathbf{S}$ is a symmetric matrix, so we calculate only the upper diagonal. The memory space required to store $\mathbf{S}$ is $m \times m \times 81 \times 4$ bytes. The CUDA grid structure consists of $m \times m$ blocks. Each block is assigned to a 9×9 submatrix in the upper diagonal, where each block calculates one $S_{ij} = U_{ij} - \sum_k Y_{ki}W_{kj}^T$. Limited by the amount of shared memory available and number of registers available per block, only 320 threads are launched. The algorithm used for computation is given in Algorithm 6.

Algorithm 6. CUDA_S_KERNEL $(\mathbf{U}^*, \mathbf{Y}, \mathbf{W}^T)$

1: **repeat** (for S_{ij})
2:     Load 320 3D Point indices (given camera set i) into shared memory
3:     Search for loaded indices in camera set j and load them into shared memory.
4:     **for all** 320 points loaded in shared memory **do**
5:         Load 10 indices of the camera set i and j from the shared memory.
6:         For each warp, compute $Y_{ki}W_{kj}^T$ and add to the partial sum for each warp in shared memory
7:     **end for**
8:     Synchronize Threads
9: **until** all the common 3D points are loaded.
10: Sum up the partial summations in the shared memory to get the final sum.
11: **if** $i == j$ **then**
12:     Compute $Y_{ii}W_{ii}^T \leftarrow U_{ii}^* - Y_{ii}W_{ii}^T$
13: **end if**
14: Store $Y_{ij}W_{ij}^T$ into global memory.

3.6   Computation of the Inverse of S

As the S Matrix is symmetric and positive definite, Cholesky decomposition is used to perform the inverse operation (Algorithm 1, line 12). Cholesky decomposition is done using the MAGMA library [19], which is highly optimized using the fine and coarse grained parallelism on GPUs as well benefits from hybrids computations by using both CPUs and GPUs. It achieves a peak performance of 282 GFlops for double precision. Since GPU's single precision performance is much higher than it's double precision performance, it used the mixed precision iterative refinement technique, in order to find inverse, which results in a speedup of more than 10 over the CPU.

3.7   Scheduling of Steps on CPU and GPU

Figure 2 shows the way CPU and GPU work together, in order to maximize the overall throughput. While the computationally intense left hand side of the equations are calculated on GPU, the relatively lighter right hand side are computed on CPU. The blocks connected by the same vertical line are calculated in parallel on CPU and GPU. The computations on the CPU and the GPU overlap. The communications are also performed asynchronously, to ensure that the GPU doesn't lie idle from the start to the finish of an iteration.

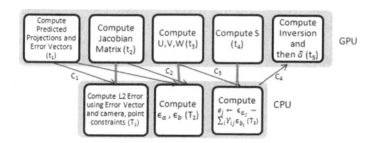

Fig. 2. Scheduling of steps on CPU and GPU. Arrows indicate data dependency between modules. Modules connected through a vertical line are computed in parallel on CPU and GPU.

4   Experimental Results

In this section, we analyze the performance of our approach and compare with the CPU implementation of Bundle Adjustment [9]. We use an Intel Core i7, 2.66GHz CPU. For the GPU, we use a quarter of an Nvidia Tesla S1070 [20] with CUDA 2.2 and an Nvidia Tesla C2050 (Fermi) with CUDA 3.2. All computations were performed in double precision, as single precision computations had correctness issues for this problem.

We used the Notre Dame 715 dataset [21] for our experiments. We ran the 3D reconstruction process on the data set and the input and output parameters $(\mathbf{P}, \mathbf{Q}, x, \mu, \delta)$ were extracted and stored for bundle adjustment. We focussed on getting good performance for a dataset of around 500 images as explained before. The redundancy is being exploited for larger data sets using a minimal skeletal subset of similar size by other researchers [2,7]. We used a 488 image subset to analyze the performance and to compare it with the popular implementation of bundle adjustment [9].

Table 1 shows the time taken for a single iteration for each major step. The **S** computation takes most of the time, followed by the **S** inverse computation. The Schur complement takes about 70% of the computation time for **S**, as it involves $\mathcal{O}(m^2 \times mnp \times pnp \times cnp \times mnvis)$ operations, where $mnvis$ is the maximum number of 3D points visible by a single camera. On the GPU, each of the m^2 blocks performs $\mathcal{O}(mnp \times pnp \times cnp \times mnvis)$ computations. 60% of **S** computation is to find the partial sums, 30% for the reduction, and 10% for the search operation. It is also limited by the amount of shared memory. The Jacobian computation is highly data parallel and maps nicely to the GPU architecture. Rest of the kernels (U, V, W and initial projection) are light.

As shown in Figure 3, the total running time on the GPU is $t = t_1 + t_2 + t_3 + t_4 + C_4 + t_5$ and on CPU is $T = T_1 + C_1 + T_2 + C_2 + T_3 + C_3$ where t_i is the time taken by GPU modules, T_i time taken by CPU modules and C_i communication time. The total time taken is $max(t, T)$. CPU-GPU parallel operations take place only when $max(t, T) < (t + T)$. For the case of 488 cameras, the time taken by GPU completely overlaps the CPU computations and communication, so that there is no idle time for the GPU. Figure 4 compares the time taken by our hybrid algorithm for each iteration of Bundle Adjustment with the CPU

Table 1. Time in seconds for each step in one iteration of Bundle Adjustment for different number of cameras on the Notre Dame data set. Total time is the time taken by hybrid implementation of BA using CPU and GPU in parallel. GPU1 is a quarter of Tesla S1070 and GPU2 is Tesla C2050.

Computation Step	Time Taken (in seconds)									
	GPU1	GPU2	GPU1	GPU2	GPU1	GPU2	GPU1	GPU2	GPU1	GPU2
	38 Cameras		104 Cameras		210 Cameras		356 Cameras		488 Cameras	
Initial Proj	0.02	0.01	0.02	0.03	0.05	0.04	0.06	0.04	0.06	0.05
Jacobian	0.1	0.04	0.2	0.07	0.32	0.12	0.39	0.16	0.45	0.17
U, V, W Mats	0.14	0.04	0.23	0.09	0.39	0.15	0.5	0.18	0.56	0.2
S Matrix	0.25	0.09	0.97	0.27	2.5	0.56	4.63	1.01	6.55	1.3
S Inverse	0.01	0	0.09	0.02	0.28	0.08	0.87	0.19	1.74	0.39
L2 Err (CPU)	0		0.01		0.01		0.01		0.02	
ϵa, ϵb (CPU)	0.05		0.12		0.17		0.21		0.24	
e (CPU)	0.03		0.05		0.08		0.1		0.11	
Total Time	**0.52**	**0.19**	**1.51**	**0.51**	**3.54**	**0.97**	**6.44**	**1.61**	**9.36**	**2.15**

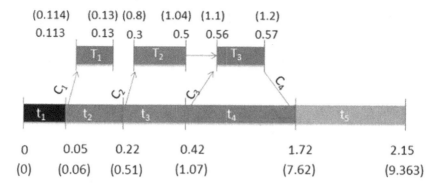

Fig. 3. Starting and ending times for each step including memory transfer for one iteration using 488 cameras. Times in paranthesis are for the use of the S1070 and others for the C2050.

only implementation on the Notre Dame dataset. The hybrid version with Tesla C2050 gets a speedup of 30-40 times over the CPU implementation.

Memory Requirements: The total memory used can be a limiting factor in the scalability of bundle adjustment for large scale 3D reconstruction. As we can see in Figure 5, the total memory requirement is high due to temporary requirements in the segmented scan [18] operation on the earlier GPU. The extra memory required is of the size $3 \times nnz \times 81 \times 4$ bytes which is used to store the data, flag and the final output arrays for the segmented scan operation. The permanent memory used to store the permanent arrays such as $\mathbf{J}$, $\mathbf{U}$, $\mathbf{V}$, $\mathbf{W}$, and $\mathbf{S}$ is only a moderate fraction of the total memory required. The Fermi has

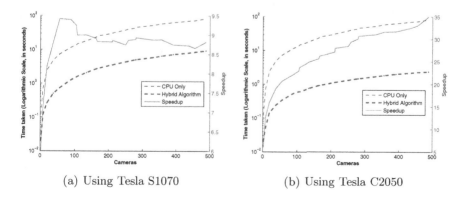

(a) Using Tesla S1070   (b) Using Tesla C2050

Fig. 4. Time and speedup for one iteration of Bundle Adjustment on the CPU using Tesla S1070 and Tesla S2050.

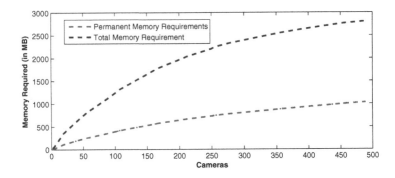

Fig. 5. Memory required (in MB) on the GPU for different number of cameras.

a larger shared memory and the reduction is performed in the shared memory itself. Thus, the total memory requirement is the same as the permanent memory requirement when using Tesla C2050.

5   Conclusions and Future Work

In this paper, we introduced a hybrid algorithm using the GPU and the CPU to perform practical time bundle adjustment. The time taken for each iteration for 488 cameras on using our approach is around 2 seconds on Tesla C2050 and 9 seconds on Tesla S1070, compared to 81 seconds on the CPU. This can reduce the computation time of a week on CPU to less than 10 hours. This can make processing larger datasets practical. Most of the computations in our case is limited by the amount of available shared memory, registers and the limit on number of threads. The double precision performance is critical to the GPU computation; the better performance using Fermi GPUs may also be due to this.

Faster bundle adjustment will enable processing of much larger data sets in the future. One option is to explore better utilization of the CPU. Even the single-core CPU is not used fully in our implementation currently. The 4-core and 8-core CPUs that are freely available can do more work, and will need a relook at the distribution of the tasks between the CPU and the GPU. The use of multiple GPUs to increase the available parallelism is another option. Expensive steps like the computation of **S** matrix can be split among multiple GPUs without adding enormous communication overheas. This will further change the balance between what can be done on the CPU and on the GPU.

References

1. Snavely, N., Seitz, S.M., Szeliski, R.: Photo tourism: exploring photo collections in 3d. ACM Trans. Graph 25, 835–846 (2006)
2. Agarwal, S., Snavely, N., Simon, I., Seitz, S.M., Szeliski, R.: Building rome in a day. In: International Conference on Computer Vision, ICCV (2009)

3. Fung, J., Mann, S.: Openvidia: parallel gpu computer vision. In: MULTIMEDIA 2005: Proceedings of the 13th Annual ACM International Conference on Multimedia, pp. 849–852 (2005)
4. Vineet, V., Narayanan, P.J.: Cuda cuts: Fast graph cuts on the gpu. In: Computer Vision and Pattern Recognition Workshop (2008)
5. Sinha, S.N., Michael Frahm, J., Pollefeys, M., Genc, Y.: Gpu-based video feature tracking and matching. Technical report. In: Workshop on Edge Computing Using New Commodity Architectures (2006)
6. Frahm, J.-M., Fite-Georgel, P., Gallup, D., Johnson, T., Raguram, R., Wu, C., Jen, Y.-H., Dunn, E., Clipp, B., Lazebnik, S., Pollefeys, M.: Building Rome on a Cloudless Day. In: Daniilidis, K., Maragos, P., Paragios, N. (eds.) ECCV 2010, Part IV. LNCS, vol. 6314, pp. 368–381. Springer, Heidelberg (2010)
7. Snavely, N., Seitz, S.M., Szeliski, R.: Skeletal graphs for efficient structure from motion. In: CVPR (2008)
8. Brown, M., Lowe, D.G.: Unsupervised 3d object recognition and reconstruction in unordered datasets. In: 3DIM 2005: Proceedings of the Fifth International Conference on 3-D Digital Imaging and Modeling, pp. 56–63 (2005)
9. Lourakis, M.A., Argyros, A.: SBA: A Software Package for Generic Sparse Bundle Adjustment. ACM Trans. Math. Software 36, 1–30 (2009)
10. Ni, K., Steedly, D., Dellaert, F.: Out-of-core bundle adjustment for large-scale 3d reconstruction. In: International Conference on Computer Vision, ICCV (2007)
11. Lourakis, M.: levmar: Levenberg-marquardt nonlinear least squares algorithms in C/C++ (July 2004), http://www.ics.forth.gr/~lourakis/levmar/
12. Byröd, M., Åström, K.: Bundle adjustment using conjugate gradients with multiscale preconditioning. In: BMVC (2009)
13. Cao, J., Novstrup, K.A., Goyal, A., Midkiff, S.P., Caruthers, J.M.: A parallel levenberg-marquardt algorithm. In: ICS 2009: Proceedings of the 23rd International Conference on Supercomputing, pp. 450–459 (2009)
14. Triggs, B., McLauchlan, P.F., Hartley, R.I., Fitzgibbon, A.W.: Bundle adjustment - a modern synthesis. In: Proceedings of the International Workshop on Vision Algorithms: Theory and Practice, ICCV 1999 (2000)
15. Ranganathan, A.: The levenberg-marquardt algorithm. Technical Report Honda Research Institute (2004), http://www.ananth.in/docs/lmtut.pdf
16. Nielsen, H.: Damping parameter in marquardt's method. Technical Report hbn, Technical University of Denmark (1999), http://www.imm.dtu.dk/~hbn
17. Dongarra, J.: Compressed column storage (1995), http://netlib2.cs.utk.edu/linalg/html_templates/node92.html
18. Sengupta, S., Harris, M., Garland, M.: Efficient parallel scan algorithms for gpus. Technical report, NVIDIA Technical Report (2008)
19. Ltaief, H., Tomov, S., Nath, R., Dongarra, J.: Hybrid multicore cholesky factorization with multiple gpu accelerators. Technical report, University of Tennessee (2010)
20. Lindholm, E., Nickolls, J., Oberman, S., Montrym, J.: Nvidia tesla: A unified graphics and computing architecture. IEEE Micro 28, 39–55 (2008)
21. Snavely, N.: Notre dame dataset (2009), http://phototour.cs.washington.edu/datasets/

Accelerating Visual Categorization with the GPU

Koen E.A. van de Sande, Theo Gevers, and Cees G.M. Snoek

Intelligent Systems Lab Amsterdam (ISLA),
University of Amsterdam,
Science Park 904, 1098 XH Amsterdam, The Netherlands
ksande@uva.nl

Abstract. Visual categorization is important to manage large collections of digital images and video, where textual meta-data is often incomplete or simply unavailable. The bag-of-words model has become the most powerful method for visual categorization of images and video. Despite its high accuracy, a severe drawback of this model is its high computational cost. As the trend to increase computational power in newer CPU and GPU architectures is to increase their level of parallelism, exploiting this parallelism becomes an important direction to handle the computational cost of the bag-of-words approach. In this paper, we analyze the bag-of-words model for visual categorization in terms of computational cost and identify two major bottlenecks: the quantization step and the classification step. We address these two bottlenecks by proposing two efficient algorithms for quantization and classification by exploiting the GPU hardware and the CUDA parallel programming model. The algorithms are designed to keep categorization accuracy intact and give the same numerical results.

In the experiments on large scale datasets it is shown that, by using a parallel implementation on the GPU, quantization is 28 times faster and classification is 35 faster than a single-threaded CPU version, while giving the exact same numerical results. The GPU accelerations are applicable to both the learning phase and the testing phase of visual categorization systems. For software visit http://www.colordescriptors.com/.[1]

1   Introduction

Visual categorization aims to determine whether objects or scene types are visually present in images or video segments. This is a useful prerequisite to manage large collections of digital images and video, where textual meta-data is often incomplete or simply unavailable [2]. Letting humans annotate such meta-data is expensive and infeasible for large datasets. While automatic visual categorization is not yet as accurate as a human annotation, it is a useful tool to manage large collections. The bag-of-words model [3] has become the most powerful method today for visual categorization [4,5,6,7,8,9,10,11]. The bag-of-words model computes image descriptors at specific points in the image. These descriptors are then quantized against a codebook of prototypical descriptors to obtain a fixed-length representation of an image. Although

---

[1] Since the workshop, an extended version of this paper has been accepted for publication in IEEE Transactions on Multimedia [1].

K.N. Kutulakos (Ed.): ECCV 2010 Workshops, Part II, LNCS 6554, pp. 436–449, 2012.

the bag-of-words model is a powerful mechanism for accurate visual categorization, a severe drawback is its high computational cost. Current state-of-the-art in visual categorization benchmarks such as TRECVID 2009 [12] require weeks of compute time on compute clusters to process 380 hours of video. However, even with weeks of compute time, most systems are still only able to process a limited subset of about 250,000 frames. In the future, more and more data needs to be processed as datasets continue to grow. To address the problem of computation, the two directions are *faster approximate methods* and *larger compute clusters*. Faster to compute descriptors (such as SURF [13,14]) and indexing mechanisms (tree-based codebooks [15,16]) have been developed. Another direction is to use large compute clusters with many CPUs [11,10] to solve the computational problem using brute force. However, both directions have their drawbacks. Faster methods will (1) suffer from reduced accuracy when they resort to increasingly coarse approximations and (2) suffer from increased complexity in the form of additional parameters and thresholds to control the approximations, all of which need to be hand-tuned. Brute force solutions based on compute clusters have the problem that (1) compute clusters are available in limited supply and (2) are expensive.

Recently, another direction for acceleration has opened up: *computing on consumer graphics hardware*. Cornelis and Van Gool [17] have implemented SURF on the GPU (Graphics Processing Unit) and obtained an order of magnitude speedup compared to a CPU implementation. These GPU implementations [17,18] build on the trend of increased parallelism. Whereas commodity CPUs currently have up to 4 cores, commodity GPUs have hundreds of cores at their disposal [19]. Together, the increased programmability and computational power of GPUs provides ample opportunities for acceleration of algorithms which can be parallelized [19]. Compared to faster approximate methods, algorithms for the GPU do not need to approximate for speedups, if they are able to exploit the parallel nature of the GPU. Compared to compute clusters, the main advantages of the GPU are their wide availability and their potential to be more energy-efficient.

When optimizing a system based on the bag-of-words model, the goal is to minimize the time it takes to process batches of images. Individual components of the bag-of-words model, such as the point sampling strategy, descriptor computation and SVM model training, have been independently studied on the GPU before [17,20,21]. These studies accelerate specific algorithms with the GPU. However, it remains unclear whether those algorithms are the real bottlenecks in accurate visual categorization with the bag-of-words model. In our overview of related work on visual categorization with the GPU, we observe that quantization and classification have remained CPU-bound so far, despite being computationally very expensive. Therefore, in this paper, the goal is to combine GPU hardware and a parallel programming model to accelerate the quantization and classification components of a visual categorization architecture. Two algorithms are proposed to accelerate these two components. The algorithms are designed to keep categorization accuracy intact and give the same numerical results.

2   Overview of Visual Categorization

The aim of this paper is to speed up state-of-the-art visual categorization systems using GPUs. In visual categorization [22], the visual presence of an object or scene of specified type is determined. In Figure 1, an overview of the components of a visual categorization system is shown. A trained visual categorization system takes an image as input and returns the likelihood that one or more visual categories are present in the image. Visual categorization systems break down into a number of common steps:

- *Image Feature Extraction*, which takes an image as input and outputs a fixed-length feature vector representing the image.
- *Category Model Learning*, learns one model per visual category by taking all vector representations of images from the train set and the category labels associated with those images.
- *Test Image Classification*, which takes vector representations of images from the test set and applies the visual category models to these images. The output of this step is a likelihood score for each image and each visual category.

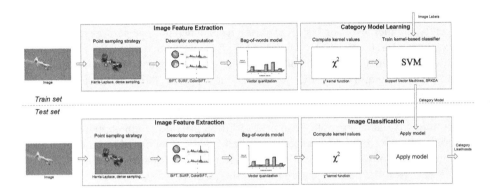

Fig. 1. The components of a state-of-the-art visual categorization system. For all images in both the train set and the test set, visual features are extracted in a number of steps. First, a point sampling method is applied to the image. Then, for every point a descriptor is computed over the area around the point. All the descriptors of an image are subsequently vector quantized against a codebook of prototypical descriptors. This results in a fixed-length feature vector representing the image. Next, the visual categorization system is trained based on the feature vectors of all training images and their category labels. To learn kernel-based classifiers, similarities between training images are needed. These similarities are computed using a kernel function. To apply a trained model to test images, the kernel function values are also needed. Given these values between a test image and the images in the train set, the category models are applied and category likelihoods are obtained.

2.1   Image Feature Extraction

Visual categorization systems which achieve state-of-the-art results on the PASCAL VOC benchmarks [5,9,6] use the bag-of-words model [3] as the underlying representation model. This model first extracts specific points in an image using a point sampling strategy. Over the area around these points, descriptors are computed which represent the local area. The bag-of-words model performs vector quantization of the descriptors in an image against a visual codebook. A descriptor is assigned to the codebook element which is closest in Euclidean space. Figure 1 gives an overview of the steps for the bag-of-words model in the image feature extraction blocks. In Table 1, the computation times of different steps within the bag-of-words model are listed. For every step, multiple options are available. Next, we will discuss these options, their presence in related work and their computation times on the CPU and GPU.

Table 1. Computation times of different steps within the bag-of-words model on both the CPU and the GPU. For every step, multiple choices are available. CPU times obtained on AMD Opteron 250 @ 2.4GHz. GPU times obtained from the literature. One of the contributions of this paper is substantially accelerating the vector quantization step using the GPU.

Image Feature Extraction	Times (s)	
	CPU	*GPU*
1) Point Sampling Strategy		
• Dense Sampling	< 0.01	< 0.01
• Difference-of-Gaussians	1.4 [23]	< 0.1 [17]
• Harris-Laplace	4.4 [24]	< 0.5 [25]
2) Descriptors		
• SIFT	1.4 [23]	< 0.1 [18]
• SURF	< 1.0 [13]	< 0.01 [17]
• ColorSIFT	4.0 [6]	< 0.3 [18]
3) Bag-of-Words		
• Tree-based Codebook	< 0.5 [15,16]	< 0.01 [20]
• Vector Quantization	**5.0** [3]	**< 0.1 this paper**

Point Sampling Strategy. As a point sampling strategy, there are two commonly used techniques in state-of-the-art systems [9,6]: dense sampling and salient point methods. Dense sampling samples points regularly over the image at fixed pixel intervals. As it does not depend on the image contents, it is a trivial operation to perform. Typically, around 10,000 points are sampled per image. Two examples of salient point methods are the Harris-Laplace salient point detector [24] and the Difference-of-Gaussians detector [23]. See Table 1 for computation times of these point sampling strategies. The Harris-Laplace detector uses the Harris corner detector to find scale-invariant interest points. It then selects a subset of these points for which the Laplacian-of-Gaussians reaches a maximum over scale. Using recursive Gaussian filters [25], the computation of Gaussian derivatives at multiple scale required for these steps is possible at a rate of multiple images per second: computational complexity of recursive Gaussian filters is independent of the scale. As has been shown by Cornelis and Van Gool [17], running the Difference-of-Gaussians detector is possible in real-time, using a scale-space pyramid to limit computational complexity.

Descriptor Computation. To describe the area around the sampled points, the SIFT descriptor [23] and the SURF descriptor [13] are the most popular choices. Sinha *et al.* [18] compute SIFT descriptors at 10 frames per second for 640x480 images. Cornelis and Van Gool [17] compute SURF descriptors at 100 frames per second for 640x480 images. Both of these papers show that descriptor computation runs with excellent performance on the GPU, because one thread can be assigned per pixel or per descriptor, and thereby performing operations in parallel. The standard SIFT descriptor has a length of 128. Following Everingham *et al.* [5], color extensions of SIFT [6] would form a reasonable state-of-the-art baseline for future VOC challenges, due to their increased classification accuracy. ColorSIFT increases the descriptor length to 384 and the required computation time is also tripled.

Bag-of-Words. Vector quantization is computationally the most expensive part of the bag-of-words model. With n descriptors of length d in an image, the quantization against a codebook with m elements requires the full $(n \times m)$ distance matrix between all descriptors and codebook elements. For values which are common for visual categorization, $n = 10,000$, $d = 128$ and codebook size $m = 4,000$, a CPU implementation takes approximately 5 seconds per image, as the complexity is $O(ndm)$ per image. When d increases to 384, as is the case for ColorSIFT, the CPU implementation slows down to more than 10 seconds per image, which makes this a computational bottleneck.

One approach to address this bottleneck is to index using a tree-based codebook structure [15,16,14], instead of a standard codebook. A tree-based codebook replaces the comparison of each descriptor with all m codebook elements by a comparison against $\log(m)$ codebook elements. As a result, algorithmic complexity is reduced to $O(nd \log(m))$. Tree-based methods have been shown to run in real-time on the GPU [20]. However, for a tree-based codebook generally the accuracy is lower [14], especially for high-dimensional descriptors such as ColorSIFT. Therefore, tree-based codebooks conflict with our goal of keeping accuracy intact. The same argument applies to other indexing structures such as miniBOF (mini bag-of-features) [26]: accuracy is sacrificed in return for faster computation. Another drawback of tree-based codebooks and miniBOFs is that soft assignment [7,27], which improves accuracy by 5% by assigning weight to more than just the closest codebook element, requires the full distance matrix instead of only the closest elements. These methods are unable to provide this matrix. Therefore, this paper studies how to accelerate the vector quantization step using normal codebooks on the GPU, as the same accelerations are then also applicable to soft assignment.

In conclusion, in a state-of-the-art setup of the bag-of-words model, the most expensive part is the vector quantization step. Approximate methods are unable to satisfy our requirement to maintain accuracy.

2.2 Category Model Learning

To learn visual category models, supervised kernel-based learning algorithms such as Support Vector Machines (SVM) and Spectral Regression Kernel Discriminant Analysis [28] have shown good results [4,6]. Key property of a kernel-based classifier is that it does not require the actual vector representation of the feature vector F, but only a kernel function $k(F, F')$ which is related to the distance between the feature vectors. This is sometimes referred to as the 'kernel trick'. It has been shown experimentally [4] that the non-linear χ^2 kernel function is the best choice [9,6] for accurate visual categorization. While typical implementations compute the values of this kernel function on-the-fly and only keep a cache of the most recent evaluations, it is more efficient to compute all values in advance and store them, because then the values can be re-used for every parameter setting and for every visual category. The total number of kernel values to be computed in advance is the number of pair-wise distances between all training images, *e.g.* , it is quadratic with respect to the number of images. The benefit of precomputing kernel values is illustrated in Table 2.

Table 2. Computation times of the different steps in visual categorization. The times listed are for an image dataset (PASCAL VOC 2008), which has a training set of size 4332 and test set of size 4133. Classification times are totals for all 20 visual categories. CPU times obtained on AMD Opteron 250 @ 2.4GHz. This paper substantially accelerates the precomputation of kernel values (shown in bold) using the GPU.

Category Model Learning	**Times (s)**	
	CPU	*GPU*
Category Model Learning (without precomputed)		
Parameter Tuning (length $F = 4,000$)	$> 1,000,000$ [29]	$> 10,000$ [21]
Train Classifier (length $F = 4,000$)	$> 100,000$ [29]	$> 1,000$ [21]
Category Model Learning (with precomputed)		
Precompute Kernel Values (length $F = 4,000$)	**660**	**9** this paper
Precompute Kernel Values (length $F = 32,000$)	**3,600**	**64** this paper
Precompute Kernel Values (length $F = 320,000$)	**36,000**	**650** this paper
Parameter Tuning	1,050 [29]	60 [21]
Train Classifier	240 [29]	10 [21]
Test Image Classification (with precomputed)		
Precompute Kernel Values (length $F = 4,000$)	**600**	**8** this paper
Apply Classifier	< 5 [29]	< 1 [21]

The kernel-based SVM algorithm has been ported to the GPU by [30,21]. In [30], specific optimizations are made in the GPU version such that only linear kernel functions are supported. For visual categorization, however, support for the more accurate non-linear χ^2 kernel function is needed to maintain accuracy. Catanzaro *et al.* [21] perform a selection of the training samples under consideration for SVM, resulting in a speedup of up to 35 times for training models. Further speedups are possible if this GPU-SVM implementation is combined with the precomputation of kernel values. The precomputation of kernel values itself has not been investigated yet. Therefore, in section 3.3, we propose an algorithm to precompute the kernel values and investigate the speedup possibilities offered by precomputing these values.

Table 2 gives an overview of computation times on the PASCAL VOC 2008 dataset for different feature vector lengths, where the learning of visual category models is split into a precomputation of kernel values and the actual model learning. Because the ground truth labels of all images and their extracted features are needed before training can start, it is an inherently offline process. When multiple features are used, more than 90% of computation time is spent on precomputing the kernel values. This makes it the most expensive step in category model learning.

In conclusion, the learning of category models can be split into two steps, kernel value computation and classifier training. The classifier training has been accelerated with the GPU before, but the kernel value computation is the most expensive step. This paper will study how to accelerate the computation of the kernel values on the GPU.

2.3 Test Image Classification

To classify images from a test set, feature extraction first has to be applied to the images, similar to the train set. Therefore, speed-ups obtained in the image feature extraction stage are useful for both the train set and the test set. To apply the visual category models, pair-wise kernel values between the feature vectors of the train set and those of the test set are needed. Therefore, when accelerating the computation of kernel values, this speedup will apply to both the training phase and the test phase of a visual categorization system. This speedup is made possible by processing the test set in small batches, instead of one image at a time. Timings in Table 2 show that for the test set, again, the computation of kernel values takes up the most time.

In conclusion, the speedups obtained using GPU vector quantization and GPU precomputation of kernel values also directly apply to the classification of images/frames from the test set.

3   GPU Accelerated Categorization

We start with discussing the CUDA programming model with an example of parallel programming for the GPU in section 3.1. Next, we discuss the GPU-accelerated versions of vector quantization (section 3.2) and kernel value precomputation (section 3.3). Both of these visual categorization steps take large numbers of vectors as input, and therefore are ideally suited for the data parallelism offered by the GPU.

3.1   CUDA Programming Model

A CUDA program is organized into a normal C/C++ host program, running sequentially on the host CPU, and one or more parallel procedures that are suitable for execution on a parallel processing device like the GPU. A parallel procedure[2] is a simple sequential program which is executed simultaneously on a set of parallel threads. The programmer organizes these threads into thread blocks. The threads within a thread block are allowed to synchronize and support inter-thread communication through a high-speed shared memory. Threads from different blocks coordinate only through global memory. CUDA

---

[2] In the CUDA documentation, parallel procedures are called parallel kernels. In this paper, we refer to them as parallel procedures to avoid using the word kernel in two different contexts.

requires that thread blocks are independent, meaning that a parallel procedure must execute correctly no matter the order in which blocks are run. This restriction on the dependencies between blocks of a parallel procedure provides scalability.

Figure 2 shows a basic example of parallel programming with CUDA. The example shows a common parallelization pattern, where a serial loop with independent iterations is executed in parallel across many threads. The results of the various threads are gathered through a parallel reduction [31], also known as the 'butterfly pattern'. With a parallel reduction, n elements are summed in $\log n$ steps.

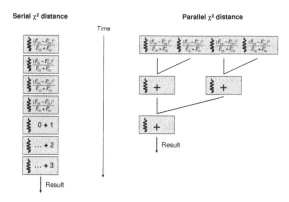

Fig. 2. Simple serial and parallel implementations of the χ^2 distance function $\frac{1}{2} \sum_{i=1} \frac{(F_i - F'_i)^2}{F_i + F'_i}$ for given vectors F and F' consisting of 4 floating point numbers. The serial version on the left is a simple loop. The parallel procedure on the right executes independent iterations in parallel.

3.2 Algorithm 1: GPU-Accelerated Vector Quantization

In section 2.1, we have shown that vector quantization is computationally the most expensive step in image feature extraction. Therefore, in this section, the GPU implementation of vector quantization for an image with n descriptors against a codebook of m elements is proposed. The descriptor length is d. Quantization against a codebook requires the full $(n \times m)$ distance matrix between all descriptors and codebook elements. A descriptor is then assigned to the column which has the lowest distance in a row. By counting the number of minima occurring in each column, the vector quantized representation of the image is obtained. To be robust against changes in the number of descriptors in an image, these counts are divided by the number of descriptors n for the final feature vector.

The most expensive computational step in vector quantization is the calculation of the distance matrix. Typically, the Euclidean distance is employed:

$$||a - b|| = \sqrt{(a_1 - b_1)^2 + (a_2 - b_2)^2 + ... + (a_q - b_q)^2}. \tag{1}$$

This formula for the Euclidean distance can be directly implemented on the GPU using loops [32]. However, such a naive implementation is not very efficient, because the same result is obtained with fewer operations by simply vectorizing the Euclidean distance. This well-known trick [21] computes the Euclidean distance in vector form:

$$||a - b|| = \sqrt{||a||^2 + ||b||^2 - 2a \cdot b}. \tag{2}$$

The advantage of the vector form of the Euclidean distance is that it allows us to decompose the computation of a distance matrix between sets of vectors into several smaller steps which are faster to compute. The dot products $a \cdot b$ in (2) between sets of vectors can be rewritten as a matrix multiplication: AB^T contains all the dot products required for the full distance matrix, with A the matrix with all image descriptors as rows and B the matrix with all codebook elements as rows. Highly optimized BLAS linear algebra libraries exist for both the CPU and the GPU which contain matrix multiplication. On the CPU we use the ATLAS library, which we tune for every CPU architecture used. Another key insight when implementing this operation is that the squared vector lengths $||a||^2$ and $||b||^2$ are used multiple times and can be cached. After the compute distance matrix has been computed, assigning the descriptors to codebook elements is a matter of finding the codebook element with the lowest distance to a descriptor, which is a simple minimization over the rows of the distance matrix.

In conclusion, vector quantization involves computing the pair-wise Euclidean distances between n descriptors and m codebook elements. By simply vectorizing the computation of the Euclidean distance, the computation can be decomposed into steps which can be efficiently executed on the GPU.

3.3   Algorithm 2: GPU-Accelerated Kernel Value Precomputation

To compute kernel function values, we use the kernel function based on the χ^2 distance, which has shown the most accurate results in visual categorization (see section 2.2). Our contribution is evaluating the χ^2 kernel function on the GPU efficiently, even for very large datasets which do not fit into memory. The χ^2 distance between feature vectors F and F' is:

$$dist_{\chi^2}(F, F') = \frac{1}{2} \sum_{i=1}^{s} \frac{(F_i - F_i')^2}{F_i + F_i'}, \tag{3}$$

with s the size of the feature vectors. For notational convenience, $\frac{0}{0}$ is assumed to be equal to 0 iff $F_i = F_i' = 0$.

The kernel function based on this χ^2 distance then is:

$$k(F, F') = e^{-\frac{1}{D} dist(F, F')}, \tag{4}$$

where D is an optional scalar to normalizes the distances [4]. Because the χ^2 distance is already constrained to lie between 0 and 1, this normalization is unnecessary and we therefore fix D to 1.

For vector quantization, discussed in the previous section, all input data and the resulting output fits into computer memory. For kernel value precomputation, memory usage is an important problem. For example, for a dataset with $50,000$ images, the input data is 12 GB and the output data is 19 GB. Therefore, special care must be taken when designing the implementation, to avoid holding all data in memory simultaneously. We divide the processing into evenly sized chunks. Each chunk corresponds to a square 1024x1024 subblock of the kernel matrix with all kernel function values. Because the final kernel function values only depend on the subset of feature vectors involved in the chunk, the operations are performed for every chunk separately. For every feature j, compute the χ^2 distances D between the 1024 vectors $F_{(j)}$ and the 1024 vectors $F'_{(j)}$. To compute the pair-wise distances between all these vectors, one thread block is created per pair (*e.g.* 1024x1024 thread blocks): F is the first input and F' is the second input to (3). The parallel procedure applied to every thread block to compute $dist_{\chi^2}(F, F')$ follows the parallelization pattern shown in Fig 2: one thread is assigned per data element. After the distances have been computed, they are divided by D and their exponent with base e is taken (see (4)). Repeat this operation for all chunks and the complete kernel matrix has been computed.

4 Experimental Setup

4.1 Experiment 1: Vector Quantization Speed

We measure the relative speed of two vector quantization implementations: CPU and GPU versions of the vectorized approach from section 3.2. Measured times are the median of 25 runs; an initial warm-up run is discarded to exclude initialization effects. For the experiments, realistic data sizes are used, following the state-of-the-art [6]: a codebook of size $m = 4,000$; up to $20,000$ descriptors per image and descriptor lengths of $d = 128$ (SIFT) and $d = 384$ (ColorSIFT). Because CPU architectures still improve with every generation, we include multiple CPU architectures in our comparison of CPU and GPU versions, to show the rate of development in CPU compute speeds.

4.2 Experiment 2: Kernel Value Precomputation Speed

To measure the speed of kernel value computation, we compare a CPU version and a GPU version based on the approach from section 3.3. An alternative approach besides the GPU would be to compute the kernel values on a compute cluster. Therefore, for reference, we include an MPI version which can execute on such a cluster. We compare the GPU version on the Geforce GTX275 to the single-threaded CPU version on the Xeon X5570 and the Opteron 250. To demonstrate the execution speed relative to that of a compute cluster, we also show results using 4, 16, 25, 36 and 49 Opteron CPUs. To obtain timings results, we have chosen the large Mediamill Challenge training set of 30 993 frames [33] with realistic feature vector lengths: from a single feature (total feature vector length $4,000$) up to 10 features (total feature vector length $128,000$). For a real system, the number of features might be even higher [6,10].

5 Results

5.1 Experiment 1: Vector Quantization Speed

Figure 3 shows the vector quantization speeds for SIFT descriptors using different hardware platforms and implementations. From the results, it is shown that vector quantization on CPUs takes more time than on GPUs. The difference between the fastest

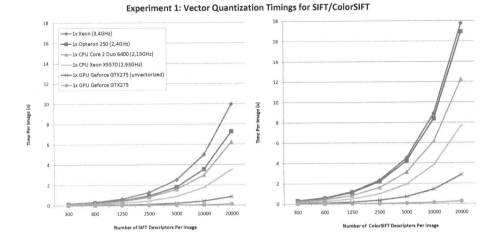

Fig. 3. Vector quantization speeds for a varying number of SIFT descriptors (on the left) or ColorSIFT descriptors (on the right). Each line represents a different hardware configuration plus appropriate implementation (CPU, GPU). The difference between the fastest single CPU core and the GPU is a factor 28.

single-threaded CPU and the fastest GPU is a factor of 28; both are using a vectorized implementation. An unvectorized GPU implementation is 6 times slower than a vectorized GPU implementation. For a typical number of SIFT descriptors per frame, 10,000, this is the difference between $0.6s$ and $0.06s$ spent *per image* in vector quantization. In the ColorSIFT results, we see the same speedup: from $1.2s$ to $0.13s$. When processing datasets of thousands or even millions of images, this is a crucial acceleration.

An interesting observation is that the CPU times can be used to roughly order them by release date. The 2004 Xeon takes about 1.4 times longer than a 2006 Core 2 Duo and 2.8 times longer than a 2009 Xeon X5570.

In conclusion, the speedup through parallelization obtained for vector quantization is an important acceleration when processing large image datasets. When combined with GPU versions of the other image feature extraction stages (see Table 1), even the most expensive feature can still be extracted in less than 1 second per image. Without GPU vector quantization, this would require an order of magnitude longer.

5.2 Experiment 2: Kernel Value Precomputation Speed

Figure 4 shows the kernel value precomputation speeds on different hardware platforms. The difference between a single GTX275 and a single Opteron CPU is a factor 90! The difference between the more recent Xeon X5570 CPU and the GPU is a factor 35. When using a bag-of-words model with features computed for four spatial pyramid levels (a total feature vector length of $120,000$), this is the difference between 2250 minutes and 170 minutes. Again, the GPU architecture results in a substantial acceleration.

When comparing the GPU implementation on a single Geforce GTX275 to the distributed CPU implementation, we see that a compute cluster with 49 Opteron CPUs is

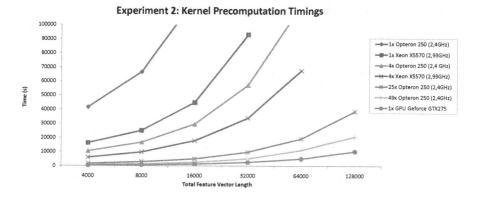

Fig. 4. Timings of kernel value precomputation on different hardware for various feature vector lengths. The difference between a single GTX275 and a single Opteron CPU is a factor 90. The difference between the more recent Xeon X5570 CPU and the GPU is a factor 35. Furthermore, a single GPU outperforms a compute cluster with 49 Opteron CPUs by a factor of 2.

still outperformed by the GPU with a factor 2. This implies that a medium-size compute cluster is insufficient to beat a single GPU when precomputing kernel values. For large datasets, consisting of tens of thousands of training images (*e.g.*, TRECVID 2009 [12], Mediamill Challenge [33]), this allows the category learning step to be performed using a single machine, instead of using an expensive compute cluster. Alternatively, the improved efficiency could be used to include more visual features (which implies even longer feature vectors) or to process additional frames from a video.

6   Conclusions

This paper provides an efficiency analysis of a state-of-the-art visual categorization pipeline based on the bag-of-words model. In this analysis, two large bottlenecks were identified: the vector quantization step in the image feature extraction and the kernel value computation in the category classification. By using a vectorized GPU implementation of vector quantization, it is 28 times faster than when it is computed on a CPU. For the classification, we exploit the intrinsic property of kernel-based classifiers that only kernel values are needed. By precomputing these kernel values, the parameter tuning and model learning stages can reuse these values, instead of computing them on the fly for every visual category and parameter setting. Also, computing these kernel values on the GPU accelerates it by a factor of 35, while giving the exact same results for visual categorization. The latter GPU acceleration is applicable to both the learning phase and the test phase. In the future, we will look at applying our GPU accelerations to other problems, such as k-means clustering and text retrieval.

References

1. van de Sande, K.E.A., Gevers, T., Snoek, C.G.M.: Empowering visual categorization with the GPU. IEEE Transactions on Multimedia (2011) (in press)

2. Hollink, L., Huurnink, B., van Liempt, M., Oomen, J., de Jong, A., de Rijke, M., Schreiber, G., Smeulders, A.W.M.: A multidisciplinary approach to unlocking television broadcast archives. Interdisciplinary Science Reviews 34, 253–267 (2009)
3. Sivic, J., Zisserman, A.: Video Google: A text retrieval approach to object matching in videos. In: IEEE International Conference on Computer Vision, pp. 1470–1477 (2003)
4. Zhang, J., Marszałek, M., Lazebnik, S., Schmid, C.: Local features and kernels for classification of texture and object categories: A comprehensive study. International Journal of Computer Vision 73, 213–238 (2007)
5. Everingham, M., Van Gool, L., Williams, C., Winn, J., Zisserman, A.: The pascal visual object classes (VOC) challenge. International Journal of Computer Vision 88, 303–338 (2010)
6. van de Sande, K.E.A., Gevers, T., Snoek, C.G.M.: Evaluating color descriptors for object and scene recognition. IEEE Transactions on Pattern Analysis and Machine Intelligence 32, 1582–1596 (2010)
7. Jiang, Y.G., Yang, J., Ngo, C.W., Hauptmann, A.: Representations of keypoint-based semantic concept detection: A comprehensive study. IEEE Transactions on Multimedia 12, 42–53 (2010)
8. van de Sande, K.E.A., Gevers, T.: University of Amsterdam at the Visual Concept Detection and Annotation Tasks. The Information Retrieval Series: Image CLEF, vol. 32, ch. 18, pp. 343–358. Springer (2010)
9. Gaidon, A., Marszałek, M., Schmid, C.: The PASCAL visual object classes challenge 2008 submission. Technical report, INRIA-LEAR (2008)
10. Snoek, C.G.M., van de Sande, K.E.A., de Rooij, O., Huurnink, B., Uijlings, J.R.R., van Liempt, M., Bugalho, M., Trancoso, I., Yan, F., Tahir, M.A., Mikolajczyk, K., Kittler, J., de Rijke, M., Geusebroek, J.M., Gevers, T., Worring, M., Koelma, D.C., Smeulders, A.W.M.: The MediaMill TRECVID 2009 semantic video search engine. In: Proceedings of the TRECVID Workshop (2009)
11. Wang, D., Liu, X., Luo, L., Li, J., Zhang, B.: Video diver: generic video indexing with diverse features. In: ACM International Workshop on Multimedia Information Retrieval, pp. 61–70 (2007)
12. Smeaton, A.F., Over, P., Kraaij, W.: Evaluation campaigns and TRECVid. In: ACM International Workshop on Multimedia Information Retrieval, pp. 321–330 (2006)
13. Bay, H., Ess, A., Tuytelaars, T., Van Gool, L.: Speeded-up robust features (SURF). Computer Vision and Image Understanding 110, 346–359 (2008)
14. Uijlings, J.R.R., Smeulders, A.W.M., Scha, R.J.H.: Real-time bag-of-words, approximately. In: ACM International Conference on Image and Video Retrieval (2009)
15. Chang, C.C., Li, Y.C., Yeh, J.B.: Fast codebook search algorithms based on tree-structured vector quantization. Pattern Recognition Letters 27, 1077–1086 (2006)
16. Moosmann, F., Triggs, B., Jurie, F.: Fast discriminative visual codebooks using randomized clustering forests. In: Neural Information Processing Systems, pp. 985–992 (2006)
17. Cornelis, N., Van Gool, L.: Fast scale invariant feature detection and matching on programmable graphics hardware. In: IEEE Computer Vision and Pattern Recognition Workshops (2008)
18. Sinha, S.N., Frahm, J.M., Pollefeys, M., Genc, Y.: Feature tracking and matching in video using programmable graphics hardware. Machine Vision and Applications (2007)
19. Owens, J.D., Houston, M., Luebke, D., Green, S., Stone, J.E., Phillips, J.C.: GPU computing. Proceedings of the IEEE 96, 879–899 (2008)
20. Sharp, T.: Implementing Decision Trees and Forests on a GPU. In: Forsyth, D., Torr, P., Zisserman, A. (eds.) ECCV 2008, Part IV. LNCS, vol. 5305, pp. 595–608. Springer, Heidelberg (2008)

21. Catanzaro, B., Sundaram, N., Keutzer, K.: Fast support vector machine training and classification on graphics processors. In: International Conference on Machine Learning, pp. 104–111 (2008)
22. Datta, R., Joshi, D., Li, J., Wang, J.Z.: Image retrieval: Ideas, influences, and trends of the new age. ACM Computing Surveys 40, 1–60 (2008)
23. Lowe, D.G.: Distinctive image features from scale-invariant keypoints. International Journal of Computer Vision 60, 91–110 (2004)
24. Mikolajczyk, K., et al.: A comparison of affine region detectors. International Journal of Computer Vision 65, 43–72 (2005)
25. Geusebroek, J.M., Smeulders, A.W.M., van de Weijer, J.: Fast anisotropic gauss filtering. IEEE Transactions on Image Processing 12, 938–943 (2003)
26. Jégou, H., Douze, M., Schmid, C.: Packing bag-of-features. In: IEEE International Conference on Computer Vision (2009)
27. van Gemert, J.C., Veenman, C.J., Smeulders, A.W.M., Geusebroek, J.M.: Visual word ambiguity. IEEE Transactions on Pattern Analysis and Machine Intelligence 32, 1271–1283 (2010)
28. Cai, D., He, X., Han, J.: Efficient kernel discriminant analysis via spectral regression. In: IEEE International Conference on Data Mining, pp. 427–432 (2007)
29. Chang, C.C., Lin, C.J.: LIBSVM: a library for support vector machines. (2001) Software available at http://www.csie.ntu.edu.tw/~cjlin/libsvm
30. Do, T.-N., Nguyen, V.-H., Poulet, F.: Speed Up SVM Algorithm for Massive Classification Tasks. In: Tang, C., Ling, C.X., Zhou, X., Cercone, N.J., Li, X. (eds.) ADMA 2008. LNCS (LNAI), vol. 5139, pp. 147–157. Springer, Heidelberg (2008)
31. Sengupta, S., Harris, M., Zhang, Y., Owens, J.D.: Scan primitives for GPU computing. In: Graphics Hardware, pp. 97–106 (2007)
32. Chang, D., Jones, N.A., Li, D., Ouyang, M.: Compute pairwise euclidean distances of data points with GPUs. In: Intelligent Systems and Control, pp. 278–283 (2008)
33. Snoek, C.G.M., Worring, M., van Gemert, J.C., Geusebroek, J.M., Smeulders, A.W.M.: The challenge problem for automated detection of 101 semantic concepts in multimedia. In: ACM International Conference on Multimedia, pp. 421–430 (2006)

Parallel Generalized Thresholding Scheme for Live Dense Geometry from a Handheld Camera

Jan Stühmer[1,2], Stefan Gumhold[2], and Daniel Cremers[1]

[1] Department of Computer Science, TU Munich, Germany
[2] Department of Computer Science, TU Dresden, Germany

Abstract. Inspired by recent successes in parallelized optic flow estimation, we propose a variational method which allows to directly estimate dense depth fields from a single hand-held camera in real-time conditions. In particular we show how the central ingredient of the corresponding optic flow method, namely a thresholding scheme, can be generalized to the problem of geometric reconstruction considered in this paper and how it can be parallelized on recent graphics cards. We compare alternative parallelization strategies and experimentally validate that high-quality depth maps can be computed in a few milliseconds from a hand-held camera.

1 Introduction

1.1 From Optic Flow to Geometric Reconstruction

Over the last years parallel algorithms accelerated by means of graphics hardware have revolutionized many areas of Computer Vision, bringing computationally intense challenges within the realm of real-time applications. One of the major breakthroughs in this context was the acceleration of variational optical flow algorithms [1] which allow to compute highly accurate dense motion fields at 640×480 pixels with speeds well above 60 frames per second.

For many computer vision problems the optical flow between two frames provides a correspondence between pairs of pixels in either image which is then further processed, for example to track articulated object models [2] or to reconstruct the depth field of a scene [3]. Yet, in many such cases one is not directly interested in the estimated flow field: For example when reconstructing a static scene from a moving camera as recently done in [3], the estimation of a motion vector field seems entirely unnecessary since apart from the 6-parameter camera motion everything else is static. One may therefore ask: How can we exploit the drastic accelerations of such parallel algorithms without actually computing a flow field?

Recently Stühmer et al. [4] proposed a variational approach to compute dense depth maps from a handheld camera. The estimation of dense geometry from a handheld camera is formulated as a variational approach that can be solved by algorithms that are quite reminiscent of optical flow approaches. Yet rather than computing a vector field that assigns a velocity to each pixel, the geometry

K.N. Kutulakos (Ed.): ECCV 2010 Workshops, Part II, LNCS 6554, pp. 450–462, 2012.

of the scene is directly determined in a coarse-to-fine manner. In particular, the central algorithmic component, namely the thresholding scheme proposed in [1] for computing the primal variables can be generalized to the geometry reconstruction problem. In this paper, we revisit this formulation and show how the arising thresholding scheme can be efficiently implemented on graphics cards.

1.2 Related Work

The reconstruction of dense geometry from images is a major challenge in computer vision. Several methods for stereo reconstruction have been suggested, that compute a disparity map from two images. By using GPU-accelerated algorithms, some of these approaches are even realtime capable, for example those based on belief propagation [5]. More precise and very detailed results can be obtained by using multiple input images [6,7]. Because existing multiview stereo approaches usually require calibrated input images from known camera positions and because of the computational complexity, these methods cannot be used in realtime-applications and therefore have been restricted to offline processing.

Recent developments of keyframe based structure from motion algorithms allow highly accurate camera pose estimation in realtime [8]. However, these approaches represent the scene as a sparse point cloud and do not allow a dense reconstruction of the geometry in front of the camera.

Two early precursors of variational approaches to estimate dense depth maps were proposed in [9,10] One of the central differences of our approach is that it makes use of quadratic relaxation and an efficient primal dual optimization strategy and allows to use robust error norms both for the data term and the regularizer.

The usage of graphics hardware as processing platform for computer vision problems has lead to realtime variational approaches in the field of optic flow computation. By parallelizing the computation on the GPU, even sophisticated PDE methods can be implemented in realtime. Highly accurate dense optic flow can be computed by using a total variation regularizer and a robust L^1-norm error measure for the data term [1]. Because both the regularizer and the data term are not continuously differentiable, the minimization of the energy functional involves some computational difficulties. For the minimization of the L^1-norm data term, a so called thresholding scheme has to be used.

In this paper we will provide a generalization of the thresholding scheme used in optic flow computation, that allows live reconstruction of dense geometry from multiple images. We show in detail how the generalized thresholding scheme can be parallelized and therefore efficiently computed on the GPU. A combination of our method with realtime camera tracking allows live dense geometry reconstruction from the images of a handheld camera.

1.3 Variational Methods for Realtime Optic Flow

Zach et al. [1] suggested the following energy functional for the estimation of dense optic flow

$$E(u) = \int_{\Omega} \left\{ |\nabla u| + \lambda |I_1 (\mathbf{x} + u(\mathbf{x})) - I_0 (\mathbf{x})| \right\} d\mathbf{x}, \tag{1}$$

where Ω is the image domain, I_0 and I_1 are two given images and u is the sought vector field that describes the optic flow between both images. The weighting parameter λ controls the influence of the data term in relation to the total variation regularizer.

This functional is not continuously differentiable, and therefore cannot be minimized directly using the Euler-Lagrange formalism. The authors propose to decouple the data term and the regularizer, as it has been previously suggested by Aujol et al. [11]. This leads to the following convex approximation

$$E_{\theta} = \int_{\Omega} \left\{ |\nabla u| + \frac{1}{2\theta}(u - v)^2 + \lambda |\rho(v, \mathbf{x})| \right\} d\mathbf{x}, \tag{2}$$

where $\theta > 0$ is a small constant. With ρ we denote the residual of the linearized data term

$$\rho(v, \mathbf{x}) := I_1(\mathbf{x} + u_0) + \langle \nabla I_1(\mathbf{x} + u_0), v - u_0 \rangle - I_0(\mathbf{x}), \tag{3}$$

where u_0 is a given flow field.

Because the regularizer and data term are decoupled and do not share any variables, a solution of Eq. 2 can be obtained with an alternating minimization scheme. The first step of this alternating scheme is the minimization of Eq. 2 for u. This sub problem is also known as the ROF energy model for image denoising [12] and can be solved using Chambolle's algorithm [13]. By minimizing Eq. 2 for v we obtain the update step of the data term. This update can be computed with a relatively simple thresholding scheme that follows directly from the three possible cases $\rho(v) > 0$, $\rho(v) < 0$ and $\rho(v) = 0$.

By subsequently solving the convex minimization problem and taking each new solution as point u_0 for the linearization of the data term, the flow field can be computed in an iterative warping scheme.

2   Dense Depthmap Estimation from Multiple Images

Instead of estimating a vector field of two-dimensional optic flow vectors, we will provide a method for dense geometry reconstruction from multiple images by minimizing the functional

$$E(h) = \lambda \int_{\Omega_0} \sum_{i \in \mathcal{I}(\mathbf{x})} |I_i (\pi (g_i(h \cdot \mathbf{x}))) - I_0 (\mathbf{x})| \, d\mathbf{x} + \int_{\Omega_0} |\nabla h| \, d\mathbf{x} \tag{4}$$

with respect to a scalar depth field $h : \Omega \rightarrow \mathbb{R}$. Here $\mathbf{x}$ denotes the 2D image location in homogeneous coordinates, $h \cdot \mathbf{x}$ denotes the corresponding 3D coordinate and g_i the rigid body transformation into the camera frame i, and π is the projection from homogeneous coordinates to pixel coordinates regarding a

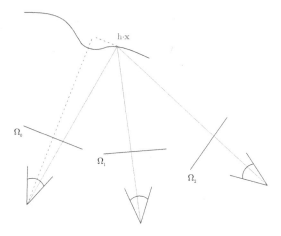

Fig. 1. The depthmap h is defined for the coordinate frame of camera 0. The 3D-point $h \cdot \mathbf{x}$ lies on the surface of the depthmap.

calibrated camera model, in the simplest case this is the perspective projection $\pi \left(x\ y\ z \right) = \left(x/z\ y/z\ 1 \right)$.

The set $\mathcal{I}(\mathbf{x})$ contains the indices of all images for which $\pi(g_i(h \cdot \mathbf{x}))$ is inside the image boundaries of I_i. In the following we will use the short form $I_i(h, \mathbf{x})$ for $I_i \left(\pi(g_i(h \cdot \mathbf{x})) \right)$.

This functional is inspired by variational optic flow methods where a robust regularizer allows to preserve discontinuities in the displacement field. By using the L^1 error measure also in the data term, outliers can be handled robustly. In our case we expect similar advantages: The total variation regularizer enables the reconstruction of dense continuous surfaces while preserving discontinuities at object boundaries. The sum of L^1-norm error measures in the data term is motivated by robust statistics and provides robustness against outliers that arise from sensor noise, illumination changes and occlusion. However, using these robust error norms gives rise to some difficulties when solving the functional, that we will address in the following.

We linearize the images I_i by using a first order Taylor expansion, i.e.

$$I_i(h, \mathbf{x}) = I_i(h_0, \mathbf{x}) + (h - h_0) \left. \frac{d}{dh} I_i(h, \mathbf{x}) \right|_{h_0} \tag{5}$$

where h_0 is a given depth map. Because this linearization only holds for small innovations of the depthmap, the whole minimization process is embedded into a coarse-to-fine warping strategy [14,15].

The derivative $\frac{d}{dh} I_i(h, \mathbf{x})$ can be considered as a directional derivative in direction of a differential vector on the image plane of I_i that results from a variation of h. By using the chain rule, this derivative can be expressed as the scalar product of the gradient of $I_i(h, \mathbf{x})$ with the mentioned differential vector, i.e.

$$\frac{d}{dh} I_i(h, \mathbf{x}) = \nabla I_i(h, \mathbf{x}) \cdot \frac{d}{dh} \pi(g_i(h \cdot \mathbf{x})). \tag{6}$$

The differential vector

$$\frac{d}{dh} \pi(g_i(h \cdot \mathbf{x})) = \begin{pmatrix} \frac{d}{dh} x' \\ \frac{d}{dh} y' \end{pmatrix} \tag{7}$$

needs to be computed with respect to the chosen camera model.

With above linear approximation for $I_i(h, \mathbf{x})$ we can express the current residual of the data term for input image i as

$$\rho_i(h, \mathbf{x}) := I_i(h_0, \mathbf{x}) + (h - h_0) \left. \frac{d}{dh} I_i(h, \mathbf{x}) \right|_{h_0} - I_0(\mathbf{x}) \tag{8}$$

Inserting this expression into the original energy functional (Eq. 4) gives

$$E(h) = \lambda \int_\Omega \sum_{i \in \mathcal{I}(\mathbf{x})} |\rho_i(h, \mathbf{x})| \; d\mathbf{x} + \int_\Omega |\nabla h| \; d\mathbf{x}. \tag{9}$$

This functional is still difficult to minimize, because it is not continuously differentiable and therefore the Euler-Lagrange formalism cannot be used directly. By decoupling the data term and the regularizer [11] we get the following convex approximation of Eq. 4:

$$E_\theta = \int_\Omega \left\{ |\nabla u| + \frac{1}{2\theta} (u - h)^2 + \lambda \sum_{i \in \mathcal{I}(\mathbf{x})} |\rho_i(h, \mathbf{x})| \right\} d\mathbf{x}. \tag{10}$$

The proposed approximation Eq. 10 is convex, thus the functional can be minimized using an alternating minimization procedure in u and h:

1. For fixed h solve Eq. 10 for u

$$\min_u \int_\Omega \left\{ |\nabla u| + \frac{1}{2\theta} (u - h)^2 \right\} d\mathbf{x}. \tag{11}$$

This optimization problem is exactly the ROF model [12], with θ as regularization parameter. We can use Chambolle's projected gradient descend method to solve this problem [13].

2. For fixed u solve Eq. 10 for h

$$\min_h \int_\Omega \left\{ \frac{1}{2\theta} (u - h)^2 + \lambda \sum_{i \in \mathcal{I}(\mathbf{x})} |\rho_i(h, \mathbf{x})| \right\} d\mathbf{x}. \tag{12}$$

This minimization problem can be solved point-wise, because it does not depend on any spatial derivatives of u any more. We will show in the following, how this minimization problem can be solved efficiently with a generalized thresholding scheme.

3   Generalized Thresholding Scheme

The second step of the alternation scheme offers some difficulties, because the sum of absolute valued functions results in multiple critical points, where the whole data term is not differentiable. Thus, a simple thresholding scheme as in the optical flow problem cannot be used. Nevertheless we will provide a generalization of the thresholding scheme that allows a closed-form solution of Eq. 12, that is a further generalization of the concept presented in [7].

For fixed h_0 and $\mathbf{x}$ the linearized data term ρ_i for each image Eq. 8 can be written in the general form of a linear function

$$\rho_i(h, \mathbf{x}) = a_i\, h + b_i, \tag{13}$$

where

$$a_i := I_i^h(\mathbf{x}) \quad \text{and} \quad b_i := I_i(h, \mathbf{x}_0) - h_0\, I_i^h(\mathbf{x}) - I_0(\mathbf{x}). \tag{14}$$

In the following we will consider h_0 and $\mathbf{x}$ as fixed and therefore we simplify our notation and omit the dependencies of a_i and b_i from these fixed values.

The absolute valued functions $|\rho_i(h)|$ are differentiable with respect to h except at their critical points, where one of the ρ_i equals zero and changes its sign. Let us denote these critical points as

$$t_i := -\frac{b_i}{a_i} = -\frac{I_i(h, \mathbf{x}_0) - h_0\, I_i^h(\mathbf{x}) - I_0(\mathbf{x})}{I_i^h(\mathbf{x})}, \tag{15}$$

where $i \in \mathcal{I}(\mathbf{x})$.

At these points Eq. 11 is not differentiable, as the corresponding ρ_i changes its sign. Without loss of generality we can assume that $t_i \leq t_{i+1}$, i.e. we obtain a sorted sequence of $\{\rho_i : i \in \mathcal{I}(\mathbf{x})\}$, that is sorted by the values of their critical points. In order to avoid special cases we add $t_0 = -\infty$ and $t_{|\mathcal{I}(\mathbf{x})|+1} = +\infty$ to this sequence.

Proposition 1. *The minimizer of Eq. 12 can be found using the following strategy: If the stationary point*

$$h_1 := u - \lambda\theta \left(\sum_{i\in\mathcal{I}(\mathbf{x}):i\leq k} I_i^h(\mathbf{x}) - \sum_{j\in\mathcal{I}(\mathbf{x}):j>k} I_j^h(\mathbf{x}) \right) \tag{16}$$

lies in the interior of (t_k, t_{k+1}) for some $k \in \mathcal{I}(\mathbf{x})$, then $h = h_1$. Else the minimizer of Eq. 12 can be found among the set of critical points:

$$h = \arg\min_{h_2\in\{t_i\}} \left(\frac{1}{2\theta}(u - h_2)^2 + \lambda \sum_{i\in\mathcal{I}(\mathbf{x})} |\rho_i(h_2, \mathbf{x})| \right). \tag{17}$$

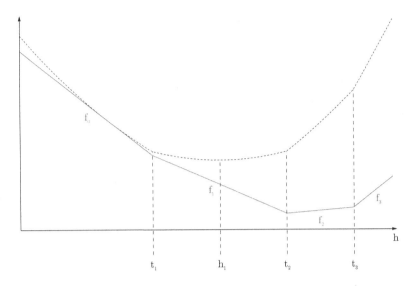

Fig. 2. The minimizations problem in the second step of the alternation scheme Eq. 12 (blue) can be written as the sum of a quadratic function and a piecewise linear function (red). In the interior of the intervals (t_k, t_{k+1}) this term is differentiable with respect to h. In this illustration the minimum is at the critical point h_1 that lies in the interval (t_1, t_2).

Proof. First we show, that Eq. 12 can be written as the sum of a quadratic function with a linear function in the interior of each interval (t_k, t_{k+1}) with $k \in \{0, |\mathcal{I}(\mathbf{x})|\}$. This is also illustrated in Fig. 2. We replace the absolute value function by using the signum function

$$\sum_{i \in \mathcal{I}(\mathbf{x})} |\rho_i(h, \mathbf{x})| = \sum_{i \in \mathcal{I}(\mathbf{x})} |a_i h + b_i| \tag{18}$$

$$= \sum_{i \in \mathcal{I}(\mathbf{x})} \left\{ \mathrm{sgn}\left(\rho_i(h, \mathbf{x})\right) (a_i h + b_i) \right\} \tag{19}$$

$$= \sum_{i \in \mathcal{I}(\mathbf{x})} \left\{ \mathrm{sgn}\left(\rho_i(h, \mathbf{x})\right) a_i \right\} h + \sum_{i \in \mathcal{I}(\mathbf{x})} \left\{ \mathrm{sgn}\left(\rho_i(h, \mathbf{x})\right) b_i \right\}. \tag{20}$$

In order to write above equation in the general form of linear functions, we need to eliminate the signum functions. Let us consider the interior of an interval (t_k, t_{k+1}) with $k \in \{0, |\mathcal{I}(\mathbf{x})|\}$. If h' lies in the interior of the interval (t_k, t_{k+1}), i.e. $h' > t_k$ and $h' < t_{k+1}$, then by definition of the sorted sequence $\{\rho_i\}$ it holds that

$$\mathrm{sgn}\left(\rho_i(h', \mathbf{x})\right) = +1 \text{ if } i < k \tag{21}$$

$$\mathrm{sgn}\left(\rho_i(h', \mathbf{x})\right) = -1 \text{ if } i \geq k. \tag{22}$$

By replacing the signum functions with above expressions the data term can be written in the general form of a linear function f_k for each interval $k \in \{0, |\mathcal{I}(\mathbf{x})|\}$

$$\sum_{i \in \mathcal{I}(\mathbf{x})} |\rho_i(h', \mathbf{x})| = \tilde{a}_k \, h' + \tilde{b}_k =: f_k(h') \tag{23}$$

with

$$\tilde{a}_k = \sum_{i \in \mathcal{I}(\mathbf{x}):i<k} a_i - \sum_{j \in \mathcal{I}(\mathbf{x}):j\geq k} a_j \tag{24}$$

and

$$\tilde{b}_k = \sum_{i \in \mathcal{I}(\mathbf{x}):i<k} b_i - \sum_{j \in \mathcal{I}(\mathbf{x}):j\geq k} b_j. \tag{25}$$

As a result Eq. 12 can be written as

$$\frac{1}{2\theta}(u - h')^2 + \lambda \, f_k(h'), \tag{26}$$

where h' lies in the interior of (t_k, t_{k+1}).

By differentiating above equation with respect to h' we get the stationary point

$$h_1 = u - \lambda \theta \, \tilde{a}_k \tag{27}$$

$$= u - \lambda \theta \left(\sum_{i \in \mathcal{I}(\mathbf{x}):i<k} a_i - \sum_{j \in \mathcal{I}(\mathbf{x}):j\geq k} a_j \right) \tag{28}$$

$$= u - \lambda \theta \left(\sum_{i \in \mathcal{I}(\mathbf{x}):i\leq k} I_i^h(\mathbf{x}) - \sum_{j \in \mathcal{I}(\mathbf{x}):j>k} I_j^h(\mathbf{x}) \right) \tag{29}$$

Such a stationary point h_1 exists, if it stays inside the interval (t_k, t_{k+1}) for some $k \in \{0, |\mathcal{I}(\mathbf{x})|\}$. If no stationary point can be found for any of the intervals, the minimizer of Eq. 12 resides on the boundary of one of the intervals, i.e. the minimizer can be found among the set of critical points $\{t_i\}$. $\qquad \square$

4 Generalized Thresholding Scheme on the GPU

We implemented the proposed method on the GPU using the CUDA (Compute Unified Device Architecture) framework. For the computation of the generalized thresholding scheme first we need a sequence of the coefficients of ρ_i, that is sorted by the critical points t_i. This sorting operation needs to be performed only once for each linearization of the data term, because the values of t_i and the coefficients do not depend on the further iterations. This step can be computed in a parallel-sequential manner on the graphics hardware, i.e. for each pixel of the depthmap, one thread (x, y) sorts the coefficients of all ρ_i at this point (x, y). Because the number of images is rather small a simple bubblesort algorithm is used in each thread.

The output of this sorting step is the sorted sequence of critical points t_k, the sum of the derivatives

$$e_k := \sum_{i \in \mathcal{I}(\mathbf{x}):i \le k} I_i^h(\mathbf{x}) - \sum_{j \in \mathcal{I}(\mathbf{x}):j > k} I_j^h(\mathbf{x}),$$

and

$$f_k := \sum_{i \in \mathcal{I}(\mathbf{x})} |\rho_i(\mathbf{x}, t_k)|, \tag{30}$$

the residuals of the data terms at the critical points. With these coefficients the values of h_1 (Eq. 16) and h_2 (Eq. 17) can be computed efficiently in every iteration of the minimization scheme.

5   Experimental Results

We evaluated two different GPU implementations of the general thresholding scheme. The first (implementation A) is a parallel sequential implementation, where one thread is assigned to each pixel of the depthmap. This thread takes the data of the views $I_1 \ldots I_n$ as input and iteratively determines the minimizer by sequential processing of the data of each view.

Because each thread can stop any further computation when the first stationary point is found, the amount of computation varies for each thread. This

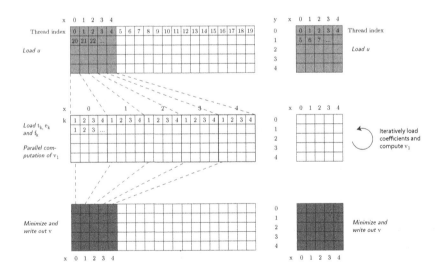

Fig. 3. Two different implementations of the generalized thresholding scheme. The implementation on the left is higher parallelized and allows a better performance balancing when the number of views increases. In the implementation on the right each thread processes the data sequentially.

usually results in suboptimal performance and lower occupancy of the GPU. Therefore we evaluated a second implementation, that is highly parallelized and has a deterministic computational load for each thread. By assigning multiple threads to each pixel of the depthmap, the data of all views I_i can be processed in parallel. While all necessary computations to find the stationary points can be performed highly parallelized, only the last step, the determination of the minimal value, involves sequential processing. In the following we will refer to this kind of implementation as implementation B. The difference of both implementations is depicted in Fig. 3.

5.1   Comparison of Different GPU Implementations

We optimized the block sizes for both algorithms by searching values of the power of two for the block-width and -height. For the parallelized implementation A, we expected that the optimal block-size would depend on the amount of data that is processed in parallel, in this case on the number of input images. The results show, that the optimal block-size is determined by the size of the small block in Fig. 3, that contains the pixels of the depthmap. While the size of the bigger block where the values of h_1 are actually computed depends on the number of images, the optimal size of the small block stays constant. The dependency between runtime performance and the size of this small block is shown in Fig. 4a for different number of input images. A size of 32×1 outperforms all other tested configurations on a NVidia Tesla C1060. On a recent GTX 480 the optimal size is 64×1.

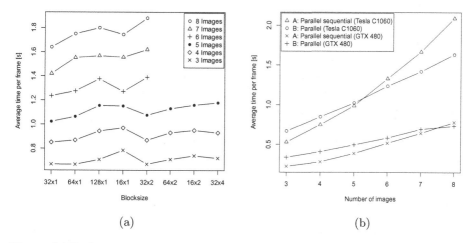

(a)   (b)

Fig. 4. (a) Performance of algorithm B on a Tesla C1060 for different sizes of the part of the depthmap that is processed in parallel. (b) Comparison of both implementation strategies for different number of input images. When the amount of input data increases, the higher parallelized algorithm B is faster than algorithm A.

(a) Reference camera image (b) Reconstructed geometry   (c) Synthesized View

Fig. 5. Dense depthmaps estimated from a single moving camera

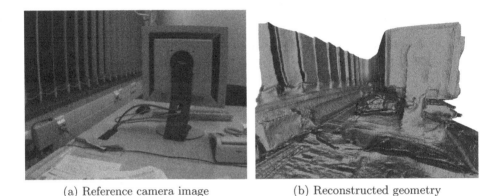

(a) Reference camera image   (b) Reconstructed geometry

Fig. 6. Note the accurate reconstruction of small-scale details like the network socket and cords.

We also compared the performance of both implementations for different number of input images. While the parallel sequential implementation A is faster for smaller number of input images, the parallelized implementation B shows a better performance for higher numbers. The exact number of input images, for which implementation B performs better than A, depends on the specific hardware configuration. The parallelized algorithm B shows a linear dependency between runtime performance and the number if input images. The images and the reconstructed depthmap in both experiments are of size 450×375.

5.2   Real World Data

The combination with a recently proposed method for realtime camera tracking [8] allows the reconstruction of dense geometry with a single hand-held camera. Figure 5 shows the input image of the reference camera, the reconstructed geometry and a synthesized view. Another example is shown in figure 6. The proposed method computes a dense geometry rather than the location of sparse

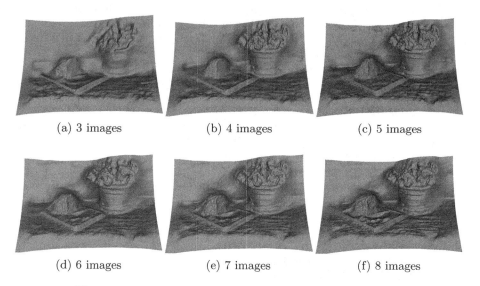

(a) 3 images   (b) 4 images   (c) 5 images

(d) 6 images   (e) 7 images   (f) 8 images

Fig. 7. Multiple images allow a more detailed reconstruction.

feature points. Increasing the number of input images allows a finer and more detailed reconstruction as shown in figure 7.

6   Conclusion

In this paper we adapted state-of-the-art variational optic flow algorithms so as to directly generate dense depth maps in a coarse-to-fine primal dual algorithm. The algorithm runs on a single GPU and allows to compute highly accurate dense geometric information within fractions of a second. In particular, we present a GPU implementation of the generalized thresholding scheme arising in the computation of the primal variables. We experimentally compare two alternative strategies of parallelization that differ with respect to the amount of balancing assured across different threads. Experimental results show that one implementation shows a higher performance when the number of views is rather small, while the other strategy is better suited when the input data increases. Highly accurate and detailed results from real world image data are presented.

References

1. Zach, C., Pock, T., Bischof, H.: A Duality Based Approach for Realtime TV-L1 Optical Flow. In: Hamprecht, F.A., Schnörr, C., Jähne, B. (eds.) DAGM 2007. LNCS, vol. 4713, pp. 214–223. Springer, Heidelberg (2007)
2. Brox, T., Rosenhahn, B., Gall, J., Cremers, D.: Combined region- and motion-based 3d tracking of rigid and articulated objects. IEEE Transactions on Pattern Analysis and Machine Intelligence (2009)

3. Newcombe, R.A., Davison, A.J.: Live dense reconstruction with a single moving camera. In: Int. Conf. on Computer Vision and Pattern Recognition (2010)

4. Stühmer, J., Gumhold, S., Cremers, D.: Real-Time Dense Geometry from a Hand-held Camera. In: Goesele, M., Roth, S., Kuijper, A., Schiele, B., Schindler, K. (eds.) DAGM 2010. LNCS, vol. 6376, pp. 11–20. Springer, Heidelberg (2010)

5. Yang, Q., Wang, L., Yang, R., Wang, S., Liao, M., Nistér, D.: Real-time global stereo matching using hierarchical belief propagation. In: British Machine Vision Association, BMVC, pp. 989–998. (2006)

6. Kolev, K., Cremers, D.: Continuous ratio optimization via convex relaxation with applications to multiview 3d reconstruction. In: Int. Conf. on Computer Vision and Pattern Recognition, pp. 1858–1864 (2009)

7. Zach, C., Pock, T., Bischof, H.: A globally optimal algorithm for robust TV-L^1 range image integration. In: IEEE Int. Conf. on Computer Vision, Rio de Janeiro, Brazil. LNCS, IEEE (2007)

8. Klein, G., Murray, D.: Parallel tracking and mapping for small AR workspaces. In: Proc. Sixth IEEE and ACM International Symposium on Mixed and Augmented Reality (ISMAR 2007), Nara, Japan (2007)

9. Robert, L., Deriche, R., Faugeras, O.D.: Dense depth recovery from stereo images. In: ECAI 1992: Proceedings of the 10th European Conference on Artificial Intelligence, pp. 821–823. John Wiley & Sons, Inc., New York (1992)

10. Robert, L., Deriche, R.: Dense Depth Map Reconstruction: A Minimization and Regularization Approach which Preserves Discontinuities. In: Buxton, B.F., Cipolla, R. (eds.) ECCV 1996. LNCS, vol. 1064, pp. 439–451. Springer, Heidelberg (1996)

11. Aujol, J.F., Gilboa, G., Chan, T., Osher, S.: Structure-texture image decomposition–modeling, algorithms, and parameter selection. Int. J. Comput. Vision 67, 111–136 (2006)

12. Rudin, L.I., Osher, S., Fatemi, E.: Nonlinear total variation based noise removal algorithms. Physica D 60, 259–268 (1992)

13. Chambolle, A.: An algorithm for total variation minimization and applications. J. Math. Im. Vis. 20, 89–97 (2004)

14. Nagel, H., Enkelmann, W.: An investigation of smoothness constraints for the estimation of displacement vector fields from image sequences. IEEE Trans. on Patt. Anal. and Mach. Intell. 8, 565–593 (1986)

15. Black, M.J., Anandan, P.: The robust estimation of multiple motions: Parametric and piecewise–smooth flow fields. Comp. Vis. Graph. Image Proc.: IU 63, 75–104 (1996)

Fast Organization of Large Photo Collections Using CUDA

Tim Johnson, Pierre Fite-Georgel, Rahul Raguram, and Jan-Michael Frahm

University of North Carolina at Chapel Hill, Department of Computer Science

Abstract. In this paper, we introduce a system for the automatic organization of photo collections consisting of millions of images downloaded from the Internet. To our knowledge, this is the first approach that tackles this problem exclusively through the use of general-purpose GPU computing techniques. By leveraging the inherent parallelism of the problem and through the use of efficient GPU-based algorithms, our system is able to effectively summarize datasets containing up to three million images in approximately 16 hours on a single PC, which is orders of magnitude faster compared to current state of the art techniques. In this paper, we present the various algorithmic considerations and design aspects of our system, and describe in detail the various steps of the processing pipeline. Additionally, we demonstrate the effectiveness of the system by showing results for a variety of real-world datasets, ranging from the scale of a single landmark, to that of an entire city.

Fig. 1. A subset of the *iconic* images automatically found by our system, for the Berlin dataset

K.N. Kutulakos (Ed.): ECCV 2010 Workshops, Part II, LNCS 6554, pp. 463–476, 2012.

1   Introduction

Organizing Internet photo collections is an important task for many computer vision applications. For instance, partitioning a large set of photographs into clusters of similar images allows for more efficient post-processing tasks, such as structure from motion [1,2]. In addition, the organization of images into semantically consistent groups can also greatly enhance the browsing experience[1]. For the summarization strategy described in this paper, we define "similar" images as those which represent the same scene or landmark, taken from nearby vantage points, and under similar lighting conditions. Given these groupings of similar images, we then automatically extract a small subset of representative or *iconic* images that represent dominant aspects of the scene, and thus provide a concise visual summary of the dataset. This approach lends itself naturally to a hierarchical organization of the dataset into a form that is suitable both for 3D reconstruction as well as browsing.

With the ever-increasing abundance of images on the Internet, photo collections for a single search term now yield datasets on the order of millions of images – for example, a query for Rome on the photo sharing website Flickr yields approximately 3.4 million images. To operate on massive datasets of this form within a reasonable time-frame, it thus becomes essential to develop efficient algorithms that are capable of elegantly scaling to *Internet-scale* datasets. This is a particularly important consideration, given that the amount of digital information is predicted to increase exponentially in the years to come[2]. In this paper, we introduce an efficient method for the automatic organization of large scale photo collections ranging from several tens of thousands of images (the scale of a single landmark) to millions of images (representing an entire city). To our knowledge, this is the first system that runs completely on the GPU and scales to datasets on the order of millions of images.

In the following sections of the paper, we present previous work leading up to our approach (Section 2), followed by a high-level overview of our system (Section 3). We then provide an in-depth look at each step of the pipeline along with a discussion of important implementation details and design decisions (Section 4). The paper concludes with a presentation of results on three challenging real-world datasets (Section 5).

2   Previous Work

Organizing large scale photo collections has been of interest to many researchers in recent years [3,4,1,5,6,2]. The various approaches can be broadly classified into two categories: the first group uses two-view geometric constraints between images to determine similarity, while the second category uses appearance cues,

---

[1] For instance, tag clusters on Flickr:
http://www.flickr.com/photos/tags/berlin/clusters/

[2] http://www.emc.com/collateral/analyst-reports/diverse-exploding-digital-universe.pdf

or constraints from object/scene recognition to measure image similarity. The notable departures from this classification are the approaches introduced in [1] and [2], which are hybrid approaches combining both appearance and geometric constraints to perform scene summarization, reconstruction and recognition. The method presented in this paper is similar in spirit to the approach of [1], but scales each of the techniques used to the true scale of internet photo collections, as in [2]. However, in addition to [2], we also propose a way to parallelize the computationally expensive two-view geometric verification step on the GPU, in addition to the appearance grouping steps.

The first work that performed 3D reconstruction of landmarks from internet photo collections containing a few thousand images was the *Photo Tourism* system [4]. This method yields high-quality reconstruction results with the help of exhaustive pairwise image matching and global bundle adjustment after inserting each new view. Both of these steps are computationally prohibitive on large scale datasets as the exhaustive matching grows exponentially and is no longer practical given contaminated real-world photo collections. To improve the performance of their system, Snavely et al. [7] find *skeletal sets* of images from the collection, whose reconstruction provides a good approximation to a reconstruction involving all the images. One remaining limitation of this work is that it still requires the exhaustive computation of all two-view relationships in the dataset as a prerequisite. Most recently, Agarwal et al. [5] address this computational challenge by using a computing cluster with up to 500 cores in order to process larger datasets. Similar to our system, the work in [5] uses image recognition techniques such as approximate nearest neighbor search [8] and query expansion [9] to reduce the number of candidate relations from the full exhaustive set. However, in contrast to Agarwal et al., our system uses a *single* PC, thereby achieving an even higher effective processing rate. The main source of the computational advantage we achieve is through the cascaded application of appearance and geometric constraints. By first using computationally cheaper 2D appearance cues, we identify consistent clusters of images that are likely to be spatially related. In turn, this leads to an overall decrease in the number of candidates to be considered for pairwise registration.

Our main goal in this work is to leverage the computing power of the GPU in order to develop a high performance system capable of efficiently organizing large image collections. Strong and Gong present such a system in [10,11], however our system differs in that it does not require a training step. Our system also scales to millions of images, whereas theirs scales to only thousands. Computation of gist vectors on the GPU was proposed in [12], however their results for large datasets were extrapolated from results on smaller datasets. Our paper presents results that were collected from actual runs on datasets of millions of images. To our knowledge, this is the first attempt that implements certain algorithms (binary code generation, RANSAC) on the GPU. In addition to these, since we operate on binary vectors, we have also developed a k-medoids implementation for the GPU, as an alternative to existing k-means implementations [13,14]. Finally, for the geometric verification step, we make use of SiftGPU, a publicly available GPU implementation of SIFT extraction and matching[3].

3   System Overview

In this section, we present a brief description of the main components of our system. At a high-level, the system operates in a hierarchical manner, using both 2D image appearance cues as well as 3D scene geometry in order to solve the task of partitioning images from large Internet photo collections into clusters of similar photographs. The input to the system is a raw Internet photo collection, downloaded using keyword searches on Flickr. It has been observed [15] that these collections can often be significantly contaminated, with a substantial fraction of the images being semantically unrelated to the query. Thus, our system has been designed with a view towards being robust to the significant amount of clutter present in community photo collections. The downloaded images are then subjected to several algorithms in a pipeline, first enforcing a loose grouping of the images based on 2D appearance cues, and subsequently refining the initial partitioning using stricter 3D constraints. This procedure allows for the efficient processing of very large datasets, since the more computationally demanding geometric verification steps are carried out only on smaller subsets of images that are already grouped together by similarity. The end result is a clustering where each image within a cluster is similar in geometric structure, vantage point, and color. The main steps in the pipeline are outlined below.

- **Global Descriptor Extraction** (Sec. 4.1):   In order to cluster images based on similarity, we first need to compute feature vectors for each image. We choose to compute gist descriptors [16] for each image, which has been shown to effectively capture perceptual similarity and has been used to retrieve structurally similar scenes [17]. We combine the gist descriptor with low resolution color descriptions of the image to produce a 368 dimensional feature vector for each image.
- **Conversion to Binary Codes** (Sec. 4.2): To efficiently store the feature vectors on the GPU, we compress them into binary codes. The compressed representation allows all of the data to be simultaneously stored on the GPU, which significantly reduces the amount of data transfer necessary between device and host during the clustering step.
- **Clustering on the Binary Codes** (Sec. 4.3): Given a set of compressed descriptor vectors, we cluster the dataset with a parallel implementation of the k-medoids algorithm [18]. This provides a rough grouping of the dataset into clusters that are similar in global appearance. In addition, this step also filters out a large fraction of unrelated images, since these fall into small and isolated clusters.
- **Geometric Verification** (Sec. 4.4): Once a loose grouping of the images has been obtained, strict geometric constraints are enforced to ensure that

---

[3] http://www.cs.unc.edu/~ccwu/siftgpu

the images within a cluster represent the same scene or structure. This step requires the extraction of SIFT features [19], followed by a RANSAC [20] procedure for estimating the pairwise epipolar geometry [21,22]. Geometrically consistent images, or images that capture the same 3D structure, are retained, while the others are discarded. This produces clean clusters that are consistent both in terms of appearance as well as geometry.

Each of the above steps is implemented in CUDA and runs on one or multiple GPUs. We also plan to make these implementations freely available on the web, for use by the community.

4   Image Organization for Internet Photo Collections

In this section we introduce the details of our proposed processing pipeline. Along with the algorithmic considerations we will discuss design decisions to ensure a efficient use of the highly parallel GPU architecture. In particular we explore the considerations made in regards to memory access patterns, maximizing hardware utilization and minimizing I/O between the host and GPU.

4.1   Global Descriptor Extraction

To boost computational efficiency, we aim at compactly describing each image with a single global image descriptor. We choose the powerful gist descriptor proposed by Oliva and Torralba [16], which was shown to achieve good results for the tasks of scene matching and retrieval [17]. The gist vector is a description of the oriented edges in an image. It is an aggregation of image convolutions that have been downsampled to a resolution of 4x4. Each convolution picks up edge responses at a certain orientation and scale. The convolution kernel used in our implementation is the Gabor filter. In our implementation, we perform a total of 20 convolutions at three different scales. The images we convolve are greyscale thumbnails with a resolution of 128x128, and are cropped accordingly to preserve their original aspect ratio. Performing these operations leads to a 320-dimensional gist vector. It is also typical to augment the gist descriptor with color information, usually by appending an additional vector that carries color information. In contrast to the downsampled L*a*b color space used to incorporate colour information as in [17], our method directly uses the RGB representation of the image. For the task of organizing image collections, we empirically found the two representations to perform comparably. Thus, a 4 × 4 RGB representation is then appended to the gist feature vector. The final descriptor has 368 dimensions, stored as floats.

Computationally, the convolution with the Gabor filter and the downsampling of the images are the most demanding tasks in this step. We improve GPU utilization during the convolution step by efficiently processing the images in batches. Since each of the input images is only of size 128×128, we combine the processing of multiple images to achieve greater occupancy of the GPU. Images are convolved in batches of 256 (determined empirically, we measure no gain with bigger batch sizes) to reduce the number of memory transfers from host to GPU. The images are laid out in row major order, one after the other and are passed to the CUDA kernel for convolution.

The CUDA kernel for convolution assigns 16x16 thread blocks to compute the convolution of some 16x16 patch of the virtual image, and each thread within a block computes one pixel of the convolved image. Prior to dispatching the CUDA kernel, the convolution kernel is transferred into a constant memory buffer. We chose to use constant memory for two main reasons. First, constant memory is cached, so reads from the buffer will be fast. Secondly, constant memory is useful for memory accesses when each thread in a half-warp accesses the same index. In this case, each thread reads from the same location in the convolution kernel simultaneously, providing a slight advantage over textured memory.

Each thread block loads its corresponding image patch into shared memory. It also needs to load in a portion of the image that borders this patch, and the size of this portion is dependent on the size of the convolution kernel. All of these memory loads are coalesced by carefully controlling which threads load a particular part of the image. Once all necessary image data is loaded into shared memory, the patches are convolved with a standard double nested loop, and the sum is written out to global memory.

Before the next convolution is performed, the current convolved images are downsampled to reduce the amount of storage necessary. Downsampling is performed on the virtual image, and care is taken to ensure that sub-image boundaries within the virtual image are preserved. Downsampling is performed in two one-dimensional passes over the virtual image. The thread blocks, accordingly, are 1-dimensional. Since each thread block outputs one downsampled pixel, the size of each thread block is determined by the level of downsampling.

The downsampling kernel essentially performs a sum reduction along a contiguous portion of the image, with a final division to achieve an average value over its portion of the image. Each thread block outputs its result to global memory buffer in a transposed fashion, so that the next pass can read in the image in a set of coalesced memory accesses. After two passes the virtual image has been downsampled in both the x and y directions, and the result remains in the row-major storage format. See Figure 2 for a pictorial explanation.

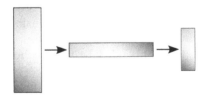

Fig. 2. Visualization of the downsampling process. It is performed in two one-dimensional passes with transpositions after each pass.

Intuitively, the extracted gist descriptors describe the viewpoint, through the edge structure, and the illumination, by means of the subsampled image, of the scene. These gist vectors can thus be leveraged to roughly group together similar images, as outlined in subsequent sections.

4.2   Conversion to Binary Codes

To group together similar images, we would like to perform a clustering procedure on the gist vectors. However, there are some important memory limitations that must be overcome in order to achieve good performance. In order to achieve efficient clustering on the GPU, we require that all feature vectors fit into the GPU memory. Given today's GPU memory limitations, we could only fit about 600K to 700K of the 368 dimensional descriptors into the GPU memory, which is significantly smaller than the dataset sizes that we seek to operate on. Processing the dataset in batches would require a large number of transfers between host and device for each iteration of the clustering algorithm, thus leading to significant overhead. To overcome this limitation, we compress each feature vector into a string of binary numbers, known as a binary code. The particular compression technique we implemented is based on the method of [23]. Since we would like to retain the appearance relationships of the gist vectors, these vectors are compressed in such a way that the Hamming distance between the resulting binary codes approximates the Euclidean distance between the original feature descriptors. Each bit of the code describes on which side of a randomly generated hyper-plane the original GIST descriptor is located. This method of compression has been compared to a simpler locality sensitive hashing method in [2], and it has been shown to preserve feature vector distances sufficiently. The ability to choose the number of bits in our binary codes provides flexibility for the clustering step. We may decrease the number of bits if we wish to manage GPU memory more conservatively, or we may increase the number of bits if we wish to approximate the feature vectors more accurately. To ensure high computational performance, our technique employs the highly optimized CUBLAS library, with the exception of a kernel for converting float vectors into binary strings. This kernel dispatches 1-dimensional thread blocks of length 32, and each thread block produces one unsigned integer of output by performing a bitwise OR reduction on 32 bits. The reduction represents the sgn of 32 floats. For Berlin, using a 512-bit binary code scheme reduces the storage requirement of the features from 3.7GB to 164MB.

4.3   Clustering

Once the binary codes have been generated we can cluster them using a parallel implementation of k-medoids. Similar to k-means, the standard k-medoids algorithm [18] takes n features as input, and outputs k clusters. It differs from k-means in that the cluster centers are the most central data elements of the respective clusters, instead of the mean of the cluster center. This accommodates our binary representation of the image descriptors for which the mean is not meaningful. Since the Hamming distance of our binary codes approximates the Euclidean distance of the original gist descriptors, our k-medoids implementation uses this as the distance metric. K-medoids consists of iterations of an assignment step and update step. It is initialized by randomly selecting k distinct binary codes as cluster centers, or *medoids*. During the assignment step, each binary code is associated with the closest medoid by Hamming distance. In the update step, the binary code that minimizes the sum of distances to all other codes in its cluster becomes the new medoid center. We define convergence as the number of medoid changes falling below a defined threshold (we use $0.01k$).

The bottleneck of the k-medoids algorithm is the computation of the Hamming distance matrices for all clusters. Distance matrices are computed in both the assignment and the update stage. In the assignment stage, an $n \times k$ matrix is computed. In the update step, k smaller matrices are computed, one for each cluster. The dimension of each matrix is square and equal to the number of elements in that cluster. Fortunately, this computation is highly parallelizable. Our kernel for computing the distance matrix dispatches as many 16x16 thread blocks as needed to cover the full distance matrix. Each thread computes one entry of the distance matrix, and does so by processing 32 bits of the binary codes at a time. This way, each thread block only requires 128 bytes of shared memory at any given time. An overview of the clustering can be found in Algorithm 1.

Algorithm 1. K-Medoids

```
for i=1 to k do
  randomly assign medoid[i] to a binary code
end for
repeat
  for i=1 to n do
    compute distance of ith binary code to medoids in parallel
    do parallel min-reduce to assign binary code i to closest medoid
  end for
  for i=1 to k do
    compute distance matrix between all elements of cluster i
    do parallel sum-reduce over rows of distance matrix
    do parallel min-reduce of result to find new cluster center
  end for
until converged
```

4.4   Geometric Verification

The initial clusters provided by k-medoids may contain still images which are close in the compressed gist space, but they still may be visually or geometrically inconsistent as shown in Figure 3. Given that the desired output of our system only consists of clusters of images which have captured a consistent geometrical scene structure, we perform a final step to remove inconsistent images. This is performed by selecting the first r images of each cluster (the medoid and the images closest to it) and estimating the epipolar geometry of each image pair within those r images. If any image has less than ρ inliers (we use $\rho = 18$ in all our experiments), they are replaced with the next closest image. Similarly, to [1] this process is repeated until r consistent images are found, or the cluster is rejected. In order to prevent extensive computation for large but inconsistent clusters, we reject a cluster if no consistent set has been found after $3r$ different images have been tested. When a cluster has been verified, the image with the most inliers over the set of r images is declared as the most representative view: the *iconic*. Afterwards, all remaining images are verified against the chosen iconic.

To compute the two-view geometry, we first extract SIFT [19] features using the efficient CUDA SiftGPU implementation. We limit the maximum number of extracted features to 4000 in the interest of computational efficiency. Following this, we compute pairwise putative matches using the CUBLAS library to perform fast matrix multiplication, followed by a distance ratio test to identify likely correspondences. The putative matches are then verified by estimating the fundamental matrix using the 7-point algorithm [24] in a RANSAC framework [20], both of which have been implemented in our system, using CUDA.

Algorithm 2. CUDA QR Decomposition Kernel

```
{Given A, compute matrices Q and R such that A = Q*R}
shared float *sR, *sQ
load A into sR, sQ = I
for k=1 to min(rows-1, cols) do
   compute kth Householder reflector in serial
   apply reflector to sR, sQ in parallel
end for
write sR, sQ to global memory
```

Due to the randomized nature of memory access patterns in RANSAC, implementing RANSAC efficiently on the GPU presents the challenge of achieving coalesced memory accesses. That is, nearby threads access nearby locations in memory. To overcome this, we push N random samples of 7 points onto the GPU, where N is the maximum number of iterations of RANSAC, set to 1024 in our experiments. This way, coalesced reads from memory can still reflect randomized reads of the data. These randomized reads of the data are used as input to the 7-point fundamental matrix estimator.

Estimating the fundamental matrix requires finding solutions to the fundamental matrix constraint $x'^T F x = 0$, where x and x' represent corresponding points across two views. At least seven of these constraints are required to solve for the fundamental matrix [24], so we randomly select 7 correspondences, which define a system of equations. The null space of this system of equations defines the fundamental matrix. To find the null space, we develop a QR decomposition algorithm in CUDA using Householder reflections. The pseudocode for our algorithm is shown in Algorithm 2. Since each thread block decomposes a separate matrix, our CUDA kernel only works for small matrices. This is not a

Fig. 3. An example cluster output from k-medoids on the Tower Bridge dataset. Note the inconsistent images near the bottom.

problem, as the system of linear equations is represented by a 7x9 matrix. The QR decomposition works by solving for one column of R at a time, and multiple columns cannot be solved simultaneously. However, all elements in one column can be solved simultaneously. Multiple blocks can be dispatched simultaneously, allowing for fast QR decompositions of multiple matrices.

Once the fundamental matrices have been generated, they must be evaluated against the entire set of correspondences. This data is stored on a GPU buffer, and we test the Sampson distance for each correspondence against a predefined threshold to identify inliers. We use the adaptive stopping criterion, where the number of iterations is updated based on the highest inlier ratio observed so far.

5   Results

In this section, we present results on three challenging real-world datasets. The experiments were run on a 2 Intel Xeon processor machine (8 available cores), with 50GB RAM and 4 Nvidia GTX 295 GPUs (8 GPU cores). The sift extraction, gist computation and RANSAC modules utilize all 8 GPUs, while the binary compression and clustering steps use 1 GPU, since multiple GPUs would require significant I/O between devices (eg., in the computation of the distance matrix). The number of clusters in k-medoids was chosen to be 10% of the dataset size, capped at a maximum of 100,000 centers.

The three datasets presented in this paper – Notre Dame (90,196 images), Tower Bridge (137,073 images), and Berlin (2,704,448 images) – were downloaded using keyword searches on Flickr. Figure 3 shows an example cluster output from k-medoids for the Tower Bridge dataset. Note that at this stage, only appearance-based cues have been employed. While the cluster demonstrates a appreciable degree of visual similarity, there exist incorrect images that are consistent in appearance, but that do not depict the same scene. Enforcing tighter geometric constraints helps "clean-up" these clusters, as shown in Figure 4.

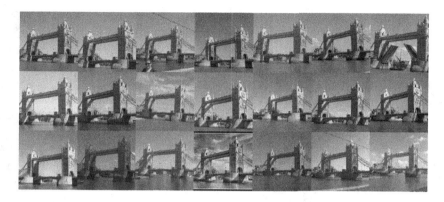

Fig. 4. The same cluster as in Fig. 3 after it has passed through geometric verification. Note how the inconsistent images have been removed.

Figures 5 shows a subset of 120 iconic images for the Notre Dame dataset. It can be seen that this provides a concise summary of the "popular" aspects and viewpoints of the landmark. These iconic images can then be used to seed a structure-from-motion system, since they capture a variety of different camera locations covering the scene. Thus, the process of 3D reconstruction may be initialized using just a small, representative subset of the dataset, thus allowing for the processing of massive image collections. In addition, the iconic images can be used as the top level of a hierarchical browsing system, where each iconic may in turn be expanded to show all the images within the corresponding cluster, which are very similar in appearance and geometry to the iconic of interest. If desired, an additional level in the browsing hierarchy may be formed by grouping together iconic images into related "components" as in [1], thereby providing a three-level organization of the image collection.

To demonstrate some of the advantages of a GPU-based approach, we compared the performance of the proposed GPU RANSAC algorithm versus a very high performance real-time robust estimation technique called ARRSAC [25]. For this experiment, 50 random clusters were selected from the Berlin dataset and geometric verification was performed as outlined in Section 4.4. The results are tabulated in Table 1 for varying numbers of CPU and GPU cores. It can be seen from the table that the use of GPU-RANSAC for the geometric verification step results in a 2-8% improvement in speed, compared to ARRSAC. While this is not a large speedup, it should be noted that ARRSAC is a highly optimized framework, whereas our brute force implementation leaves much room for optimization.

Table 2 lists summary statistics for the complete pipeline operating on all three datasets. The table lists the number of iconics found by our system for each dataset, and it can be seen that these large datasets are efficiently reduced to a small, representative set of iconic images. The table also lists the number of geometrically consistent images that remain in the clusters following the robust geometric verification step of the processing pipeline. On average, roughly

Fig. 5. Subset of 120 iconic images for the Notre Dame dataset. The iconics denote dominant aspects of the scene or landmark, thus providing a concise but representative visual summary of the dataset.

5-35% of the images in each dataset are retained at this stage, though it must be noted this fraction can be increased through additional stages that attempt to match discarded images across different iconic clusters. Finally, Table 2 also lists runtimes for each stage of the pipeline. It can be seen that our GPU-based pipeline is able to process more than two million images in approximately 16

Table 1. Geometric verification performance: ARRSAC vs. our GPU-RANSAC. Timings were collected for different numbers of CPU and GPU cores used simultaneously.

Number of CPU/GPU cores	Geometric verification timing (seconds)	
	ARRSAC	**GPU-RANSAC**
1/1	155.38	152.40
4/4	38.5802	36.8281
8/8	28.299	25.892

Table 2. Summary statistics and timings for each processing step in the pipeline

Dataset	# Iconics	# Images Registered	Gist	Binary Code	Clustering	Geom Verif.
Notre Dame	3,566	27,496	87s	0.79s	20.4s	42min 8s
Tower Bridge	5,479	47,146	138s	1.29s	26.2s	59min 46s
Berlin	13,612	133,634	1hr 1min	28.9s	30min 46s	14hr 27min

hours, on a single PC equipped with graphics hardware. This represents an order of magnitude more data than current state of the art techniques [5].

6 Conclusion

This paper presents a high-performance GPU-based system for organizing large photo collections. The system employs recognition constraints along with 3D geometry, and exploits the underlying parallelism of the organization problem. The system is entirely implemented on the GPU in CUDA, and is capable of efficiently organizing massive image collections, containing millions of images, on a single computer while still producing high-quality results. To our knowledge, this is the first system that uses GPGPU computation to achieve the image organization task.

References

1. Li, X., Wu, C., Zach, C., Lazebnik, S., Frahm, J.-M.: Modeling and Recognition of Landmark Image Collections Using Iconic Scene Graphs. In: Forsyth, D., Torr, P., Zisserman, A. (eds.) ECCV 2008, Part I. LNCS, vol. 5302, pp. 427–440. Springer, Heidelberg (2008)
2. Frahm, J.-M., Fite-Georgel, P., Gallup, D., Johnson, T., Raguram, R., Wu, C., Jen, Y.-H., Dunn, E., Clipp, B., Lazebnik, S., Pollefeys, M.: Building Rome on a Cloudless Day. In: Daniilidis, K., Maragos, P., Paragios, N. (eds.) ECCV 2010, Part IV. LNCS, vol. 6314, pp. 368–381. Springer, Heidelberg (2010)
3. Schaffalitzky, F., Zisserman, A.: Multi-view Matching for Unordered Image Sets, or How Do I Organize My Holiday Snaps? In: Heyden, A., Sparr, G., Nielsen, M., Johansen, P. (eds.) ECCV 2002, Part I. LNCS, vol. 2350, pp. 414–431. Springer, Heidelberg (2002)
4. Snavely, N., Seitz, S.M., Szeliski, R.: Modeling the world from Internet photo collections. International Journal of Computer Vision 80, 189–210 (2008)

5. Agarwal, S., Snavely, N., Simon, I., Seitz, S.M., Szeliski, R.: Building Rome in a day. In: ICCV (2009)
6. Berg, T.L., Berg, A.C.: Finding iconic images. In: The 2nd Internet Vision Workshop at IEEE CVPR (2009)
7. Snavely, N., Seitz, S.M., Szeliski, R.: Skeletal sets for efficient structure from motion. In: CVPR (2008)
8. Arya, S., Mount, D., Netanyahu, N., Silverman, R., Wu, A.: An optimal algorithm for approximate nearest neighbor searching fixed dimensions. JACM 45, 891–923 (1998)
9. Chum, O., Philbin, J., Sivic, J., Isard, M., Zisserman, A.: Total recall: Automatic query expansion with a generative feature model for object retrieval. In: ICCV (2007)
10. Strong, G., Gong, M.: Browsing a Large Collection of Community Photos Based on Similarity on GPU. In: Bebis, G., Boyle, R., Parvin, B., Koracin, D., Remagnino, P., Porikli, F., Peters, J., Klosowski, J., Arns, L., Chun, Y.K., Rhyne, T.-M., Monroe, L. (eds.) ISVC 2008, Part II. LNCS, vol. 5359, pp. 390–399. Springer, Heidelberg (2008)
11. Strong, G., Gong, M.: Organizing and browsing photos using different feature vectors and their evaluations. In: CIVR, pp. 1–8 (2009)
12. Wang, Y., Feng, Z., Guo, H., He, C., Yang, Y.: Scene recognition acceleration using cuda and openmp. In: ICISE, pp. 1422–1425 (2009)
13. Shalom, S.A.A., Dash, M., Tue, M.: Efficient K-Means Clustering Using Accelerated Graphics Processors. In: Song, I.-Y., Eder, J., Nguyen, T.M. (eds.) DaWaK 2008. LNCS, vol. 5182, pp. 166–175. Springer, Heidelberg (2008)
14. Hall, J.D., Hart, J.C.: Abstract gpu acceleration of iterative clustering (2004)
15. Kennedy, L., Chang, S.F., Kozintsev, I.: To search or to label?: Predicting the performance of search-based automatic image classifiers. ACM MIR (2006)
16. Oliva, A., Torralba, A.: Modeling the shape of the scene: A holistic representation of the spatial envelope. IJCV 42, 145–175 (2001)
17. Hays, J., Efros, A.A.: Scene completion using millions of photographs. SIGGRAPH (2007)
18. Kaufman, L., Rousseeuw, P.J.: Finding Groups in Data An Introduction to Cluster Analysis. Wiley Interscience, New York (1990)
19. Lowe, D.: Distinctive image features from scale-invariant keypoints. IJCV 60, 91–110 (2004)
20. Fischler, M.A., Bolles, R.C.: Random sample consensus: A paradigm for model fitting with applications to image analysis and automated cartography. Communications of the ACM 24 (1981)
21. Beardsley, P., Zisserman, A., Murray, D.: Sequential updating of projective and affine structure from motion. Int. J. Computer Vision 23, 235–259 (1997)
22. Nistér, D., Naroditsky, O., Bergen, J.: Visual odometry for ground vehicle applications. Journal of Field Robotics 23 (2006)
23. Raginsky, M., Lazebnik, S.: Locality-sensitive binary codes from shift-invariant kernels. NIPS 22, 1509–1517 (2009)
24. Hartley, R.I., Zisserman, A.: Multiple View Geometry in Computer Vision, 2nd edn. Cambridge University Press (2004) ISBN: 0521540518
25. Raguram, R., Frahm, J.-M., Pollefeys, M.: A Comparative Analysis of RANSAC Techniques Leading to Adaptive Real-Time Random Sample Consensus. In: Forsyth, D., Torr, P., Zisserman, A. (eds.) ECCV 2008, Part II. LNCS, vol. 5303, pp. 500–513. Springer, Heidelberg (2008)

Author Index